THE COLLECTED WORKS OF
WILLIAM HAZLITT

EDITED BY A. R. WALLER
AND ARNOLD GLOVER

WITH AN INTRODUCTION BY
W. E. HENLEY

Lectures on the English Comic Writers
A View of the English Stage
Dramatic Essays from
'The London Magazine'

1903
LONDON: J. M. DENT & CO.
McCLURE, PHILLIPS & CO.: NEW YORK

Edinburgh : Printed by T. and A. CONSTABLE

CONTENTS

LECTURES ON THE ENGLISH COMIC WRITERS

BIBLIOGRAPHICAL NOTE

The first edition (here reprinted) was published in 1819 in one 8vo. volume (343 pp.), with the following title-page :—'Lectures on the English Comic Writers. Delivered at the Surry Institution. By William Hazlitt. "It is a very good office one man does another, when he tells him the manner of his being pleased." Steele. London : Printed for Taylor and Hessey, 93. Fleet Street. 1819.' The volume was printed by J. Miller, Noble Street, Cheapside. The 'third edition' (the second having been presumably a mere re-print of the first), edited by the author's son and published by Templeman, appeared in 1841, and included some additions collected from various sources. These additions are referred to in the notes to the present volume. The first edition was republished by Mr. W. C. Hazlitt in Bohn's Library in 1869, and the third edition has quite recently been included in the Temple Classics series 'under the immediate editorial care of Mr. Austin Dobson' (1900).

CONTENTS

LECTURES ON
THE COMIC WRITERS, Etc.
OF GREAT BRITAIN

LECTURE I.—INTRODUCTORY

ON WIT AND HUMOUR

Man is the only animal that laughs and weeps; for he is the only animal that is struck with the difference between what things are, and what they ought to be. We weep at what thwarts or exceeds our desires in serious matters: we laugh at what only disappoints our expectations in trifles. We shed tears from sympathy with real and necessary distress; as we burst into laughter from want of sympathy with that which is unreasonable and unnecessary, the absurdity of which provokes our spleen or mirth, rather than any serious reflections on it.

To explain the nature of laughter and tears, is to account for the condition of human life; for it is in a manner compounded of these two! It is a tragedy or a comedy—sad or merry, as it happens. The crimes and misfortunes that are inseparable from it, shock and wound the mind when they once seize upon it, and when the pressure can no longer be borne, seek relief in tears: the follies and absurdities that men commit, or the odd accidents that befal them, afford us amusement from the very rejection of these false claims upon our sympathy, and end in laughter. If every thing that went wrong, if every vanity or weakness in another gave us a sensible pang, it would be hard indeed: but as long as the disagreeableness of the conse-quences of a sudden disaster is kept out of sight by the immediate oddity of the circumstances, and the absurdity or unaccountableness of a foolish action is the most striking thing in it, the ludicrous prevails over the pathetic, and we receive pleasure instead of pain from the farce of life which is played before us, and which discomposes our gravity as often as it fails to move our anger or our pity!

5

LECTURES ON THE COMIC WRITERS

Tears may be considered as the natural and involuntary resource of the mind overcome by some sudden and violent emotion, before it has had time to reconcile its feelings to the change of circumstances: while laughter may be defined to be the same sort of convulsive and involuntary movement, occasioned by mere surprise or contrast (in the absence of any more serious emotion), before it has time to reconcile its belief to contradictory appearances. If we hold a mask before our face, and approach a child with this disguise on, it will at first, from the oddity and incongruity of the appearance, be inclined to laugh; if we go nearer to it, steadily, and without saying a word, it will begin to be alarmed, and be half inclined to cry: if we suddenly take off the mask, it will recover from its fears, and burst out a-laughing; but if, instead of presenting the old well-known countenance, we have concealed a satyr's head or some frightful caricature behind the first mask, the suddenness of the change will not in this case be a source of merriment to it, but will convert its surprise into an agony of consternation, and will make it scream out for help, even though it may be convinced that the whole is a trick at bottom.

The alternation of tears and laughter, in this little episode in common life, depends almost entirely on the greater or less degree of interest attached to the different changes of appearance. The mere suddenness of the transition, the mere baulking our expectations, and turning them abruptly into another channel, seems to give additional liveliness and gaiety to the animal spirits; but the instant the change is not only sudden, but threatens serious consequences, or calls up the shape of danger, terror supersedes our disposition to mirth, and laughter gives place to tears. It is usual to play with infants, and make them laugh by clapping your hands suddenly before them; but if you clap your hands too loud, or too near their sight, their countenances immediately change, and they hide them in the nurse's arms. Or suppose the same child, grown up a little older, comes to a place, expecting to meet a person it is particularly fond of, and does not find that person there, its countenance suddenly falls, its lips begin to quiver, its cheek turns pale, its eye glistens, and it vents its little sorrow (grown too big to be concealed) in a flood of tears. Again, if the child meets the same person unexpectedly after long absence, the same effect will be produced by an excess of joy, with different accompaniments; that is, the surprise and the emotion excited will make the blood come into his face, his eyes sparkle, his tongue falter or be mute, but in either case the tears will gush to his relief, and lighten the pressure about his heart. On the other hand, if a child is playing at hide-and-seek, or blindman's-buff, with persons it is ever so fond of, and either misses them where it had made sure of finding

6

them, or suddenly runs up against them where it had least expected it, the shock or additional impetus given to the imagination by the disappointment or the discovery, in a matter of this indifference, will only vent itself in a fit of laughter.[1] The transition here is not from one thing of importance to another, or from a state of indifference to a state of strong excitement; but merely from one impression to another that we did not at all expect, and when we had expected just the contrary. The mind having been led to form a certain conclusion, and the result producing an immediate solution of continuity in the chain of our ideas, this alternate excitement and relaxation of the imagination, the object also striking upon the mind more vividly in its loose unsettled state, and before it has had time to recover and collect itself, causes that alternate excitement and relaxation, or irregular convulsive movement of the muscular and nervous system, which constitutes physical laughter. The *discontinuous* in our sensations produces a correspondent jar and discord in the frame. The steadiness of our faith and of our features begins to give way at the same time. We turn with an incredulous smile from a story that staggers our belief: and we are ready to split our sides with laughing at an extravagance that sets all common sense and serious concern at defiance.

To understand or define the ludicrous, we must first know what the serious is. Now the serious is the habitual stress which the mind lays upon the expectation of a given order of events, following one another with a certain regularity and weight of interest attached to them. When this stress is increased beyond its usual pitch of intensity, so as to overstrain the feelings by the violent opposition of good to bad, or of objects to our desires, it becomes the pathetic or tragical. The ludicrous, or comic, is the unexpected loosening or relaxing this stress below its usual pitch of intensity, by such an abrupt transposition of the order of our ideas, as taking the mind unawares, throws it off its guard, startles it into a lively sense of pleasure, and leaves no time nor inclination for painful reflections.

The essence of the laughable then is the incongruous, the disconnecting one idea from another, or the jostling of one feeling against another. The first and most obvious cause of laughter is to be found in the simple succession of events, as in the sudden shifting of a disguise, or some unlooked-for accident, without any absurdity of character or situation. The accidental contradiction between our expectations and the event can hardly be said, however, to amount to

---

[1] A child that has hid itself out of the way in sport, is under a great temptation to laugh at the unconsciousness of others as to its situation. A person concealed from assassins, is in no danger of betraying his situation by laughing.

the ludicrous: it is merely laughable. The ludicrous is where there is the same contradiction between the object and our expectations, heightened by some deformity or inconvenience, that is, by its being contrary to what is customary or desirable; as the ridiculous, which is the highest degree of the laughable, is that which is contrary not only to custom but to sense and reason, or is a voluntary departure from what we have a right to expect from those who are conscious of absurdity and propriety in words, looks, and actions.

Of these different kinds or degrees of the laughable, the first is the most shallow and short-lived; for the instant the immediate surprise of a thing's merely happening one way or another is over, there is nothing to throw us back upon our former expectation, and renew our wonder at the event a second time. The second sort, that is, the ludicrous arising out of the improbable or distressing, is more deep and lasting, either because the painful catastrophe excites a greater curiosity, or because the old impression, from its habitual hold on the imagination, still recurs mechanically, so that it is longer before we can seriously make up our minds to the unaccountable deviation from it. The third sort, or the ridiculous arising out of absurdity as well as improbability, that is, where the defect or weakness is of a man's own seeking, is the most refined of all, but not always so pleasant as the last, because the same contempt and disapprobation which sharpens and subtilises our sense of the impropriety, adds a severity to it inconsistent with perfect ease and enjoyment. This last species is properly the province of satire. The principle of contrast is, however, the same in all the stages, in the simply laughable, the ludicrous, the ridiculous; and the effect is only the more complete, the more durably and pointedly this principle operates.

To give some examples in these different kinds. We laugh, when children, at the sudden removing of a pasteboard mask: we laugh, when grown up, more gravely at the tearing off the mask of deceit. We laugh at absurdity; we laugh at deformity. We laugh at a bottle-nose in a caricature; at a stuffed figure of an alderman in a pantomime, and at the tale of Slaukenbergius. A giant standing by a dwarf makes a contemptible figure enough. Rosinante and Dapple are laughable from contrast, as their masters from the same principle make two for a pair. We laugh at the dress of foreigners, and they at ours. Three chimney-sweepers meeting three Chinese in Lincoln's-inn Fields, they laughed at one another till they were ready to drop down. Country people laugh at a person because they never saw him before. Any one dressed in the height of the fashion, or quite out of it, is equally an object of ridicule. One rich source of the ludicrous is distress with which we cannot sympathise from its absurdity or

8

insignificance. Women laugh at their lovers. We laugh at a damned author, in spite of our teeth, and though he may be our friend. 'There is something in the misfortunes of our best friends that pleases us.' We laugh at people on the top of a stage-coach, or in it, if they seem in great extremity. It is hard to hinder children from laughing at a stammerer, at a negro, at a drunken man, or even at a madman. We laugh at mischief. We laugh at what we do not believe. We say that an argument or an assertion that is very absurd, is quite ludicrous. We laugh to shew our satisfaction with ourselves, or our contempt for those about us, or to conceal our envy or our ignorance. We laugh at fools, and at those who pretend to be wise—at extreme simplicity, awkwardness, hypocrisy, and affectation. 'They were talking of me,' says Scrub, 'for they laughed *consumedly*.' Lord Foppington's insensibility to ridicule, and airs of ineffable self-conceit, are no less admirable; and Joseph Surface's cant maxims of morality, when once disarmed of their power to do hurt, become sufficiently ludicrous.—We laugh at that in others which is a serious matter to ourselves; because our self-love is stronger than our sympathy, sooner takes the alarm, and instantly turns our heedless mirth into gravity, which only enhances the jest to others. Some one is generally sure to be the sufferer by a joke. What is sport to one, is death to another. It is only very sensible or very honest people, who laugh as freely at their own absurdities as at those of their neighbours. In general the contrary rule holds, and we only laugh at those misfortunes in which we are spectators, not sharers. The injury, the disappointment, shame, and vexation that we feel, put a stop to our mirth; while the disasters that come home to us, and excite our repugnance and dismay, are an amusing spectacle to others. The greater resistance we make, and the greater the perplexity into which we are thrown, the more lively and *piquant* is the intellectual display of cross-purposes to the by-standers. Our humiliation is their triumph. We are occupied with the disagreeableness of the result instead of its oddity or unexpectedness. Others see only the conflict of motives, and the sudden alternation of events; we feel the pain as well, which more than counterbalances the speculative entertainment we might receive from the contemplation of our abstract situation.

You cannot force people to laugh: you cannot give a reason why they should laugh: they must laugh of themselves, or not at all. As we laugh from a spontaneous impulse, we laugh the more at any restraint upon this impulse. We laugh at a thing merely because we ought not. If we think we must not laugh, this perverse impediment makes our temptation to laugh the greater; for by endeavouring to keep the obnoxious image out of sight, it comes upon us more irresistibly and repeatedly; and the inclination to indulge our mirth, the longer it is held back, collects its force, and breaks out the more violently in peals of laughter. In like manner, any thing we must not think of makes us laugh, by its coming upon us by stealth and unawares, and from the very efforts we make to exclude it. A secret, a loose word, a wanton jest, make people laugh. Aretine laughed himself to death at hearing a lascivious story. Wickedness is often made a substitute for wit; and in most of our good old comedies, the intrigue of the plot and the double meaning of the dialogue go hand-in-hand, and keep up the ball with wonderful spirit between them. The consciousness, however it may arise, that there is something that we ought to look grave at, is almost always a signal for laughing outright: we can hardly keep our countenance at a sermon, a funeral, or a wedding. What an excellent old custom was that of throwing the stocking! What a deal of innocent mirth has been spoiled by the disuse of it!—It is not an easy matter to preserve decorum in courts of justice. The smallest circumstance that interferes with the solemnity of the proceedings, throws the whole place into an uproar of laughter. People at the point of death often say smart things. Sir Thomas More jested with his executioner. Rabelais and Wycherley both died with a *bon-mot* in their mouths.

Misunderstandings, (*malentendus*) where one person means one thing, and another is aiming at something else, are another great source of comic humour, on the same principle of ambiguity and contrast. There is a high-wrought instance of this in the dialogue between Aimwell and Gibbet, in the Beaux' Stratagem, where Aimwell mistakes his companion for an officer in a marching regiment, and Gibbet takes it for granted that the gentleman is a highwayman. The alarm and consternation occasioned by some one saying to him, in the course of common conversation, 'I apprehend you,' is the most ludicrous thing in that admirably natural and powerful performance, Mr. Emery's Robert Tyke. Again, unconsciousness in the person himself of what he is about, or of what others think of him, is also a great heightener of the sense of absurdity. It makes it come the fuller home upon us from his insensibility to it. His simplicity sets off the satire, and gives it a finer edge. It is a more extreme case still where the person is aware of being the object of ridicule, and yet seems perfectly reconciled to it as a matter of course. So wit is often the more forcible and pointed for being dry and serious, for it then seems as if the speaker himself had no intention in it, and we were the first to find it out. Irony, as a species of wit, owes its force to the same principle. In such cases it is the contrast between the appearance and the reality, the suspense of belief, and the seeming

10

incongruity, that gives point to the ridicule, and makes it enter the deeper when the first impression is overcome. Excessive impudence, as in the Liar; or excessive modesty, as in the hero of She Stoops to Conquer; or a mixture of the two, as in the Busy Body, are equally amusing. Lying is a species of wit and humour. To lay any thing to a person's charge from which he is perfectly free, shews spirit and invention; and the more incredible the effrontery, the greater is the joke.

There is nothing more powerfully humorous than what is called *keeping* in comic character, as we see it very finely exemplified in Sancho Panza and Don Quixote. The proverbial phlegm and the romantic gravity of these two celebrated persons may be regarded as the height of this kind of excellence. The deep feeling of character strengthens the sense of the ludicrous. Keeping in comic character is consistency in absurdity; a determined and laudable attachment to the incongruous and singular. The regularity completes the contradiction; for the number of instances of deviation from the right line, branching out in all directions, shews the inveteracy of the original bias to any extravagance or folly, the natural improbability, as it were, increasing every time with the multiplication of chances for a return to common sense, and in the end mounting up to an incredible and unaccountably ridiculous height, when we find our expectations as invariably baffled. The most curious problem of all, is this truth of absurdity to itself. That reason and good sense should be consistent, is not wonderful: but that caprice, and whim, and fantastical prejudice, should be uniform and infallible in their results, is the surprising thing. But while this characteristic clue to absurdity helps on the ridicule, it also softens and harmonises its excesses; and the ludicrous is here blended with a certain beauty and decorum, from this very truth of habit and sentiment, or from the principle of similitude in dissimilitude. The devotion to nonsense, and enthusiasm about trifles, is highly affecting as a moral lesson: it is one of the striking weaknesses and greatest happinesses of our nature. That which excites so lively and lasting an interest in itself, even though it should not be wisdom, is not despicable in the sight of reason and humanity. We cannot suppress the smile on the lip; but the tear should also stand ready to start from the eye. The history of hobbyhorses is equally instructive and delightful; and after the pair I have just alluded to, My Uncle Toby's is one of the best and gentlest that 'ever lifted leg!' The inconveniences, odd accidents, falls, and bruises, to which they expose their riders, contribute their share to the amusement of the spectators; and the blows and wounds that the Knight of the Sorrowful Countenance received in his many perilous

17

adventures, have applied their healing influence to many a hurt mind.
—In what relates to the laughable, as it arises from unforeseen
accidents or self-willed scrapes, the pain, the shame, the mortification,
and utter helplessness of situation, add to the joke, provided they are
momentary, or overwhelming only to the imagination of the sufferer.
Malvolio's punishment and apprehensions are as comic, from our
knowing that they are not real, as Christopher Sly's drunken transformation and short-lived dream of happiness are for the like reason.
Parson Adams's fall into the tub at the 'Squire's, or his being
discovered in bed with Mrs. Slipslop, though pitiable, are laughable
accidents: nor do we read with much gravity of the loss of his
Æschylus, serious as it was to him at the time.—A Scotch clergyman, as he was going to church, seeing a spruce conceited mechanic
who was walking before him, suddenly covered all over with dirt,
either by falling into the kennel, or by some other calamity befalling
him, smiled and passed on: but afterwards seeing the same person,
who had stopped to refit, seated directly facing him in the gallery,
with a look of perfect satisfaction and composure, as if nothing of the
sort had happened to him, the idea of his late disaster and present
self-complacency struck him so powerfully, that, unable to resist the
impulse, he flung himself back in the pulpit, and laughed till he could
laugh no longer. I remember reading a story in an odd number of
the European Magazine, of an old gentleman who used to walk out
every afternoon, with a gold-headed cane, in the fields opposite
Baltimore House, which were then open, only with foot-paths crossing
them. He was frequently accosted by a beggar with a wooden leg,
to whom he gave money, which only made him more importunate.
One day, when he was more troublesome than usual, a well-dressed
person happening to come up, and observing how saucy the fellow
was, said to the gentleman, 'Sir, if you will lend me your cane for
a moment, I 'll give him a good threshing for his impertinence.'
The old gentleman, smiling at the proposal, handed him his cane,
which the other no sooner was going to apply to the shoulders of the
culprit, than he immediately whipped off his wooden leg, and
scampered off with great alacrity, and his chastiser after him as hard
as he could go. The faster the one ran, the faster the other followed
him, brandishing the cane, to the great astonishment of the gentleman
who owned it, till having fairly crossed the fields, they suddenly
turned a corner, and nothing more was seen of either of them.

In the way of mischievous adventure, and a wanton exhibition of
ludicrous weakness in character, nothing is superior to the comic
parts of the Arabian Nights' Entertainments. To take only the set
of stories of the Little Hunchback, who was choked with a bone,

and the Barber of Bagdad and his seven brothers,—there is that of the tailor who was persecuted by the miller's wife, and who, after toiling all night in the mill, got nothing for his pains :—of another who fell in love with a fine lady who pretended to return his passion, and inviting him to her house, as the preliminary condition of her favour, had his eyebrows shaved, his clothes stripped off, and being turned loose into a winding gallery, he was to follow her, and by overtaking obtain all his wishes, but, after a turn or two, stumbled on a trap-door, and fell plump into the street, to the great astonishment of the spectators and his own, shorn of his eyebrows, naked, and without a ray of hope left :—that of the castle-building pedlar, who, in kicking his wife, the supposed daughter of an emperor, kicks down his basket of glass, the brittle foundation of his ideal wealth, his good fortune, and his arrogance :—that, again, of the beggar who dined with the Barmecide, and feasted with him on the names of wines and dishes : and, last and best of all, the inimitable story of the Impertinent Barber himself, one of the seven, and worthy to be so ; his pertinacious, incredible, teasing, deliberate, yet unmeaning folly, his wearing out the patience of the young gentleman whom he is sent for to shave, his preparations and his professions of speed, his taking out an astrolabe to measure the height of the sun while his razors are getting ready, his dancing the dance of Zimri and singing the song of Zamtout, his disappointing the young man of an assignation, following him to the place of rendezvous, and alarming the master of the house in his anxiety for his safety, by which his unfortunate patron loses his hand in the affray, and this is felt as an awkward accident. The danger which the same loquacious person is afterwards in, of losing his head for want of saying who he was, because he would not forfeit his character of being 'justly called the Silent,' is a consummation of the jest, though, if it had really taken place, it would have been carrying the joke too far. There are a thousand instances of the same sort in the Thousand and One Nights, which are an inexhaustible mine of comic humour and invention, and which, from the manners of the East which they describe, carry the principle of callous indifference in a jest as far as it can go. The serious and marvellous stories in that work, which have been so much admired and so greedily read, appear to me monstrous and abortive fictions, like disjointed dreams, dictated by a preternatural dread of arbitrary and despotic power, as the comic and familiar stories are rendered proportionably amusing and interesting from the same principle operating in a different direction, and producing endless uncertainty and vicissitude, and an heroic contempt for the untoward accidents and petty vexations of human life. It is the gaiety of despair, the mirth

13

and laughter of a respite during pleasure from death. The strongest instances of effectual and harrowing imagination, are in the story of Amine and her three sisters, whom she led by her side as a leash of hounds, and of the *goul* who nibbled grains of rice for her dinner, and preyed on human carcasses. In this condemnation of the serious parts of the Arabian Nights, I have nearly all the world, and in particular the author of the Ancient Mariner, against me, who must be allowed to be a judge of such matters, and who said, with a subtlety of philosophical conjecture which he alone possesses, 'That if I did not like them, it was because I did not dream.' On the other hand, I have Bishop Atterbury on my side, who, in a letter to Pope, fairly confesses that 'he could not read them in his old age.'

There is another source of comic humour which has been but little touched on or attended to by the critics—not the infliction of casual pain, but the pursuit of uncertain pleasure and idle gallantry. Half the business and gaiety of comedy turns upon this. Most of the adventures, difficulties, demurs, hair-breadth 'scapes, disguises, deceptions, blunders, disappointments, successes, excuses, all the dextrous manœuvres, artful inuendos, assignations, billets-doux, *double entendres,* sly allusions, and elegant flattery, have an eye to this—to the obtaining of those 'favours secret, sweet, and precious,' in which love and pleasure consist, and which when attained, and the *equivoque* is at an end, the curtain drops, and the play is over. All the attractions of a subject that can only be glanced at indirectly, that is a sort of forbidden ground to the imagination, except under severe restrictions, which are constantly broken through; all the resources it supplies for intrigue and invention; the bashfulness of the clownish lover, his looks of alarm and petrified astonishment; the foppish affectation and easy confidence of the happy man; the dress, the airs, the languor, the scorn, and indifference of the fine lady; the bustle, pertness, loquaciousness, and tricks of the chambermaid; the impudence, lies, and roguery of the valet; the match-making and unmaking; the wisdom of the wise; the sayings of the witty, the folly of the fool; 'the soldier's, scholar's, courtier's eye, tongue, sword, the glass of fashion and the mould of form,' have all a view to this. It is the closet in Blue-Beard. It is the life and soul of Wycherley, Congreve, Vanbrugh, and Farquhar's plays. It is the salt of comedy, without which it would be worthless and insipid. It makes Horner decent, and Millamant divine. It is the jest between Tattle and Miss Prue. It is the bait with which Olivia, in the Plain Dealer, plays with honest Manly. It lurks at the bottom of the catechism which Archer teaches Cherry, and which she learns by heart. It gives the finishing grace to Mrs. Amlet's confession—'Though I'm old, I'm chaste.'

14

ON WIT AND HUMOUR

Valentine and his Angelica would be nothing without it; Miss Peggy would not be worth a gallant; and Slender's 'sweet Ann Page' would be no more! 'The age of comedy would be gone, and the glory of our play-houses extinguished for ever.' Our old comedies would be invaluable, were it only for this, that they keep alive this sentiment, which still survives in all its fluttering grace and breathless palpitations on the stage.

Humour is the describing the ludicrous as it is in itself; wit is the exposing it, by comparing or contrasting it with something else. Humour is, as it were, the growth of nature and accident; wit is the product of art and fancy. Humour, as it is shewn in books, is an imitation of the natural or acquired absurdities of mankind, or of the ludicrous in accident, situation, and character: wit is the illustrating and heightening the sense of that absurdity by some sudden and unexpected likeness or opposition of one thing to another, which sets off the quality we laugh at or despise in a still more contemptible or striking point of view. Wit, as distinguished from poetry, is the imagination or fancy inverted, and so applied to given objects, as to make the little look less, the mean more light and worthless; or to divert our admiration or wean our affections from that which is lofty and impressive, instead of producing a more intense admiration and exalted passion, as poetry does. Wit may sometimes, indeed, be shewn in compliments as well as satire; as in the common epigram—

> 'Accept a miracle, instead of wit:
> See two dull lines with Stanhope's pencil writ.'

But then the mode of paying it is playful and ironical, and contradicts itself in the very act of making its own performance an humble foil to another's. Wit hovers round the borders of the light and trifling, whether in matters of pleasure or pain; for as soon as it describes the serious seriously, it ceases to be wit, and passes into a different form. Wit is, in fact, the eloquence of indifference, or an ingenious and striking exposition of those evanescent and glancing impressions of objects which affect us more from surprise or contrast to the train of our ordinary and literal preconceptions, than from anything in the objects themselves exciting our necessary sympathy or lasting hatred. The favourite employment of wit is to add littleness to littleness, and heap contempt on insignificance by all the arts of petty and incessant warfare; or if it ever affects to aggrandise, and use the language of hyperbole, it is only to betray into derision by a fatal comparison, as in the mock-heroic; or if it treats of serious passion, it must do it so as to lower the tone of intense and high-wrought sentiment, by the introduction of burlesque and familiar circumstances. To give an

15

instance or two. Butler, in his Hudibras, compares the change of night into day, to the change of colour in a boiled lobster.

> ' The sun had long since, in the lap
> Of Thetis, taken out his nap;
> And, like a lobster boil'd, the morn
> From black to red, began to turn :
> When Hudibras, whom thoughts and aching
> 'Twixt sleeping kept all night, and waking,
> Began to rub his drowsy eyes,
> And from his couch prepared to rise,
> Resolving to dispatch the deed
> He vow'd to do with trusty speed.'

Compare this with the following stanzas in Spenser, treating of the same subject :—

> ' By this the Northern Waggoner had set
> His seven-fold team behind the stedfast star,
> That was in Ocean waves yet never wet,
> But firm is fix'd and sendeth light from far
> To all that in the wide deep wand'ring are :
> And cheerful chanticleer with his note shrill,
> Had warned once that Phœbus' fiery car
> In haste was climbing up the eastern hill,
> Full envious that night so long his room did fill.
>
> At last the golden oriental gate
> Of greatest heaven 'gan to open fair,
> And Phœbus, fresh as bridegroom to his mate,
> Came dancing forth, shaking his dewy hair,
> And hurl'd his glist'ring beams through gloomy air :
> Which when the wakeful elf perceiv'd, straitway
> He started up and did himself prepare
> In sun-bright arms and battailous array,
> For with that pagan proud he combat will that day.'

In this last passage, every image is brought forward that can give effect to our natural impression of the beauty, the splendour, and solemn grandeur of the rising sun; pleasure and power wait on every line and word : whereas, in the other, the only memorable thing is a grotesque and ludicrous illustration of the alteration which takes place from darkness to gorgeous light, and that brought from the lowest instance, and with associations that can only disturb and perplex the imagination in its conception of the real object it describes. There cannot be a more witty, and at the same time degrading comparison,

16

than that in the same author, of the Bear turning round the pole-star
to a bear tied to a stake :—

> ' But now a sport more formidable
> Had raked together village rabble ;
> 'Twas an old way of recreating
> Which learned butchers call bear-baiting,
> A bold adventurous exercise
> With ancient heroes in high prize,
> For authors do affirm it came
> From Isthmian or Nemæan game ;
> Others derive it from the Bear
> That's fixed in Northern hemisphere,
> And round about his pole does make
> A circle like a bear at stake,
> That at the chain's end wheels about
> And overturns the rabble rout.'

I need not multiply examples of this sort.—Wit or ludicrous invention
produces its effect oftenest by comparison, but not always.   It
frequently effects its purposes by unexpected and subtle distinctions.
For instance, in the first kind, Mr. Sheridan's description of Mr.
Addington's administration as the fag-end of Mr. Pitt's, who had
remained so long on the treasury bench that, like Nicias in the fable,
' he left the sitting part of the man behind him,' is as fine an example
of metaphorical wit as any on record.   The same idea seems,
however, to have been included in the old well-known nickname of the
Rump Parliament.   Almost as happy an instance of the other kind of
wit, which consists in sudden retorts, in turns upon an idea, and
diverting the train of your adversary's argument abruptly and adroitly
into another channel, may be seen in the sarcastic reply of Porson,
who hearing some one observe that ' certain modern poets would be
read and admired when Homer and Virgil were forgotten,' made
answer—' And not till then ! '   Sir Robert Walpole's definition of
the gratitude of place-expectants, ' That it is a lively sense of *future*
favours,' is no doubt wit, but it does not consist in the finding out any
coincidence or likeness, but in suddenly transposing the order of time
in the common account of this feeling, so as to make the professions
of those who pretend to it correspond more with their practice.   It
is filling up a blank in the human heart with a word that explains its
hollowness at once.   Voltaire's saying, in answer to a stranger who
was observing how tall his trees grew—' That they had nothing else
to do '—was a quaint mixture of wit and humour, making it out as if
they really led a lazy, laborious life ; but there was here neither
allusion or metaphor.   Again, that master-stroke in Hudibras is

sterling wit and profound satire, where speaking of certain religious hypocrites he says, that they

> ' Compound for sins they are inclin'd to,
> By damning those they have no mind to ; '

but the wit consists in the truth of the character, and in the happy exposure of the ludicrous contradiction between the pretext and the practice; between their lenity towards their own vices, and their severity to those of others. The same principle of nice distinction must be allowed to prevail in those lines of the same author, where he is professing to expound the dreams of judicial astrology.

> ' There's but the twinkling of a star
> Betwixt a man of peace and war,
> A thief and justice, fool and knave,
> A huffing officer and a slave;
> A crafty lawyer and pickpocket;
> A great philosopher and a blockhead ;
> A formal preacher and a player;
> A learn'd physician and man slayer.'

The finest piece of wit I know of, is in the lines of Pope on the Lord Mayor's show—

> ' Now night descending, the proud scene is o'er,
> But lives in Settle's numbers one day more.'

This is certainly as mortifying an inversion of the idea of poetical immortality as could be thought of; it fixes the *maximum* of littleness and insignificance : but it is not by likeness to any thing else that it does this, but by literally taking the lowest possible duration of ephemeral reputation, marking it (as with a slider) on the scale of endless renown, and giving a rival credit for it as his loftiest praise. In a word, the shrewd separation or disentangling of ideas that seem the same, or where the secret contradiction is not sufficiently suspected, and is of a ludicrous and whimsical nature, is wit just as much as the bringing together those that appear at first sight totally different.   There is then no sufficient ground for admitting Mr. Locke's celebrated definition of wit, which he makes to consist in the finding out striking and unexpected resemblances in things so as to make pleasant pictures in the fancy, while judgment and reason, according to him, lie the clean contrary way, in separating and nicely distinguishing those wherein the smallest difference is to be found.[1]

---

[1] His words are—' If in having our ideas in the memory ready at hand consists quickness of parts, in this of having them unconfused, and being able nicely to

18

ON WIT AND HUMOUR

On this definition Harris, the author of Hermes, has very well observed that the demonstrating the equality of the three angles of a right-angled triangle to two right ones, would, upon the principle here stated, be a piece of wit instead of an act of the judgment, or understanding, and Euclid's Elements a collection of epigrams. On the contrary it has appeared, that the detection and exposure of difference, particularly where this implies nice and subtle observation, as in discriminating between pretence and practice, between appearance and reality, is common to wit and satire with judgment and reasoning, and certainly the comparing and connecting our ideas together is an essential part of reason and judgment, as well as of wit and fancy.— Mere wit, as opposed to reason or argument, consists in striking out some casual and partial coincidence which has nothing to do, or at least implies no necessary connection with the nature of the things, which are forced into a seeming analogy by a play upon words, or some irrelevant conceit, as in puns, riddles, alliteration, &c. The jest, in all such cases, lies in the sort of mock-identity, or nominal resemblance, established by the intervention of the same words expressing different ideas, and countenancing as it were, by a fatality of language, the mischievous insinuation which the person who has

distinguish one thing from another, where there is but the least difference, consists in a great measure the exactness of judgment and clearness of reason, which is to be observed in one man above another. And hence, perhaps, may be given some reason of that common observation, that men who have a great deal of wit and prompt memories, have not always the clearest judgment or deepest reason. For wit lying mostly in the assemblage of ideas, and putting them together with quickness and variety, wherein can be found any resemblance or congruity, thereby to make up pleasant pictures and agreeable visions in the fancy ; judgment, on the contrary, lies quite on the other side, in separating carefully one from another, ideas wherein can be found the least difference, thereby to avoid being misled by similitude, and by affinity to take one thing for another.' (*Essay*, vol. i. p. 143.) This definition, such as it is, Mr. Locke took without acknowledgment from Hobbes, who says in his Leviathan, 'This difference of quickness in imagining is caused by the difference of men's passions, that love and dislike some one thing, some another, and therefore some men's thoughts run one way, some another, and are held to and observe differently the things that pass through their imagination. And whereas in this succession of thoughts there is nothing to observe in the things they think on, but either in what they be like one another, or in what they be unlike, those that observe their similitudes, in case they be such as are but rarely observed by others, are said to have a good wit, by which is meant on this occasion a good fancy. But they that observe their differences and dissimilitudes, which is called distinguishing and discerning and judging between thing and thing ; in case such discerning be not easy, are said to have a good judgment ; and particularly in matter of conversation and business, wherein times, places, and persons are to be discerned, this virtue is called discretion. The former, that is, fancy, without the help of judgment, is not commended for a virtue ; but the latter, which is judgment or discretion, is commended for itself, without the help of fancy.' *Leviathan*, p. 32.

the wit to take advantage of it wishes to convey. So when the disaffected French wits applied to the new order of the *Fleur du lys* the *double entendre* of *Compagnons d' Ulysse*, or companions of Ulysses, meaning the animal into which the fellow-travellers of the hero of the Odyssey were transformed, this was a shrewd and biting intimation of a galling truth (if truth it were) by a fortuitous concourse of letters of the alphabet, jumping in 'a foregone conclusion,' but there was no proof of the thing, unless it was self-evident. And, indeed, this may be considered as the best defence of the contested maxim—*That ridicule is the test of truth* ; viz. that it does not contain or attempt a formal proof of it, but owes its power of conviction to the bare suggestion of it, so that if the thing when once hinted is not clear in itself, the satire fails of its effect and falls to the ground. The sarcasm here glanced at the character of the new or old French noblesse may not be well founded ; but it is so like truth, and 'comes in such a questionable shape,' backed with the appearance of an identical proposition, that it would require a long train of facts and laboured arguments to do away the impression, even if we were sure of the honesty and wisdom of the person who undertook to refute it. A flippant jest is as good a test of truth as a solid bribe ; and there are serious sophistries,

'Soul-killing lies, and truths that work small good,'

as well as idle pleasantries. Of this we may be sure, that ridicule fastens on the vulnerable points of a cause, and finds out the weak sides of an argument ; if those who resort to it sometimes rely too much on its success, those who are chiefly annoyed by it almost always are so with reason, and cannot be too much on their guard against deserving it. Before we can laugh at a thing, its absurdity must at least be open and palpable to common apprehension. Ridicule is necessarily built on certain supposed facts, whether true or false, and on their inconsistency with certain acknowledged maxims, whether right or wrong. It is, therefore, a fair test, if not of philosophical or abstract truth, at least of what is truth according to public opinion and common sense ; for it can only expose to instantaneous contempt that which is condemned by public opinion, and is hostile to the common sense of mankind. Or to put it differently, it is the test of the quantity of truth that there is in our favourite prejudices.—To shew how nearly allied wit is thought to be to truth, it is not unusual to say of any person—'Such a one is a man of sense, for though he said nothing, he laughed in the right place.'—Alliteration comes in here under the head of a certain sort of verbal wit ; or, by pointing the expression, sometimes points the sense. Mr. Grattan's wit or eloquence (I don't know by what name to call it) would be nothing without this accompaniment. Speaking of some ministers whom he did not like, he said, 'Their only means of government are the guinea and the gallows.' There can scarcely, it must be confessed, be a more effectual mode of political conversion than one of these applied to a man's friends, and the other to himself. The fine sarcasm of Junius on the effect of the supposed ingratitude of the Duke of Grafton at court—'The instance might be painful, but the principle would please'—notwithstanding the profound insight into human nature it implies, would hardly pass for wit without the alliteration, as some poetry would hardly be acknowledged as such without the rhyme to clench it. A quotation or a hackneyed phrase dextrously turned or wrested to another purpose, has often the effect of the liveliest wit. An idle fellow who had only fourpence left in the world, which had been put by to pay for the baking some meat for his dinner, went and laid it out to buy a new string for a guitar. An old acquaintance on hearing this story, repeated those lines out of the Allegro—

> 'And ever against *eating* cares
> Lap me in soft Lydian airs.'

The reply of the author of the periodical paper called the World to a lady at church, who seeing him look thoughtful, asked what he was thinking of—'The next World,'—is a perversion of an established formula of language, something of the same kind.—Rhymes are sometimes a species of wit, where there is an alternate combination and resolution or decomposition of the elements of sound, contrary to our usual division and classification of them in ordinary speech, not unlike the sudden separation and re-union of the component parts of the machinery in a pantomime. The author who excels infinitely the most in this way is the writer of Hudibras. He also excels in the invention of single words and names which have the effect of wit by sounding big, and meaning nothing :—'full of sound and fury, signifying nothing.' But of the artifices of this author's burlesque style I shall have occasion to speak hereafter.—It is not always easy to distinguish between the wit of words and that of things. 'For thin partitions do their bounds divide.' Some of the late Mr. Curran's *bon mots* or *jeux d'esprit*, might be said to owe their birth to this sort of equivocal generation ; or were a happy mixture of verbal wit and a lively and picturesque fancy, of legal acuteness in detecting the variable application of words, and of a mind apt at perceiving the ludicrous in external objects. 'Do you see any thing ridiculous in this wig?' said one of his brother judges to him. 'Nothing but the head,' was the answer. Now here instantaneous advantage was taken of the slight technical ambiguity in the construction of language, and the matter-of-fact is flung into the scale as a thumping makeweight. After all, verbal and accidental strokes of wit, though the most surprising and laughable, are not the best and most lasting. That wit is the most refined and effectual, which is founded on the detection of unexpected likeness or distinction in things, rather than in words. It is more severe and galling, that is, it is more unpardonable though less surprising, in proportion as the thought suggested is more complete and satisfactory, from its being inherent in the nature of the things themselves. *Hæret lateri lethalis arundo.* Truth makes the greatest libel; and it is that which barbs the darts of wit. The Duke of Buckingham's saying, 'Laws are not, like women, the worse for being old,' is an instance of a harmless truism and the utmost malice of wit united. This is, perhaps, what has been meant by the distinction between true and false wit. Mr. Addison, indeed, goes so far as to make it the exclusive test of true wit that it will bear translation into another language, that is to say, that it does not depend at all on the form of expression. But this is by no means the case. Swift would hardly have allowed of such a strait-laced theory, to make havoc with his darling conundrums; though there is no one whose serious wit is more that of things, as opposed to a mere play either of words or fancy. I ought, I believe, to have noticed before, in speaking of the difference between wit and humour, that wit is often pretended absurdity, where the person overacts or exaggerates a certain part with a conscious design to expose it as if it were another person, as when Mandrake in the Twin Rivals says, 'This glass is too big, carry it away, I 'll drink out of the bottle.' On the contrary, when Sir Hugh Evans says very innocently, ''Od's plessed will, I will not be absence at the grace,' though there is here a great deal of humour, there is no wit. This kind of wit of the humorist, where the person makes a butt of himself, and exhibits his own absurdities or foibles purposely in the most pointed and glaring lights, runs through the whole of the character of Falstaff, and is, in truth, the principle on which it is founded. It is an irony directed against one's-self. Wit is, in fact, a voluntary act of the mind, or exercise of the invention, shewing the absurd and ludicrous consciously, whether in ourselves or another. Cross-readings, where the blunders are designed, are wit: but if any one were to light upon them through ignorance or accident, they would be merely ludicrous.

It might be made an argument of the intrinsic superiority of poetry or imagination to wit, that the former does not admit of mere verbal combinations. Whenever they do occur, they are uniformly

22

blemishes. It requires something more solid and substantial to raise admiration or passion. The general forms and aggregate masses of our ideas must be brought more into play, to give weight and magnitude. Imagination may be said to be the finding out something similar in things generally alike, or with like feelings attached to them; while wit principally aims at finding out something that seems the same, or amounts to a momentary deception where you least expected it, viz. in things totally opposite. The reason why more slight and partial, or merely accidental and nominal resemblances serve the purposes of wit, and indeed characterise its essence as a distinct operation and faculty of the mind, is, that the object of ludicrous poetry is naturally to let down and lessen; and it is easier to let down than to raise up, to weaken than to strengthen, to disconnect our sympathy from passion and power, than to attach and rivet it to any object of grandeur or interest, to startle and shock our preconceptions by incongruous and equivocal combinations, than to confirm, enforce, and expand them by powerful and lasting associations of ideas, or striking and true analogies. A slight cause is sufficient to produce a slight effect. To be indifferent or sceptical, requires no effort; to be enthusiastic and in earnest, requires a strong impulse, and collective power. Wit and humour (comparatively speaking, or taking the extremes to judge of the gradations by) appeal to our indolence, our vanity, our weakness, and insensibility; serious and impassioned poetry appeals to our strength, our magnanimity, our virtue, and humanity. Any thing is sufficient to heap contempt upon an object; even the bare suggestion of a mischievous allusion to what is improper, dissolves the whole charm, and puts an end to our admiration of the sublime or beautiful. Reading the finest passage in Milton's Paradise Lost in a false tone, will make it seem insipid and absurd. The cavilling at, or invidiously pointing out, a few slips of the pen, will embitter the pleasure, or alter our opinion of a whole work, and make us throw it down in disgust. The critics are aware of this vice and infirmity in our nature, and play upon it with periodical success. The meanest weapons are strong enough for this kind of warfare, and the meanest hands can wield them. Spleen can subsist on any kind of food. The shadow of a doubt, the hint of an inconsistency, a word, a look, a syllable, will destroy our best-formed convictions. What puts this argument in as striking a point of view as any thing, is the nature of parody or burlesque, the secret of which lies merely in transposing or applying at a venture to any thing, or to the lowest objects, that which is applicable only to certain given things, or to the highest matters. 'From the sublime to the ridiculous, there is but one step.' The slightest want of unity of

23

impression destroys the sublime; the detection of the smallest incongruity is an infallible ground to rest the ludicrous upon. But in serious poetry, which aims at rivetting our affections, every blow must tell home. The missing a single time is fatal, and undoes the spell. We see how difficult it is to sustain a continued flight of impressive sentiment: how easy it must be then to travestie or burlesque it, to flounder into nonsense, and be witty by playing the fool. It is a common mistake, however, to suppose that parodies degrade, or imply a stigma on the subject: on the contrary, they in general imply something serious or sacred in the originals. Without this, they would be good for nothing; for the immediate contrast would be wanting, and with this they are sure to tell. The best parodies are, accordingly, the best and most striking things reversed. Witness the common travesties of Homer and Virgil. Mr. Canning's court parodies on Mr. Southey's popular odes, are also an instance in point (I do not know which were the cleverest); and the best of the Rejected Addresses is the parody on Crabbe, though I do not certainly think that Crabbe is the most ridiculous poet now living.

Lear and the Fool are the sublimest instance I know of passion and wit united, or of imagination unfolding the most tremendous sufferings, and of burlesque on passion playing with it, aiding and relieving its intensity by the most pointed, but familiar and indifferent illustrations of the same thing in different objects, and on a meaner scale. The Fool's reproaching Lear with ‘making his daughters his mothers,’ his snatches of proverbs and old ballads, ‘The hedge-sparrow fed the cuckoo so long, that it had its head bit off by its young,’ and ‘Whoop jug, I know when the horse follows the cart,’ are a running commentary of trite truisms, pointing out the extreme folly of the infatuated old monarch, and in a manner reconciling us to its inevitable consequences.

Lastly, there is a wit of sense and observation, which consists in the acute illustration of good sense and practical wisdom, by means of some far-fetched conceit or quaint imagery. The matter is sense, but the form is wit. Thus the lines in Pope—

> ‘ ’Tis with our judgments as our watches, none
> Go just alike; yet each believes his own——’

are witty, rather than poetical; because the truth they convey is a mere dry observation on human life, without elevation or enthusiasm, and the illustration of it is of that quaint and familiar kind that is merely curious and fanciful. Cowley is an instance of the same kind in almost all his writings. Many of the jests and witticisms in the best comedies are moral aphorisms and rules for the conduct of life,

24

sparkling with wit and fancy in the mode of expression. The ancient philosophers also abounded in the same kind of wit, in telling home truths in the most unexpected manner.—In this sense Æsop was the greatest wit and moralist that ever lived. Ape and slave, he looked askance at human nature, and beheld its weaknesses and errors transferred to another species. Vice and virtue were to him as plain as any objects of sense. He saw in man a talking, absurd, obstinate, proud, angry animal; and clothed these abstractions with wings, or a beak, or tail, or claws, or long ears, as they appeared embodied in these hieroglyphics in the brute creation. His moral philosophy is natural history. He makes an ass bray wisdom, and a frog croak humanity. The store of moral truth, and the fund of invention in exhibiting it in eternal forms, palpable and intelligible, and delightful to children and grown persons, and to all ages and nations, are almost miraculous. The invention of a fable is to me the most enviable exertion of human genius: it is the discovering a truth to which there is no clue, and which, when once found out, can never be forgotten. I would rather have been the author of Æsop's Fables, than of Euclid's Elements!— That popular entertainment, Punch and the Puppet-show, owes part of its irresistible and universal attraction to nearly the same principle of inspiring inanimate and mechanical agents with sense and consciousness. The drollery and wit of a piece of wood is doubly droll and farcical. Punch is not merry in himself, but ' he is the cause of heartfelt mirth in other men.' The wires and pulleys that govern his motions are conductors to carry off the spleen, and all ' that perilous stuff that weighs upon the heart.' If we see a number of people turning the corner of a street, ready to burst with secret satisfaction, and with their faces bathed in laughter, we know what is the matter —that they are just come from a puppet-show. Who can see three little painted, patched-up figures, no bigger than one's thumb, strut, squeak and gibber, sing, dance, chatter, scold, knock one another about the head, give themselves airs of importance, and ' imitate humanity most abominably,' without laughing immoderately? We overlook the farce and mummery of human life in little, and for nothing; and what is still better, it costs them who have to play in it nothing. We place the mirth, and glee, and triumph, to our own account; and we know that the bangs and blows they have received go for nothing, as soon as the showman puts them up in his box and marches off quietly with them, as jugglers of a less amusing description sometimes march off with the wrongs and rights of mankind in their pockets!—I have heard no bad judge of such matters say, that ' he liked a comedy better than a tragedy, a farce better than a comedy, a pantomime better than a farce, but a puppet-show best of all.' I look upon it,

25

that he who invented puppet-shows was a greater benefactor to his species, than he who invented Operas!

I shall conclude this imperfect and desultory sketch of wit and humour with Barrow's celebrated description of the same subject. He says, '—But first it may be demanded, what the thing we speak of is, or what this facetiousness doth import; to which question I might reply, as Democritus did to him that asked the definition of a man—*'tis that which we all see and know;* and one better apprehends what it is by acquaintance, than I can inform him by description. It is, indeed, a thing so versatile and multiform, appearing in so many shapes, so many postures, so many garbs, so variously apprehended by several eyes and judgments, that it seemeth no less hard to settle a clear and certain notice thereof, than to make a portrait of Proteus, or to define the figure of fleeting air. Sometimes it lieth in pat allusion to a known story, or in seasonable application of a trivial saying, or in forging an apposite tale: sometimes it playeth in words and phrases, taking advantage from the ambiguity of their sense, or the affinity of their sound: sometimes it is wrapped in a dress of luminous expression; sometimes it lurketh under an odd similitude. Sometimes it is lodged in a sly question, in a smart answer; in a quirkish reason; in a shrewd intimation; in cunningly diverting or cleverly restoring an objection: sometimes it is couched in a bold scheme of speech; in a tart irony; in a lusty hyperbole; in a startling metaphor; in a plausible reconciling of contradictions, or in acute nonsense: sometimes a scenical representation of persons or things, a counterfeit speech, a mimical look or gesture passeth for it; sometimes an affected simplicity, sometimes a presumptuous bluntness giveth it being: sometimes it riseth only from a lucky hitting upon what is strange: sometimes from a crafty wresting obvious matter to the purpose: often it consisteth in one knows not what, and springeth up one can hardly tell how. Its ways are unaccountable and inexplicable, being answerable to the numberless rovings of fancy and windings of language. It is, in short, a manner of speaking out of the simple and plain way (such as reason teacheth and knoweth things by), which by a pretty surprising uncouthness in conceit or expression doth affect and amuse the fancy, shewing in it some wonder, and breathing some delight thereto. It raiseth admiration, as signifying a nimble sagacity of apprehension, a special felicity of invention, a vivacity of spirit, and reach of wit more than vulgar: it seeming to argue a rare quickness of parts, that one can fetch in remote conceits applicable; a notable skill that he can dextrously accommodate them to a purpose before him, together with a lively briskness of humour, not apt to damp those sportful flashes of

26

ON WIT AND HUMOUR

imagination. (Whence in Aristotle such persons are termed ἐπιδέξιοι, dexterous men and εὔτροποι, men of facile or versatile manners, who can easily turn themselves to all things, or turn all things to themselves.) It also procureth delight by gratifying curiosity with its rareness or semblance of difficulty (as monsters, not for their beauty but their rarity; as juggling tricks, not for their use but their abstruseness, are beheld with pleasure;) by diverting the mind from its road of serious thoughts; by instilling gaiety and airiness of spirit; by provoking to such dispositions of spirit, in way of emulation or complaisance, and by seasoning matter, otherwise distasteful or insipid, with an unusual and thence grateful tang.'—*Barrow's Works, Serm.* 14.

I will only add by way of general caution, that there is nothing more ridiculous than laughter without a cause, nor any thing more troublesome than what are called laughing people. A professed laugher is as contemptible and tiresome a character as a professed wit: the one is always contriving something to laugh at, the other is always laughing at nothing. An excess of levity is as impertinent as an excess of gravity. A character of this sort is well personified by Spenser, in the Damsel of the Idle Lake—

'————Who did essay
To laugh at shaking of the leaves light.'

Any one must be mainly ignorant or thoughtless, who is surprised at every thing he sees; or wonderfully conceited, who expects every thing to conform to his standard of propriety. Clowns and idiots laugh on all occasions; and the common failing of wishing to be thought satirical often runs through whole families in country places, to the great annoyance of their neighbours. To be struck with incongruity in whatever comes before us, does not argue great comprehension or refinement of perception, but rather a looseness and flippancy of mind and temper, which prevents the individual from connecting any two ideas steadily or consistently together. It is owing to a natural crudity and precipitateness of the imagination, which assimilates nothing properly to itself. People who are always laughing, at length laugh on the wrong side of their faces; for they cannot get others to laugh with them. In like manner, an affectation of wit by degrees hardens the heart, and spoils good company and good manners. A perpetual succession of good things puts an end to common conversation. There is no answer to a jest, but another; and even where the ball can be kept up in this way without ceasing, it tires the patience of the by-standers, and runs the speakers out of breath. Wit is the salt of conversation, not the food.

The four chief names for comic humour out of our own language

27

are Aristophanes and Lucian among the ancients, Moliere and Rabelais among the moderns. Of the two first I shall say, for I know but little. I should have liked Aristophanes better, if he had treated Socrates less scurvily, for he has treated him most scurvily both as to wit and argument. His Plutus and his Birds are striking instances, the one of dry humour, the other of airy fancy.—Lucian is a writer who appears to deserve his full fame : he has the licentious and extravagant wit of Rabelais, but directed more uniformly to a purpose ; and his comic productions are interspersed with beautiful and eloquent descriptions, full of sentiment, such as the exquisite account of the fable of the halcyon put into the mouth of Socrates, and the heroic eulogy on Bacchus, which is conceived in the highest strain of glowing panegyric.

The two other authors I proposed to mention are modern, and French. Moliere, however, in the spirit of his writings, is almost as much an English as a French author—quite a *barbare* in all in which he really excelled. He was unquestionably one of the greatest comic geniuses that ever lived ; a man of infinite wit, gaiety, and invention—full of life, laughter, and whim. But it cannot be denied, that his plays are in general mere farces, without scrupulous adherence to nature, refinement of character, or common probability. The plots of several of them could not be carried on for a moment without a perfect collusion between the parties to wink at contradictions, and act in defiance of the evidence of their senses. For instance, take the *Medecin malgrè lui* (the Mock Doctor), in which a common wood-cutter takes upon himself, and is made successfully to support through a whole play, the character of a learned physician, without exciting the least suspicion ; and yet, notwithstanding the absurdity of the plot, it is one of the most laughable and truly comic productions that can well be imagined. The rest of his lighter pieces, the *Bourgeois Gentilhomme, Monsieur Pourceaugnac, George Dandin,* (or Barnaby Brittle,) &c. are of the same description—gratuitous assumptions of character, and fanciful and outrageous caricatures of nature. He indulges at his peril in the utmost license of burlesque exaggeration ; and gives a loose to the intoxication of his animal spirits. With respect to his two most laboured comedies, the Tartuffe and Misanthrope, I confess that I find them rather hard to get through : they have much of the improbability and extravagance of the others, united with the endless common-place prosing of French declamation. What can exceed, for example, the absurdity of the Misanthrope, who leaves his mistress, after every proof of her attachment and constancy, for no other reason than that she will not submit to the *technical formality* of going to live with him in a wilderness ? The characters, again, which Celimene gives of her female friends, near the opening of the play, are admirable satires, (as good as Pope's characters of women,) but not exactly in the spirit of comic dialogue. The strictures of Rousseau on this play, in his Letter to D'Alembert, are a fine specimen of the best philosophical criticism.—The same remarks apply in a greater degree to the Tartuffe. The long speeches and reasonings in this play tire one almost to death : they may be very good logic, or rhetoric, or philosophy, or any thing but comedy. If each of the parties had retained a special pleader to speak his sentiments, they could have appeared more verbose or intricate. The improbability of the character of Orgon is wonderful. This play is in one point of view invaluable, as a lasting monument of the credulity of the French to all verbal professions of wisdom or virtue ; and its existence can only be accounted for from that astonishing and tyrannical predominance which words exercise over things in the mind of every Frenchman. The *Ecole des Femmes*, from which Wycherley has borrowed his Country Wife, with the true spirit of original genius, is, in my judgment, the masterpiece of Moliere. The set speeches in the original play, it is true, would not be borne on the English stage, nor indeed on the French, but that they are carried off by the verse. The *Critique de l'Ecole des Femmes*, the dialogue of which is prose, is written in a very different style. Among other things, this little piece contains an exquisite, and almost unanswerable defence of the superiority of comedy over tragedy. Moliere was to be excused for taking this side of the question.

A writer of some pretensions among ourselves has reproached the French with ' an equal want of books and men.' There is a common French print, in which Moliere is represented reading one of his plays in the presence of the celebrated Ninon de l'Enclos, to a circle of the wits and first men of his own time. Among these are the great Corneille ; the tender, faultless Racine ; Fontaine, the artless old man, unconscious of immortality ; the accomplished St. Evremond ; the Duke de la Rochefocault, the severe anatomiser of the human breast ; Boileau, the flatterer of courts and judge of men ! Were these men nothing ? They have passed for men (and great ones) hitherto, and though the prejudice is an old one, I should hope it may still last our time.

Rabelais is another name that might have saved this unjust censure. The wise sayings and heroic deeds of Gargantua and Pantagruel ought not to be set down as nothing. I have already spoken my mind at large of this author ; but I cannot help thinking of him here, sitting in his easy chair, with an eye languid with excess of mirth, his lip quivering with a new-born conceit, and wiping his beard after a well-seasoned jest, with his pen held carelessly in his hand, his wine-flagons, and his books of law, of school divinity, and physic before him, which were his jest-books, whence he drew endless stores of absurdity; laughing at the world and enjoying it by turns, and making the world laugh with him again, for the last three hundred years, at his teeming wit and its own prolific follies. Even to those who have never read his works, the name of Rabelais is a cordial to the spirits, and the mention of it cannot consist with gravity or spleen!

LECTURE II

ON SHAKSPEARE AND BEN JONSON

Dr. Johnson thought Shakspeare's comedies better than his tragedies, and gives as a reason, that he was more at home in the one than in the other. That comedies should be written in a more easy and careless vein than tragedies, is but natural. This is only saying that a comedy is not so serious a thing as a tragedy. But that he shewed a greater mastery in the one than the other, I cannot allow, nor is it generally felt. The labour which the Doctor thought it cost Shakspeare to write his tragedies, only shewed the labour which it cost the critic in reading them, that is, his general indisposition to sympathise heartily and spontaneously with works of high-wrought passion or imagination. There is not in any part of this author's writings the slightest trace of his having ever been 'smit with the love of sacred song,' except some passages in Pope. His habitually morbid temperament and saturnine turn of thought required that the string should rather be relaxed than tightened, that the weight upon the mind should rather be taken off than have any thing added to it. There was a sluggish moroseness about his moral constitution that refused to be roused to any keen agony of thought, and that was not very safely to be trifled with in lighter matters, though this last was allowed to pass off as the most pardonable offence against the gravity of his pretensions. It is in fact the established rule at present, in these cases, to speak highly of the Doctor's authority, and to dissent from almost every one of his critical decisions. For my own part, I so far consider this preference given to the comic genius of the poet as erroneous and unfounded, that I should say that he is the only tragic poet in the world in the highest sense, as being on a par with, and the same as Nature, in her greatest heights and depths of

30

action and suffering. There is but one who durst walk within that mighty circle, treading the utmost bound of nature and passion, shewing us the dread abyss of woe in all its ghastly shapes and colours, and laying open all the faculties of the human soul to act, to think, and suffer, in direst extremities; whereas I think, on the other hand, that in comedy, though his talents there too were as wonderful as they were delightful, yet that there were some before him, others on a level with him, and many close behind him. I cannot help thinking, for instance, that Moliere was as great, or a greater comic genius than Shakspeare, though assuredly I do not think that Racine was as great, or a greater tragic genius. I think that both Rabelais and Cervantes, the one in the power of ludicrous description, the other in the invention and perfect keeping of comic character, excelled Shakspeare; that is, they would have been greater men, if they had had equal power with him over the stronger passions. For my own reading, I like Vanbrugh's City Wives' Confederacy as well, or ('not to speak it profanely') better than the Merry Wives of Windsor, and Congreve's Way of the World as well as the Comedy of Errors or Love's Labour Lost. But I cannot say that I know of any tragedies in the world that make even a tolerable approach to Hamlet, or Lear, or Othello, or some others, either in the sum total of their effect, or in their complete distinctness from every thing else, by which they take not only unquestioned, but undivided possession of the mind, and form a class, a world by themselves, mingling with all our thoughts like a second being. Other tragedies tell for more or less, are good, bad, or indifferent, as they have more or less excellence of a kind common to them with others: but these stand alone by themselves; they have nothing common-place in them; they are a new power in the imagination, they tell for their whole amount, they measure from the ground. There is not only nothing so good (in my judgment) as Hamlet, or Lear, or Othello, or Macbeth, but there is nothing like Hamlet, or Lear, or Othello, or Macbeth. There is nothing, I believe, in the majestic Corneille, equal to the stern pride of Coriolanus, or which gives such an idea of the crumbling in pieces of the Roman grandeur, 'like an unsubstantial pageant faded,' as the Antony and Cleopatra. But to match the best serious comedies, such as Moliere's Misanthrope and his Tartuffe, we must go to Shakspeare's tragic characters, the Timon of Athens or honest Iago, when we shall more than succeed. He put his strength into his tragedies, and played with comedy. He was greatest in what was greatest; and his *forte* was not trifling, according to the opinion here combated, even though he might do that as well as any body else, unless he could do it better than any body else.—I would not be understood to say that there are not scenes or whole characters in Shakspeare equal in wit and drollery to any thing upon record. Falstaff alone is an instance which, if I would, I could not get over. 'He is the leviathan of all the creatures of the author's comic genius, and tumbles about his unwieldy bulk in an ocean of wit and humour.' But in general it will be found (if I am not mistaken) that even in the very best of these, the spirit of humanity and the fancy of the poet greatly prevail over the mere wit and satire, and that we sympathise with his characters oftener than we laugh at them. His ridicule wants the sting of ill-nature. He had hardly such a thing as spleen in his composition. Falstaff himself is so great a joke, rather from his being so huge a mass of enjoyment than of absurdity. His re-appearance in the Merry Wives of Windsor is not 'a consummation devoutly to be wished,' for we do not take pleasure in the repeated triumphs over him.—Mercutio's quips and banter upon his friends shew amazing gaiety, frankness, and volubility of tongue, but we think no more of them when the poet takes the words out of his mouth, and gives the description of Queen Mab. Touchstone, again, is a shrewd biting fellow, a lively mischievous wag : but still what are his gibing sentences and chopped logic to the fine moralising vein of the fantastical Jacques, stretched beneath 'the shade of melancholy boughs ?' Nothing. That is, Shakspeare was a greater poet than wit : his imagination was the leading and master-quality of his mind, which was always ready to soar into its native element : the ludicrous was only secondary and subordinate. In the comedies of gallantry and intrigue, with what freshness and delight we come to the serious and romantic parts ! What a relief they are to the mind, after those of mere ribaldry or mirth ! Those in Twelfth Night, for instance, and Much Ado about Nothing, where Olivia and Hero are concerned, throw even Malvolio and Sir Toby, and Benedick and Beatrice, into the shade. They 'give a very echo to the seat where love is throned.' What he has said of music might be said of his own poetry—

> 'Oh ! it came o'er the ear like the sweet south
> Breathing upon a bank of violets,
> Stealing and giving odour.'

How poor, in general, what a falling-off, these parts seem in mere comic authors ; how ashamed we are of them ; and how fast we hurry the blank verse over, that we may get upon safe ground again, and recover our good opinion of the author ! A striking and lamentable instance of this may be found (by any one who chooses) in the high-flown speeches in Sir Richard Steele's Conscious Lovers. —As good an example as any of this informing and redeeming power in our author's genius might be taken from the comic scenes in both parts of Henry IV. Nothing can go much lower in intellect or morals than many of the characters. Here are knaves and fools in abundance, of the meanest order, and stripped stark-naked. But genius, like charity, 'covers a multitude of sins:' we pity as much as we despise them; in spite of our disgust we like them, because they like themselves, and because we are made to sympathise with them; and the ligament, fine as it is, which links them to humanity, is never broken. Who would quarrel with Wart or Feeble, or Mouldy or Bull-calf, or even with Pistol, Nym, or Bardolph? None but a hypocrite. The severe censurers of the morals of imaginary characters can generally find a hole for their own vices to creep out at; and yet do not perceive how it is that the imperfect and even deformed characters in Shakspeare's plays, as done to the life, by forming a part of our personal consciousness, claim our personal forgiveness, and suspend or evade our moral judgment, by bribing our self-love to side with them. Not to do so, is not morality, but affectation, stupidity, or ill-nature. I have more sympathy with one of Shakspeare's pick-purses, Gadshill or Peto, than I can possibly have with any member of the Society for the Suppression of Vice, and would by no means assist to deliver the one into the hands of the other. Those who cannot be persuaded to draw a veil over the foibles of ideal characters, may be suspected of wearing a mask over their own! Again, in point of understanding and attainments, Shallow sinks low enough; and yet his cousin Silence is a foil to him; he is the shadow of a shade, glimmers on the very verge of downright imbecility, and totters on the brink of nothing. 'He has been merry twice or once ere now,' and is hardly persuaded to break his silence in a song. Shallow has 'heard the chimes at midnight,' and roared out glees and catches at taverns and inns of court, when he was young. So, at least, he tells his cousin Silence, and Falstaff encourages the loftiness of his pretensions. Shallow would be thought a great man among his dependents and followers; Silence is nobody— not even in his own opinion: yet he sits in the orchard, and eats his carraways and pippins among the rest. Shakspeare takes up the meanest subjects with the same tenderness that we do an insect's wing, and would not kill a fly. To give a more particular instance of what I mean, I will take the inimitable and affecting, though most absurd and ludicrous dialogue, between Shallow and Silence, on the death of old Double.

' *Shallow*. Come on, come on, come on ; give me your hand, Sir; give me your hand, Sir ; an early stirrer, by the rood. And how doth my good cousin Silence ?

Silence. Good morrow, good cousin Shallow.

Shallow. And how doth my cousin, your bedfellow ? and your fairest daughter, and mine, my god-daughter Ellen ?

Silence. Alas, a black ouzel, cousin Shallow.

Shallow. By yea and nay, Sir ; I dare say, my cousin William is become a good scholar : he is at Oxford still, is he not ?

Silence. Indeed, Sir, to my cost.

Shallow. He must then to the Inns of Court shortly. I was once of Clement's-Inn ; where, I think, they will talk of mad Shallow yet.

Silence. You were called lusty Shallow then, cousin.

Shallow. I was called any thing, and I would have done any thing indeed, and roundly too. There was I, and little John Doit of Stafford-shire, and black George Bare, and Francis Pickbone, and Will Squele a Cotswold man, you had not four such swinge-bucklers in all the Inns of Court again ; and, I may say to you, we knew where the bona-robas were, and had the best of them all at commandment. Then was Jack Falstaff (now Sir John, a boy,) and page to Thomas Mowbray, Duke of Norfolk.

Silence. This Sir John, cousin, that comes hither anon about soldiers ?

Shallow. The same Sir John, the very same : I saw him break Schoggan's head at the court-gate, when he was a crack, not thus high ; and the very same day did I fight with one Sampson Stockfish, a fruiterer, behind Gray's-Inn. O, the mad days that I have spent ! and to see how many of mine old acquaintance are dead !

Silence. We shall all follow, cousin.

Shallow. Certain, 'tis certain, very sure, very sure : death (as the Psalmist saith) is certain to all, all shall die.—How a good yoke of bullocks at Stamford fair ?

Silence. Truly, cousin, I was not there.

Shallow. Death is certain. Is old Double of your town living yet ?

Silence. Dead, Sir.

Shallow. Dead ! see, see ! he drew a good bow : and dead ? he shot a fine shoot. John of Gaunt loved him well, and betted much money on his head. Dead ! he would have clapped i'th' clout at twelve score ; and carried you a forehand shaft a fourteen and fourteen and a half, that it would have done a man's heart good to see.—How a score of ewes now ?

Silence. Thereafter as they be : a score of good ewes may be worth ten pounds.

Shallow. And is old Double dead ? '

There is not any thing more characteristic than this in all Shakspeare. A finer sermon on mortality was never preached. We see the frail condition of human life, and the weakness of the human understanding in Shallow's reflections on it ; who, while the past is sliding from beneath his feet, still clings to the present. The meanest circumstances are shewn through an atmosphere of abstraction that dignifies them : their very insignificance makes them more affecting, for they instantly put a check on our aspiring thoughts, and remind us that, seen through that dim perspective, the difference between the great and little, the wise and foolish, is not much. 'One touch of nature makes the whole world kin:' and old Double, though his exploits had been greater, could but have had his day. There is a pathetic *naiveté* mixed up with Shallow's common-place reflections and impertinent digressions. The reader laughs (as well he may) in reading the passage, but he lays down the book to think. The wit, however diverting, is social and humane. But this is not the distinguishing characteristic of wit, which is generally provoked by folly, and spends its venom upon vice.

The fault, then, of Shakspeare's comic Muse is, in my opinion, that it is too good-natured and magnanimous. It mounts above its quarry. It is 'apprehensive, quick, forgetive, full of nimble, fiery, and delectable shapes:' but it does not take the highest pleasure in making human nature look as mean, as ridiculous, and contemptible as possible. It is in this respect, chiefly, that it differs from the comedy of a later, and (what is called) a more refined period. Genteel comedy is the comedy of fashionable life, and of artificial character and manners. The most pungent ridicule, is that which is directed to mortify vanity, and to expose affectation; but vanity and affectation, in their most exorbitant and studied excesses, are the ruling principles of society, only in a highly advanced state of civilisation and manners. Man can hardly be said to be a truly contemptible animal, till, from the facilities of general intercourse, and the progress of example and opinion, he becomes the ape of the extravagances of other men. The keenest edge of satire is required to distinguish between the true and false pretensions to taste and elegance; its lash is laid on with the utmost severity, to drive before it the common herd of knaves and fools, not to lacerate and terrify the single stragglers. In a word, it is when folly is epidemic, and vice worn as a mark of distinction, that all the malice of wit and humour is called out and justified to detect the imposture, and prevent the contagion from spreading. The fools in Wycherley and Congreve are of their own, or one another's making, and deserve to be well scourged into common sense and decency: the fools in Shakspeare are of his own or nature's making; and it would be unfair to probe to the quick, or hold up to unqualified derision, the faults which are involuntary and incorrigible, or those which you yourself encourage and exaggerate, from the pleasure you take in witnessing them. Our later comic writers represent a state of manners, in which to be a man of wit and pleasure about town was become the fashion, and in which the swarms of egregious pretenders in both kinds openly kept one another in countenance, and were become a public nuisance. Shakspeare, living in a state of greater rudeness and simplicity, chiefly gave certain characters which were a kind of *grotesques*, or solitary excrescences growing up out of their native soil without affectation, and which he undertook kindly to pamper for the public entertainment. For instance, Sir Andrew Aguecheek is evidently a creature of the poet's own fancy. The author lends occasion to his absurdity to shew itself as much as he pleases, devises antics for him which would not enter into his own head, makes him 'go to church in a galliard, and return home in a coranto;' adds fuel to his folly, or throws cold water on his courage; makes his puny extravagances venture out or slink into corners without asking his leave; encourages them into indiscreet luxuriance, or checks them in the bud, just as it suits him for the jest's sake. The gratification of the fancy, 'and furnishing matter for innocent mirth,' are, therefore, the chief object of this and other characters like it, rather than reforming the moral sense, or indulging our personal spleen. But Tattle and Sparkish, who are fops cast not in the mould of fancy, but of fashion, who have a tribe of forerunners and followers, who catch certain diseases of the mind on purpose to communicate the infection, and are screened in their preposterous eccentricities by their own conceit and by the world's opinion, are entitled to no quarter, and receive none. They think themselves objects of envy and admiration, and on that account are doubly objects of our contempt and ridicule.—We find that the scenes of Shakspeare's comedies are mostly laid in the country, or are transferable there at pleasure. The genteel comedy exists only in towns, and crowds of borrowed characters, who copy others as the satirist copies them, and who are only seen to be despised. 'All beyond Hyde Park is a desart to it:' while there the pastoral and poetic comedy begins to vegetate and flourish, unpruned, idle, and fantastic. It is hard to 'lay waste a country gentleman' in a state of nature, whose humours may have run a little wild or to seed, or to lay violent hands on a young booby 'squire, whose absurdities have not yet arrived at years of discretion: but my Lord Foppington, who is 'the prince of coxcombs,' and 'proud of being at the head of so prevailing a party,' deserves his fate. I am not for going so far as to pronounce Shakspeare's 'manners damnable, because he had not seen the court;' but I think that comedy does not find its richest harvest till individual infirmities have passed into general manners, and it is the example of courts, chiefly, that stamps folly with credit and currency, or glosses over vice with meretricious lustre. I conceive,

36

ON SHAKSPEARE AND BEN JONSON

therefore, that the golden period of our comedy was just after the age of Charles II. when the town first became tainted with the affectation of the manners and conversation of fashionable life, and before the distinction between rusticity and elegance, art and nature, was lost (as it afterwards was) in a general diffusion of knowledge, and the reciprocal advantages of civil intercourse. It is to be remarked, that the union of the three gradations of artificial elegance and courtly accomplishments in one class, of the affectation of them in another, and of absolute rusticity in a third, forms the highest point of perfection of the comedies of this period, as we may see in Vanbrugh's Lord Foppington, Sir Tunbelly Clumsy, and Miss Hoyden; Lady Townly, Count Basset, and John Moody; in Congreve's Millamant, Lady Wishfort, Witwoud, Sir Wilful Witwoud, and the rest.

In another point of view, or with respect to that part of comedy which relates to gallantry and intrigue, the difference between Shakspeare's comic heroines and those of a later period may be referred to the same distinction between natural and artificial life, between the world of fancy and the world of fashion. The refinements of romantic passion arise out of the imagination brooding over 'airy nothing,' or over a favourite object, where 'love's golden shaft hath killed the flock of all affections else:' whereas the refinements of this passion in genteel comedy, or in every-day life, may be said to arise out of repeated observation and experience, diverting and frittering away the first impressions of things by a multiplicity of objects, and producing, not enthusiasm, but fastidiousness or giddy dissipation. For the one a comparatively rude age and strong feelings are best fitted; for 'there the mind must minister to itself:' to the other, the progress of society and a knowledge of the world are essential; for here the effect does not depend on leaving the mind concentred in itself, but on the wear and tear of the heart, amidst the complex and rapid movements of the artificial machinery of society, and on the arbitrary subjection of the natural course of the affections to every the slightest fluctuation of fashion, caprice, or opinion. Thus Olivia, in Twelfth Night, has but one admirer of equal rank with herself, and but one love, to whom she innocently plights her hand and heart; or if she had a thousand lovers, she would be the sole object of their adoration and burning vows, without a rival. The heroine of romance and poetry sits secluded in the bowers of fancy, sole queen and arbitress of all hearts; and as the character is one of imagination, 'of solitude and melancholy musing born,' so it may be best drawn from the imagination. Millamant, in the Way of the World, on the contrary, who is the fine lady or heroine of comedy, has so many lovers, that she surfeits on admiration, till it becomes indifferent to her; so many rivals, that she is forced to put on a thousand airs of languid affectation to mortify and vex them more; so many offers, that she at last gives her hand to the man of her heart, rather to escape the persecution of their addresses, and out of levity and disdain, than from any serious choice of her own. This is a comic character; its essence consists in making light of things from familiarity and use, and as it is formed by habit and outward circumstances, so it requires actual observation, and an acquaintance with the modes of artificial life, to describe it with the utmost possible grace and precision. Congreve, who had every other opportunity, was but a young man when he wrote this character; and that makes the miracle the greater.

I do not, in short, consider comedy as exactly an affair of the heart or the imagination; and it is for this reason only that I think Shakspeare's comedies deficient. I do not, however, wish to give a preference of any comedies over his; but I do perceive a difference between his comedies and some others that are, notwithstanding, excellent in their way, and I have endeavoured to point out in what this difference consists, as well as I could. Finally, I will not say that he had not as great a natural genius for comedy as any one; but I may venture to say, that he had not the same artificial models and regulated mass of fashionable absurdity or elegance to work upon.

The superiority of Shakspeare's natural genius for comedy cannot be better shewn than by a comparison between his comic characters and those of Ben Jonson. The matter is the same: but how different is the manner! The one gives fair-play to nature and his own genius, while the other trusts almost entirely to imitation and custom. Shakspeare takes his groundwork in individual character and the manners of his age, and raises from them a fantastical and delightful superstructure of his own: the other takes the same ground-work in matter-of-fact, but hardly ever rises above it; and the more he strives, is but the more enveloped 'in the crust of formality' and the crude circumstantials of his subject. His genius (not to profane an old and still venerable name, but merely to make myself under-stood) resembles the grub more than the butterfly, plods and grovels on, wants wings to wanton in the idle summer's air, and catch the golden light of poetry. Ben Jonson is a great borrower from the works of others, and a plagiarist even from nature; so little freedom is there in his imitations of her, and he appears to receive her bounty like an alms. His works read like translations, from a certain cramp manner, and want of adaptation. Shakspeare, even when he takes whole passages from books, does it with a spirit, felicity, and mastery over his subject, that instantly makes them his own; and shews more

38

independence of mind and original thinking in what he plunders without scruple, than Ben Jonson often did in his most studied passages, forced from the sweat and labour of his brain.   His style is as dry, as literal, and meagre, as Shakspeare's is exuberant, liberal, and unrestrained.   The one labours hard, lashes himself up, and produces little pleasure with all his fidelity and tenaciousness of purpose : the other, without putting himself to any trouble, or thinking about his success, performs wonders,—

> ' Does mad and fantastic execution,
> Engaging and redeeming of himself,
> With such a careless force and forceless[1] care,
> As if that luck, in very spite of cunning,
> Bade him win all.'

There are people who cannot taste olives—and I cannot much relish Ben Jonson, though I have taken some pains to do it, and went to the task with every sort of good will.   I do not deny his power or his merit ; far from it : but it is to me of a repulsive and unamiable kind.   He was a great man in himself, but one cannot readily sympathise with him.   His works, as the characteristic productions of an individual mind, or as records of the manners of a particular age, cannot be valued too highly ; but they have little charm for the mere general reader.   Schlegel observes, that whereas Shakspeare gives the springs of human nature, which are always the same, or sufficiently so to be interesting and intelligible ; Jonson chiefly gives the *humours* of men, as connected with certain arbitrary or conventional modes of dress, action, and expression, which are intelligible only while they last, and not very interesting at any time.   Shakspeare's characters are men ; Ben Jonson's are more like machines, governed by mere routine, or by the convenience of the poet, whose property they are. In reading the one, we are let into the minds of his characters, we see the play of their thoughts, how their humours flow and work : the author takes a range over nature, and has an eye to every object or occasion that presents itself to set off and heighten the ludicrous character he is describing.   His humour (so to speak) bubbles, sparkles, and finds its way in all directions, like a natural spring.   In Ben Jonson it is, as it were, confined in a leaden cistern, where it stagnates and corrupts ; or directed only through certain artificial pipes and conduits, to answer a given purpose.   The comedy of this author is far from being ' lively, audible, and full of vent : ' it is for the most part obtuse, obscure, forced, and tedious.   He wears out a jest to the last shred and coarsest grain.   His imagination fastens

[1] Unforced.

instinctively on some one mark or sign by which he designates the individual, and never lets it go, for fear of not meeting with any other means to express himself by.   A cant phrase, an odd gesture, an old-fashioned regimental uniform, a wooden leg, a tobacco-box, or a hacked sword, are the standing topics by which he embodies his characters to the imagination.   They are cut and dried comedy; the letter, not the spirit of wit and humour.   Each of his characters has a particular cue, a professional badge which he wears and is known by, and by nothing else.   Thus there is no end of Captain Otter, his Bull, his Bear, and his Horse, which are no joke at first, and do not become so by being repeated twenty times.   It is a mere matter of fact, that some landlord of his acquaintance called his drinking cups by these ridiculous names; but why need we be told so more than once, or indeed at all?   There is almost a total want of variety, fancy, relief, and of those delightful transitions which abound, for instance, in Shakspeare's tragi-comedy.   In Ben Jonson, we find ourselves generally in low company, and we see no hope of getting out of it.   He is like a person who fastens upon a disagreeable subject, and cannot be persuaded to leave it.   His comedy, in a word, has not what Shakspeare somewhere calls 'bless'd conditions.'   It is cross-grained, mean, and mechanical.   It is handicraft wit.   Squalid poverty, sheer ignorance, bare-faced impudence, or idiot imbecility, are his dramatic common-places—things that provoke pity or disgust, instead of laughter.   His portraits are caricatures by dint of their very likeness, being extravagant tautologies of themselves; as his plots are improbable by an excess of consistency; for he goes thorough-stitch with whatever he takes in hand, makes one contrivance answer all purposes, and every obstacle give way to a predetermined theory. For instance, nothing can be more incredible than the mercenary conduct of Corvino, in delivering up his wife to the palsied embraces of Volpone; and yet the poet does not seem in the least to boggle at the incongruity of it: but the more it is in keeping with the absurdity of the rest of the fable, and the more it advances it to an incredible catastrophe, the more he seems to dwell upon it with complacency and a sort of wilful exaggeration, as if it were a logical discovery or corollary from well-known premises.   He would no more be baffled in the working out a plot, than some people will be baffled in an argument.   'If to be wise were to be obstinate,' our author might have laid signal claim to this title.   Old Ben was of a scholastic turn, and had dealt a little in the occult sciences and controversial divinity.   He was a man of strong crabbed sense, retentive memory, acute observation, great fidelity of description and keeping in character, a power of working out an idea so as to make it painfully true and

40

oppressive, and with great honesty and manliness of feeling, as well as directness of understanding : but with all this, he wanted, to my thinking, that genial spirit of enjoyment and finer fancy, which constitute the essence of poetry and of wit. The sense of reality exercised a despotic sway over his mind, and equally weighed down and clogged his perception of the beautiful or the ridiculous. He had a keen sense of what was true and false, but not of the difference between the agreeable and disagreeable ; or if he had, it was by his understanding rather than his imagination, by rule and method, not by sympathy, or intuitive perception of 'the gayest, happiest attitude of things.' There was nothing spontaneous, no impulse or ease about his genius : it was all forced, up-hill work, making a toil of a pleasure. And hence his overweening admiration of his own works, from the effort they had cost him, and the apprehension that they were not proportionably admired by others, who knew nothing of the pangs and throes of his Muse in child-bearing. In his satirical descriptions he seldom stops short of the lowest and most offensive point of meanness ; and in his serious poetry he seems to repose with complacency only on the pedantic and far-fetched, the *ultima Thule* of his knowledge. He has a conscience of letting nothing escape the reader that he knows. *Aliquando sufflaminandus erat,* is as true of him as it was of Shakspeare, but in a quite different sense. He is doggedly bent upon fatiguing you with a favourite idea ; whereas, Shakspeare overpowers and distracts attention by the throng and indiscriminate variety of his. His Sad Shepherd is a beautiful fragment. It was a favourite with the late Mr. Horne Tooke : indeed it is no wonder, for there was a sort of sympathy between the two men. Ben was like the modern wit and philosopher, a grammarian and a hard-headed thinker.—There is an amusing account of Ben Jonson's private manners in Howel's Letters, which is not generally known, and which I shall here extract.

       '*From James Howel, Esq. to Sir Thomas Hawk, Kt.*

'Sir,   *Westminster, 5th April,* 1636.

    'I was invited yesternight to a solemn supper by B. J. where were deeply remembered ; there was good company, excellent cheer, choice wines, and jovial welcome : one thing intervened, which almost spoiled the relish of the rest, that B. began to engross all the discourse, to vapour extremely of himself, and, by vilifying others, to magnify his own Muse. T. Ca. (Tom Carew) buzzed me in the ear, that though Ben had barrelled up a great deal of knowledge, yet it seems he had not read the ethics, which, among other precepts of morality, forbid self-commendation, declaring it to be an ill-favoured solecism in good manners. It made me think upon the lady (not very young) who having a good while given her

4 1

LECTURES ON THE COMIC WRITERS

guests neat entertainment, a capon being brought upon the table, instead of a spoon, she took a mouthful of claret, and spouted into the hollow bird: such an accident happened in this entertainment: you know—*Propria laus sordet in ore*: be a man's breath ever so sweet, yet it makes one's praise stink, if he makes his own mouth the conduit-pipe of it. But for my part I am content to dispense with the Roman infirmity of Ben, now that time hath snowed upon his pericranium. You know Ovid and (your) Horace were subject to this humour, the first bursting out into—

> *Jamque opus exegi, quod nec Jovis ira nec ignis,* &c.

the other into—

> *Exegi monumentum ære perennius,* &c.

As also Cicero, while he forced himself into this hexameter: *O fortunatam natam, me consule Romam!* There is another reason that excuseth B. which is, that if one be allowed to love the natural issue of his body, why not that of the brain, which is of a spiritual and more noble extraction?'

The concurring testimony of all his contemporaries agrees with his own candid avowal, as to Ben Jonson's personal character. He begins, for instance, an epistle to Drayton in these words—

> 'Michael, by some 'tis doubted if I be
> A friend at all; or if a friend, to thee.'

Of Shakspeare's comedies I have already given a detailed account, which is before the public, and which I shall not repeat of course: but I shall give a cursory sketch of the principal of Ben Jonson's.— The Silent Woman is built upon the supposition of an old citizen disliking noise, who takes to wife Epicene (a supposed young lady) for the reputation of her silence, and with a view to disinherit his nephew, who has laughed at his infirmity; when the ceremony is no sooner over than the bride turns out a very shrew, his house becomes a very Babel of noises, and he offers his nephew his own terms to unloose the matrimonial knot, which is done by proving that Epicene is no woman. There is some humour in the leading character, but too much is made out of it, not in the way of Moliere's exaggerations, which, though extravagant, are fantastical and ludicrous, but of serious, plodding, minute prolixity. The first meeting between Morose and Epicene is well managed, and does not 'o'erstep the modesty of nature,' from the very restraint imposed by the situation of the parties—by the affected taciturnity of the one, and the other's singular dislike of noise. The whole story, from the beginning to the end, is a gratuitous assumption, and the height of improbability. The author, in sustaining the weight of his plot, seems like a balance-master who supports a number of people, piled one upon another, on his hands, his knees, his shoulders, but with a

42

great effort on his own part, and with a painful effect to the beholders. The scene between Sir Amorous La Foole and Sir John Daw, in which they are frightened by a feigned report of each other's courage, into a submission to all sorts of indignities, which they construe into flattering civilities, is the same device as that in Twelfth Night between Sir Andrew Aguecheek and Viola, carried to a paradoxical and revolting excess. Ben Jonson had no idea of decorum in his dramatic fictions, which Milton says is the principal thing, but went on caricaturing himself and others till he could go no farther in extravagance, and sink no lower in meanness. The titles of his *dramatis personæ*, such as Sir Amorous La Foole, Truewit, Sir John Daw, Sir Politic Would-be, &c. &c. which are significant and knowing, shew his determination to overdo every thing by thus letting you into their characters beforehand, and afterwards proving their pretensions by their names. Thus Peregrine, in Volpone, says, 'Your name, Sir? *Politick.* My name is Politick Would-be.' To which Peregrine replies, 'Oh, that speaks him.' How it should, if it was his real name, and not a nick-name given him on purpose by the author, is hard to conceive. This play was Dryden's favourite. It is indeed full of sharp, biting sentences against the women, of which he was fond. The following may serve as a specimen. Truewit says, 'Did I not tell thee, Dauphine? Why, all their actions are governed by crude opinion, without reason or cause: they know not why they do any thing; but, as they are informed, believe, judge, praise, condemn, love, hate, and in emulation one of another, do all these things alike. Only they have a natural inclination sways 'em generally to the worst, when they are left to themselves.' This is a cynical sentence; and we may say of the rest of his opinions, that 'even though we should hold them to be true, yet it is slander to have them so set down.' The women in this play indeed justify the author's severity; they are altogether abominable. They have an utter want of principle and decency, and are equally without a sense of pleasure, taste, or elegance. Madame Haughty, Madame Centaur, and Madame Mavis, form the College, as it is here pedantically called. They are a sort of candidates for being upon the town, but cannot find seducers, and a sort of blue-stockings, before the invention of letters. Mistress Epicene, the silent gentlewoman, turns out not to be a woman at all; which is not a very pleasant *denouement* of the plot, and is itself an incident apparently taken from the blundering blindman's-buff conclusion of the Merry Wives of Windsor. What Shakspeare might introduce by an accident, and as a mere passing jest, Ben Jonson would set about building a whole play upon. The directions for making love given by Truewit, the author's favourite, discover great knowledge and shrewdness of observation, mixed with the acuteness of malice, and approach to the best style of comic dialogue. But I must refer to the play itself for them.

The Fox, or Volpone, is his best play. It is prolix and improbable, but intense and powerful. It is written *con amore*. It is made up of cheats and dupes, and the author is at home among them. He shews his hatred of the one and contempt for the other, and makes them set one another off to great advantage. There are several striking dramatic contrasts in this play, where the Fox lies *perdue* to watch his prey, where Mosca is the dextrous go-between outwitting his gulls, his employer, and himself, and where each of the gaping legacy-hunters, the lawyer, the merchant, and the miser, eagerly occupied with the ridiculousness of the other's pretensions, is blind only to the absurdity of his own : but the whole is worked up too mechanically, and our credulity overstretched at last revolts into scepticism, and our attention overtasked flags into drowsiness. This play seems formed on the model of Plautus, in unity of plot and interest ; and old Ben, in emulating his classic model, appears to have done his best. There is the same caustic unsparing severity in it as in his other works. His patience is tried to the utmost. His words drop gall.

> ' Hood an ass with reverend purple,
>   So you can hide his too ambitious ears,
>   And he shall pass for a cathedral doctor.'

The scene between Volpone, Mosca, Voltore, Corvino, and Corbaccio, at the outset, will shew the dramatic power in the conduct of this play, and will be my justification in what I have said of the literal tenaciousness (to a degree that is repulsive) of the author's imaginary descriptions.

Every Man in his Humour, is a play well-known to the public. This play acts better than it reads. The pathos in the principal character, Kitely, is ' as dry as the remainder biscuit after a voyage.' There is, however, a certain good sense, discrimination, or logic of passion in the part, which affords excellent hints for an able actor, and which, if properly pointed, gives it considerable force on the stage. Bobadil is the only actually striking character in the play, and the real hero of the piece. His well-known proposal for the pacification of Europe, by killing some twenty of them, each his man a day, is as good as any other that has been suggested up to the present moment. His extravagant affectation, his blustering and cowardice, are an entertaining medley ; and his final defeat and

44

ON SHAKSPEARE AND BEN JONSON

exposure, though exceedingly humorous, are the most affecting part of the story. Brain-worm is a particularly dry and abstruse character. We neither know his business nor his motives : his plots are as intricate as they are useless, and as the ignorance of those he imposes upon is wonderful. This is the impression in reading it. Yet from the bustle and activity of this character on the stage, the changes of dress, the variety of affected tones and gipsy jargon, and the limping affected gestures, it is a very amusing theatrical exhibition. The rest, Master Matthew, Master Stephen, Cob and Cob's wife, were living in the sixteenth century. That is all we all know of them. But from the very oddity of their appearance and behaviour, they have a very droll and even picturesque effect when acted. It seems a revival of the dead. We believe in their existence when we see them. As an example of the power of the stage in giving reality and interest to what otherwise would be without it, I might mention the scene in which Brain-worm praises Master Stephen's leg. The folly here is insipid from its being seemingly carried to an excess, till we see it ; and then we laugh the more at it, the more incredible we thought it before.

Bartholomew Fair is chiefly remarkable for the exhibition of odd humours and tumbler's tricks, and is on that account amusing to read once.—The Alchymist is the most famous of this author's comedies, though I think it does not deserve its reputation. It contains all that is quaint, dreary, obsolete, and hopeless in this once-famed art, but not the golden dreams and splendid disappointments. We have the mere circumstantials of the sublime science, pots and kettles, aprons and bellows, crucibles and diagrams, all the refuse and rubbish, not the essence, the true *elixir vitæ*. There is, however, one glorious scene between Surly and Sir Epicure Mammon, which is the finest example I know of dramatic sophistry, or of an attempt to prove the existence of a thing by an imposing description of its effects ; but compared with this, the rest of the play is a *caput mortuum*. The scene I allude to is the following :

' *Mammon.* Come on, Sir. Now, you set your foot on shore,
In *Novo Orbe*; here's the rich Peru :
And there within, Sir, are the golden mines,
Great Solomon's Ophir ! He was sailing to 't
Three years, but we have reached it in ten months.
This is the day wherein, to all my friends,
I will pronounce the happy word, BE RICH;
This day you shall be Spectatissimi.
You shall no more deal with the hollow dye,
Or the frail card. * * * * * * * *

45

You shall start up young viceroys,
And have your punks and punketees, my Surly,
And unto thee, I speak it first, BE RICH.
Where is my Subtle, there ?   Within, ho !
  Face. [*within*] Sir, he 'll come to you, by and by.
  Mam. That is his Firedrake,
His Lungs, his Zephyrus, he that puffs his coals,
Till he firk nature up in her own centre.
You are not faithful, Sir.   This night I 'll change
All that is metal in my house to gold :
And early in the morning, will I send
To all the plumbers and the pewterers
And buy their tin and lead up ; and to Lothbury,
For all the copper.
  Surly.   What, and turn that too ?
  Mam. Yes, and I 'll purchase Devonshire and Cornwall,
And make them perfect Indies !   You admire now ?
  Surly. No, faith.
  Mam. But when you see th' effects of the great medicine,
Of which one part projected on a hundred
Of Mercury, or Venus, or the Moon,
Shall turn it to as many of the Sun ;
Nay, to a thousand, so *ad infinitum* ;
You will believe me.
  Surly. Yes, when I see't, I will—
  Mam. Ha ! why ?
Do you think I fable with you ?   I assure you,
He that has once the flower of the Sun,
The perfect ruby, which we call Elixir,
Not only can do that, but, by its virtue,
Can confer honour, love, respect, long life ;
Give safety, valour, yea, and victory,
To whom he will.   In eight and twenty days,
I 'll make an old man of fourscore, a child.
  Surly. No doubt ; he 's that already.
  Mam. Nay, I mean,
Restore his years, renew him, like an eagle,
To the fifth age ; make him get sons and daughters,
Young giants ; as our philosophers have done,
The ancient patriarchs, afore the flood,
But taking, once a week, on a knife's point,
The quantity of a grain of mustard of it ;
Become stout Marses, and beget young Cupids.
*   *   *   *   *   *   *   *
You are incredulous.
  Surly. Faith, I have a humour,
I would not willingly be gull'd.   Your stone
Cannot transmute me.
  Mam. Pertinax Surly,

46

ON SHAKSPEARE AND BEN JONSON

Will you believe antiquity ? records ?
I 'll shew you a book where Moses and his sister,
And Solomon have written of the art;
Ay, and a treatise penn'd by Adam—
    Surly. How !
    Mam. Of the philosopher's stone, and in High Dutch.
    Surly. Did Adam write, Sir, in High Dutch ?
    Mam. He did;
Which proves it was the primitive tongue.
*   *   *   *   *   *   *   *
                                [Enter Face, as a servant.
                How now !
Do we succeed ?   Is our day come, and holds it ?
    Face. The evening will set red upon you, Sir:
You have colour for it, crimson; the red ferment
Has done his office: three hours hence prepare you
To see projection.
    Mam. Pertinax, my Surly,
Again I say to thee, aloud, Be rich.
This day thou shalt have ingots; and to-morrow
Give lords the affront.   *   *   *   *   Where 's thy master ?
    Face. At his prayers, Sir, he ;
Good man, he 's doing his devotions
For the success.
    Mam. Lungs, I will set a period
To all thy labours ; thou shalt be the master
Of my seraglio . . .
For I do mean
To have a list of wives and concubines
Equal with Solomon :   *   *   *
I will have all my beds blown up, not stuft:
Down is too hard ; and then, mine oval room
Fill'd with such pictures as Tiberius took
From Elephantis, and dull Aretine
But coldly imitated.   Then, my glasses
Cut in more subtle angles, to disperse
And multiply the figures, as I walk.   *   *   *   My mists
I 'll have of perfume, vapoured about the room
To lose ourselves in; and my baths, like pits
To fall into : from whence we will come forth,
And roll us dry in gossamer and roses.
Is it arriv'd at ruby ?   Where I spy
A wealthy citizen, or a rich lawyer,
Have a sublimed pure wife, unto that fellow
I 'll send a thousand pound to be my cuckold.
    Face. And I shall carry it ?
    Mam. No.   I 'll have no bawds.
But fathers and mothers.   They will do it best,
Best of all others.   And my flatterers

47

Shall be the pure and gravest of divines
That I can get for money.
We will be brave, Puffe, now we have the medicine.
My meat shall all come in, in Indian shells,
Dishes of agat set in gold, and studded
With emeralds, sapphires, hyacinths, and rubies.
The tongues of carps, dormice, and camel's heels
Boil'd in the spirit of Sol, and dissolv'd pearl,
Apicius' diet, 'gainst the epilepsy;
And I will eat these broths with spoons of amber,
Headed with diamond and carbuncle.
My footboys shall eat pheasants, calver'd salmons,
Knots, godwits, lampreys; I myself will have
The beards of barbels serv'd instead of salads;
Oil'd mushrooms; and the swelling unctuous paps
Of a fat pregnant sow, newly cut off,
Drest with an exquisite and poignant sauce;
For which I'll say unto my cook, *There's gold,*
Go forth, and be a knight.
    Face. Sir, I'll go look
A little, how it heightens.
    Mam. Do. My shirts
I'll have of taffeta-sarsnet, soft and light,
As cobwebs; and for all my other raiment,
It shall be such as might provoke the Persian,
Were he to teach the world riot anew.
My gloves of fishes and birds' skins, perfum'd
With gums of Paradise and eastern air.
    Surly. And do you think to have the stone with this?
    Mam. No, I do think t' have all this with the stone.
    Surly. Why, I have heard, he must be *homo frugi,*
A pious, holy, and religious man,
One free from mortal sin, a very virgin.
    Mam. That makes it, Sir, he is so; but I buy it.
My venture brings it me. He, honest wretch,
A notable, superstitious, good soul,
Has worn his knees bare, and his slippers bald,
With prayer and fasting for it, and, Sir, let him
Do it alone, for me, still; here he comes;
Not a profane word afore him: 'tis poison.'

                                    Act II. *scene* I.

I have only to add a few words on Beaumont and Fletcher. Rule a Wife and Have a Wife, the Chances, and the Wild Goose Chase, the original of the Inconstant, are superior in style and execution to any thing of Ben Jonson's. They are, indeed, some of the best comedies on the stage; and one proof that they are so, is, that they still hold possession of it. They shew the utmost alacrity of invention in contriving ludicrous distresses, and the utmost spirit in bearing up against, or impatience and irritation under them. Don John, in the Chances, is the heroic in comedy. Leon, in Rule a Wife and Have a Wife, is a fine exhibition of the born gentleman and natural fool : the Copper Captain is sterling to this hour : his mistress, Estifania, only died the other day with Mrs. Jordan : and the two grotesque females, in the same play, act better than the Witches in Macbeth.

LECTURE III

ON COWLEY, BUTLER, SUCKLING, ETHEREGE, &c.

The metaphysical poets or wits of the age of James and Charles I. whose style was adopted and carried to a more dazzling and fantastic excess by Cowley in the following reign, after which it declined, and gave place almost entirely to the poetry of observation and reasoning, are thus happily characterised by Dr. Johnson.

'The metaphysical poets were men of learning, and to show their learning was their whole endeavour : but unluckily resolving to show it in rhyme, instead of writing poetry, they only wrote verses, and very often such verses as stood the trial of the finger better than of the ear ; for the modulation was so imperfect, that they were only found to be verses by counting the syllables.

'If the father of criticism has rightly denominated poetry $\tau \acute{\epsilon} \chi \nu \eta$ $\mu \iota \mu \eta \tau \iota \kappa \acute{\eta}$, an imitative art, these writers will, without great wrong, lose their right to the name of poets, for they cannot be said to have imitated any thing ; they neither copied nature nor life ; neither painted the forms of matter, nor represented the operations of intellect.'

The whole of the account is well worth reading : it was a subject for which Dr. Johnson's powers both of thought and expression were better fitted than any other man's. If he had had the same capacity for following the flights of a truly poetic imagination, or for feeling the finer touches of nature, that he had felicity and force in detecting and exposing the aberrations from the broad and beaten path of propriety and common sense, he would have amply deserved the reputation he has acquired as a philosophical critic.

The writers here referred to (such as Donne, Davies, Crashaw, and others) not merely mistook learning for poetry—they thought any thing was poetry that differed from ordinary prose and the natural impression of things, by being intricate, far fetched, and improbable. Their style was not so properly learned as metaphysical ;

that is to say, whenever, by any violence done to their ideas, they could make out an abstract likeness or possible ground of comparison, they forced the image, whether learned or vulgar, into the service of the Muses. Any thing would do to ' hitch into a rhyme,' no matter whether striking or agreeable, or not, so that it would puzzle the reader to discover the meaning, and if there was the most remote circumstance, however trifling or vague, for the pretended comparison to hinge upon. They brought ideas together not the most, but the least like ; and of which the collision produced not light, but obscurity—served not to strengthen, but to confound. Their mystical verses read like riddles or an allegory. They neither belong to the class of lively or severe poetry. They have not the force of the one, nor the gaiety of the other ; but are an ill-assorted, unprofitable union of the two together, applying to serious subjects that quaint and partial style of allusion which fits only what is light and ludicrous, and building the most laboured conclusions on the most fantastical and slender premises. The object of the poetry of imagination is to raise or adorn one idea by another more striking or more beautiful : the object of these writers was to match any one idea with any other idea, *for better for worse,* as we say, and whether any thing was gained by the change of condition or not. The object of the poetry of the passions again is to illustrate any strong feeling, by shewing the same feeling as connected with objects or circumstances more palpable and touching ; but here the object was to strain and distort the immediate feeling into some barely possible consequence or recondite analogy, in which it required the utmost stretch of misapplied ingenuity to trace the smallest connection with the original impression. In short, the poetry of this period was strictly the poetry not of ideas, but of *definitions* : it proceeded in mode and figure, by *genus* and specific difference ; and was the logic of the schools, or an oblique and forced construction of dry, literal matter-of-fact, decked out in a robe of glittering conceits, and clogged with the halting shackles of verse. The imagination of the writers, instead of being conversant with the face of nature, or the secrets of the heart, was lost in the labyrinths of intellectual abstraction, or entangled in the technical quibbles and impertinent intricacies of language. The complaint so often made, and here repeated, is not of the want of power in these men, but of the waste of it ; not of the absence of genius, but the abuse of it. They had (many of them) great talents committed to their trust, richness of thought, and depth of feeling ; but they chose to hide them (as much as they possibly could) under a false shew of learning and unmeaning subtlety. From the style which they had systematically adopted, they thought nothing done till they had perverted simplicity into affectation, and

spoiled nature by art. They seemed to think there was an irreconcileable opposition between genius, as well as grace, and nature;
tried to do without, or else constantly to thwart her; left nothing to
her outward 'impress,' or spontaneous impulses, but made a point of
twisting and torturing almost every subject they took in hand, till
they had fitted it to the mould of their self-opinion and the previous
fabrications of their own fancy, like those who pen acrostics in the
shape of pyramids, and cut out trees into the shape of peacocks.
Their chief aim is to make you wonder at the writer, not to interest
you in the subject; and by an incessant craving after admiration, they
have lost what they might have gained with less extravagance and
affectation. So Cowper, who was of a quite opposite school, speaks
feelingly of the misapplication of Cowley's poetical genius.

> 'And though reclaim'd by modern lights
> From an erroneous taste,
> I cannot but lament thy splendid wit
> Entangled in the cobwebs of the schools.'

Donne, who was considerably before Cowley, is without his fancy,
but was more recondite in his logic, and rigid in his descriptions.
He is hence led, particularly in his satires, to tell disagreeable
truths in as disagreeable a way as possible, or to convey a pleasing
and affecting thought (of which there are many to be found in his
other writings) by the harshest means, and with the most painful
effort. His Muse suffers continual pangs and throes. His thoughts
are delivered by the Cæsarean operation. The sentiments, profound
and tender as they often are, are stifled in the expression; and
'heaved pantingly forth,' are 'buried quick again' under the ruins
and rubbish of analytical distinctions. It is like poetry waking from
a trance: with an eye bent idly on the outward world, and half-
forgotten feelings crowding about the heart; with vivid impressions,
dim notions, and disjointed words. The following may serve as
instances of beautiful or impassioned reflections losing themselves in
obscure and difficult applications. He has some lines to a Blossom,
which begin thus:

> 'Little think'st thou, poor flow'r,
> Whom I have watched six or seven days,
> And seen thy birth, and seen what every hour
> Gave to thy growth, thee to this height to raise,
> And now dost laugh and triumph on this bough,
> Little think'st thou
> That it will freeze anon, and that I shall
> To-morrow find thee fall'n, or not at all.'

LECTURES ON THE COMIC WRITERS

This simple and delicate description is only introduced as a foundation for an elaborate metaphysical conceit as a parallel to it, in the
next stanza.

> ' Little think'st thou (poor heart
> That labour'st yet to nestle thee,
> And think'st by hovering here to get a part
> In a forbidden or forbidding tree,
> And hop'st her stiffness by long siege to bow :)
>   Little think'st thou,
> That thou to-morrow, ere the sun doth wake,
> Must with this sun and me a journey take.'

This is but a lame and impotent conclusion from so delightful a
beginning.—He thus notices the circumstance of his wearing his
late wife's hair about his arm, in a little poem which is called the
Funeral :

> ' Whoever comes to shroud me, do not harm
>   Nor question much
> That subtle wreath of hair, about mine arm ;
> The mystery, the sign you must not touch.'

The scholastic reason he gives quite dissolves the charm of tender
and touching grace in the sentiment itself—

> ' For 'tis my outward soul,
> Viceroy to that, which unto heaven being gone,
>   Will leave this to control,
> And keep these limbs, her provinces, from dissolution.'

Again, the following lines, the title of which is Love's Deity, are
highly characteristic of this author's manner, in which the thoughts
are inlaid in a costly but imperfect mosaic-work.

> ' *I long to talk with some old lover's ghost,*
> *Who died before the God of Love was born* :
> I cannot think that he, who then lov'd most,
> Sunk so low, as to love one which did scorn.
> But since this God produc'd a destiny,
> And that vice-nature, custom, lets it be ;
> I must love her that loves not me.'

The stanza in the Epithalamion on a Count Palatine of the Rhine,
has been often quoted against him, and is an almost irresistible
illustration of the extravagances to which this kind of writing,
which turns upon a pivot of words and possible allusions, is liable.

52

ON COWLEY, BUTLER, SUCKLING, ETC.

Speaking of the bride and bridegroom he says, by way of serious compliment—

> ' Here lies a she-Sun, and a he-Moon there,
> She gives the best light to his sphere;
> Or each is both and all, and so
> They unto one another nothing owe.'

His love-verses and epistles to his friends give the most favourable idea of Donne. His satires are too clerical. He shews, if I may so speak, too much disgust, and, at the same time, too much contempt for vice. His dogmatical invectives hardly redeem the nauseousness of his descriptions, and compromise the imagination of his readers more than they assist their reason. The satirist does not write with the same authority as the divine, and should use his poetical privileges more sparingly. ' To the pure all things are pure,' is a maxim which a man like Dr. Donne may be justified in applying to himself; but he might have recollected that it could not be construed to extend to the generality of his readers, *without benefit of clergy*.

Bishop Hall's Satires are coarse railing in verse, and hardly that. Pope has, however, contrived to avail himself of them in some of his imitations.

Sir John Davies is the author of a poem on the Soul, and of one on Dancing. In both he shews great ingenuity, and sometimes terseness and vigour. In the last of these two poems his fancy *pirouettes* in a very lively and agreeable manner, but something too much in the style of a French opera-dancer, with sharp angular turns, and repeated deviations from the faultless line of simplicity and nature.

Crashaw was a writer of the same ambitious stamp, whose imagination was rendered still more inflammable by the fervors of fanaticism, and who having been converted from Protestantism to Popery (a weakness to which the ' seething brains ' of the poets of this period were prone) by some visionary appearance of the Virgin Mary, poured out his devout raptures and zealous enthusiasm in a torrent of poetical hyperboles. The celebrated Latin Epigram on the miracle of our Saviour, ' The water blushed into wine,' is in his usual *hectic* manner. His translation of the contest between the Musician and the Nightingale is the best specimen of his powers.

Davenant's Gondibert is a tissue of stanzas, all aiming to be wise and witty, each containing something in itself, and the whole together amounting to nothing. The thoughts separately require so much attention to understand them, and arise so little out of the narrative, that they with difficulty sink into the mind, and have no common feeling of interest to recal or link them together afterwards. The general style may be judged of by these two memorable lines in the description of the skeleton-chamber.

> ' Yet on that wall hangs he too, who so thought,
> And she dried by him whom that he obeyed.'

Mr. Hobbes, in a prefatory discourse, has thrown away a good deal of powerful logic and criticism in recommendation of the plan of his friend's poem. Davenant, who was poet-laureate to Charles ii. wrote several masques and plays which were well received in his time, but have not come down with equal applause to us.

Marvel (on whom I have already bestowed such praise as I could, for elegance and tenderness in his descriptive poems) in his satires and witty pieces was addicted to the affected and involved style here reprobated, as in his Flecknoe (the origin of Dryden's Macflecknoe) and in his satire on the Dutch. As an instance of this forced, far-fetched method of treating his subject, he says, in ridicule of the Hollanders, that when their dykes overflowed, the fish used to come to table with them,

> ' And sat not as a meat, but as a guest.'

There is a poem of Marvel's on the death of King Charles i. which I have not seen, but which I have heard praised by one whose praise is never high but of the highest things, for the beauty and pathos, as well as generous frankness of the sentiments, coming, as they did, from a determined and incorruptible political foe.

Shadwell was a successful and voluminous dramatic writer of much the same period. His Libertine (taken from the celebrated Spanish story) is full of spirit; but it is the spirit of licentiousness and impiety. At no time do there appear to have been such extreme speculations afloat on the subject of religion and morality, as there were shortly after the Reformation, and afterwards under the Stuarts, the differences being widened by political irritation; and the Puritans often over-acting one extreme out of grimace and hypocrisy, as the king's party did the other out of *bravado*.

Carew is excluded from his pretensions to the laureateship in Suckling's Sessions of the Poets, on account of his slowness. His verses are delicate and pleasing, with a certain feebleness, but with very little tincture of the affectation of this period. His masque (called *Cœlum Britannicum*) in celebration of a marriage at court, has not much wit nor fancy, but the accompanying prose directions and commentary on the mythological story, are written with

54

wonderful facility and elegance, in a style of familiar dramatic dialogue approaching nearer the writers of Queen Anne's reign than those of Queen Elizabeth's.

Milton's name is included by Dr. Johnson in the list of metaphysical poets on no better authority than his lines on Hobson the Cambridge Carrier, which he acknowledges were the only ones Milton wrote on this model. Indeed, he is the great contrast to that style of poetry, being remarkable for breadth and massiness, or what Dr. Johnson calls 'aggregation of ideas,' beyond almost any other poet. He has in this respect been compared to Michael Angelo, but not with much reason: his verses are

> ———'inimitable on earth
> By model, or by shading pencil drawn.'

Suckling is also ranked, without sufficient warrant, among the metaphysical poets. Sir John was of 'the court, courtly;' and his style almost entirely free from the charge of pedantry and affectation. There are a few blemishes of this kind in his works, but they are but few. His compositions are almost all of them short and lively effusions of wit and gallantry, written in a familiar but spirited style, without much design or effort. His shrewd and taunting address to a desponding lover will sufficiently vouch for the truth of this account of the general cast of his best pieces.

> ' Why so pale and wan, fond lover ?
> Pr'ythee why so pale ?
> Will, when looking well can't move her,
> Looking ill prevail ?
> Pr'ythee why so pale ?
>
> Why so dull and mute, young sinner ?
> Pr'ythee why so mute ?
> Will, when speaking well, can't win her,
> Saying nothing do 't ?
> Pr'ythee why so mute ?
>
> Quit, quit for shame, this will not move,
> This cannot take her ;
> If of herself she will not love,
> Nothing can make her ;
> The Devil take her.'

The two short poems against Fruition, that beginning, ' There never yet was woman made, nor shall, but to be curst,'—the song, ' I pr'ythee, spare me, gentle boy, press me no more for that slight toy, that foolish trifle of a heart,'—another, ' 'Tis now, since I sat

55

down before, that foolish fort, a heart,'—*Lutea Alanson*—the set of similes, 'Hast thou seen the down in the air, when wanton winds have tost it,'—and his 'Dream,' which is of a more tender and romantic cast, are all exquisite in their way. They are the origin of the style of Prior and Gay in their short fugitive verses, and of the songs in the Beggar's Opera. His Ballad on a Wedding is his masterpiece, and is indeed unrivalled in that class of composition, for the voluptuous delicacy of the sentiments, and the luxuriant richness of the images. I wish I could repeat the whole, but that, from the change of manners, is impossible. The description of the bride is (half of it) as follows : the story is supposed to be told by one countryman to another :—

> ' Her finger was so small, the ring
>   Would not stay on, which they did bring ;
>   It was too wide a peck :
>   And to say truth (for out it must)
>   It look'd like the great collar (just)
>   About our young colt's neck.
>
>   Her feet beneath her petticoat,
>   Like little mice, stole in and out,
>   As if they fear'd the light :
>   But oh ! she dances such a way !
>   No sun upon an Easter-day
>   Is half so fine a sight.
>
> *   *   *   *   *   *
>
>   Her cheeks so rare a white was on,
>   No daisy makes comparison,
>   (Who sees them is undone)
>   For streaks of red were mingled there,
>   Such as are on a Cath'rine pear,
>   (The side that 's next the sun.)
>
>   Her lips were red ; and one was thin,
>   Compar'd to that was next her chin ;
>   (Some bee had stung it newly)
>   But (Dick) her eyes so guard her face,
>   I durst no more upon them gaze,
>   Than on the sun in July.
>
>   Her mouth so small, when she does speak,
>   Thoud'st swear her teeth her words did break,
>   That they might passage get ;
>   But she so handled still the matter,
>   They came as good as ours, or better,
>   And are not spent a whit.'

ON COWLEY, BUTLER, SUCKLING, ETC.

There is to me in the whole of this delightful performance a freshness and purity like the first breath of morning. Its sportive irony never trespasses on modesty, though it sometimes (laughing) threatens to do so! Suckling's Letters are full of habitual gaiety and good sense. His Discourse on Reason in Religion is well enough meant. Though he excelled in the conversational style of poetry, writing verse with the freedom and readiness, vivacity and unconcern, with which he would have talked on the most familiar and sprightly topics, his peculiar powers deserted him in attempting dramatic dialogue. His comedy of the *Goblins* is equally defective in plot, wit, and nature; it is a wretched list of *exits* and *entrances,* and the whole business of the scene is taken up in the unaccountable seizure, and equally unaccountable escapes, of a number of persons from a band of robbers in the shape of goblins, who turn out to be noblemen and gentlemen in disguise. Suckling was not a Grub-street author; or it might be said, that this play is like what he might have written after dreaming all night of duns and a spunging-house. His tragedies are no better: their titles are the most interesting part of them, Aglaura, Brennoralt, and the Sad One.

Cowley had more brilliancy of fancy and ingenuity of thought than Donne, with less pathos and sentiment. His mode of illustrating his ideas differs also from Donne's in this: that whereas Donne is contented to analyse an image into its component elements, and resolve it into its most abstracted species; Cowley first does this, indeed, but does not stop till he has fixed upon some other prominent example of the same general class of ideas, and forced them into a metaphorical union, by the medium of the generic definition. Thus he says—

> 'The Phœnix Pindar is a vast species alone.'

He means to say that he stands by himself: he is then 'a vast species alone:' then by applying to this generality the *principium individuationis*, he becomes a Phœnix, because the Phœnix is the only example of a species contained in an individual. Yet this is only a literal or metaphysical coincidence: and literally and metaphysically speaking, Pindar was not a species by himself, but only seemed so by pre-eminence or excellence; that is, from qualities of mind appealing to and absorbing the imagination, and which, therefore, ought to be represented in poetical language, by some other obvious and palpable image exhibiting the same kind or degree of excellence in other things, as when Gray compares him to the Theban eagle,

> 'Sailing with supreme dominion
> Through the azure deep of air.'

Again, he talks in the Motto, or Invocation to his Muse, of 'marching the Muse's Hannibal' into undiscovered regions. That is, he thinks first of being a leader in poetry, and then he immediately, by virtue of this abstraction, becomes a Hannibal; though no two things can really be more unlike in all the associations belonging to them, than a leader of armies and a leader of the tuneful Nine. In like manner, he compares Bacon to Moses; for in *his* verses extremes are sure to meet. The Hymn to Light, which forms a perfect contrast to Milton's Invocation to Light, in the commencement of the third book of Paradise Lost, begins in the following manner :—

> ' First-born of Chaos, who so fair didst come
> From the old negro's darksome womb!
> Which, when it saw the lovely child,
> The melancholy mass put on kind looks, and smil'd.'
> * * * * * * * *

And soon after

> ' 'Tis, I believe, this archery to show
> That so much cost in colours thou,
> And skill in painting, dost bestow,
> Upon thy ancient arms, the gaudy heav'nly bow.
>
> Swift as light thoughts their empty career run,
> Thy race is finish'd when begun;
> Let a post-angel start with thee,
> And thou the goal of earth shalt reach as soon as he.'

The conceits here are neither wit nor poetry; but a burlesque upon both, made up of a singular metaphorical jargon, verbal generalities, and physical analogies. Thus his calling Chaos, or Darkness, 'the old negro,' would do for abuse or jest, but is too remote and degrading for serious poetry, and yet it is meant for such. The 'old negro' is at best a nickname, and the smile on its face loses its beauty in such company. The making out the rainbow to be a species of heraldic painting, and converting an angel into a post-boy, shew the same rage for comparison; but such comparisons are as odious as they are unjust. Dr. Johnson has multiplied instances of the same false style, in its various divisions and subdivisions.[1] Of Cowley's serious poems, the Complaint is the one I like the best; and some of his translations in the Essays, as those on Liberty and Retirement, are exceedingly good. The Odes to Vandyke, to the Royal Society, to Hobbes, and to the latter Brutus, beginning

---

[1] See his Lives of the British Poets, Vol. i.

ON COWLEY, BUTLER, SUCKLING, ETC.

'Excellent Brutus,' are all full of ingenious and high thoughts, impaired by a load of ornament and quaint disguises. The Chronicle, or list of his Mistresses, is the best of his original lighter pieces: but the best of his poems are the translations from Anacreon, which remain, and are likely to remain unrivalled. The spirit of wine and joy circulates in them; and though they are lengthened out beyond the originals, it is by fresh impulses of an eager and inexhaustible feeling of delight. Here are some of them:—

DRINKING

'The thirsty earth soaks up the rain,
And drinks, and gapes for drink again.
The plants suck in the earth, and are
With constant drinking fresh and fair.
The sea itself, which one would think
Should have but little need of drink,
Drinks twice ten thousand rivers up,
So fill'd that they o'erflow the cup.
The busy sun (and one would guess
By 's drunken fiery face no less)
Drinks up the sea, and, when he 'as done,
The moon and stars drink up the sun.
They drink and dance by their own light,
They drink and revel all the night.
Nothing in nature 's sober found,
But an eternal health goes round.
Fill up the bowl then, fill it high,
Fill all the glasses there; for why
Should every creature drink but I;
Why, man of morals, tell me why?'

This is a classical intoxication; and the poet's imagination, giddy with fancied joys, communicates its spirit and its motion to inanimate things, and makes all nature reel round with it. It is not easy to decide between these choice pieces, which may be reckoned among the *delights of human kind*; but that to the Grasshopper is one of the happiest as well as most serious:—

'Happy insect, what can be
In happiness compar'd to thee?
Fed with nourishment divine,
The dewy morning's gentle wine!
Nature waits upon thee still,
And thy verdant cup does fill;
'Tis filled wherever thou dost tread,
Nature's self thy Ganymede.
Thou dost drink, and dance, and sing;
Happier than the happiest king!

59

All the fields which thou dost see,
All the plants, belong to thee;
All that summer-hours produce,
Fertile made with early juice.
Man for thee does sow and plough,
Farmer he, and landlord thou!
Thou dost innocently joy;
Nor does thy luxury destroy;
The shepherd gladly heareth thee,
More harmonious than he.
Thee country hinds with gladness hear,
Prophet of the ripen'd year!
Thee Phœbus loves, and does inspire;
Phœbus is himself thy sire.
To thee, of all things upon earth,
Life is no longer than thy mirth.
Happy insect, happy thou!
Dost neither age nor winter know;
But, when thou'st drunk, and danc'd, and sung
Thy fill, the flowery leaves among,
(Voluptuous and wise withal,
Epicurean animal!)
Sated with thy summer feast,
Thou retir'st to endless rest.'

Cowley's Essays are among the most agreeable prose-compositions in our language, being equally recommended by sense, wit, learning, and interesting personal history, and written in a style quite free from the faults of his poetry. It is a pity that he did not cultivate his talent for prose more, and write less in verse, for he was clearly a man of more reflection than imagination. The Essays on Agriculture, on Liberty, on Solitude, and on Greatness, are all of them delightful. From the last I may give his account of Senecio as an addition to the instances of the ludicrous, which I have attempted to enumerate in the introductory Lecture; whose ridiculous affectation of grandeur Seneca the elder (he tells us) describes to this effect: 'Senecio was a man of a turbid and confused wit, who could not endure to speak any but mighty words and sentences, till this humour grew at last into so notorious a habit, or rather disease, as became the sport of the whole town: he would have no servants, but huge, massy fellows; no plate or household stuff, but thrice as big as the fashion: you may believe me, for I speak it without raillery, his extravagancy came at last into such a madness, that he would not put on a pair of shoes, each of which was not big enough for both his feet: he would eat nothing but what was great, nor touch any fruit but horse-plums and pound-pears: he kept a mistress that was a very giantess, and made her walk too always in chiopins, till, at last, he got the surname of Senecio Grandio.' This was certainly the most absurd person we read of in antiquity. Cowley's character of Oliver Cromwell, which is intended as a satire, (though it certainly produces a very different impression on the mind), may vie for truth of outline and force of colouring with the masterpieces of the Greek and Latin historians. It may serve as a contrast to the last extract. 'What can be more extraordinary, than that a person of mean birth, no fortune, no eminent qualities of body, which have sometimes, or of mind, which have often, raised men to the highest dignities, should have the courage to attempt, and the happiness to succeed in, so improbable a design, as the destruction of one of the most ancient and most solidly-founded monarchies upon the earth ? That he should have the power or boldness to put his prince and master to an open and infamous death ; to banish that numerous and strongly-allied family ; to do all this under the name and wages of a Parliament ; to trample upon them too as he pleased, and spurn them out of doors when he grew weary of them ; to raise up a new and unheard-of monster out of their ashes; to stifle that in the very infancy, and set up himself above all things that ever were called sovereign in England ; to oppress all his enemies by arms, and all his friends afterwards by artifice ; to serve all parties patiently for a while, and to command them victoriously at last ; to over-run each corner of the three nations, and overcome with equal facility both the riches of the south and the poverty of the north ; to be feared and courted by all foreign princes, and adopted a brother to the gods of the earth ; to call together Parliaments with a word of his pen, and scatter them again with the breath of his mouth ; to be humbly and daily petitioned that he would please to be hired, at the rate of two millions a-year, to be the master of those who had hired him before to be their servant ; to have the estates and lives of three kingdoms as much at his disposal, as was the little inheritance of his father, and to be as noble and liberal in the spending of them ; and lastly, (for there is no end of all the particulars of his glory) to bequeath all this with one word to his posterity ; to die with peace at home, and triumph abroad ; to be buried among kings, and with more than regal solemnity ; and to leave a name behind him, not to be extinguished, but with the whole world ; which as it is now too little for his praises, so might have been too for his conquests, if the short line of his human life could have been stretched out to the extent of his immortal designs ! '

Cowley has left one comedy, called Cutter of Coleman Street, which met with an unfavourable reception at the time, and is now (not undeservedly) forgotten. It contains, however, one good scene, which is rich both in fancy and humour, that between the puritanical bride, Tabitha, and her ranting royalist husband. It is said that this play was originally composed, and afterwards revived, as a satire upon the Presbyterian party; yet it was resented by the court party as a satire upon itself. A man must, indeed, be sufficiently blind with party-prejudice, to have considered this as a compliment to his own side of the question. 'Call you this backing of your friends?' The cavaliers are in this piece represented as reduced to the lowest shifts in point of fortune, and sunk still lower in point of principle.

The greatest single production of wit of this period, I might say of this country, is Butler's Hudibras. It contains specimens of every variety of drollery and satire, and those specimens crowded together into almost every page. The proof of this is, that nearly one half of his lines are got by heart, and quoted for mottos. In giving instances of different sorts of wit, or trying to recollect good things of this kind, they are the first which stand ready in the memory; and they are those which furnish the best tests and most striking illustrations of what we want. Dr. Campbell, in his Philosophy of Rhetoric, when treating of the subject of wit, which he has done very neatly and sensibly, has constant recourse to two authors, Pope and Butler, the one for ornament, the other more for use. Butler is equally in the hands of the learned and the vulgar; for the sense is generally as solid, as the images are amusing and grotesque. Whigs and Tories join in his praise. He could not, in spite of himself,

———'narrow his mind,
'And to party give up what was meant for mankind.'

Though his subject was local and temporary, his fame was not circumscribed within his own age. He was admired by Charles ii. and has been rewarded by posterity. It is the poet's fate! It is not, perhaps, to be wondered at, that arbitrary and worthless monarchs like Charles ii. should neglect those who pay court to them. The idol (if it had sense) would despise its worshippers. Indeed, Butler hardly merited any thing on the score of loyalty to the house of Stuart. True wit is not a parasite plant. The strokes which it aims at folly and knavery on one side of a question, tell equally home on the other. Dr. Zachary Grey, who added notes to the poem, and abused the leaders of Cromwell's party by name, would be more likely to have gained a pension for his services than Butler, who was above such petty work. A poem like Hudibras could not be *made to order of a court*. Charles might very well have reproached the author with wanting to shew his own wit and sense rather than to favour a tottering cause; and he has even been suspected, in parts of his poem, of glancing at majesty itself.   He in general ridicules not persons, but things, not a party, but their principles, which may belong, as time and occasion serve, to one set of solemn pretenders or another.   This he has done most effectually, in every possible way, and from every possible source, learned or unlearned.   He has exhausted the moods and figures of satire and sophistry.[1]   It would be possible to deduce the different forms of syllogism in Aristotle, from the different violations or mock-imitations of them in Butler.   He fulfils every one of Barrow's conditions of wit, which I have enumerated in the first Lecture. He makes you laugh or smile by comparing the high to the low,[2] or by pretending to raise the low to the lofty ; [3] he succeeds equally in the familiarity of his illustrations,[4] or their incredible extravagance,[5] by comparing things that are alike or not alike.   He surprises equally

[1] 'And have not two saints power to use
A greater privilege than three Jews ? '
     *   *   *   *   *
'Her voice, the music of the spheres,
So loud it deafens mortals' ears,
As wise philosophers have thought,
And that's the cause we hear it not.'

[2] 'No Indian prince has to his palace
More followers than a thief to the gallows.'

[3] 'And in his nose, like Indian king,
He (Bruin) wore for ornament a ring.'

[4] 'Whose noise whets valour sharp, like beer
By thunder turned to vinegar.'

[5] 'Replete with strange hermetic powder,
That wounds nine miles point-blank would solder.'
     *   *   *   *   *
'His tawny beard was th' equal grace
Both of his wisdom and his face ;
In cut and die so like a tile,
A sudden view it would beguile :
The upper part thereof was whey,
The nether orange mixed with grey.
This hairy meteor did denounce
The fall of sceptres and of crowns ;
With grisly type did represent
Declining age of government ;
And tell with hieroglyphic spade
Its own grave and the state's were made.'
     *   *   *   *   *
'This sword a dagger had his page,
That was but little for his age ;
And therefore waited on him so,
As dwarfs upon knight errants do.'

by his coincidences or contradictions, by spinning out a long-winded
flimsy excuse, or by turning short upon you with the point-blank
truth. His rhymes are as witty as his reasons, equally remote from
what common custom would suggest;[1] and he startles you sometimes
by an empty sound like a blow upon a drum-head,[2] by a pun upon
one word,[3] and by splitting another in two at the end of a verse,
with the same alertness and power over the odd and unaccountable
in the combinations of sounds as of images.[4]

There are as many shrewd aphorisms in his works, clenched by
as many quaint and individual allusions, as perhaps in any author
whatever. He makes none but palpable hits, that may be said to
give one's understanding a rap on the knuckles.[5] He is, indeed,
sometimes too prolific, and spins his antithetical sentences out, one
after another, till the reader, not the author, is wearied. He is,
however, very seldom guilty of repetitions or wordy paraphrases of
himself; but he sometimes comes rather too near it; and interrupts
the thread of his argument (for narrative he has none) by a tissue of
epigrams, and the tagging of points and conundrums without end.
The fault, or original sin of his genius, is, that from too much leaven
it ferments and runs over; and there is, unfortunately, nothing in his
subject to restrain and keep it within compass. He has no story
good for any thing; and his characters are good for very little.
They are too low and mechanical, or too much one thing, personifications, as it were, of nicknames, and bugbears of popular prejudice
and vulgar cant, unredeemed by any virtue, or difference or variety
of disposition. There is no relaxation or shifting of the parts; and
the impression in some degree fails of its effect, and becomes
questionable from its being always the same. The satire looks, at
length, almost like special-pleading: it has nothing to confirm it in

---

[1] 'And straight another with his flambeau,
Gave Ralpho o'er the eyes a damn'd blow.'
*   *   *   *   *
'That deals in destiny's dark counsels,
And sage opinions of the moon sells.'

[2] 'The mighty Tottipottimoy
Sent to our elders an envoy.'

[3] 'For Hebrew *roots*, although they're found
To flourish most in barren ground.'

[4] 'Those wholesale critics that in coffee-
Houses cry down all philosophy.'

[5] 'This we among ourselves may speak,
But to the wicked or the weak
We must be cautious to declare
Perfection-truths, such as these are.'

the apparent good humour or impartiality of the writer. It is something revolting to see an author persecute his characters, the cherished offspring of his brain, in this manner, without mercy. Hudibras and Ralpho have immortalised Butler; and what has he done for them in return, but set them up to be 'pilloried on infamy's high and lasting stage?' This is ungrateful!

The rest of the characters have, in general, little more than their names and professions to distinguish them. We scarcely know one from another, Cerdon, or Orsin, or Crowdero, and are often obliged to turn back, to connect their several adventures together. In fact, Butler drives only at a set of obnoxious opinions, and runs into general declamations. His poem in its essence is a satire, or didactic poem. It is not virtually dramatic, or narrative. It is composed of digressions by the author. He instantly breaks off in the middle of a story, or incident, to comment upon and turn it into ridicule. He does not give characters but topics, which would do just as well in his own mouth without agents, or machinery of any kind. The long digression in Part III. in which no mention is made of the hero, is just as good and as much an integrant part of the poem as the rest. The conclusion is lame and impotent, but that is saying nothing; the beginning and middle are equally so as to historical merit. There is no keeping in his characters, as in Don Quixote; nor any enjoyment of the ludicrousness of their situations, as in Hogarth. Indeed, it requires a considerable degree of sympathy to enter into and describe to the life even the ludicrous eccentricities of others, and there is no appearance of sympathy or liking to his subject in Butler. His humour is to his wit, 'as one grain of wheat in a bushel of chaff: you shall search all day, and when you find it, it is not worth the trouble.' Yet there are exceptions. The most decisive is, I think, the description of the battle between Bruin and his foes, Part I. Canto iii., and again of the triumphal procession in Part II. Canto ii. of which the principal features are copied in Hogarth's election print, the Chairing of the successful candidate. The account of Sidrophel and Whackum is another instance, and there are some few others, but rarely sprinkled up and down.[1]

---

[1] The following are nearly all I can remember.—

> 'Thus stopp'd their fury and the basting
> Which towards Hudibras was hasting.'

It is said of the bear, in the fight with the dogs—

> 'And setting his right foot before,
> He raised himself to shew how tall
> His person was above them all,'
> *   *   *   *   *

The widow, the termagant heroine of the poem, is still more disagreeable than her lover; and her sarcastic account of the passion of
love, as consisting entirely in an attachment to land and houses, goods
and chattels, which is enforced with all the rhetoric the author is
master of, and hunted down through endless similes, is evidently
false. The vulgarity and meanness of sentiment which Butler
complains of in the Presbyterians, seems at last from long familiarity and close contemplation to have tainted his own mind. Their
worst vices appear to have taken root in his imagination. Nothing
but what was selfish and groveling sunk into his memory, in the
depression of a menial situation under his supposed hero. He has,
indeed, carried his private grudge too far into his general speculations.
He even makes out the rebels to be cowards and well beaten, which
does not accord with the history of the times. In an excess of zeal
for church and state, he is too much disposed to treat religion as a
cheat, and liberty as a farce. It was the cant of that day (from

> ' At this the knight grew high in chafe,
> And staring furiously on Ralph,
> He trembled and look'd pale with ire,
> Like ashes first, then red as fire.'
>   *   *   *   *   *
> ' The knight himself did after ride,
> Leading Crowdero by his side,
> And tow'd him if he lagged behind,
> Like boat against the tide and wind.'
>   *   *   *   *   *
> ' And rais'd upon his desperate foot,
> On stirrup-side he gazed about.'
>   *   *   *   *   *
> 'And Hudibras, who used to ponder
> On such sights with judicious wonder.'
>   *   *   *   *   *

The beginning of the account of the procession in Part ii. is as follows :—

> ' Both thought it was the wisest course
> To wave the fight and mount to horse,
> And to secure by swift retreating,
> Themselves from danger of worse beating :
> Yet neither of them would disparage
> By uttering of his mind his courage.
> Which made 'em stoutly keep their ground,
> With horror and disdain wind-bound.
> And now the cause of all their fear
> By slow degrees approach'd so near,
> They might distinguish different noise
> Of horns and pans, and dogs and boys,
> And kettle-drums, whose sullen dub
> Sounds like the hooping of a tub.'

66

which he is not free) to cry down sanctity and sobriety as marks of disaffection, as it is the cant of this, to hold them up as proofs of loyalty and staunch monarchical principles. Religion and morality are, in either case, equally made subservient to the spirit of party, and a stalking-horse to the love of power. Finally, there is a want of pathos and humour, but no want of interest in Hudibras. It is difficult to lay it down. One thought is inserted into another; the links in the chain of reasoning are so closely rivetted, that the attention seldom flags, but is kept alive (without any other assistance) by the mere force of writing. There are occasional indications of poetical fancy, and an eye for natural beauty; but these are kept under or soon discarded, judiciously enough, but it should seem, not for lack of power, for they are certainly as masterly as they are rare. Such are the burlesque description of the stocks, or allegorical prison, in which first Crowdero, and then Hudibras, is confined: the passage beginning—

> 'As when an owl that's in a barn,
> Sees a mouse creeping in the corn,
> Sits still and shuts his round blue eyes,
> As if he slept,' &c.

And the description of the moon going down in the early morning, which is as pure, original, and picturesque as possible :—

> 'The queen of night, whose large command
> Rules all the sea and half the land,
> And over moist and crazy brains
> In high spring-tides at midnight reigns,
> Was now declining to the west,
> To go to bed and take her rest.'

Butler is sometimes scholastic, but he makes his learning tell to good account; and for the purposes of burlesque, nothing can be better fitted than the scholastic style.

Butler's Remains are nearly as good and full of sterling genius as his principal poem. Take the following ridicule of the plan of the Greek tragedies as an instance.

> —'Reduce all tragedy, by rules of art,
> Back to its ancient theatre, a cart,
> And make them henceforth keep the beaten roads
> Of reverend choruses and episodes;
> Reform and regulate a puppet-play,
> According to the true and ancient way;
> That not an actor shall presume to squeak,
> Unless he have a license for 't in Greek :

67

Nor devil in the puppet-play be allowed
To roar and spit fire, but to fright the crowd,
Unless some god or demon chance to have piques
Against an ancient family of Greeks;
That other men may tremble and take warning
How such a fatal progeny they're born in;
For none but such for tragedy are fitted,
That have been ruined only to be pitied:
And only those held proper to deter,
Who have th' ill luck against their wills to err;
Whence only such as are of middling sizes,
Betwixt morality and venial vices,
Are qualified to be destroyed by fate,
For other mortals to take warning at.'

Upon Critics.

His ridicule of Milton's Latin style is equally severe, but not so well founded.

I have only to add a few words respecting the dramatic writers about this time, before we arrive at the golden period of our comedy. Those of Etherege [1] are good for nothing, except The Man of Mode, or Sir Fopling Flutter, which is, I think, a more exquisite and airy picture of the manners of that age than any other extant. Sir Fopling himself is an inimitable coxcomb, but pleasant withal. He is a suit of clothes personified. Dorimant (supposed to be Lord Rochester) is the genius of grace, gallantry, and gaiety. The women in this courtly play have very much the look and air (but something more demure and significant) of Sir Peter Lely's beauties. Harriet, the mistress of Dorimant, who 'tames his wild heart to her loving hand,' is the flower of the piece. Her natural, untutored grace and spirit, her meeting with Dorimant in the Park, bowing and mimicking him, and the luxuriant description which is given of her fine person, altogether form one of the *chef d'œuvres* of dramatic painting. I should think this comedy would bear reviving; and if Mr. Liston were to play Sir Fopling, the part would shine out with double lustre, 'like the morn risen on mid-noon.'—Dryden's comedies have all the point that there is in ribaldry, and all the humour that there is in extravagance. I am sorry I can say nothing better of them. He was not at home in this kind of writing, of which he was himself conscious. His play was *horse-play*. His wit (what there is of it) is ingenious and scholar-like, rather than natural and dramatic. Thus Burr, in the Wild Gallant, says to Failer, 'She shall sooner cut an atom than part us.'—His plots are pure *voluntaries* in absurdity,

[1] Love in a Tub, and She Would if She Could.

that bend and shift to his purpose without any previous notice or reason, and are governed by final causes. Sir Martin Mar-all, which was taken from the Duchess of Newcastle, is the best of his plays, and the origin of the Busy Body. Otway's comedies do no sort of credit to him: on the contrary, they are as desperate as his fortunes. The Duke of Buckingham's famous Rehearsal, which has made, and deservedly, so much noise in the world, is in a great measure taken from Beaumont and Fletcher's Knight of the Burning Pestle, which was written in ridicule of the London apprentices in the reign of Elizabeth, who had a great hand in the critical decisions of that age. There were other dramatic writers of this period, noble and plebeian. I shall only mention one other piece, the Committee, I believe by Sir Robert Howard, which has of late been cut down into the farce called Honest Thieves, and which I remember reading with a great deal of pleasure many years ago.

One cause of the difference between the immediate reception and lasting success of dramatic works at this period may be, that after the court took the play-houses under its particular protection, every thing became very much an affair of private patronage. If an author could get a learned lord or a countess-dowager to bespeak a box at his play, and applaud the doubtful passages, he considered his business as done. On the other hand, there was a reciprocity between men of letters and their patrons; critics were 'mitigated into courtiers, and submitted,' as Mr. Burke has it, 'to the soft collar of social esteem,' in pronouncing sentence on the works of lords and ladies. How ridiculous this seems now! What a hubbub it would create, if it were known that a particular person of fashion and title had taken a front-box in order to decide on the fate of a first play! How the newspaper critics would laugh in their sleeves! How the public would sneer! But at this time there was no public. I will not say, therefore, that these times are better than those; but they are better, I think, in this respect. An author now-a-days no longer hangs dangling on the frown of a lord, or the smile of a lady of quality (the one governed perhaps by his valet, and the other by her waiting-maid), but throws himself boldly, making a lover's leap of it, into the broad lap of public opinion, on which he falls like a feather-bed; and which, like the great bed of Ware, is wide enough to hold us all very comfortably!

LECTURES ON THE COMIC WRITERS

LECTURE IV

ON WYCHERLEY, CONGREVE, VANBRUGH, AND FARQUHAR

COMEDY is a 'graceful ornament to the civil order; the Corinthian capital of polished society.' Like the mirrors which have been added to the sides of one of our theatres, it reflects the images of grace, of gaiety, and pleasure double, and completes the perspective of human life. To read a good comedy is to keep the best company in the world, where the best things are said, and the most amusing happen. The wittiest remarks are always ready on the tongue, and the luckiest occasions are always at hand to give birth to the happiest conceptions. Sense makes strange havoc of nonsense. Refinement acts as a foil to affectation, and affectation to ignorance. Sentence after sentence tells. We don't know which to admire most, the observation, or the answer to it. We would give our fingers to be able to talk so ourselves, or to hear others talk so. In turning over the pages of the best comedies, we are almost transported to another world, and escape from this dull age to one that was all life, and whim, and mirth, and humour. The curtain rises, and a gayer scene presents itself, as on the canvass of Watteau. We are admitted behind the scenes like spectators at court, on a levee or birth-day; but it is the court, the gala day of wit and pleasure, of gallantry and Charles II! What an air breathes from the name! what a rustling of silks and waving of plumes! what a sparkling of diamond ear-rings and shoe-buckles! What bright eyes, (ah, those were Waller's Sacharissa's as she passed!) what killing looks and graceful motions! How the faces of the whole ring are dressed in smiles! how the repartee goes round! how wit and folly, elegance and awkward imitation of it, set one another off! Happy, thoughtless age, when kings and nobles led purely ornamental lives; when the utmost stretch of a morning's study went no farther than the choice of a sword-knot, or the adjustment of a side-curl; when the soul spoke out in all the pleasing eloquence of dress; and beaux and belles, enamoured of themselves in one another's follies, fluttered like gilded butterflies, in giddy mazes, through the walks of St. James's Park!

The four principal writers of this style of comedy (which I think the best) are undoubtedly Wycherley, Congreve, Vanbrugh, and Farquhar. The dawn was in Etherege, as its latest close was in Sheridan.—It is hard to say which of these four is best, or in what each of them excels, they had so many and such great excellences.

70

Congreve is the most distinct from the others, and the most easily defined, both from what he possessed, and from what he wanted. He had by far the most wit and elegance, with less of other things, of humour, character, incident, &c. His style is inimitable, nay perfect. It is the highest model of comic dialogue. Every sentence is replete with sense and satire, conveyed in the most polished and pointed terms. Every page presents a shower of brilliant conceits, is a tissue of epigrams in prose, is a new triumph of wit, a new conquest over dulness. The fire of artful raillery is nowhere else so well kept up. This style, which he was almost the first to introduce, and which he carried to the utmost pitch of classical refinement, reminds one exactly of Collins's description of wit as opposed to humour,

> ' Whose jewels in his crisped hair
> Are placed each other's light to share.'

Sheridan will not bear a comparison with him in the regular antithetical construction of his sentences, and in the mechanical artifices of his style, though so much later, and though style in general has been so much studied, and in the mechanical part so much improved since then. It bears every mark of being what he himself in the dedication of one of his plays tells us that it was, a spirited copy taken off and carefully revised from the most select society of his time, exhibiting all the sprightliness, ease, and anima-tion of familiar conversation, with the correctness and delicacy of the most finished composition. His works are a singular treat to those who have cultivated a taste for the niceties of English style: there is a peculiar flavour in the very words, which is to be found in hardly any other writer. To the mere reader his writings would be an irreparable loss: to the stage they are already become a dead letter, with the exception of one of them, Love for Love. This play is as full of character, incident, and stage-effect, as almost any of those of his contemporaries, and fuller of wit than any of his own, except perhaps the Way of the World. It still acts, and is still acted well. The effect of it is prodigious on the well-informed spectator. In particular, Munden's Foresight, if it is not just the thing, is a wonderfully rich and powerful piece of comic acting. His look is planet-struck ; his dress and appearance like one of the signs of the Zodiac taken down. Nothing can be more bewildered ; and it only wants a little more helplessness, a little more of the doating querulous garrulity of age, to be all that one conceives of the superannuated, star-gazing original. The gay, unconcerned opening of this play, and the romantic generosity of the conclusion, where

Valentine, when about to resign his mistress, declares—'I never valued fortune, but as it was subservient to my pleasure; and my only pleasure was to please this lady,'—are alike admirable. The peremptory bluntness and exaggerated descriptions of Sir Sampson Legend are in a vein truly oriental, with a Shakespearian cast of language, and form a striking contrast to the quaint credulity and senseless superstitions of Foresight. The remonstrance of his son to him, 'to divest him, along with his inheritance, of his reason, thoughts, passions, inclinations, affections, appetites, senses, and the huge train of attendants which he brought into the world with him,' with his valet's accompanying comments, is one of the most eloquent and spirited specimens of wit, pathos, and morality, that is to be found. The short scene with Trapland, the money-broker, is of the first water. What a picture is here drawn of Tattle! 'More misfortunes, Sir!' says Jeremy. *Valentine.* 'What, another dun?' *Jeremy.* 'No, Sir, but Mr. Tattle is come to wait upon you.' What an introduction to give of an honest gentleman in the shape of a misfortune! The scenes between him, Miss Prue, and Ben, are of a highly coloured description. Mrs. Frail and Mrs. Foresight are 'sisters every way;' and the bodkin which Mrs. Foresight brings as a proof of her sister's levity of conduct, and which is so convincingly turned against her as a demonstration of her own— 'Nay, if you come to that, where did you find that bodkin?'—is one of the trophies of the moral justice of the comic drama. The Old Bachelor and Double Dealer are inferior to Love for Love, but one is never tired of reading them. The fault of the last is, that Lady Touchwood approaches, in the turbulent impetuosity of her character, and measured tone of her declamation, too near to the tragedy-queen; and that Maskwell's plots puzzle the brain by their intricacy, as they stagger our belief by their gratuitous villainy. Sir Paul and Lady Pliant, and my Lord and Lady Froth, are also scarcely credible in the extravagant insipidity and romantic vein of their follies, in which they are notably seconded by the lively Mr. Brisk and 'dying Ned Careless.'

The Way of the World was the author's last and most carefully finished performance. It is an essence almost too fine; and the sense of pleasure evaporates in an aspiration after something that seems too exquisite ever to have been realised. After inhaling the spirit of Congreve's wit, and tasting 'love's thrice reputed nectar' in his works, the head grows giddy in turning from the highest point of rapture to the ordinary business of life; and we can with difficulty recal the truant Fancy to those objects which we are fain to take up with here, *for better, for worse.* What can be more

72

enchanting than Millamant and her morning thoughts, her *doux sommeils*? What more provoking than her reproach to her lover, who proposes to rise early, ' Ah! idle creature!' The meeting of these two lovers after the abrupt dismissal of Sir Wilful, is the height of careless and voluptuous elegance, as if they moved in air, and drank a finer spirit of humanity.

> ' *Millamant*. Like Phœbus sung the no less amorous boy.
> *Mirabell*. Like Daphne she, as lovely and as coy.'

Millamant is the perfect model of the accomplished fine lady :

> ' Come, then, the colours and the ground prepare,
> Dip in the rainbow, trick her off in air ;
> Choose a firm cloud, before it falls, and in it
> Catch ere she change, the Cynthia of a minute.'

She is the ideal heroine of the comedy of high life, who arrives at the height of indifference to every thing from the height of satisfaction; to whom pleasure is as familiar as the air she draws ; elegance worn as a part of her dress ; wit the habitual language which she hears and speaks ; love, a matter of course ; and who has nothing to hope or to fear, her own caprice being the only law to herself, and rule to those about her. Her words seem composed of amorous sighs—her looks are glanced at prostrate admirers or envious rivals.

> ' If there 's delight in love, 'tis when I see
> That heart that others bleed for, bleed for me.'

She refines on her pleasures to satiety ; and is almost stifled in the incense that is offered to her person, her wit, her beauty, and her fortune. Secure of triumph, her slaves tremble at her frown : her charms are so irresistible, that her conquests give her neither surprise nor concern. ' Beauty the lover's gift?' she exclaims, in answer to Mirabell—' Dear me, what is a lover that it can give? Why one makes lovers as fast as one pleases, and they live as long as one pleases, and they die as soon as one pleases ; and then if one pleases, one makes more.' We are not sorry to see her tamed down at last, from her pride of love and beauty, into a wife. She is good-natured and generous, with all her temptations to the contrary ; and her behaviour to Mirabell reconciles us to her treatment of Witwoud and Petulant, and of her country admirer, Sir Wilful.

Congreve has described all this in his character of Millamant, but he has done no more ; and if he had, he would have done wrong. He has given us the finest idea of an artificial character of this kind ; but it is still the reflection of an artificial character. The springs of nature, passion, or imagination are but feebly touched. The impressions appealed to, and with masterly address, are habitual, external, and conventional advantages: the ideas of birth, of fortune, of connexions, of dress, accomplishment, fashion, the opinion of the world, of crowds of admirers, continually come into play, flatter our vanity, bribe our interest, soothe our indolence, fall in with our prejudices;—it is these that support the goddess of our idolatry, with which she is every thing, and without which she would be nothing. The mere fine lady of comedy, compared with the heroine of romance or poetry, when stripped of her adventitious ornaments and advantages, is too much like the doll stripped of its finery. In thinking of Millamant, we think almost as much of her dress as of her person: it is not so with respect to Rosalind or Perdita. The poet has painted them differently; in colours which 'nature's own sweet and cunning hand laid on,' with health, with innocence, with gaiety, 'wild wit, invention ever new;' with pure red and white, like the wilding's blossoms; with warbled wood-notes, like the feathered choir's; with thoughts fluttering on the wings of imagination, and hearts panting and breathless with eager delight. The interest we feel is in themselves; the admiration they excite is for themselves. They do not depend upon the drapery of circumstances. It is nature that 'blazons herself' in them. Imogen is the same in a lonely cave as in a court; nay more, for she there seems something heavenly—a spirit or a vision; and, as it were, shames her destiny, brighter for the foil of circumstances. Millamant is nothing but a fine lady; and all her airs and affectation would be blown away with the first breath of misfortune. Enviable in drawing-rooms, adorable at her toilette, fashion, like a witch, has thrown its spell around her; but if that spell were broken, her power of fascination would be gone. For that reason I think the character better adapted for the stage: it is more artificial, more theatrical, more meretricious. I would rather have seen Mrs. Abington's Millamant, than any Rosalind that ever appeared on the stage. Some how, this sort of acquired elegance is more a thing of costume, of air and manner; and in comedy, or on the comic stage, the light and familiar, the trifling, superficial, and agreeable, bears, perhaps, rightful sway over that which touches the affections, or exhausts the fancy.—There is a callousness in the worst characters in the Way of the World, in Fainall, and his wife and Mrs. Marwood, not very pleasant; and a grossness in the absurd ones, such as Lady Wishfort and Sir Wilful, which is not a little amusing. Witwoud wishes to declaim, as far as he can, his relationship to this last character, and says, 'he's but his half-brother;' to which Mirabell makes answer— 'Then, perhaps, he's but half a fool.' Peg is an admirable caricature of rustic awkwardness and simplicity, which is carried to excess without any offence, from a sense of contrast to the refinement of the chief characters in the play. The description of Lady Wishfort's face is a perfect piece of painting. The force of style in this author at times amounts to poetry. Waitwell, who personates Sir Rowland, and Foible, his accomplice in the matrimonial scheme upon her mistress, hang as a dead weight upon the plot. They are mere tools in the hands of Mirabell, and want life and interest. Congreve's characters can all of them speak well, they are mere machines when they come to act. Our author's superiority deserted him almost entirely with his wit. His serious and tragic poetry is frigid and jejune to an unaccountable degree. His *forte* was the description of actual manners, whether elegant or absurd ; and when he could not deride the one or embellish the other, his attempts at romantic passion or imaginary enthusiasm are forced, abortive, and ridiculous, or common-place. The description of the ruins of a temple in the beginning of the Mourning Bride, was a great stretch of his poetic genius. It has, however, been over-rated, particularly by Dr. Johnson, who could have done nearly as well himself for a single passage in the same style of moralising and sentimental description. To justify this general censure, and to shew how the lightest and most graceful wit degenerates into the heaviest and most bombastic poetry, I will give one description out of his tragedy, which will be enough. It is the speech which Gonsalez addresses to Almeria :

> ' Be every day of your long life like this.
> The sun, bright conquest, and your brighter eyes
> Have all conspired to blaze promiscuous light,
> And bless this day with most unequal lustre.
> Your royal father, my victorious lord,
> Loaden with spoils, and ever-living laurel,
> Is entering now, in martial pomp, the palace.
> Five hundred mules precede his solemn march,
> Which groan beneath the weight of Moorish wealth.
> Chariots of war, adorn'd with glittering gems,
> Succeed ; and next, a hundred neighing steeds,
> White as the fleecy rain on Alpine hills;
> That bound, and foam, and champ the golden bit,
> As they disdain'd the victory they grace.
> Prisoners of war in shining fetters follow :
> And captains of the noblest blood of Afric
> Sweat by his chariot-wheels, and lick and grind,
> With gnashing teeth, the dust his triumphs raise.
> The swarming populace spread every wall,
> And cling, as if with claws they did enforce

75

Their hold, through clifted stones stretching and staring
As if they were all eyes, and every limb
Would feed its faculty of admiration,
While you alone retire, and shun this sight;
This sight, which is indeed not seen (though twice
The multitude should gaze) in absence of your eyes.'

This passage seems, in part, an imitation of Bolingbroke's entry into London. The style is as different from Shakspeare, as it is from that of Witwoud and Petulant. It is plain that the imagination of the author could not raise itself above the burlesque. His Mask of Semele, Judgment of Paris, and other occasional poems, are even worse. I would not advise any one to read them, or if I did, they would not.

Wycherley was before Congreve; and his Country Wife will last longer than any thing of Congreve's as a popular acting play. It is only a pity that it is not entirely his own; but it is enough so to do him never-ceasing honour, for the best things are his own. His humour is, in general, broader, his characters more natural, and his incidents more striking than Congreve's. It may be said of Congreve, that the workmanship overlays the materials: in Wycherley, the casting of the parts and the fable are alone sufficient to ensure success. We forget Congreve's characters, and only remember what they say: we remember Wycherley's characters, and the incidents they meet with, just as if they were real, and forget what they say, comparatively speaking. Miss Peggy (or Mrs. Margery Pinchwife) is a character that will last for ever, I should hope; and even when the original is no more, if that should ever be, while self-will, curiosity, art, and ignorance are to be found in the same person, it will be just as good and as intelligible as ever in the description, because it is built on first principles, and brought out in the fullest and broadest manner. Agnes, in Moliere's play, has a great deal of the same unconscious impulse and heedless *naïveté*, but hers is sentimentalised and varnished over (in the French fashion) with long-winded apologies and analytical distinctions. It wants the same simple force and *home* truth. It is not so direct and downright. Miss Peggy is not even a novice in casuistry: she blurts out her meaning before she knows what she is saying, and she speaks her mind by her actions oftener than by her words. The outline of the plot is the same; but the point-blank hits and master-strokes, the sudden thoughts and delightful expedients, such as her changing the letters, the meeting her husband plump in the Park, as she is running away from him as fast as her heels can carry her, her being turned out of doors by her jealous booby of a husband, and sent by him to her lover disguised as Alicia, her sister-

76

in-law—occur first in the modern play. There are scarcely any incidents or situations on the stage, which tell like these for panto-mimic effect, which give such a tingling to the blood, or so completely take away the breath with expectation and surprise. Miss Prue, in Love for Love, is a lively reflection of Miss Peggy, but without the bottom and weight of metal. Hoyden is a match for her in consti-tution and complete effect, as Corinna, in the Confederacy, is in mischief, but without the wit. Mrs. Jordan used to play all these characters; and as she played them, it was hard to know which was best. Pinchwife, or Moody, (as he is at present called) is, like others of Wycherley's moral characters, too rustic, abrupt, and cynical. He is a more disagreeable, but less tedious character than the husband of Agnes, and both seem, by all accounts, to have been rightly served. The character of Sparkish is quite new, and admirably hit off. He is an exquisite and suffocating coxcomb; a pretender to wit and letters, without common understanding, or the use of his senses. The class of character is thoroughly exposed and understood; but he persists in his absurd conduct so far, that it becomes extravagant and disgusting, if not incredible, from mere weakness and foppery. Yet there is something in him that we are inclined to tolerate at first, as his professing that ' with him a wit is the first title to respect;' and we regard his unwillingness to be pushed out of the room, and coming back, in spite of their teeth, to keep the company of wits and raillers, as a favourable omen. But he utterly disgraces his pretensions before he has done. With all his faults and absurdities, he is, however, a much less offensive character than Tattle.—Horner is a stretch of probability in the first concoction of that ambiguous character, (for he does not appear at present on the stage as Wycherley made him) but notwithstanding the indecency and indirectness of the means he employs to carry his plans into effect, he deserves every sort of consideration and forgiveness, both for the display of his own ingenuity, and the deep insight he discovers into human nature—such as it was in the time of Wycherley. The author has commented on this character, and the double meaning of the name in his Plain Dealer, borrowing the remarks, and almost the very words of Moliere, who has brought forward and defended his own work against the objections of the precise part of his audience, in his *Critique de l'Ecole des Femmes*. There is no great harm in these occasional plagiarisms, except that they make one uncomfortable at other times, and distrustful of the originality of the whole.—The Plain Dealer is Wycherley's next best work; and is a most severe and poignant moral satire. There is a heaviness about it, indeed, an extravagance, an overdoing both in the style, the plot, and characters, but the truth of feeling and the force of interest prevail over every objection. The character of Manly, the Plain Dealer, is violent, repulsive, and uncouth, which is a fault, though one that seems to have been intended for the sake of contrast; for the portrait of consummate, artful hypocrisy in Olivia, is, perhaps, rendered more striking by it. The indignation excited against this odious and pernicious quality by the masterly exposure to which it is here subjected, is 'a discipline of humanity.' No one can read this play attentively without being the better for it as long as he lives. It penetrates to the core; it shews the immorality and hateful effects of duplicity, by shewing it fixing its harpy fangs in the heart of an honest and worthy man. It is worth ten volumes of sermons. The scenes between Manly after his return, Olivia, Plausible, and Novel, are instructive examples of unblushing impudence, of shallow pretensions to principle, and of the most mortifying reflections on his own situation, and bitter sense of female injustice and ingratitude, on the part of Manly. The devil of hypocrisy and hardened assurance seems worked up to the highest pitch of conceivable effrontery in Olivia, when, after confiding to her cousin the story of her infamy, she, in a moment, turns round upon her for some sudden purpose, and affecting not to know the meaning of the other's allusions to what she has just told her, reproaches her with forging insinuations to the prejudice of her character, and in violation of their friendship. 'Go! you 're a censorious ill woman.' This is more trying to the patience than any thing in the Tartuffe. The name of this heroine, and her overtures to Fidelia, as the page, seem to have been suggested by Twelfth Night. It is curious to see how the same subject is treated by two such different authors as Shakspeare and Wycherley. The widow Blackacre and her son are like her lawsuit—everlasting. A more lively, palpable, bustling, ridiculous picture cannot be drawn. Jerry is a hopeful lad, though undutiful and gets out of bad hands into worse. Goldsmith evidently had an eye to these two precious characters, in She Stoops to Conquer. Tony Lumpkin and his mother are of the same family, and the incident of the theft of the casket of jewels, and the bag of parchments, is nearly the same in both authors. Wycherley's other plays are not so good. The Gentleman Dancing Master is a long, foolish farce, in the exaggerated manner of Moliere, but without his spirit or whimsical invention. Love in a Wood, though not what one would wish it to be for the author's sake or our own, is much better, and abounds in several rich and highly-coloured scenes, particularly those in which Miss Lucy, her mother Crossbite, Dapperwit, and Alderman Gripe are concerned. Some of the subordinate characters and intrigues in this comedy are grievously spun out. Wycherley, when he got hold of a good thing, or sometimes even of a bad one, was determined to make the most of it; and might have said with Dogberry, truly enough, 'Had I the tediousness of a king, I could find in my heart to bestow it all upon your worships.' In reading this author's best works, those which one reads most frequently over, and knows almost by heart, one cannot help thinking of the treatment he received from Pope about his verses. It was hardly excusable in a boy of sixteen to an old man of seventy.

Vanbrugh comes next, and holds his own fully with the best. He is no writer at all, as to mere authorship; but he makes up for it by a prodigious fund of comic invention and ludicrous description, bordering somewhat on caricature. Though he did not borrow from him, he was much more like Moliere in genius than Wycherley was, who professedly imitated him. He has none of Congreve's graceful refinement, and as little of Wycherley's serious manner and studied insight into the springs of character; but his exhibition of it in dramatic contrast and unlooked-for situations, where the different parties play upon one another's failings, and into one another's hands, keeping up the jest like a game at battledore and shuttlecock, and urging it to the utmost verge of breathless extravagance, in the mere eagerness of the fray, is beyond that of any other of our writers. His fable is not so profoundly laid, nor his characters so well digested as Wycherley's (who, in these respects, bore some resemblance to Fielding). Vanbrugh does not lay the same deliberate train from the outset to the conclusion, so that the whole may hang together, and tend inevitably from the combination of different agents and circumstances to the same decisive point: but he works out scene after scene, on the spur of the occasion, and from the immediate hold they take of his imagination at the moment, without any previous bias or ultimate purpose, much more powerfully, with more *verve*, and in a richer vein of original invention. His fancy warms and burnishes out as if he were engaged in the real scene of action, and felt all his faculties suddenly called forth to meet the emergency. He has more nature than art: what he does best, he does because he cannot help it. He has a masterly eye to the advantages which certain accidental situations of character present to him on the spot, and he executes the most difficult and rapid theatrical movements at a moment's warning. Of this kind are the inimitable scenes in the Provoked Wife, between Razor and Mademoiselle, where they repeat and act over again the rencontre in the Mulberry-walk between Constant and his mistress, than which nothing was ever more happily conceived, or done to more absolute perfection; that again in the Relapse, where Loveless pushes

79

Berinthia into the closet; the sudden meeting in the Confederacy between Dick and Mrs. Amlet; the altercation about the letter between Flippanta and Corinna, in the same play, and that again where Brass, at the house of Gripe the money-scrivener, threatens to discover his friend and accomplice, and by talking louder and louder to him, as he tries to evade his demands, extorts a grudging submission from him. This last scene is as follows :—

'*Dick.* I wish my old hobbling mother han't been blabbing something here she should not do.

Brass. Fear nothing, all's safe on that side yet. But how speaks young mistress's epistle ? soft and tender ?

Dick. As pen can write.

Brass. So you think all goes well there ?

Dick. As my heart can wish.

Brass. You are sure on 't ?

Dick. Sure on 't !

Brass. Why then, ceremony aside—[*Putting on his hat*]—you and I must have a little talk, Mr. Amlet.

Dick. Ah, Brass, what art thou going to do ? wo't ruin me?

Brass. Look you, Dick, few words; you are in a smooth way of making your fortune ; I hope all will roll on. But how do you intend matters shall pass 'twixt you and me in this business?

Dick. Death and furies ! What a time does take to talk on 't ?

Brass. Good words, or I betray you ; they have already heard of one Mr. Amlet in the house.

Dick. Here's a son of a whore.   [*Aside.*

Brass. In short, look smooth, and be a good prince. I am your valet, 'tis true : your footman, sometimes, which I 'm enraged at ; but you have always had the ascendant I confess : when we were schoolfellows, you made me carry your books, make your exercise, own your rogueries, and sometimes take a whipping for you. When we were fellow-'prentices, though I was your senior, you made me open the shop, clean my master's shoes, cut last at dinner, and eat all the crust. In our sins too, I must own you still kept me under; you soar'd up to adultery with the mistress, while I was at humble fornication with the maid. Nay, in our punishments you still made good your post ; for when once upon a time I was sentenced but to be whipp'd, I cannot deny but you were condemn'd to be hang'd. So that in all times, I must confess, your inclinations have been greater and nobler than mine ; however, I cannot consent that you should at once fix fortune for life, and I dwell in my humilities for the rest of my days.

Dick. Hark thee, Brass, if I do not most nobly by thee, I 'm a dog.

Brass. And when?

Dick. As soon as ever I am married.

Brass. Ay, the plague take thee.

Dick. Then you mistrust me ?

Brass. I do, by my faith. Look you, Sir, some folks we mistrust,

80

because we don't know them: others we mistrust, because we do know them: and for one of these reasons I desire there may be a bargain beforehand: if not [*raising his voice*] look ye, Dick Amlet—

Dick. Soft, my dear friend and companion. The dog will ruin me [*Aside*]. Say, what is 't will content thee?

Brass. O ho!

Dick. But how canst thou be such a barbarian?

Brass. I learnt it at Algiers.

Dick. Come, make thy Turkish demand then.

Brass. You know you gave me a bank-bill this morning to receive for you.

Dick. I did so, of fifty pounds; 'tis thine. So, now thou art satisfied all is fixed.

Brass. It is not indeed. There's a diamond necklace you robb'd your mother of e'en now.

Dick. Ah, you Jew!

Brass. No words.

Dick. My dear Brass!

Brass. I insist.

Dick. My old friend!

Brass. Dick Amlet [*raising his voice*] I insist.

Dick. Ah, the cormorant [*Aside*].—Well, 'tis thine: thou'lt never thrive with it.

Brass. When I find it begins to do me mischief, I'll give it you again. But I must have a wedding suit.

Dick. Well.

Brass. A stock of linen.

Dick. Enough.

Brass. Not yet——a silver-hilted sword.

Dick. Well, thou shalt have that too. Now thou hast every thing.

Brass. Heav'n forgive me, I forgot a ring of remembrance. I would not forget all these favours for the world: a sparkling diamond will be always playing in my eye, and put me in mind of them.

Dick. This unconscionable rogue! [*Aside*]—Well, I'll bespeak one for thee.

Brass. Brilliant.

Dick. It shall. But if the thing don't succeed after all—

Brass. I am a man of honour and restore: and so, the treaty being finish'd, I strike my flag of defiance, and fall into my respects again.'

[*Takes off his hat.*

The Confederacy is a comedy of infinite contrivance and intrigue, with a matchless spirit of impudence. It is a fine careless *exposé* of heartless want of principle: for there is no anger or severity against vice expressed in it, as in Wycherley. The author's morality in all cases (except his Provoked Wife, which was undertaken as a penance for past peccadillos) sits very loose upon him. It is a little upon the turn; 'it does somewhat smack.' Old Palmer, as Dick Amlet, asking his mother's blessing on his knee, was the very idea of a graceless son.—His sweetheart Corinna is a Miss Prue, but nature works in her more powerfully.—Lord Foppington, in the Relapse, is a most splendid caricature: he is a personification of the foppery and folly of dress and external appearance in full feather. He blazes out and dazzles sober reason with ridiculous ostentation. Still I think this character is a copy from Etherege's Sir Fopling Flutter, and upon the whole, perhaps, Sir Fopling is the more natural grotesque of the two. His soul is more in his dress; he is a more disinterested coxcomb. The lord is an ostentatious, strutting, vain-glorious blockhead: the knight is an unaffected, self-complacent, serious admirer of his equipage and person. For instance, what they severally say on the subject of contemplating themselves in the glass, is a proof of this. Sir Fopling thinks a looking-glass in the room 'the best company in the world;' it is another self to him: Lord Foppington merely considers it as necessary to adjust his appearance, that he may make a figure in company. The finery of the one has an imposing air of grandeur about it, and is studied for effect: the other is really in love with a laced suit, and is hand and glove with the newest-cut fashion. He really thinks his tailor or peruke-maker the greatest man in the world, while his lordship treats them familiarly as necessary appendages of his person. Still this coxcomb-nobleman's effeminacy and mock-heroic vanity are admirably depicted, and held up to unrivalled ridicule; and his courtship of Miss Hoyden is excellent in all its stages, and ends oracularly.

Lord Foppington.—'Now, for my part, I think the wisest thing a man can do with an aching heart, is to put on a serene countenance; for a philosophical air is the most becoming thing in the world to the face of a person of quality: I will therefore bear my disgrace like a great man, and let the people see I am above an affront. [*then turning to his brother*] Dear Tam, since things are thus fallen out, pr'ythee give me leave to wish thee joy, I do it *de bon cœur*, strike me dumb: you have married a woman beautiful in her person, charming in her airs, prudent in her conduct, constant in her inclinations, and of a nice morality—stap my vitals!'

Poor Hoyden fares ill in his lordship's description of her, though she could expect no better at his hands for her desertion of him. She wants sentiment, to be sure, but she has other qualifications—she is a fine bouncing piece of flesh and blood. Her first announcement is decisive—'Let loose the greyhound, and lock up Hoyden.' Her declaration, 'It's well they've got me a husband, or ecod, I'd marry the baker,' comes from her mouth like a shot from a culverin, and leaves no doubt, by its effect upon the ear, that she would have made

it good in the sequel, if she had not been provided for. Her
indifference to the man she is to marry, and her attachment to the
finery and the title, are justified by an attentive observation of nature
in its simplest guise. There is, however, no harm in Hoyden; she
merely wishes to consult her own inclination: she is by no means
like Corinna in the Confederacy, 'a devilish girl at the bottom,' nor
is it her great delight to plague other people.—Sir Tunbelly Clumsy
is the right worshipful and worthy father of so delicate an offspring.
He is a coarse, substantial contrast to the flippant and flimsy Lord
Foppington. If the one is not without reason 'proud to be at the
head of so prevailing a party' as that of coxcombs, the other may
look big and console himself (under some affronts) with being a very
competent representative, a knight of the shire, of the once formidable,
though now obsolete class of country squires, who had no idea
beyond the boundaries of their own estates, or the circumference of
their own persons. His unwieldy dulness gives, by the rule of
contraries, a lively sense of lightness and grace: his stupidity answers
all the purposes of wit. His portly paunch repels a jest like a wool-
sack: a sarcasm rebounds from him like a ball. His presence is a
cure for gravity; and he is a standing satire upon himself and the
class in natural history to which he belonged.—Sir John Brute, in
the Provoked Wife, is an animal of the same English growth, but of
a cross-grained breed. He has a spice of the demon mixed up with
the brute; is mischievous as well as stupid; has improved his natural
parts by a town education and example; opposes the fine-lady airs
and graces of his wife by brawling oaths, impenetrable surliness, and
pot-house valour; overpowers any tendency she might have to
vapours or hysterics, by the fumes of tobacco and strong beer; and
thinks to be master in his own house by roaring in taverns, reeling
home drunk every night, breaking lamps, and beating the watch.
He does not, however, find this lordly method answer. He turns
out to be a coward as well as a bully, and dares not resent the
injuries he has provoked by his unmanly behaviour. This was
Garrick's favourite part; and I have heard that his acting in the
drunken scene, in which he was disguised not as a clergyman, but as
a woman of the town, which was an alteration of his own to suit the
delicacy of the times, was irresistible. The ironical conversations in
this play between Belinda and Lady Brute, as well as those in the
Relapse between Amanda and her cousin Berinthia, will do to compare with Congreve in the way of wit and studied raillery, but they
will not stand the comparison. Araminta and Clarissa keep up the
ball between them with more spirit, for their conversation is very like
that of kept mistresses; and the mixture of fashionable *slang* and

professed want of principle gives a sort of zest and high seasoning to their confidential communications, which Vanbrugh could supply as well as any body. But he could not do without the taint of grossness and licentiousness. Lady Townly is not the really vicious character, nor quite the fine lady, which the author would have her to be. Lady Grace is so far better; she is what she pretends to be, merely *sober* and insipid.—Vanbrugh's *forte* was not the sentimental or didactic; his genius flags and grows dull when it is not put into action, and wants the stimulus of sudden emergency, or the fortuitous collision of different motives, to call out all its force and vivacity. His antitheses are happy and brilliant contrasts of character; his *double entendres* equivocal situations; his best jokes are practical devices, not epigrammatic conceits. His wit is that which is emphatically called *mother-wit*. It brings those who possess it, or to whom he lends it, into scrapes by its restlessness, and brings them out of them by its alacrity. Several of his favourite characters are knavish, adroit adventurers, who have all the gipsy jargon, the cunning impudence, cool presence of mind, selfishness, and indefatigable industry; all the excuses, lying, dexterity, the intellectual juggling and legerdemain tricks, necessary to fit them for this sort of predatory warfare on the simplicity, follies, or vices of mankind. He discovers the utmost dramatic generalship in bringing off his characters at a pinch, and by an instantaneous *ruse de guerre*, when the case seems hopeless in any other hands. The train of his associations, to express the same thing in metaphysical language, lies in following the suggestions of his fancy into every possible connexion of cause and effect, rather than into every possible combination of likeness or difference. His ablest characters shew that they are so by displaying their ingenuity, address, and presence of mind in critical junctures, and in their own affairs, rather than their wisdom or their wit ' in intellectual gladiatorship,' or in speculating on the affairs and characters of other people.

Farquhar's chief characters are also adventurers; but they are adventurers of a romantic, not a knavish stamp, and succeed no less by their honesty than their boldness. They conquer their difficulties, and effect their ' hair-breadth 'scapes ' by the impulse of natural enthusiasm and the confidence of high principles of gallantry and honour, as much as by their dexterity and readiness at expedients. They are real gentlemen, and only pretended impostors. Vanbrugh's upstart heroes are without ' any relish of salvation,' without generosity, virtue, or any pretensions to it. We have little sympathy for them, and no respect at all. But we have every sort of good-will towards Farquhar's heroes, who have as many peccadillos to answer for, and play as many rogue's tricks, but are honest fellows at bottom. I know little other difference between these two capital writers and copyists of nature, than that Farquhar's nature is the better nature of the two. We seem to like both the author and his favourites. He has humour, character, and invention, in common with the other, with a more unaffected gaiety and spirit of enjoyment, which over-flows and sparkles in all he does. He makes us laugh from pleasure oftener than from malice. He somewhere prides himself in having introduced on the stage the class of comic heroes here spoken of, which has since become a standard character, and which represents the warm-hearted, rattle-brained, thoughtless, high-spirited young fellow, who floats on the back of his misfortunes without repining, who forfeits appearances, but saves his honour—and he gives us to understand that it was his own. He did not need to be ashamed of it. Indeed there is internal evidence that this sort of character is his own, for it pervades his works generally, and is the moving spirit that informs them. His comedies have on this account probably a greater appearance of truth and nature than almost any others. His incidents succeed one another with rapidity, but without premeditation; his wit is easy and spontaneous; his style animated, unembarrassed, and flowing; his characters full of life and spirit, and never overstrained so as to 'o'erstep the modesty of nature,' though they sometimes, from haste and carelessness, seem left in a crude, unfinished state. There is a constant ebullition of gay, laughing invention, cordial good humour, and fine animal spirits, in his writings.

Of the four writers here classed together, we should perhaps have courted Congreve's acquaintance most, for his wit and the elegance of his manners; Wycherley's, for his sense and observation on human nature; Vanbrugh's, for his power of farcical description and telling a story; Farquhar's, for the pleasure of his society, and the love of good fellowship. His fine gentlemen are not gentlemen of fortune and fashion, like those in Congreve; but are rather 'God Almighty's gentlemen.' His valets are good fellows: even his chambermaids are some of them disinterested and sincere. But his fine ladies, it must be allowed, are not so amiable, so witty, or accomplished, as those in Congreve. Perhaps they both described women in high-life as they found them: Congreve took their conversation, Farquhar their conduct. In the way of fashionable vice and petrifying affecta-tion, there is nothing to come up to his Lady Lurewell, in the Trip to the Jubilee. She by no means makes good Mr. Burke's courtly and chivalrous observation, that the evil of vice consists principally in its want of refinement; and one benefit of the dramatic exhibition of such characters is, that they overturn false maxims of morality, and

85

settle accounts fairly and satisfactorily between theory and practice. Her lover, Colonel Standard, is indeed an awkward incumbrance upon so fine a lady: it was a character that the poet did not like; and he has merely sketched him in, leaving him to answer for himself as well as he could, which is but badly. We have no suspicion, either from his conduct, or from any hint dropped by accident, that he is the first seducer and the possessor of the virgin affections of Lady Lurewell. The double transformation of this virago from vice to virtue, and from virtue to vice again, her plausible pretensions and artful wiles, her violent temper and dissolute passions, shew a thorough knowledge of the effects both of nature and habit in making up human character. Farquhar's own heedless turn for gallantry would be likely to throw him upon such a character; and his goodness of heart and sincerity of disposition would teach him to expose its wanton duplicity and gilded rottenness. Lurewell is almost as abandoned a character as Olivia, in the Plain Dealer; but the indignation excited against her is of a less serious and tragic cast. Her peevish disgust and affected horror at every thing that comes near her, form a very edifying picture. Her dissatisfaction and *ennui* are not mere airs and graces worn for fashion's sake; but are real and tormenting inmates of her breast, arising from a surfeit of pleasure and the consciousness of guilt. All that is hateful in the caprice, ill humour, spite, *hauteur*, folly, impudence, and affectation of the complete woman of quality, is contained in the scene between her and her servants in the first act. The depravity would be intolerable, even in imagination, if the weakness were not ludicrous in the extreme. It shews, in the highest degree, the power of circumstances and example to pervert the understanding, the imagination, and even the senses. The manner in which the character of the gay, wild, free-hearted, but not altogether profligate or unfeeling Sir Harry Wildair is played off against the designing, vindictive, imperious, uncontrolable, and unreasonable humours of Lurewell, in the scene where she tries to convince him of his wife's infidelity, while he stops his ears to her pretended proofs, is not surpassed in modern comedy. I shall give it here :—

'*Wildair.* Now, dear madam, I have secur'd my brother, you have dispos'd of the colonel, and we'll rail at love till we ha'n't a word more to say.

Lurewell. Ay, Sir Harry. Please to sit a little, Sir. You must know I'm in a strange humour of asking you some questions. How did you like your lady, pray, Sir?

Wild. Like her! Ha, ha, ha. So very well, faith, that for her very sake I'm in love with every woman I meet.

Lure. And did matrimony please you extremely?

Wild. So very much, that if polygamy were allow'd, I would have a new wife every day.

Lure. Oh, Sir Harry ! this is raillery. But your serious thoughts upon the matter, pray.

Wild. Why, then, Madam, to give you my true sentiments of wedlock : I had a lady that I married by chance, she was virtuous by chance, and I lov'd her by great chance. Nature gave her beauty, education an air ; and fortune threw a young fellow of five-and-twenty in her lap. I courted her all day, lov'd her all night ; she was my mistress one day, and my wife another : I found in one the variety of a thousand, and the very confinement of marriage gave me the pleasure of change.

Lure. And she was very virtuous.

Wild. Look ye, Madam, you know she was beautiful. She had good nature about her mouth, the smile of beauty in her cheeks, sparkling wit in her forehead, and sprightly love in her eyes.

Lure. Pshaw ! I knew her very well ; the woman was well enough. But you don't answer my question, Sir.

Wild. So, Madam, as I told you before, she was young and beautiful, I was rich and vigorous ; my estate gave a lustre to my love, and a swing to our enjoyment ; round, like the ring that made us one, our golden pleasures circled without end.

Lure. Golden pleasures ! Golden fiddlesticks. What d 'ye tell me of your canting stuff ? Was she virtuous, I say ?

Wild. Ready to burst with envy ; but I will torment thee a little. [*Aside.*] So, Madam, I powder'd to please her, she dress'd to engage me ; we toy'd away the morning in amorous nonsense, loll'd away the evening in the Park or the playhouse, and all the night—hem !

Lure. Look ye, Sir, answer my question, or I shall take it ill.

Wild. Then, Madam, there was never such a pattern of unity. Her wants were still prevented by my supplies ; my own heart whisper'd me her desires, 'cause she herself was there ; no contention ever rose, but the dear strife of who should most oblige : no noise about authority ; for neither would stoop to command, 'cause both thought it glory to obey.

Lure. Stuff ! stuff ! stuff ! I won't believe a word on 't.

Wild. Ha, ha, ha. Then, Madam, we never felt the yoke of matrimony, because our inclinations made us one ; a power superior to the forms of wedlock. The marriage torch had lost its weaker light in the bright flame of mutual love that join'd our hearts before ; then—

Lure. Hold, hold, Sir ; I cannot bear it ; Sir Harry, I 'm affronted.

Wild. Ha, ha, ha. Affronted !

Lure. Yes, Sir ; 'tis an affront to any woman to hear another commended ; and I will resent it.—In short, Sir Harry, your wife was a—

Wild. Buz, Madam—no detraction ! I 'll tell you what she was. So much an angel in her conduct, that though I saw another in her arms, I should have thought the devil had rais'd the phantom, and my more conscious reason had given my eyes the lie.

Lure. Very well ! Then I a'n't to be believ'd, it seems. But, d 'ye hear, Sir ?

Wild. Nay, Madam, do you hear ! I tell you, 'tis not in the power of malice to cast a blot upon her fame; and though the vanity of our sex, and the envy of yours, conspir'd both against her honour, I would not hear a syllable.   [*Stopping his ears.*

Lure. Why then, as I hope to breathe, you shall hear it.   The picture! the picture! the picture!   [*Bawling aloud.*

Wild. Ran, tan, tan.   A pistol-bullet from ear to ear.

Lure. That picture which you had just now from the French marquis for a thousand pound; that very picture did your very virtuous wife send to the marquis as a pledge of her very virtuous and dying affection.   So that you are both robb'd of your honour, and cheated of your money.

[*Aloud.*

Wild. Louder, louder, Madam.

Lure. I tell you, Sir, your wife was a jilt; I know it, I'll swear it. She virtuous! she was a devil!

Wild. [*Sings.*] Tal, al, deral.

Lure. Was ever the like seen!   He won't hear me.   I burst with malice, and now he won't mind me!   Won't you hear me yet?

Wild. No, no, Madam.

Lure. Nay, then I can't bear it.   [*Bursts out a crying.*]   Sir, I must say that you're an unworthy person, to use a woman of quality at this rate, when she has her heart full of malice; I don't know but it may make me miscarry.   Sir, I say again and again, that she was no better than one of us, and I know it; I have seen it with my eyes, so I have.

Wild. Good heav'ns deliver me, I beseech thee.   How shall I 'scape!

Lure. Will you hear me yet?   Dear Sir Harry, do but hear me; I'm longing to speak.

Wild. Oh! I have it.—Hush, hush, hush.

Lure. Eh! what's the matter?

Wild. A mouse! a mouse! a mouse!

Lure. Where? where? where?

Wild. Your petticoats, your petticoats, Madam.   [*Lurewell shrieks and runs.*]   O my head!   I was never worsted by a woman before.   But I have heard so much to know the marquis to be a villain.   [*Knocking.*]   Nay, then, I must run for't.   [*Runs out, and returns.*]   The entry is stopt by a chair coming in; and something there is in that chair that I will discover, if I can find a place to hide myself.   [*Goes to the closet door.*]   Fast! I have keys about me for most locks about St. James's.   Let me see.   [*Tries one key.*]   No, no; this opens my Lady Planthorn's back-door.   [*Tries another.*]   Nor this; this is the key to my Lady Stakeall's garden.   [*Tries a third.*]   Ay, ay, this does it, faith.   [*Goes into the closet.*]'

The dialogue between Cherry and Archer, in the Beaux' Stratagem, in which she repeats her well-conned love catechism, is as good as this, but not so fit to be repeated any where but on the stage.   The Beaux' Stratagem is the best of his plays, as a whole; infinitely lively, bustling, and full of point and interest.   The assumed disguise of the two principal characters, Archer and Aimwell, is a perpetual amusement to the mind.   Scrub is an indispensable appendage to a country gentleman's kitchen, and an exquisite confidant for the secrets of young ladies. The Recruiting Officer is not one of Farquhar's best comedies, though it is light and entertaining. It contains chiefly sketches and hints of characters; and the conclusion of the plot is rather lame. He informs us, in the dedication to the published play, that it was founded on some local and personal circumstances that happened in Shropshire, where he was himself a recruiting officer; and it seems not unlikely, that most of the scenes actually took place at the foot of the Wrekin. The Inconstant is much superior to it. The romantic interest and impressive catastrophe of this play I thought had been borrowed from the more poetical and tragedy-practised muse of Beaumont and Fletcher; but I find they are taken from an actual circumstance which took place in the author's knowledge, at Paris. His other pieces, Love and a Bottle, and the Twin Rivals, are not on a par with these; and are no longer in possession of the stage. The public are, after all, not the worst judges.—Farquhar's Letters, prefixed to the collection of his plays, are lively, good humoured, and sensible; and contain, among other things, an admirable exposition of the futility of the dramatic unities of time and place. This criticism preceded Dennis's remarks on that subject, in his Strictures on Mr. Addison's Cato; and completely anticipates all that Dr. Johnson has urged so unanswerably on the subject, in his preface to Shakspeare.

We may date the decline of English comedy from the time of Farquhar. For this several causes might be assigned in the political and moral changes of the times; but among other minor ones, Jeremy Collier, in his View of the English Stage, frightened the poets, and did all he could to spoil the stage, by pretending to reform it; that is, by making it an echo of the pulpit, instead of a reflection of the manners of the world. He complains bitterly of the profaneness of the stage; and is for fining the actors for every oath they utter, to put an end to the practice; as if common swearing had been an invention of the poets and stage-players. He cannot endure that the fine gentlemen drink, and the fine ladies intrigue, in the scenes of Congreve and Wycherley, when things so contrary to law and gospel happened nowhere else. He is vehement against duelling, as a barbarous custom, of which the example is suffered with impunity nowhere but on the stage. He is shocked at the number of fortunes that are irreparably ruined by the vice of gaming on the boards of the theatres. He seems to think that every breach of the ten commandments begins and ends there. He complains that the tame husbands of his time are laughed at on the stage, and that the successful gallants triumph, which was without precedent either in the city or the court. He does not think it enough that the stage 'shews vice its own image, scorn its own feature,' unless they are damned at the same instant, and carried off (like Don Juan) by real devils to the infernal regions, before the faces of the spectators. It seems that the author would have been contented to be present at a comedy or a farce, like a Father Inquisitor, if there was to be an *auto da fe* at the end, to burn both the actors and the poet. This sour, nonjuring critic has a great horror and repugnance at poor human nature, in nearly all its shapes; of the existence of which he appears only to be aware through the stage: and this he considers as the only exception to the practice of piety, and the performance of the whole duty of man; and seems fully convinced, that if this nuisance were abated, the whole world would be regulated according to the creed and the catechism.—This is a strange blindness and infatuation! He forgets, in his overheated zeal, two things: First, That the stage must be copied from real life, that the manners represented there must exist elsewhere, and 'denote a foregone conclusion,' to satisfy common sense.—Secondly, That the stage cannot shock common decency, according to the notions that prevail of it in any age or country, because the exhibition is public. If the pulpit, for instance, had banished all vice and imperfection from the world, as our critic would suppose, we should not have seen the offensive reflection of them on the stage, which he resents as an affront to the cloth, and an outrage on religion. On the contrary, with such a sweeping reformation as this theory implies, the office of the preacher, as well as of the player, would be gone; and if the common peccadillos of lying, swearing, intriguing, fighting, drinking, gaming, and other such obnoxious dramatic common-places, were once fairly got rid of in reality, neither the comic poet would be able to laugh at them on the stage, nor our good-natured author to consign them over to damnation elsewhere. The work is, however, written with ability, and did much mischief: it produced those *do-me-good*, lack-a-daisical, whining, make-believe comedies in the next age, (such as Steele's Conscious Lovers, and others,) which are enough to set one to sleep, and where the author tries in vain to be merry and wise in the same breath; in which the utmost stretch of licentiousness goes no farther than the gallant's being suspected of keeping a mistress, and the highest proof of courage is given in his refusing to accept a challenge.

In looking into the old editions of the comedies of the last age, I find the names of the best actors of those times, of whom scarcely any record is left but in Colley Cibber's Life, and the monument to Mrs. Oldfield, in Westminster Abbey; which Voltaire reckons

among the proofs of the liberality, wisdom, and politeness of the
English nation :—

> 'Let no rude hand deface it,
> And its forlorn *hic jacet*.'

Authors after their deaths live in their works; players only in their
epitaphs and the breath of common tradition. They 'die and leave
the world no copy.' Their uncertain popularity is as short-lived as
it is dazzling: and in a few years nothing is known of them but that
they were.

LECTURE V

ON THE PERIODICAL ESSAYISTS

'THE PROPER STUDY OF MANKIND IS MAN'

I now come to speak of that sort of writing which has been so
successfully cultivated in this country by our periodical Essayists, and
which consists in applying the talents and resources of the mind to
all that mixed mass of human affairs, which, though not included
under the head of any regular art, science, or profession, falls under
the cognizance of the writer, and 'comes home to the business and
bosoms of men.' *Quicquid agunt homines nostri farrago libelli,* is the
general motto of this department of literature. It does not treat of
minerals or fossils, of the virtues of plants, or the influence of planets;
it does not meddle with forms of belief, or systems of philosophy, nor
launch into the world of spiritual existences; but it makes familiar
with the world of men and women, records their actions, assigns
their motives, exhibits their whims, characterises their pursuits in
all their singular and endless variety, ridicules their absurdities,
exposes their inconsistencies, 'holds the mirror up to nature, and
shews the very age and body of the time its form and pressure;'
takes minutes of our dress, air, looks, words, thoughts, and actions;
shews us what we are, and what we are not; plays the whole game
of human life over before us, and by making us enlightened spectators
of its many-coloured scenes, enables us (if possible) to become
tolerably reasonable agents in the one in which we have to perform
a part. 'The act and practic part of life is thus made the mistress
of our theorique.' It is the best and most natural course of study.
It is in morals and manners what the experimental is in natural
philosophy, as opposed to the dogmatical method. It does not deal
in sweeping clauses of proscription and anathema, but in nice

91

distinctions and liberal constructions. It makes up its general
accounts from details, its few theories from many facts. It does
not try to prove all black or all white as it wishes, but lays on the
intermediate colours, (and most of them not unpleasing ones,) as it
finds them blended with 'the web of our life, which is of a mingled
yarn, good and ill together.' It inquires what human life is and has
been, to shew what it ought to be. It follows it into courts and
camps, into town and country, into rustic sports or learned disputa-
tions, into the various shades of prejudice or ignorance, of refinement
or barbarism, into its private haunts or public pageants, into its
weaknesses and littlenesses, its professions and its practices—before
it pretends to distinguish right from wrong, or one thing from
another. How, indeed, should it do so otherwise?

> 'Quid sit pulchrum, quid turpe, quid utile, quid non,
> Plenius et melius Chrysippo et Crantore dicit.'

The writers I speak of are, if not moral philosophers, moral historians,
and that's better: or if they are both, they found the one character
upon the other; their premises precede their conclusions; and we
put faith in their testimony, for we know that it is true.

Montaigne was the first person who in his Essays led the way
to this kind of writing among the moderns. The great merit of
Montaigne then was, that he may be said to have been the first who
had the courage to say as an author what he felt as a man. And
as courage is generally the effect of conscious strength, he was
probably led to do so by the richness, truth, and force of his own
observations on books and men. He was, in the truest sense, a
man of original mind, that is, he had the power of looking at things
for himself, or as they really were, instead of blindly trusting to,
and fondly repeating what others told him that they were. He got
rid of the go-cart of prejudice and affectation, with the learned
lumber that follows at their heels, because he could do without
them. In taking up his pen he did not set up for a philosopher,
wit, orator, or moralist, but he became all these by merely daring
to tell us whatever passed through his mind, in its naked simplicity
and force, that he thought any ways worth communicating. He
did not, in the abstract character of an author, undertake to say all
that could be said upon a subject, but what in his capacity as an
inquirer after truth he happened to know about it. He was neither
a pedant nor a bigot. He neither supposed that he was bound to
know all things, nor that all things were bound to conform to what
he had fancied or would have them to be. In treating of men and
manners, he spoke of them as he found them, not according to pre-

92

conceived notions and abstract dogmas; and he began by teaching us what he himself was. In criticising books he did not compare them with rules and systems, but told us what he saw to like or dislike in them. He did not take his standard of excellence ' according to an exact scale' of Aristotle, or fall out with a work that was good for any thing, because 'not one of the angles at the four corners was a right one.' He was, in a word, the first author who was not a book-maker, and who wrote not to make converts of others to established creeds and prejudices, but to satisfy his own mind of the truth of things. In this respect we know not which to be most charmed with, the author or the man. There is an inexpressible frankness and sincerity, as well as power, in what he writes. There is no attempt at imposition or concealment, no juggling tricks or solemn mouthing, no laboured attempts at proving himself always in the right, and every body else in the wrong; he says what is uppermost, lays open what floats at the top or the bottom of his mind, and deserves Pope's character of him, where he professes to

> '——pour out all as plain
> As downright Shippen, or as old Montaigne.'[1]

He does not converse with us like a pedagogue with his pupil, whom he wishes to make as great a blockhead as himself, but like a philosopher and friend who has passed through life with thought and observation, and is willing to enable others to pass through it with pleasure and profit. A writer of this stamp, I confess, appears to me as much superior to a common bookworm, as a library of real books is superior to a mere book-case, painted and lettered on the outside with the names of celebrated works. As he was the first to attempt this new way of writing, so the same strong natural impulse which prompted the undertaking, carried him to the end of his career. The same force and honesty of mind which urged him to throw off the shackles of custom and prejudice, would enable him to complete his triumph over them. He has left little for his successors to achieve in the way of just and original speculation on human life. Nearly all the thinking of the two last centuries of that kind which the French denominate *morale observatrice*, is to be found in Montaigne's Essays: there is the germ, at least, and generally much more. He sowed the seed and cleared away the rubbish, even where others have reaped the fruit, or cultivated and decorated the soil to a greater degree of nicety and perfection.

[1] Why Pope should say in reference to him, ' Or *more wise* Charron,' is not easy to determine.

LECTURES ON THE COMIC WRITERS

There is no one to whom the old Latin adage is more applicable than to Montaigne, ' *Pereant isti qui ante nos nostra dixerunt.*' There has been no new impulse given to thought since his time. Among the specimens of criticisms on authors which he has left us, are those on Virgil, Ovid, and Boccaccio, in the account of books which he thinks worth reading, or (which is the same thing) which he finds he can read in his old age, and which may be reckoned among the few criticisms which are worth reading at any age.[1]

Montaigne's Essays were translated into English by Charles Cotton, who was one of the wits and poets of the age of Charles II ; and Lord Halifax, one of the noble critics of that day, declared it to be 'the book in the world he was the best pleased with.' This mode of familiar Essay-writing, free from the trammels of the schools, and the airs of professed authorship, was successfully imitated, about the same time, by Cowley and Sir William Temple, in their miscellaneous Essays, which are very agreeable and learned talking upon paper. Lord Shaftesbury, on the contrary, who aimed at the same easy, *degagé* mode of communicating his thoughts to the world, has quite spoiled his matter, which is sometimes valuable, by his manner, in which he carries a certain flaunting, flowery, figurative, flirting style of amicable condescension to the reader, to an excess more tantalising than the most starched and ridiculous

---

[1] As an instance of his general power of reasoning, I shall give his chapter entitled *One Man's Profit is another's Loss,* in which he has nearly anticipated Mandeville's celebrated paradox of private vices being public benefits :—

'Demades, the Athenian, condemned a fellow-citizen, who furnished out funerals, for demanding too great a price for his goods : and if he got an estate, it must be by the death of a great many people : but I think it a sentence ill grounded, forasmuch as no profit can be made, but at the expense of some other person, and that every kind of gain is by that rule liable to be condemned. The tradesman thrives by the debauchery of youth, and the farmer by the dearness of corn ; the architect by the ruin of buildings, the officers of justice by quarrels and law-suits ; nay, even the honour and function of divines is owing to our mortality and vices. No physician takes pleasure in the health even of his best friends, said the ancient Greek comedian, nor soldier in the peace of his country ; and so of the rest. And, what is yet worse, let every one but examine his own heart, and he will find that his private wishes spring and grow up at the expense of some other person. Upon which consideration this thought came into my head, that nature does not hereby deviate from her general policy ; for the naturalists hold, that the birth, nourishment, and increase of any one thing is the decay and corruption of another :

> *Nam quodcunque suis mutatum finibus exit,*
> *Continuo hoc mors est illius, quod fuit ante.* i.e.

> For what from its own confines chang'd doth pass,
> Is straight the death of what before it was.'

Vol. I. *Chap.* xxi.

formality of the age of James I. There is nothing so tormenting as the affectation of ease and freedom from affectation.

The ice being thus thawed, and the barrier that kept authors at a distance from common sense and feeling broken through, the transition was not difficult from Montaigne and his imitators, to our Periodical Essayists. These last applied the same unrestrained expression of their thoughts to the more immediate and passing scenes of life, to temporary and local matters; and in order to discharge the invidious office of *Censor Morum* more freely, and with less responsibility, assumed some fictitious and humorous disguise, which, however, in a great degree corresponded to their own peculiar habits and character. By thus concealing their own name and person under the title of the Tatler, Spectator, &c. they were enabled to inform us more fully of what was passing in the world, while the dramatic contrast and ironical point of view to which the whole is subjected, added a greater liveliness and *piquancy* to the descriptions. The philosopher and wit here commences newsmonger, makes himself master of 'the perfect spy o' th' time,' and from his various walks and turns through life, brings home little curious specimens of the humours, opinions, and manners of his contemporaries, as the botanist brings home different plants and weeds, or the mineralogist different shells and fossils, to illustrate their several theories, and be useful to mankind.

The first of these papers that was attempted in this country was set up by Steele in the beginning of the last century; and of all our periodical Essayists, the *Tatler* (for that was the name he assumed) has always appeared to me the most amusing and agreeable. Montaigne, whom I have proposed to consider as the father of this kind of personal authorship among the moderns, in which the reader is admitted behind the curtain, and sits down with the writer in his gown and slippers, was a most magnanimous and undisguised egotist; but Isaac Bickerstaff, Esq. was the more disinterested gossip of the two. The French author is contented to describe the peculiarities of his own mind and constitution, which he does with a copious and unsparing hand. The English journalist good-naturedly lets you into the secret both of his own affairs and those of others. A young lady, on the other side Temple Bar, cannot be seen at her glass for half a day together, but Mr. Bickerstaff takes due notice of it; and he has the first intelligence of the symptoms of the *belle* passion appearing in any young gentleman at the West-end of the town. The departures and arrivals of widows with handsome jointures, either to bury their grief in the country, or to procure a second husband in town, are punctually recorded in his pages. He

is well acquainted with the celebrated beauties of the preceding age
at the court of Charles II.; and the old gentleman (as he feigns
himself) often grows romantic in recounting 'the disastrous strokes
which his youth suffered' from the glances of their bright eyes, and
their unaccountable caprices.   In particular, he dwells with a secret
satisfaction on the recollection of one of his mistresses, who left him
for a richer rival, and whose constant reproach to her husband, on
occasion of any quarrel between them, was 'I, that might have
married the famous Mr. Bickerstaff, to be treated in this manner!'
The club at the Trumpet consists of a set of persons almost as well
worth knowing as himself.   The cavalcade of the justice of the
peace, the knight of the shire, the country squire, and the young
gentleman, his nephew, who came to wait on him at his chambers,
in such form and ceremony, seem not to have settled the order of
their precedence to this hour; [1] and I should hope that the upholsterer
and his companions, who used to sun themselves in the Green Park,
and who broke their rest and fortunes to maintain the balance of
power in Europe, stand as fair a chance for immortality as some
modern politicians.   Mr. Bickerstaff himself is a gentleman and a
scholar, a humourist, and a man of the world; with a great deal of
nice easy *naïveté* about him.   If he walks out and is caught in a
shower of rain, he makes amends for this unlucky accident by a
criticism on the shower in Virgil, and concludes with a burlesque
copy of verses on a city-shower.   He entertains us, when he dates
from his own apartment, with a quotation from Plutarch, or a moral
reflection; from the Grecian coffee-house with politics; and from
Wills', or the Temple, with the poets and players, the beaux and
men of wit and pleasure about town.   In reading the pages of the
Tatler, we seem as if suddenly carried back to the age of Queen
Anne, of toupees and full-bottomed periwigs.   The whole appearance
of our dress and manners undergoes a delightful metamorphosis.   The
beaux and the belles are of a quite different species from what they
are at present; we distinguish the dappers, the smarts, and the pretty
fellows, as they pass by Mr. Lilly's shop-windows in the Strand; we
are introduced to Betterton and Mrs. Oldfield behind the scenes;
are made familiar with the persons and performances of Will Estcourt
or Tom Durfey; we listen to a dispute at a tavern, on the merits
of the Duke of Marlborough, or Marshal Turenne; or are present
at the first rehearsal of a play by Vanbrugh, or the reading of a new
poem by Mr. Pope.   The privilege of thus virtually transporting
ourselves to past times, is even greater than that of visiting distant

---

[1] No. 125.

places in reality. London, a hundred years ago, would be much better worth seeing than Paris at the present moment.

It will be said, that all this is to be found, in the same or a greater degree, in the Spectator. For myself, I do not think so; or at least, there is in the last work a much greater proportion of common-place matter. I have, on this account, always preferred the Tatler to the Spectator. Whether it is owing to my having been earlier or better acquainted with the one than the other, my pleasure in reading these two admirable works is not in proportion to their comparative reputation. The Tatler contains only half the number of volumes, and, I will venture to say, nearly an equal quantity of sterling wit and sense. 'The first sprightly runnings' are there; it has more of the original spirit, more of the freshness and stamp of nature. The indications of character and strokes of humour are more true and frequent; the reflections that suggest themselves arise more from the occasion, and are less spun out into regular dissertations. They are more like the remarks which occur in sensible conversation, and less like a lecture. Something is left to the understanding of the reader. Steele seems to have gone into his closet chiefly to set down what he observed out of doors. Addison seems to have spent most of his time in his study, and to have spun out and wire-drawn the hints, which he borrowed from Steele, or took from nature, to the utmost. I am far from wishing to depreciate Addison's talents, but I am anxious to do justice to Steele, who was, I think, upon the whole, a less artificial and more original writer. The humorous descriptions of Steele resemble loose sketches, or fragments of a comedy; those of Addison are rather comments or ingenious para-phrases on the genuine text. The characters of the club not only in the Tatler, but in the Spectator, were drawn by Steele. That of Sir Roger de Coverley is among the number. Addison has, how-ever, gained himself immortal honour by his manner of filling up this last character. Who is there that can forget, or be insensible to, the inimitable nameless graces and varied traits of nature and of old English character in it—to his unpretending virtues and amiable weaknesses—to his modesty, generosity, hospitality, and eccentric whims—to the respect of his neighbours, and the affection of his domestics—to his wayward, hopeless, secret passion for his fair enemy, the widow, in which there is more of real romance and true delicacy, than in a thousand tales of knight-errantry—(we perceive the hectic flush of his cheek, the faltering of his tongue in speaking of her bewitching airs and 'the whiteness of her hand')—to the havoc he makes among the game in his neighbourhood—to his speech from the bench, to shew the Spectator what is thought of him in the country—to his unwillingness to be put up as a sign-post, and his having his own likeness turned into the Saracen's head—to his gentle reproof of the baggage of a gipsy that tells him ' he has a widow in his line of life '—to his doubts as to the existence of witch-craft, and protection of reputed witches—to his account of the family pictures, and his choice of a chaplain—to his falling asleep at church, and his reproof of John Williams, as soon as he recovered from his nap, for talking in sermon-time. The characters of Will, Wimble, and Will. Honeycomb are not a whit behind their friend, Sir Roger, in delicacy and felicity. The delightful simplicity and good-humoured officiousness in the one, are set off by the graceful affectation and courtly pretension in the other. How long since I first became acquainted with these two characters in the Spectator! What old-fashioned friends they seem, and yet I am not tired of them, like so many other friends, nor they of me! How airy these abstractions of the poet's pen stream over the dawn of our acquaint-ance with human life! how they glance their fairest colours on the prospect before us! how pure they remain in it to the last, like the rainbow in the evening-cloud, which the rude hand of time and experience can neither soil nor dissipate! What a pity that we cannot find the reality, and yet if we did, the dream would be over. I once thought I knew a Will. Wimble, and a Will. Honeycomb, but they turned out but indifferently ; the originals in the Spectator still read, word for word, the same that they always did. We have only to turn to the page, and find them where we left them!—Many of the most exquisite pieces in the Tatler, it is to be observed, are Addison's, as the Court of Honour, and the Personification of Musical Instruments, with almost all those papers that form regular sets or series. I do not know whether the picture of the family of an old college acquaintance, in the Tatler, where the children run to let Mr. Bickerstaff in at the door, and where the one that loses the race that way, turns back to tell the father that he is come; with the nice gradation of incredulity in the little boy, who is got into Guy of Warwick, and the Seven Champions, and who shakes his head at the improbability of Æsop's Fables, is Steele's or Addison's, though I believe it belongs to the former. The account of the two sisters, one of whom held up her head higher than ordinary, from having on a pair of flowered garters, and that of the married lady who complained to the Tatler of the neglect of her husband, with her answers to some *home* questions that were put to her, are unquestionably Steele's.—If the Tatler is not inferior to the Spectator as a record of manners and character, it is superior to it in the interest of many of the

98

stories. Several of the incidents related there by Steele have never been surpassed in the heart-rending pathos of private distress. I might refer to those of the lover and his mistress, when the theatre, in which they were, caught fire; of the bridegroom, who by accident kills his bride on the day of their marriage; the story of Mr. Eustace and his wife; and the fine dream about his own mistress when a youth. What has given its superior reputation to the Spectator, is the greater gravity of its pretensions, its moral dissertations and critical reasonings, by which I confess myself less edified than by other things, which are thought more lightly of. Systems and opinions change, but nature is always true. It is the moral and didactic tone of the Spectator which makes us apt to think of Addison (according to Mandeville's sarcasm) as 'a parson in a tie-wig.' Many of his moral Essays are, however, exquisitely beautiful and quite happy. Such are the reflections on cheerfulness, those in Westminster Abbey, on the Royal Exchange, and particularly some very affecting ones on the death of a young lady in the fourth volume. These, it must be allowed, are the perfection of elegant sermonising. His critical Essays are not so good. I prefer Steele's occasional selection of beautiful poetical passages, without any affectation of analysing their beauties, to Addison's finer-spun theories. The best criticism in the Spectator, that on the Cartoons of Raphael, of which Mr. Fuseli has availed himself with great spirit in his Lectures, is by Steele.[1] I owed this acknowledgment to a writer who has so often put me in good humour with myself, and every thing about me, when few things else could, and when the tomes of casuistry and ecclesiastical history, with which the little duodecimo volumes of the Tatler were overwhelmed and surrounded, in the only library to which I had access when a boy, had tried their tranquillising effects upon me in vain. I had not long ago in my hands, by favour of a friend, an original copy of the quarto edition of the Tatler, with a list of the subscribers. It is curious to see some names there which we should hardly think of, (that of Sir Isaac Newton is among them,) and also to observe the degree of interest excited by those of the different persons, which is not determined according to the rules of the Herald's College. One literary name lasts as long as a whole race of heroes and their descendants! The Guardian, which followed the Spectator, was, as may be supposed, inferior to it.

The dramatic and conversational turn which forms the distin-

---

[1] The antithetical style and verbal paradoxes which Burke was so fond of, in which the epithet is a seeming contradiction to the substantive, such as 'proud submission and dignified obedience,' are, I think, first to be found in the Tatler.

guishing feature and greatest charm of the Spectator and Tatler, is quite lost in the Rambler by Dr. Johnson. There is no reflected light thrown on human life from an assumed character, nor any direct one from a display of the author's own. The Tatler and Spectator are, as it were, made up of notes and memorandums of the events and incidents of the day, with finished studies after nature, and characters fresh from the life, which the writer moralises upon, and turns to account as they come before him : the Rambler is a collection of moral Essays, or scholastic theses, written on set subjects, and of which the individual characters and incidents are merely artificial illustrations, brought in to give a pretended relief to the dryness of didactic discussion. The Rambler is a splendid and imposing common-place-book of general topics, and rhetorical declamation on the conduct and business of human life. In this sense, there is hardly a reflection that had been suggested on such subjects which is not to be found in this celebrated work, and there is, perhaps, hardly a reflection to be found in it which had not been already suggested and developed by some other author, or in the common course of conversation. The mass of intellectual wealth here heaped together is immense, but it is rather the result of gradual accumulation, the produce of the general intellect, labouring in the mine of knowledge and reflection, than dug out of the quarry, and dragged into the light by the industry and sagacity of a single mind. I am not here saying that Dr. Johnson was a man without originality, compared with the ordinary run of men's minds, but he was not a man of original thought or genius, in the sense in which Montaigne or Lord Bacon was. He opened no new vein of precious ore, nor did he light upon any single pebbles of uncommon size and unrivalled lustre. We seldom meet with any thing to 'give us pause ; ' he does not set us thinking for the first time. His reflections present themselves like reminiscences ; do not disturb the ordinary march of our thoughts ; arrest our attention by the stateliness of their appearance, and the costliness of their garb, but pass on and mingle with the throng of our impressions. After closing the volumes of the Rambler, there is nothing that we remember as a new truth gained to the mind, nothing indelibly stamped upon the memory ; nor is there any passage that we wish to turn to as embodying any known principle or observation, with such force and beauty that justice can only be done to the idea in the author's own words. Such, for instance, are many of the passages to be found in Burke, which shine by their own light, belong to no class, have neither equal nor counterpart, and of which we say that no one but the author could have written them ! There is neither the same boldness of design, nor mastery of execution in Johnson. In the one, the spark of genius seems to have met with its congenial matter : the shaft is sped ; the forked lightning dresses up the face of nature in ghastly smiles, and the loud thunder rolls far away from the ruin that is made. Dr. Johnson's style, on the contrary, resembles rather the rumbling of mimic thunder at one of our theatres ; and the light he throws upon a subject is like the dazzling effect of phosphorus, or an *ignis fatuus* of words. There is a wide difference, however, between perfect originality and perfect common-place : neither ideas nor expressions are trite or vulgar because they are not quite new. They are valuable, and ought to be repeated, if they have not become quite common ; and Johnson's style both of reasoning and imagery holds the middle rank between startling novelty and vapid common-place. Johnson has as much originality of thinking as Addison ; but then he wants his familiarity of illustration, knowledge of character, and delightful humour.—What most distinguishes Dr. Johnson from other writers is the pomp and uniformity of his style. All his periods are cast in the same mould, are of the same size and shape, and consequently have little fitness to the variety of things he professes to treat of. His subjects are familiar, but the author is always upon stilts. He has neither ease nor simplicity, and his efforts at playfulness, in part, remind one of the lines in Milton :—

'———— The elephant
To make them sport wreath'd his proboscis lithe.'

His Letters from Correspondents, in particular, are more pompous and unwieldy than what he writes in his own person. This want of relaxation and variety of manner has, I think, after the first effects of novelty and surprise were over, been prejudicial to the matter. It takes from the general power, not only to please, but to instruct. The monotony of style produces an apparent monotony of ideas. What is really striking and valuable, is lost in the vain ostentation and circumlocution of the expression ; for when we find the same pains and pomp of diction bestowed upon the most trifling as upon the most important parts of a sentence or discourse, we grow tired of distinguishing between pretension and reality, and are disposed to confound the tinsel and bombast of the phraseology with want of weight in the thoughts. Thus, from the imposing and oracular nature of the style, people are tempted at first to imagine that our author's speculations are all wisdom and profundity : till having found out their mistake in some instances, they suppose that there is nothing but common place in them, concealed under verbiage and pedantry ; and in both they are wrong. The fault of Dr. Johnson's style is, that it reduces all things to the same artificial and unmeaning level. It destroys all shades of difference, the association between words and things. It is a perpetual paradox and innovation. He condescends to the familiar till we are ashamed of our interest in it: he expands the little till it looks big. 'If he were to write a fable of little fishes,' as Goldsmith said of him, 'he would make them speak like great whales.' We can no more distinguish the most familiar objects in his descriptions of them, than we can a well-known face under a huge painted mask. The structure of his sentences, which was his own invention, and which has been generally imitated since his time, is a species of rhyming in prose, where one clause answers to another in measure and quantity, like the tagging of syllables at the end of a verse; the close of the period follows as mechanically as the oscillation of a pendulum, the sense is balanced with the sound; each sentence, revolving round its centre of gravity, is contained with itself like a couplet, and each paragraph forms itself into a stanza. Dr. Johnson is also a complete balance-master in the topics of morality. He never encourages hope, but he counteracts it by fear; he never elicits a truth, but he suggests some objection in answer to it. He seizes and alternately quits the clue of reason, lest it should involve him in the labyrinths of endless error: he wants confidence in himself and his fellows. He dares not trust himself with the immediate impressions of things, for fear of compromising his dignity; or follow them into their consequences, for fear of committing his prejudices. His timidity is the result, not of ignorance, but of morbid apprehension. 'He runs the great circle, and is still at home.' No advance is made by his writings in any sentiment, or mode of reasoning. Out of the pale of established authority and received dogmas, all is sceptical, loose, and desultory: he seems in imagination to strengthen the dominion of prejudice, as he weakens and dissipates that of reason; and round the rock of faith and power, on the edge of which he slumbers blindfold and uneasy, the waves and billows of uncertain and dangerous opinion roar and heave for evermore. His Rasselas is the most melancholy and debilitating moral speculation that ever was put forth. Doubtful of the faculties of his mind, as of his organs of vision, Johnson trusted only to his feelings and his fears. He cultivated a belief in witches as an out-guard to the evidences of religion; and abused Milton, and patronised Lauder, in spite of his aversion to his countrymen, as a step to secure the existing establishment in church and state. This was neither right feeling nor sound logic.

The most triumphant record of the talents and character of

ON THE PERIODICAL ESSAYISTS

Johnson is to be found in Boswell's Life of him. The man was superior to the author. When he threw aside his pen, which he regarded as an incumbrance, he became not only learned and thoughtful, but acute, witty, humorous, natural, honest; hearty and determined, 'the king of good fellows and wale of old men.' There are as many smart repartees, profound remarks, and keen invectives to be found in Boswell's 'inventory of all he said,' as are recorded of any celebrated man. The life and dramatic play of his conversation forms a contrast to his written works. His natural powers and undisguised opinions were called out in convivial intercourse. In public, he practised with the foils on : in private, he unsheathed the sword of controversy, and it was 'the Ebro's temper.' The eagerness of opposition roused him from his natural sluggishness and acquired timidity; he returned blow for blow; and whether the trial were of argument or wit, none of his rivals could boast much of the encounter. Burke seems to have been the only person who had a chance with him : and it is the unpardonable sin of Boswell's work, that he has purposely omitted their combats of strength and skill. Goldsmith asked, 'Does he wind into a subject like a serpent, as Burke does?' And when exhausted with sickness, he himself said, 'If that fellow Burke were here now, he would kill me.' It is to be observed, that Johnson's colloquial style was as blunt, direct, and downright, as his style of studied composition was involved and circuitous. As when Topham Beauclerc and Langton knocked him up at his chambers, at three in the morning, and he came to the door with the poker in his hand, but seeing them, exclaimed, 'What, is it you, my lads? then I'll have a frisk with you!' and he afterwards reproaches Langton, who was a literary milksop, for leaving them to go to an engagement 'with some *un-idead* girls.' What words to come from the mouth of the great moralist and lexicographer! His good deeds were as many as his good sayings. His domestic habits, his tenderness to servants, and readiness to oblige his friends; the quantity of strong tea that he drank to keep down sad thoughts; his many labours reluctantly begun, and irresolutely laid aside; his honest acknowledgement of his own, and indulgence to the weaknesses of others; his throwing himself back in the post-chaise with Boswell, and saying, 'Now I think I am a good-humoured fellow,' though nobody thought him so, and yet he was; his quitting the society of Garrick and his actresses, and his reason for it ; his dining with Wilkes, and his kindness to Goldsmith; his sitting with the young ladies on his knee at the Mitre, to give them good advice, in which situation, if not explained, he might be taken for Falstaff; and last and noblest, his carrying the unfortunate victim of disease and dissipation on his back up through Fleet Street, (an act which realises the parable of the good Samaritan)—all these, and innumerable others, endear him to the reader, and must be remembered to his lasting honour. He had faults, but they lie buried with him. He had his prejudices and his intolerant feelings; but he suffered enough in the conflict of his own mind with them. For if no man can be happy in the free exercise of his reason, no wise man can be happy without it. His were not time-serving, heartless, hypocritical prejudices; but deep, inwoven, not to be rooted out but with life and hope, which he found from old habit necessary to his own peace of mind, and thought so to the peace of mankind. I do not hate, but love him for them. They were between himself and his conscience; and should be left to that higher tribunal, ' where they in trembling hope repose, the bosom of his Father and his God.' In a word, he has left behind him few wiser or better men.

The herd of his imitators shewed what he was by their disproportionate effects. The Periodical Essayists, that succeeded the Rambler, are, and deserve to be, little read at present. The Adventurer, by Hawksworth, is completely trite and vapid, aping all the faults of Johnson's style, without any thing to atone for them. The sentences are often absolutely unmeaning; and one half of each might regularly be left blank. The World, and Connoisseur, which followed, are a little better; and in the last of these there is one good idea, that of a man in indifferent health, who judges of every one's title to respect from their possession of this blessing, and bows to a sturdy beggar with sound limbs and a florid complexion, while he turns his back upon a lord who is a valetudinarian.

Goldsmith's Citizen of the World, like all his works, bears the stamp of the author's mind. It does not ' go about to cozen reputation without the stamp of merit.' He is more observing, more original, more natural and picturesque than Johnson. His work is written on the model of the Persian Letters; and contrives to give an abstracted and somewhat perplexing view of things, by opposing foreign prepossessions to our own, and thus stripping objects of their customary disguises. Whether truth is elicited in this collision of contrary absurdities, I do not know; but I confess the process is too ambiguous and full of intricacy to be very amusing to my plain understanding. For light summer reading, it is like walking in a garden full of traps and pitfalls. It necessarily gives rise to paradoxes, and there are some very bold ones in the Essays, which would subject an author less established to no very agreeable sort of *censura literaria*. Thus the Chinese philosopher exclaims very unadvisedly, ' The bonzes and priests of all religions keep up superstition and imposture:

104

all reformations begin with the laity.' Goldsmith, however, was staunch in his practical creed, and might bolt speculative extravagances with impunity. There is a striking difference in this respect between him and Addison, who, if he attacked authority, took care to have common sense on his side, and never hazarded any thing offensive to the feelings of others, or on the strength of his own discretional opinion. There is another inconvenience in this assumption of an exotic character and tone of sentiment, that it produces an inconsistency between the knowledge which the individual has time to acquire, and which the author is bound to communicate. Thus the Chinese has not been in England three days before he is acquainted with the characters of the three countries which compose this kingdom, and describes them to his friend at Canton, by extracts from the newspapers of each metropolis. The nationality of Scotchmen is thus ridiculed :—' *Edinburgh*. We are positive when we say, that Sanders Macgregor, lately executed for horse-stealing, is not a native of Scotland, but born at Carrickfergus.' Now this is very good ; but how should our Chinese philosopher find it out by instinct ? Beau Tibbs, a prominent character in this little work, is the best comic sketch since the time of Addison ; unrivalled in his finery, his vanity, and his poverty.

I have only to mention the names of the Lounger and the Mirror, which are ranked by the author's admirers with Sterne for sentiment, and with Addison for humour. I shall not enter into that : but I know that the story of La Roche is not like the story of Le Fevre, nor one hundredth part so good. Do I say this from prejudice to the author ? No : for I have read his novels. Of the Man of the World I cannot think so favourably as some others ; nor shall I here dwell on the picturesque and romantic beauties of Julia de Roubigné, the early favourite of the author of Rosamond Gray ; but of the Man of Feeling I would speak with grateful recollections : nor is it possible to forget the sensitive, irresolute, interesting Harley : and that lone figure of Miss Walton in it, that floats in the horizon, dim and ethereal, the day-dream of her lover's youthful fancy—better, far better than all the realities of life !

LECTURES ON THE COMIC WRITERS

LECTURE VI

ON THE ENGLISH NOVELISTS

THERE is an exclamation in one of Gray's Letters—'Be mine to read eternal new romances of Marivaux and Crebillon!'—If I did not utter a similar aspiration at the conclusion of the last new novel which I read (I would not give offence by being more particular as to the name) it was not from any want of affection for the class of writing to which it belongs: for, without going so far as the celebrated French philosopher, who thought that more was to be learnt from good novels and romances than from the gravest treatises on history and morality, yet there are few works to which I am oftener tempted to turn for profit or delight, than to the standard productions in this species of composition. We find there a close imitation of men and manners; we see the very web and texture of society as it really exists, and as we meet with it when we come into the world. If poetry has 'something more divine in it,' this savours more of humanity. We are brought acquainted with the motives and characters of mankind, imbibe our notions of virtue and vice from practical examples, and are taught a knowledge of the world through the airy medium of romance. As a record of past manners and opinions, too, such writings afford the best and fullest information. For example, I should be at a loss where to find in any authentic documents of the same period so satisfactory an account of the general state of society, and of moral, political, and religious feeling in the reign of George II. as we meet with in the Adventures of Joseph Andrews and his friend Mr. Abraham Adams. This work, indeed, I take to be a perfect piece of statistics in its kind. In looking into any regular history of that period, into a learned and eloquent charge to a grand jury or the clergy of a diocese, or into a tract on controversial divinity, we should hear only of the ascendancy of the Protestant succession, the horrors of Popery, the triumph of civil and religious liberty, the wisdom and moderation of the sovereign, the happiness of the subject, and the flourishing state of manufactures and commerce. But if we really wish to know what all these fine-sounding names come to, we cannot do better than turn to the works of those, who having no other object than to imitate nature, could only hope for success from the fidelity of their pictures; and were bound (in self-defence) to reduce the boasts of vague theorists and the exaggerations of angry disputants to the mortifying standard of reality. Extremes are said to meet: and the works of imagination, as they are called, sometimes come the nearest to truth and nature. Fielding in speaking on this subject, and vindicating the use and dignity of the style of writing in which he excelled against the loftier pretensions of professed historians, says, that in their productions nothing is true but the names and dates, whereas in his every thing is true but the names and dates. If so, he has the advantage on his side.

I will here confess, however, that I am a little prejudiced on the point in question; and that the effect of many fine speculations has been lost upon me, from an early familiarity with the most striking passages in the work to which I have just alluded. Thus nothing can be more captivating than the description somewhere given by Mr. Burke of the indissoluble connection between learning and nobility; and of the respect universally paid by wealth to piety and morals. But the effect of this ideal representation has always been spoiled by my recollection of Parson Adams sitting over his cup of ale in Sir Thomas Booby's kitchen. Echard 'On the Contempt of the Clergy' is, in like manner, a very good book, and 'worthy of all acceptation:' but, somehow, an unlucky impression of the reality of Parson Trulliber involuntarily checks the emotions of respect, to which it might otherwise give rise: while, on the other hand, the lecture which Lady Booby reads to Lawyer Scout on the immediate expulsion of Joseph and Fanny from the parish, casts no very favourable light on the flattering accounts of our practical jurisprudence which are to be found in Blackstone or De Lolme. The most moral writers, after all, are those who do not pretend to inculcate any moral. The professed moralist almost unavoidably degenerates into the partisan of a system; and the philosopher is too apt to warp the evidence to his own purpose. But the painter of manners gives the facts of human nature, and leaves us to draw the inference: if we are not able to do this, or do it ill, at least it is our own fault.

The first-rate writers in this class, of course, are few; but those few we may reckon among the greatest ornaments and best benefactors of our kind. There is a certain set of them who, as it were, take their rank by the side of reality, and are appealed to as evidence on all questions concerning human nature. The principal of these are Cervantes and Le Sage, who may be considered as having been naturalised among ourselves; and, of native English growth, Fielding, Smollett, Richardson, and Sterne.[1] As this is a depart-

---

[1] It is not to be forgotten that the author of Robinson Crusoe was also an Englishman. His other works, such as the Life of Colonel Jack, &c., are of the same cast, and leave an impression on the mind more like that of things than words.

ment of criticism which deserves more attention than has been usually bestowed upon it, I shall here venture to recur (not from choice, but necessity) to what I have said upon it in a well known periodical publication; and endeavour to contribute my mite towards settling the standard of excellence, both as to degree and kind, in these several writers.

I shall begin with the history of the renowned Don Quixote de la Mancha; who presents something more stately, more romantic, and at the same time more real to the imagination than any other hero upon record. His lineaments, his accoutrements, his pasteboard vizor, are familiar to us; and Mambrino's helmet still glitters in the sun! We not only feel the greatest veneration and love for the knight himself, but a certain respect for all those connected with him, the curate and Master Nicolas the barber, Sancho and Dapple, and even for Rosinante's leanness and his errors.—Perhaps there is no work which combines so much whimsical invention with such an air of truth. Its popularity is almost unequalled; and yet its merits have not been sufficiently understood. The story is the least part of them; though the blunders of Sancho, and the unlucky adventures of his master, are what naturally catch the attention of the majority of readers. The pathos and dignity of the sentiments are often disguised under the ludicrousness of the subject; and provoke laughter when they might well draw tears. The character of Don Quixote himself is one of the most perfect disinterestedness. He is an enthusiast of the most amiable kind; of a nature equally open, gentle, and generous; a lover of truth and justice; and one who had brooded over the fine dreams of chivalry and romance, till they had robbed him of himself, and cheated his brain into a belief of their reality. There cannot be a greater mistake than to consider Don Quixote as a merely satirical work, or as a vulgar attempt to explode 'the long-forgotten order of chivalry.' There could be no need to explode what no longer existed. Besides, Cervantes himself was a man of the most sanguine and enthusiastic temperament; and even through the crazed and battered figure of the knight, the spirit of chivalry shines out with undiminished lustre; as if the author had half-designed to revive the example of past ages, and once more 'witch the world with noble horsemanship.' Oh! if ever the mouldering flame of Spanish liberty is destined to break forth, wrapping the tyrant and the tyranny in one consuming blaze, that the spark of generous sentiment and romantic enterprise, from which it must be kindled, has not been quite extinguished, will perhaps be owing to thee, Cervantes, and to thy Don Quixote!

108

ON THE ENGLISH NOVELISTS

The character of Sancho is not more admirable in itself, than as a relief to that of the knight. The contrast is as picturesque and striking as that between the figures of Rosinante and Dapple. Never was there so complete a *partie quarrée*:—they answer to one another at all points. Nothing need surpass the truth of physiognomy in the description of the master and man, both as to body and mind; the one lean and tall, the other round and short; the one heroical and courteous, the other selfish and servile; the one full of high-flown fancies, the other a bag of proverbs; the one always starting some romantic scheme, the other trying to keep to the safe side of custom and tradition. The gradual ascendancy, however, obtained by Don Quixote over Sancho, is as finely managed as it is characteristic. Credulity and a love of the marvellous are as natural to ignorance, as selfishness and cunning. Sancho by degrees becomes a kind of lay-brother of the order; acquires a taste for adventures in his own way, and is made all but an entire convert, by the discovery of the hundred crowns in one of his most comfortless journeys. Towards the end, his regret at being forced to give up the pursuit of knight-errantry, almost equals his master's; and he seizes the proposal of Don Quixote for them to turn shepherds with the greatest avidity—still applying it in his own fashion; for while the Don is ingeniously torturing the names of his humble acquaintance into classical terminations, and contriving scenes of gallantry and song, Sancho exclaims, ' Oh, what delicate wooden spoons shall I carve! what crumbs and cream shall I devour!'—forgetting, in his milk and fruits, the pullets and geese at Camacho's wedding.

This intuitive perception of the hidden analogies of things, or, as it may be called, this *instinct of the imagination*, is, perhaps, what stamps the character of genius on the productions of art more than any other circumstance: for it works unconsciously, like nature, and receives its impressions from a kind of inspiration. There is as much of this indistinct keeping and involuntary unity of purpose in Cervantes, as in any author whatever. Something of the same unsettled, rambling humour extends itself to all the subordinate parts and characters of the work. Thus we find the curate confidentially informing Don Quixote, that if he could get the ear of the government, he has something of considerable importance to propose for the good of the state; and our adventurer afterwards (in the course of his peregrinations) meets with a young gentleman who is a candidate for poetical honours, with a mad lover, a forsaken damsel, a Mahometan lady converted to the Christian faith, &c.—all delineated with the same truth, wildness, and delicacy of fancy. The whole work breathes that air of romance, that aspiration after imaginary good, that indescribable longing after something more than we possess, that in all places and in all conditions of life,

> '——still prompts the eternal sigh,
> For which we wish to live, or dare to die!'

The leading characters in Don Quixote are strictly individuals; that is, they do not so much belong to, as form a class by themselves. In other words, the actions and manners of the chief *dramatis personæ* do not arise out of the actions and manners of those around them, or the situation of life in which they are placed, but out of the peculiar dispositions of the persons themselves, operated upon by certain impulses of caprice and accident. Yet these impulses are so true to nature, and their operation so exactly described, that we not only recognise the fidelity of the representation, but recognise it with all the advantages of novelty superadded. They are in the best sense *originals,* namely, in the sense in which nature has her originals. They are unlike any thing we have seen before—may be said to be purely ideal; and yet identify themselves more readily with our imagination, and are retained more strongly in memory, than perhaps any others: they are never lost in the crowd. One test of the truth of this ideal painting, is the number of allusions which Don Quixote has furnished to the whole of civilised Europe; that is to say, of appropriate cases and striking illustrations of the universal principles of our nature. The detached incidents and occasional descriptions of human life are more familiar and obvious; so that we have nearly the same insight here given us into the characters of innkeepers, barmaids, ostlers, and puppet-show men, that we have in Fielding. There is much greater mixture, however, of the pathetic and sentimental with the quaint and humorous, than there ever is in Fielding. I might instance the story of the countryman whom Don Quixote and Sancho met in their doubtful search after Dulcinea, driving his mules to plough at break of day, and 'singing the ancient ballad of Ronscevalles!' The episodes, which are frequently introduced, are excellent, but have, upon the whole, been overrated. They derive their interest from their connexion with the main story. We are so pleased with that, that we are disposed to receive pleasure from every thing else. Compared, for instance, with the serious tales in Boccaccio, they are slight and somewhat superficial. That of Marcella, the fair shepherdess, is, I think, the best. I shall only add, that Don Quixote was, at the time it was published, an entirely original work in its kind, and that the author claims the highest honour which can belong to one, that of being the inventor of a new style of writing. I have never read his Galatea, nor his Loves of

ON THE ENGLISH NOVELISTS

Persiles and Sigismunda, though I have often meant to do it, and I hope to do so yet. Perhaps there is a reason lurking at the bottom of this dilatoriness: I am quite sure the reading of these works could not make me think higher of the author of Don Quixote, and it might, for a moment or two, make me think less.

There is another Spanish novel, Gusman D'Alfarache, nearly of the same age as Don Quixote, and of great genius, though it can hardly be ranked as a novel or a work of imagination. It is a series of strange, unconnected adventures, rather drily told, but accompanied by the most severe and sarcastic commentary. The satire, the wit, the eloquence and reasoning, are of the most potent kind : but they are didactic rather than dramatic. They would suit a homily or a pasquinade as well or better than a romance. Still there are in this extraordinary book occasional sketches of character and humorous descriptions, to which it would be difficult to produce any thing superior. This work, which is hardly known in this country except by name, has the credit, without any reason, of being the original of Gil Blas. There is one incident the same, that of the unsavoury ragout, which is served up for supper at the inn. In all other respects these two works are the very reverse of each other, both in their excellences and defects.—Lazarillo de Tormes has been more read than the Spanish Rogue, and is a work more readable, on this account among others, that it is contained in a duodecimo instead of a folio volume. This, however, is long enough, considering that it treats of only one subject, that of eating, or rather the possibility of living without eating. Famine is here framed into an art, and feasting is banished far hence. The hero's time and thoughts are taken up in a thousand shifts to procure a dinner ; and that failing, in tampering with his stomach till supper time, when being forced to go supperless to bed, he comforts himself with the hopes of a breakfast the next morning, of which being again disappointed, he reserves his appetite for a luncheon, and then has to stave it off again by some meagre excuse or other till dinner ; and so on, by a perpetual adjournment of this necessary process, through the four and twenty hours round. The quantity of food proper to keep body and soul together is reduced to a *minimum* ; and the most uninviting morsels with which Lazarillo meets once a week as a God's-send, are pampered into the most sumptuous fare by a long course of inanition. The scene of this novel could be laid nowhere so properly as in Spain, that land of priestcraft and poverty, where hunger seems to be the ruling passion, and starving the order of the day.

Gil Blas has, next to Don Quixote, been more generally read and admired than any other novel ; and in one sense, deservedly so : for it is at the head of its class, though that class is very different from, and I should say inferior to the other. There is little individual character in Gil Blas. The author is a describer of manners, and not of character. He does not take the elements of human nature, and work them up into new combinations (which is the excellence of Don Quixote); nor trace the peculiar and shifting shades of folly and knavery as they are to be found in real life (like Fielding): but he takes off, as it were, the general, habitual impression which circumstances make on certain conditions of life, and moulds all his characters accordingly. All the persons whom he introduces, carry about with them the badge of their profession; and you see little more of them than their costume. He describes men as belonging to distinct classes in society; not as they are in themselves, or with the individual differences which are always to be discovered in nature. His hero, in particular, has no character but that of the successive circumstances in which he is placed. His priests are only described as priests: his valets, his players, his women, his courtiers and his sharpers, are all alike. Nothing can well exceed the monotony of the work in this respect :—at the same time that nothing can exceed the truth and precision with which the general manners of these different characters are preserved, nor the felicity of the particular traits by which their common foibles are brought out. Thus the Archbishop of Grenada will remain an everlasting memento of the weakness of human vanity; and the account of Gil Blas' legacy, of the uncertainty of human expectations. This novel is also deficient in the fable as well as in the characters. It is not a regularly constructed story; but a series of amusing adventures told with equal gaiety and good sense, and in the most graceful style imaginable.

It has been usual to class our own great novelists as imitators of one or other of these two writers. Fielding, no doubt, is more like Don Quixote than Gil Blas; Smollett is more like Gil Blas than Don Quixote; but there is not much resemblance in either case. Sterne's Tristram Shandy is a more direct instance of imitation. Richardson can scarcely be called an imitator of any one; or if he is, it is of the sentimental refinement of Marivaux, or of the verbose gallantry of the writers of the seventeenth century.

There is very little to warrant the common idea that Fielding was an imitator of Cervantes, except his own declaration of such an intention in the title-page of Joseph Andrews, the romantic turn of the character of Parson Adams (the only romantic character in his works), and the proverbial humour of Partridge, which is kept up only for a few pages. Fielding's novels are, in general, thoroughly his own; and they are thoroughly English. What they are most remarkable for, is neither sentiment, nor imagination, nor wit, nor even humour, though there is an immense deal of this last quality; but profound knowledge of human nature, at least of English nature; and masterly pictures of the characters of men as he saw them existing. This quality distinguishes all his works, and is shown almost equally in all of them. As a painter of real life, he was equal to Hogarth; as a mere observer of human nature, he was little inferior to Shakspeare, though without any of the genius and poetical qualities of his mind. His humour is less rich and laughable than Smollett's; his wit as often misses as hits; he has none of the fine pathos of Richardson or Sterne; but he has brought together a greater variety of characters in common life, marked with more distinct peculiarities, and without an atom of caricature, than any other novel writer whatever. The extreme subtlety of observation on the springs of human conduct in ordinary characters, is only equalled by the ingenuity of contrivance in bringing those springs into play, in such a manner as to lay open their smallest irregularity. The detection is always complete, and made with the certainty and skill of a philosophical experiment, and the obviousness and familiarity of a casual observation. The truth of the imitation is indeed so great, that it has been argued that Fielding must have had his materials ready-made to his hands, and was merely a transcriber of local manners and individual habits. For this conjecture, however, there seems to be no foundation. His representations, it is true, are local and individual; but they are not the less profound and conclusive. The feeling of the general principles of human nature operating in particular circumstances, is always intense, and uppermost in his mind; and he makes use of incident and situation only to bring out character.

It is scarcely necessary to give any illustrations. Tom Jones is full of them. There is the account, for example, of the gratitude of the elder Blifil to his brother, for assisting him to obtain the fortune of Miss Bridget Alworthy by marriage; and of the gratitude of the poor in his neighbourhood to Alworthy himself, who had done so much good in the country that he had made every one in it his enemy. There is the account of the Latin dialogues between Partridge and his maid, of the assault made on him during one of these by Mrs. Partridge, and the severe bruises he patiently received on that occasion, after which the parish of Little Baddington rung with the story, that the school-master had killed his wife. There is the exquisite keeping in the character of Blifil, and the want of it in that of Jones. There is the gradation in the lovers of Molly Seagrim; the philosopher Square succeeding to Tom Jones, who again finds that he himself had succeeded to the accomplished Will. Barnes, who had the first possession of her person, and had still possession of her heart, Jones being only the instrument of her vanity, as Square was of her interest. Then there is the discreet honesty of Black George, the learning of Thwackum and Square, and the profundity of Squire Western, who considered it as a physical impossibility that his daughter should fall in love with Tom Jones. We have also that gentleman's disputes with his sister, and the inimitable appeal of that lady to her niece.—'I was never so handsome as you, Sophy: yet I had something of you formerly. I was called the cruel Parthenissa. Kingdoms and states, as Tully Cicero says, undergo alteration, and so must the human form!' The adventure of the same lady with the highwayman, who robbed her of her jewels, while he complimented her beauty, ought not to be passed over, nor that of Sophia and her muff, nor the reserved coquetry of her cousin Fitzpatrick, nor the description of Lady Bellaston, nor the modest overtures of the pretty widow Hunt, nor the indiscreet babblings of Mrs. Honour. The moral of this book has been objected to, without much reason; but a more serious objection has been made to the want of refinement and elegance in two principal characters. We never feel this objection, indeed, while we are reading the book: but at other times, we have something like a lurking suspicion that Jones was but an awkward fellow, and Sophia a pretty simpleton. I do not know how to account for this effect, unless it is that Fielding's constantly assuring us of the beauty of his hero, and the good sense of his heroine, at last produces a distrust of both. The story of Tom Jones is allowed to be unrivalled: and it is this circumstance, together with the vast variety of characters, that has given the history of a Foundling so decided a preference over Fielding's other novels. The characters themselves, both in Amelia and Joseph Andrews, are quite equal to any of those in Tom Jones. The account of Miss Matthews and Ensign Hibbert, in the former of these; the way in which that lady reconciles herself to the death of her father; the inflexible Colonel Bath; the insipid Mrs. James, the complaisant Colonel Trent, the demure, sly, intriguing, equivocal Mrs. Bennet, the lord who is her seducer, and who attempts afterwards to seduce Amelia by the same mechanical process of a concert-ticket, a book, and the disguise of a great coat; his little, fat, short-nosed, red-faced, good-humoured accomplice, the keeper of the lodging-house, who, having no pretensions to gallantry herself, has a disinterested delight in forwarding the intrigues and pleasures of others, (to say nothing of honest Atkinson, the story of the miniature-picture of Amelia, and the hashed mutton, which are in a different style,) are masterpieces of description. The whole scene at the lodging-house, the masquerade, &c. in Amelia, are equal in interest to the parallel scenes in Tom Jones, and even more refined in the knowledge of character. For instance, Mrs. Bennet is superior to Mrs. Fitzpatrick in her own way. The uncertainty, in which the event of her interview with her former seducer is left, is admirable. Fielding was a master of what may be called the *double entendre* of character, and surprises you no less by what he leaves in the dark, (hardly known to the persons themselves) than by the unexpected discoveries he makes of the real traits and circumstances in a character with which, till then, you find you were unacquainted. There is nothing at all heroic, however, in the usual style of his delineations. He does not draw lofty characters or strong passions; all his persons are of the ordinary stature as to intellect; and possess little elevation of fancy, or energy of purpose. Perhaps, after all, Parson Adams is his finest character. It is equally true to nature, and more ideal than any of the others. Its unsuspecting simplicity makes it not only more amiable, but doubly amusing, by gratifying the sense of superior sagacity in the reader. Our laughing at him does not once lessen our respect for him. His declaring that he would willingly walk ten miles to fetch his sermon on vanity, merely to convince Wilson of his thorough contempt of this vice, and his consoling himself for the loss of his Æschylus, by suddenly recollecting that he could not read it if he had it, because it is dark, are among the finest touches of *naïveté*. The night-adventures at Lady Booby's with Beau Didapper, and the amiable Slipslop, are the most ludicrous; and that with the huntsman, who draws off the hounds from the poor Parson, because they would be spoiled by following *vermin*, the most profound. Fielding did not often repeat himself; but Dr. Harrison, in Amelia, may be considered as a variation of the character of Adams: so also is Goldsmith's Vicar of Wakefield; and the latter part of that work, which sets out so delightfully, an almost entire plagiarism from Wilson's account of himself, and Adams's domestic history.

Smollett's first novel, Roderick Random, which is also his best, appeared about the same time as Fielding's Tom Jones; and yet it has a much more modern air with it: but this may be accounted for, from the circumstance that Smollett was quite a young man at the time, whereas Fielding's manner must have been formed long before. The style of Roderick Random is more easy and flowing than that of Tom Jones; the incidents follow one another more rapidly (though, it must be confessed, they never come in such a throng, or are brought out with the same dramatic effect); the humour is broader, and as effectual; and there is very nearly, if not quite, an equal interest excited by the story. What then is it that gives the superiority to Fielding? It is the superior insight into the springs of human character, and the constant developement of that character through every change of circumstance. Smollett's humour often arises from the situation of the persons, or the peculiarity of their external appearance; as, from Roderick Random's carrotty locks, which hung down over his shoulders like a pound of candles, or Strap's ignorance of London, and the blunders that follow from it. There is a tone of vulgarity about all his productions. The incidents frequently resemble detached anecdotes taken from a newspaper or magazine; and, like those in Gil Blas, might happen to a hundred other characters. He exhibits the ridiculous accidents and reverses to which human life is liable, not 'the stuff' of which it is composed. He seldom probes to the quick, or penetrates beyond the surface; and, therefore, he leaves no stings in the minds of his readers, and in this respect is far less interesting than Fielding. His novels always enliven, and never tire us : we take them up with pleasure, and lay them down without any strong feeling of regret. We look on and laugh, as spectators of a highly amusing scene, without closing in with the combatants, or being made parties in the event. We read Roderick Random as an entertaining story; for the particular accidents and modes of life which it describes have ceased to exist : but we regard Tom Jones as a real history; because the author never stops short of those essential principles which lie at the bottom of all our actions, and in which we feel an immediate interest—*intus et in cute*. Smollett excels most as the lively caricaturist : Fielding as the exact painter and profound metaphysician. I am far from maintaining that this account applies uniformly to the productions of these two writers; but I think that, as far as they essentially differ, what I have stated is the general distinction between them. Roderick Random is the purest of Smollett's novels : I mean in point of style and description. Most of the incidents and characters are supposed to have been taken from the events of his own life; and are, therefore, truer to nature. There is a rude conception of generosity in some of his characters, of which Fielding seems to have been incapable, his amiable persons being merely good-natured. It is owing to this that Strap is superior to Partridge; as there is a heartiness and warmth of feeling in some of the scenes between Lieutenant Bowling and his nephew, which is beyond Fielding's power of impassioned writing. The whole of the scene on ship-board is a most admirable and striking picture, and, I imagine, very little if at all exaggerated, though the interest it excites is of a very unpleasant kind, because the irritation and resistance to petty oppression can be of no avail. The picture of the little profligate French friar, who was Roderick's travelling companion, and of whom he always kept to the windward, is one of Smollett's most masterly sketches.—Peregrine Pickle is no great favourite of mine, and Launcelot Greaves was not worthy of the genius of the author.

Humphry Clinker and Count Fathom are both equally admirable in their way. Perhaps the former is the most pleasant gossiping novel that ever was written ; that which gives the most pleasure with the least effort to the reader. It is quite as amusing as going the journey could have been ; and we have just as good an idea of what happened on the road, as if we had been of the party. Humphry Clinker himself is exquisite ; and his sweetheart, Winifred Jenkins, not much behind him. Matthew Bramble, though not altogether original, is excellently supported, and seems to have been the prototype of Sir Anthony Absolute in the Rivals. But Lismahago is the flower of the flock. His tenaciousness in argument is not so delightful as the relaxation of his logical severity, when he finds his fortune mellowing in the wintry smiles of Mrs. Tabitha Bramble. This is the best preserved, and most severe of all Smollett's characters. The resemblance to Don Quixote is only just enough to make it interesting to the critical reader, without giving offence to any body else. The indecency and filth in this novel, are what must be allowed to all Smollett's writings.—The subject and characters in Count Fathom are, in general, exceedingly disgusting : the story is also spun out to a degree of tediousness in the serious and sentimental parts ; but there is more power of writing occasionally shewn in it than in any of his works. I need only to refer to the fine and bitter irony of the Count's address to the country of his ancestors on his landing in England ; to the robber scene in the forest, which has never been surpassed ; to the Parisian swindler who personates a raw English country squire (Western is tame in the comparison) ; and to the story of the seduction in the west of England. It would be difficult to point out, in any author, passages written with more force and mastery than these.

It is not a very difficult undertaking to class Fielding or Smollett ; —the one as an observer of the characters of human life, the other as a describer of its various eccentricities. But it is by no means so easy to dispose of Richardson, who was neither an observer of the one, nor a describer of the other ; but who seemed to spin his materials entirely out of his own brain, as if there had been nothing existing in the world beyond the little room in which he sat writing. There is an artificial reality about his works, which is no where else to be met with. They have the romantic air of a pure fiction, with the literal minuteness of a common diary. The author had the strongest matter-of-fact imagination that ever existed, and wrote the oddest mixture of poetry and prose. He does not appear to have taken advantage of any thing in actual nature, from one end of his works to the other ; and yet, throughout all his works, voluminous as they are—(and this, to be sure, is one reason why they are so,)—he sets about describing every object and transaction, as if the whole had been given in on evidence by an eye-witness. This kind of high finishing from imagination is an anomaly in the history of human genius ; and, certainly, nothing so fine was ever produced by the same accumulation of minute parts. There is not the least distraction, the least forgetfulness of the end : every circumstance is made to tell. I cannot agree that this exactness of detail produces heaviness ; on the contrary, it gives an appearance of truth, and a positive interest to the story ; and we listen with the same attention as we should to the particulars of a confidential communication. I at one time used to think some parts of Sir Charles Grandison rather trifling and tedious, especially the long description of Miss Harriet Byron's wedding clothes, till I was told of two young ladies who had severally copied out the whole of that very description for their own private gratification. After that, I could not blame the author.

The effect of reading this work is like an increase of kindred. You find yourself all of a sudden introduced into the midst of a large family, with aunts and cousins to the third and fourth generation, and grandmothers both by the father's and mother's side ;—and a very odd set of people they are, but people whose real existence and personal identity you can no more dispute than your own senses, for you see and hear all that they do or say. What is still more extraordinary, all this extreme elaborateness in working out the story, seems to have cost the author nothing ; for it is said, that the published works are mere abridgments. I have heard (though this I suspect must be a pleasant exaggeration) that Sir Charles Grandison was originally written in eight and twenty volumes.

Pamela is the first of Richardson's productions, and the very child of his brain. Taking the general idea of the character of a modest and beautiful country girl, and of the ordinary situation in which she is placed, he makes out all the rest, even to the smallest circumstance, by the mere force of a reasoning imagination. It would seem as if a step lost, would be as fatal here as in a mathematical demonstration. The developement of the character is the most simple, and comes the nearest to nature that it can do, without being the same thing. The interest of the story increases with the dawn of understanding and reflection in the heroine : her sentiments gradually expand themselves,

118

like opening flowers. She writes better every time, and acquires a confidence in herself, just as a girl would do, writing such letters in such circumstances; and yet it is certain *that no girl would write such letters in such circumstances.* What I mean is this:—Richardson's nature is always the nature of sentiment and reflection, not of impulse or situation. He furnishes his characters, on every occasion, with the presence of mind of the author. He makes them act, not as they would from the impulse of the moment, but as they might upon reflection, and upon a careful review of every motive and circumstance in their situation. They regularly sit down to write letters: and if the business of life consisted in letter-writing, and was carried on by the post (like a Spanish game at chess), human nature would be what Richardson represents it. All actual objects and feelings are blunted and deadened by being presented through a medium which may be true to reason, but is false in nature. He confounds his own point of view with that of the immediate actors in the scene; and hence presents you with a conventional and factitious nature, instead of that which is real. Dr. Johnson seems to have preferred this truth of reflection to the truth of nature, when he said that there was more knowledge of the human heart in a page of Richardson, than in all Fielding. Fielding, however, saw more of the practical results, and understood the principles as well; but he had not the same power of speculating upon their possible results, and combining them in certain ideal forms of passion and imagination, which was Richardson's real excellence.

It must be observed, however, that it is this mutual good understanding, and comparing of notes between the author and the persons he describes; his infinite circumspection, his exact process of ratiocination and calculation, which gives such an appearance of coldness and formality to most of his characters,—which makes prudes of his women, and coxcombs of his men. Every thing is too conscious in his works. Every thing is distinctly brought home to the mind of the actors in the scene, which is a fault undoubtedly: but then it must be confessed, every thing is brought home in its full force to the mind of the reader also; and we feel the same interest in the story as if it were our own. Can any thing be more beautiful or more affecting than Pamela's reproaches to her 'lumpish heart,' when she is sent away from her master's at her own request; its lightness, when she is sent for back; the joy which the conviction of the sincerity of his love diffuses in her heart, like the coming on of spring; the artifice of the stuff gown; the meeting with Lady Davers after her marriage; and the trial-scene with her husband? Who ever remained insensible to the passion of Lady Clementina, except Sir Charles Grandison himself, who was the object of it? Clarissa is, however, his masterpiece, if we except Lovelace. If she is fine in herself, she is still finer in his account of her. With that foil, her purity is dazzling indeed: and she who could triumph by her virtue, and the force of her love, over the regality of Lovelace's mind, his wit, his person, his accomplishments, and his spirit, conquers all hearts. I should suppose that never sympathy more deep or sincere was excited than by the heroine of Richardson's romance, except by the calamities of real life. The links in this wonderful chain of interest are not more finely wrought, than their whole weight is overwhelming and irresistible. Who can forget the exquisite gradations of her long dying-scene, or the closing of the coffin-lid, when Miss Howe comes to take her last leave of her friend; or the heart-breaking reflection that Clarissa makes on what was to have been her wedding-day? Well does a certain writer exclaim—

> ' Books are a real world, both pure and good,
> Round which, with tendrils strong as flesh and blood,
> Our pastime and our happiness may grow!'

Richardson's wit was unlike that of any other writer—his humour was so too. Both were the effect of intense activity of mind—laboured, and yet completely effectual. I might refer to Lovelace's reception and description of Hickman, when he calls out Death in his ear, as the name of the person with whom Clarissa had fallen in love; and to the scene at the glove-shop. What can be more magnificent than his enumeration of his companions—' Belton, so pert and so pimply—Tourville, so fair and so foppish!' &c. In casuistry this author is quite at home; and, with a boldness greater even than his puritanical severity, has exhausted every topic on virtue and vice. There is another peculiarity in Richardson, not perhaps so uncommon, which is, his systematically preferring his most insipid characters to his finest, though both were equally his own invention, and he must be supposed to have understood something of their qualities. Thus he preferred the little, selfish, affected, insignificant Miss Byron, to the divine Clementina; and again, Sir Charles Grandison, to the nobler Lovelace. I have nothing to say in favour of Lovelace's morality; but Sir Charles is the prince of coxcombs, —whose eye was never once taken from his own person, and his own virtues; and there is nothing which excites so little sympathy as this excessive egotism.

It remains to speak of Sterne; and I shall do it in few words. There is more of *mannerism* and affectation in him, and a more immediate reference to preceding authors; but his excellences, where he is excellent, are of the first order. His characters are intellectual and inventive, like Richardson's; but totally opposite in the execution. The one are made out by continuity, and patient repetition of touches: the others, by glancing transitions and graceful apposition. His style is equally different from Richardson's: it is at times the most rapid, the most happy, the most idiomatic of any that is to be found. It is the pure essence of English conversational style. His works consist only of *morceaux*—of brilliant passages. I wonder that Goldsmith, who ought to have known better, should call him 'a dull fellow.' His wit is poignant, though artificial; and his characters (though the groundwork of some of them had been laid before) have yet invaluable original differences; and the spirit of the execution, the master-strokes constantly thrown into them, are not to be surpassed. It is sufficient to name them;—Yorick, Dr. Slop, Mr. Shandy, My Uncle Toby, Trim, Susanna, and the Widow Wadman. In these he has contrived to oppose, with equal felicity and originality, two characters, one of pure intellect, and the other of pure good nature, in My Father and My Uncle Toby. There appears to have been in Sterne a vein of dry, sarcastic humour, and of extreme tenderness of feeling; the latter sometimes carried to affectation, as in the tale of Maria, and the apostrophe to the recording angel: but at other times pure, and without blemish. The story of Le Fevre is perhaps the finest in the English language. My Father's restlessness, both of body and mind, is inimitable. It is the model from which all those despicable performances against modern philosophy ought to have been copied, if their authors had known any thing of the subject they were writing about. My Uncle Toby is one of the finest compliments ever paid to human nature. He is the most unoffending of God's creatures; or, as the French express it, *un tel petit bon homme*! Of his bowling-green, his sieges, and his amours, who would say or think any thing amiss!

It is remarkable that our four best novel-writers belong nearly to the same age. We also owe to the same period (the reign of George II.) the inimitable Hogarth, and some of our best writers of the middle style of comedy. If I were called upon to account for this coincidence, I should wave the consideration of more general causes, and ascribe it at once to the establishment of the Protestant ascendancy, and the succession of the House of Hanover. These great events appear to have given a more popular turn to our literature and genius, as well as to our government. It was found high time that the people should be represented in books as well as in Parliament. They wished to see some account of themselves in what they

any other idea. It has been said of Shakspeare, that you may always assign his speeches to the proper characters;—and you may infallibly do the same thing with Madame D'Arblay's, for they always say the same thing. The Branghtons are the best. Mr. Smith is an exquisite city portrait. Evelina is also her best novel, because it is the shortest; that is, it has all the liveliness in the sketches of character, and smartness of common dialogue and repartee, without the tediousness of the story, and endless affectation of sentiment which disfigures the others.

Women, in general, have a quicker perception of any oddity or singularity of character than men, and are more alive to every absurdity which arises from a violation of the rules of society, or a deviation from established custom. This partly arises from the restraints on their own behaviour, which turn their attention constantly on the subject, and partly from other causes. The surface of their minds, like that of their bodies, seems of a finer texture than ours; more soft, and susceptible of immediate impulses. They have less muscular strength; less power of continued voluntary attention—of reason, passion, and imagination: but they are more easily impressed with whatever appeals to their senses or habitual prejudices. The intuitive perception of their minds is less disturbed by any abstruse reasonings on causes or consequences. They learn the idiom of character and manners, as they acquire that of language, by rote, without troubling themselves about the principles. Their observation is not the less accurate on that account, as far as it goes; for it has been well said, that 'there is nothing so true as habit.'

There is little other power in Miss Burney's novels, than that of immediate observation: her characters, whether of refinement or vulgarity, are equally superficial and confined. The whole is a question of form, whether that form is adhered to or infringed upon. It is this circumstance which takes away dignity and interest from her story and sentiments, and makes the one so teazing and tedious, and the other so insipid. The difficulties in which she involves her heroines are too much 'Female Difficulties'; they are difficulties created out of nothing. The author appears to have no other idea of refinement than that it is the reverse of vulgarity; but the reverse of vulgarity is fastidiousness and affectation. There is a true and a false delicacy. Because a vulgar country Miss would answer 'yes' to a proposal of marriage in the first page, Madame D'Arblay makes it a proof of an excess of refinement, and an indispensable point of etiquette in her young ladies, to postpone the answer to the end of five volumes, without the smallest reason for their doing so, and with every reason to the contrary. The reader is led every moment to expect a *denouement,* and is as often disappointed on some trifling pretext. The whole artifice of her fable consists in coming to no conclusion. Her ladies ' stand so upon the order of their going,' that they do not go at all. They will not abate an ace of their punctilio in any circumstances, or on any emergency. They would consider it as quite indecorous to run down stairs though the house were in flames, or to move an inch off the pavement though a scaffolding was falling. She has formed to herself an abstract idea of perfection in common behaviour, which is quite as romantic and impracticable as any other idea of the sort : and the consequence has naturally been, that she makes her heroines commit the greatest improprieties and absurdities in order to avoid the smallest. In opposition to a maxim in philosophy, they constantly act from the weakest motive, or rather from pure contradiction. The whole tissue of the fable is, in general, more wild and chimerical than any thing in Don Quixote, without the poetical truth or elevation. Madame D'Arblay has woven a web of difficulties for her heroines, something like the green silken threads in which the shepherdesses entangled the steed of Cervantes's hero, who swore, in his fine enthusiastic way, that he would sooner cut his passage to another world than disturb the least of those beautiful meshes. To mention the most painful instance—the Wanderer, in her last novel, raises obstacles, lighter than ' the gossamer that idles in the wanton summer air,' into insurmountable barriers ; and trifles with those that arise out of common sense, reason, and necessity. Her conduct is not to be accounted for directly out of the circumstances in which she is placed, but out of some factitious and misplaced refinement on them. It is a perpetual game at cross-purposes. There being a plain and strong motive why she should pursue any course of action, is a sufficient reason for her to avoid it ; and the perversity of her conduct is in proportion to its levity—as the lightness of the feather baffles the force of the impulse that is given to it, and the slightest breath of air turns it back on the hand from which it is thrown. We can hardly consider this as the perfection of the female character !

I must say I like Mrs. Radcliffe's romances better, and think of them oftener ;—and even when I do not, part of the impression with which I survey the full-orbed moon shining in the blue expanse of heaven, or hear the wind sighing through autumnal leaves, or walk under the echoing archways of a Gothic ruin, is owing to a repeated perusal of the Romance of the Forest and the Mysteries of Udolpho. Her descriptions of scenery, indeed, are vague and wordy to the last degree ; they are neither like Salvator nor Claude, nor nature nor art; and she dwells on the effects of moonlight till we are sometimes weary of them: her characters are insipid, the shadows of a shade, continued on, under different names, through all her novels: her story comes to nothing. But in harrowing up the soul with imaginary horrors, and making the flesh creep, and the nerves thrill, with fond hopes and fears, she is unrivalled among her fair country-women. Her great power lies in describing the indefinable, and embodying a phantom. She makes her readers twice children: and from the dim and shadowy veil which she draws over the objects of her fancy, forces us to believe all that is strange, and next to impossible, of their mysterious agency :—whether it is the sound of the lover's lute borne o'er the distant waters along the winding shores of Provence, recalling, with its magic breath, some long-lost friendship, or some hopeless love; or the full choir of the cloistered monks, chaunting their midnight orgies, or the lonely voice of an unhappy sister in her pensive cell, like angels' whispered music; or the deep sigh that steals from a dungeon on the startled ear; or the dim apparition of ghastly features; or the face of an assassin hid beneath a monk's cowl; or the robber gliding through the twilight gloom of the forest. All the fascination that links the world of passion to the world unknown, is hers, and she plays with it at her pleasure: she has all the poetry of romance, all that is obscure, visionary, and objectless, in the imagination. It seems that the simple notes of Clara's lute, which so delighted her youthful heart, still echo among the rocks and mountains of the Valois; the mellow tones of the minstrel's songs still mingle with the noise of the dashing oar, and the rippling of the silver waves of the Mediterranean; the voice of Agnes is heard from the haunted tower; and Schedoni's form still stalks through the frowning ruins of Palinzi. The greatest treat, however, which Mrs. Radcliffe's pen has provided for the lovers of the marvellous and terrible, is the Provençal tale which Ludovico reads in the Castle of Udolpho, as the lights are beginning to burn blue, and just before the faces appear from behind the tapestry that carry him off, and we hear no more of him. This tale is of a knight, who being engaged in a dance at some high festival of old romance, was summoned out by another knight clad in complete steel; and being solemnly adjured to follow him into the mazes of the neighbouring wood, his conductor brought him at length to a hollow glade in the thickest part, where he pointed to the murdered corse of another knight, and lifting up his beaver, shewed him by the gleam of moonlight which fell on it, that it had the face of his spectre-guide! The dramatic power in the character of Schedoni, the Italian monk, has been much admired and praised; but the effect does not depend upon the character, but the situations;

not upon the figure, but upon the back-ground.—The Castle of Otranto (which is supposed to have led the way to this style of writing) is, to my notion, dry, meagre, and without effect. It is done upon false principles of taste. The great hand and arm, which are thrust into the court-yard, and remain there all day long, are the pasteboard machinery of a pantomime; they shock the senses, and have no purchase upon the imagination. They are a matter-of-fact impossibility; a fixture, and no longer a phantom. *Quod sic mihi ostendis, incredulus odi.* By realising the chimeras of ignorance and fear, begot upon shadows and dim likenesses, we take away the very grounds of credulity and superstition; and, as in other cases, by facing out the imposture, betray the secret to the contempt and laughter of the spectators. The Recess and the Old English Baron are also 'dismal treatises,' but with little in them ' at which our fell of hair is likely to rouse and stir as life were in it.' They are dull and prosing, without the spirit of fiction, or the air of tradition to make them interesting. After Mrs. Radcliffe, Monk Lewis was the greatest master of the art of freezing the blood. The robber-scene in the Monk is only inferior to that in Count Fathom, and perfectly new in the circumstances and cast of the characters. Some of his descriptions are chargeable with unpardonable grossness, but the pieces of poetry interspersed in this far-famed novel, such as the fight of Ronscevalles and the Exile, in particular, have a romantic and delightful harmony, such as might be chaunted by the moonlight pilgrim, or might lull the dreaming mariner on summer-seas.

If Mrs. Radcliffe touched the trembling chords of the imagination, making wild music there, Mrs. Inchbald has no less power over the springs of the heart. She not only moves the affections, but melts us into ' all the luxury of woe.' Her ' Nature and Art ' is one of the most pathetic and interesting stories in the world. It is, indeed, too much so; or the distress is too naked, and the situations hardly to be borne with patience. I think nothing, however, can exceed in delicacy and beauty the account of the love-letter which the poor girl, who is the subject of the story, receives from her lover, and which she is a fortnight in spelling out, sooner than shew it to any one else; nor the dreadful catastrophe of the last fatal scene, in which the same poor creature, as her former seducer, now become her judge, is about to pronounce sentence of death upon her, cries out in agony—' Oh, not from you! ' The effect of this novel upon the feelings, is not only of the most distressing, but withering kind. It blights the sentiments, and haunts the memory. The Simple Story is not much better in this respect: the gloom, however, which hangs over it, is of a more fixed and tender kind: we are not now lifted to ecstacy, only to be plunged in madness; and besides the sweetness and dignity of some of the characters, there are redeeming traits, retrospective glances on the course of human life, which brighten the backward stream, and smile in hope or patience to the last. Such is the account of Sandford, her stern and inflexible adviser, sitting by the bedside of Miss Miller, and comforting her in her dying moments; thus softening the worst pang of human nature, and reconciling us to the best, but not most shining virtues in human character. The conclusion of Nature and Art, on the contrary, is a scene of heartless desolation, which must effectually deter any one from ever reading the book twice. Mrs. Inchbald is an instance to confute the assertion of Rousseau, that women fail whenever they attempt to describe the passion of love.

I shall conclude this Lecture, by saying a few words of the author of Caleb Williams, and the author of Waverley. I shall speak of the last first. In knowledge, in variety, in facility, in truth of painting, in costume and scenery, in freshness of subject and in untired interest, in glancing lights and the graces of a style passing at will from grave to gay, from lively to severe, at once romantic and familiar, having the utmost force of imitation and apparent freedom of invention; these novels have the highest claims to admiration. What lack they yet? The author has all power given him from without—he has not, perhaps, an equal power from within. The intensity of the feeling is not equal to the distinctness of the imagery. He sits like a magician in his cell, and conjures up all shapes and sights to the view; and with a little variation we might apply to him what Spenser says of Fancy:—

> ' His chamber was dispainted all within
> With sundry colours, in the which were writ
> Infinite shapes of things dispersed thin;
> Some such as in the world were never yet;
> Some daily seen and knowen by their names,
> Such as in idle fantasies do flit;
> Infernal hags, centaurs, fiends, hippodames,
> Apes, lions, eagles, owls, fools, lovers, children, dames.'

In the midst of all this phantasmagoria, the author himself never appears to take part with his characters, to prompt our affection to the good, or sharpen our antipathy to the bad. It is the perfection of art to conceal art; and this is here done so completely, that while it adds to our pleasure in the work, it seems to take away from the merit of the author. As he does not thrust himself forward in the foreground, he loses the credit of the performance. The copies are so true to nature, that they appear like tapestry figures

128

taken off by the pattern; the obvious patchwork of tradition and history. His characters are transplanted at once from their native soil to the page which we are reading, without any traces of their having passed through the hot-bed of the author's genius or vanity. He leaves them as he found them; but this is doing wonders. The Laird and the Baillie of Bradwardine, the idiot rhymer David Gellatly, Miss Rose Bradwardine, and Miss Flora Mac Ivor, her brother the Highland Jacobite chieftain, Vich Ian Vohr, the Highland rover, Donald Bean Lean, and the worthy page Callum Beg, Bothwell, and Balfour of Burley, Claverhouse and Macbriar, Elshie, the Black Dwarf, and the Red Reever of Westburn Flat, Hobbie and Grace Armstrong, Ellen Gowan and Dominie Sampson, Dirk Hatteraick and Meg Merrilees, are at present 'familiar in our mouths as household names,' and whether they are actual persons or creations of the poet's pen, is an impertinent inquiry. The picturesque and local scenery is as fresh as the lichen on the rock: the characters are a part of the scenery. If they are put in action, it is a moving picture: if they speak, we hear their dialect and the tones of their voice. If the humour is made out by dialect, the character by the dress, the interest by the facts and documents in the author's possession, we have no right to complain, if it is made out; but sometimes it hardly is, and then we have a right to say so. For instance, in the Tales of my Landlord, Canny Elshie is not in himself so formidable or petrific a person as the real Black Dwarf, called David Ritchie, nor are his acts or sayings so staggering to the imagination. Again, the first introduction of this extraordinary personage, groping about among the hoary twilight ruins of the Witch of Micklestane Moor and her Grey Geese, is as full of preternatural power and bewildering effect (according to the tradition of the country) as can be; while the last decisive scene, where the Dwarf, in his resumed character of Sir Edward Mauley, comes from the tomb in the chapel, to prevent the forced marriage of the daughter of his former betrothed mistress with the man she abhors, is altogether powerless and tame. No situation could be imagined more finely calculated to call forth an author's powers of imagination and passion; but nothing is done. The assembly is dispersed under circumstances of the strongest natural feeling, and the most appalling preternatural appearances, just as if the effect had been produced by a peace-officer entering for the same purpose. These instances of a falling off are, however, rare; and if this author should not be supposed by fastidious critics to have original genius in the highest degree, he has other qualities which supply its place so well, his materials are so rich and varied, and he uses them so lavishly, that the reader is no loser by the exchange. We are not in fear that he should publish another novel; we are under no apprehension of his exhausting himself, for he has shewn that he is inexhaustible.

Whoever else is, it is pretty clear that the author of Caleb Williams and St. Leon is not the author of Waverley. Nothing can be more distinct or excellent in their several ways than these two writers. If the one owes almost every thing to external observation and traditional character, the other owes every thing to internal conception and contemplation of the possible workings of the human mind. There is little knowledge of the world, little variety, neither an eye for the picturesque, nor a talent for the humorous in Caleb Williams, for instance, but you cannot doubt for a moment of the originality of the work and the force of the conception. The impression made upon the reader is the exact measure of the strength of the author's genius. For the effect, both in Caleb Williams and St. Leon, is entirely made out, neither by facts, nor dates, by black-letter or magazine learning, by transcript nor record, but by intense and patient study of the human heart, and by an imagination projecting itself into certain situations, and capable of working up its imaginary feelings to the height of reality. The author launches into the ideal world, and must sustain himself and the reader there by the mere force of imagination. The sense of power in the writer thus adds to the interest of the subject.—The character of Falkland is a sort of apotheosis of the love of fame. The gay, the gallant Falkland lives only in the good opinion of good men; for this he adorns his soul with virtue, and tarnishes it with crime; he lives only for this, and dies as he loses it. He is a lover of virtue, but a worshipper of fame. Stung to madness by a brutal insult, he avenges himself by a crime of the deepest die, and the remorse of his conscience and the stain upon his honour prey upon his peace and reason ever after. It was into the mouth of such a character that a modern poet has well put the words,

> '—— Action is momentary,
> The motion of a muscle, this way or that;
> Suffering is long, obscure, and infinite.'

In the conflict of his feelings, he is worn to a skeleton, wasted to a shadow. But he endures this living death to watch over his undying reputation, and to preserve his name unsullied and free from suspicion. But he is at last disappointed in this his darling object, by the very means he takes to secure it, and by harassing and goading Caleb Williams (whose insatiable, incessant curiosity had wormed itself into his confidence) to a state of desperation, by employing every sort of persecution, and by trying to hunt him from society like an infection, makes him turn upon him, and betray the inmost secret of his soul. The last moments of Falkland are indeed sublime : the spark of life and the hope of imperishable renown are extinguished in him together; and bending his last look of forgiveness on his victim and destroyer, he dies a martyr to fame, but a confessor at the shrine of virtue! The re-action and play of these two characters into each other's hands (like Othello and Iago) is inimitably well managed, and on a par with any thing in the dramatic art ; but Falkland is the hero of the story, Caleb Williams is only the instrument of it. This novel is utterly unlike any thing else that ever was written, and is one of the most original as well as powerful productions in the English language. —St. Leon is not equal to it in the plot and ground-work, though perhaps superior in the execution. In the one Mr. Godwin has hit upon the extreme point of the perfectly natural and perfectly new ; in the other he ventures into the preternatural world, and comes nearer to the world of common place. Still the character is of the same exalted intellectual kind. As the ruling passion of the one was the love of fame, so in the other the sole business of life is thought. Raised by the fatal discovery of the philosopher's stone above mortality, he is cut off from all participation with its pleasures. He is a limb torn from society. In possession of eternal youth and beauty, he can feel no love ; surrounded, tantalized, tormented with riches, he can do no good. The races of men pass before him as in a *speculum* ; but he is attached to them by no common tie of sympathy or suffering. He is thrown back into himself and his own thoughts. He lives in the solitude of his own breast,—without wife or child, or friend, or enemy in the world. His is the solitude of the soul,—not of woods, or seas, or mountains,—but the desart of society, the waste and desolation of the heart. He is himself alone. His existence is purely contemplative, and is therefore intolerable to one who has felt the rapture of affection or the anguish of woe. The contrast between the enthusiastic eagerness of human pursuits and their blank disappointment, was never, perhaps, more finely pourtrayed than in this novel. Marguerite, the wife of St. Leon, is an instance of pure and disinterested affection in one of the noblest of her sex. It is not improbable that the author found the model of this character in nature.—Of Mandeville, I shall say only one word. It appears to me to be a falling off in the subject, not in the ability. The style and declamation are even more powerful than ever. But unless an author surpasses himself, and surprises the public as much the fourth or fifth time as he did the first, he is said to fall off, because there is not the same stimulus of novelty. A great deal is here made out of nothing, or out of a very disagreeable subject. I cannot agree that the story is out of nature. The feeling is very common indeed; though carried to an unusual and improbable excess, or to one with which from the individuality and minuteness of the circumstances, we cannot readily sympathise.

It is rare that a philosopher is a writer of romances. The union of the two characters in this author is a sort of phenomenon in the history of letters; for I cannot but consider the author of Political Justice as a philosophical reasoner of no ordinary stamp or pretensions. That work, whatever its defects may be, is distinguished by the most acute and severe logic, and by the utmost boldness of thinking, founded on a love and conviction of truth. It is a system of ethics, and one that, though I think it erroneous myself, is built on following up into its fair consequences, a very common and acknowledged principle, that abstract reason and general utility are the only test and standard of moral rectitude. If this principle is true, then the system is true: but I think that Mr. Godwin's book has done more than any thing else to overturn the sufficiency of this principle by abstracting, in a strict metaphysical process, the influence of reason or the understanding in moral questions and relations from that of habit, sense, association, local and personal attachment, natural affection, &c.; and by thus making it appear how necessary the latter are to our limited, imperfect, and mixed being, how impossible the former as an exclusive guide of action, unless man were, or were capable of becoming, a purely intellectual being. Reason is no doubt one faculty of the human mind, and the chief gift of Providence to man; but it must itself be subject to and modified by other instincts and principles, because it is not the only one. This work then, even supposing it to be false, is invaluable as demonstrating an important truth by the *reductio ad absurdum*; or it is an *experimentum crucis* in one of the grand and trying questions of moral philosophy.—In delineating the character and feelings of the hermetic philosopher St. Leon, perhaps the author had not far to go from those of a speculative philosophical Recluse. He who deals in the secrets of magic, or in the secrets of the human mind, is too often looked upon with jealous eyes by the world, which is no great conjuror; he who pours out his intellectual wealth into the lap of the public, is hated by those who cannot understand how he came by it; he who thinks beyond his age, cannot expect the feelings of his contemporaries to go along with him; he whose mind is of no age or country, is seldom properly recognised during his life-time, and must wait, in order to have justice done him, for the late but lasting award of posterity:—'Where his treasure is, there his heart is also.'

ON THE WORKS OF HOGARTH, ETC.

LECTURE VII

ON THE WORKS OF HOGARTH.——ON THE GRAND AND FAMILIAR STYLE OF PAINTING

IF the quantity of amusement, or of matter for more serious reflection which their works have afforded, is that by which we are to judge of precedence among the intellectual benefactors of mankind, there are, perhaps, few persons who can put in a stronger claim to our gratitude than Hogarth. It is not hazarding too much to assert, that he was one of the greatest comic geniuses that ever lived, and he was certainly one of the most extraordinary men this country has produced. The wonderful knowledge which he possessed of human life and manners, is only to be surpassed (if it can be) by the power of invention with which he has combined and contrasted his materials in the most ludicrous and varied points of view, and by the mastery of execution with which he has embodied and made tangible the very thoughts and passing movements of the mind. Critics sometimes object to the style of Hogarth's pictures, or to the class to which they belong. First, he belongs to no class, or if he does, it is to the same class as Fielding, Smollett, Vanbrugh, and Moliere. Besides, the merit of his pictures does not depend on the nature of the subject, but on the knowledge displayed of it, on the number of ideas they excite, on the fund of thought and observation contained in them. They are to be studied as works of science as well as of amusement; they satisfy our love of truth; they fill up the void in the mind; they form a series of plates in natural history, and of that most interesting part of natural history, the history of our own species. Make what deductions you please for the vulgarity of the subject, yet in the research, the profundity, the absolute truth and precision of the delineation of character; in the invention of incident, in wit and humour; in the life with which they are 'instinct in every part;' in everlasting variety and originality; they never have, and probably never will be surpassed. They stimulate the faculties as well as soothe them. 'Other pictures we see, Hogarth's we read.'

The public had not long ago an opportunity of viewing most of Hogarth's pictures, in the collection made of them at the British Gallery. The superiority of the original paintings to the common prints, is in a great measure confined to the Marriage a-la-Mode, with which I shall begin my remarks.

Boccaccio, the most refined and sentimental of all the novel-writers, has been stigmatised as a mere inventor of licentious tales, because readers in general have only seized on those things in his works which were suited to their own taste, and have thus reflected their own gross-ness back upon the writer. So it has happened, that the majority of critics having been most struck with the strong and decided expression in Hogarth, the extreme delicacy and subtle gradations of character in his pictures have almost entirely escaped them. In the first picture of the *Marriage a-la-Mode*, the three figures of the young Nobleman, his intended Bride, and her Inamorato, the Lawyer, shew how much Hogarth excelled in the power of giving soft and effeminate expression. They have, however, been less noticed than the other figures, which tell a plainer story, and convey a more palpable moral. Nothing can be more finely managed than the differences of character in these delicate personages. The beau sits smiling at the looking-glass with a reflected simper of self-admiration, and a languishing inclination of the head, while the rest of his body is perked up on his high heels with a certain air of tip-toe elevation. He is the Narcissus of the reign of George II.; whose powdered peruke, ruffles, gold-lace, and patches, divide his self-love unequally with his own person—the true *Sir Plume* of his day;

> ' Of amber-lidded snuff box justly vain,
> And the nice conduct of a clouded cane.'

Again we find the same felicity in the figure and attitude of the Bride, courted by the Lawyer. There is the utmost flexibility, and yielding softness in her whole person, a listless languor and tremulous suspense in the expression of her face. It is the precise look and air which Pope has given to his favourite Belinda, just at the moment of the *Rape of the Lock*. The heightened glow, the forward intelli-gence, and loosened soul of love in the same face, in the Assignation scene before the masquerade, form a fine and instructive contrast to the delicacy, timidity, and coy reluctance expressed in the first. The Lawyer in both pictures is much the same, perhaps too much so; though even this unmoved, unaltered appearance may be designed as characteristic. In both cases he has 'a person, and a smooth dispose, framed to make women false.' He is full of that easy good-humour, and easy good opinion of himself, with which the sex are often delighted. There is not a sharp angle in his face to obstruct his success, or give a hint of doubt or difficulty. His whole aspect is round and rosy, lively and unmeaning, happy without the least expense of thought, careless and inviting; and conveys a perfect idea of the uninterrupted glide and pleasing murmur of the soft periods that flow from his tongue.

The expression of the Bride in the Morning Scene is the most highly seasoned, and at the same time the most vulgar in the series. The figure, face, and attitude of the husband, are inimitable. Hogarth has with great skill contrasted the pale countenance of the husband with the yellow whitish colour of the marble chimney-piece behind him, in such a manner as to preserve the fleshy tone of the former. The airy splendour of the view of the inner-room in this picture is probably not exceeded by any of the productions of the Flemish school.

The young girl in the third picture, who is represented as the victim of fashionable profligacy, is unquestionably one of the artist's *chef-d'œuvres*. The exquisite delicacy of the painting is only surpassed by the felicity and subtlety of the conception. Nothing can be more striking than the contrast between the extreme softness of her person, and the hardened indifference of her character. The vacant stillness, the docility to vice, the premature suppression of youthful sensibility, the doll-like mechanism of the whole figure, which seems to have no other feeling but a sickly sense of pain—shew the deepest insight into human nature, and into the effects of those refinements in depravity, by which it has been good-naturedly asserted, that ' vice loses half its evil in losing all its grossness.' The story of this picture is in some parts very obscure and enigmatical. It is certain that the nobleman is not looking strait forward to the quack, whom he seems to have been threatening with his cane ; but that his eyes are turned up with an ironical leer of triumph to the procuress. The commanding attitude and size of this woman, the swelling circumference of her dress, spread out like a turkey-cock's feathers, the fierce, ungovernable, inveterate malignity of her countenance, which hardly needs the comment of the clasp-knife to explain her purpose, all are admirable in themselves, and still more so, as they are opposed to the mute insensibility, the elegant negligence of dress, and the childish figure of the girl who is supposed to be her *protegée.* —As for the Quack, there can be no doubt entertained about him. His face seems as if it were composed of salve, and his features exhibit all the chaos or confusion of the most gross, ignorant, and impudent empiricism. The gradations of ridiculous affectation in the Music scene are finely imagined and preserved. The preposterous, overstrained admiration of the lady of quality ; the sentimental, insipid, patient delight of the man, with his hair in papers, and sipping his tea : the pert, smirking, conceited, half-distorted approbation of the figure next to him ; the transition to the total insensibility of the round face in profile, and then to the wonder of the negro-boy at the rapture of his mistress, form a perfect whole. The sanguine complexion and flame-coloured hair of the female virtuoso throw an additional light on the character. This is lost in the print. The continuing the red colour of the hair into the back of the chair, has been pointed out as one of those instances of what may be termed alliteration in colouring, of which these pictures are every where full. The gross bloated appearance of the Italian singer is well relieved by the hard features of the instrumental performer behind him, which might be carved of wood. The negro-boy holding the chocolate, both in expression, colour, and execution, is a masterpiece. The gay, lively derision of the other negro-boy playing with the Acteon, is an ingenious contrast to the profound amazement of the first. Some account has already been given of the two lovers in this picture. It is curious to observe the infinite activity of mind which the artist displays on every occasion. An instance occurs in the present picture. He has so contrived the papers in the hair of the bride, as to make them look almost like a wreath of half-blown flowers; while those which he has placed on the head of the musical amateur, very much resemble a *cheveux-de-fris* of horns, which adorn and fortify the lack lustre expression, and mild resignation of the face beneath.

The Night Scene is inferior to the rest of the series. The attitude of the husband, who is just killed, is one in which it would be impossible for him to stand or even to fall. It resembles the loose pasteboard figures they make for children. The characters in the last picture, in which the wife dies, are all masterly. I would particularly refer to the captious, petulant, self-sufficiency of the Apothecary, whose face and figure are constructed on exact physiognomical principles; and to the fine example of passive obedience and non-resistance in the servant, whom he is taking to task, and whose coat, of green and yellow livery, is as long and as melancholy as his face. The disconsolate look and haggard eyes, the open mouth, the comb sticking in the hair, the broken gapped teeth, which, as it were, hitch in an answer, every thing about him denotes the utmost perplexity and dismay. The harmony and gradations of colour in this picture are uniformly preserved with the greatest nicety, and are well worthy the attention of the artist.— I have so far attempted to point out the fund of observation, physical and moral, contained in one set of these pictures, the *Marriage-a-la-Mode*. The rest would furnish as many topics to descant upon, were the patience of the reader as inexhaustible as the painter's invention. But as this is not the case, I shall content myself with barely referring to some of those figures in the other pictures, which appear to me the most striking, and which we see not only while we are looking at them, but which we have before us at all other times. For instance, who, having seen, can easily forget that exquisite frost-piece of religion and morality, the antiquated Prude in the Morning Scene; or that striking commentary on the *good old times*, the little wretched appendage of a Foot-boy, who crawls, half famished and half frozen, behind her? The French man and woman in the Noon, are the perfection of flighty affectation and studied grimace; the amiable *fraternization* of the two old women saluting each other, is not enough to be admired; and in the little Master, in the same national group, we see the early promise and personification of that eternal principle of wondrous self-complacency, proof against all circumstances, and which makes the French the only people who are vain even of being cuckolded and being conquered! Or shall we prefer to this the outraged distress and unmitigated terrors of the Boy who has dropped his dish of meat, and who seems red all over with shame and vexation, and bursting with the noise he makes? Or what can be better than the good housewifery of the Girl underneath, who is devouring the lucky fragments; or than the plump, ripe, florid, luscious look of the Servant-wench near her, embraced by a greasy rascal of an Othello, with her pye-dish tottering like her virtue, and with the most precious part of its contents running over? Just—no, not quite—as good is the joke of the Woman overhead, who, having quarrelled with her Husband, is throwing their Sunday's dinner out of the window, to complete this chapter of accidents of baked-dishes. The Husband in the Evening Scene is certainly as meek as any recorded in history; but I cannot say that I admire this picture, or the Night Scene after it. But then, in the Taste in High-Life, there is that inimitable pair, differing only in sex, congratulating and delighting one another by 'all the mutually reflected charities' of folly and affectation, with the young Lady, coloured like a rose, dandling her little, black, pug-faced, white-teethed, chuckling favourite; and with the portrait of Monsieur Des Noyers in the back-ground, dancing in a grand ballet, surrounded by butterflies. And again, in the Election Dinner, is the immortal Cobbler, surrounded by his Peers, who,

> '—— frequent and full,
> In *loud* recess and *brawling* conclave sit'——

the Jew in the second picture, a very Jew in grain; innumerable fine sketches of heads in the Polling for Votes, of which the Nobleman overlooking the Caricaturist is the second best, and the Blind-man going up to vote, the best; and then the irresistible, tumultuous display of broad humour in the Chairing the Member, which is, perhaps, of all Hogarth's pictures, the most full of laughable incidents

137

and situations; the yellow, rusty-faced Thresher, with his swinging flail breaking the head of one of the chairmen; and his redoubted antagonist, the Sailor, with his oak-stick, and stumping wooden-leg, a supplemental cudgel; the persevering ecstasy of the hobbling Blind Fiddler, who, in the fray, appears to have been trod upon by the artificial excrescence of the honest tar; Monsieur, the monkey, with piteous aspect, speculating the impending disaster of the triumphant Candidate, and his brother Bruin, appropriating the paunch; the precipitous flight of the Pigs, souse over head into the water; the fine Lady fainting, with vermilion lips; and the two Chimney Sweepers, satirical young rogues!—I had almost forgot the Politician, who is burning a hole through his hat with a candle in reading a newspaper; and the Chickens, in the *March to Finchley*, wandering in search of their lost dam, who is found in the pocket of the Serjeant. Of the pictures in the *Rake's Progress*, exhibited in this collection, I shall not here say any thing, because I think them on the whole inferior to the prints, and because they have already been criticised by a writer, to whom I could add nothing, in a paper which ought to be read by every lover of Hogarth and of English genius—I mean, Mr. Lamb's Essay on the works of Hogarth. I shall at present proceed to form some estimate of the style of art in which this painter excelled.

What distinguishes his compositions from all others of the same general kind, is, that they are equally remote from caricature, and from mere still life. It of course happens in subjects taken from common life, that the painter can procure real models, and he can get them to sit as long as he pleases. Hence, in general, those attitudes and expressions have been chosen which could be assumed the longest; and in imitating which, the artist by taking pains and time might produce almost as complete *fac-similes* as he could of a flower or a flower-pot, of a damask curtain or a china-vase. The copy was as perfect and as uninteresting in the one case as in the other. On the contrary, subjects of drollery and ridicule affording frequent examples of strange deformity and peculiarity of features, these have been eagerly seized by another class of artists, who, without subjecting themselves to the laborious drudgery of the Dutch school and their imitators, have produced our popular caricatures, by rudely copying or exaggerating the casual irregularities of the human countenance. Hogarth has equally avoided the faults of both these styles: the insipid tameness of the one, and the gross extravagance of the other, so as to give to the productions of his pencil equal solidity and effect. For his faces go to the very verge of caricature, and yet never (I believe in any single instance) go beyond it: they

138

take the very widest latitude, and yet we always see the links which
bind them to nature : they bear all the marks, and carry all the conviction of reality with them, as if we had seen the actual faces for
the first time, from the precision, consistency, and good sense with
which the whole and every part is made out. They exhibit the
most uncommon features, with the most uncommon expressions :
but which yet are as familiar and intelligible as possible, because with
all the boldness, they have all the truth of nature. Hogarth has left
behind him as many of these memorable faces, in their memorable
moments, as, perhaps, most of us remember in the course of our
lives, and has thus doubled the quantity of our experience.

It will assist us in forming a more determinate idea of the peculiar
genius of Hogarth, to compare him with a deservedly admired artist
in our own times. The highest authority on art in this country, I
understand, has pronounced that Mr. Wilkie united the excellences
of Hogarth to those of Teniers. I demur to this decision in both
its branches ; but in demurring to authority, it is necessary to give
our reasons. I conceive that this ingenious and attentive observer
of nature has certain essential, real, and indisputable excellences of
his own ; and I think it, therefore, the less important to clothe him
with any vicarious merits which do not belong to him. Mr. Wilkie's
pictures, generally speaking, derive almost their whole value from
their *reality*, or the truth of the representation. They are works of
pure imitative art ; and the test of this style of composition is to
represent nature faithfully and happily in its simplest combinations.
It may be said of an artist like Mr. Wilkie, that *nothing human is indifferent to him*. His mind takes an interest in, and it gives an
interest to, the most familiar scenes and transactions of life. He
professedly gives character, thought, and passion, in their lowest
degrees, and in their every-day forms. He selects the commonest
events and appearances of nature for his subjects ; and trusts to their
very commonness for the interest and amusement he is to excite.
Mr. Wilkie is a serious, prosaic, literal narrator of facts ; and his
pictures may be considered as diaries, or minutes of what is passing
constantly about us. Hogarth, on the contrary, is essentially a
comic painter ; his pictures are not indifferent, unimpassioned descriptions of human nature, but rich, exuberant satires upon it. He
is carried away by a passion for the *ridiculous*. His object is 'to
shew vice her own feature, scorn her own image.' He is so far from
contenting himself with still-life, that he is always on the verge of
caricature, though without ever falling into it. He does not represent folly or vice in its incipient, or dormant, or *grub* state ; but
full grown, with wings, pampered into all sorts of affectation, airy,

ostentatious, and extravagant. Folly is there seen at the height—the moon is at the full; it is 'the very error of the time.' There is a perpetual collision of eccentricities—a tilt and tournament of absurdities; the prejudices and caprices of mankind are let loose, and set together by the ears, as in a bear-garden. Hogarth paints nothing but comedy, or tragi-comedy. Wilkie paints neither one nor the other. Hogarth never looks at any object but to find out a moral or a ludicrous effect. Wilkie never looks at any object but to see that it is there. Hogarth's pictures are a perfect jest-book, from one end to the other. I do not remember a single joke in Wilkie's, except one very bad one of the boy in the Blind Fiddler, scraping the gridiron, or fire-shovel, I forget which it is.[1] In looking at Hogarth, you are ready to burst your sides with laughing at the unaccountable jumble of odd things which are brought together; you look at Wilkie's pictures with a mingled feeling of curiosity, and admiration at the accuracy of the representation. For instance, there is a most admirable head of a man coughing in the Rent-day; the action, the keeping, the choaked sensation, are inimitable: but there is nothing to laugh at in a man coughing. What strikes the mind is the difficulty of a man's being painted coughing, which here certainly is a masterpiece of art. But turn to the blackguard Cobbler in the Election Dinner, who has been smutting his neighbour's face over, and who is lolling out his tongue at the joke, with a most surprising obliquity of vision; and immediately 'your lungs begin to crow like chanticleer.' Again, there is the little boy crying in the Cut Finger, who only gives you the idea of a cross, disagreeable, obstinate child in pain: whereas the same face in Hogarth's Noon, from the ridiculous perplexity it is in, and its extravagant, noisy, unfelt distress, at the accident of having let fall the pye-dish, is quite irresistible. Mr. Wilkie, in his picture of the Ale-house door, I believe, painted Mr. Liston as one of the figures, without any great effect. Hogarth would have given any price for such a subject, and would have made it worth any money. I have never seen any thing, in the expression of comic humour, equal to Hogarth's pictures, but Liston's face!

Mr. Wilkie paints interiors: but still you generally connect them with the country. Hogarth, even when he paints people in the open air, represents them either as coming from London, as in the polling for votes at Brentford, or as returning to it, as the dyer and his wife at Bagnigge Wells. In this last picture, he has contrived to convert a common rural image into a type and emblem of city honours. In

[1] The Waiter drawing the cork, in the Rent-day, is another exception, and quite Hogarthian.

ON THE WORKS OF HOGARTH, ETC.

fact, I know no one who had a less pastoral imagination than Hogarth. He delights in the thick of St. Giles's or St. James's. His pictures breathe a certain close, greasy, tavern air. The fare he serves up to us consists of high-seasoned dishes, ragouts and olla podridas, like the supper in Gil Blas, which it requires a strong stomach to digest. Mr. Wilkie presents us with a sort of lenten fare, very good and wholesome, but rather insipid than overpowering! Mr. Wilkie's pictures are, in general, much better painted than Hogarth's; but the Marriage-a-la-Mode is superior both in colour and execution to any of Wilkie's. I may add here, without any disparagement, that, as an artist, Mr. Wilkie is hardly to be mentioned with Teniers. Neither in truth and brilliant clearness of colouring, nor in facility of execution, is there any comparison. Teniers was a perfect master in all these respects; and our own countryman is positively defective, notwithstanding the very laudable care with which he finishes every part of his pictures. There is an evident smear and dragging of the paint, which is also of a bad purple, or puttyish tone, and which never appears in the pictures of the Flemish artist, any more than in a looking-glass. Teniers, probably from his facility of execution, succeeded in giving a more local and momentary expression to his figures. They seem each going on with his particular amusement or occupation; Wilkie's have, in general, more a look of sitting for their pictures. Their compositions are very different also: and in this respect, I believe, Mr. Wilkie has the advantage. Teniers's boors are usually amusing themselves at skittles, or dancing, or drinking, or smoking, or doing what they like, in a careless, desultory way; and so the composition is loose and irregular. Wilkie's figures are all drawn up in a regular order, and engaged in one principal action, with occasional episodes. The story of the Blind Fiddler is the most interesting, and the best told. The two children standing before the musician are delightful. The Card-players is the best coloured of his pictures, if I am not mistaken. The Village Politicians, though excellent as to character and composition, is inferior as a picture to those which Mr. Wilkie has since painted. His latest pictures, however, do not appear to me to be his best. There is something of manner and affectation in the grouping of the figures, and a pink and rosy colour spread over them, which is out of place. The hues of Rubens and Sir Joshua do not agree with Mr. Wilkie's subjects. One of his last pictures, that of Duncan Gray, is equally remarkable for sweetness and simplicity in colour, composition, and expression. I must here conclude this very general account; for to point out the particular beauties of every one of his pictures in detail, would require an Essay by itself.

LECTURES ON THE COMIC WRITERS

I have promised to say something in this Lecture on the difference between the grand and familiar style of painting; and I shall throw out what imperfect hints I have been able to collect on this subject, so often attempted, and never yet succeeded in, taking the examples and illustrations from Hogarth, that is, from what he possessed or wanted in each kind.

And first, the difference is not that between imitation and invention : for there is as much of this last quality in Hogarth, as in any painter or poet whatever. As, for example, to take two of his pictures only, I mean the Enraged Musician and the Gin Lane ;—in one of which every conceivable variety of disagreeable and discordant sound—the razor-grinder turning his wheel; the boy with his drum, and the girl with her rattle momentarily suspended; the pursuivant blowing his horn; the shrill milkwoman; the inexorable ballad-singer, with her squalling infant; the pewterer's shop close by; the fishwomen; the chimey-sweepers at the top of a chimney, and the two cats in melodious concert on the ridge of the tiles; with the bells ringing in the distance, as we see by the flags flying :—and in the other, the complicated forms and signs of death and ruinous decay—the woman on the stairs of the bridge asleep, letting her child fall over; her ghastly companion opposite, next to death's door, with hollow, famished cheeks and staring ribs; the dog fighting with the man for the bare shin-bone; the man hanging himself in a garret; the female corpse put into a coffin by the parish beadle; the men marching after a funeral, seen through a broken wall in the back ground; and the very houses reeling as if drunk and tumbling about the ears of the infatuated victims below, the pawnbroker's being the only one that stands firm and unimpaired—enforce the moral meant to be conveyed by each of these pieces with a richness and research of combination and artful contrast not easily paralleled in any production of the pencil or the pen. The clock pointing to four in the morning, in Modern Midnight Conversation, just as the immoveable Parson Ford is filling out another glass from a brimming punch-bowl, while most of his companions, with the exception of the sly Lawyer, are falling around him 'like leaves in October;' and again, the extraordinary mistake of the man leaning against the post, in the Lord Mayor's Procession—shew a mind capable of seizing the most rare and transient coincidences of things, of imagining what either never happened at all, or of instantly fixing on and applying to its purpose what never happened but once. So far, the invention shewn in the great style of painting is poor in the comparison. Indeed, grandeur is supposed (whether rightly or not, I shall not here inquire) to imply a

142

simplicity inconsistent with this inexhaustible variety of incident and circumstantial detail.

Secondly, the difference between the ideal and familiar style is not to be explained by the difference between the genteel and vulgar; for it is evident that Hogarth was almost as much at home in the genteel comedy, as in the broad farce of his pictures. He excelled not only in exhibiting the coarse humours and disgusting incidents of low life, but in exhibiting the vices, follies, and frivolity of the fashionable manners of his time: his fine ladies hardly yield the palm to his waiting-maids, and his lords and his footmen are on a respectable footing of equality. There is no want, for example, in the Marriage-a-la-Mode, or in Taste in High Life, of affectation verging into idiotism, or of languid sensibility, that might—

'Die of a rose in aromatic pain.'

In short, Hogarth was a painter, not of low but of actual life; and the ridiculous and prominent features of high or low life, of the great vulgar or the small, lay equally open to him. The Country Girl, in the first plate of the Harlot's Progress, coming out of the waggon, is not more simple and ungainly, than the same figure, in the second, is thoroughly initiated into the mysteries of her art, and suddenly accomplished in all the airs and graces of affectation, ease, and impudence. The affected languor and imbecility of the same girl afterwards, when put to beat hemp in Bridewell, is exactly in keeping with the character she has been taught to assume. Sir Joshua could do nothing like it in his line of portrait, which differed chiefly in the back ground. The fine gentleman at his levee, in the Rake's Progress, is also a complete model of a person of rank and fortune, surrounded by needy and worthless adventurers, fiddlers, poetasters and virtuosi, as was the custom in those days. Lord Chesterfield himself would not have been disgraced by sitting for it. I might multiply examples to shew that Hogarth was not characteristically deficient in that kind of elegance which arises from an habitual attention to external appearance and deportment. I will only add as instances, among his women, the two *élégantes* in the Bedlam scene, which are dressed (allowing for the difference of not quite a century) in the manner of Ackerman's dresses for May; and among the men, the Lawyer in Modern Midnight Conversation, whose gracious significant leer and sleek lubricated countenance exhibit all the happy finesse of his profession, when a silk gown has been added, or is likely to be added to it; and several figures in the Cockpit, who are evidently, at the first glance, gentlemen of the old school, and where the mixture of the blacklegs with the higher character is a still further test of the discriminating skill of the painter.

Again, Hogarth had not only a perception of fashion, but a sense of natural beauty. There are as many pleasing faces in his pictures as in Sir Joshua. Witness the girl picking the Rake's pocket in the Bagnio scene, whom we might suppose to be 'the Charming Betsy Careless;' the Poet's wife, handsomer than falls to the lot of most poets, who are generally more intent upon the idea in their own minds than on the image before them, and are glad to take up with Dulcineas of their own creating; the theatrical heroine in the Southwark Fair, who would be an accession to either of our play-houses; the girl asleep, ogled by the clerk in church time, and the sweetheart of the Good Apprentice in the reading desk in the second of that series, almost an ideal face and expression; the girl in her cap selected for a partner by the footman in the print of Morning, very handsome; and many others equally so, scattered like 'stray-gifts of love and beauty' through these pictures. Hogarth was not then exclusively the painter of deformity. He painted beauty or ugliness indifferently, as they came in his way; and was not by nature confined to those faces which are painful and disgusting, as many would have us believe.

Again, neither are we to look for the solution of the difficulty in the difference between the comic and the tragic, between loose laughter and deep passion. For Mr. Lamb has shewn unanswerably that Hogarth is quite at home in scenes of the deepest distress, in the heart-rending calamities of common life, in the expression of ungovernable rage, silent despair, or moody madness, enhanced by the tenderest sympathy, or aggravated by the frightful contrast of the most impenetrable and obdurate insensibility, as we see strikingly exemplified in the latter prints of the Rake's Progress. To the unbeliever in Hogarth's power over the passions and the feelings of the heart, the characters there speak like 'the hand-writing on the wall.' If Mr. Lamb has gone too far in paralleling some of these appalling representations with Shakespear, he was excusable in being led to set off what may be considered as a staggering paradox against a rooted prejudice. At any rate, the inferiority of Hogarth (be it what it may) did not arise from a want of passion and intense feeling; and in this respect he had the advantage over Fielding, for instance, and others of our comic writers, who excelled only in the light and ludicrous. There is in general a distinction, almost an impassable one, between the power of embodying the serious and the ludicrous; but these contradictory faculties were reconciled in Hogarth, as they were in Shakspeare, in Chaucer; and as it is said that they were in another extraordinary and later instance, Garrick's acting.

None of these then will do : neither will the most masterly and entire keeping of character lead us to an explanation of the grand and ideal style; for Hogarth possessed the most complete and absolute mastery over the truth and identity of expression and features in his subjects. Every stroke of his pencil tells according to a preconception in his mind. If the eye squints, the mouth is distorted; every feature acts, and is acted upon by the rest of the face ; even the dress and attitude are such as could be proper to no other figure : the whole is under the influence of one impulse, that of truth and nature. Look at the heads in the Cockpit, already mentioned, one of the most masterly of his productions in this way, where the workings of the mind are seen in every muscle of the face ; and the same expression, more intense or relaxed, of hope or of fear, is stamped on each of the characters, so that you could no more transpose any part of one countenance to another, than you could change a profile to a front face. Hogarth was, in one sense, strictly an historical painter : that is, he represented the manners and humours of mankind in action, and their characters by varied expression. Every thing in his pictures has life and motion in it. Not only does the business of the scene never stand still, but every feature is put into full play ; the exact feeling of the moment is brought out, and carried to its utmost height, and then instantly seized and stamped on the canvass for ever. The expression is always taken *en passant*, in a state of progress or change, and, as it were, at the salient point. Besides the excellence of each individual face, the reflection of the expression from face to face, the contrast and struggle of particular motives and feelings in the different actors in the scene, as of anger, contempt, laughter, compassion, are conveyed in the happiest and most lively manner. His figures are not like the back-ground on which they are painted : even the pictures on the wall have a peculiar look of their own. All this is effected by a few decisive and rapid touches of the pencil, careless in appearance, but infallible in their results ; so that one great criterion of the grand style insisted on by Sir Joshua Reynolds, that of leaving out the details, and attending to general character and outline, belonged to Hogarth. He did not indeed arrive at middle forms or neutral expression, which Sir Joshua makes another test of the ideal; for Hogarth was not insipid. That was the last fault with which he could be charged. But he had breadth and boldness of manner, as well as any of them ; so that neither does that constitute the *ideal*.

What then does ? We have reduced this to something like the last remaining quantity in an equation, where all the others have been ascertained. Hogarth had all the other parts of an original and accomplished genius except this, but this he had not. He had an intense feeling and command over the impressions of sense, of habit, of character, and passion, the serious and the comic, in a word, of nature, as it fell within his own observation, or came within the sphere of his actual experience; but he had little power beyond that sphere, or sympathy with that which existed only *in idea*. He was 'conformed to this world, not transformed.' If he attempted to paint Pharaoh's daughter, and Paul before Felix, he lost himself. His mind had feet and hands, but not wings to fly with. There is a mighty world of sense, of custom, of every-day action, of accidents and objects coming home to us, and interesting because they do so; the gross, material, stirring, noisy world of common life and selfish passion, of which Hogarth was absolute lord and master: there is another mightier world, that which exists only in conception and in power, the universe of thought and sentiment, that surrounds and is raised above the ordinary world of reality, as the empyrean surrounds this nether globe, into which few are privileged to soar with mighty wings outspread, and in which, as power is given them to embody their aspiring fancies, to 'give to airy nothing a local habitation and a name,' to fill with imaginary shapes of beauty or sublimity, and make the dark abyss pregnant, bringing that which is remote home to us, raising themselves to the lofty, sustaining themselves on the refined and abstracted, making all things like not what we know and feel in ourselves, in this 'ignorant present' time, but like what they must be in themselves, or in our noblest idea of them, and stamping that idea with reality, (but chiefly clothing the best and the highest with grace and grandeur): this is the ideal in art, in poetry, and in painting. There are things which are cognisable only to sense, which interest only our more immediate instincts and passions; the want of food, the loss of a limb, or a sum of money: there are others that appeal to different and nobler faculties; the wants of the mind, the hunger and thirst after truth and beauty; that is, to faculties commensurate with objects greater and of greater refinement, which to be grand must extend beyond ourselves to others, and our interests in which must be refined in proportion as they do so.[1] The interest in these subjects is in proportion to the power of conceiving them and the power of conceiving them is in proportion to the interest and

---

[1] When Meg Merrilies says in her dying moments—'Nay, nay, lay my head to the East,' what was the East to her? Not a reality but an idea of distant time and the land of her forefathers; the last, the strongest, and the best that occurred to her in this world. Her gipsy slang and dress were quaint and grotesque; her attachment to the Kaim of Derncleugh and the wood of Warrock was romantic; her worship of the East was *ideal*.

146

affection for them, to the innate bias of the mind to elevate itself above every thing low, and purify itself from every thing gross. Hogarth only transcribes or transposes what was tangible and visible, not the abstracted and intelligible. You see in his pictures only the faces which you yourself have seen, or others like them ; none of his characters are thinking of any person or thing out of the picture : you are only interested in the objects of their contention or pursuit, because they themselves are interested in them. There is nothing remote in thought, or comprehensive in feeling. The whole is intensely personal and local : but the interest of the ideal and poetical style of art, relates to more permanent and universal objects ; and the characters and forms must be such as to correspond with and sustain that interest, and give external grace and dignity to it. Such were the subjects which Raphael chose ; faces imbued with unalterable sentiment, and figures, that stand in the eternal silence of thought. He places before you objects of everlasting interest, events of greatest magnitude, and persons in them fit for the scene and action—warriors and kings, princes and nobles, and, greater yet, poets and philosophers ; and mightier than these, patriarchs and apostles, prophets and founders of religion, saints and martyrs, angels and the Son of God. We know their importance and their high calling, and we feel that they do not belie it. We see them as they were painted, with the eye of faith. The light which they have kindled in the world, is reflected back upon their faces : the awe and homage which has been paid to them, is seated upon their brow, and encircles them like a glory. All those who come before them, are conscious of a superior presence. For example, the beggars, in the Gate Beautiful, are impressed with this ideal borrowed character. Would not the cripple and the halt feel a difference of sensation, and express it outwardly in such circumstances ? And was the painter wrong to transfer this sense of preternatural power and the confidence of a saving faith to his canvass ? Hogarth's Pool of Bethesda, on the contrary, is only a collection of common beggars receiving an alms. The waters may be stirred, but the mind is not stirred with them. The fowls, again, in the Miraculous Draught of Fishes, exult and clap their wings, and seem lifted up with some unusual cause of joy. There is not the same expansive, elevated principle in Hogarth. He has amiable and praise-worthy characters, indeed, among his bad ones. The Master of the Industrious and Idle Apprentice is a good citizen and a virtuous man ; but his benevolence is mechanical and confined : it extends only to his shop, or, at most, to his ward. His face is not ruffled by passion, nor is it inspired by thought. To give another instance, the face of the faithful Female, fainting in the prison-scene in the Rake's Progress, is more one of effeminate softness than of distinguished tenderness, or heroic constancy. But in the pictures of the Mother and Child, by Raphael and Leonard da Vinci, we see all the tenderness purified from all the weakness of maternal affection, and exalted by the prospects of religious faith ; so that the piety and devotion of future generations seems to add its weight to the expression of feminine sweetness and parental love, to press upon the heart, and breathe in the countenance. This is the *ideal*, passion blended with thought and pointing to distant objects, not debased by grossness, not thwarted by accident, nor weakened by familiarity, but connected with forms and circumstances that give the utmost possible expansion and refinement to the general sentiment. With all my admiration of Hogarth, I cannot think him equal to Raphael. I do not know whether, if the port-folio were opened, I would not as soon look over the prints of Hogarth as those of Raphael ; but, assuredly, if the question were put to me, I would sooner never have seen the prints of Hogarth than never have seen those of Raphael. It is many years ago since I first saw the prints of the Cartoons hanging round the old-fashioned parlour of a little inn in a remote part of the country. I was then young : I had heard of the fame of the Cartoons, but this was the first time I had ever been admitted face to face into the presence of those divine guests. 'How was I then uplifted!' Prophets and Apostles stood before me as in a dream, and the Saviour of the Christian world, with his attributes of faith and power; miracles were working on the walls ; the hand of Raphael was there ; and as his pencil traced the lines, I saw godlike spirits and lofty shapes descend and walk visibly the earth, but as if their thoughts still lifted them above the earth. There I saw the figure of St. Paul, pointing with noble fervour to 'temples not made with hands, eternal in the heavens ; ' and that finer one of Christ in the boat, whose whole figure seems sustained by meekness and love ; and that of the same person surrounded by his disciples, like a flock of sheep listening to the music of some divine shepherd. I knew not how enough to admire them.—Later in life, I saw other works of this great painter (with more like them) collected in the Louvre : where Art, at that time, lifted up her head, and was seated on her throne, and said, 'All eyes shall see me, and all knees shall bow to me ! ' Honour was done to her and all hers. There was her treasure, and there the inventory of all she had. There she had gathered together her pomp, and there was her shrine, and there her votaries came and worshipped as in a temple. The crown she wore was brighter than that of kings. Where the struggles for human liberty had been, there were the triumphs of human genius. For there, in the Louvre, were the precious monu-

148

ments of art :—There ' stood the statue that enchants the world; '
there was Apollo, the Laocoon, the Dying Gladiator, the head of
the Antinous, Diana with her Fawn, the Muses and the Graces in
a ring, and all the glories of the antique world :—

> ' There was old Proteus coming from the sea,
> And wreathed Triton blew his winding horn.'

There, too, were the two St. Jeromes, Correggio's, and Domeni-
chino's; there was Raphael's Transfiguration; the St. Mark of
Tintoret; Paul Veronese's Marriage of Cana; the Deluge of
Poussin; and Titian's St. Peter Martyr. It was there that I
learned to become an enthusiast of the lasting works of the great
painters, and of their names no less magnificent; grateful to the
heart as the sound of celestial harmony from other spheres, waking
around us (whether heard or not) from youth to age; the stay, the
guide, and anchor of our purest thoughts; whom, having once seen,
we always remember, and who teach us to see all things through
them; without whom life would be to begin again, and the earth
barren; of Raphael, who lifted the human form half way to heaven;
of Titian, who painted the mind in the face, and unfolded the soul
of things to the eye; of Rubens, around whose pencil gorgeous shapes
thronged numberless, startling us by the novel accidents of form and
colour, putting the spirit of motion into the universe, and weaving
a gay fantastic round and Bacchanalian dance with nature; of
Rembrandt, too, who ' smoothed the raven down of darkness till it
smiled,' and tinged it with a light like streaks of burning ore: of
these, and more than these, of whom the world was scarce worthy,
and for the loss of whom nothing could console me—not even the
works of Hogarth!

LECTURE VIII

ON THE COMIC WRITERS OF THE LAST CENTURY

THE question which has been often asked, *Why there are comparatively
so few good modern Comedies?* appears in a great measure to answer
itself. It is because so many excellent comedies have been written,
that there are none written at present. Comedy naturally wears itself
out—destroys the very food on which it lives; and by constantly
and successfully exposing the follies and weaknesses of mankind
to ridicule, in the end leaves itself nothing worth laughing at. It
holds the mirror up to nature; and men, seeing their most striking
peculiarities and defects pass in gay review before them, learn either

to avoid or conceal them. It is not the criticism which the public taste exercises upon the stage, but the criticism which the stage exercises upon public manners, that is fatal to comedy, by rendering the subject-matter of it tame, correct, and spiritless. We are drilled into a sort of stupid decorum, and forced to wear the same dull uniform of outward appearance; and yet it is asked, why the Comic Muse does not point, as she was wont, at the peculiarities of our gait and gesture, and exhibit the picturesque contrasts of our dress and costume, in all that graceful variety in which she delights. The genuine source of comic writing,

'Where it must live, or have no life at all,'

is undoubtedly to be found in the distinguishing peculiarities of men and manners. Now this distinction can subsist, so as to be strong, pointed, and general, only while the manners of different classes are formed almost immediately by their particular circumstances, and the characters of individuals by their natural temperament and situation, without being everlastingly modified and neutralized by intercourse with the world—by knowledge and education. In a certain stage of society, men may be said to vegetate like trees, and to become rooted to the soil in which they grow. They have no idea of any thing beyond themselves and their immediate sphere of action; they are, as it were, circumscribed, and defined by their particular circumstances; they are what their situation makes them, and nothing more. Each is absorbed in his own profession or pursuit, and each in his turn contracts that habitual peculiarity of manners and opinions which makes him the subject of ridicule to others, and the sport of the Comic Muse. Thus the physician is nothing but a physician, the lawyer is a mere lawyer, the scholar degenerates into a pedant, the country squire is a different species of being from the fine gentleman, the citizen and the courtier inhabit a different world, and even the affectation of certain characters, in aping the follies or vices of their betters, only serves to shew the immeasurable distance which custom or fortune has placed between them. Hence the earlier comic writers, taking advantage of this mixed and solid mass of ignorance, folly, pride, and prejudice, made those deep and lasting incisions into it,— have given those sharp and nice touches, that bold relief to their characters,—have opposed them in every variety of contrast and collision, of conscious self-satisfaction and mutual antipathy, with a power which can only find full scope in the same rich and inexhaustible materials. But in proportion as comic genius succeeds in taking off the mask from ignorance and conceit, as it teaches us

'To see ourselves as others see us,'—

in proportion as we are brought out on the stage together, and our prejudices clash one against the other, our sharp angular points wear off; we are no longer rigid in absurdity, passionate in folly, and we prevent the ridicule directed at our habitual foibles by laughing at them ourselves.

If it be said, that there is the same fund of absurdity and prejudice in the world as ever—that there are the same unaccountable perversities lurking at the bottom of every breast,—I should answer, Be it so: but at least we keep our follies to ourselves as much as possible; we palliate, shuffle, and equivocate with them; they sneak into bye-corners, and do not, like *Chaucer's Canterbury Pilgrims*, march along the high road, and form a procession; they do not entrench themselves strongly behind custom and precedent; they are not embodied in professions and ranks in life; they are not organized into a system; they do not openly resort to a standard, but are a sort of straggling non-descripts, that, like *Wart*, 'present no mark to the foeman.' As to the gross and palpable absurdities of modern manners, they are too shallow and barefaced, and those who affect are too little *serious* in them, to make them worth the detection of the Comic Muse. They proceed from an idle, impudent affectation of folly in general, in the dashing *bravura* style, not from an infatuation with any of its characteristic modes. In short, the proper object of ridicule is *egotism*: and a man cannot be a very great egotist, who every day sees himself represented on the stage. We are deficient in comedy, because we are without characters in real life—as we have no historical pictures, because we have no faces proper for them.

It is, indeed, the evident tendency of all literature to generalise and *dissipate* character, by giving men the same artificial education, and the same common stock of ideas; so that we see all objects from the same point of view, and through the same reflected medium;—we learn to exist, not in ourselves, but in books;—all men become alike mere readers—spectators, not actors in the scene, and lose their proper personal identity. The templar, the wit, the man of pleasure, and the man of fashion, the courtier and the citizen, the knight and the squire, the lover and the miser—*Lovelace, Lothario, Will Honeycomb*, and *Sir Roger de Coverley, Sparkish* and *Lord Foppington, Western* and *Tom Jones, My Father* and *My Uncle Toby, Millamant* and *Sir Sampson Legend, Don Quixote* and *Sancho, Gil Blas* and *Guzman d'Alfarache, Count Fathom* and *Joseph Surface*,—have met and exchanged common-places on the barren plains of the *haute littérature* toil slowly on to the temple of science, 'seen a long way off upon a level,' and end in one dull compound of politics, criticism, and metaphysics !

151

LECTURES ON THE COMIC WRITERS

We cannot expect to reconcile opposite things. If, for example, any of us were to put ourselves into the stage-coach from Salisbury to London, it is more than probable we should not meet with the same number of odd accidents, or ludicrous distresses on the road, that befel *Parson Adams*; but why, if we get into a common vehicle, and submit to the conveniences of modern travelling, should we complain of the want of adventures? Modern manners may be compared to a modern stage-coach; our limbs may be a little cramped with the confinement, and we may grow drowsy, but we arrive safe, without any very amusing or very sad accident, at our journey's end.

In this theory I have, at least, the authority of Sterne and the Tatler on my side, who attribute the greater variety and richness of comic excellence in our writers, to the greater variety and distinctness of character among ourselves; the roughness of the texture and the sharp angles not being worn out by the artificial refinements of intellect, or the frequent collision of social intercourse.—It has been argued on the other hand, indeed, that this circumstance makes against me; that the suppression of the grosser indications of absurdity ought to stimulate and give scope to the ingenuity and penetration of the comic writer who is to detect them; and that the progress of wit and humour ought to keep pace with critical distinctions and metaphysical niceties. Some theorists, indeed, have been sanguine enough to expect a regular advance from grossness to refinement on the stage and in real life, marked on a graduated scale of human perfectibility, and have been hence led to imagine that the best of our old comedies were no better than the coarse jests of a set of country clowns—a sort of *comedies bourgeoises*, compared with the admirable productions which might, but have not, been written in our times. I must protest against this theory altogether, which would go to degrade genteel comedy from a high court lady into a literary prostitute. I do not know what these persons mean by refinement in this instance. Do they find none in Millamant and her morning dreams, in Sir Roger de Coverley and his widow? Did not Etherege, Wycherley, and Congreve, approach tolerably near

'——the ring
Of mimic statesmen and their merry king?'

Is there no distinction between an Angelica and a Miss Prue, a Valentine, a Tattle, and a Ben? Where, in the annals of modern literature, shall we find any thing more refined, more deliberate, more abstracted in vice, than the nobleman in Amelia? Are not the compliments which Pope paid to his friends equal in taste and elegance to any which have been paid since? Are there no traits in Sterne? Is

152

not Richardson minute enough? Must we part with Sophia Western and her muff, and Clarissa Harlowe's 'preferable regards' for the loves of the plants and the triangles? Or shall we say that the Berinthias and Alitheas of former times were little rustics, because they did not, like our modern belles, subscribe to circulating libraries, read Beppo, prefer Gertrude of Wyoming to the Lady of the Lake, or the Lady of the Lake to Gertrude of Wyoming, differ in their sentiments on points of taste or systems of mineralogy, and deliver dissertations on the arts with Corinna of Italy? They had something else to do and to talk about. They were employed in reality, as we see them on the stage, in setting off their charms to the greatest advantage, in mortifying their rivals by the most pointed irony, and trifling with their lovers with infinite address. The height of comic elegance and refinement is not to be found in the general diffusion of knowledge and civilization, which tends to level and neutralize, but in the pride of individual distinction, and the contrast between the conflicting pretensions of different ranks in society.

For this reason I conceive that the alterations which have taken place in coversation and dress, in consequence of the change of manners in the same period, have been by no means favourable to comedy. The present prevailing style of conversation is not *personal*, but critical and analytical. It consists almost entirely in the discussion of general topics, in ascertaining the merits of authors and their works : and Congreve would be able to derive no better hints from the conversations of our toilettes or drawing-rooms, for the exquisite raillery or poignant repartee of his dialogues, than from a deliberation of the Royal Society. In manner, the extreme simplicity and graceful uniformity of modern dress, however favourable to the arts, has certainly stript comedy of one of its richest ornaments and most expressive symbols. The sweeping pall and buskin, and nodding plume, were never more serviceable to tragedy, than the enormous hoops and stiff stays worn by the belles of former days, were to the intrigues of comedy. They assisted wonderfully in heightening the mysteries of the passion, and adding to the intricacy of the plot. Wycherley and Vanbrugh could not have spared the dresses of Vandyke. These strange fancy-dresses, perverse disguises, and counterfeit shapes, gave an agreeable scope to the imagination. 'That sevenfold fence' was a sort of foil to the lusciousness of the dialogue, and a barrier against the sly encroachments of *double entendre*. The greedy eye and bold hand of indiscretion were repressed, which gave a greater license to the tongue. The senses were not to be gratified in an instant. Love was entangled in the folds of the swelling handkerchief, and the desires might wander for ever round the circumference of a quilted petticoat, or find a rich lodging in the flowers of a damask stomacher. There was room for years of patient contrivance, for a thousand thoughts, schemes, conjectures, hopes, fears, and wishes. There seemed no end of obstacles and delays; to overcome so many difficulties was the work of ages. A mistress was an angel, concealed behind whalebone, flounces, and brocade. What an undertaking to penetrate through the disguise! What an impulse must it give to the blood, what a keenness to the invention, what a volubility to the tongue! 'Mr. Smirk, you are a brisk man,' was then the most significant commendation; but now-a-days—a woman can be *but undressed!*—Again, the character of the fine gentleman is at present a little obscured on the stage, nor do we immediately recognise it elsewhere, for want of the formidable *insignia* of a bag-wig and sword. Without these outward credentials, the public must not only be unable to distinguish this character intuitively, but it must be 'almost afraid to know itself.' The present simple disguise of a gentleman is like the *incognito* of kings. The opinion of others affects our opinion of ourselves; and we can hardly expect from a modern man of fashion that air of dignity and superior gracefulness of carriage, which those must have assumed who were conscious that all eyes were upon them, and that their lofty pretensions continually exposed them either to public scorn or challenged public admiration. A lord who should take the wall of the plebeian passengers without a sword by his side, would hardly have his claim of precedence acknowledged; nor could he be supposed to have that obsolete air of self-importance about him, which should alone clear the pavement at his approach. It is curious how an ingenious actor of the present day (Mr. Farren) should play Lord Ogleby so well as he does, having never seen any thing of the sort in reality. A nobleman in full costume, and in broad day, would be a phenomenon like the lord mayor's coach. The attempt at getting up genteel comedy at present is a sort of Galvanic experiment, a revival of the dead.[1]

I have observed in a former Lecture, that the most spirited æra of

---

[1] I have only to add, by way of explanation on this subject, the following passage from the Characters of Shakspeare's Plays : 'There is a certain stage of society in which people become conscious of their peculiarities and absurdities, affect to disguise what they are, and set up pretensions to what they are not. This gives rise to a corresponding style of comedy, the object of which is to detect the disguises of self-love, and to make reprisals on these preposterous assumptions of vanity, by marking the contrast between the real and the affected character as severely as possible, and denying to those, who would impose on us for what they are not, even the merit which they have. This is the comedy of artificial life, of wit and satire, such as we see it in Congreve, Wycherley, Vanbrugh, &c. To this succeeds a state of society from which the same sort of affectation and pretence are

our comic drama was that which reflected the conversation, tone, and manners of the profligate, but witty age of Charles II. With the graver and more business-like turn which the Revolution probably gave to our minds, comedy stooped from her bolder and more fantastic flights; and the ferocious attack made by the nonjuring divine, Jeremy Collier, on the immorality and profaneness of the plays then chiefly in vogue, nearly frightened those unwarrantable liberties of wit and humour from the stage, which were no longer countenanced at court nor copied in the city. Almost the last of our writers who ventured to hold out in the prohibited track, was a female adventurer, Mrs. Centlivre, who seemed to take advantage of the privilege of her sex, and to set at defiance the cynical denunciations of the angry puritanical reformist. Her plays have a provoking spirit and volatile salt in them, which still preserves them from decay. Congreve is said to have been jealous of their success at the time, and that it was one cause which drove him in disgust from the stage. If so, it was without any good reason: for these plays have great and intrinsic merit in them, which entitled them to their popularity (and it is only spurious and undeserved popularity which should excite a feeling of jealousy in any well-regulated mind): and besides, their merit was of a kind entirely different from his own. The Wonder and the Busy Body are properly comedies of intrigue. Their interest depends chiefly on the intricate involution and artful *denouement* of the plot, which has a strong tincture of mischief in it, and the wit is seasoned by the archness of the humour and sly allusion to the most delicate points. They are plays evidently written by a very clever woman, but still by a woman: for I hold, in spite of any fanciful theories to the contrary, that there is a distinction discernible in the minds of women as well as in their faces. The Wonder is one of the best of our acting plays. The passion of jealousy in Don Felix is managed in such a way as to give as little offence as possible to the audience, for every appearance combines to excite and confirm his worst suspicions, while we, who are in the secret, laugh at his ground-

banished by a greater knowledge of the world, or by their successful exposure on the stage ; and which by neutralizing the materials of comic character, both natural and artificial, leaves no comedy at all—but *the sentimental*. Such is our modern comedy. There is a period in the progress of manners anterior to both these, in which the foibles and follies of individuals are of nature's planting, not the growth of art or study ; in which they are therefore unconscious of them themselves, or care not who knows them, if they can but have their whim out ; and in which, as there is no attempt at imposition, the spectators rather receive pleasure from humouring the inclinations of the persons they laugh at, than wish to give them pain by exposing their absurdity. This may be called the comedy of nature, and it is the comedy which we generally find in Shakspeare.' P. 256.

155

less uneasiness and apprehensions. The ambiguity of the heroine's situation, which is like a continued practical *equivoque*, gives rise to a quick succession of causeless alarms, subtle excuses, and the most hair-breadth 'scapes. The scene near the end, in which Don Felix, pretending to be drunk, forces his way out of Don Manuel's house, who wants to keep him a prisoner, by producing his marriage-contract in the shape of a pocket-pistol, with the terrors and confusion into which the old gentleman is thrown by this sort of *argumentum ad hominem*, is one of the richest treats the stage affords, and calls forth incessant peals of laughter and applause. Besides the two principal characters (Violante and Don Felix) Lissardo and Flippanta come in very well to carry on the under-plot; and the airs and graces of an amorous waiting-maid and conceited man-servant, each copying after their master and mistress, were never hit off with more natural volubility or affected *nonchalance* than in this enviable couple. Lissardo's playing off the diamond ring before the eyes of his mortified Dulcinea, and aping his master's absent manner while repeating—'Roast me these Violantes,' as well as the jealous quarrel of the two waiting-maids, which threatens to end in some very extraordinary discoveries, are among the most amusing traits in this comedy. Colonel Breton, the lover of Clara, is a spirited and enterprising soldier of fortune; and his servant Gibby's undaunted, incorrigible blundering, with a dash of nationality in it, tells in a very edifying way.—The Busy Body is inferior, in the interest of the story and characters, to the Wonder; but it is full of bustle and gaiety from beginning to end. The plot never stands still; the situations succeed one another like the changes of machinery in a pantomime. The nice dove-tailing of the incidents, and cross-reading in the situations, supplies the place of any great force of wit or sentiment. The time for the entrance of each person on the stage is the moment when they are least wanted, and when their arrival makes either themselves or somebody else look as foolish as possible. The laughableness of this comedy, as well as of the Wonder, depends on a brilliant series of mistimed exits and entrances. Marplot is the whimsical hero of the piece, and a standing memorial of unmeaning vivacity and assiduous impertinence.

The comedies of Steele were the first that were written expressly with a view not to imitate the manners, but to reform the morals of the age. The author seems to be all the time on his good behaviour, as if writing a comedy was no very creditable employment, and as if the ultimate object of his ambition was a dedication to the queen. Nothing can be better meant, or more inefficient. It is almost a misnomer to call them comedies; they are rather homilies in dialogue,

in which a number of very pretty ladies and gentlemen discuss the
fashionable topics of gaming, of duelling, of seduction, of scandal, &c.
with a sickly sensibility, that shews as little hearty aversion to vice,
as sincere attachment to virtue.   By not meeting the question fairly
on the ground of common experience, by slubbering over the objections, and varnishing over the answers, the whole distinction between
virtue and vice (as it appears in evidence in the comic drama) is
reduced to verbal professions, and a mechanical, infantine goodness.
The sting is, indeed, taken out of what is bad ; but what is good, at
the same time, loses its manhood and nobility of nature by this
enervating process.   I am unwilling to believe that the only difference
between right and wrong is mere cant, or *make-believe ;* and I imagine,
that the advantage which the moral drama possesses over mere
theoretical precept or general declamation is this, that by being left
free to imitate nature as it is, and not being referred to an ideal
standard, it is its own voucher for the truth of the inferences it draws,
for its warnings, or its examples ; that it brings out the higher, as
well as lower principles of action, in the most striking and convincing
points of view ; satisfies us that virtue is not a mere shadow ; clothes
it with passion, imagination, reality, and, if I may so say, translates
morality from the language of theory into that of practice.   But
Steele, by introducing the artificial mechanism of morals on the stage,
and making his characters act, not from individual motives and
existing circumstances, the truth of which every one must feel, but
from vague topics and general rules, the truth of which is the very
thing to be proved in detail, has lost that fine 'vantage ground which
the stage lends to virtue ; takes away from it its best grace, the grace
of sincerity ; and, instead of making it a test of truth, has made it an
echo of the doctrine of the schools—and 'the one cries *Mum,* while
t'other cries *Budget!* '   The comic writer, in my judgment, then,
ought to open the volume of nature and the world for his living
materials, and not take them out of his ethical common-place book ;
for in this way, neither will throw any additional light upon the
other.   In all things there is a division of labour ; and I am as little
for introducing the tone of the pulpit or reading-desk on the stage, as
for introducing plays and interludes in church-time, according to the
good old popish practice.   It was a part, indeed, of Steele's plan, 'by
the politeness of his style and the genteelness of his expressions,'[1] to
bring about a reconciliation between things which he thought had
hitherto been kept too far asunder, to wed the graces to the virtues,
and blend pleasure with profit.   And in this design he succeeded

[1] See Mandeville's Fable of the Bees.

admirably in his Tatler, and some other works; but in his comedies he has failed. He has confounded, instead of harmonising—has taken away its gravity from wisdom, and its charm from gaiety. It is not that in his plays we find 'some soul of goodness in things evil;' but they have no soul either of good or bad. His Funeral is as trite, as tedious, and full of formal grimace, as a procession of mutes and undertakers. The characters are made either affectedly good and forbearing, with 'all the milk of human kindness;' or purposely bad and disgusting, for the others to exercise their squeamish charities upon them. The Conscious Lovers is the best; but that is far from good, with the exception of the scene between Mr. Thomas and Phillis, who are fellow-servants, and commence lovers from being set to clean the window together. We are here once more in the company of our old friend, Isaac Bickerstaff, Esq. Indiana is as listless, and as insipid, as a drooping figure on an Indian screen; and Mr. Myrtle and Mr. Bevil only just disturb the still life of the scene. I am sorry that in this censure I should have Parson Adams against me; who thought the Conscious Lovers the only play fit for a Christian to see, and as good as a sermon. For myself, I would rather have read, or heard him read, one of his own manuscript sermons: and if the volume which he left behind him in his saddle-bags was to be had in print, for love or money, I would at any time walk ten miles on foot only to get a sight of it.

Addison's Drummer, or the Haunted House, is a pleasant farce enough; but adds nothing to our idea of the author of the Spectator.

Pope's joint after-piece, called 'An Hour after Marriage,' was not a successful attempt. He brought into it 'an alligator stuff'd,' which disconcerted the ladies, and gave just offence to the critics. Pope was too fastidious for a farce-writer; and yet the most fastidious people, when they step out of their regular routine, are apt to become the grossest. The smallest offences against probability or decorum are, to their habitual scrupulousness, as unpardonable as the greatest. This was the rock on which Pope probably split. The affair was, however, hushed up; and he wreaked his discreet vengeance at leisure on the 'odious endeavours,' and more odious success of Colley Cibber in the line in which he had failed.

Gay's 'What-d'ye-call-it,' is not one of his happiest things. His 'Polly' is a complete failure, which, indeed, is the common fate of second parts. If the original Polly, in the Beggar's Opera, had not had more winning ways with her, she would hardly have had so many Countesses for representatives as she has had, from her first appearance up to the present moment.

Fielding was a comic writer, as well as a novelist; but his comedies

158

are very inferior to his novels : they are particularly deficient both in plot and character. The only excellence which they have is that of the style, which is the only thing in which his novels are deficient. The only dramatic pieces of Fielding that retain possession of the stage are, the Mock Doctor (a tolerable translation from Moliere's *Medecin malgrè lui*), and his Tom Thumb, a very admirable piece of burlesque. The absurdities and bathos of some of our celebrated tragic writers could hardly be credited, but for the notes at the bottom of this preposterous medley of bombast, containing his authorities and the parallel passages. Dryden, Lee, and Shadwell, make no very shining figure there. Mr. Liston makes a better figure in the text. His Lord Grizzle is prodigious. What a name, and what a person! It has been said of this ingenious actor, that 'he is very great in Liston;' but he is even greater in Lord Grizzle. What a wig is that he wears! How flighty, flaunting, and fantastical! Not 'like those hanging locks of young Apollo,' nor like the serpent-hair of the Furies of Æschylus; but as troublous, though not as tragical as the one—as imposing, though less classical than the other. '*Que terribles sont ces cheveux gris*,' might be applied to Lord Grizzle's most valiant and magnanimous curls. This sapient courtier's 'fell of hair does at a dismal treatise rouse and stir as if life were in 't.' His wits seem flying away with the disorder of his flowing locks, and to sit as loosely on our hero's head as the caul of his peruke. What a significant vacancy in his open eyes and mouth! what a listlessness in his limbs! what an abstraction of all thought or purpose! With what an headlong impulse of enthusiasm he throws himself across the stage when he is going to be married, crying, 'Hey for Doctor's Commons,' as if the genius of folly had taken whole-length possession of his person! And then his dancing is equal to the discovery of a sixth sense—which is certainly very different from *common sense*! If this extraordinary personage cuts a great figure in his life, he is no less wonderful in his death and burial. 'From the sublime to the ridiculous there is but one step;' and this character would almost seem to prove, that there is but one step from the ridiculous to the sublime.—Lubin Log, however inimitable in itself, is itself an imitation of something existing elsewhere; but the Lord Grizzle of this truly original actor, is a pure invention of his own. His Caper, in the Widow's Choice, can alone dispute the palm with it in incoherence and volatility; for that, too, 'is high fantastical,' almost as full of emptiness, in as grand a gusto of insipidity, as profoundly absurd, as elaborately nonsensical! Why does not Mr. Liston play in some of Moliere's farces? I heartily wish that the author of Love, Law, and Physic, would launch him on the London boards in Monsieur Jourdain, or Monsieur Pourceaugnac. The genius of Liston and Moliere together—

> '——Must bid a gay defiance to mischance.'

Mr. Liston is an actor hardly belonging to the present age. Had he lived, unfortunately for us, in the time of Colley Cibber, we should have seen what a splendid niche he would have given him in his Apology.

Cibber is the hero of the Dunciad; but it cannot be said of him, that he was 'by merit raised to that bad eminence.' He was pert, not dull; a coxcomb, not a blockhead; vain, but not malicious. Pope's unqualified abuse of him was mere spleen; and the most obvious provocation to it seems to have been an excess of flippant vivacity in the constitution of Cibber. That Cibber's Birth-day Odes were dull, is true; but this was not peculiar to him. It is an objection which may be made equally to Shadwell's, to Whitehead's, to Warton's, to Pye's, and to all others, except those which of late years have *not* been written! In his Apology for his own Life, Cibber is a most amusing biographer: happy in his own good opinion, the best of all others; teeming with animal spirits, and uniting the self-sufficiency of youth with the garrulity of age. His account of his waiting as a page behind the chair of the old Duchess of Marlborough, at the time of the Revolution, who was then in the bloom of youth and beauty, which seems to have called up in him the secret homage of 'distant, enthusiastic, respectful love,' fifty years after, and the compliment he pays to her (then in her old age), 'a great grandmother without grey hairs,' is as delightful as any thing in fiction or romance; and is the evident origin of Mr. Burke's celebrated apostrophe to the Queen of France. Nor is the political confession of faith which he makes on this occasion, without a suitable mixture of vanity and sincerity: the vanity we may ascribe to the player, the sincerity to the politician. The self-complacency with which he talks of his own success both as a player and a writer, is not greater than the candour and cordiality with which he does heaped justice to the merits of his theatrical contemporaries and predecessors. He brings down the history of the stage, either by the help of observation or tradition, from the time of Shakspeare to his own; and quite dazzles the reader with a constellation of male and female, of tragic and comic, of past and present excellence. He gives portraits at full length of Kynaston, of Betterton, of Booth, of Estcourt, of Penkethman and Dogget, of Mohun and Wilks, of Nokes and Sandford, of Mrs. Montford, of Mrs. Oldfield, of Mrs. Barry and Mrs. Bracegirdle, and of others of equal note; with delectable criticisms on their several performances, and anecdotes of their private lives, with scarcely a single particle of jealousy or ill-nature, or any other motive than to expatiate in the delight of talking of the ornaments of his art, and a wish to share his pleasure with the reader. I wish I could quote some of these theatrical sketches; but the time presses. The latter part of his work is less entertaining when he becomes Manager, and gives us an exact statement of his squabbles with the Lord Chamberlain, and the expense of his ground-rent, his repairs, his scenery, and his dresses.—In his plays, his personal character perhaps predominates too much over the inventiveness of his Muse; but so far from being dull, he is every where light, fluttering, and airy. His pleasure in himself made him desirous to please; but his fault was, that he was too soon satisfied with what he did, that his indolence or want of thought led him to indulge in the vein that flowed from him with most ease, and that his vanity did not allow him to distinguish between what he did best and worst. His Careless Husband is a very elegant piece of agreeable, thoughtless writing; and the incident of Lady Easy throwing her handkerchief over her husband, whom she finds asleep in a chair by the side of her waiting-woman, was an admirable contrivance, taken, as he informs us, from real life. His Double Gallant, which has been lately revived, though it cannot rank in the first, may take its place in the second or third class of comedies. It abounds in character, bustle, and stage-effect. It belongs to what may be called the composite style; and very happily mixes up the comedy of intrigue, such as we see it in Mrs. Centlivre's Spanish plots, with a tolerable share of the wit and spirit of Congreve and Vanbrugh. As there is a good deal of wit, there is a spice of wickedness in this play, which was a privilege of the good old style of comedy, not altogether abandoned in Cibber's time. The luscious vein of the dialogue is stopped short in many of the scenes of the revived play, though not before we perceive its object—

'—— In hidden mazes running,
With wanton haste and giddy cunning.'

These imperfect hints of double meanings, however, pass off without any marks of reprobation; for unless they are insisted on, or made pretty broad, the audience, from being accustomed to the cautious purity of the modern drama, are not very expert in decyphering the equivocal allusion, for which they are not on the look-out. To what is this increased nicety owing? Was it that vice, from being formerly less common (though more fashionable) was less catching than at present? The first inference is by no means in our favour; for though I think that the grossness of manners prevailing in our fashionable comedies was a direct transcript of the manners of the court at the time, or in the period immediately preceding, yet the same grossness of expression and allusion existed long before, as in the plays of Shakspeare and Ben Jonson, when there was not this grossness of manners, and it has of late years been gradually refining away. There is a certain grossness or freedom of expression, which may arise as often from unsuspecting simplicity as from avowed profligacy. Whatever may be our progress either in virtue or vice since the age of Charles II. certain it is, that our manners are not mended since the time of Elizabeth and Charles I. Is it, then, that vice was formerly a thing more to be wondered at than imitated; that behind the rigid barriers of religion and morality it might be exposed freely, without the danger of any serious practical consequences—whereas now that the safeguards of wholesome authority and prejudice are removed, we seem afraid to trust our eyes or ears with a single situation or expression of a loose tendency, as if the mere mention of licentiousness implied a conscious approbation of it, and the extreme delicacy of our moral sense would be debauched by the bare suggestion of the possibility of vice? But I shall not take upon me to answer this question. The characters in the Double Gallant are well kept up: At-All and Lady Dainty are the two most prominent characters in this comedy, and those into which Cibber has put most of his own nature and genius. They are the essence of active impertinence and fashionable frivolity. Cibber, in short, though his name has been handed down to us as a bye-word of impudent pretension and impenetrable dulness by the classical pen of his accomplished rival, who, unfortunately, did not admit of any merit beyond the narrow circle of wit and friendship in which he himself moved, was a gentleman and a scholar of the old school; a man of wit and pleasantry in conversation, a diverting mimic, an excellent actor, an admirable dramatic critic, and one of the best comic writers of his age. His works, instead of being a *caput mortuum* of literature, had a great deal of the spirit, with a little too much of the froth. His Nonjuror was taken from Moliere's Tartuffe, and has been altered to the Hypocrite. Love's Last Shift appears to have been his own favourite; and he received the compliments of Sir John Vanbrugh and old Mr. Southern upon it:—the latter said to him, ' Young man, your play is a good one; and it will succeed, if you do not spoil it by your acting.' His plays did not always take equally. It is ludicrous to hear him complaining of the ill success of one of them, Love in a Riddle, a pastoral comedy, ' of a nice morality,' and well spoken sentiments, which he wrote in opposition to the Beggar's Opera, at the time when its worthless and vulgar rival was carrying every thing triumphantly before it. Cibber brings this, with much pathetic *naïveté*, as an instance of the lamentable want of taste in the town!

The Suspicious Husband by Hoadley, the Jealous Wife by Colman, and the Clandestine Marriage by Colman and Garrick, are excellent plays of the middle style of comedy; which are formed rather by judgment and selection, than by any original vein of genius; and have all the parts of a good comedy in degree, without having any one prominent, or to excess. The character of Ranger, in the Suspicious Husband, is only a variation of those of Farquhar, of the same class as his Sir Harry Wildair and others, without equal spirit. A great deal of the story of the Jealous Wife is borrowed from Fielding; but so faintly, that the resemblance is hardly discernible till you are apprised of it. The Jealous Wife herself is, however, a dramatic *chef-d'œuvre*, and worthy of being acted as often, and better than it is. Sir Harry Beagle is a true fox-hunting English squire. The Clandestine Marriage is nearly without a fault; and has some lighter theatrical graces, which I suspect Garrick threw into it. *Canton* is, I should think, his; though this classification of him among the ornamental parts of the play may seem whimsical. Garrick's genius does not appear to have been equal to the construction of a solid drama; but he could retouch and embellish with great gaiety and knowledge of the technicalities of his art. Garrick not only produced joint-pieces and after-pieces, but often set off the plays of his friends and contemporaries with the garnish, the *sauce piquant*, of prologues and epilogues, at which he had an admirable knack.—The elder Colman's translation of Terence, I may here add, has always been considered, by good judges, as an equal proof of the author's knowledge of the Latin language, and taste in his own.

Bickerstaff's plays and comic operas are continually acted: they come under the class of mediocrity, generally speaking. Their popularity seems to be chiefly owing to the unaffected ease and want of pretension with which they are written, with a certain humorous *naïveté* in the lower characters, and an exquisite adaptation of the music to the songs. His Love in a Village is one of the most delightful comic operas on the stage. It is truly pastoral; and the sense of music hovers over the very scene like the breath of morning. In his alteration of the Tartuffe he has spoiled the Hypocrite, but he has added Maw-worm.

Mrs. Cowley's comedy of the Belles' Stratagem, Who's the Dupe, and others, are of the second or third class: they are rather *refaccimentos* of the characters, incidents, and materials of former writers, got up with considerable liveliness and ingenuity, than original compositions, with marked qualities of their own.

LECTURES ON THE COMIC WRITERS

Goldsmith's Good-natured Man is inferior to She Stoops to Conquer; and even this last play, with all its shifting vivacity, is rather a
sportive and whimsical effusion of the author's fancy, a delightful and
delicately managed caricature, than a genuine comedy.

Murphy's plays of All in the Wrong and Know Your Own Mind,
are admirably written; with sense, spirit, and conception of character:
but without any great effect of the humorous, or that truth of feeling
which distinguishes the boundary between the absurdities of natural
character and the gratuitous fictions of the poet's pen. The heroes
of these two plays, Millamour and Sir Benjamin Constant, are too
ridiculous in their caprices to be tolerated, except in farce; and yet
their follies are so flimsy, so motiveless, and fine-spun, as not to be
intelligible, or to have any effect in their only proper sphere. Both his
principal pieces are said to have suffered by their similarity, first, to
Colman's Jealous Wife, and next to the School for Scandal, though
in both cases he had the undoubted priority. It is hard that the fate
of plagiarism should attend upon originality: yet it is clear that the
elements of the School for Scandal are not sparingly scattered in
Murphy's comedy of Know your own Mind, which appeared before
the latter play, only to be eclipsed by it. This brings me to speak of
Sheridan.

Mr. Sheridan has been justly called 'a dramatic star of the first
magnitude:' and, indeed, among the comic writers of the last
century, he 'shines like Hesperus among the lesser lights.' He has
left four several dramas behind him, all different or of different kinds,
and all excellent in their way;—the School for Scandal, the Rivals,
the Duenna, and the Critic. The attraction of this last piece is,
however, less in the mock-tragedy rehearsed, than in the dialogue of
the comic scenes, and in the character of Sir Fretful Plagiary, which
is supposed to have been intended for Cumberland. If some of the
characters in the School for Scandal were contained in Murphy's
comedy of Know your own Mind (and certainly some of Dashwoud's
detached speeches and satirical sketches are written with quite as firm
and masterly a hand as any of those given to the members of the
scandalous club, Mrs. Candour or Lady Sneerwell), yet they were
buried in it for want of grouping and relief, like the colours of a well-
drawn picture sunk in the canvass. Sheridan brought them out, and
exhibited them in all their glory. If that gem, the character of
Joseph Surface, was Murphy's, the splendid and more valuable setting
was Sheridan's. He took Murphy's Malvil from his lurking-place
in the closet, and 'dragged the struggling monster into day' upon
the stage. That is, he gave interest, life, and action, or, in other
words, its dramatic being, to the mere conception and written

specimens of a character. This is the merit of Sheridan's comedies, that every thing in them *tells*; there is no labour in vain. His Comic Muse does not go about prying into obscure corners, or collecting idle curiosities, but shews her laughing face, and points to her rich treasure—the follies of mankind. She is garlanded and crowned with roses and vine-leaves. Her eyes sparkle with delight, and her heart runs over with good-natured malice. Her step is firm and light, and her ornaments consummate! The School for Scandal is, if not the most original, perhaps the most finished and faultless comedy which we have. When it is acted, you hear people all around you exclaiming, ' Surely it is impossible for any thing to be cleverer.' The scene in which Charles sells all the old family pictures but his uncle's, who is the purchaser in disguise, and that of the discovery of Lady Teazle when the screen falls, are among the happiest and most highly wrought that comedy, in its wide and brilliant range, can boast. Besides the wit and ingenuity of this play, there is a genial spirit of frankness and generosity about it, that relieves the heart as well as clears the lungs. It professes a faith in the natural goodness, as well as habitual depravity of human nature. While it strips off the mask of hypocrisy, it inspires a confidence between man and man. As often as it is acted, it must serve to clear the air of that low, creeping, pestilent fog of cant and mysticism, which threatens to confound every native impulse, or honest conviction, in the nauseous belief of a perpetual lie, and the laudable profession of systematic hypocrisy.—The character of Lady Teazle is not well made out by the author; nor has it been well represented on the stage since the time of Miss Farren.—The Rivals is a play of even more action and incident, but of less wit and satire than the School for Scandal. It is as good as a novel in the reading, and has the broadest and most palpable effect on the stage. If Joseph Surface and Charles have a smack of Tom Jones and Blifil in their moral constitution, Sir Anthony Absolute and Mrs. Malaprop remind us of honest Matthew Bramble and his sister Tabitha, in their tempers and dialect. Acres is a distant descendant of Sir Andrew Ague-cheek. It must be confessed of this author, as Falstaff says of some one, that ' he had damnable iteration in him ! ' The Duenna is a perfect work of art. It has the utmost sweetness and point. The plot, the characters, the dialogue, are all complete in themselves, and they are all his own; and the songs are the best that ever were written, except those in the Beggar's Opera. They have a joyous spirit of intoxication in them, and a strain of the most melting tenderness. Compare the softness of that beginning,

' Had I heart for falsehood framed,'

with the spirited defiance to Fortune in the lines,

> ' Half thy malice youth could bear,
> And the rest a bumper drown.'

It would have been too much for the author of these elegant and classic productions not to have had some drawbacks on his felicity and fame. But even the applause of nations and the favour of princes cannot always be enjoyed with impunity.—Sheridan was not only an excellent dramatic writer, but a first-rate parliamentary speaker. His characteristics as an orator were manly, unperverted good sense, and keen irony. Wit, which has been thought a two-edged weapon, was by him always employed on the same side of the question—I think, on the right one. His set and more laboured speeches, as that on the Begum's affairs, were proportionably abortive and unimpressive : but no one was equal to him in replying, on the spur of the moment, to pompous absurdity, and unravelling the web of flimsy sophistry. He was the last accomplished debater of the House of Commons.—His character will, however, soon be drawn by one who has all the ability, and every inclination to do him justice; who knows how to bestow praise and to deserve it; by one who is himself an ornament of private and of public life ; a satirist, beloved by his friends ; a wit and a patriot to-boot ; a poet, and an honest man.

Macklin's Man of the World has one powerfully written character, that of Sir Pertinax Macsycophant, but it required Cooke's acting to make it thoroughly effectual.

Mr. Holcroft, in his Road to Ruin, set the example of that style of comedy, in which the *slang* phrases of jockey-noblemen and the humours of the four-in-hand club are blended with the romantic sentiments of distressed damsels and philosophic waiting-maids, and in which he has been imitated by the most successful of our living writers, unless we make a separate class for the school of Cumberland, who was almost entirely devoted to the *comedie larmoyante*, and who, passing from the light, volatile spirit of his West-Indian to the mawkish sensibility of the Wheel of Fortune, linked the Muse of English comedy to the genius of German tragedy, where she has since remained, like Christabel fallen asleep in the Witch's arms, and where I shall leave her, as I have not the poet's privilege to break the spell.

There are two other writers whom I have omitted to mention, but not forgotten : they are our two immortal farce-writers, the authors of the Mayor of Garratt and the Agreeable Surprise. If Foote has been called our English Aristophanes, O'Keeffe might well be called our English Moliere. The scale of the modern writer was smaller, but the spirit is the same. In light, careless laughter, and pleasant exaggerations of the humorous, we have had no one equal to him. There is no labour or contrivance in his scenes, but the drollery of his subject seems to strike irresistibly upon his fancy, and run away with his discretion as it does with ours. His Cowslip and Lingo are Touchstone and Audrey revived. He is himself a Modern Antique. His fancy has all the quaintness and extravagance of the old writers, with the ease and lightness which the moderns arrogate to themseves. All his pieces are delightful, but the Agreeable Surprise is the most so. There are in this some of the most felicitous blunders in situation and character that can be conceived ; and in Lingo's superb replication, ' A scholar ! I was a master of scholars,' he has hit the height of the ridiculous. Foote had more dry, sarcastic humour, and more knowledge of the world. His farces are bitter satires, more or less personal, as it happened. Mother Cole, in the Minor, and Mr. Smirk the Auctioneer, in Taste, with their coadjutors, are rich cut-and-come-again, 'pleasant, though wrong.' But the Mayor of Garratt is his *magnum opus* in this line. Some comedies are long farces : this farce is a comedy in little. It is also one of the best acted farces that we have. The acting of Dowton and Russell, in Major Sturgeon and Jerry Sneak, cannot be too much praised : Foote himself would have been satisfied with it. The strut, the bluster, the hollow swaggering, and turkey-cock swell of the Major ; and Jerry's meekness, meanness, folly, good-nature, and hen-pecked air, are assuredly done to the life. The latter character is even better than the former, which is saying a bold word. Dowton's art is only an imitation of art, of an affected or assumed character ; but in Russell's Jerry you see the very soul of nature, in a fellow that is ' pigeon-livered and lacks gall,' laid open and anatomized. You can see that his heart is no bigger than a pin, and his head as soft as a pippin. His whole aspect is chilled and frightened, as if he had been dipped in a pond ; and yet he looks as if he would like to be snug and comfortable, if he durst. He smiles as if he would be friends with you upon any terms ; and the tears come in his eyes because you will not let him. The tones of his voice are prophetic as the cuckoo's under-song. His words are made of water-gruel. The scene in which he tries to make a confidant of the Major is great ; and his song of ' Robinson Crusoe ' as melancholy as the island itself. The reconciliation-scene with his wife, and his exclamation over her, ' to think that I should make my Molly *veep* ! ' are pathetic, if the last stage of human infirmity is so. This farce appears to me to be both moral and entertaining ; yet it does not take. It is considered as an unjust satire on the city, and the country at large; and there is a very frequent repetition of the word 'nonsense' in the house, during the performance. Mr. Dowton was even hissed, either from the upper boxes or gallery, in his speech recounting the marching of his corps 'from Brentford to Ealing, and from Ealing to Acton;' and several persons in the pit, who thought the whole *low*, were for going out. This shows well for the progress of civilization. I suppose the manners described in the Mayor of Garratt have, in the last forty years, become obsolete, and the characters ideal: we have no longer either hen-pecked or brutal husbands, or domineering wives; the Miss Molly Jollops no longer wed Jerry Sneaks, or admire the brave Major Sturgeons on the other side of Temple-bar; all our soldiers have become heroes, and our magistrates respectable, and the farce of life is o'er.

One more name, and I have done. It is that of Peter Pindar. The historian of Sir Joseph Banks and the Emperor of Morocco, of the Pilgrims and the Peas, of the Royal Academy, and of Mr. Whitbread's brewing-vat, the bard in whom the nation and the king delighted, is old and blind, but still merry and wise:—remembering how he has made the world laugh in his time, and not repenting of the mirth he has given; with an involuntary smile lighted up at the mad pranks of his Muse, and the lucky hits of his pen—'faint picture of those flashes of his spirit, that were wont to set the table in a roar;' like his own Expiring Taper, bright and fitful to the last; tagging a rhyme or conning his own epitaph; and waiting for the last summons, GRATEFUL and CONTENTED ! [1]

I have thus gone through the history of that part of our literature, which I had proposed to myself to treat of. I have only to add, by way of explanation, that in some few parts I had anticipated myself in fugitive or periodical publications; and I thought it better to repeat what I had already stated to the best of my ability, than alter it for the worse. These parts bear, however, a very small proportion to the whole; and I have used such diligence and care as I could, in adding to them whatever appeared necessary to complete the general view of the subject, or make it (as far as lay in my power) interesting to others.

[1] This ingenious and popular writer is since dead.

End of LECTURES ON THE ENGLISH COMIC WRITERS

A VIEW OF THE ENGLISH STAGE

OR

A SERIES OF DRAMATIC CRITICISMS

BIBLIOGRAPHICAL NOTE

Published in one 8vo volume in 1818 with the following title-page : ' A View of the English Stage ; or, a Series of Dramatic Criticisms. By William Hazlitt. "For I am nothing if not critical." London : Printed for Robert Stodart, 81, Strand ; Anderson and Chase, 40, West Smithfield ; and Bell and Bradfute, Edinburgh. 1818.' The volume was printed by B. M'Millan, Bow Street, Covent Garden. The work was re-issued in 1821 with a fresh half-title, ' Dramatic Criticisms,' and a fresh title-page bearing the imprint : ' London : John Warren, Old Bond-Street. MDCCCXXI.' Selections from the volume have been made and published along with other dramatic criticisms of Hazlitt's, but the entire work has never been republished. See the notes at the end of this volume for particulars as to these volumes of selections. It is sufficient to state here that the so-called ' second edition,' published by the author's son in 1851 under the title of 'Criticisms and Dramatic Essays, of the English Stage,' contains only a selection from the essays published in *A View of the English Stage*. The present edition is reprinted from that of 1818, with the addition of a Table of Contents. For the sake of convenience the name of the journal from which the essay is taken and the date of the journal are printed at the beginning of each essay. Hazlitt himself gave the dates (very inaccurately), but not the names of the journals. In some cases he gave the name of the theatre at the head of an essay.

CONTENTS

A VIEW OF THE ENGLISH STAGE

PREFACE

THE Stage is one great source of public amusement, not to say instruction. A good play, well acted, passes away a whole evening delightfully at a certain period of life, agreeably at all times; we read the account of it next morning with pleasure, and it generally furnishes one leading topic of conversation for the afternoon. The disputes on the merits or defects of the last new piece, or of a favourite performer, are as common, as frequently renewed, and carried on with as much eagerness and skill, as those on almost any other subject. Rochefoucault, I believe, it was, who said that the reason why lovers were so fond of one another's company was, that they were always talking about themselves. The same reason almost might be given for the interest we feel in talking about plays and players; they are 'the brief chronicles of the time,' the epitome of human life and manners. While we are talking about them, we are thinking about ourselves. They 'hold the mirror up to Nature'; and our thoughts are turned to the Stage as naturally and as fondly as a fine lady turns to contemplate her face in the glass. It is a glass too, in which the wise may see themselves; but in which the vain and superficial see their own virtues, and laugh at the follies of others. The curiosity which every one has to know how his voice and manner can be mimicked, must have been remarked or felt by most of us. It is no wonder then, that we should feel the same sort of curiosity and interest, in seeing those whose business it is to 'imitate humanity' in general, and who do it sometimes 'abominably,' at other times admirably. Of these, some record is due to the world; but the player's art is one that perishes with him, and leaves no traces of itself, but in the faint descriptions of the pen or pencil. Yet how eagerly do we stop to look at the prints from Zoffany's pictures of Garrick and Weston! How much we are vexed, that so much of Colley Cibber's Life is taken up with the accounts of his own managership, and so little with those inimitable portraits which he has occasionally given of the actors of his time! How fortunate we think ourselves, when we can meet with any person who remembers the principal performers of the last age, and who can give us some distant idea of Garrick's nature, or of an Abington's grace! We are always indignant at Smollett, for having introduced a perverse caricature of the English Roscius, which staggers our faith in his faultless excellence while reading it. On the contrary, we are pleased to collect anecdotes of this celebrated actor, which shew his power over the human heart, and enable us to measure his genius with that of others by its effects. I have heard, for instance, that once, when Garrick was acting Lear, the spectators in the front row of the pit, not being able to see him well in the kneeling scene, where he utters the curse, rose up, when those behind them, not willing to interrupt the scene by remonstrating, immediately rose up too, and in this manner, the whole pit rose up, without uttering a syllable, and so that you might hear a pin drop. At another time, the crown of straw which he wore in the same character fell off, or was discomposed, which would have produced a burst of laughter at any common actor to whom such an accident had happened; but such was the deep interest in the character, and such the power of rivetting the attention possessed by this actor, that not the slightest notice was taken of the circumstance, but the whole audience remained bathed in silent tears. The knowledge of circumstances like these, serves to keep alive the memory of past excellence, and to stimulate future efforts. It was thought that a work containing a detailed account of the Stage in our own times—a period not unfruitful in theatrical genius—might not be wholly without its use.

The volume here offered to the public, is a collection of Theatrical Criticisms which have appeared with little interruption, during the last four years, in different newspapers—the *Morning Chronicle*, the *Champion*, the *Examiner*, and lastly, the *Times*. How I came to be regularly transferred from one of these papers to the other, sometimes formally and sometimes without ceremony, till I was forced to quit the last-mentioned by want of health and leisure, would make rather an amusing story, but that I do not chuse to tell 'the secrets of the prison-house.' I would, however, advise any one who has an ambition to write, and to write *his best*, in the periodical press, to get if possible 'a situation' in the *Times* newspaper, the Editor of which is a man of business, and not of letters. He may write there as long and as good articles as he can, without being turned out for it,—unless he should be too prolix on the subject of the Bourbons, and in that case he may set up an opposition paper on his own account—as 'one who loved not wisely but too well.'

The first, and (as I think) the best articles in this series, appeared originally in the *Morning Chronicle*. They are those relating to Mr. Kean. I went to see him the first night of his appearing in

174

PREFACE

Shylock. I remember it well. The boxes were empty, and the pit not half full : 'some quantity of barren spectators and idle renters were thinly scattered to make up a show.' The whole presented a dreary, hopeless aspect. I was in considerable apprehension for the result. From the first scene in which Mr. Kean came on, my doubts were at an end. I had been told to give as favourable an account as I could : I gave a true one. I am not one of those who, when they see the sun breaking from behind a cloud, stop to ask others whether it is the moon. Mr. Kean's appearance was the first gleam of genius breaking athwart the gloom of the Stage, and the public have since gladly basked in its ray, in spite of actors, managers, and critics. I cannot say that my opinion has much changed since that time. Why should it ? I had the same eyes to see with that I have now, the same ears to hear with, and the same understanding to judge with. Why then should I not form the same judgment? My opinions have been sometimes called singular : they are merely sincere. I say what I think : I think what I feel. I cannot help receiving certain impressions from things ; and I have sufficient courage to declare (somewhat abruptly) what they are. This is the only singularity I am conscious of. I do not shut my eyes to extraordinary merit because I hate it, and refuse to open them till the clamours of others make me, and then affect to wonder extravagantly at what I have before affected hypocritically to despise. I do not make it a common practice, to think nothing of an actor or an author, because all the world have not pronounced in his favour, and after they have, to persist in condemning him, as a proof not of imbecility and ill-nature, but of independence of taste and spirit. Nor do I endeavour to communicate the infection of my own dulness, cowardice, and spleen to others, by chilling the coldness of their constitutions by the poisonous slime of vanity or interest, and setting up my own conscious inability or unwillingness to form an opinion on any one subject, as the height of candour and judgment.—I did not endeavour to persuade Mr. Perry that Mr. Kean was an actor that would not last, merely because he had not lasted ; nor that Miss Stephens knew nothing of singing, because she had a sweet voice. On the contrary, I did all I could to counteract the effect of these safe, not very sound, insinuations, and 'screw the courage' of one principal organ of public opinion 'to the sticking-place.' I do not repent of having done so.

With respect to the spirit of partisanship in which the controversy respecting Mr. Kean's merits as an actor was carried on, there were two or three things remarkable. One set of persons, out of the excess of their unbounded admiration, furnished him with all sorts of

A VIEW OF THE ENGLISH STAGE

excellences which he did not possess or pretend to, and covered his defects from the wardrobe of their own fancies. With this class of persons,

> 'Pritchard's genteel, and Garrick's six feet high!'

I never enlisted in this corps of Swiss bodyguards; I was even suspected of disloyalty and *leze-majesté*, because I did not cry out—*Quand meme!*—to all Mr. Kean's stretches of the prerogatives of genius, and was placed out of the pale of theatrical orthodoxy, for not subscribing implicitly to all the articles of belief imposed upon my senses and understanding. If you had not been to see the little man twenty times in Richard, and did not deny his being hoarse in the last act, or admire him for being so, you were looked on as a luke-warm devotee, or half an infidel. On the other hand, his detractors constantly argued not from what he was, but from what he was not. 'He was not tall. He had not a fine voice. He did not play at Covent-Garden. He was not John Kemble.' This was all you could get from them, and this they thought quite sufficient to prove that he was not any thing, because he was not something quite different from himself. They did not consider that an actor might have the eye of an eagle with the voice of a raven, a 'pigmy body,' and 'a fiery soul that o'er-informed its tenement'; that he might want grace and dignity, and yet have enough nature and passion in his breast to set up a whole corps of regular stagers. They did not enquire whether this was the case with respect to Mr. Kean, but took it for granted that it was not, for no other reason, than because the question had not been settled by the critics twenty or thirty years ago, and admitted by the town ever since, that is, before Mr. Kean was born. A royal infant may be described as 'un haut et puissant prince, agé d'un jour,'[1] but a great and powerful actor cannot be known till he arrives at years of discretion, and he must be first a candidate for theatrical reputation before he can be a veteran. This is a truism, but it is one that our prejudices constantly make us not only forget, but frequently combat with all the spirit of martyrdom. I have (as it will be seen in the following pages) all along spoken freely of Mr. Kean's faults, or what I considered such, physical as well as intellectual; but the balance inclines decidedly to the favour-able side, though not more I think than his merits exceed his defects. It was also the more necessary to dwell on the claims of an actor to public support, in proportion as they were original, and to the illiberal opposition they unhappily had to encounter. I endeavoured to prove

[1] See the Fudge Family, edited by Thomas Brown, jun.

176

(and with some success), that he was not 'the very worst actor in the world.' His Othello is what appears to me his master-piece. To those who have seen him in this part, and think little of it, I have nothing farther to say. It seems to me, as far as the mind alone is concerned, and leaving the body out of the question, fully equal to any thing of Mrs. Siddons's. But I hate such comparisons; and only make them on strong provocation.

Though I do not repent of what I have said in praise of certain actors, yet I wish I could retract what I have been obliged to say in reprobation of others. Public reputation is a lottery, in which there are blanks as well as prizes. The Stage is an arduous profession, requiring so many essential excellences and accidental advantages, that though it is an honour and a happiness to succeed in it, it is only a misfortune, and not a disgrace, to fail in it. Those who put themselves upon their trial, must, however, submit to the verdict; and the critic in general does little more than prevent a lingering death, by anticipating, or putting in immediate force, the sentence of the public. The victims of criticism, like the victims of the law, bear no good will to their executioners; and I confess I have often been heartily tired of so thankless an office. What I have said of any actor, has never arisen from private pique of any sort. Indeed the only person on the stage with whom I have ever had any personal intercourse, is Mr. Liston, and of him I have not spoken 'with the malice of a friend.' To Mr. Conway and Mr. Bartley my apologies are particularly due: I have accused the one of being tall, and the other of being fat. I have also said that Mr. Young plays not only like a scholar, but like 'a master of scholars'; that Miss O'Neill shines more in tragedy than comedy; and that Mr. Mathews is an excellent mimic. I am sorry for these disclosures, which were extorted from me, but I cannot retract them. There is one observation which has been made, and which is true, that public censure hurts actors in a pecuniary point of view; but it has been forgotten, that public praise assists them in the same manner. Again, I never understood that the applauded actor thought himself personally obliged to the newspaper critic; the latter was merely supposed to do his duty. Why then should the critic be held responsible to the actor whom he *damns* by virtue of his office? Besides, as the mimic caricatures absurdity off the Stage, why should not the critic sometimes caricature it on the Stage? The children of Momus should not hold themselves sacred from ridicule. Though the colours may be a little heightened, the outline may be correct; and truth may be conveyed, and the public taste improved, by an alliteration or a quibble that wounds the self-love of an individual. Authors must live as well as actors; and the *insipid* must at all events be avoided as that which the public abhors most.

I am not aware of any thing necessary to be added to this Preface, but to apologize for some repetitions to be found in the work; I mean some passages and criticisms that have been transferred to other publications, such as the account of the Beggar's Opera, Coriolanus, &c. In fact, I have come to this determination in my own mind, that a work is as good as *manuscript*, and is invested with all the same privileges, till it appears in a second edition—a rule which leaves me at liberty to make what use I please of what I have hitherto written, with the single exception of THE CHARACTERS OF SHAKESPEAR'S PLAYS.

W. HAZLITT.

April 24, 1818.

A VIEW OF THE ENGLISH STAGE

MR. KEAN'S SHYLOCK

The Morning Chronicle.   *January* 27, 1814.

Mr. Kean (of whom report had spoken highly) last night made his appearance at Drury-Lane Theatre in the character of Shylock. For voice, eye, action, and expression, no actor has come out for many years at all equal to him. The applause, from the first scene to the last, was general, loud, and uninterrupted. Indeed, the very first scene in which he comes on with Bassanio and Antonio, shewed the master in his art, and at once decided the opinion of the audience. Perhaps it was the most perfect of any. Notwithstanding the complete success of Mr. Kean in the part of Shylock, we question whether he will not become a greater favourite in other parts. There was a lightness and vigour in his tread, a buoyancy and elasticity of spirit, a fire and animation, which would accord better with almost any other character than with the morose, sullen, inward, inveterate, inflexible malignity of Shylock. The character of Shylock is that of a man brooding over one idea, that of its wrongs, and bent on one unalterable purpose, that of revenge. In conveying a profound impression of this feeling, or in embodying the general conception of rigid and uncontroulable self-will, equally proof against every sentiment of humanity or prejudice of opinion, we have seen actors more successful than Mr. Kean; but in giving effect to the conflict of passions arising out of the contrasts of situation, in varied vehemence of declamation, in keenness of sarcasm, in the rapidity of his transitions from one tone and feeling to another, in propriety and novelty of action, presenting a succession of striking pictures, and giving perpetually fresh shocks of delight and surprise, it would be difficult to single out a competitor. The fault of his acting was (if we may hazard the objection), an over-display of the resources of the art, which gave too much relief to the hard, impenetrable, dark ground-work of the character of Shylock. It would be endless to point out individual beauties, where almost every passage was received with equal and deserved applause. We thought, in one or two instances,

A VIEW OF THE ENGLISH STAGE

the pauses in the voice were too long, and too great a reliance placed on the expression of the countenance, which is a language intelligible only to a part of the house.

The rest of the play was, upon the whole, very respectably cast. It would be an equivocal compliment to say of Miss Smith, that her acting often reminds us of Mrs. Siddons. Rae played Bassanio; but the abrupt and harsh tones of his voice are not well adapted to the mellifluous cadences of Shakespear's verse.

The Morning Chronicle.   *February 2, 1814.*

Mr. Kean appeared again in Shylock, and by his admirable and expressive manner of giving the part, fully sustained the reputation he had acquired by his former representation of it, though he laboured under the disadvantage of a considerable hoarseness. He assumed a greater appearance of age and feebleness than on the first night, but the general merit of his playing was the same. His style of acting is, if we may use the expression, more significant, more pregnant with meaning, more varied and alive in every part, than any we have almost ever witnessed. The character never stands still; there is no vacant pause in the action; the eye is never silent. For depth and force of conception, we have seen actors whom we should prefer to Mr. Kean in Shylock; for brilliant and masterly execution, none. It is not saying too much of him, though it is saying a great deal, that he has all that Mr. Kemble *wants* of perfection. He reminds us of the descriptions of the 'far-darting eye' of Garrick. We are anxious to see him in Norval and Richard, and anticipate more complete satisfaction from his performance of the latter part, than from the one in which he has already stamped his reputation with the public

Miss Smith played Portia with much more animation than the last time we saw her, and in delivering the fine apostrophe on Mercy, in the trial-scene, was highly impressive.

MR. KEAN'S RICHARD

The Morning Chronicle.   *February, 15, 1814.*

Mr. Kean's manner of acting this part has one peculiar advantage; it is entirely his own, without any traces of imitation of any other actor. He stands upon his own ground, and he stands firm upon it. Almost every scene had the stamp and freshness of nature. The excellences and defects of his performance were in general the same
180

A VIEW OF THE ENGLISH STAGE

as those which he discovered in Shylock; though, as the character of Richard is the most difficult, so we think he displayed most power in it. It is possible to form a higher conception of this character (we do not mean from seeing other actors, but from reading Shakespear) than that given by this very admirable tragedian; but we cannot imagine any character represented with greater distinctness and precision, more perfectly *articulated* in every part. Perhaps, indeed, there is too much of this; for we sometimes thought he failed, even from an exuberance of talent, and dissipated the impression of the character by the variety of his resources. To be perfect, it should have a little more solidity, depth, sustained, and impassioned feeling, with somewhat less brilliancy, with fewer glancing lights, pointed transitions, and pantomimic evolutions.

The Richard of Shakespear is towering and lofty, as well as aspiring; equally impetuous and commanding; haughty, violent, and subtle; bold and treacherous; confident in his strength, as well as in his cunning; raised high by his birth, and higher by his genius and his crimes; a royal usurper, a princely hypocrite, a tyrant, and a murderer of the House of Plantagenet.

> ' But I was born so high ;
> Our airy buildeth in the cedar's top,
> And dallies with the wind, and scorns the sun.'

The idea conveyed in these lines (which are omitted in the miserable medley acted for Richard III.) is never lost sight of by Shakespear, and should not be out of the actor's mind for a moment. The restless and sanguinary Richard is not a man striving to be great, but to be greater than he is; conscious of his strength of will, his powers of intellect, his daring courage, his elevated station, and making use of these advantages, as giving him both the means and the pretext to commit unheard-of crimes, and to shield himself from remorse and infamy.

If Mr. Kean does not completely succeed in concentrating all the lines of the character, as drawn by Shakespear, he gives an animation, vigour, and relief to the part, which we have never seen surpassed. He is more refined than Cooke; more bold, varied, and original than Kemble, in the same character. In some parts, however, we thought him deficient in dignity; and particularly in the scenes of state business, there was not a sufficient air of artificial authority. The fine assumption of condescending superiority, after he is made king—'Stand all apart—Cousin of Buckingham,' &c. was not given with the effect which it might have received. There was also at times, a sort of tip-toe elevation, an enthusiastic rapture in his expectations of obtaining the crown, instead of a gloating expression of sullen delight, as if he already clutched the bauble, and held it within his grasp. This was the precise expression which Mr. Kean gave with so much effect to the part where he says, that he already feels

'The golden rigol bind his brows.'

In one who *dares* so much, there is little indeed to blame. The only two things which appeared to us decidedly objectionable, were the sudden letting down of his voice when he says of Hastings, 'chop off his head,' and the action of putting his hands behind him, in listening to Buckingham's account of his reception by the citizens. His courtship scene with Lady Anne was an admirable exhibition of smooth and smiling villainy. The progress of wily adulation, of encroaching humility, was finely marked throughout by the action, voice, and eye. He seemed, like the first tempter, to approach his prey, certain of the event, and as if success had smoothed the way before him. We remember Mr. Cooke's manner of representing this scene was more violent, hurried, and full of anxious uncertainty. This, though more natural in general, was, we think, less in character. Richard should woo not as a lover, but as an actor—to shew his mental superiority, and power to make others the playthings of his will. Mr. Kean's attitude in leaning against the side of the stage before he comes forward in this scene, was one of the most graceful and striking we remember to have seen. It would have done for Titian to paint. The opening scene in which Richard descants on his own deformity, was conceived with perfect truth and character, and delivered in a fine and varied tone of natural recitation. Mr. Kean did equal justice to the beautiful description of the camps the night before the battle, though, in consequence of his hoarseness, he was obliged to repeat the whole passage in an under-key.[1] His manner of bidding his friends good night, and his pausing with the point of his sword, drawn slowly backward and forward on the ground, before he retires to his tent, received shouts of applause. He gave to all the busy scenes of the play the greatest animation and effect. He filled every part of the stage. The concluding scene, in which he is killed by Richmond, was the most brilliant. He fought like one drunk with wounds: and the attitude in which he stands with his hands stretched out, after his sword is taken from him, had a preternatural and terrific grandeur, as if his will could not be disarmed, and the very phantoms of his despair had a withering power.

[1] The defects in the upper tones of Mr. Kean's voice were hardly perceptible in his performance of Shylock, and were at first attributed to hoarseness.

182

A VIEW OF THE ENGLISH STAGE

The Morning Chronicle.   *February* 21, 1814.

The house was crowded at an early hour in every part, to witness Mr. Kean's second representation of Richard. His admirable acting received that meed of applause, which it so well deserved. His voice had not entirely recovered its tone and strength; and when (after the curtain had dropped, amidst a tumult of approbation), Mr. Rae came forward to announce the play for Monday, cries of ' No, no,' from every part of the house, testified the sense entertained by the audience, of the impropriety of requiring the repetition of this extraordinary effort, till every physical disadvantage had been completely removed.

We have little to add to our former remarks, for Mr. Kean went through the part nearly as before, and we saw no reason to alter our opinion. The dying scene was the most varied, and, we think, for the worse. In pronouncing the words in Richard's soliloquy, ' I am myself alone,' Mr. Kean gave a quick and hurried movement to his voice, as if it was a thought that suddenly struck him, or which he wished to pass over ; whereas it is the deep and rooted sentiment of his breast. The reduplication of the words in Shakespear points out the manner in which the voice should dwell upon, and as it were, brood over the feeling, loth to part with the bitter consolation. Where he says to Buckingham, ' I am not i' the vein,' the expression should, we imagine, be that of stifled hatred, and cold contempt, instead of sarcastic petulance. The scene tells for itself, without being pointed by the manner. In general, perhaps, if Mr. Kean were to give to the character less of the air of an ostentatious hypocrite, of an intelligible villain, it would be more correct, and would accord better with Shakespear's idea of the part. The description which he has put into the mouth of Hastings, is a perfect study for the actor.

> ' His grace looks cheerfully and smooth this morning :
> There 's some conceit or other likes him well,
> When that he bids good-morrow with such spirit.
> I think there 's ne'er a man in Christendom
> Can lesser hide his hate or love than he,
> For by his face straight shall you know his heart.'

In the scene with Lady Anne, in the sudden alteration of his manner to the messenger who brings him the news of Edward's illness, in the interview with Buckingham, where he desires the death of the children, in his infinitely spirited expostulation with Lord Stanley, in his triumph at the death of Buckingham, in the parting scene with his friends before the battle, in his treatment of the paper sent to Norfolk, and in all the tumult and glowing interest of the last scenes of the play, we had fresh cause for admiration. It were in vain, however, to point out particular beauties; for the research, the ingenuity, and the invention manifested throughout the character are endless. We have said before, and we still think so, that there is even too much effect given, too many significant hints, too much appearance of study. There is a tone in acting, as well as in painting, which is the chief and master excellence. Our highest conception of an actor is, that he shall assume the character once for all, and be it throughout, and trust to this conscious sympathy for the effect produced. Mr. Kean's manner of acting is, on the contrary, rather a perpetual assumption of his part, always brilliant and successful, almost always true and natural, but yet always a distinct effort in every new situation, so that the actor does not seem entirely to forget himself, or to be identified with the character. The extreme elaboration of the parts injures the broad and massy effect; the general impulse of the machine is retarded by the variety and intricacy of the movements. But why do we try this actor by an ideal theory? Who is there that will stand the same test? It is, in fact, the last forlorn hope of criticism, for it shews that we have nothing else to compare him with. 'Take him for all in all,' it will be long, very long, before we 'look upon his like again,' if we are to wait as long as we *have* waited.

We wish the introduction of the ghosts through the trap-doors of the stage were altogether omitted. The speeches, which they address to Richard, might be delivered just as well from behind the scenes. These sort of exhibitions are only proper for a superstitious age; and in an age not superstitious, excite ridicule instead of terror. Mr. Wroughton makes a very substantial ghost, and Miss Boyce retains the same ruddy appearance of flesh and blood, and the same graceful *embonpoint*, which so well became her in the scene where she was wooed by Richard. Mrs. Glover's Queen was more natural and impressive than on the first night, because it was less turbulent; and if she would use still less vociferation, she would produce a still greater effect—'For in the very torrent and whirlwind of the passion, you should acquire a temperance that may give it smoothness.'

Mr. Kean's acting in Richard, as we before remarked in his Shylock, presents a perpetual succession of striking pictures. He bids fair to supply us with the best Shakespear Gallery we have had!

A VIEW OF THE ENGLISH STAGE

MR. KEAN'S HAMLET

The Morning Chronicle.   *March* 14, 1814.

That which distinguishes the dramatic productions of Shakespear from all others, is the wonderful variety and perfect individuality of his characters. Each of these is as much itself, and as absolutely independent of the rest, as if they were living persons, not fictions of the mind. The poet appears for the time being, to be identified with the character he wishes to represent, and to pass from one to the other, like the same soul, successively animating different bodies. By an art like that of the ventriloquist, he throws his imagination out of himself, and makes every word appear to proceed from the very mouth of the person whose name it bears. His plays alone are properly expressions of the passions, not descriptions of them. His characters are real beings of flesh and blood; they speak like men, not like authors. One might suppose that he had stood by at the time, and had overheard what passed. Each object and circumstance seems to exist in his mind as it existed in nature; each several train of thought and feeling goes on of itself without effort or confusion; in the world of his imagination every thing has a life, a place and being of its own.

These remarks are, we think, as applicable to Hamlet, as to any of Shakespear's tragedies. It is, if not the finest, perhaps the most inimitable of all his productions. Lear is first, for the profound intensity of the passion: Macbeth, for the wildness of the imagination, and the glowing rapidity of the action: Othello, for the progressive interest, and rapid alternations of feeling: Hamlet, for perfect dramatic truth, and the unlooked-for development of sentiment and character. Shakespear has in this play shewn more of the magnanimity of genius, than in any other. There is no attempt to force an interest, but every thing is left to time and circumstances. The interest is excited without premeditation or effort, the events succeed each other as matters of course, the characters think, and speak and act just as they would do, if they were left to themselves. The whole play is an exact transcript of what might have taken place at the Court of Denmark five hundred years ago, before the modern refinements in morality and manners.

The character of Hamlet is itself a pure effusion of genius. It is not a character marked by strength of passion or will, but by refinement of thought and feeling. Hamlet is as little of the hero as a man can well be; but he is 'a young and princely novice,' full of high enthusiasm and quick sensibility—the sport of circumstances, questioning with fortune, and refining on his own feelings, and forced from the natural bias of his character, by the strangeness of his situation. He seems incapable of deliberate action, and is only hurried into extremities on the spur of the occasion, when he has no time to reflect, as in the scene where he kills Polonius, and where he alters the letters which Rosencrantz and Guildenstern take with them. At other times, he remains puzzled, undecided, and sceptical, dallies with his purposes till the occasion is lost, and always finds some reason to relapse into indolence and thoughtfulness again. For this reason he refuses to kill the King when he is at his prayers, and by a refinement in malice, which is only an excuse for his own want of resolution, defers his revenge to some more fatal opportunity, when he shall be engaged in some act 'that has no relish of salvation in it.' So he scruples to trust the suggestions of the Ghost, contrives the scene of the play to have surer proof of his uncle's guilt, and then rests satisfied with this confirmation of his suspicions, and the success of his experiment, instead of acting upon it. The moral perfection of this character has been called in question. It is more natural than conformable to rules; and if not more amiable, is certainly more dramatic on that account. Hamlet is not, to be sure, a Sir Charles Grandison. In general, there is little of the drab-coloured quakerism of morality in the ethical delineations of 'that noble and liberal casuist,' as Shakespear has been well called. He does not set his heroes in the stocks of virtue, to make mouths at their own situation. His plays are not transcribed from the Whole Duty of Man! We confess, we are a little shocked at the want of refinement in those, who are shocked at the want of refinement in Hamlet. The want of punctilious exactness of behaviour either partakes of the 'license of the time,' or belongs to the very excess of intellectual refinement in the character, which makes the common rules of life, as well as his own purposes, sit loose upon him. He may be said to be amenable only to the tribunal of his own thoughts, and is too much occupied with the airy world of contemplation, to lay as much stress as he ought on the practical consequences of things. His habitual principles of action are unhinged, and 'out of joint' with the time.

This character is probably of all others the most difficult to personate on the stage. It is like the attempt to embody a shadow.

> 'Come then, the colours and the ground prepare,
> Dip in the rainbow, trick her off in air,
> Chuse a firm cloud, before it falls, and in it
> Catch, 'ere she change, the Cynthia of a minute.'

Such nearly is the task which the actor imposes on himself in the
186

part of Hamlet. It is quite remote from hardness and dry precision. The character is spun to the finest thread, yet never loses its continuity. It has the yielding flexibility of 'a wave of the sea.' It is made up of undulating lines, without a single sharp angle. There is no set purpose, no straining at a point. The observations are suggested by the passing scene—the gusts of passion come and go, like the sounds of music borne on the wind. The interest depends not on the action, but on the thoughts—on 'that within which passeth shew.' Yet, in spite of these difficulties, Mr. Kean's representation of the character had the most brilliant success. It did not indeed come home to our feelings, as Hamlet (that very Hamlet whom we read of in our youth, and seem almost to remember in our after-years), but it was a most striking and animated rehearsal of the part.

High as Mr. Kean stood in our opinion before, we have no hesitation in saying, that he stands higher in it (and, we think, will in that of the public), from the powers displayed in this last effort. If it was less perfect as a whole, there were parts in it of a higher cast of excellence than any part of his Richard. We will say at once, in what we think his general delineation of the character wrong. It was too strong and pointed. There was often a severity, approaching to virulence, in the common observations and answers. There is nothing of this in Hamlet. He is, as it were, wrapped up in the cloud of his reflections, and only *thinks aloud*. There should therefore be no attempt to impress what he says upon others by any exaggeration of emphasis or manner, no talking *at* his hearers. There should be as much of the gentleman and scholar as possible infused into the part, and as little of the actor. A pensive air of sadness should sit unwillingly upon his brow, but no appearance of fixed and sullen gloom. He is full of 'weakness and melancholy,' but there is no harshness in his nature. Hamlet should be the most amiable of misanthropes. There is no one line in this play, which should be spoken like any one line in Richard; yet Mr. Kean did not appear to us to keep the two characters always distinct. He was least happy in the last scene with Guildenstern and Rosencrantz. In some of these more familiar scenes he displayed more energy than was requisite; and in others where it would have been appropriate, did not rise equal to the exigency of the occasion. In particular, the scene with Laertes, where he leaps into the grave, and utters the exclamation, ''Tis I, Hamlet the Dane,' had not the tumultuous and overpowering effect we expected from it. To point out the defects of Mr. Kean's performance of the part, is a less grateful but a much shorter task, than to enumerate the many striking beauties which he

A VIEW OF THE ENGLISH STAGE

gave to it, both by the power of his action and by the true feeling of nature. His surprise when he first sees the Ghost, his eagerness and filial confidence in following it, the impressive pathos of his action and voice in addressing it, 'I'll call thee Hamlet, *Father*, Royal Dane,' were admirable.

Mr. Kean has introduced in this part a *new reading*, as it is called, which we think perfectly correct. In the scene where he breaks from his friends to obey the command of his father, he keeps his sword pointed behind him, to prevent them from following him, instead of holding it before him to protect him from the Ghost. The manner of his taking Guildenstern and Rosencrantz under each arm, under pretence of communicating his secret to them, when he only means to trifle with them, had the finest effect, and was, we conceive, exactly in the spirit of the character. So was the suppressed tone of irony in which he ridicules those who gave ducats for his uncle's picture, though they would 'make mouths at him,' while his father lived. Whether the way in which Mr. Kean hesitates in repeating the first line of the speech in the interview with the player, and then, after several ineffectual attempts to recollect it, suddenly hurries on with it, 'The rugged Pyrrhus,' &c. is in perfect keeping, we have some doubts: but there was great ingenuity in the thought; and the spirit and life of the execution was beyond every thing. Hamlet's speech in describing his own melancholy, his instructions to the players, and the soliloquy on death, were all delivered by Mr. Kean in a tone of fine, clear, and natural recitation. His pronunciation of the word 'contumely' in the last of these, is, we apprehend, not authorized by custom, or by the metre.

Both the closet scene with his mother, and his remonstrances to Ophelia, were highly impressive. If there had been less vehemence of effort in the latter, it would not have lost any of its effect. But whatever nice faults might be found in this scene, they were amply redeemed by the manner of his coming back after he has gone to the extremity of the stage, from a pang of parting tenderness to press his lips to Ophelia's hand. It had an electrical effect on the house. It was the finest commentary that was ever made on Shakespear. It explained the character at once (as he meant it), as one of disappointed hope, of bitter regret, of affection suspended, not obliterated, by the distractions of the scene around him! The manner in which Mr. Kean acted in the scene of the Play before the King and Queen was the most daring of any, and the force and animation which he gave to it, cannot be too highly applauded. Its extreme boldness 'bordered on the verge of all we hate,' and the effect it produced, was a test of the extraordinary powers of this extraordinary actor.

188

A VIEW OF THE ENGLISH STAGE

We cannot speak too highly of Mr. Raymond's representation of the Ghost. It glided across the stage with the preternatural grandeur of a spirit. His manner of speaking the part was not equally excellent. A spirit should not whine or shed tears.

Mr. Dowton's Polonius was unworthy of so excellent an actor. The part was mistaken altogether. Polonius is not exceedingly wise, but he is not quite a fool; or if he is, he is at the same time a courtier, and a courtier of the old school. Mr. Dowton made nothing, or worse than nothing, of the part.

MR. KEAN'S OTHELLO

The Morning Chronicle.   *May* 6, 1814.

Othello was acted at Drury-Lane last night, the part of Othello by Mr. Kean. His success was fully equal to the arduousness of the undertaking. In general, we might observe that he displayed the same excellences and the same defects as in his former characters. His voice and person were not altogether in consonance with the character, nor was there throughout, that noble tide of deep and sustained passion, impetuous, but majestic, that 'flows on to the Propontic, and knows no ebb,' which raises our admiration and pity of the lofty-minded Moor. There were, however, repeated bursts of feeling and energy which we have never seen surpassed. The whole of the latter part of the third act was a master-piece of profound pathos and exquisite conception, and its effect on the house was electrical. The tone of voice in which he delivered the beautiful apostrophe, 'Then, oh farewell!' struck on the heart and the imagination like the swelling notes of some divine music. The look, the action, the expression of voice, with which he accompanied the exclamation, 'Not a jot, not a jot;' the reflection, 'I felt not *Cassio's kisses* on her lips;' and his vow of revenge against Cassio, and abandonment of his love for Desdemona, laid open the very tumult and agony of the soul. In other parts, where we expected an equal interest to be excited, we were disappointed; and in the common scenes, we think Mr. Kean's manner, as we have remarked on other occasions, had more point and emphasis than the sense or character required.[1]

The rest of the play was by no means judiciously cast; indeed, almost every individual appeared to be out of his proper place.

[1] For a fuller account of Mr. Kean's Othello, see one of the last articles in this volume.

A VIEW OF THE ENGLISH STAGE

MR. KEAN'S IAGO

The Morning Chronicle.   *May* 9, 1814.

The part of Iago was played at Drury-Lane on Saturday by Mr. Kean, and played with admirable facility and effect. It was the most faultless of his performances, the most consistent and entire. Perhaps the accomplished hypocrite was never so finely, so adroitly pourtrayed —a gay, light-hearted monster, a careless, cordial, comfortable villain. The preservation of character was so complete, the air and manner were so much of a piece throughout, that the part seemed more like a detached scene or single *trait*, and of shorter duration than it usually does. The ease, familiarity, and tone of nature with which the text was delivered, were quite equal to any thing we have seen in the best comic acting. It was the least overdone of all his parts, though full of point, spirit, and brilliancy. The odiousness of the character was in fact, in some measure, glossed over by the extreme grace, alacrity and rapidity of the execution. Whether this effect were 'a consummation of the art devoutly to be wished,' is another question, on which we entertain some doubts. We have already stated it as our opinion, that Mr. Kean is not a literal transcriber of his author's text; he translates his characters with great freedom and ingenuity into a language of his own; but at the same time we cannot help preferring his liberal and spirited dramatic versions, to the dull, literal, common-place monotony of his competitors. Besides, after all, in the conception of the part, he may be right, and we may be wrong. We have before complained that Mr. Kean's Richard was not gay enough, and we should now be disposed to complain that his Iago is not grave enough.

Mr. Sowerby's Othello, we are sorry to add, was a complete failure, and the rest of the play was very ill got up.

ANTONY AND CLEOPATRA

The Morning Chronicle.   *Nov.* 16, 1813.

Shakespear's tragedy of Antony and Cleopatra was brought out last night at Covent-Garden with alterations, and with considerable additions from Dryden's All for Love. The piece seems to have been in some measure got up for the occasion, as there are several claptraps in the speeches, which admit of an obvious allusion to passing characters and events, and which were eagerly seized by the audience. Of the execution of the task which the compiler has imposed upon himself, we cannot speak in terms of much praise.

190

Almost all the transpositions of passages which he has attempted, are, we think, injudicious and injurious to the effect. Thus the rich and poetical description of the person of Cleopatra, in the beginning of the second act—'The barge she sat in, like a burnished throne, burnt on the water,' &c. which prepares the way for, and almost seems to justify the subsequent infatuation of Antony, is here postponed till near the catastrophe, where it answers no end, and excites little interest. It would also have been much better, if the author had contented himself merely with omitting certain passages, which he might deem objectionable to a modern audience, without encumbering either the plot or dialogue with any foreign interpolation. He might have separated the gold of Shakespear from the alloy which at times accompanies it, but he ought not to have mixed it up with the heavy tinsel of Dryden. We cannot approve of the attempt to effect 'an amalgamation of the wonderful powers' of these writers, who are, in the preface to the printed play, classed together as 'two of England's greatest poets.' There is not the slightest comparison between them, either in kind or degree. There is all the difference between them, that can subsist between artificial and natural passion. Dryden never goes out of himself: he is a man of strong sense and powerful feeling, reasoning upon what he should feel in certain situations, and expressing himself in studied declamation, in general topics, expanding and varying the stock of his own ideas, so as to produce a tolerable resemblance to those of mankind in different situations, and building up, by the aid of logic and rhetoric—that is, by means of certain truths and images, generally known and easily applied, a stately and impressive poem. Whereas Shakespear does not suppose himself to be others, but at once *becomes* them. His imagination passes out of himself into them, and as it were, transmits to him their feelings and circumstances. Nothing is made out by inference and analogy, by climax and antithesis, but all comes immediately from nature—the thoughts, the images, the very words are hers. His plays can only be compared with Nature—they are unlike every thing else.

Antony and Cleopatra, though not in the first order of Shakespear's productions, is one of the best of his historical plays. It is every where full of that pervading comprehensive power, by which the poet seemed to identify himself with time and nature. The pomp and voluptuous charms of Cleopatra are displayed in all their force and lustre, as well as the effeminate grandeur of the soul of Mark Antony. The repentance of Enobarbus after his treachery to his master, the most beautiful and affecting part of the play, is here, for some reason, entirely omitted. Nothing can have more local truth and perfect character than the passage in which Cleopatra is represented as conjecturing what were the employments of Antony in his absence. 'He's speaking now, or murmuring—where's my serpent of old Nile?' Or again, when she says to Antony, after the defeat of Actium, and his resolution to risk another fight—'It is my birth-day; I had thought to have held it poor, but since my Lord is Antony again, I will be Cleopatra.' The transition, in the present compilation, from these flashes of genius which lay open the inmost soul, to the forced mechanical style and architectural dialogue of Dryden, is abrupt and painful.

The play was got up with every advantage of external pomp and decoration. Mr. Young, as Mark Antony, exhibited a just and impressive picture of the Roman hero, struggling between the dictates of his love and honour. Mrs. M'Gibbon was a respectable and interesting representative of Octavia. Mrs. Faucit's Cleopatra conveyed at least a reflex image of the voluptuous magnificence of the Queen of Egypt. In the ironical scenes with Antony, her manner sometimes bordered too much on the affected levity of a modern fine lady, and wanted the passion and dignity of the enamoured and haughty sovereign. In the part of Ventidius, we are sorry to say, that we think Mr. Terry was by no means successful. His manner had all the turbulent ferocity of a gloomy savage, none of the lofty firmness of the Roman Senator. The expression of the passion was every where too coarse and too physical; his muscles assumed a preternatural rigidity, and the mode in which he articulated every sentence was distinct, almost to dislocation. The house, however, seemed to be of a different opinion; for, in the several scenes with Mr. Young, he was loudly and tumultuously applauded.

ARTAXERXES

The Morning Chronicle.   *Oct.* 18, 1813.

Miss Stephens made her appearance again on Saturday at Covent-Garden, as Mandane, in Artaxerxes. She becomes more and more a favourite with the public. Her singing is delicious; but admired as it is, it is not yet admired as it ought to be. Oh, if she had been wafted to us from Italy!—A voice more sweet, varied, and flexible, was perhaps never heard on an English stage. In 'The Soldier tired,' her voice, though it might be said to cleave the very air, never once lost its sweetness and clearness. 'Let not rage thy bosom firing' was deservedly and rapturously encored. But if we were to express a preference, it would be to her singing the lines, 'What was my pride is now my shame,' &c. in which the notes seemed to fall from her lips like the liquid drops from the bending flower, and her voice fluttered and died away with the expiring conflict of passion in her bosom. We know, and have felt the divine power and impassioned tones of Catalani—the lightning of her voice and of her eye—but we doubt whether she would give the ballad style of the songs in Artaxerxes, simple but elegant, chaste but full of expression, with equal purity, taste, and tenderness.

Mr. Liston's acting in Love, Law, and Physic, was as excellent as it always is. It is hard to say, whether the soul of Mr. Liston has passed into Mr. Lubin Log, or that of Mr. Lubin Log into Mr. Liston:—but a most wonderful congeniality and mutual good understanding there is between them. A more perfect personation we never witnessed. The happy compound of meanness, ignorance, vulgarity, and conceit, was given with the broadest effect, and with the nicest discrimination of feeling. Moliere would not have wished for a richer representative of his *Gentilhomme Bourgeois*. We insist the more on this point, because of all imitations we like the imitation of nature best. The marked *cockneyism* of pronouncing the V for the W, was the only circumstance to which we could object, and this is an interpolation on the part since we first saw it, suggested (we suppose) by friends. It is a hackneyed and cheap way of producing a laugh, unworthy of the true comic genius of Liston.

THE BEGGAR'S OPERA

The Morning Chronicle.   *Oct.* 23, 1813.

The Beggar's Opera was acted at Covent-Garden last night, for the purpose of introducing Miss Stephens in the character of Polly. The play itself is among the most popular of our dramas, and one which the public are always glad to have some new excuse for seeing acted again. Its merits are peculiarly its own. It not only delights, but instructs us, without our knowing how, and though it is at first view equally offensive to good taste and common decency. The materials, indeed, of which it is composed, the scenes, characters, and incidents, are in general of the lowest and most disgusting kind; but the author, by the sentiments and reflections which he has put into the mouths of highwaymen, turnkeys, their wives and daughters, has converted the motley groupe into a set of fine gentlemen and ladies, satirists, and philosophers. What is still more extraordinary, he has effected this transformation without once violating probability, or ' o'erstepping the modesty of nature.' In fact, Gay has in this instance turned the tables on the critics; and by the assumed license of the mock-heroic style, has enabled himself to *do justice to nature,* that is, to give all the force, truth, and locality of real feeling to the thoughts and expressions, without being called to the bar of false taste, and affected delicacy. We might particularly refer to Polly's description of the death of her lover, and to the song, 'Woman is like the fair flower in its lustre,' the extreme beauty and feeling of which are only equalled by their characteristic propriety and *naivete.* Every line of this sterling Comedy sparkles with wit, and is fraught with the keenest and bitterest invective.

It has been said by a great moralist, 'There is some soul of goodness in things evil;' and The Beggar's Opera is a good-natured, but severe comment on this text. The poet has thrown all the gaiety and sunshine of the imagination, the intoxication of pleasure, and the vanity of despair, round the short-lived existence of his heroes, while Peachum and Lockitt are seen in the back ground, parcelling out their months and weeks between them. The general view of human life is of the most refined and abstracted kind. With the happiest art, the author has brought out the good qualities and interesting emotions almost inseparable from humanity in the lowest situations, and with the same penetrating glance, has detected the disguises which rank and circumstance lend to exalted vice. It may be said that the moral of the piece (which some respectable critics have been at a loss to discover), *is to shew the vulgarity of vice*; or that the sophisms with which the great and powerful palliate their violations of integrity and decorum, are, in fact, common to them with the vilest, most abandoned and contemptible of the species. What can be more galling than the arguments used by these would-be politicians, to prove that in hypocrisy, selfishness, and treachery, they are far behind some of their betters? The exclamation of Mrs. Peachum, when her daughter marries Macheath, 'Hussey, hussey, you will be as ill used and as much neglected as if you had married a Lord,' is worth all Miss Hannah More's laboured invectives on the laxity of the manners of high life!

The innocent and amiable Polly found a most interesting representative in Miss Stephens. Her acting throughout was simple, unaffected, graceful, and full of tenderness. Her tones in speaking, though low, and suited to the gentleness of the character, were distinct, and varied with great flexibility. She will lose by her performance of this part, none of the reputation she has gained in Mandane. The manner in which she gave the song in the first act, 'But he so teazed me,' &c. was sweetness itself: the notes undulated through the house, amidst murmurs of rapturous applause. She gave equal animation and feeling to the favourite air, 'Cease your funning.'

194

A VIEW OF THE ENGLISH STAGE

To this, however, as well as to some other of the songs, a more dramatic effect might perhaps be given. There is a severity of feeling, and a plaintive sadness, both in the words and music of the songs in this Opera, on which too much stress cannot be laid.

Oct. 30.

Miss Stephens made her appearance again last night at Covent-Garden, in Polly, with additional lustre. Her timidity was overcome, and her voice was exerted in all its force and sweetness. We find so much real taste, elegance, and feeling, in this very delightful singer, that we cannot help repeating our praise of her, though, perhaps, by so doing, we shall only irritate the sullen fury of certain formidable critics, at the appearance of a new favourite of the public. We are aware that there is a class of connoisseurs whose envy it might be prudent to disarm, by some compromise with their perverted taste; who are horror-struck at grace and beauty, and who can only find relief and repose in the consoling thoughts of deformity and defect; whose blood curdles into poison at deserved reputation, who shudder at every temptation *to admire*, as an unpardonable crime, and shrink from whatever gives delight to others, with more than monkish self-denial. These kind of critics are well described by Molière, as displaying, on all occasions, an invincible hatred for what the rest of the world admire, and an inconceivable partiality for those perfections which none but themselves can discover. The secret both of their affection and enmity is the same—their pride is mortified with whatever can give pleasure, and soothed with what excites only pity or indifference. They search out with scrupulous malice, the smallest defect or excess of every kind : it is only when it becomes painfully oppressive to every one else, that they are reconciled to it. A critic of this order is dissatisfied with the *embonpoint* of Miss Stephens; while his eye reposes with perfect self-complacency on the little round graces of Mrs. Liston's person !

RICHARD CŒUR DE LION

The Morning Chronicle.   *May* 27, 1814.

Richard Cœur de Lion was brought out last night at Covent-Garden, in which Miss Stephens made her appearance in the character of Matilda. She looked and spoke the part well, but the favourite pathetic air of 'Oh, Richard ! oh, my love,' was omitted, we suppose in consequence of indisposition.

The new farce, called 'Tricking's fair in Love,' followed, but

195

with little success; for after being heard out with great fairness, it was decidedly condemned at last, notwithstanding some inimitable acting by Liston as Count Hottentot. We never saw his face in a state of higher keeping. It was quite rich and unctuous.

A young lady (Miss Foote) afterwards made her first appearance in Amanthis. Her face and figure excited the liveliest interest as soon as she appeared; which her manner of executing the part did not diminish, but increased as she proceeded. Her voice possesses great clearness and sweetness, and her enunciation is exceedingly distinct and articulate, without any appearance of labour. Her features are soft and regular. She perfectly answered to the idea which we form of youth, beauty, grace, and artless innocence in the original character. She seemed to be, indeed, the Child of Nature, such as

'Youthful poets fancy when they love.'

Her reception throughout was flattering in the highest degree.

DIDONE ABANDONNATA

The Champion. *August* 14, 1814.

The Opera closed for the season on Saturday last. We attended on this farewell occasion, without any strong feelings of regret for the past, or of sanguine expectations for the future. The Opera, from its constant and powerful appeals to the senses, by imagery, by sound, and motion, is well calculated to amuse or stimulate the intellectual languor of those classes of society, on whose support it immediately depends. This is its highest aim, and its appropriate use. But, without the aid of luxurious pomp, what can there be to interest in this merely artificial vehicle of show, and dance, and song, which is purposely constructed so as to lull every effort of the understanding and feeling of the heart in the soft, soothing effeminacy of sensual enjoyment? The Opera Muse is not a beautiful virgin who can hope to charm by simplicity and sensibility; but a tawdry courtesan, who, when her paint and patches, her rings and jewels are stripped off, can excite only disgust and ridicule. This is the state to which she has been reduced by dissentions among her keepers for the last season.— Nothing could be more unpleasant than the impression produced on our minds by the exhibition of Saturday last. Tattered hanging fragments of curtains, disjointed machinery, silver pannels turned black, a few thin y scattered lamps badly lighted, were among the various circumstances which threw a damp over our spirits. Bank-

196

ruptcy every where stared us in the face. The general *coup d'œil* of the theatre had no affinity with gaiety or grandeur. The whole had the melancholy appearance, without any of the sublimity, of some relic of eastern magnificence.

The Opera was Didone Abandonnata, in which Madame Grassini performed the part of the unfortunate Queen, and Signor Tramezzani (appearing for the last time on the English stage), that of the faithless Æneas. During the greater part of the first act, there was hardly any body in the pit, and nobody in the boxes. The performance evidently partook of the apathy of the public. We do not know otherwise how to account for the undress manner in which Madame Grassini acted the part of Dido. She walked through it with the most perfect indifference, or as if she had been at a morning rehearsal before empty benches. The graceful dignity of the character never left her, but it was the habitual grace of a queen surrounded by her maids of honour, not the impassioned energy of a queen enamoured of the son of a goddess, and courted by Numidian kings. Even after the desertion of Æneas, and when the flames of her capital were surrounding her, the terror and agitation she displayed did not amount to the anxiety of a common assignation-scene; her trills and quavers very artfully mimicked the uncertain progress of the tremulous flames; and she at last left the stage, not as if rushing in an agony of despair to her fate, but with the hurry and alarm of a person who is afraid of being detected in a clandestine correspondence. In some passages, however, both of the recitative and the songs, the beauty of the movement or the force of the sentiment drew from her tones of mingled grace and energy, which 'might create a soul under the ribs of death.' This effect seemed to be purely involuntary, and not to proceed from any desire to gratify the audience, or to do justice to the part she had to sustain.

The same objections cannot be applied to the acting of Signor Tramezzani, in which there was no want of animation or effort. We are not among this gentleman's enthusiastic admirers; at the same time we would not wish to speak of him more contemptuously than he deserves. There is, we think, in general, considerable propriety in his conception, and great spirit in his execution; but it is almost universally carried into grimace and caricature. His heroes have the fierceness of bullies; his lovers are the fondest creatures;—his frowns and his smiles seem alike fated to kill. Signor Tramezzani is really too prodigal of his physical accomplishments: his acting is quite of the amatory kind. We see no reason why Æneas, because Dido takes him by the hand, should ogle the sweet heavens with such tender glances, nor why his lips should feed on the imagination of a kiss, as if he had tasted marmalade. Signor Tramezzani's amorous raptures put us in mind of the pious ardours of a female saint, who sighs out her soul at some divine man at a conventicle. We hate such fulsome fooleries.

After the Opera 'God save the King' was sung. The first verse was given by Madame Grassini, with that ease and simplicity which are natural to her. The second was torn to tatters by Signor Tramezzani with every preposterous accompaniment of imitative action. Into the homely couplet,

> 'Scatter his enemies,
> And make them fall,'

he introduced as much heroic action, as if Jove, in the first line, had had to shake a thousand thunderbolts from his hand, and in the next to transfix the giants to the earth. The bow with which this celebrated actor quitted the stage was endless and inimitable. The Genius of Scotland would have turned pale with envy at the sight! Of the other performers we shall say nothing. M. Vestris made an able-bodied representative of Zephyr in the ballet.

MISS O'NEILL'S JULIET

The Champion.   *Oct.* 16, 1814.

We occasionally see something on the stage that reminds us a little of Shakespear. Miss O'Neill's Juliet, if it does not correspond exactly with our idea of the character, does not degrade it. We never saw Garrick ; and Mrs. Siddons was the only person who ever embodied our idea of high tragedy. Her mind and person were both fitted for it. The effect of her acting was greater than could be conceived before-hand. It perfectly filled and overpowered the mind. The first time of seeing this great artist was an epoch in every one's life, and left impressions which could never be forgotten. She appeared to belong to a superior order of beings, to be surrounded with a personal awe, like some prophetess of old, or Roman matron, the mother of Coriolanus or the Gracchi. Her voice answered to her form, and her expression to both. Yet she was a pantomime actress. Her common recitation was faulty. It was in bursts of indignation, or grief, in sudden exclamations, in apostrophes and inarticulate sounds, that she raised the soul of passion to its height, or sunk it in despair.

We remember her manner in the Gamester, when Stukeley, (it

198

was then played by Palmer), declares his love to her. The look, first of incredulity and astonishment, then of anger, then passing suddenly into contempt, and ending in bitter scorn, and a convulsive burst of laughter, all given in a moment, and laying open every movement of the soul, produced an effect which we shall never forget. Her manner of rubbing her hands, in the night scene in Macbeth, and of dismissing the guests at the banquet, were among her finest things. We have, many years ago, wept outright during the whole time of her playing Isabella, and this we take to have been a higher employment of the critical faculties than doubling down the book in dog-ears to make out a regular list of critical common-places. To the tears formerly shed on such occasions, we may apply the words of a modern dashing orator, ' Sweet is the dew of their memory, and pleasant the balm of their recollection.'

We have, we believe, been betrayed into this digression, because Miss O'Neill, more than any late actress, reminded us in certain passages, and in a faint degree, of Mrs. Siddons. This young lady, who will probably become a favourite with the public, is rather tall; and though not *of the first order of fine forms*, her figure is of that respectable kind, which will not interfere with the characters she represents. Her deportment is not particularly graceful : there is a heaviness, and want of firmness about it. Her features are regular, and the upper part of her face finely expressive of terror or sorrow. It has that mixture of beauty and passion which we admire so much in some of the antique statues. The lower part of her face is not equally good. From a want of fulness or flexibility about the mouth, her laugh is not at any time pleasing, and where it is a laugh of terror, is distorted and painful. Her voice, without being musical, is distinct, powerful, and capable of every necessary exertion. Her action is impressive and simple. She looks the part she has to perform, and fills up the pauses in the words, by the varied expression of her countenance or gestures, without any thing artificial, pointed, or far-fetched.

In the silent expression of feeling, we have seldom witnessed any thing finer than her acting, where she is told of Romeo's death, her listening to the Friar's story of the poison, and her change of manner towards the Nurse, when she advises her to marry Paris. Her delivery of the speeches in the scenes where she laments Romeo's banishment, and anticipates her waking in the tomb, marked the fine play and undulation of natural sensibility, rising and falling with the gusts of passion, and at last worked up into an agony of despair, in which imagination approaches the brink of frenzy. Her actually screaming at the imaginary sight of Tybalt's ghost, appeared to us the only instance of extravagance or caricature. Not only is there a distinction to be kept up between physical and intellectual horror, (for the latter becomes more general, internal, and absorbed, in proportion as it becomes more intense), but the scream, in the present instance, startled the audience, as it preceded the speech which explained its meaning. Perhaps the emphasis given to the exclamation, '*And Romeo banished*,' and to the description of Tybalt, '*festering in his shroud*,' was too much in that epigrammatic, pointed style, which we think inconsistent with the severe and simple dignity of tragedy.

In the last scene, at the tomb with Romeo, which, however, is not from Shakespear, though it tells admirably on the stage, she did not produce the effect we expected. Miss O'Neill seemed least successful in the former part of the character, in the garden scene, &c. The expression of tenderness bordered on hoydening, and affectation. The character of Juliet is a pure effusion of nature. It is as serious, and as much in earnest, as it is frank and susceptible. It has all the exquisite voluptuousness of youthful innocence.—There is not the slightest appearance of coquetry in it, no sentimental languor, no meretricious assumption of fondness to take her lover by surprise. She ought not to laugh, when she says, 'I have forgot why I did call thee back,' as if conscious of the artifice, nor hang in a fondling posture over the balcony. Shakespear has given a fine idea of the composure of the character, where he first describes her at the window, leaning her cheek upon her arm. The whole expression of her love should be like the breath of flowers.

Mr. Jones's Mercutio was lively farce. Of Mr. Conway's Romeo, we cannot speak with patience. He bestrides the stage like a Colossus, throws his arms into the air like the sails of a windmill, and his motion is as unwieldy as that of a young elephant. His voice breaks in thunder on the ear like Gargantua's, but when he pleases to be soft, he is 'the very beadle to an amorous sigh.' Mr. Coates's absurdities are tame and trifling in comparison.—*Quere*, Why does he not marry?

MR. KEAN'S RICHARD.

The Champion.   *Oct.* 9, 1814.

We do not think Mr. Kean at all improved by his Irish expedition. As this is a point in which we feel a good deal of interest, both on Mr. Kean's account and our own, we shall state briefly our objections to some alterations in his mode of acting, which appear to us for the worse. His pauses are twice as long as they were, and the rapidity with which he hurries over other parts of the dialogue is twice as great as it was. In both these points, his style of acting always bordered on the very verge of extravagance ; and we suspect it has at present passed the line. There are, no doubt, passages in which the pauses can hardly be too long, or too marked ;—these must be, however, of rare occurrence, and it is in the finding out these exceptions to the general rule, and in daring to give them all their effect, that the genius of an actor discovers itself. But the most common-place drawling monotony is not more mechanical or more offensive, than the converting these exceptions into a general rule, and making every sentence an alternation of dead pauses and rapid transitions.[1] It is not in extremes that dramatic genius is shewn, any more than skill in music consists in passing continually from the highest to the lowest note. The quickness of familiar utterance with which Mr. Kean pronounced the anticipated doom of Stanley, 'chop off his head,' was quite ludicrous. Again, the manner in which, after his nephew said, 'I fear no uncles dead,' he suddenly turned round, and answered, 'And I hope none living, sir,' was, we thought, quite out of character. The motion was performed, and the sounds uttered, in the smallest possible time in which a puppet could be made to mimic or gabble the part. For this we see not the least reason ; and can only account for it, from a desire to give excessive effect by a display of the utmost dexterity of execution.

It is almost needless to observe, that executive power in acting, as in all other arts, is only valuable as it is made subservient to truth and nature. Even some want of mechanical skill is better than the perpetual affectation of shewing it. The absence of a quality is often less provoking than its abuse, because less voluntary.

The part which was least varied was the scene with Lady Anne. This is, indeed, nearly a perfect piece of acting. In leaning against the pillar at the commencement of the scene, Mr. Kean did not go through exactly the same regular evolution of graceful attitudes, and we regretted the omission. He frequently varied the execution of many of his most striking conceptions, and the attempt in general failed, as it naturally must do. We refer particularly to his manner of resting on the point of his sword before he retires to his tent, to

[1] An old gentleman, riding over Putney-bridge, turned round to his servant, and said, 'Do you like eggs, John ?' 'Yes, sir.' Here the conversation ended. The same gentleman riding over the same bridge that day year, again turned round, and said, 'How ?' 'Poached, sir,' was the answer.—This is the longest pause upon record, and has something of a dramatic effect, though it could not be transferred to the stage. Perhaps an actor might go so far, on the principle of indefinite pauses, as to begin a sentence in one act, and finish it in the next.

A VIEW OF THE ENGLISH STAGE

his treatment of the letter sent to Norfolk, and to his dying scene with Richmond.

Mr. Kean's *bye-play* is certainly one of his greatest excellences, and it might be said, that if Shakespear had written marginal directions to the players, in the manner of the German dramatists, he would often have directed them to do what Mr. Kean does. Such additions to the text are, however, to be considered as lucky hits, and it is not to be supposed that an actor is to provide an endless variety of these running accompaniments, which he is not in strictness bound to provide at all. In general, we think it a rule, that an actor ought to vary his part as little as possible, unless he is convinced that his former mode of playing it is erroneous. He should make up his mind as to the best mode of representing the part, and come as near to this standard as he can, in every successive exhibition. It is absurd to object to this mechanical uniformity as studied and artificial. All acting is studied or artificial. An actor is no more called upon to vary his gestures or articulation at every new rehearsal of the character, than an author can be required to furnish various readings to every separate copy of his work. To a new audience it is quite unnecessary; to those who have seen him before in the same part, it is worse than useless. They may at least be presumed to have come to a second representation, because they approved of the first, and will be sure to be disappointed in almost every alteration. The attempt is endless, and can only produce perplexity and indecision in the actor himself. He must either return perpetually in the same narrow round, or if he is determined to be always new, he may at last fancy that he ought to perform the part standing on his head instead of his feet. Besides, Mr. Kean's style of acting is not in the least of the unpremeditated, *improvisatori* kind: it is throughout elaborate and systematic, instead of being loose, off-hand, and accidental. He comes upon the stage as little unprepared as any actor we know. We object particularly to his varying the original action in the dying scene. He at first held out his hands in a way which can only be conceived by those who saw him—in motionless despair,—or as if there were some preternatural power in the mere manifestation of his will:—he now actually fights with his doubled fists, after his sword is taken from him, like some helpless infant.

We have been quite satisfied with the attempts we have seen to ape Mr. Kean in this part, without wishing to see him ape himself in it. There is no such thing as trick in matters of genius. All poetical licenses, however beautiful in themselves, by being parodied, instantly become ridiculous. It is because beauties of this kind have no clue

202

to them, and are reducible to no standard, that it is the peculiar province of genius to detect them ; by making them common, and reducing them to a rule, you make them perfectly mechanical, and perfectly absurd into the bargain.

To conclude our hypercritical remarks : we really think that Mr. Kean was, in a great many instances, either too familiar, too emphatical, or too energetic. In the latter scenes, perhaps his energy could not be too great ; but he gave the energy of action alone. He merely gesticulated, or at best vociferated the part. His articulation totally failed him. We doubt, if a single person in the house, not acquainted with the play, understood a single sentence that he uttered. It was 'inexplicable dumb show and noise.'—We wish to throw the fault of most of our objections on the managers. Their conduct has been marked by one uniform character, a paltry attention to their own immediate interest, a distrust of Mr. Kean's abilities to perform more than the character he had succeeded in, and a contempt for the wishes of the public. They have spun him tediously out in every character, and have forced him to display the variety of his talents in the same, instead of different characters. They kept him back in Shylock, till he nearly failed in Richard from a cold. Why not bring him out in Macbeth, which was at one time got up for him ? Why not bring him out at once in a variety of characters, as the Dublin managers have done ? It does not appear that either they or he suffered by it. It seems, by all we can find, that versatility is, perhaps, Mr. Kean's greatest excellence. Why, then, not give him his range ? Why tantalize the public ? Why extort from them their last shilling for the twentieth repetition of the same part, instead of letting them make their election for themselves, of what they like best ? It is really very pitiful.

Ill as we conceive the London managers have treated him, the London audiences have treated him well, and we wish Mr. Kean, for some years at least, to stick to them. They are his best friends ; and he may assuredly account us, who have made these sorry remarks upon him, not among his worst. After he has got through the season here well, we see no reason why he should make himself hoarse with performing Hamlet at twelve o'clock, and Richard at six, at Kidderminster. At his time of life, and with his prospects, the improvement of his fortune is not the principal thing. A training under Captain Barclay would do more towards strengthening his mind and body, his fame and fortune, than sharing bumper receipts with the Dublin managers, or carousing with the whole Irish bar. Or, if Mr. Kean does not approve of this rough regimen, he might devote the summer vacation to the Muses. To a man of genius, leisure is the first of benefits, as well as of luxuries; where, 'with her best nurse, Contemplation,' the mind

> 'Can plume her feathers, and let grow her wings,
> That in the various bustle of resort
> Were all too ruffled, and sometimes impaired.'

It was our first duty to point out Mr. Kean's excellences to the public, and we did so with no sparing hand; it is our second duty to him, to ourselves, and the public, to distinguish between his excellences and defects, and to prevent, if possible, his excellences from degenerating into defects.

MR. KEAN'S MACBETH

The Champion.   *Nov.* 13, 1814.

The genius of Shakespear was as much shewn in the subtlety and nice discrimination, as in the force and variety of his characters. The distinction is not preserved more completely in those which are the most opposite, than in those which in their general features and obvious appearance most nearly resemble each other. It has been observed, with very little exaggeration, that not one of his speeches could be put into the mouth of any other character than the one to which it is given, and that the transposition, if attempted, might be always detected from some circumstance in the passage itself. If *to invent according to nature,* be the true definition of genius, Shakespear had more of this quality than any other writer. He might be said to have been a joint-worker with Nature, and to have created an imaginary world of his own, which has all the appearance and the truth of reality. His mind, while it exerted an absolute controul over the stronger workings of the passions, was exquisitely alive to the slightest impulses and most evanescent shades of character and feeling. The broad distinctions and governing principles of human nature are presented not in the abstract, but in their immediate and endless application to different persons and things. The local details, the particular accidents have the fidelity of history, without losing any thing of their general effect.

It is the business of poetry, and indeed of all works of imagination, to exhibit the species through the individual. Otherwise, there can be no opportunity for the exercise of the imagination, without which the descriptions of the painter or the poet are lifeless, unsubstantial, and vapid. If some modern critics are right, with their sweeping

A VIEW OF THE ENGLISH STAGE

generalities and vague abstractions, Shakespear was quite wrong. In the French dramatists, only the class is represented, never the individual: their kings, their heroes, and their lovers are all the same, and they are all French—that is, they are nothing but the mouth-pieces of certain rhetorical common-place sentiments on the favourite topics of morality and the passions. The characters in Shakespear do not declaim like pedantic school-boys, but speak and act like men, placed in real circumstances, with ' real hearts of flesh and blood beating in their bosoms.' No two of his characters are the same, more than they would be so in nature. Those that are the most alike, are distinguished by positive differences, which accompany and modify the leading principle of the character through its most obscure ramifications, embodying the habits, gestures, and almost the looks of the individual. These touches of nature are often so many, and so minute, that the poet cannot be supposed to have been distinctly aware of the operation of the springs by which his imagination was set at work: yet every one of the results is brought out with a truth and clearness, as if his whole study had been directed to that peculiar trait of character, or subordinate train of feeling.

Thus Macbeth, and Richard the Third, King Henry the Sixth, and Richard the Second,—characters that, in their general description, and in common hands, would be merely repetitions of the same idea—are distinguished by traits as precise, though of course less violent, than those which separate Macbeth from Henry the Sixth, or Richard the Third from Richard the Second. Shakespear has, with wonderful accuracy, and without the smallest appearance of effort, varied the portraits of imbecility and effeminacy in the two deposed monarchs. With still more powerful and masterly strokes, he has marked the different effects of ambition and cruelty, operating on different dispositions in different circumstances, in his Macbeth and Richard the Third. Both are tyrants and usurpers, both violent and ambitious, both cruel and treacherous. But, Richard is cruel from nature and constitution. Macbeth becomes so from accidental circumstances. He is urged to the commission of guilt by golden opportunity, by the instigations of his wife, and by prophetic warnings. 'Fate and metaphysical aid,' conspire against his virtue and loyalty. Richard needs no prompter, but wades through a series of crimes to the height of his ambition, from ungovernable passions and the restless love of mischief. He is never gay but in the prospect, or in the success of his villanies : Macbeth is full of horror at the thoughts of the murder of Duncan, and of remorse after its perpetration. Richard has no mixture of humanity in his composition, no tie which binds him to the kind; he owns no fellowship with others, but is himself alone.   Macbeth is not without feelings of sympathy, is accessible to pity, is even the dupe of his uxoriousness, and ranks the loss of friends and of his good name among the causes that have made him sick of life.   He becomes more callous indeed as he plunges deeper in guilt, 'direness is thus made familiar to his slaughterous thoughts,' and he anticipates his wife in the boldness and bloodiness of his enterprises, who, for want of the same stimulus of action, is 'troubled with thick-coming fancies,' walks in her sleep, goes mad, and dies.   Macbeth endeavours to escape from reflection on his crimes, by repelling their consequences, and banishes remorse for the past, by meditating future mischief.   This is not the principle of Richard's cruelty, which resembles the cold malignity of a fiend, rather than the frailty of human nature.   Macbeth is goaded on by necessity; to Richard, blood is a pastime.—

There are other essential differences.   Richard is a man of the world, a vulgar, plotting, hardened villain, wholly regardless of every thing but his own ends, and the means to accomplish them.   Not so Macbeth.   The superstitions of the time, the rude state of society, the local scenery and customs, all give a wildness and imaginary grandeur to his character.   From the strangeness of the events which surround him, he is full of amazement and fear, and stands in doubt between the world of reality and the world of fancy.   He sees sights not shewn to mortal eye, and hears unearthly music.   All is tumult and disorder within and without his mind.   In thought, he is absent and perplexed, desperate in act : his purposes recoil upon himself, are broken, and disjointed : he is the double thrall of his passions and his evil destiny.   He treads upon the brink of fate, and grows dizzy with his situation.   Richard is not a character of imagination, but of pure will or passion.   There is no conflict of opposite feelings in his breast.   The apparitions which he sees are in his sleep, nor does he live like Macbeth, in a waking dream.

Such, at least, is our conception of the two characters, as drawn by Shakespear.   Mr. Kean does not distinguish them so completely as he might.   His Richard comes nearer to the original than his Macbeth.   He was deficient in the poetry of the character.   He did not look like a man who had encountered the Weird Sisters.   There should be nothing tight or compact in Macbeth, no tenseness of fibre, nor pointed decision of manner.   He has, indeed, energy and manliness of soul, but 'subject to all the skyey influences.'   He is sure of nothing.   All is left at issue.   He runs a-tilt with fortune, and is baffled with preternatural riddles.   The agitation of his mind resembles the rolling of the sea in a storm; or, he is like a lion in the toils—fierce, impetuous, and ungovernable. In the fifth act in particular, which is in itself as busy and turbulent as possible, there was not that giddy whirl of the imagination—the character did not burnish out on all sides with those flashes of genius, of which Mr. Kean had given so fine an earnest in the conclusion of his Richard. The scene stood still—the parts might be perfect in themselves, but they were not joined together; they wanted vitality. The pauses in the speeches were too long—the actor seemed to be studying the part, rather than performing it—striving to make every word more emphatic than the last, and 'lost too poorly in himself,' instead of being carried away with the grandeur of his subject. The text was not given accurately. Macbeth is represented in the play, arming before the castle, which adds to the interest of the scene.

In the delivery of the beautiful soliloquy, 'My way of life is fallen into the sear, the yellow leaf,' Mr. Kean was unsuccessful. That fine thoughtful melancholy did not seem to come over his mind, which characterises Mr. Kemble's recitation of these lines. The very tone of Mr. Kemble's voice has something retrospective in it—it is an echo of the past. Mr. Kean in his dress was occasionally too much docked and curtailed for the gravity of the character. His movements were too agile and mercurial, and he fought more like a modern fencing-master than a Scottish chieftain of the eleventh century. He fell at last finely, with his face downwards, as if to cover the shame of his defeat. We recollect that Mr. Cooke discovered the great actor both in the death-scene in Macbeth, and in that of Richard. He fell like the ruin of a state, like a king with his regalia about him.

The two finest things that Mr. Kean has ever done, are his recitation of the passage in Othello, 'Then, oh, farewell the tranquil mind,' and the scene in Macbeth after the murder. The former was the highest and most perfect effort of his art. To enquire whether his manner in the latter scene was that of a king who commits a murder, or of a man who commits a murder to become a king, would be 'to consider too curiously.' But, as a lesson of common humanity, it was heart-rending. The hesitation, the bewildered look, the coming to himself when he sees his hands bloody; the manner in which his voice clung to his throat, and choaked his utterance; his agony and tears, the force of nature overcome by passion—beggared description. It was a scene, which no one who saw it can ever efface from his recollection.

A VIEW OF THE ENGLISH STAGE

MR. KEAN'S ROMEO

The Champion. *January* 8, 1815.

Mr. Kean appeared at Drury-Lane in the character of Romeo, for the first time on Monday last. The house was crowded at an early hour, and neither those who went to admire, nor those who went to find fault, could go away disappointed. He discovered no new and unlooked-for excellences in the part, but displayed the same extraordinary energies which he never fails to do on every occasion. There is, indeed, a set of ingenious persons, who having perceived on Mr. Kean's first appearance, that he was a little man with an inharmonious voice, and no very great dignity or elegance of manner, go regularly to the theatre to confirm themselves in this singular piece of sagacity ; and finding that the object of their contempt and wonder has not, since they last saw him, ' added a cubit to his stature,'—that his tones have not become ' as musical as is Apollo's lute,' and that there is still an habitual want of grace about him, are determined, till such a metamorphosis is effected, not to allow a particle of genius to the actor, or of taste or common sense to those who are not stupidly blind to every thing but his defects. That an actor with very moderate abilities, having the advantages of voice, person and graceful-ness of manner on his side, should acquire a very high reputation, is what we can understand, and have seen some instances of ; but that an actor with almost every physical disadvantage against him, should, without very extraordinary powers and capacities indeed, be able to excite the most enthusiastic and general admiration, would, we conceive, be a phenomenon in the history of public imposture, totally without example. In fact, the generality of critics who undertake to give the tone to public opinion, have neither the courage nor discernment to decide on the merits of a truly excellent and original actor, and are equally without the candour to acknowledge their error, after they find themselves in the wrong.

In going to see Mr. Kean in any new character, we do not go in the expectation of seeing either a perfect actor or perfect acting ; because this is what we have not yet seen, either in him or in any one else. But we go to see (what he never disappoints us in) great spirit, ingenuity, and originality given to the text in general, and an energy and depth of passion given to certain scei, s and passages, which we should in vain look for from any other actor on the stage. In every character that he has played, in Shylock, in Richard, in Hamlet, in Othello, in Iago, in Luke, and in Macbeth, there has been either a dazzling repetition of master-strokes of art and nature, or if at any time (from a want of physical adaptation, or sometimes

208

of just conception of the character) the interest has flagged for a considerable interval, the deficiency has always been redeemed by some collected and overpowering display of energy or pathos, which electrified at the moment, and left a lasting impression on the mind afterwards. Such, for instance, were the murder-scene in Macbeth, the third act of his Othello, the interview with Ophelia in Hamlet, and, lastly, the scene with Friar Lawrence, and the death-scene in Romeo.

Of the characters that Mr. Kean has played, Hamlet and Romeo are the most like one another, at least in adventitious circumstances; those to which Mr. Kean's powers are least adapted, and in which he has failed most in general truth of conception and continued interest. There is in both characters the same strong tincture of youthful enthusiasm, of tender melancholy, of romantic thought and sentiment; but we confess we did not see these qualities in Mr. Kean's performance of either. His Romeo had nothing of the lover in it. We never saw any thing less ardent or less voluptuous. In the Balcony-scene in particular, he was cold, tame, and unimpressive. It was said of Garrick and Barry in this scene, that the one acted it as if he would jump up to the lady, and the other as if he would make the lady jump down to him. Mr. Kean produced neither of these effects. He stood like a statue of lead. Even Mr. Conway might feel taller on the occasion, and Mr. Coates wonder at the taste of the public. The only time in this scene when he attempted to give any thing like an effect, was when he smiled on over-hearing Juliet's confession of her passion. But the smile was less like that of a fortunate lover who unexpectedly hears his happiness confirmed, than of a discarded lover, who hears of the disappointment of a rival.—The whole of this part not only wanted 'the silver sound of lovers' tongues by night' to recommend it, but warmth, tenderness,—every thing which it should have possessed. Mr. Kean was like a man waiting to receive a message from his mistress through her confidante, not like one who was pouring out his rapturous vows to the idol of his soul. There was neither glowing animation, nor melting softness in his manner; his cheek was not flushed, no sigh breathed involuntary from his overcharged bosom : all was forced and lifeless. His acting sometimes reminded us of the scene with Lady Anne, and we cannot say a worse thing of it, considering the difference of the two characters. Mr. Kean's imagination appears not to have the principles of joy, or hope, or love in it. He seems chiefly sensible to pain, or to the passions that spring from it, and to the terrible energies of mind or body, which are necessary to grapple with, or to avert it. Even over the world of passion he holds but a divided sway : he either does not feel, or

one of the most extraordinary exhibitions on the stage. There is no one within our remembrance, who has so completely foiled the critics as this celebrated actor : one sagacious person imagines that he must perform a part in a certain manner ; another virtuoso chalks out a different path for him ; and when the time comes, he does the whole off in a way, that neither of them had the least conception of, and which both of them are therefore very ready to condemn as entirely wrong. It was ever the trick of genius to be thus. We confess that Mr. Kean has thrown us out more than once. For instance, we are very much inclined to persist in the objection we before made, that his Richard is not gay enough, and that his Iago is not grave enough. This he may perhaps conceive to be the mere caprice of captious criticism ; but we will try to give our reasons, and shall leave them to Mr. Kean's better judgment.

It is to be remembered, then, that Richard was a princely villain, borne along in a sort of triumphal car of royal state, buoyed up with the hopes and privileges of his birth, reposing even on the sanctity of religion, trampling on his devoted victims without remorse, and who looked out and laughed from the high watch-tower of his confidence and his expectations, on the desolation and misery he had caused around him. He held on his way, unquestioned, 'hedged in with the divinity of kings,' amenable to no tribunal, and abusing his power *in contempt of mankind.* But as for Iago, we conceive differently of him. He had not the same natural advantages. He was a mere adventurer in mischief, a pains-taking, plodding knave, without patent or pedigree, who was obliged to work his uphill way by wit, not by will, and to be the founder of his own fortune. He was, if we may be allowed a vulgar allusion, a true prototype of modern Jacobinism, who thought that talents ought to decide the place ; a man of 'morbid sensibility' (in the fashionable phrase), full of distrust, of hatred, of anxious and corroding thoughts, and who, though he might assume a temporary superiority over others by superior adroitness, and pride himself in his skill, could not be supposed to assume it as a matter of course, as if he had been entitled to it from his birth.

We do not here mean to enter into the characters of the two men, but something must be allowed to the difference of their situations. There might be the same indifference in both as to the end in view, but there could not well be the same security as to the success of the means. Iago had to pass through a different ordeal : he had no appliances and means to boot ; no royal road to the completion of his tragedy. His pretensions were not backed by authority ; they were not baptized at the font ; they were not holy-water proof. He had the whole to answer for in his own person, and could not shift the

A VIEW OF THE ENGLISH STAGE

responsibility to the heads of others. Mr. Kean's Richard was therefore, we think, deficient in something of that regal jollity and reeling triumph of success which the part would bear; but this we can easily account for, because it is the traditional common-place idea of the character, that he is to 'play the dog—to bite and snarl.'— The extreme unconcern and laboured levity of his Iago, on the contrary, is a refinement and original device of the actor's own mind, and deserves a distinct consideration. The character of Iago, in fact, belongs to a class of characters common to Shakespear, and at the same time peculiar to him, namely, that of great intellectual activity, accompanied with a total want of moral principle, and therefore displaying itself at the constant expence of others, making use of reason as a pander to will—employing its ingenuity and its resources to palliate its own crimes, and aggravate the faults of others, and seeking to confound the practical distinctions of right and wrong, by referring them to some overstrained standard of speculative refinement.

Some persons more nice than wise, have thought the whole of the character of Iago unnatural. Shakespear, who was quite as good a philosopher as he was a poet, thought otherwise. He knew that the love of power, which is another name for the love of mischief, was natural to man. He would know this as well or better than if it had been demonstrated to him by a logical diagram, merely from seeing children paddle in the dirt, or kill flies for sport. We might ask those who think the character of Iago not natural, why they go to see it performed—but from the interest it excites, the sharper edge which it sets on their curiosity and imagination? Why do we go to see tragedies in general? Why do we always read the accounts in the newspapers, of dreadful fires and shocking murders, but for the same reason? Why do so many persons frequent executions and trials; or why do the lower classes almost universally take delight in barbarous sports and cruelty to animals, but because there is a natural tendency in the mind to strong excitement, a desire to have its faculties roused and stimulated to the utmost? Whenever this principle is not under the restraint of humanity or the sense of moral obligation, there are no excesses to which it will not of itself give rise, without the assistance of any other motive, either of passion or self-interest. Iago is only an extreme instance of the kind; that is, of diseased intellectual activity, with an almost perfect indifference to moral good or evil, or rather with a preference of the latter, because it falls more in with his favourite propensity, gives greater zest to his thoughts and scope to his actions. Be it observed, too, (for the sake of those who are for squaring all human actions by the maxims of Rochefoucault), that he is quite or nearly as indifferent to his own fate as to that of others; that he runs all risks for a trifling and doubtful advantage; and is himself the dupe and victim of his ruling passion—an incorrigible love of mischief—an insatiable craving after action of the most difficult and dangerous kind. Our Ancient is a philosopher, who fancies that a lie that kills, has more point in it than an alliteration or an antithesis; who thinks a fatal experiment on the peace of a family a better thing than watching the palpitations in the heart of a flea in an air-pump; who plots the ruin of his friends as an exercise for his understanding, and stabs men in the dark to prevent *ennui*. Now this, though it be sport, yet it is dreadful sport. There is no room for trifling and indifference, nor scarcely for the appearance of it; the very object of his whole plot is to keep his faculties stretched on the rack, in a state of watch and ward, in a sort of breathless suspense, without a moment's interval of repose. He has a desperate stake to play for, like a man who fences with poisoned weapons, and has business enough on his hands to call for the whole stock of his sober circumspection, his dark duplicity, and insidious gravity. He resembles a man who sits down to play at chess, for the sake of the difficulty and complication of the game, and who immediately becomes absorbed in it. His amusements, if they are amusements, are severe and saturnine—even his wit blisters. His gaiety arises from the success of his treachery; his ease from the sense of the torture he has inflicted on others. Even if other circumstances permitted it, the part he has to play with Othello requires that he should assume the most serious concern, and something of the plausibility of a confessor. 'His cue is villanous melancholy, with a sigh like Tom o' Bedlam.' He is repeatedly called 'honest Iago,' which looks as if there were something suspicious in his appearance, which admitted a different construction. The tone which he adopts in the scenes with Roderigo, Desdemona, and Cassio, is only a relaxation from the more arduous business of the play. Yet there is in all his conversation, an inveterate misanthropy, a licentious keenness of perception, which is always sagacious of evil, and snuffs up the tainted scent of its quarry with rancorous delight. An exuberance of spleen is the essence of the character. The view which we have here taken of the subject, (if at all correct) will not therefore justify the extreme alteration which Mr. Kean has introduced into the part.

Actors in general have been struck only with the wickedness of the character, and have exhibited an assassin going to the place of execution. Mr. Kean has abstracted the wit of the character, and makes Iago appear throughout an excellent good fellow, and lively

A VIEW OF THE ENGLISH STAGE

bottle-companion. But though we do not wish him to be represented as a monster, or a fiend, we see no reason why he should instantly be converted into a pattern of comic gaiety and good humour. The light which illumines the character, should rather resemble the flashes of lightning in the mirky sky, which make the darkness more terrible. Mr. Kean's Iago is, we suspect, too much in the sun. His manner of acting the part would have suited better with the character of Edmund in King Lear, who, though in other respects much the same, has a spice of gallantry in his constitution, and has the favour and countenance of the ladies, which always gives a man the smug appearance of a bridegroom!—We shall in another article, illustrate these remarks by a reference to some passages in the text itself.

MR KEAN'S IAGO.
(concluded)
The Examiner.   *Aug.* 7, 1814.

The general groundwork of the character of Iago, as it appears to us, is not absolute malignity, but a want of moral principle, or an indifference to the real consequences of the actions, which the meddling perversity of his disposition and love of immediate excitement lead him to commit. He is an amateur of tragedy in real life; and instead of exercising his ingenuity on imaginary characters, or forgotten incidents, he takes the bolder and more desperate course of getting up his plot at home, casts the principal parts among his nearest friends and connections, and rehearses it in downright earnest, with steady nerves and unabated resolution. The character is a complete abstraction of the intellectual from the moral being; or, in other words, consists in an absorption of every common feeling in the virulence of his understanding, the deliberate wilfulness of his purposes, and in his restless, untamable love of mischievous contrivance. We proceed to quote some particular passages in support of this opinion.

In the general dialogue and reflections, which are an accompaniment to the progress of the catastrophe, there is a constant overflowing of gall and bitterness. The acuteness of his malice fastens upon every thing alike, and pursues the most distant analogies of evil with a provoking sagacity. He by no means forms an exception to his own rule :—

> 'Who has that breast so pure,
> But some uncleanly apprehensions
> Keep leets and law-days, and in sessions sit
> With meditations lawful?'

215

His mirth is not natural and cheerful, but forced and extravagant, partaking of the intense activity of mind and cynical contempt of others in which it originates. Iago is not, like Candide, a believer in optimism, but seems to have a thorough hatred or distrust of every thing of the kind, and to dwell with gloating satisfaction on whatever can interrupt the enjoyment of others, and gratify his moody irritability. One of his most characteristic speeches is that immediately after the marriage of Othello :—

> ' *Roderigo*. What a full fortune does the thick-lips owe,
> If he can carry her thus ?
>   *Iago*. Call up her father :
> Rouse him [*Othello*], make after him, poison his delight,
> Proclaim him in the streets, incense her kinsmen,
> And tho' he in a fertile climate dwell,
> Plague him with flies : tho' that his joy be joy,
> Yet throw such changes of vexation on't,
> As it may lose some colour.'

The pertinacious logical following up of his favourite principle in this passage, is admirable. In the next, his imagination runs riot in the mischief he is plotting, and breaks out into the wildness and impetuosity of real enthusiasm :—

> ' *Roderigo*. Here is her father's house, I 'll call aloud.
>   *Iago*. Do, with like timorous accent and dire yell,
> As when, by night and negligence, the fire
> Is spied in populous cities.'

There is nothing here of the trim levity and epigrammatic conciseness of Mr. Kean's manner of acting the part ; which is no less paradoxical than Mrs. Greville's celebrated Ode to Indifference. Iago was a man of genius, and not a *petit maitre*. One of his most frequent topics, on which he is rich indeed, and in descanting on which, his spleen serves him for a muse, is the disproportionate match between Desdemona and the Moor. This is brought forward in the first scene, and is never lost sight of afterwards.

> ' *Brabantio*. What is the reason of this terrible summons ?
>   *Iago*. Sir, you 're robb'd ; for shame, put on your gown ;
> Your heart is burst, you have lost half your soul :
> ————————————————Arise, arise,
> Awake the snorting citizens with the bell,
> Or else the devil will make a grandsire of you.
> Arise, I say.'—[*And so on to the end of the passage.*]

Now, all this goes on springs well oiled : Mr. Kean's mode of
216

giving the passage had the tightness of a drumhead, and was muffled (perhaps purposely so) into the bargain.

This is a clue to the character of the lady which Iago is not at all ready to part with. He recurs to it again in the second act, when in answer to his insinuations against Desdemona, Roderigo says,—

> 'I cannot believe that in her—she's full of most bless'd conditions.
>
> *Iago.* Bless'd fig's end. The wine she drinks is made of grapes. If she had been bless'd, she would never have loved the Moor.'

And again, with still more effect and spirit afterwards, when he takes advantage of this very suggestion arising in Othello's own breast :—

> '*Othello.* And yet how nature erring from itself—
>
> *Iago.* Aye, there's the point ;—as, to be bold with you,
> Not to affect many proposed matches,
> Of her own clime, complexion, and degree,
> Whereto we see in all things, Nature tends ;
> Foh ! one may smell in such, a will most rank,
> Foul disproportions, thoughts unnatural.'

This is probing to the quick. 'Our Ancient' here turns the character of poor Desdemona, as it were, inside out. It is certain that nothing but the genius of Shakespear could have preserved the entire interest and delicacy of the part, and have even drawn an additional elegance and dignity from the peculiar circumstances in which she is placed. The character indeed has always had the greatest charm for minds of the finest sensibility.

For our own part, we are a little of Iago's council in this matter ; and all circumstances considered, and platonics out of the question, if we were to cast the complexion of Desdemona physiognomically, we should say that she had a very fair skin, and very light auburn hair, inclining to yellow ! We at the same time give her infinite credit for purity and delicacy of sentiment ; but it so happens that purity and grossness sometimes

> 'nearly are allied,
> And thin partitions do their bounds divide.'

Yet the reverse does not hold ; so uncertain and undefinable a thing is moral character ! It is no wonder that Iago had some contempt for it, 'who knew all quantities of human dealings, with a learned spirit.' There is considerable gaiety and ease in his dialogue with Emilia and Desdemona on their landing. It is then holiday time with him ; but yet the general satire will be acknowledged (at least by one half of our readers) to be biting enough, and his idea of his own character is finely expressed in what he says to Desdemona, when she asks him how he would praise her—

> ' Oh gentle lady, do not put me to it,
> For I am nothing, if not critical.'

Mr. Kean's execution of this part we thought admirable; but he was quite as much at his ease in every other part of the play, which was done (we know not why) in a single key.

The habitual licentiousness of Iago's conversation is not to be traced to the pleasure he takes in gross or lascivious images, but to a desire of finding out the worst side of every thing, and of proving himself an over-match for appearances. He has none of ' the milk of human kindness ' in his composition. His imagination refuses every thing that has not a strong infusion of the most unpalatable ingredients, and his moral constitution digests only poisons. Virtue, or goodness, or whatever has the least ' relish of salvation in it,' is, to his depraved appetite, sickly and insipid; and he even resents the good opinion entertained of his own integrity, as if it were an affront cast on the masculine sense and spirit of his character. Thus, at the meeting between Othello and Desdemona, he exclaims—' Oh, you are well tuned now: but I'll set down the pegs that make this music, *as honest as I am*'—deriving an indirect triumph over the want of penetration in others from the consciousness of his own villainy.

In most of the passages which we have hitherto quoted, Iago gives a loose to his passion for theoretical evil: in the scenes with Othello, where he has to put his theory in practice, with great risk to himself, and with dreadful consequences to others, he is proportionably guarded, insidious, dark and deliberate. In the very first scene with Othello, he takes a very different tone;—that tone of hypocritical virtue and affected delicacy, which always betrays the want of the reality.

> ' *Enter Othello, Iago, and Attendants.*
>
> *Iago.* Though in the trade of war I have slain men,
> Yet do I hold it very stuff o' th' conscience,
> To do no contriv'd murder. I lack iniquity
> Sometimes to do me service. Nine or ten times
> I thought to have jerk'd him here under the ribs.
>   *Othello.* 'Tis better as it is.
>   *Iago.* Nay, but he prated,
> And spoke such scurvy and provoking terms
> Against your honour, that with the little godliness I have
> I did full hard forbear him.'

A VIEW OF THE ENGLISH STAGE

But the part in which, according to our conception, Mr. Kean failed most, was in the third act with Othello, where ' comes the tug of war.' The following passage is, we think, decisive to our purpose :—

> ' *Iago.* My noble lord.
> *Othello.* What dost thou say, Iago ?
> *Iago.* Did Michael Cassio,
> When you woo'd my lady, know of your love ?
> *Othello.* He did from first to last.
> Why dost thou ask ?
> *Iago.* But for a satisfaction of my thought,
> No further harm.
> *Othello.* Why of thy thought, Iago ?
> *Iago.* I did not think he had been acquainted with it.
> *Othello.* O yes, and went between us very oft—
> *Iago.* Indeed !
> *Othello.* Indeed ! Ay, indeed. Discern'st thou aught of that ?
> Is he not honest ?
> *Iago.* Honest, my Lord ?
> *Othello.* Honest ? Ay, honest.
> *Iago.* My Lord, for aught I know.
> *Othello.* What dost thou think ?
> *Iago.* Think, my Lord !
> *Othello.* Think, my Lord ! Alas, thou echo'st me,
> As if there were some monster in thy thought
> Too hideous to be shewn. Thou dost mean something :
> I heard thee say even now, thou lik'dst not that—
> When Cassio left my wife. What did'st not like ?
> And when I told thee, he was of my counsel,
> Of my whole course of wooing ; thou criedst, indeed !
> And didst contract and purse thy brow together,
> As if thou then hadst shut up in thy brain
> Some horrible conceit : If thou dost love me,
> Shew me thy thought.
> *Iago.* My Lord, you know I love you.
> *Othello.* I think thou dost :
> And for I know thou 'rt full of love and honesty,
> And weigh'st thy words before thou giv'st them breath,
> Therefore these stops of thine fright me the more :
> For such things in a false disloyal knave
> Are tricks of custom : but in a man that 's just,
> They 're cold dilations working from the heart,
> Which passion cannot rule.'

Now, if there is any thing of superficial gaiety or heedlessness in this, ' it is not written in the bond : '—the breaks and stops, the pursing and knitting of the brow together, the deep internal working of hypocrisy under the mask of love and honesty, escaped us on the stage.—The same observation applies to what he says afterwards of himself :—

> ' Though I perchance am vicious in my guess,
> As I confess it is my nature's plague
> To spy into abuses, and oft my jealousy
> Shapes faults that are not.'

The candour of this confession would hardly be extorted from him, if it did not correspond with the moody dissatisfaction, and suspicious, creeping, cat-like watchfulness of his general appearance. The anxious suspense, the deep artifice, the collected earnestness, and, if we may so say, the *passion* of hypocrisy, are decidedly marked in every line of the whole scene, and are worked up to a sort of paroxysm afterwards, in that inimitably characteristic apostrophe :—

> ' O Grace ! O Heaven forgive me !
> Are you a man ?   Have you a soul or sense ?
> God be wi' you : take mine office.   O wretched fool
> That lov'st to make thine honesty a vice !
> Oh monstrous world ! take note, take note, O world !
> To be direct and honest, is not safe.
> I thank you for this profit, and from hence
> I 'll love no friend, since love breeds such offence.'

This burst of hypocritical indignation might well have called forth all Mr. Kean's powers, but it did not. We might multiply passages of the same kind, if we had time.

The philosophy of the character is strikingly unfolded in the part where Iago gets the handkerchief :—

> ' This may do something.
> The Moor already changes with my poisons,
> Which at the first are scarce found to distaste,
> But with a little act upon the blood,
> Burn like the mines of sulphur.'

We here find him watching the success of his experiment, with the sanguine anticipation of an alchemist at the moment of projection.

> ' I did say so :
> Look where he comes '—[*Enter Othello*]—' Not poppy
> nor mandragora,
> Nor all the drowsy syrups of the world,
> Shall ever medicine thee to that sweet sleep
> Which thou ow'dst yesterday.'

Again he says :—

> ' Work on :
> My medicine works; thus credulous fools are caught,
> And many worthy and chaste dames even thus
> All guiltless meet reproach.'

So that after all, he would persuade us that his object is only to give an instructive example of the injustice that prevails in the world.

If he is bad enough when he has business on his hands, he is still worse when his purposes are suspended, and he has only to reflect on the misery he has occasioned. His indifference when Othello falls in a trance, is perfectly diabolical, but perfectly in character :—

> ' *Iago.* How is it, General ? Have you not hurt your head ?
> *Othello.* Dost thou mock me ?
> *Iago.* I mock you not, by heaven,' &c.

The callous levity which Mr. Kean seems to consider as belonging to the character in general, is proper here, because Iago has no feelings connected with humanity; but he has other feelings and other passions of his own, which are not to be trifled with.

We do not, however, approve of Mr. Kean's pointing to the dead bodies after the catastrophe. It is not in the character of the part, which consists in the love of mischief, not as an end, but as a means, and when that end is attained, though he may feel no remorse, he would feel no triumph. Besides, it is not the text of Shakespear. Iago does not point to the bed, but Ludovico bids him look at it :—' Look on the tragic loading of this bed,' &c.

We have already noticed that Edmund the Bastard is like an episode of the same character, placed in less difficult circumstances. Zanga is a vulgar caricature of it.

MR. KEAN'S RICHARD II.

The Examiner. *March* 19, 1815.

We are not in the number of those who are anxious in recommending the getting-up of Shakespear's plays in general, as a duty which our stage-managers owe equally to the author, and the reader of those wonderful compositions. The representing the very finest of them on the stage, even by the best actors, is, we apprehend, an abuse of the genius of the poet, and even in those of a second-rate class, the quantity of sentiment and imagery greatly outweighs the immediate impression of the situation and story. Not only are the more refined poetical beauties and minuter strokes of character lost to the audience, but the most striking and impressive passages, those which having once read we can never forget, fail comparatively of their effect, except in one or two rare instances indeed. It is only the *pantomime* part of tragedy, the exhibition of immediate and physical distress, that which gives the greatest opportunity for 'inexpressible dumb-show and noise,' which is sure to tell, and tell completely on the stage. All the rest, all that appeals to our profounder feelings, to reflection and imagination, all that affects us most deeply in our closets, and in fact constitutes the glory of Shakespear, is little else than an interruption and a drag on the business of the stage. *Segnius per aures demissa,* &c. Those parts of the play on which the reader dwells the longest, and with the highest relish in the perusal, are hurried through in the performance, while the most trifling and exceptionable are obtruded on his notice, and occupy as much time as the most important. We do not mean to say that there is less knowledge or display of mere stage-effect in Shakespear than in other writers, but that there is a much greater knowledge and display of other things, which divide the attention with it, and to which it is not possible to give an equal force in the representation. Hence it is, that the reader of the plays of Shakespear is almost always disappointed in seeing them acted ; and, for our own parts, we should never go to see them acted, if we could help it.

Shakespear has embodied his characters so very distinctly, that he stands in no need of the actor's assistance to make them more distinct ; and the representation of the character on the stage almost uniformly interferes with our conception of the character itself. The only exceptions we can recollect to this observation, are Mrs. Siddons and Mr. Kean—the former of whom in one or two characters, and the latter, not certainly in any one character, but in very many passages, have raised our imagination of the part they acted. It may be asked then, why all great actors chuse characters from Shakespear to come out in ; and again, why these become their favourite parts ? First, it is not that they are able to exhibit their author, but that he enables them to shew themselves off. The only way in which Shakespear appears to greater advantage on the stage than common writers is, that he stimulates the faculties of the actor more. If he is a sensible man, he perceives how much he has to do, the inequalities he has to contend with, and he exerts himself accordingly ; he puts himself at full speed, and lays all his resources under contribution ; he attempts more, and makes a greater number of brilliant failures ; he plays off all the tricks of his art to mimic the poet ; he does all he can, and bad is often the best. We have before said that there are some few exceptions. If the genius of Shakespear does not shine out undiminished in the actor, we perceive certain effects and refractions of it in him. If the oracle does not speak quite intelligibly, yet we perceive that the priest at the altar is inspired with the god, or possessed with a demon. To speak our minds at once, we believe that in acting Shakespear there is a greater number of good things marred than in acting any other author. In fact, in going to see the plays of Shakespear, it would be ridiculous to suppose, that any one ever went to see Hamlet or Othello represented by Kean or Kemble; we go to see Kean or Kemble in Hamlet or Othello. On the contrary, Miss O'Neill and Mrs. Beverley are, we take it, one and the same person. As to the second point, viz. that Shakespear's characters are decidedly favourites on the stage in the same proportion as they are in the closet, we deny it altogether. They either do not tell so much, or very little more than many others. Mrs. Siddons was quite as great in Mrs. Beverley and Isabella as in Lady Macbeth or Queen Katherine: yet no one, we apprehend, will say that the poetry is equal. It appears, therefore, not that the most intellectual characters excite most interest on the stage, but that they are objects of greater curiosity; they are nicer tests of the skill of the actor, and afford greater scope for controversy, how far the sentiment is 'overdone or come tardy of.' There is more in this circumstance than people in general are aware of. We have no hesitation in saying, for instance, that Miss O'Neill has more popularity *in the house* than Mr. Kean. It is quite as certain, that he is more thought of *out of it.* The reason is, that she is not 'food for the critics,' whereas Mr. Kean notoriously is; there is no end of the topics he affords for discussion —for praise and blame.

All that we have said of acting in general applies to his Richard ii. It has been supposed that this is his finest part: this is, however, a total misrepresentation. There are only one or two electrical shocks given in it; and in many of his characters he gives a much greater number.—The excellence of his acting is in proportion to the number of hits, for he has not equal truth or purity of style. Richard ii. was hardly given correctly as to the general outline. Mr. Kean made it a character of *passion*, that is, of feeling combined with energy; whereas it is a character of *pathos*, that is to say, of feeling combined with weakness. This, we conceive, is the general fault of Mr. Kean's acting, that it is always energetic or nothing. He is always on full stretch—never relaxed. He expresses all the violence, the extravagance, and fierceness of the passions, but not their mis-givings, their helplessness, and sinkings into despair. He has too much of that strong nerve and fibre that is always equally elastic. We might instance to the present purpose, his dashing the glass down with all his might, in the scene with Hereford, instead of letting it fall out of his hands, as from an infant's; also, his manner of expostulating with Bolingbroke, 'Why on thy knee, thus low, &c.' which was altogether fierce and heroic, instead of being sad, thoughtful, and melancholy. If Mr. Kean would look into some passages in this play, into that in particular, 'Oh that I were a mockery king of snow, to melt away before the sun of Bolingbroke,' he would find a clue to this character, and to human nature in general, which he seems to have missed—how far feeling is connected with the sense of weakness as well as of strength, or the power of imbecility, and the force of passiveness.

We never saw Mr. Kean look better than when we saw him in Richard II. and his voice appeared to us to be stronger. We saw him near, which is always in his favour; and we think one reason why the Editor of this Paper[1] was disappointed in first seeing this celebrated actor, was his being at a considerable distance from the stage. We feel persuaded that on a nearer and more frequent view of him, he will agree that he is a perfectly original, and sometimes a perfectly natural actor; that if his conception is not always just or profound, his execution is masterly; that where he is not the very character he assumes, he makes a most brilliant rehearsal of it: that he never wants energy, ingenuity, and animation, though he is often deficient in dignity, grace, and tenderness; that if he frequently disappoints us in those parts where we expect him to do most, he as frequently surprises us by striking out unexpected beauties of his own; and that the objectionable parts of his acting arise chiefly from the physical impediments he has to overcome.

Of the other characters of the play, it is needless to say much. Mr. Pope was respectable in John of Gaunt. Mr. Holland was lamentable in the Duke of York, and Mr. Elliston indifferent in Bolingbroke. This alteration of Richard II. is the best that has been attempted; for it consists entirely of omissions, except one or two scenes which are idly tacked on to the conclusion.

THE UNKNOWN GUEST

The Examiner.   *April 2,* 1815.

The English Drama has made an acquisition of no less than three new pieces in the course of the week. The Unknown Guest (said to be from the pen of Mr. Arnold, the Manager) is, we suppose, to

[1] The Examiner.

be considered as a dramatic trifle : it is one of the longest and dullest trifles we almost ever remember to have sat out. We think in general, that the practice of making the Manager bring out his own pieces on the stage, is a custom which would be 'more honoured in the breach than the observance : ' it is offering a premium for the rejection of better pieces than his own. In the present instance, it would be a compliment to say, that the author has failed in wit, character, incident, or sentiment ; for he has not attempted any thing of the kind. The dialogue bears no proportion in quantity to the songs ; and chiefly serves as a vehicle to tack together a certain number of unmeaning lines, arranged for different voices, and set in our opinion to very indifferent music. The music of this Opera professes to be by Mr. Kelly and Mr. Braham, except that of one song, which is modestly said to be—selected ;—a title which we apprehend might be extended to the whole. We do not recollect a single movement in the airs composed by Mr. Kelly, which was not familiar even to vulgarity ; and the style of Mr. Braham's songs has no other object than to pamper him in his peculiar vices, and to produce that *mannerism*, which is the destruction of all excellence in art. There are two or three favourite passages which seem to dwell upon his ear, and to which he gives a striking expression ; these he combines and repeats with laborious foolery ; and in fact, sings nothing but himself over and over continually. Nothing can be worse than this affected and selfish monotony. Instead of acquiring new and varied resources, by lending his imagination to the infinite combinations of which music is susceptible, and by fairly entering into his subject, all his ideas of excellence are taken from, and confined to the sound of his own voice. It is on this account that we listen to Mr. Braham's singing with less pleasure than we formerly did. It is not assuredly that Mr. Braham has fallen off in his singing ; on the contrary, he has improved and perfected his particular talent, but we constantly know what we have to expect, or rather to apprehend, for this anticipation at last amounts to apprehension : we perceive a limit, and this perception is always painful, where it seems to arise from any thing wilful or systematic. Those who first hear Mr. Braham, are struck with a noble simplicity and fervour in his manner of expressing certain emotions, in the eagerness with which he seems to fling himself into his subject, disdaining the rules of art, like the combatant who rushes without his armour to the battle : the sounds he utters, appear to rend his own bosom, or at other times, linger in fluttering accents on his lips. The communication between the voice and the feelings is immediate, instantaneous, irresistible ; and the language of music seems the language of nature and passion.

But when the sound becomes not only an echo to the sense, but to itself—when the same alternation of bursts of heroic passion, and thrillings of sentimental tenderness is constantly played off upon us —when there is nothing but this trite transition from the *con furio*, *con strepito*, to the *affettuoso* and *adagio* style, in their greatest extremes —we then begin to perceive something like a trick, and are little more affected than by reading the marginal directions in a music book. The inspiration of genius is fled ; that which before breathed the very soul of music, becomes little better than a puppet, and like all other puppets, is good only according to its compass, and the number of evolutions it performs. We have here spoken of directness and simplicity of style, as Mr. Braham's *forte* in singing ; for though we agree that he has too much ornament (a very little is too much), yet we can by no means allow that this can be made an unqualified objection to his style, for he has much less than other singers.

Of Mr. Phillips we would not wish to speak ; but as he puts himself forward and is put forward by others, we must say something. He is said to be an imitator of Mr. Braham ; if so, the imitation is a vile one. This gentleman has one qualification, which has been said to be the great secret of pleasing others, that he is evidently pleased with himself. But he does not produce a corresponding effect upon us ; we have not one particle of sympathy with his wonderful self-complacency. We should wish never to hear him sing again ; or, if he must sing, at least, we should hope never to see him act : let him not top his part—why should he sigh, and ogle, and languish, and display all his accomplishments—he should spare the side-boxes !—Mrs. Dickons never appeared to us any thing but an ordinary musical instrument, and at present, she is very much out of tune. We do not well understand what has been said of this piece having called forth all the musical strength of the house : except Braham's, there was not a single song sung so as not to give pain, even to a moderately cultivated ear. In this censure, we do not (of course) include Miss Kelly ; in seeing her, we never think of her singing. The comic parts of this Opera (if such they can be called) were sustained by Miss Kelly, Mr. Munden, and Mr. Knight. Miss Kelly did the little she had to do, with that fine unobtrusive good sense, and reluctant *naiveté*, which distinguish all her performances. If she carries her shyness of the audience and of her profession to a fault, not so Mr. Munden. He out-caricatures caricature, and outgrimaces himself. We have seen him twice lately in the same character of a drunken confidant, and were both times heartily tired. He is not only perfectly conscious what he is about, but has a thorough understanding with the audience all along. He makes his face up into a bad joke, and flings it right in the teeth of the spectators. The expression of the masks hanging out at the shop-windows, is less extravagant and distorted. There is no one on the stage who can, or at least who does, draw up his eyebrows, roll his eyes, thrust out his tongue, or drop his under jaw, in so astonishing a manner as Mr. Munden; and if acting consisted in making wry faces, he would be the greatest actor on the stage, instead of which he is, on these occasions, only a bad clown. His over-desire to produce effect, destroys all effect on our minds.[1]—Mr. Knight played the servant very well; but in general, there is too much an appearance in his acting, as if he was moved by wires. His feeling always flies to the extremities: his vivacity is in his feet and finger-ends. He is a very lively automaton.

March 30.

The farce of Love in Limbo, brought out at Covent-Garden Theatre, has no other merit than the plot, which, however, is neither very laughable nor very probable.—The melo-drame of Zembuca, besides the attractions of the scenery and music, has considerable neatness of point in the dialogue, to which Liston gave its full effect.

MR. KEAN'S ZANGA

The Examiner. *May 28, 1815.*

Mr. Kean played for his benefit on Wednesday, the character of Zanga, in the Revenge (which he is to repeat), and the character of Abel Drugger from the Alchymist, (we are sorry to say for that night only). The house was crowded to excess. The play of the Revenge is an obvious transposition of Othello: the two principal characters are the same; only their colours are reversed. The giving the dark, treacherous, fierce, and remorseless character to the Moor, is an alteration, which is more in conformity to our prejudices, as well as to historical truth. We have seen Mr. Kean in no part, to which his general style of acting is so completely adapted as to this, or to which he has given greater spirit and effect. He had all the wild impetuosity of barbarous revenge, the glowing energy of the untamed children of the sun, whose blood drinks up the radiance of fiercer skies. He was like a man stung with rage, and bursting with stifled passions. His hurried motions had the restlessness of the panther's: his wily caution, his cruel eye, his quivering visage, his

[1] It will be seen, that this severe censure of Munden is nearly reversed in the sequel of these remarks, and on a better acquaintance with this very able actor in characters more worthy of his powers.

violent gestures, his hollow pauses, his abrupt transitions, were all in character. The very vices of Mr. Kean's general acting might almost be said to assist him in the part. What in our judgment he wants, is dignified repose, and deep internal sentiment. But in Zanga, nothing of this kind is required. The whole character is violent; the whole expression is in action. The only passage which struck us as one of calm and philosophical grandeur, and in which Mr. Kean failed from an excess of misplaced energy, was the one in the conclusion, where he describes the tortures he is about to undergo, and expresses his contempt for them. Certainly, the predominant feeling here is that of stern, collected, impenetrable fortitude, and the expression given to it should not be that of a pantomimic exaggeration of the physical horrors to which he professes to rise superior. The mind in such a situation recoils upon itself, summons up its own powers and resources, and should seem to await the blow of fate with the stillness of death. The scene in which he discloses himself to Alonzo, and insults over his misery, was terrific: the attitude in which he tramples on the body of his prostrate victim, was not the less dreadful from its being perfectly beautiful. Among the finest instances of natural expression, were the manner in which he interrupts himself in his relation to Alonzo, 'I knew you could not bear it,' and his reflection when he sees that Alonzo is dead—'And so is my revenge.' The play should end here: the soliloquy afterwards is a mere drawling piece of common-place morality. We ought to add, that Mr. Rae acted the part of Alonzo with great force and feeling.

Mr. Kean's Abel Drugger was an exquisite piece of ludicrous *naiveté*. The first word he utters, '*Sure*,' drew bursts of laughter and applause. The mixture of simplicity and cunning in the character could not be given with a more whimsical effect. First, there was the wonder of the poor Tobacconist, when he is told by the Conjurer that his name is Abel, and that he was born on a Wednesday; then the conflict between his apprehensions and his cupidity, as he becomes more convinced that Subtle is a person who has dealings with the devil; and lastly, his contrivances to get all the information he can, without paying for it. His distress is at the height, when the two-guinea pocket-piece is found upon him: 'He had received it from his grandmother, and would fain save it for his grand-children.' The battle between him and Face (Oxberry) was irresistible; and he went off after he had got well through it, strutting, and fluttering his cloak about, much in the same manner that a game cock flaps his wings after a victory. We wish he would do it again!

228

A VIEW OF THE ENGLISH STAGE

MR. BANNISTER'S FAREWELL

The Examiner.   *June* 4, 1815.

Mr. Bannister had the comedy of The World, and the after-piece of The Children in the Wood, for his benefit on Thursday last, at Drury-Lane. Mr. Gattie, in consequence of the indisposition of Mr. Dowton, undertook the part of Index in the play. This alteration occasioned a short interruption; but after the usual explanation, the piece proceeded, and in our opinion, Mr. Gattie made a very excellent representative of the busy, whiffling, insignificant, but good-natured character which he personated. The figure and manner of this actor are certainly better fitted for the part than those of Dowton, who has too much weight and sturdiness of mind and body, to run about on ladies' errands, and take an interest in every thing that does not concern him. He is not a Will Wimble. Mr. Bannister played the character of Echo, which is a whimsical mixture of simplicity, affectation, and good-nature, with his usual excellence. Mr. Elliston's Cheviot is one of his best characters. Whatever requires spirit, animation, or the lively expression of natural feelings, he does well. Sentimental comedy is the equivocal reflection of tragedy in common life, and Mr. Elliston can rehearse the one just well enough to play the other. The coincidence is complete. He raises his voice to a pitch of romantic rapture, or lowers it to the tones of sullen despondence and disappointment, with the happiest effect. The Duke, in the Honey-Moon, is the *assumption* of an impassioned character. The Comedy of the World, is one of the most ingenious and amusing of the modern stage. It has great neatness of dialogue, and considerable originality, as well as sprightliness of character. It is, however, chargeable with a grossness which is common to modern plays, we mean, the grossness of fashionable life in the men, and the grossness of fine sentiment in the women. Mrs. Davison did not soften down the exuberant qualities of Lady Bloomfield into any thing like decency; and the two fashionable loungers, Loiter and Dauntless, were certainly done to the life by Decamp and R. Palmer. Between the acts, Mr. Braham sung Robin Adair, and The Death of Nelson, in his most delightful style.

In the after-piece, Mr. Bannister played the favourite part of Walter, in the Children in the Wood, for the last time.

He then came forward to take his leave of the Stage, in a Farewell Address, in which he expressed his thanks for the long and flattering patronage he had received from the public. We do not wonder that his feelings were overpowered on this occasion: our own (we confess it) were nearly so too. We remember him in the first hey-day of our youthful spirits, in The Prize—which he played so delightfully with that fine old croaker Suett, and Madame Storace—in the farce of My Grandmother, in the Son-in-Law, in Autolycus, and in Scrub, in which our satisfaction was at its height.   At that time, King, and Parsons, and Dodd, and Quick, and Edwin, were in the full vigour of their reputation, who are now all gone!   We still feel the vivid delight with which we used to see their names in the play-bills, as we went along to the theatre.   Bannister was almost the last of these that remained; and we parted with him as we should with one of our oldest and best friends.   The most pleasant feature in the profession of a player, and which is peculiar to it, is, that we not only admire the talents of those who adorn it, but we contract a personal intimacy with them.   There is no class of society whom so many persons regard with affection as actors.   We greet them on the stage; we like to meet them in the streets; they always recall to us pleasant associations; and we feel our gratitude excited, without the uneasiness of a sense of obligation.   The very gaiety and popularity, however, which surrounds the life of a favourite performer, makes the retiring from it a very serious business.   It glances a mortifying reflection on the shortness of human life, and the vanity of human pleasures. Something reminds us, that ' all the world's a stage, and all the men and women merely players.'

COMUS

The Examiner.   *June 11, 1815.*

Comus has been got up at Covent-Garden Theatre with great splendour, and has had as much success as was to be expected.   The genius of Milton was essentially *undramatic*: he saw all objects from his own point of view, and with certain exclusive preferences.   Shakespear, on the contrary, had no personal character, and no moral principle, except that of good-nature.   He took no part in the scene he describes, but gave fair play to all his characters, and left virtue and vice, folly and wisdom, right and wrong, to fight it out between themselves, just as they do on their ' old prize-fighting stage '—the world.   He is only the vehicle for the sentiments of his characters. Milton's characters are only a vehicle for his own.   Comus is a didactic poem, or a dialogue in verse, on the advantages or disadvantages of virtue and vice.   It is merely a discussion of general topics, but with a beauty of language and richness of illustration, that in the perusal leave no feeling of the want of any more powerful interest.   On the stage, the poetry of course lost above half of its

230

effect: but this was compensated to the audience by every advantage of scenery and decoration. By the help of dance and song, 'of mask and antique pageantry,' this most delightful poem went off as well as any common pantomime. Mr. Conway topped the part of Comus with his usual felicity, and seemed almost as if the genius of a maypole had inspired a human form. He certainly gives a totally new idea of the character. We allow him to be 'a marvellous proper man,' but we see nothing of the magician, or the son of Bacchus and Circe in him. He is said to make a very handsome Comus: so he would make a very handsome Caliban; and the common sense of the transformation would be the same. Miss Stephens played the First Nymph very prettily and insipidly; and Miss Matthews played the Second Nymph with appropriate significance of nods and smiles. Mrs. Faucit, as the Lady, rehearsed the speeches in praise of virtue very well, and acted the scene of the Enchanted Chair admirably. She seemed changed into a statue of alabaster. Miss Foote made a very elegant Younger Brother.—It is only justice to add, that Mr. Duruset gave the songs of the Spirit with equal taste and effect; and in particular, sung the final invocation to Sabrina in a full and powerful tone of voice, which we have seldom heard surpassed.

These kind of allegorical compositions are necessarily unfit for actual representation. Every thing on the stage takes a literal, palpable shape, and is embodied to the sight. So much is done by the senses, that the imagination is not prepared to eke out any deficiency that may occur. We resign ourselves, as it were, to the illusion of the scene: we take it for granted, that whatever happens within that 'magic circle' is real; and whatever happens without it, is nothing. The eye of the mind cannot penetrate through the glare of lights which surround it, to the pure empyrean of thought and fancy; and the whole world of imagination fades into a dim and refined abstraction, compared with that part of it, which is brought out dressed, painted, moving, and breathing, a speaking pantomime before us. Whatever is seen or done, is sure to tell: what is heard only, unless it relates to what is seen or done, has little or no effect. All the fine writing in the world, therefore, which does not find its immediate interpretation in the objects or situations before us, is at best but elegant impertinence. We will just take two passages out of Comus, to shew how little the beauty of the poetry adds to the interest on the stage: the first is from the speech of the Spirit as Thyrsis:—

> 'This evening late, by then the chewing flocks
> Had ta'en their supper on the savoury herb

Of knot-grass dew-besprent, and were in fold,
I sat me down to watch upon a bank
With ivy canopied, and interwove
With flaunting honeysuckle, and began,
Wrapt in a pleasing fit of melancholy,
To meditate my rural minstrelsy,
Till Fancy had her fill; but ere a close,
The wonted roar was up amidst the woods,
And filled the air with barbarous dissonance:
At which I ceased, and listen'd them a while,
Till an unusual stop of sudden silence
Gave respite to the drowsy-flighted steeds
That draw the litter of close-curtain'd sleep:
At last a soft and solemn breathing sound
Rose like a steam of rich distill'd perfumes,
And stole upon the air, that even Silence
Was took ere she was 'ware, and wished she might
Deny her nature, and be never more
Still to be so displaced.'

This passage was recited by Mr. Duruset; and the other, which
we proposed to quote, equally became the mouth of Mr. Conway :—

'Two such I saw, what time the labour'd ox
In his loose traces from the furrow came,
And the swinkt hedger at his supper sat ;
I saw them under a green mantling vine
That crawls along the side of yon small hill,
Plucking ripe clusters from the tender shoots:
Their port was more than human as they stood :
I took it for a fairy vision
Of some gay creatures of the element,
That in the colours of the rainbow live
And play in th' plighted clouds. I was awe-struck,
And as I pass'd, I worshipp'd.'

To those of our readers who may not be acquainted with Comus,
these exquisite passages will be quite new, though they may have
lately heard them on the stage.

There was an evident want of adaptation to theatrical representation in the last scene, where Comus persists in offering the Lady the
cup, which she as obstinately rejects, without any *visible* reason. In
the poetical allegory, it is the poisoned cup of pleasure : on the stage,
it is a goblet filled with wine, which it seems strange she should
refuse, as the person who presents it to her, has certainly no appearance of any dealings with the devil.

Milton's Comus is not equal to Lycidas, nor to Samson Agonistes.

232

It wants interest and passion, which both the others have. Lycidas is a fine effusion of classical sentiment in a youthful scholar: his Samson Agonistes is almost a canonisation of all the high moral and religious prejudices of his maturer years. *We* have no less respect for the memory of Milton as a patriot than as a poet. Whether he was a *true* patriot, we shall not enquire: he was at least a *consistent* one. He did not retract his defence of the people of England; he did not say that his sonnets to Vane or Cromwell were meant ironically; he was not appointed Poet-Laureat to a Court which he had reviled and insulted; he accepted neither place nor pension; nor did he write paltry sonnets upon the 'Royal fortitude' of the House of Stuart, by which, however, they really lost something.[1]

MR. KEAN'S LEON

The Examiner.   *July 2, 1815.*

We went to see Mr. Kean in Leon, at Drury-Lane, and, on the whole, liked him less in it than we formerly liked Mr. Kemble in the same part. This preference, however, relates chiefly to personal considerations. In the first scenes of the play, Mr. Kemble's face and figure had a nobleness in them, which formed a contrast to the assumed character of the idiot, and thus carried off the disgusting effect of the part. Mr. Kean both acted and looked it too well. At the same time, we must do justice to the admirable comic talents displayed by Mr. Kean on this occasion. We never saw or heard looks or tones more appropriate and ludicrous. The house was in a roar. His alarm on being first introduced to his mistress, his profession of being 'very loving,' his shame after first saluting the lady, and his chuckling half-triumph on the repetition of the ceremony, were complete acting. Above all, we admired the careless self-complacent idiotcy with which he marched in, carrying his wife's fan, and holding up her hand. It was the triumph of folly. Even Mr. Liston, with all his inimitable graces in that way, could not have bettered it. In the serious part of the character he appeared to us less perfect. There was not repose enough, not enough of dignity. Leon, we apprehend, ought to be the man of spirit, but still more the gentleman. He has to stand in general upon the

---

[1] In the last edition of the works of a modern Poet, there is a Sonnet to the King, complimenting him on 'his royal fortitude.' The story of the Female Vagrant, which very beautifully and affectingly describes the miseries brought on the lower classes by war, in bearing which the said 'royal fortitude' is so nobly exercised, is very properly struck out of the collection.

defensive, upon his own rights, upon his own ground, and need not bluster, or look fierce. We will mention one instance in particular. Where he tells the Duke to leave the house, which we think he should do with perfect coolness and confidence, he pointed with his finger to the door, 'There, there,' with the same significant inveteracy of manner, as where, in Iago, he points to the dead body of Othello. The other parts of the play were well supported. Mrs. Glover deserves great praise for her Estifania. Mr. Bartley shewed both judgment and humour in the Copper Captain; and yet we were not satisfied with his performance. There is a thinness in his voice, and a plumpness in his person, neither of which is to our taste. His laughing when he finds that Cacafogo had been cheated by Estifania, was perfectly well done; but there was an effeminacy in his voice which took away from the hearty effect which Bannister used to give to this scene. Knight, in the old woman, was excellent. His reiteration of 'What?' in answer to the Copper Captain's questions, had the startling effect produced by letting off a pistol close at one's ears. It evidently proceeded from a person blest with 'double deafness' of body and mind. The morality of this excellent comedy is very indifferent; and having been prompted by the observations of some persons of fashion near us, we got into a train of agreeable reflections on the progressive refinement of this our age and country, which it was our intention to have communicated to our readers,— but that we dropt them in the lobbies!

THE TEMPEST

The Examiner.   *July* 23, 1815.

As we returned some evenings ago from seeing the Tempest at Covent-Garden, we almost came to the resolution of never going to another representation of a play of Shakespear's as long as we lived; and we certainly did come to this determination, that we never would go *by choice*. To call it a representation, is indeed an abuse of language: it is travestie, caricature, any thing you please, but a representation. Even those daubs of pictures, formerly exhibited under the title of the Shakespear Gallery, had a less evident tendency to disturb and distort all the previous notions we had imbibed from reading Shakespear. In the first place, it was thought fit and necessary, in order to gratify the sound sense, the steady, sober judgment, and natural unsophisticated feelings of Englishmen a hundred years ago, to modernize the original play, and to disfigure its simple and beautiful structure, by loading it with the common-place, clap-trap sentiments,

234

artificial contrasts of situations and character, and all the heavy tinsel and affected formality which Dryden had borrowed from the French school. And be it observed, further, that these same anomalous, unmeaning, vulgar, and ridiculous additions, are all that *take* in the present farcical representation of the Tempest. The beautiful, the exquisitely beautiful descriptions in Shakespear, the still more refined, and more affecting sentiments, are not only not applauded as they ought to be (what fine murmur of applause should do them justice?) —they are not understood, nor are they even heard. The lips of the actors are seen to move, but the sounds they utter exciting no corresponding emotions in the breast, are no more distinguished than the repetition of so many cabalistical words. The ears of the audience are not prepared to drink in the music of the poet; or grant that they were, the bitterness of disappointment would only succeed to the stupor of indifference.

Shakespear has given to Prospero, Ariel, and the other characters in this play, language such as wizards and spirits, 'the gay creatures of the element,' might want to express their thoughts and purposes, and this language is here put into the mouth of Messrs. Young, Abbott, and Emery, and of Misses Matthews, Bristow, and Booth. ''Tis much.' Mr. Young is in general what is called a respectable actor. Now, as this is a phrase which does not seem to be very clearly understood by those who most frequently use it, we shall take this opportunity to define it. A respectable actor then, is one who seldom gratifies, and who seldom offends us; who never disappoints us, because we do not expect any thing from him, and who takes care never to rouse our dormant admiration by any unlooked-for strokes of excellence. In short, an actor of this class (not to speak it profanely) is a mere machine, who walks and speaks his part; who, having a tolerable voice, face, and figure, reposes entirely and with a prepossessing self-complacency on these natural advantages: who never risks a failure, because he never makes an effort; who keeps on the safe side of custom and decorum, without attempting improper liberties with his art; and who has not genius or spirit enough to do either well or ill. A respectable actor is on the stage, much what a pretty woman is in private life, who trusts to her outward attractions, and does not commit her taste or understanding, by hazardous attempts to shine in conversation. So we have generals, who leave every thing to be done by their men; patriots, whose reputation depends on their estates; and authors, who live on the stock of ideas they have in common with their readers.

Such is the best account we can give of the class of actors to which Mr. Young belongs, and of which he forms a principal ornament. As long as he contents himself to play indifferent characters, we shall say nothing: but whenever he plays Shakespear, we must be excused if we take unequal revenge for the martyrdom which our feelings suffer. His Prospero was good for nothing; and consequently, was indescribably bad. It was grave without solemnity, stately without dignity, pompous without being impressive, and totally destitute of the wild, mysterious, preternatural character of the original. Prospero, as depicted by Mr. Young, did not appear the potent wizard brooding in gloomy abstraction over the secrets of his art, and around whom spirits and airy shapes throng numberless 'at his bidding;' but seemed himself an automaton, stupidly prompted by others: his lips moved up and down as if pulled by wires, not governed by the deep and varied impulses of passion; and his painted face, and snowy hair and beard, reminded us of the masks for the representation of Pantaloon. In a word, Mr. Young did not personate Prospero, but a pedagogue teaching his scholars how to recite the part, and not teaching them well.

Of one of the actors who assisted at this sacrifice of poetical genius, Emery, we think as highly as any one can do: he is indeed, in his way, the most perfect actor on the stage. His representations of common rustic life have an absolute identity with the thing represented. But the power of his mind is evidently that of imitation, not that of creation. He has nothing romantic, grotesque, or imaginary about him. Every thing in his hands takes a local and habitual shape. Now, Caliban is a mere creation; one of the wildest and most abstracted of all Shakespear's characters, whose deformity is only redeemed by the power and truth of the imagination displayed in it. It is the essence of grossness, but there is not the smallest vulgarity in it. Shakespear has described the brutal mind of this man-monster in contact with the pure and original forms of nature; the character grows out of the soil where it is rooted uncontrouled, uncouth, and wild, uncramped by any of the meannesses of custom. It is quite remote from any thing provincial; from the manners or dialect of any county in England. Mr. Emery had nothing of Caliban but his gaberdine, which did not become him. (We liked Mr. Grimaldi's Orson much better, which we saw afterwards in the pantomime.) Shakespear has, by a process of imagination usual with him, drawn off from Caliban the elements of every thing etherial and refined, to compound them into the unearthly mould of Ariel. Nothing was ever more finely conceived than this contrast between the material and the spiritual, the gross and delicate. Miss Matthews played and sung Ariel. She is to be sure a very 'tricksy spirit:' and all that we can say in her praise is, that she is a better representative of the sylph-like form of the character, than the light and portable Mrs. Bland, who used formerly to play it. She certainly does not sing the songs so well. We do not however wish to hear them sung, though never so well; no music can add any thing to their magical effect.—The words of Shakespear would be sweet, even 'after the songs of Apollo!'

MY WIFE! WHAT WIFE?

The Examiner. *July 30, 1815.*

The Haymarket is the most sociable of all our theatres. A wonderful concentration of interest, and an agreeable equality of pretension reign here. There is an air of unusual familiarity between the audience and the actors; the pit shakes hands with the boxes, and the galleries descend, from the invisible height to which they are raised at the other theatres, half-way into the orchestra. Now we have certain remains of a sneaking predilection for this mode of accommodating differences between all parts of the house; this average dissemination of comfort, and immediate circulation of enjoyment; and we take our places (just as it happens), on the same good terms with ourselves and our neighbours, as we should in sitting down to an ordinary at an inn. Every thing, however, has its drawbacks; and the Little Theatre in the Haymarket is not without them. If, for example, a party of elderly gentlewomen should come into a box close at your elbow, and immediately begin to talk loud, with an evident disregard of those around them, your only chance is either to quit the house altogether, or (if you really wish to hear the play), to remove to the very opposite side of it; for the ill-breeding of persons of that class, sex, and time of life, is incorrigible. At the great Theatres, it is sometimes very difficult to hear, for the noise and quarrelling in the gallery; here the only interruption to the performance is from the overflowing garrulity and friendly tittle-tattle of the boxes. The gods (as they are called), at Drury-lane and Covent-garden, we suspect, 'keep such a dreadful pudder o'er our heads,' from their impatience at not being able to hear what is passing below; and, at the minor theatres, are the most quiet and attentive of the audience.

It is the immemorial practice of the Haymarket Theatre to bring out, every season, a number of new pieces, good, bad, or indifferent. To this principle we are indebted for an odd play, with an odd title, 'My Wife! What Wife?' and whether it belongs to the class of good, bad, or indifferent, we could not make up our minds at the time, and it has nearly escaped our memory since. Whether from its excellences or its absurdities, it is altogether very amusing. The best part of it is a very unaccountable, easy, impudent, blundering Irish footman, admirably represented by Mr. Tokely, whom we here take the liberty of introducing to the notice of our readers. 'Good Mr. Tokely, we desire better acquaintance with you.' We do not know whether this gentleman is himself an Irishman, but he has a wonderful sympathy with the manners and peculiarities of the character he had to represent. The ease, the ignorance, the impudence, the simplicity, the cunning, the lying, the good-nature, the absurdity, and the wit of the common character of the Irish, were depicted with equal fidelity and *naiveté* by this very lively actor; and his *brogue* was throughout a complete accompaniment to the sense. It floated up and down, and twisted round, and rose and fell, and started off or rattled on, just as the gusts of passion led.

The Irish and the Scotch brogue are very characteristic. In the one, the words are tumbled out altogether: in the other, every syllable is held fast between the teeth and kept in a sort of undulating suspense, lest circumstances should require a retractation before the end of the sentence. The Irish character is impetuous: the Scotch circumspect. The one is extreme unconsciousness, the other extreme consciousness. The one depends almost entirely on animal spirits, the other on will; the one on the feeling of the moment, the other on the calculation of consequences. The Irish character is therefore much more adapted for the stage: it presents more heterogeneous materials, and it is only unconscious absurdity that excites laughter. We seldom see a Scotchman introduced into an English farce: whereas an Irishman is always ready to be served up, and it is a standing dish at this kind of entertainment. Mr. Tokely sung two songs in the afterpiece with great effect. The laughing song was a thing of pure execution, made out of nothing but the feeling of humour in the actor.

Mr. Terry played the principal serious character in 'My Wife! What Wife?' He is a very careful and judicious actor: but his execution overlays the character. He is a walking grievance on the stage; a robust personification of the *comedie larmoyante*; a rock dropping tears of crystal; an iron figure, 'in the likeness of a sigh.' Mr. Jones was intended as a lively set-off to Mr. Terry. It was but a diversity of wretchedness. Mr. Jones is no favourite of ours. He is always the same Mr. Jones, who shews his teeth, and rolls his eyes,—

'And looks like a jackdaw just caught in a snare.'

A VIEW OF THE ENGLISH STAGE

Mr. Meggett has played Octavian twice at this theatre. He is a very decent, disagreeable actor, of the second or third-rate, who takes a great deal of pains to do ill. He did not, however, deserve to be hissed, and he only deserves to be applauded, because he was hissed undeservedly. He is a Scotch edition of Conway, without his beauty, and without his talent for noisy declamation.

Our play-houses are just now crowded with French people, with or without white cockades. A very intelligent French man and woman sat behind us the other evening at the representation of the Mountaineers, (one of the best of our modern plays) who were exceedingly shocked at the constant transitions from tragic to comic in this piece. It is strange that a people who have no keeping in themselves, should be offended at our want of keeping in theatrical representations. But it is an old remark, that the manners of every nation and their dramatic taste are opposite to each other. In the present instance, there can be no question, but that the distinguishing character of the English is gravity, and of the French levity. How then is it that this is reversed on the stage? Because the English wish to relieve the continuity of their feelings by something light and even farcical, and the French cannot afford to offer the same temptation to their natural levity. They become grave only by system, and the formality of their artificial style is resorted to as a preservative against the infection of their national disposition. One quaint line in a thousand sad ones, operating on their mercurial and volatile spirits, would turn the whole to farce. The English are sufficiently tenacious of strong passion to retain it in spite of other feelings: the French are only tragic by the force of dulness, and every thing serious would fly at the appearance of a jest.

MR. HARLEY'S FIDGET

The Examiner.   *August* 6, 1815.

Mr. Harley is an addition to the comic strength of the Lyceum. We have not seen him in the part of Leatherhead, in The Blue Stocking, in which he has been much spoken of; but as an intriguing knave of a servant, he was the life of a very dull and incredible farce, which came out the other night under the title of My Aunt; and we afterwards liked him still better as Fidget, in The Boarding House, where he had more scope for his abilities. He gave the part with all the liveliness, insinuating complaisance, and volubility of speech and motion, which belong to it. He has a great deal of vivacity, archness, and that quaint extravagance,

239

which constitutes the most agreeable kind of buffoonery   We think it likely he will become a considerable favourite with the public; and the more so, because he is not only a very amusing actor, but also possesses those recommendations of face, person, and manner, which go a great way in conciliating public favour.   These are the more necessary in those burlesque characters, which have little foundation in real life, and which, as they serve chiefly to furnish opportunities for the drollery of the actor to display itself, bring him constantly before us in his personal capacity.

We are really glad to be pleased whenever we can, and we were pleased with Peter Fidget.   His dress and his address are equally comic and in character.   He wears a white morning jean coat, and a white wig, the curls of which hang down like lappets over his shoulders, and form a good contrast with the plump, rosy, shining face beneath it.   He comes bolt upon the stage, and jumps into the good graces of the audience before they have time to defend themselves.   Peter Fidget, 'master of a boarding-house, with a green door—brass knocker—No. 1, round the corner—facing the Steyne—Brighton'—is a very impudent, rattling fellow, with a world of business and cares on his back, which however it seems broad enough to bear, the lightness of whose head gets the better of the heaviness of his heels, and whose person thrives in proportion to his custom.   It is altogether a very laughable exaggeration, and lost none of its effect in the hands of Mr. Harley.

In the new farce of My Aunt, Mr. Wallack played the character of a fashionable rake, and he is said to have played it well.   If this is a good specimen of the class, we can only say we do not wish to extend our acquaintance with it; for we never saw any thing more disagreeable.   Miss Poole played the Niece to Mrs. Harlowe's Aunt; and seemed a very proper niece for such an aunt.   Mr. Pyne 'warbled his love-lorn ditties all night long;'—for a despairing lover, we never saw any one look better, or flushed with a more purple grace—'as one incapable of his own distress.'   He appears to have taken a hint from Sir John Suckling;—

> 'Prythee, why so pale, fond lover,
>   Prythee why so pale?
> Will, if looking well won't win her,
>   Looking ill prevail?
> Prythee, why so pale?'

We went to the Haymarket Theatre on Thursday, to see Mr. Meggett in the Iron Chest, with that laudable desire which we always feel to find out any error in our former opinions; but in this desire, as it generally happens, we were disappointed. We however consider Mr. Meggett's Sir Edward Mortimer as a much more successful delineation than his Octavian. The character is taken from Falkland, in Mr. Godwin's Caleb Williams, which is unquestionably the best modern novel. The character, as it is treated by Colman, is one of much less genius and elevation than the original. It is harsh, heavy, fierce, and painfully irritable, but at the same time forcible and affecting. Such, at least, was the impression we received from Mr. Meggett's representation of it. What this actor wants is genial expression, and a certain general impulse which is inseparable from all passion. The tide of feeling in him frets itself away in narrow nooks and estuaries. His habitual manner is too hard and dry—he makes too dead a set at every thing. He grinds his words out between his teeth as if he had a lockjaw, and his action is clenched till it resembles the commencement of a fit of the epilepsy. He strains his muscles till he seems to have lost the use of them. If Mr. Kemble was hard, Mr. Meggett is rigid, to a petrifying degree. We however think that he gave considerable force and feeling to the part, by the justness of his conception, and by the energy of his execution. But neither energy nor good sense is sufficient to make the great actor:—it requires genius, which nothing can give. Study may teach us to distinguish the forms and classes of things; but it is genius alone which puts us in possession of the powers of art or nature. This play, when it first came out, excited a great deal of idle controversy and vulgar abuse. It appears to us to be a play of great interest; but that interest depends upon the sentiment, and not on the story or situations, and consequently is very little understood by a mixed audience.

Miss Greville made an interesting representative of Helen, the mistress of Sir Edward Mortimer. Mr. Barnard had considerable merit in Wilford, the Caleb Williams of the piece; though he seemed somewhat too insignificant an instrument to produce such terrible effects. Mr. Tokely played the ruffian (Orson) admirably well. Mrs. Belfield, his Dulcinea in the gang of robbers, perfectly frightened us in the cave-scene. We felt as much disconcerted by the uncalled-for phrensy of this theatrical amazon, as the Squire of Dames in Spenser did, when he was carried off by the giantess, Ogygia; or, as Mr. Capel Lofft must have done the other day, when Mrs. Mary Ann Bulmer pounced upon him in the Chronicle.

Mr. Foote was the brother of Sir Edward Mortimer. This gentleman is of the Wroughton school; that is, he belongs to the old English class of honest country gentlemen, who abound more in good nature than good sense, and who have a most plentiful lack of gall and wit. Mr. Foote does not discredit this branch of the profession. These persons are always very comfortable in themselves, and busy about other people. This is exceedingly provoking. They speak with good emphasis and discretion, and are in general of a reasonable corpulence. Whenever we see an actor of this class, with a hat and feather, a gold belt, and more than ordinary merit, we are strangely reminded of our old friend Mr. Gyngell, the celebrated itinerant manager, and the only showman in England, who, after the festivity of the week, makes a point of staying the Sunday over, and goes with all his family to church.

LIVING IN LONDON

The Examiner. *August* 13, 1815.

A new Comedy, called Living in London, by the author (as it appears) of Love and Gout, has been brought forward at the Haymarket Theatre. It is in three acts. The first act promised exceedingly well. The scenes were well-contrived, and the dialogue was neat and pointed. But in the second and third, the comic invention of the writer seemed to be completely exhausted; his plot became entangled and ridiculous, and he strove to relieve the wearied attention of the audience, by some of the most desperate attempts at *double entendre* we ever remember. Thus a servant is made to say, that ' no one can *bring up* his master's dinner but himself.' We are told by very good authority, that ' want of decency is want of sense.' The plot is double, and equally ill-supported in both its branches. A lady of fashion (who was made as little disgusting as the part would permit by Miss Greville) makes overtures of love to a nobleman, (Lord Clamourcourt, Mr. Foote), by publishing an account of a supposed intrigue between herself and him in the newspapers. The device is new, at least. The same nobleman is himself made jealous of his wife by the assumption of her brother's name (Neville) by a coxcomb of his acquaintance, by the circumstance of a letter directed to the real Neville having been received by the pretended one, and by the blunders which follow from it. The whole developement of the plot is carried on by letters, and there is hardly a scene towards the conclusion, in which a footman does not come in, as the bearer of some alarming piece of intelligence. Lord Clamourcourt, just as he is sitting down to dinner with his wife, receives a letter from his mistress; he hurries away, and his Lady

242

having no appetite left, orders the dinner back. Lord Clamourcourt is no sooner arrived at the place of assignation than he receives an anonymous letter, informing him that Neville is at his house, and he flies back on the wings of jealousy, as he had come on those of love. All this is very artificial and improbable. *Quod sic mihi ostendis incredulus odi.*

We were a good deal disappointed in this play, as from the commencement we had augured very favourably of it. There was not much attempt to draw out the particular abilities of the actors; and the little that there was, did not succeed. Matthews, who is in general exceedingly amusing, did not appear at all to advantage. The author did not seem to understand what use to make of him. He was an automaton put into his hands, of which he did not know how to turn the pegs. He is shoved on, and then shoved off the stage to no purpose, as if his exit or his entrance made the jest. One person twirls him round by the flap of his coat, and another jerks him back again by the tail of his perriwig. He is first a stupid servant, and is next metamorphosed, without taking his degrees, into an ignorant doctor. He changes his dress, but the same person remains. He has nothing to do but to run about like a dog to fetch and carry, or to fidget over the stage like the dolls that dance (to please the children) to the barrel-organs in the street. For our own parts, we had rather see Punch and the puppet-shew.

THE KING'S PROXY

The Examiner.   *Aug.* 27, 1815.

A new Opera was brought out at the Lyceum, last week, called The King's Proxy; or Judge for yourself. If we were to judge for ourselves, we should conceive that Mr. Arnold must have dreamt this opera. It might be called the Manager's Opera. It is just what might be supposed to occur to him, nodding and half asleep in his arm-chair after dinner, having fatigued himself all the morning with ransacking the refuse of the theatre for the last ten years. In this dozing state, it seems that from the wretched fragments strewed on the floor, the essence of four hundred rejected pieces flew up and took possession of his brain, with all that is thread-bare in plot, life-less in wit, and sickly in sentiment. Plato, in one of his immortal dialogues, supposes a man to be shut up in a cave with his back to the light, so that he sees nothing but the shadows of men passing and repassing on the wall of his prison. The Manager of the Lyceum Theatre appears to be much in the same situation. He does not get

243

a single glimpse of life or nature, but as he has seen it represented on his own boards, or conned it over in his manuscripts. The apparitions of gilded sceptres, painted groves and castles, wandering damsels, cruel fathers and tender lovers, float in incessant confusion before him. His characters are the shadows of a shade; but he keeps a very exact inventory of his scenery and dresses, and can always command the orchestra.

Mr. Arnold may be safely placed at the head of a very prevailing class of poets. He writes with the fewest ideas possible; his meaning is more nicely balanced between sense and nonsense, than that of any of his competitors; he succeeds from the perfect insignificance of his pretensions, and fails to offend through downright imbecility. The story of the present piece, (built on the well-known tradition of the Saxon King who was deceived by one of his courtiers in the choice of his wife), afforded ample scope for striking situation and effect; but Mr. Arnold has perfectly neutralised all interest in it. In this he was successfully seconded by those able associates, Mr. and Mrs. T. Cooke, Mr. Pyne, Mr. Wallack, by the sturdy pathos of Fawcett, and Miss Poole's elegant dishabille. One proof of talent the author has shewn, we allow—and that is, he has contrived to make Miss Kelly disagreeable in the part of Editha. The only good thing in the play was a dance by Miss Luppino and Miss C. Bristow.

THE MAID AND THE MAGPIE

The Examiner. *Sept.* 3, 1815.

A piece has been brought out at the Lyceum, called the Maid and the Magpie, translated from the French, and said to be founded on a true story of a girl having been condemned for a theft, which was discovered after her death to have been committed by a magpie. The catastrophe is here altered. The play itself is a very delightful little piece. It unites a great deal of lightness and gaiety with an equal degree of interest. The dialogue is kept up with spirit, and the story never flags. The incidents, though numerous and complicated with a number of minute circumstances, are very clearly and artfully connected together. The spirit of the French stage is manifest through the whole performance, as well as its superiority to the general run of our present dramatic productions. The superiority of our old comedy to the French (if we make the single exception of Moliere) is to be traced to the greater variety and originality of our national characters. The French, however, have the advantage of us in playing with the common-place surface of comedy, in the harlequinade of surprises and escapes, in the easy gaiety of the dialogue, and in the delineation of character, neither insipid nor overcharged.

The whole piece was excellently cast. Miss Kelly was the life of it. Oxberry made a very good Jew. Mrs. Harlowe was an excellent representative of the busy, bustling, scolding housewife; and Mr. Gattie played the Justice of the Peace with good emphasis and discretion. The humour of this last actor, if not exceedingly powerful, is always natural and easy. Knight did not make so much of his part as he usually does.

THE HYPOCRITE

The Examiner.   *(Drury-Lane) Sept.* 17, 1815.

The Tartuffe, the original of the Hypocrite, is a play that we do not very well understand. Still less do we understand the Hypocrite, which is taken from it. In the former, the glaring improbability of the plot, the absurdity of a man's imposing on the credulity of another in spite of the evidence of his senses, and without any proof of the sincerity of a religious charlatan but his own professions, is carried off by long formal speeches and dull pompous casuistry. We find our patience tired out, and our understanding perplexed, as if we were sitting by in a court of law. If there is nothing of nature, at least there is enough of art, in the French play. But in the Hypocrite (we mean the principal character itself), there is neither the one nor the other. Tartuffe is a plausible, fair-spoken, long-winded knave, who if he does not convince, confounds his auditors.

In the Hypocrite of Bickerstaff, the insidious, fawning, sophistical, accomplished French Abbé is modernised into a low-lived, canting, impudent Methodist preacher; and this was the character which Mr. Dowton represented, we must say, too well. Dr. Cantwell is a sturdy beggar, and nothing more: he is not an impostor, but a bully. There is not in any thing that he says or does, in his looks, words or actions, the least reason that Sir John Lambert should admit him into his house and friendship, suffer him to make love to his wife and daughter, disinherit his son in his favour, and refuse to listen to any insinuation or proof offered against the virtue and piety of his treacherous inmate. In the manners and institutions of the old French *regime,* there was something to account for the blind ascendancy acquired by the good priest over his benefactor, who might have submitted to be cuckolded, robbed, cheated, and insulted, as a tacit proof of his religion and loyalty. The inquisitorial power exercised by the

245

Church was then so great, that a man who refused to be priest-ridden, might very soon be suspected of designs against the state. This is at least the best account we can give of the tameness of Orgon. But in this country, nothing of the kind could happen. A fellow like Dr. Cantwell could only have got admittance into the kitchen of Sir John Lambert—or to the ear of old Lady Lambert. The animal magnetism of such spiritual guides, is with us directed against the weaker nerves of our female devotees.

We discovered nothing in Mr. Dowton's manner of giving the part to redeem its original improbability, or gloss over its obvious deformity. His locks are combed down smooth over his shoulders; but he does not sufficiently 'sleek o'er his rugged looks.' His tones, except where he assumes the whining twang of the conventicle, are harsh and abrupt. He sometimes exposes his true character prematurely and unnecessarily, as where he is sent to Charlotte with a message from her father. He is a very vulgar, coarse, *substantial* hypocrite. His hypocrisy appears to us of that kind which arises from ignorance and grossness, without any thing of refinement or ability, which yet the character requires. The cringing, subtle, accomplished master-villain, the man of talent and of the world, was wanting. It is, in a word, just that sort of hypocrisy which might supply a lazy adventurer in the place of work, which he might live and get fat upon, but which would not enable him to conduct plots and conspiracies in high life. We do not say that the fault is in Mr. Dowton. The author has attempted to amalgamate two contradictory characters, by engrafting our vulgar Methodist on the courtly French impostor; and the error could not perhaps be remedied in the performance. The only scene which struck us as in Mr. Dowton's best manner, as truly masterly, was that in which he listens with such profound indifference and unmoved gravity to the harangue of Mawworm. Mr. Dowton's general excellence is in hearty ebullitions of generous and natural feeling, or in a certain swelling pride and vain-glorious exaggerated ostentation, as in Major Sturgeon, and not in constrained and artificial characters.

Mawworm, which is a purely local and national caricature, was admirably personated by Oxberry. Mrs. Sparks's old Lady Lambert, is, we think, one of the finest exhibitions of character on the stage. The attention which she pays to Dr. Cantwell, her expression of face and her fixed uplifted hands, were a picture which Hogarth might have copied. The effects of the *spirit* in reviving the withered ardour of youth, and giving a second birth to forgotten raptures, were never better exemplified. Mrs. Orger played young Lady Lambert as well as the equivocal nature of the part would

246

admit; and Miss Kelly was as lively and interesting as usual in Charlotte. Of Mr. Wallack we cannot speak so favourably as some of our contemporaries. This gentleman 'has honours thrust upon him' which he does not deserve, and which, we should think, he does not wish. He has been declared, by the first authority, to stand at the head of his profession in the line of genteel comedy. It is usual, indeed, to congratulate us on the accession of Mr. Wallack at the expence of Mr. Decamp, but it is escaping from Scylla to Charybdis. We are glad to have parted with Mr. Decamp, and should not be inconsolable for the loss of Mr. Wallack.

The best thing we remember in Mr. Coleridge's tragedy of Remorse, and which gave the greatest satisfaction to the audience, was that part in which Decamp was precipitated into a deep pit, from which, by the elaborate description which the poet had given of it, it was plainly impossible he should ever rise again. If Mr. Wallack is puffed off and stuck at the top of his profession at this unmerciful rate, it would almost induce us to wish Mr. Coleridge to write another tragedy, to dispose of him in the same way as his predecessor.

MR. EDWARDS'S RICHARD III

The Examiner.   *Oct.* 1, 1815.

A Mr. Edwards, who has occasionally played at private theatricals, appeared at Covent-Garden Theatre in the character of Richard the Third. It was one of those painful failures, for which we are so often indebted to the managers. How these profound judges, who exercise 'sole sway and sovereignty' over this department of the public amusements, who have it in their power to admit or reject without appeal, whose whole lives have been occupied in this one subject, and whose interest (to say nothing of their reputation) must prompt them to use their very best judgment in deciding on the pretensions of the candidates for public favour, should yet be so completely ignorant of their profession, as to seem not to know the difference between the *best* and the *worst*, and frequently to bring forward in the most arduous characters, persons whom the meanest critic in the pit immediately perceives to be totally disqualified for the part they have undertaken—is a problem which there would be some difficulty in solving. It might suggest to us also, a passing suspicion that the same discreet arbiters of taste suppress real excellence in the same manner as they obtrude incapacity on the notice of the public, if genius were not a thing so much rarer than the want of it.

A VIEW OF THE ENGLISH STAGE

If Mr. Edwards had shewn an extreme ignorance of the author, but had possessed the peculiar theatrical requisites of person, voice, and manner, we should not have been surprised at the managers having been deceived by imposing appearances. But Mr. Edwards failed, less from a misapprehension of his part, than from an entire defect of power to execute it. If every word had been uttered with perfect propriety (which however was very far from being the case) his gestures and manner would have made it ridiculous. Of personal defects of this kind, a man cannot be a judge of himself; and his friends will not tell him. The managers of a play-house are the only persons who can screen any individual, possessed with an unfortunate theatrical *mania*, from exposing himself to public mortification and disgrace for the want of those professional qualifications of which they are supposed to be infallible judges.

At the same Theatre, a lady of the name of Hughes has been brought out in Mandane, in the favourite Opera of Artaxerxes—we should hope, not in the place of Miss Stephens. We do not say this for the sake of any invidious comparison, but for our own sakes, and for the sake of the public. Miss Hughes is, we believe, a very accomplished singer, with a fine and flexible voice, with considerable knowledge and execution. But where is the sweetness, the simplicity, the melting soul of music? There was a voluptuous delicacy, a *naiveté* in Miss Stephens's singing, which we have never heard before nor since, and of which we should be loth to be deprived. Her songs in Mandane lingered on the ear like an involuntary echo to the music—as if the sentiment were blended with and trembled on her voice. This was particularly the case in the two delightful airs, ' If o'er the cruel tyrant love,' and ' Let not rage thy bosom firing.' In the former of these, the notes faultered and fell from her lips like drops of dew from surcharged flowers. If it is impossible to be a judge of music without understanding it as a science, it is still more impossible to be so without understanding the sentiment it is intended to convey. Miss Hughes declaimed and acted these two songs, instead of singing them. She lisps, and smiles, and bows, and overdoes her part constantly. We do not think Mandane is at all the heroine she represents her—or, if she is, we do not wish to see her. This lady would do much better at the Opera.

Mr. Duruset sung ' Fair Semira ' with taste and feeling. We wish, in hearing the song ' In infancy our hope and fears,' we could have forgotten Miss Rennell's simple, but sustained and impressive execution of it.—Mr. Taylor played Arbaces, instead of Mr. Incledon.

A VIEW OF THE ENGLISH STAGE

LOVERS' VOWS

The Examiner.   *October* 8, 1815.

Lovers' Vows has been brought forward at Drury-Lane Theatre, and a young lady of the name of Mardyn has appeared in the character of Amelia Wildenheim. Much has been said in her praise, and with a great deal of justice. Her face is handsome, and her figure is good, bordering (but not too much), on *embonpoint*. There is, also, a full luscious sweetness in her voice, which was in harmony with the sentiments she had to express. The whole of this play, which is of German origin, carries the romantic in sentiment and story to the extreme verge of decency as well as probability. The character of Amelia Wildenheim is its principal charm. The open, undisguised simplicity of this character is, however, so enthusiastically extravagant, as to excite some little surprise and incredulity on an English stage. The portrait is too naked, but still it is the nakedness of innocence. She lets us see into the bottom of her heart, but there is nothing there which she need wish to disguise. Mrs. Mardyn did the part very delightfully —with great spirit, truth, and feeling. She, perhaps, gave it a greater maturity of consciousness than it is supposed to possess. Her action is, in general, graceful and easy, but her movements were, at times, too youthful and unrestrained, and too much like *waltzing*.

Mrs. Glover and Mr. Pope did ample justice to the principal *moral* characters in the drama; and we were perfectly satisfied with Mr. Wallack in Anhalt, the tutor and lover of Amelia. Some of the situations in this popular play (let the critics say what they will of their extravagance), are very affecting, and we will venture our opinion, that more tears were shed on this one occasion, than there would be at the representation of Hamlet, Othello, Lear, and Macbeth, for a whole season. This is not the fault of Shakespeare, but neither is it the fault of Kotzebue.

Mr. Dowton came out for the first time in the character of Shylock, in the Merchant of Venice. Our own expectations were not raised very high on this occasion, and they were not disappointed. All the first part of the character, the habitual malignity of Shylock, his keen sarcasms and general invectives, were fully understood, and given with equal force and discrimination. His manner of turning the bond into a 'merry jest,' and his ironical indifference about it, were an improvement which Mr. Dowton had borrowed from the comic art. But when the character is brought into action, that is, when the passions are let loose, and excited to the highest pitch of malignity, joy, or agony, he failed, not merely from the breaking down of his voice, but from the want of that movement and tide of passion, which overcomes every external disadvantage, and bears down every thing in its course. We think Mr. Dowton was wrong in several of his conceptions in the trial scene and other places, by attempting too many of those significant distinctions, which are only natural and proper when the mind remains in its ordinary state, and in entire possession of its faculties. Passion requires the broadest and fullest manner possible. In fine, Mr. Dowton gave only the prosaic side of the character of Shylock, without the poetical colouring which belongs to it and is the essence of tragic acting. Mr. Lovegrove was admirable in Launcelot Gobbo. The scene between him and Wewitzer, as Old Gobbo, was one of the richest we have seen for a long time. Pope was respectable as Antonio. Mr. Penley's Gratiano was more remarkable for an appearance of folly than of gaiety.

THE SCHOOL FOR SCANDAL

The Examiner.   (*Covent Garden*) *October* 15, 1815.

Why can we not always be young, and seeing the School for Scandal? This play used to be one of our great theatrical treats in our early play-going days. What would we not give to see it once more, as it was then acted, and with the same feelings with which we saw it then? Not one of our old favourites is left, except little Simmons, who only served to put us in mind more strongly of what we have lost! Genteel comedy cannot be acted at present. Little Moses, the money-lender, was within a hair's-breadth of being the only person in the piece who had the appearance or manners of a gentleman. There was a *retenu* in the conduct of his cane and hat, a precision of dress and costume, an idiomatic peculiarity of tone, an exact propriety both in his gestures and sentiments, which reminded us of the good old times when every one belonged to a marked class in society, and maintained himself in his characteristic absurdities by a *cheveux-de-fris* of prejudices, forms, and ceremonies. Why do our patriots and politicians rave for ever about the restoration of the good old times? Till they can persuade the beaux in Bond-street to resume their swords and bag-wigs, they will never succeed.

When we go to see a Comedy of the past age acted on the modern stage, we too almost begin to ' cast some longing, lingering looks behind,' at the departed sword-knots and toupees of the age 'of Louis xiv. We never saw a play more completely vulgarised in the acting than this. What shall we say of Fawcett, who played Sir Peter Teazle with such formidable breadth of shoulders and strength of lungs? Or to Mrs. Dobbs, who made such a pretty, insipid little rustic of Lady Teazle, shewing her teeth like the painted dolls in a peruke-maker's window? Or to Mrs. Gibbs, who converted the delicacy of Mrs. Candour into the coarseness of a bar-maid? Or to Mr. Blanchard, whose face looked so red, and his eyes so fierce in Old Crabtree, and who seemed to have mistaken one of his stable-boys for his nephew, Sir Benjamin? Or (not to speak it profanely) to Mr. Young's Joseph Surface? Never was there a less prepossessing hypocrite. Mr. Young, indeed, puts on a long, disagreeable, whining face, but he does not hide the accomplished, plausible villain beneath it. Jack Palmer was the man. No one ever came so near the idea of what the women call ' a fine man.' With what an air he trod the stage!—With what pomp he handed Lady Teazle to a chair! With what elaborate duplicity he knelt to Maria! Mr. Young ought never to condescend to play comedy, nor aspire to play tragedy. Sentimental pantomime is his forte. Charles Kemble made the best Charles Surface we have seen. He acted this difficult character (difficult because it requires a union of so many requisites, a good face and figure, easy manners, evident good nature, animation and sensibility) in such a way as to make it truly interesting and delightful. The only fault we can find with him is, that he was not well dressed.—Mrs. Faucit was respectable in Lady Sneerwell. Mr. Terry, as Sir Oliver Surface, wore a great coat with yellow buttons. Mr. Farley, in Trip, had a large bouquet: and why should we refuse to do justice to Mr. Claremont, who was dressed in black? The School for Scandal is one of the best Comedies in our language (a language abounding in good Comedies), and it deserves either to be well acted, or not acted at all. The wit is inferior to Congreve's, and the allusions much coarser. Its great excellence is in the invention of comic situations,[1] and the lucky contrast of different characters. The satirical conversation at Lady Sneerwell's, is an indifferent imitation of The Way of the World, and Sir Benjamin Backbite a foolish superfluity from the older comedy. He did not need the aid of Mr. Tokely to make him ridiculous. We have already spoken well of this actor's talents for low humour, but if he wishes to remain on the establishment, we are afraid he must keep in the kitchen.

[1] The scene where the screen falls and discovers Lady Teazle, is without a rival. Perhaps the discovery is delayed rather too long.

A VIEW OF THE ENGLISH STAGE

MRS. ALSOP'S ROSALIND

The Examiner.   *October 22, 1815.*

A Lady of the name of Alsop, a daughter of Mrs. Jordan (by a former husband), has appeared at Covent-Garden Theatre, in the character of Rosalind. Not only the circumstance of her relationship to that excellent actress, but the accounts in the papers, raised our curiosity and expectations very high. We were unwillingly disappointed. The truth is, Mrs. Alsop is a very nice little woman, who acts her part very sensibly and cleverly, and with a certain degree of arch humour, but 'no more like her mother than we to Hercules.' When we say this, we mean no disparagement to this lady's talents, who is a real acquisition to the stage in correct and chaste acting, but simply to prevent comparisons, which can only end in disappointment. Mrs. Alsop would make a better Celia than Rosalind. Mrs. Jordan's excellences were all natural to her. It was not as an actress but as herself, that she charmed every one. Nature had formed her in her most prodigal humour: and when nature is in the humour to make a woman all that is delightful, she does it most effectually. Mrs. Jordan was the same in all her characters, and inimitable in all of them, because there was no one else like her. Her face, her tones, her manner were irresistible. Her smile had the effect of sunshine, and her laugh did one good to hear it. Her voice was eloquence itself: it seemed as if her heart was always at her mouth. She was all gaiety, openness, and good-nature. She rioted in her fine animal spirits, and gave more pleasure than any other actress, because she had the greatest spirit of enjoyment in herself. Her Nell—but we will not tantalize ourselves or our readers. Mrs. Alsop has nothing luxurious about her, and Mrs. Jordan was nothing else. Her voice is clear and articulate, but not rich or flowing. In person she is small, and her face is not prepossessing. Her delivery of the speeches was correct and excellent as far as it went, but without much richness or power. Lively good sense is what she really possesses. She also sung the Cuckoo Song very pleasingly.

Charles Kemble made an interesting Orlando. Mr. Young spoke the 'Seven Ages' with propriety, and some effect. Mr. Fawcett's Touchstone was decent; and Mrs. Gibbs in Audrey, the very thing itself.

Mrs. Mardyn appeared at Drury-Lane Theatre in the play of The Will. We like her better than ever. She has still an exuberance

252

in her manner and action, which might be spared. She almost *dances* the character. She is, or she looks, very handsome; is perfectly well made, and has a very powerful voice, of which she makes full use. With a little more elegance, a little more decorum, a little more restraint upon the display of her charms, she would be the most fascinating comic actress on the stage. We cannot express the only fault we have to find with her better than by saying, that we think her manner was perfectly in character in her boy's clothes. The scene with Deborah, where she was frightened by the supposed ghost, had wonderful effect. Mr. Wallack played the young tutor as if he had been chaplain to a bishop. Lovegrove's humour in the old steward was feeble: it would not reach the galleries.

JOHN DU BART

The Examiner.   *October* 29, 1815.

John Du Bart is said to have made a great noise in his life-time; but it was nothing to the noise he makes at present at Covent-Garden Theatre, with his good ship Fame, and his gallant son Francis. We very much doubt, whether the vessel in which the great John forced his way out of Dunkirk harbour, was equal in size to the one in which Mr. Farley pipes all hands on board, and assaults the chandeliers and side-boxes of the Theatre-Royal. The ladies, like so many Andromedas, were thrown into evident consternation at the approach of this sea-monster. To what a degree of perfection the useful and elegant arts must have been carried in a country, where a real ship, as large as the life, can be brought on the stage, to the amazement and confusion of the audience! Speaking within compass, the man of war which is now got up at Covent-Garden, is full as large as any of the flotilla which last year ploughed the bosom of the Serpentine River, and the sea-fight with which the Managers have favoured us before Christmas, is as interesting as that which took place in Hyde Park, between the English and American squadrons, under the tasteful direction of the Prince Regent. We pronounce this the most nonsensical farce (with the exception perhaps of the one just alluded to) we were ever present at. The utmost that the poet or the mechanist could have aspired to, must have been to produce the effects of a first sea-voyage. There lay the ship of John Du Bart for half an hour, rocking about on crape waves, with the sun rising on one side, and night coming on in a thunder-storm on the other, guns firing, and the orchestra playing; Mr. Farley on board, bawling himself hoarse, looking like the

253

master of a Dutch squabber, or still more like the figure at the mast-head; Miss Booth as busy as she could make herself; Mr. Treby and Mr. Truman doing nothing; Mr. Hamerton with a hat and feathers, as the Crown Prince of Poland; Mr. Tokely very much at home drinking punch, and Mr. Liston (the only sensible man on board) wishing himself in any other situation. If any thing were wanting to complete the dizziness of brain produced by all this, it was supplied by the music of Mr. Bishop, who kept firing a perpetual broadside on the ears of the audience. From the overture to the finale, we heard nothing but

'Guns, drums, trumpets, blunderbuss, and thunder!'

Never since the invention of French Operas was there such an explosion of dissonant sounds. If this is music, then the clashing of bells, the letting off of rockets and detonating balls, or the firing a pistol close at your ear on an illumination night, is music. John Du Bart is taken from the French; and from the plot and sentiments, it is not difficult to guess the date of the French piece. It turns upon the preference due to an elected over an hereditary prince; and the chief actors are made to utter such sentiments as this, that 'treason consists in supporting a monarch on the throne in opposition to the voice of the people.' We wonder it is suffered to be acted —since *the hundred days* are over!

THE BEGGAR'S OPERA

The Examiner.   *November 6, 1815.*

We are glad to announce another interesting Polly at Drury-Lane Theatre, in the person of Miss Nash, from the Theatre-Royal, Bath. We are glad of every thing that facilitates the frequent representation of that inimitable play, the Beggar's Opera, which unites those two good things, sense and sound, in a higher degree than any other performance on the English or (or as far as we know) on any other stage. It is to us the best proof of the good sense as well as real delicacy of the British public, to see the most beautiful women in the boxes and the most veteran critics in the pit, whenever it is acted. All sense of humanity must be lost before the Beggar's Opera can cease to fill the mind with delight and admiration.

Miss Nash is tall, elegantly formed, in the bloom of youth, and with a very pretty face. Her voice has great sweetness, flexibility, and depth. Her execution is scientific, but gracefully simple; and she sang the several songs with equal taste and feeling. Her action, though sufficiently chaste and correct, wanted ease and spirit, so that the general impression left on the spectator's imagination was that of a very beautiful alabaster figure which had been taught to sing. She was greeted in the most encouraging manner on her first appearance, and rapturously applauded throughout. Indeed the songs and the music are so exquisite in themselves, that if given with their genuine characteristic simplicity, they cannot fail to delight the most insensible ear. The songs to which she gave most sweetness and animation were those beginning, ' But he so teazed me '—' Why how now, saucy Jade '—and ' Cease your funning.' Her mode of executing the last was not certainly so delightful as the way in which Miss Stephens sings it, but it was still infinitely delightful. Her low notes are particularly fine. They have a deep, mellow richness, which we have never heard before in a female voice. The sound is like the murmuring of bees.

Miss Kelly played Lucy, and we need hardly add, that she played it well. She is a charming little vixen: has the most agreeable pout in the world, and the best-humoured smile; shews all the insolence of lively satisfaction, and when she is in her airs, the blood seems to tingle at her fingers' ends. Her expression of triumph when Macheath goes up to her rival, singing ' Tol de rol lol,' and her vexation and astonishment when he turns round upon her in the same manner, were admirable. Her acting in this scene was encored; that is to say, Mr. Cooke's song was encored for the sake of the acting. She is the best Lucy we have seen, except Mrs. Charles Kemble, who, though she did not play the part more naturally, did it with a higher spirit and greater *gusto*.

Of Mr. T. Cooke's Macheath, we cannot say any thing favourable. Indeed, we do not know any actor on the stage who is enough of the fine gentleman to play it. Perhaps the elder Kemble might, but then he is no singer ! It would be an experiment for Mr. Kean : but we don't think he could do it. This is a paradox; but we will explain. As close a resemblance, then, as the dress of the ladies in the private boxes bears to that of that of the ladies in the boxes which are not private, so nearly should the manners of Gay's Macheath resemble those of the fine gentleman. Mr. Harley's Filch is not good. Filch is a serious, contemplative, conscientious character. This Simmons perfectly understands, as he does every character that he plays. He sings the song, ' 'Tis woman that seduces all mankind,' as if he had a pretty girl in one eye, and the gallows in the other. Mr. Harley makes a joke of it. Mrs. Sparkes's Mrs. Peachum we hardly think so good as Mrs. Davenport's.

A VIEW OF THE ENGLISH STAGE

Munden spoils Peachum, by lowering the character into broad farce. He does not utter a single word without a nasal twang, and a distortion of his face and body. Peachum is an old rogue, but not a buffoon. Mr. Dowton's Lockitt was good, but it is difficult to play this part after Emery, who in the hard, dry, and impenetrable, has no rival. The scene where Dowton and Munden quarrel, and exchange wigs in the scuffle, was the best. They were admirably dressed. A hearty old gentleman in the pit, one of the old school, enthusiastically called out, ' Hogarth, by G—d ! ' The ladies in the scene at the tavern with Macheath were genteeler than usual. This we were pleased to see; for a great deal depends on the casting of that scene. How Gay must have chuckled, when he found it once fairly over, and the house in a roar! They leave it out at Covent-Garden, from the systematic attention which is paid there to the morals of the town!

MISS O'NEILL'S ELWINA

The Examiner.   *November* 19, 1815.

During the last week Miss O'Neill has condescended to play the character of Elwina, in Miss Hannah More's tragedy of Percy. ' Although this production,' says a critic in the Times, ' like every other of the excellent and enlightened author, affords equal pleasure and instruction in the perusal, we are not sure that it was ever calculated to obtain very eminent success upon the stage. The language is undoubtedly classical and flowing; the sentiment character-istically natural and pure ; the fable uninterrupted ; the catastrophe mournful ; and the moral of unquestionable utility and truth. With all these requisites to dramatic fortune, the tragedy of Percy does not so strongly rivet the attention, as some other plays less free from striking faults, and composed by writers of far less distinguished talent. Though the versification be sufficiently musical, and in many passages conspicuous for nerve as well as cadence, there is no splendid burst of imagery, nor lofty strain of poetical inspiration. Taste and intelligence have decked their lines in every grace of sculptured beauty : we miss but the presence of that Promethean fire, which could bid the statue ' speak.' It may be objected, moreover, to this drama, that its incidents are too few, and too little diversified. The grand interest which belongs to the unlooked-for preservation of Percy's life, is, perhaps, too soon elicited and expended : and if we mistake not, there is room for doubting whether, at length, he fairly met his death, or was ensnared once more by some unworthy treachery of Douglas. Neither do we think the passions which are called into play by the solemn events of a history so calamitous, have been very minutely traced, intensely coloured, or powerfully illustrated. We have a general impression that Douglas is racked by jealousy—Elwina by grief—and Percy by disappointment. But we fain would have the home touches of Shakespear.'

Thus far the Times critic : from all which it appears that Miss Hannah More is not like Shakespear. The writer afterwards tries his hand at a comparison between Miss More and Virgil ; and the result, after due deliberation, is, that Virgil was the wiser man. The part, however, to which the learned commentator has the most decided objection, is that 'where Elwina steps out of her way to preach rather a lengthy sermon to her father, against war in general, as offensive to the Prince of Peace.'—Now if this writer had thought proper, he might have discovered that the whole play is 'a lengthy sermon,' without poetry or interest, and equally deficient in 'sculptured grace, and Promethean fire.'—We should not have made these remarks, but that the writers in the above paper have a greater knack than any others, of putting a parcel of tall opaque words before them, to blind the eyes of their readers, and hoodwink their own understandings. There is one short word which might be aptly inscribed on its swelling columns—it is the word which Burchell applies to the conversation of some high-flown female critics in the Vicar of Wakefield.

But to have done with this subject. We shall not readily forgive Miss Hannah More's heroine Elwina, for having made us perceive what we had not felt before, that there is a considerable degree of manner and monotony in Miss O'Neill's acting. The peculiar excellence which has been ascribed to Miss O'Neill (indeed over every other actress) is that of *faultless nature*. Mrs. Siddons's acting is said to have greater grandeur, to have possessed loftier flights of passion and imagination ; but then it is objected, that it was not a pure imitation of nature. Miss O'Neill's recitation is indeed nearer the common standard of level speaking, as her person is nearer the common size, but we will venture to say that there is as much a tone, a certain stage sing-song in her delivery as in Mrs. Siddons's. Through all the tedious speeches of this play, she preserved the same balanced artificial cadence, the same melancholy tone, as if her words were the continued echo of a long-drawn sigh. There is the same pitch-key, the same alternation of sad sounds in almost every line. We do not insist upon perfection in any one, nor do we mean to decide how far this intonation may be proper in tragedy ; but we contend, that Miss O'Neill does not in general speak in a natural tone of voice, nor as people speak in conversation. Her great excellence is extreme natural sensibility; that is, she perfectly conceives and expresses what would be generally felt by the female mind in the extraordinary and overpowering situations in which she is placed. In truth, in beauty, and in that irresistible pathos, which goes directly to the heart, she has at present no equal, and can have no superior. There were only one or two opportunities for the display of her delightful powers in the character of Elwina, but of these she made the fullest use. The expression of mute grief, when she hears of the death of Percy, in the last act, was as fine as possible: nor could any thing be more natural, more beautiful or affecting, than the manner in which she receives his scarf, and hurries out with it, tremulously clasping it to her bosom. It was one of those moments of still, and breathless passion, in which the tongue is silent, while the heart breaks. We did not approve of her dying scene at all. It was a mere convulsive struggle for breath, the representation of a person in the act of suffocation—one of those agonies of human nature, which, as they do not appeal to the imagination, should not certainly be obtruded on the senses. Once or twice Miss O'Neill dropped her voice so low, and articulated so internally, that we gathered what she said rather from the motion of her lips, than from distinguishing the sound. This in Mr. Kean would be called extravagance. We were heartily glad when the play was over. From the very construction of the plot, it is impossible that any good can come of it till all the parties are dead; and when this catastrophe took place, the audience seemed perfectly satisfied.

WHERE TO FIND A FRIEND

The Examiner.   *November* 26, 1815.

A new Comedy, entitled Where to find a Friend, and said to be from the pen of a Mr. Leigh, has been brought out at Drury-Lane Theatre. The Dramatis Personæ are as follows:

General Torrington	Mr. BARTLEY.
Sir Harry Moreden	Mr. WALLACK.
Heartly	Mr. DOWTON.
Young Bustle	Mr. KNIGHT.
Barney	Mr. JOHNSTONE.
Tim	Mr. OXBERRY.
Lady Moreden	Mrs. DAVISON.
Maria	Miss KELLY.
Mrs. Bustle	Mrs. SPARKS.

The story is not easily told, for it is a story almost destitute of events. Sir Harry Moreden has been for some years married to an heiress, a woman of exemplary principles and amiable feelings; but who, as it appears, through no other misconduct than a little playful gaiety of manner, has so far provoked the capricious and irritable temper of her husband, that he writes off to General Torrington, her guardian, gravely proposing a separation. This letter brings the General down from London, in order to learn from the Baronet his real cause of quarrel with his wife; and a singular conversation ensues, in which, to every conjecture of the General's as to the nature of Lady M.'s offences, the unaccountable husband answers in the negative, leaving it to the discernment of her guardian to find out the actual source of his disquietude. This, it appears, in the course of the play, is a certain fashionable levity and sportiveness of manner, with which it is rather extraordinary that Sir Harry should be displeased, as another objection on which he sometimes dwells is the rusticity of his wife's taste, in not having any inclination for the dissipation and frivolities of a town life. Some improbable scenes are however introduced to explain the merits of this matrimonial question, in which the studied levity on one side is contrasted with the unconscious violence on the other, until at length Lady Moreden, hearing from her guardian that her husband is much embarrassed in his circumstances, and almost on the point of ruin, reproaches herself with her thoughtless habit of tormenting him; and prevails upon the General to concur with her in applying her own large fortune, left to her separately by her father's will, to the relief of her husband's distresses: at the moment when Sir Harry is complaining of his not knowing 'where to find a friend,' all his applications to those whom he had considered such having proved unsuccessful, her guardian introduces his wife to him, which produces the reconciliation between them, and gives rise to the title of the play.

In the progress and developement of this story there is very little to interest or surprise: the sentimental part of the comedy is founded on the story of Heartly, whose daughter Maria has run away from him, and been privately married to a man of fashion, but who having, for family reasons, enjoined secresy upon her in his absence abroad, subjects her, in her father's eyes, to the supposed disgrace of a criminal connection. Old Heartly retires into the country in a melancholy state of mind, and Maria, finding herself unexpectedly near to his cottage, determines to throw herself upon his forgiveness, prevails upon an honest old servant to admit her to his presence, supplicates for pardon, and is again received into his affections. This reconciliation is not well brought about. Her seeking the interview with her father through the connivance of a servant, after the repeated rejection of every application to his tenderness, and when she has an advocate in General Torrington, an old friend of Heartly's, who has undertaken to bring about a reconciliation, is not exceedingly probable. After her clandestine introduction by the servant, the reconciliation is first effected between Heartly and Maria, on the supposition of her guilt, and is afterwards acted as it were twice over, when the sight of a ring on her finger leads to the discovery of her innocence. The comedy opens with the arrival of Maria at a country inn, near Moreden-hall, kept by the widow Bustle. The introductory scene between this veteran lady of the old school, and her son Jack Bustle, who is infected with the modern cant of humanity, and is besides very indecorous in his manners, is tediously long. Maria's depositing the hundred pounds in the hands of Mrs. Bustle is a gratuitous improbability; and it is with some difficulty that the notes are retrieved for the use of the right owner by the busy interference of Mr. Jack Bustle and the generosity of Mr. Barney O'Mulchesen, an honest Irishman, who at the beginning of the play is the ostler, but at the end of it, as he himself informs us, becomes 'the mistress of the Black Lion.'

Johnstone gave great spirit, and an appearance of cordial good humour, to this last character. He has a great deal of 'the milk of human kindness' in all his acting. There is a rich genial suavity of manner, a laughing confidence, a fine oily impudence about him, which must operate as a saving grace to any character he is concerned in, and would make it difficult to hiss him off the stage. In any other hands we think Mr. Barney O'Mulchesen would have stood some chance of being damned. Oxberry's Tim was excellent: in those kind of loose dangling characters, in which the limbs do not seem to hang to the body nor the body to the mind, in which he has to display meanness and poverty of spirit together with a natural love of good fellowship and good cheer, there is nobody equal to Oxberry. His scene with Dowton, his master, who comes home, and finds him just returning from the fair, from the passionateness of the master and the meekness of the man, had a very comic effect. This was the best scene in the play, and the only one in it, which struck us as containing any thing like originality in the conception of humour and character. Of Mrs. Davison's Lady Moreden, we cannot speak favourably, if we are to speak what we think. Her acting is said to have much playfulness about it; if so, it is *horse-play*.

A singularity in the construction of the scenes of this comedy is, that they are nearly an uninterrupted series of tête-à-têtes: the

A VIEW OF THE ENGLISH STAGE

personages of the drama regularly come on in couples, and the two persons go off the stage to make room for two others to come on, just like the procession to Noah's Ark. Perhaps this principle might be improved upon, by making an entire play of nothing but soliloquies.

Covent-Garden.

Cymon, an opera, by Garrick, was brought out on Monday. It is not very interesting, either in itself or the music. Mr. Duruset played Cymon very naturally, though the compliment is, perhaps, somewhat equivocal. Miss Stephens looked very prettily in Sylvia; but the songs had not any great effect: 'Sweet Passion of Love' was the best of them.

'It is silly sooth, and dallies with the innocence of love.'

Mrs. Liston, who played a little old woman, was encored in the burlesque song, 'Now I am seventy-two.' Mr. Liston's Justice Dorus is a rich treat: his face is certainly a prodigious invention in physiognomy.

MISS O'NEILL'S BELVIDERA

The Examiner. *December 10, 1815.*

Miss O'Neill repeated her usual characters last week. We saw her in Belvidera, and were disappointed. We do not think she plays it so well as she did last year. We thought her representation of it then as near perfection as possible; and her present acting we think chargeable in many instances, with affectation and extravagance. She goes into the two extremes of speaking so loud as to 'split the ears of the groundlings' and so low as not to be heard. She has (or we mistake) been taking a bad lesson of Mr. Kean: in our opinion, the excellences of genius are not communicable. A second-rate actor may learn of a first; but all imitation in the latter must prove a source of error: for the power with which great talent works, can only be regulated by its own suggestions and the force of nature. The bodily energy which Mr. Kean exhibits cannot be transferred to female characters, without making them disgusting instead of impressive. Miss O'Neill during the two last acts of Belvidera, is in a continual convulsion. But the intention of tragedy is to exhibit mental passion and not bodily agony, or the last only as a necessary concomitant of the former. Miss O'Neill clings so long about Jaffier, and with such hysterical violence, before she leaps upon his neck and

261

calls for the fatal blow, that the connection of the action with the sentiment is lost in the pantomime exhibition before us. We are not fastidious ; nor do we object to having the painful worked up with the catastrophe to the utmost pitch of human suffering ; but we must object to a constant recurrence of such extreme agony, as a convenient common-place or trick to bring down thunders of applause. Miss O'Neill twice, if we remember, seizes her forehead with her clenched fists, making a hissing noise through her teeth, and twice is thrown into a fit of agonized choking. Neither is her face fine enough in itself not to become unpleasant by such extreme and repeated distortion. Miss O'Neill's freedom from mannerism was her great charm, and we should be sorry to see her fall into it. Mr. C. Kemble's Jaffier had very considerable effect. Mr. Young's Pierre is his best character.

A new Farce was brought out here on Monday week, the title of which is What's a Man of Fashion? a question which it does not solve. A young lady (Miss Mathews) is left a fortune by her father, on condition of her marrying a man of fashion within a year of his death. Her aunt (Mrs. Davenport) is left her guardian, and locks her up to prevent her marrying any one, that the fortune may devolve to her. Old Project (personated by Fawcett) is instigated by the young lady, through the key-hole of the door where she is locked up, to find her a husband who shall also be a man of fashion ; and just as the old gentleman, who is a very strange mixture of the sailor, fox-hunter, and Bond-street lounger, has undertaken this laudable task, he meets his nephew (Mr. Jones), whom he fixes upon as the candidate for the young lady and for fifty thousand pounds. The whole business of the piece arises out of the attempts of Old Project to bring them together, and the schemes of the aunt to prevent the conclusion of the marriage before the expiration of the year, that is, before it strikes twelve o'clock at night. After many trifling and improbable adventures, Old Project and his nephew succeed. The clock strikes twelve, but the man of fashion and his mistress have been married a few minutes before, though nobody knows how. We do not think this farce a bit better than some we have lately noticed. The author seems to have sat down to write it without a plot. There is neither dialogue nor character in it, nor has it any thing to make it amusing, but the absurdity of the incidents.

We have seen Miss O'Neill in the Orphan, and almost repent of

262

what we have said above. Her Monimia is a piece of acting as beautiful as it is affecting. We never wish to see it acted otherwise or better. She is the Orphan that Otway drew.

> ' With pleas'd attention 'midst his scenes we find
> Each glowing thought that warms the female mind ;
> Each melting sigh and every tender tear,
> The lover's wishes, and the virgin's fear,
> His every strain the Smiles and Graces own.'

This idea of the character, which never leaves the mind in reading the play, was delightfully represented on the stage. Miss O'Neill did not once overstep the limits of propriety, and was interesting in every part. Her conversation with the page was delicately familiar and playful. Her death was judiciously varied, and did not affect the imagination less, because it gave no shock to the senses. Her greatest effort, however, was in the scene with Polydore, where she asks him, ' Where did you rest last night ? ' and where she falls senseless on the floor at his answer. The breathless expectation, the solemn injunction, the terror which the discovery strikes to her heart as if she had been struck with lightning, had an irresistible effect. Nothing could be pourtrayed with greater truth and feeling. We liked Charles Kemble's Castalio not much, and Mr. Conway's Polydore not at all. It is impossible that this gentleman should become an actor, unless he could take ' a cubit from his stature.' Mr. Young's Chamont was quite as good as the character deserves.

Mr. Kean's appearance at Drury-Lane on Tuesday, in the Duke Aranza, in the Honey Moon, excited considerable expectations in the public. Our own were not fulfilled. We think this the least brilliant of all his characters. It was Duke and no Duke. It had severity without dignity ; and was deficient in ease, grace, and gaiety. He played the feigned character as if it were reality. Now we believe that a spirit of raillery should be thrown over the part, so as to carry off the gravity of the imposture. There is in Mr. Kean an infinite variety of talent, with a certain monotony of genius. He has not the same ease in doing common things that he has energy on great occasions. We seldom entirely lose sight of his Richard, and to a certain degree, in all his acting, ' *he still plays the dog.*' His dancing was encored. George II. encored Garrick in the *Minuet de la Cour* : Mr. Kean's was not like court dancing. It had more alacrity than ease.

A VIEW OF THE ENGLISH STAGE

THE MERCHANT OF BRUGES

The Examiner.   *December* 17, 1815.

The Merchant of Bruges; or, The Beggars' Bush, altered from
Beaumont and Fletcher, was brought out at Drury-Lane on Thursday,
with great preparation, applause, and effect. Contrary, we believe,
to Green-room expectation, it answered completely. This, assuredly,
is not a classical drama; but the spirit of poetry constantly peeps out
from beneath the rags, and patches, and miserable disguise, in which
it is clothed. Where the eye was most offended by the want of
costume, songs and music came to its relief. The airs selected by
Mr. T. Cooke were admirably adapted to the situations, and we need
not remind the critical reader, that the lyrical effusions in Beaumont
and Fletcher are master-pieces in their kind. They are exactly
fitted to be either 'said or sung' under the green-wood tree. One or
two of these were sung separately, with a good deal of sweetness and
characteristic *naiveté*, by Miss L. Kelly, who is one of the supposed
beggars, but a princess in disguise. Either we mistook certain
significant intimations, or she wished to make this appear before the
proper time. One of the oddest transformations in the Beggars'
Bush, was, that it inspired Mr. Holland with no small degree of
animation and fancy; for he depicted the worthy Clause, who is
at the same time the King of the Beggars, the Father of the
Merchant of Bruges, and the old Earl of Flanders, inimitably
well.

Again, Mr. Oxberry and Harley were most respectable Beggars,
and had their cues perfect (which was more than Mr. Pope had in
the prologue); Mr. Kean topped his part as the Merchant-Earl,
Mr. Munden was not far behind him as the drunken Burgo-master,
and Mr. S. Penley, Mr. Rae, and Mr. Raymond, served to fill the
stage. The scenes from which this play derived its interest, and
which both for sentiment and situation were admirable, are those in
which Mr. Kean vindicates his character as a Merchant and his love
for Gertrude against the arrogant assumptions of her uncle
(Raymond), and disarms the latter in the fight. His retort upon
the noble baron, who accuses him of being a barterer of pepper and
sugar, 'that every petty lord lived upon his rents or the sale of his
beves, his poultry, his milk and his butter,' made a forcible appeal to
John Bull, nor did the manner in which Munden, who is bottle-
holder on the occasion, vociferated, 'Don't forget butter,' take away
from the effect. The whole of this scene is (if not in the best) in
the most peculiar and striking manner of Beaumont and Fletcher. It

264

is the very petulance of youthful ardour and aspiring self-opinion, defying and taunting the frigid prejudices of age and custom. If Mr. Kean's voice failed him, his expression and his action did full justice to the heroic spirit and magnanimity of conception of the poet, where he says to his mistress, after depriving his antagonist of his sword, 'Within these arms thou art safe as in a wall of brass,' and again, folding her to his breast, exclaims, 'Come, kiss me, love,' and afterwards rising in his extravagant importunity, 'Come, say before all these, say that thou lov'st me.' We do not think any of the German dramatic paradoxes come up to this in spirit, and in acting as it were up to the feeling of the moment, irritated by a triumph over long-established and insolent pretension. The scene between Mr. Kean and Gertrude (Mrs. Horn), where he is in a manner distracted between his losses and his love, had great force and feeling. We have seen him do much the same thing before. There is a very fine pulsation in the veins of his forehead on these occasions, an expression of nature which we do not remember in any other actor. One of the last scenes, in which *Clause* brings in the money-bags to the creditors, and Kean bends forward pointing to them, and Munden after him, repeating the same attitude, but caricaturing it, was a perfect *coup-de-théatre*. The last scene rather disappointed our expectations; but the whole together went off admirably, and every one went away satisfied.

The story of the Merchant of Bruges is founded on the usurped authority of Woolmar, as Earl of Flanders, to the exclusion of Gerald, the rightful heir, and his infant son Floris; the latter of whom, on his father being driven out by the usurper, has been placed with a rich merchant of Bruges; whilst the father, with his infant daughter, takes refuge among a band of Beggars, whose principal resort is in a wood near the town of Bruges. Young Floris is brought up by the merchant as his own son; and on the death of his protector, whom he considers as his real father, succeeds to his property, and becomes the principal merchant in Bruges. Gerald, in the mean time, is elected King of the Beggars; and, by the influence which his authority gives him over the fraternity, he is enabled to assist his son with a large sum of money at a time when he is on the verge of bankruptcy, owing to the non-arrival of several vessels richly laden, and which are detained by contrary winds. This circumstance gives the supposed Beggar considerable influence over the actions of his son, who declares himself ready to pay him the duties of a son, without being at all suspicious that it is indeed his real parent whom he is thus obeying; and Gerald, determining to reveal to his son the mystery of his birth, appoints an interview with him at midnight, near the Beggar's Bush, in the Forest. In the mean time Woolmar, having learnt that Gerald and Floris, whom he supposes dead, are still living, and that Gerald is concealed amongst the Beggars, goes with a troop of horse at midnight to the Beggar's Bush, for the purpose of surprising him. His plan is, however, circumvented by Hubert, a nobleman at the court of Woolmar, but who is secretly attached to the right heir. Hubert conveys intelligence of the intended attempt of Woolmar to Gerald, and a strong band of the Beggars are armed, and set in readiness to seize him on his entering a particular part of the forest, to which he is enticed by Hubert, under pretence of leading him to the spot where Gerald is concealed. Here they arrive just at the time Floris, by appointment, meets his father Gerald. Woolmar falls into the trap prepared for him, and is, with his principal confidant, Hemskirk, secured. An explanation takes place, and Gerald resigning his pretensions to his son, Floris, the Merchant is restored to the possession of the earldom of Flanders, and Woolmar, the usurping Earl, is banished for life.

SMILES AND TEARS

The Examiner.   *December* 24, 1815.

A new piece in five acts, called Smiles and Tears; or the Widow's Stratagem, has been produced, with very considerable success, at Covent-Garden Theatre. The Dramatis Personæ are :

Mr. Fitzharding	. . .	Mr. YOUNG.
Sir Henry Chomley	. . .	Mr. C. KEMBLE.
Colonel O'Donolan	. . .	Mr. JONES.
Mr. Stanley	. . .	Mr. FAWCETT.
Mr. Delaval	. . .	Mr. ABBOTT.
Lady Emily	. . .	Mrs. C. KEMBLE.
Mrs. Belmore	. . .	Mrs. FAUCIT.
Miss Fitzharding	. . .	Miss FOOTE.

The plot is as follows : Lady Emily, a young widow supposed to possess every amiable quality of body and mind, has for her intimate friend Mrs. Belmore, who is also a widow, and engaged in a law-suit with Sir Henry Chomley, by which she is likely to lose her whole fortune. Sir Henry has by chance met Lady Emily at a masquerade, where he has become deeply enamoured of her figure, wit, and vivacity, without having ever seen her face; and having at length obtained information who she is, and where she resides, writes to her, soliciting an interview, and declaring the impression which her person

266

and conversation had made on his heart. Lady Emily being herself sincerely attached to Colonel O'Donolan, determines to convert the passion of Sir Henry to the advantage of her friend Mrs. Belmore; and as they have never seen each other, to introduce Mrs. Belmore to Sir Henry as Lady Emily: but, aware that Mrs. Belmore will not receive Sir Henry's addresses, whom she regards as her enemy, on account of the law-suit between them, she writes to Sir Henry that she will admit his visits, but that it must, for particular reasons, be under the assumed name of Grenville; and as Mr. Grenville, she prevails on Mrs. Belmore to receive him in the name of Lady Emily, assigning as her reason for this request, her fear of seeing him herself, lest the Colonel's jealousy should be excited. Several interviews take place between Sir Henry and Mrs. Belmore, who conceive so warm an attachment for each other, under their assumed characters, that when the widow's stratagem is discovered, they gladly agree to put an end to their law-suit by a matrimonial union. The other, and the most afflicting part of the plot, turns on a stratagem conceived by Lady Emily (who it must be allowed is fruitful in stratagems), to restore Fitzharding to his reason, and his daughter to his affections, both of which had been lost by the dishonourable conduct of Delaval, who had first seduced, and then deserted the lovely and unsuspecting Cicely Fitzharding.

All that is particularly good in this play arises from the mistakes and surprises produced by the double confusion of the names of the principal characters concerned in the Widow's Stratagem. The scene between Charles Kemble and Jones, when the former acquaints him with his success with the supposed Lady Emily, and in which Jones testifies a resentment against his rival as violent as it is in reality groundless, was in the true spirit of comedy. Jones's scene with the Widow Belmore (Mrs. Faucit), in which the mystery is cleared up to him, is also conceived and executed with great spirit and effect. The character which Jones represents, an Irish Colonel, is one of the most misplaced and absurd we remember to have seen, and the only excuse for whose blunders, rudeness, officiousness, and want of common sense, is (as far as we could learn), that he is a countryman of Lord Wellington. This is but an indifferent compliment to his Grace, and perhaps no great one to Colonel O'Donolan. There were two direct clap-traps aimed directly at the Duke's popularity, which did not take. The truth, we suspect, is, that his Lordship is not very popular at present in either of his two great characters, as liberator of Ferdinand VII. or as keeper of Louis XVIII. Charles Kemble played the part of Sir Henry Chomley with that gentlemanly ease, gaiety, and good nature, which always gain him the entire favour of the

267

audience in such characters. He indeed did as much for this play
as if it had been his own. Mrs. Faucit played Mrs. Belmore
exceedingly well. There was something that reminded us of a
jointure and a view to a second match in her whole look and air. We
cannot speak a word of praise of Mrs. C. Kemble's Lady Emily.
Neither her person nor her manner at all suited the character, nor the
description of it which is several times interlarded in the dialogue.
Her walk is not the fine lady; she is nearly the worst actress we
ever saw in the artificial *mimmine-pimmine* style of Miss Farren. We
hope she will discontinue such characters, and return to nature; or
she will make us forget her Lucy Lockitt, or what we should hope
never to forget, her acting in Julio in Deaf and Dumb.

There is a great deal of affectation of gentility, and a great deal of
real indecorum, in the comic dialogue of this play. The tragic part
is violent and vulgar in the extreme. Mr. Young is brought forward
as a downright common madman, just broke loose from a madhouse
at Richmond, and is going with a club to dash out the brains of his
daughter, Miss Foote, and her infant. This infant is no other than
a large wooden doll: it fell on the floor the other evening without
receiving any hurt, at which the audience laughed. This dreadful
interlude is taken, we suppose, from Mrs. Opie's tale of Father and
Daughter, of which we thought never to have heard or seen any thing
more. As the whole of this part is conceived without the smallest
poetical feeling, so Mr. Young did not contrive to throw one ray of
genius over it. Miss Foote behaved throughout very prettily,
dutifully and penitently; and in the last scene, where, to bring
back her father's senses, she is made to stand in a frame and to
represent her own portrait playing on the harp, she looked a
perfect picture.

GEORGE BARNWELL

The Examiner.   *December* 31, 1815.

George Barnwell has been acted as usual at both Theatres during
the Christmas week. Whether this is 'a custom more honoured in
the breach or the observance,' we shall not undertake to decide. But
there is one error on this subject which we wish to correct; which
is, that its defects arise from its being too natural. It is one of the
most improbable and purely arbitrary fictions we have ever seen.
Lillo is by some people considered as a kind of natural Shakespear,
and Shakespear as a poetical Lillo. We look upon Shakespear to
have been a greater man than the Ordinary of Newgate; and we

268

at the same time conceive that there is not any one of the stories in the Newgate Calendar so badly told as this tragedy of Lillo's. Lillo seems to have proceeded on the old Scotch proverb,

'The kirk is gude, and the gallows is gude.'

He comes with his moral lessons and his terrible examples; a sermon in the morning and an execution at night; the tolling of the bell for Tyburn follows hard upon the bell that knolls to church. Nothing can be more virtuous or prudent than George Barnwell at the end of the first act, or a more consummate rogue and fool than he is at the beginning of the second. This play is a piece of wretched cant; it is an insult on the virtues and the vices of human nature; it supposes that the former are relinquished and the others adopted without common sense or reason, for the sake of a Christmas catastrophe, of a methodistical moral. The account of a young unsuspecting man being seduced by the allurements of an artful prostitute is natural enough, and something might have been built on this foundation, but all the rest is absurd, and equally senseless as poetry or prose. It is a caricature on the imbecility of goodness, and of the unprovoked and gratuitous depravity of vice. Shakespear made 'these odds more even;' that is, he drew from nature, and did not drag the theatre into the service of the conventicle. George Barnwell first robs his master at Milwood's instigation: (this lady has the merit of being what Dr. Johnson would have called 'a good hater'). He then, being in want of money, proceeds to rob and murder somebody; and in the way of deliberation and selection fixes upon his uncle, his greatest friend and benefactor, as if he were the only man in the world who carried a purse. He therefore goes to seek him in his solitary walks, where, good man, he is reading a book on the short-ness and uncertainty of human life, bursting out, as he reads, into suitable comments, which, as his ungracious nephew, who watches behind him in crape, says, shews that 'he is the fitter for heaven.' Well, he turns round, and sees that he is way-laid by some one; but his nephew, at the sight of his benign and well-known aspect, drops the pistol, but presently after stabs him to the heart. This is no sooner effected without remorse or pity, but the instant it is over, he loses all thought of the purpose which had instigated him to the act, the securing his property (not that it appears he had any about him), and this raw, desperate convert to vice returns to his mistress, to say that he had committed the murder, and omitted the robbery. On being questioned as to the *proceeds* of so nefarious a business, our retro-spective enthusiast asks, 'Could he lay sacrilegious hands on the body he had just murdered?' to which his cooler and more rational accomplice replies, 'That as he had robbed him of his life, which was no doubt precious to him, she did not see why he should not rifle his pockets of that which, being dead, could be of no farther use to him.' However, Barnwell makes such a noise with his virtue and his penitence, that she is alarmed for the consequences; and anticipating a discovery of the whole, calls in the constable, and gives up her companion as a measure of precaution. Her maid, however, who is her confidante, has been before-hand with her, and she is also taken into custody, and both are hanged. Such is the morality of this piece.

THE BUSY BODY

The Examiner.   *January* 7, 1816.

The admirable Comedy of the Busy Body was brought out at Drury-Lane Theatre on Wednesday, for the purpose of introducing Mrs. Mardyn in Miranda. She acted the part very delightfully, and without at all overdoing it. We seem to regret her former luxuriance of manner, and think she might take greater liberties with the public, without offence. Though she has lost some of the heyday vivacity of her natural spirits, she looks as charmingly as ever.

Mr. Dowton's Gripe was not one of his best performances. It is very much a character of grimace, and Munden perhaps would do it better on this account, for he is the greatest caricaturist on the stage. It was the character in which he originally appeared. We never saw him in it, but in several parts we missed his broad shining face, the orbicular rolling of his eye, and the alarming drop of his chin. Mr. Dowton, however, gave the whining tones and the dotage of fondness very well, and 'his voice pipes and whistles in the sound, like second childishness.' If any thing, he goes too far in this, and drawls out his ecstasies too much into the tabernacle sing-song.

Mr. Harley played Marplot in a very lively and amusing manner. He presented a very laughable picture of blundering vivacity and blank stupidity. This gentleman is the most *moveable* actor on the stage. He runs faster and stops shorter than any body else. There was but one fault in his delineation of the character. The officious Marplot is a gentleman, a foolish one, to be sure; but Harley played it like a footman. We observed also, that when Mr. Harley got very deserved applause by his manner of strutting, and sidling, and twisting himself about in the last scene, where he fights, he continued to repeat the same gestures over again, as if he had been *encored* by the audience.

We cannot close these remarks, without expressing the satisfaction which we received from this play. It is not so profound in wit or character as some other of the old Comedies, but it is nothing but bustle and gaiety from beginning to end. The plot never ceases. The ingenuity of contrivance is admirable. The developement of the story is an uninterrupted series of what the French call *coups de théatre*, and the situations succeed one another like the changes of machinery in a pantomime. It is a true comic pantomime.

A lady of the name of Barnes has appeared in Desdemona at this Theatre. Her voice is powerful, her face is pretty, but her person is too *petite* and undignified for tragedy. Her conception of the part was good, and she gave to some of the scenes considerable feeling and effect; but who shall represent 'the divine Desdemona?'

Mr. Kean's Othello is his best character, and the highest effort of genius on the stage. We say this without any exception or reserve. Yet we wish it was better than it is. In parts, we think he rises as high as human genius can go: at other times, though powerful, the whole effort is thrown away in a wrong direction, and disturbs our idea of the character. There are some technical objections. Othello was tall; but that is nothing: he was black, but that is nothing. But he was not fierce, and that is every thing. It is only in the last agony of human suffering that he gives way to his rage and his despair, and it is in working his noble nature up to that extremity, that Shakespear has shewn his genius and his vast power over the human heart. It was in raising passion to its height, from the lowest beginnings and in spite of all obstacles, in shewing the conflict of the soul, the tug and war between love and hatred, rage, tenderness, jealousy, remorse, in laying open the strength and the weaknesses of human nature, in uniting sublimity of thought with the anguish of the keenest woe, in putting in motion all the springs and impulses which make up this our mortal being, and at last blending them in that noble tide of deep and sustained passion, impetuous, but majestic, 'that flows on to the Propontic and knows no ebb,' that the great excellence of Shakespear lay. Mr. Kean is in general all passion, all energy, all relentless will. He wants imagination, that faculty which contemplates events, and broods over feelings with a certain calmness and grandeur; his feelings almost always hurry on to action, and hardly ever repose upon themselves. He is too often in the highest key of passion, too uniformly on the verge of extravagance, too constantly on the rack. This does very well in certain characters, as Zanga or Bajazet, where there is merely a physical passion, a boiling of the blood to be expressed, but it is not so in the lofty-minded and generous Moor.

We make these remarks the more freely, because there were parts of the character in which Mr. Kean shewed the greatest sublimity and pathos, by laying aside all violence of action. For instance, the tone of voice in which he delivered the beautiful apostrophe, ' Then, oh, farewell ! ' struck on the heart like the swelling notes of some divine music, like the sound of years of departed happiness. Why not all so, or all that is like it ? why not speak the affecting passage —' I found not Cassio's kisses on her lips '—why not speak the last speech, in the same manner ? They are both of them, we do most strenuously contend, speeches of pure pathos, of thought, and feeling, and not of passion, venting itself in violence of action or gesture. Again, the look, the action, the expression of voice, with which he accompanied the exclamation, ' Not a jot, not a jot,' was perfectly heart-rending. His vow of revenge against Cassio, and his abandonment of his love for Desdemona, were as fine as possible. The whole of the third act had an irresistible effect upon the house, and indeed is only to be paralleled by the murder scene in Macbeth. Mr. Pope's Iago was better acted than usual, but he does not look the character. Mr. Holland's drunken scene was, as it always is, excellent.

A NEW WAY TO PAY OLD DEBTS

The Examiner.   *January* 14, 1816.

Massinger's play of A New Way to Pay Old Debts, which has been brought out at Drury-Lane Theatre to introduce Mr. Kean in the part of Sir Giles Overreach, must have afforded a rich treat to theatrical amateurs. There is something in a good play well acted, a peculiar charm, that makes us forget ourselves and all the world.

It has been considered as the misfortune of great talents for the stage, that they leave no record behind them, except that of vague rumour, and that the genius of a great actor perishes with him, ' leaving the world no copy.' This is a misfortune, or at least a mortifying reflection, to actors ; but it is, we conceive, an advantage to the stage. It leaves an opening to originality. The stage is always beginning anew ; the candidates for theatrical reputation are always setting out afresh, unincumbered by the affectation of the faults or excellences of their predecessors. In this respect, we conceive that the average quantity of dramatic talent remains more nearly the same than that in any other walk of art. In the other arts, (as

272

A VIEW OF THE ENGLISH STAGE

painting and poetry), it may be supposed that what has been well done already, by giving rise to endless vapid imitations, is an obstacle to what might be done hereafter: that the models or *chef d'œuvres* of art, where they are accumulated, choke up the path to excellence; and that the works of genius, where they can be rendered permanent, and transmitted from age to age, not only prevent, but render superfluous, future productions of the same kind. We have not, neither do we want, two Shakespears, two Miltons, two Raphaels, two Popes, any more than we require two suns in the same sphere. Even Miss O'Neill stands a little in the way (and it is paying her a great compliment to say so) of our recollections of Mrs. Siddons. But Mr. Kean is an excellent substitute for the memory of Garrick, whom we never saw! When an author dies, it is no matter, for his works remain. When a great actor dies, there is a void produced in society, a gap which requires to be filled up. Who does not go to see Kean? Who, if Garrick were alive, would go to see him? At least, either one or the other must have quitted the stage; 'For two at a time there's no mortal could bear.' Again, we know that Mr. Kean cannot have been spoiled by Garrick. He might indeed have been spoiled by Mr. Kemble or Mr. Cooke, but he fortunately has not. The stage is a place where genius is sure to come upon its legs in a generation or two. We cannot conceive of better actors than some of those we now have. In Comedy, Liston is as good as Edwin was when we were school-boys. We grant that we are deficient in genteel comedy; we have no fine gentlemen or ladies on the stage—nor off it. That which is merely artificial and local is a matter of mimicry, and must exist, to be well copied. Players, however, have little reason to complain of their hard-earned, short-lived popularity. One thunder of applause from pit, boxes, and galleries, is equal to a whole immortality of posthumous fame; and when we hear an actor whose modesty is equal to his merit, declare that he would like to see a dog wag his tail in approbation, what must he feel when he sets the whole house in a roar? Besides, Fame, as if their reputation had been entrusted to her alone, has been particularly careful of the renown of her theatrical favourites; she forgets one by one, and year by year, those who have been great lawyers, great statesmen, and great warriors in their day; but the name of Garrick still survives, with the works of Reynolds and of Johnson.

We do not know any one now-a-days, who could write Massinger's Comedy of A New Way to Pay Old Debts, though we do not believe that it was better acted at the time it was first brought out, than it is at present. We cannot conceive of any one's doing Mr. Kean's part of Sir Giles Overreach so well as himself. We have seen others in the part, superior in the look and costume, in hardened, clownish, rustic insensibility; but in the soul and spirit, no one equal to him. He is a truly great actor. This is one of his very best parts. He was not at a single fault. The passages which we remarked as particularly striking and original, were those where he expresses his surprise at his nephew's answers, 'His fortune swells him!—'Tis rank, he's married!' and again, where, after the exposure of his villanies, he calls to his accomplice Marall in a half-wheedling, half-terrific tone, 'Come hither Marall, come hither.' Though the speech itself is absurd and out of character, his manner of stopping when he is running at his foes, 'I'm feeble, some widow's curse hangs on my sword,' was exactly as if his arm had been suddenly withered, and his powers shrivelled up on the instant. The conclusion was quite overwhelming. Mr. Kean looked the part well, and his voice does not fail as it used to do. Mr. Munden's Marall was an admirable piece of acting, and produced some of the most complete comic contrasts we ever saw. He overdoes his parts sometimes, and sometimes gets into parts for which he is not fit: but he has a fine broad face and manner which tells all the world over. His manner of avoiding the honour of a salute from the Lady Allworth, was a most deliberate piece of humour; and the account of the unexpected good fortune of young Welborn almost converts his eyes into saucers, and chokes him with surprise.

Mr. Oxberry's Justice Greedy was very entertaining, both from the subject and from his manner of doing it. Oxberry is a man of a practical imagination, and the apparitions of fat turkeys, chines of bacon, and pheasants dressed in toast and butter, evidently floated in rapturous confusion before his senses. There is nothing that goes down better than what relates to eating and drinking, on the stage, in books, or in real life. Mr. Harley's Welborn was indifferent, but he is upon the whole a very pleasant actor. Mrs. Glover, as Lady Allworth, puts on some very agreeable frowns; and Mr. Holland's Lord Lovell was one continued smile, without any meaning that we could discover, unless this actor, after his disguise in the Beggar's Bush, was delighted with the restoration of his hat and feather.

THE MIDSUMMER NIGHT'S DREAM

The Examiner.   *January* 21, 1816.

We hope we have not been accessory to murder, in recommending a delightful poem to be converted into a dull pantomime; for such is the fate of the Midsummer Night's Dream. We have found to our cost, once for all, that the regions of fancy and the boards of Covent-Garden are not the same thing. All that is fine in the play, was lost in the representation. The spirit was evaporated, the genius was fled; but the spectacle was fine: it was that which saved the play-Oh, ye scene-shifters, ye scene-painters, ye machinists and dress-makers, ye manufacturers of moon and stars that give no light, ye musical composers, ye men in the orchestra, fiddlers and trumpeters and players on the double drum and loud bassoon, rejoice! This is your triumph; it is not ours: and ye full-grown, well-fed, substantial, real fairies, Messieurs Treby, and Truman, and Atkins, and Misses Matthews, Carew, Burrell, and Mac Alpine, we shall remember you: we shall believe no more in the existence of your fantastic tribe. Flute the bellows-mender, Snug the joiner, Starveling the tailor, farewell! you have lost the charm of your names; but thou, Nic Bottom, thou valiant Bottom, what shall we say to thee? Thou didst console us much; thou didst perform a good part well; thou didst top the part of Bottom the weaver! He comes out of thy hands as clean and clever a fellow as ever. Thou art a person of exquisite whim and humour; and thou didst hector over thy companions well, and fall down flat before the Duke, like other bullies, well; and thou didst sing the song of the Black Ousel well; but chief, thou didst noddle thy ass's head, which had been put upon thee, well; and didst seem to say, significantly, to thy new attendants, Peaseblossom, Cobweb, Moth, and Mustard-seed, 'Gentlemen, I can present you equally to my friends, and to my enemies!'[1]

All that was good in this piece (except the scenery) was Mr. Liston's Bottom, which was an admirable and judicious piece of acting. Mr. Conway was Theseus. Who would ever have taken this gentleman for the friend and companion of Hercules? Miss Stephens played the part of Hermia, and sang several songs very delightfully, which however by no means assisted the progress or interest of the story. Miss Foote played Helena. She is a very sweet girl, and not at all a bad actress; yet did any one feel or even hear her address to Hermia? To shew how far asunder the closet and the stage are, we give it here once more entire:

> 'Injurious Hermia, most ungrateful maid,
> Have you conspired, have you with these contriv'd
> To bait me with this foul derision?
> Is all the counsel that we two have shar'd,

---

[1] What Louis xviii. said to his new National Guards.

> The sisters' vows, the hours that we have spent,
> When we have chid the hasty-footed time
> For parting us—Oh! and is all forgot?
> All school days' friendship, childhood innocence?
> We, Hermia, like two artificial Gods,
> Created with our needles both one flower,
> Both on one sampler, sitting on one cushion;
> Both warbling of one song, both in one key;
> As if our hands, our sides, voices and minds,
> Had been incorporate. So we grew together,
> Like to a double cherry, seeming parted,
> But yet an union in partition.
> And will you rend our ancient love asunder,
> And join with men in scorning your poor friend?
> It is not friendly, 'tis not maidenly:
> Our sex as well as I may chide you for it,
> Though I alone do feel the injury.'

In turning to Shakespear to look for this passage, the book opened at the Midsummer Night's Dream, the title of which half gave us back our old feeling; and in reading this one speech twice over, we have completely forgot all the noise we have heard and the sights we have seen. Poetry and the stage do not agree together. The attempt to reconcile them fails not only of effect, but of decorum. The *ideal* has no place upon the stage, which is a picture without perspective; every thing there is in the foreground. That which is merely an airy shape, a dream, a passing thought, immediately becomes an unmanageable reality. Where all is left to the imagination, every circumstance has an equal chance of being kept in mind, and tells according to the mixed impression of all that has been suggested. But the imagination cannot sufficiently qualify the impressions of the senses. Any offence given to the eye is not to be got rid of by explanation. Thus Bottom's head in the play is a fantastic illusion, produced by magic spells: on the stage it is an ass's head, and nothing more; certainly a very strange costume for a gentleman to appear in. Fancy cannot be represented any more than a simile can be painted; and it is as idle to attempt it as to personate Wall or Moonshine. Fairies are not incredible, but fairies six feet high are so. Monsters are not shocking, if they are seen at a proper distance. When ghosts appear in mid-day, when apparitions stalk along Cheapside, then may the Midsummer Night's Dream be represented at Covent-Garden or at Drury-Lane; for we hear, that it is to be brought out there also, and that we have to undergo another crucifixion.

Mrs. Faucit played the part of Titania very well, but for one circumstance—that she is a woman. The only glimpse which we caught of the possibility of acting the imaginary scenes properly, was from the little girl who dances before the fairies (we do not know her name), which seemed to shew that the whole might be carried off in the same manner—by a miracle.

Drury-Lane.

The admirable comedy of a New Way to Pay Old Debts, continues to be acted with increased effect. Mr. Kean is received with shouts of applause in Sir Giles Overreach. We have heard two objections to his manner of doing this part, one of which we think right and the other not. When he is asked, 'Is he not moved by the orphan's tears, the widow's curse?' he answers—'Yes—as rocks by waves, or the moon by howling wolves.' Mr. Kean, in speaking the latter sentence, dashes his voice about with the greatest violence, and howls out his indignation and rage. Now we conceive this is wrong: for he has to express not violence, but firm, inflexible resistance to it,— not motion, but rest. The very pause after the word *yes*, points out the cool deliberate way in which it should be spoken. The other objection is to his manner of pronouncing the word 'Lord,—Right Honourable Lord,' which Mr. Kean uniformly does in a drawling tone, with a mixture of fawning servility and sarcastic contempt. This has been thought inconsistent with the part, and with the desire which Sir Giles has to ennoble his family by alliance with a 'Lord, a Right Honourable Lord.' We think Mr. Kean never shewed more genius than in pronouncing this single word, *Lord*. It is a complete exposure (produced by the violence of the character), of the elementary feelings which make up the common respect excited by mere rank. This is nothing but a cringing to power and opinion, with a view to turn them to our own advantage with the world. Sir Giles is one of those knaves, who 'do themselves homage.' He makes use of Lord Lovell merely as the stalking-horse of his ambition. In other respects, he has the greatest contempt for him, and the necessity he is under of paying court to him for his own purposes, infuses a double portion of gall and bitterness into the expression of his self-conscious superiority. No; Mr. Kean was perfectly right in this, he spoke the word 'Lord' *con amore*. His praise of the kiss, 'It came twanging off—I like it,' was one of his happiest passages. It would perhaps be as well, if in the concluding scene he would contrive not to frighten the ladies into hysterics. But the whole together is admirable.

A VIEW OF THE ENGLISH STAGE

LOVE FOR LOVE

The Examiner.   *January* 28, 1816.

Congreve's Comedy of Love for Love is, in wit and elegance, perhaps inferior to the Way of the World; but it is unquestionably the best-acting of all his plays. It abounds in dramatic situation, in incident, in variety of character. Still (such is the power of good writing) we prefer reading it in the closet, to seeing it on the stage. As it was acted the other night at Drury-Lane Theatre, many of the finest traits of character were lost. Though Love for Love is much less a tissue of epigrams than his other plays, the author has not been able to keep his wit completely under. Jeremy is almost as witty and learned as his master.—The part which had the greatest effect in the acting was Munden's Foresight. We hardly ever saw a richer or more powerful piece of comic acting. It was done to the life, and indeed somewhat over; but the effect was irresistible. His look was planet-struck, his dress and appearance like one of the signs of the Zodiac taken down. We never saw any thing more bewildered. Parsons, if we remember right, gave more imbecility, more of the doating garrulity of age, to the part, and blundered on with a less determined air of stupidity.—Mr. Dowton did not make much of Sir Sampson Legend. He looked well, like a hale, hearty old gentleman, with a close bob-wig, and bronze complexion;—but that was all. We were very much amused with Mr. Harley's *Tattle*. His indifference in the scene where he breaks off his engagement with Miss Prue, was very entertaining. In the scene in which he teaches her how to make love, he was less successful: he delivered his lessons to his fair disciple with the air of a person giving good advice, and did not seem to have a proper sense of his good fortune. 'Desire to please, and you will infallibly please,' is an old maxim, and Mr. Harley is an instance of the truth of it. This actor is always in the best possible humour with himself and the audience. He is as happy as if he had jumped into the very part which he liked the best of all others. Mr. Rae, on the contrary, who played Valentine, apparently feels as little satisfaction as he communicates. He always acts with an air of injured excellence.

Mrs. Mardyn's Miss Prue was not one of her most successful characters. It was a little hard and coarse. It was not fond and yielding enough. Miss Prue is made of the most susceptible materials. She played the hoydening parts best, as where she cries out, 'School's up, school's up!'—and she knocked off Mr. Bartley's hat with great good-will.—Mr. Bartley was Ben; and we confess we think Miss Prue's distaste to him very natural. We cannot make up

278

our minds to like this actor; and yet we have no fault to find with him. For instance, he played the character of Ben very properly; that is, just like 'a great sea-porpoise.' There is an art of qualifying such a part in a manner to carry off its disagreeableness, which Mr. Bartley wants.—Mrs. Harlowe's Mrs. Frail was excellent: she appeared to be the identical Mrs. Frail, with all her airs of mincing affectation, and want of principle. The character was seen quite in dishabille. The scene between her and her sister Mrs. Foresight, about the discovery of the pin—'And pray sister where did you find that pin?'—was managed with as much coolness as any thing of this sort that ever happened in real life.—Mrs. Orger played Mrs. Foresight with much ease and natural propriety. She in general reposes too much on her person, and does not display all the animation of which the character is susceptible. She is also too much in female parts, what the *walking fine gentleman* of the stage used to be in male. Mr. Barnard played Jeremy with a smart shrug in his shoulders, and the trusty air of a valet in his situation.

THE ANGLADE FAMILY

The Examiner.   *February* 4, 1816.

The well known collection of French trials, under the title of *Causes Celebres*, has served as the ground-work of a new piece, brought out on Thursday at Drury-Lane Theatre, called Accusation, or The Anglade Family. The old historical materials are rather scanty, consisting only of a narrative of a robbery committed on a nobleman by some members of his own household, for which a M. D'Anglade, who with his family occupied part of the same hotel, was condemned on false evidence to the gallies, where grief and mortification put a period to his life before his innocence was discovered. On this foundation an interesting drama has been raised by the French author. M. Valmore is introduced as a lover of Madame D'Anglade, who rejects his unlawful passion. In revenge, he agrees with a worthless valet to rob his aunt, who resides under the same roof with the family of M. D'Anglade, in whose hands part of the stolen property (consisting of bank-notes—a trifling anachronism) is treacherously deposited by an accomplice of Hubert, Valmore's servant, under pretence of paying for jewels which D'Anglade is compelled to dispose of to satisfy the demands made upon him by a relation who was supposed to have been dead, and whose estate he had inherited. He is seized under strong circum-

279

stances of suspicion by the police, and conveyed to prison; but the agents of Valmore are detected in stealing away with part of the property from the place where it had been secreted: they are stopped separately by the domestics of the injured person—each is made to believe that his accomplice has betrayed him—and on the manifestation of D'Anglade's innocence and of his own guilt, Valmore, unable to escape the pursuit of the officers of justice, puts an end to his existence with a pistol, in a summer-house in which he has in vain tried to conceal himself.

The interest excited is much of the same kind as in the Maid and the Magpye: and we think the piece will be almost as great a favourite with the public. There is a great deal of ingenuity shewn in the developement of the plot; the scenic effect is often beautiful, and the situations have real pathos.

The acting was upon the whole excellent. Miss Kelly, as the wife of the unfortunate D'Anglade, gave a high degree of interest to the story. She was only less delightful in this character than in that of the Maid of Paliseau, because she has less to do in it. Mr. Rae was the hero of the present drama, and he acquitted himself in it with considerable applause. We never saw Mr. Bartley to so much advantage as in the rough, honest character of the relation of D'Anglade, (we forget the name), who comes to claim restitution of his fortune, to try the integrity of his old friend, but who generously offers him his assistance as soon as he finds him plunged in distress. Mr. Wallack was Valmore, and there was a scene of really fine acting between him and Mrs. Glover, (the Countess of Servan, his aunt), where she tries to probe the guilty conscience of her nephew, and to induce him to release D'Anglade from his dangerous situation, by a confession of the treachery of which he has been made the victim. Mr. S. Penley played the part of the unprincipled valet very unexceptionably, and Mr. Barnard made an admirable accomplice, in the character of a strolling Italian musician. Knight, as the raw country lad by whose means the plot is chiefly discovered, was as natural as he always is in such characters. He perhaps has got too much of a habit of expressing his joy by running up and down the stage with his arms spread out like a pair of wings. Mr. Powell, as the faithful old servant of the Anglade family, was highly respectable. One sentiment in the play, 'The woman who follows her husband to a prison, to share or to alleviate his misfortunes, is an ornament to her sex, and an honour to human nature,' was highly applauded—we do not know for what particular reason.[1]

[1] It was about this time that Madame Lavalette assisted her husband to escape from prison.

A VIEW OF THE ENGLISH STAGE

Covent-Garden.

The same drama has been abridged and brought out here as an After-piece. We cannot speak highly of the alteration. The senti-mental French romance is cut down into an English farce, in which both the interest of the story and the *naiveté* of the characters are lost. The two characters of the Valet and the Italian stroller are confounded in the same person, and played by Mathews, who is death to the pathetic! Charles Kemble played the Count D'Anglade in a very gentlemanly manner. Farley was the most turbulent Valet we have ever seen.

MEASURE FOR MEASURE

The Examiner.   *February* 11, 1816.

In the 'Lectures on Dramatic Literature by William Schlegel,' the German translator of Shakespear, is the following criticism on Measure for Measure, which has been just acted at Covent-Garden Theatre: 'In Measure for Measure, Shakespear was compelled, by the nature of the subject, to make his poetry more familiar with criminal justice than is usual with him. All kinds of proceedings connected with the subject, all sorts of active or passive persons, pass in review before us; the hypocritical Lord Deputy, the compassionate Provost, and the hard-hearted Hangman; a young man of quality who is to suffer for the seduction of his mistress before marriage, loose wretches brought in by the police, nay, even a hardened criminal whom the preparations for his execution cannot awake out of his callousness. But yet, notwithstanding this convincing truth, how tenderly and mildly the whole is treated! The piece takes improperly its name from the punishment: the sense of the whole is properly the triumph of mercy over strict justice, no man being him-self so secure from errors as to be entitled to deal it out among his equals. The most beautiful ornament of the composition is the character of Isabella, who, in the intention of taking the veil, allows herself to be again prevailed on by pious love to tread the perplexing ways of the world, while the heavenly purity of her mind is not even stained with one unholy thought by the general corruption. In the humble robes of the novice of a nunnery, she is a true angel of light. When the cold and hitherto unsullied Angelo, whom the Duke has commissioned to restrain the excess of dissolute immorality by a rigid administration of the laws during his pretended absence, is even him-self tempted by the virgin charms of Isabella, as she supplicates for

281

A VIEW OF THE ENGLISH STAGE

her brother Claudio; when he first insinuates, in timid and obscure language, but at last impudently declares his readiness to grant the life of Claudio for the sacrifice of her honour; when Isabella repulses him with a noble contempt; when she relates what has happened to her brother, and the latter at first applauds her, but at length, overpowered by the dread of death, wishes to persuade her to consent to her dishonour; in these masterly scenes Shakespear has sounded the depth of the human heart. The interest here reposes altogether on the action; curiosity constitutes no part of our delight; for the Duke, in the disguise of a monk, is always present to watch over his dangerous representatives, and to avert every evil which could possibly be apprehended: we look here with confidence to the solemn decision. The Duke acts the part of the Monk naturally, even to deception; he unites in his person the wisdom of the priest and the prince. His wisdom is merely too fond of roundabout ways; his vanity is flattered with acting invisibly like an earthly providence; he is more entertained with overhearing his subjects than governing them in the customary manner. As he at last extends pardon to all the guilty, we do not see how his original purpose of restoring the strictness of the laws by committing the execution of them to other hands, has been in any wise accomplished. The poet might have had this irony in view—that of the numberless slanders of the Duke, told him by the petulant Lucio, without knowing the person to whom he spoke, what regarded his singularities and whims was not wholly without foundation.

'It is deserving of remark, that Shakespear, amidst the rancour of religious parties, takes a delight in representing the condition of a monk, and always represents his influence as beneficial. We find in him none of the black and knavish monks, which an enthusiasm for the Protestant Religion, rather than poetical inspiration, has suggested to some of our modern poets. Shakespear merely gives his monks an inclination to busy themselves in the affairs of others, after renouncing the world for themselves; with respect, however, to privy frauds, he does not represent them as very conscientious. Such are the parts acted by the Monk in Romeo and Juliet, and another in Much ado about Nothing, and even by the Duke, whom, contrary to the well known proverb, "the cowl seems really to make a monk."' Vol. ii. p. 169.

This is, we confess, a very poor criticism on a very fine play; but we are not in the humour (even if we could) to write a better. A very obvious beauty, which has escaped the critic, is the admirable description of life, as poetical as it is metaphysical, beginning, 'If I do lose thee, I do lose a thing,' &c. to the truth and justice of which

282

Claudio assents, contrasted almost immediately afterwards with his
fine description of death as the worst of ills:

> 'To lie in cold obstruction, and to rot;
> This sensible warm motion to become
> A kneaded clod, and the delighted spirit
> To bathe in fiery floods, or to reside
> In thrilling regions of thick-ribbed ice.
> —————— 'Tis too horrible!
> The weariest and most loathed worldly life
> That age, ache, penury, imprisonment,
> Can lay on nature, is a paradise
> To what we fear of death.'—

Neither has he done justice to the character of Master Barnardine,
one of the finest (and that's saying a bold word) in all Shakespear.
He calls him a hardened criminal. He is no such thing. He is
what he is by nature, not by circumstance, 'careless, reckless, and
fearless of past, present, and to come.' He is Caliban transported to
the forests of Bohemia, or the prisons of Vienna. He has, however,
a sense of the natural fitness of things: 'He has been drinking hard
all night, and he will not be hanged that day,' and Shakespear has
let him off at last. Emery does not play it well, for Master
Barnardine is not the representative of a Yorkshireman, but of an
universal class in nature. We cannot say that the Clown Pompey
suffered in the hands of Mr. Liston; on the contrary, he played it
inimitably well. His manner of saying 'a dish of some three-pence'
was worth any thing. In the scene of his examination before the
Justice, he delayed, and dallied, and dangled in his answers, in the
true spirit of the genius of his author.

We do not understand why the philosophical critic, whom we have
quoted above, should be so severe on those pleasant persons Lucio,
Pompey, and Master Froth, as to call them 'wretches.' They seem
all mighty comfortable in their occupations, and determined to pursue
them, 'as the flesh and fortune should serve.' Shakespear was the
least moral of all writers; for morality (commonly so called) is made
up of antipathies, and his talent consisted in sympathy with human
nature, in all its shapes, degrees, elevations, and depressions. The
object of the pedantic moralist is to make the worst of every thing;
his was to make the best, according to his own principle, 'There is
some soul of goodness in things evil.' Even Master Barnardine is
not left to the mercy of what others think of him, but when he comes
in, he speaks for himself. We would recommend it to the Society
for the Suppression of Vice to read Shakespear.

Mr. Young played the Duke tolerably well. As to the cant

introduced into Schlegel's account of the Duke's assumed character of a Monk, we scout it altogether. He takes advantage of the good-nature of the poet to impose on the credulity of mankind. Chaucer spoke of the Monks historically, Shakespear poetically. It was not in the nature of Shakespear to insult over 'the enemies of the human race' just after their fall. We however object to them entirely in this age of the revival of Inquisitions and Protestant massacres. We have not that stretch of philosophical comprehension which, in German metaphysics, unites popery and free-thinking together, loyalty and regicide, and which binds up the Bible and Spinoza in the same volume!—Mr. Jones did not make a bad Lucio. Miss O'Neill's Isabella, though full of merit, disappointed us; as indeed she has frequently done of late. Her 'Oh fie, fie,' was the most spirited thing in her performance. She did not seize with much force the spirit of her author, but she seemed in complete possession of a certain conventicle twang. She whined and sang out her part in that querulous tone that has become unpleasant to us by ceaseless repetition. She at present plays all her parts in the Magdalen style. We half begin to suspect that she represents the bodies, not the souls of women, and that her *forte* is in tears, sighs, sobs, shrieks, and hysterics. She does not play either Juliet or Isabella finely. She must stick to the common-place characters of Otway, Moore, and Miss Hannah More, or she will ruin herself. As Sir Joshua Reynolds concluded his last lecture with the name of Michael Angelo, as Vetus wished the name of the Marquis Wellesley to conclude his last letter, so we will conclude this article with a devout apostrophe to the name of Mrs. Siddons.

MR. KEAN'S SIR GILES OVERREACH

The Examiner. *February* 18, 1816.

We saw Mr. Kean's Sir Giles Overreach on Friday night from the boxes at Drury-Lane Theatre, and are not surprised at the incredulity as to this great actor's powers, entertained by those persons who have only seen him from that elevated sphere. We do not hesitate to say, that those who have only seen him at that distance, have not seen him at all. The expression of his face is quite lost, and only the harsh and grating tones of his voice produce their full effect on the ear. The same recurring sounds, by dint of repetition, fasten on the attention, while the varieties and finer modulations are lost in their passage over the pit. All you discover is an abstraction of his defects, both of person, voice, and manner. He appears to be a little man in a great passion. The accompaniment of expression is

284

absolutely necessary to explain his tones and gestures : and the outline which he gives of the character, in proportion as it is bold and
decided, requires to be filled up and modified by all the details of
execution. Without seeing the workings of his face, through which
you read the movements of his soul, and anticipate their violent effects
on his utterance and action, it is impossible to understand or feel
pleasure in the part. All strong expression, deprived of its gradations and connecting motives, unavoidably degenerates into caricature.
This was the effect uniformly produced on those about us, who kept
exclaiming, 'How extravagant, how odd,' till the last scene, where
the extreme and admirable contrasts both of voice and gesture in
which Mr. Kean's genius shews itself, and which are in their nature
more obviously intelligible, produced a change of opinion in his favour.

As a proof of what we have above advanced, it was not possible to
discover in the last scene, where he is lifted from the ground by the
attendants, and he rivets his eyes in dreadful despair upon his daughter,
whether they were open or closed. The action of advancing to the
middle of the stage, and his faultering accent in saying, 'Marall,
come hither, Marall,' could not be mistaken. The applause, however,
came almost constantly from those who were near the orchestra, and
circulated in eddies round the house. It is unpleasant to see a play
from the boxes. There is no part of the house which is so thoroughly
wrapped up in itself, and fortified against any impression from what
is passing on the stage ; which seems so completely weaned from all
superstitious belief in dramatic illusion ; which takes so little interest
in all that is interesting. Not a cravat nor a muscle was discomposed,
except now and then by some gesticulation of Mr. Kean, which
violated the decorum of fashionable indifference, or by some expression
of the author, two hundred years old. Mr. Kean's acting is not, we
understand, much relished in the upper circles. It is thought too
obtrusive and undisguised a display of nature. Neither was Garrick's
at all relished at first, by the old Nobility, till it became the fashion
to admire him. The court dresses, the drawing-room strut, and the
sing-song declamation, which he banished from the stage, were
thought much more dignified and imposing.

THE RECRUITING OFFICER

The Examiner.   *March* 3, 1816.

Farquhar's Comedy of the Recruiting Officer was revived at Drury-
Lane Theatre on Tuesday, when Mrs. Mardyn appeared as Sylvia.
She looked very charmingly in it while she continued in her female

dress, and displayed some good acting, particularly in the scene where Plume gives her his will to read; but we did not like her at all as Young Wilful, with her jockey coat, breeches, and boots. Her dress seemed as if contrived on purpose to hide the beauties of her natural shape, and discover its defects. A woman in Hessian boots can no more move gracefully under such an additional and unusual incumbrance to her figure, than a man could with a clog round each leg. We hope that she will re-cast her male attire altogether, if she has not already done it. The want of vivacity and elegance in her appearance gave a flatness to the latter part of the comedy, which was not relieved by the circumstance of Mr. Rae's forgetting his part. We do not think he played the airy, careless, lively Captain Plume well; and Mr. Harley did not play *Captain* Brazen, but *Serjeant* Brazen. Johnstone's Serjeant Kite was not very happy. Johnstone's impudence is good-humoured and natural, Serjeant Kite's is knavish impudence. Johnstone is not exactly fitted for any character, the failings of which do not lean to the amiable side. There was one speech which entirely suited him, and that was where he says to his Captain, ' The mob are so pleased with your Honour, and the justices and better sort of people are so delighted with me, that we shall soon do our business! ' Munden's Costar Pearmain, and Knight's Thomas Appletree, were a double treat. Knight's fixed, rivetted look at the guinea, accompanied with the exclamation, ' Oh the wonderful works of Nature! ' and Munden's open-mouthed, reeling wonder, were in the best style of broad comic acting. If any thing, this scene was even surpassed by that in which Munden, after he has listed with Plume, makes his approximations to his friend, who is whimpering, and casting at him a most inviting ogle, with an expression of countenance all over oily and lubricated, emphatically ejaculates, ' Well, Tummy! ' We have no wish to see better acting than this. This actor has won upon our good opinion, and we here retract openly all that we have said disrespectfully of his talents, generally speaking. Miss Kelly's Rose was played *con amore ;* it was an exquisite exhibition of rustic *naiveté.* Her riding on the basket as a side-saddle, was very spirited and well contrived. Passion expresses itself in such characters by a sort of uneasy bodily vivacity, which no actress gives so well as Miss Kelly. We ought not to omit, that she cries her chickens in a good shrill huswifely market-voice, as if she would drive a good bargain with them. Mr. Powell played Justice Balance as well as if he had been the Justice himself.

The Recruiting Officer is not one of Farquhar's best comedies, though it is lively and entertaining. It contains merely sketches of characters, and the conclusion of the plot is rather lame. He informs us in the dedication to the published play, that it was founded on some local and personal circumstances that happened in Shropshire, where he was a recruiting officer, and it seems not unlikely that most of the scenes actually took place near the foot of the Wrekin.

THE FAIR PENITENT

The Examiner.   *(Covent-Garden) March* 10, 1816.

The Fair Penitent is a tragedy which has been found fault with both on account of its poetry and its morality. Notwithstanding these objections, it still holds possession of the stage, where morality is not very eagerly sought after, and poetry but imperfectly understood. We conceive, that for every purpose of practical criticism, that is a good tragedy which draws tears without moving laughter. Rowe's play is founded on one of Massinger's, the Fatal Dowry, in which the characters are a good deal changed, and the interest not increased. The genius of Rowe was slow and timid, and loved the ground: he had not 'a Muse of fire to ascend the brightest heaven of invention:' but he had art and judgment enough to accommodate the more daring flights of a ruder age to the polished well-bred mediocrity of the age he lived in. We may say of Rowe as Voltaire said of Racine: 'All his lines are equally good.' The compliment is after all equivocal; but it is one which may be applied generally to all poets, who in their productions are always thinking of what they shall say, and of what others have said, and who are never hurried into excesses of any kind, good or bad, by trusting implicitly to the impulse of their own genius or of the subject. The excellent author of Tom Jones, in one of his introductory chapters, represents Rowe as an awkward imitator of Shakespear. He was rather an imitator of the style and tone of sentiment of that age,—a sort of modernizer of antiquity. The character of Calista is quite in the *bravura* style of Massinger. She is a heroine, a virago, fair, a woman of high spirit and violent resolutions, any thing but a penitent. She dies indeed at last, not from remorse for her vices, but because she can no longer gratify them. She has not the slightest regard for her virtue, and not much for her reputation; but she would brand with scorn, and blast with the lightning of her indignation, the friend who wishes to stop her in the career of her passions in order to save her from destruction and infamy. She has a strong sentiment of respect and attachment to her father, but she will sooner consign his grey hairs to shame and death

287

than give up the least of her inclinations, or sacrifice her sullen gloom to the common decencies of behaviour. She at last pretends conversion from her errors, in a soft whining address to her husband, and after having deliberately and wantonly done all the mischief in her power, with her eyes open, wishes that she had sooner known better, that she might have acted differently! We do not however for ourselves object to the morality of all this: for we apprehend that morality is little more than truth; and we think that Rowe has given a very true and striking picture of the nature and consequences of that wilful selfishness of disposition, 'which to be hated needs but to be seen.' We do not think it necessary that the spectator should wait for the reluctant conversion of the character itself, to be convinced of its odiousness or folly, or that the only instruction to be derived from the drama is, not from the insight it gives us into the nature of human character and passion, but from some artificial piece of patch-work morality tacked to the end. However, Rowe has so far complied with the rules.

After what we have said of the character of Calista, Miss O'Neill will perhaps excuse us if we do not think that she was a very perfect representative of it. The character, as she gave it, was a very fine and impressive piece of acting, but it was not quite Calista. She gave the pathos, but not the spirit of the character. Her grief was sullen and sad, not impatient and ungovernable. Calista's melancholy is not a settled dejection, but a feverish state of agitation between conflicting feelings. Her eyes should look bright and sparkling through her tears. Her action should be animated and aspiring. Her present woes should not efface the traces of past raptures. There should be something in her appearance of the intoxication of pleasure, mixed with the madness of despair. The scene in which Miss O'Neill displayed most power, was that in which she is shewn her letter to Lothario by Horatio, her husband's friend. The rage and shame with which her bosom seemed labouring were truly dreadful. This is the scene in which the poet has done most for the imagination, and it is the characteristic excellence of Miss O'Neill's acting, that it always rises with the expectations of the audience. She also repeated the evasive answer, 'It was the day in which my father gave my hand to Altamont—as such I shall remember it for ever,' in a tone of deep and suppressed emotion. It is needless to add, that she played the part with a degree of excellence which no other actress could approach, and that she was only inferior to herself in it, because there is not the same opportunity for the display of her inimitable powers, as in some of her other characters.

A VIEW OF THE ENGLISH STAGE

THE DUKE OF MILAN

The Examiner.   *March* 17, 1816.

We do not think the Duke of Milan will become so great a favourite as Sir Giles Overreach, at Drury-Lane Theatre. The first objection to this play is, that it is an arbitrary falsification of history. There is nothing in the life of Sforza, the supposed hero of the piece, to warrant the account of the extravagant actions and tragical end which are here attributed to him, to say nothing of political events. In the second place, his resolution to destroy his wife, to whom he is passionately attached, rather than bear the thought of her surviving him, is as much out of the verge of nature and probability, as it is unexpected and revolting from the want of any circumstances of palliation leading to it. It stands out alone, a piece of pure voluntary atrocity, which seems not the dictate of passion but a start of phrenzy. From the first abrupt mention of this design to his treacherous accomplice, Francesco, he loses the favour, and no longer excites the sympathy of the audience. Again, Francesco is a person whose actions we are at a loss to explain, till the last act of the piece, when the attempt to account for them from motives originally amiable and generous, only produces a double sense of incongruity, and instead of satisfying the mind, renders it totally incredulous. He endeavours to debauch the wife of his benefactor, he then attempts her death, slanders her foully, and wantonly causes her to be slain by the hand of her husband, and has him poisoned by a deliberate stratagem ; and all this to appease a high sense of injured honour, ' which felt a stain like a wound,' and from the tender overflowings of fraternal affection ; his sister having, it appears, been formerly betrothed to, and afterwards deserted by the Duke.

In the original play, the Duke is killed by a poison which is spread by Francesco over the face of the deceased Duchess, whose lips her husband fondly kisses, though cold in death, in the distracted state into which he is plunged by remorse for his rash act. But in the acted play, it is so contrived, that the sister of Francesco personates the murdered Duchess, and poisons the Duke (as it is concerted with her brother), by holding a flower in her hand, which, as he squeezes it, communicates the infection it has received from some juice in which it has been steeped. How he is to press the flower in her hand, in such a manner as not to poison her as well as himself, is left unexplained. The lady, however, does not die, and a reconciliation takes place between her and her former lover.

We hate these sickly sentimental endings, without any meaning in them.

The peculiarity of Massinger's vicious characters seems in general to be, that they are totally void of moral sense, and have a gloating pride and disinterested pleasure in their villanies, unchecked by the common feelings of humanity. Francesco, in the present play, holds it out to the last, defies his enemies, and is 'proud to die what he was born.' At other times, after the poet has carried on one of these hardened unprincipled characters for a whole play, he is seized with a sudden qualm of conscience, and his villain is visited with a judicial remorse. This is the case with Sir Giles Overreach, whose hand is restrained in the last extremity of his rage by 'some widow's curse that hangs upon it,' and whose heart is miraculously melted 'by orphan's tears.' We will not, however, deny that such may be a true picture of the mixed barbarity and superstition of the age in which Massinger wrote. We have no doubt that his Sir Giles Overreach, which some have thought an incredible exaggeration, was an actual portrait. Traces of such characters are still to be found in some parts of the country, and in classes to which modern refinement and modern education have not penetrated;—characters that not only make their own selfishness and violence the sole rule of their actions, but triumph in the superiority which their want of feeling and of principle gives them over their opponents or dependants. In the time of Massinger, philosophy had made no progress in the minds of country gentlemen: nor had the theory of moral sentiments, in the community at large, been fashioned and moulded into shape by systems of ethics continually pouring in upon us from the Universities of Glasgow, Edinburgh, and Aberdeen. Persons in the situation, and with the dispositions of Sir Giles, cared not what wrong they did, nor what was thought of it, if they had only the power to maintain it. There is no calculating the advantages of civilization and letters, in taking off the hard, coarse edge of rusticity, and in softening social life. The vices of refined and cultivated periods are *personal* vices, such as proceed from too unrestrained a pursuit of pleasure in ourselves, not from a desire to inflict pain on others.

Mr. Kean's Sforza is not his most striking character; on the contrary, it is one of his least impressive, and least successful ones. The mad scene was fine, but we have seen him do better. The character is too much at cross-purposes with itself, and before the actor has time to give its full effect to any impulse of passion, it is interrupted and broken off by some caprice or change of object. In Mr. Kean's representation of it, our expectations were often excited, but never thoroughly satisfied, and we were teased with a sense of littleness in every part of it. It entirely wants the breadth, force, and grandeur of his Sir Giles.

One of the scenes, a view of the court-house at Milan, was most beautiful. Indeed, the splendour of the scenery and dresses frequently took away from the effect of Mr. Kean's countenance.

MISS O'NEILL'S LADY TEAZLE

The Examiner.   *March* 24, 1816.

Miss O'Neill's Lady Teazle at Covent-Garden Theatre appears to us to be a complete failure. It was not comic; it was not elegant; it was not easy; it was not dignified; it was not playful; it was not any thing that it ought to be. All that can be said of it is, that it was not tragedy. It seemed as if all the force and pathos which she displays in interesting situations had left her, but that not one spark of gaiety, one genuine expression of delight, had come in their stead. It was a piece of laboured heavy *still-life*. The only thing that had an air of fashion about her was the feather in her hat. It was not merely that she did not succeed as Miss O'Neill; it would have been a falling off in the most common-place actress who had ever done any thing tolerably. She gave to the character neither the complete finished air of fashionable indifference, which was the way in which Miss Farren played it, if we remember right, nor that mixture of artificial refinement and natural vivacity, which appears to be the true idea of the character (which however is not very well made out), but she seemed to have been thrust by some injudicious caprice of fortune, into a situation for which she was fitted neither by nature nor education. There was a perpetual affectation of the wit and the fine lady, with an evident conscious-ness of effort, a desire to please without any sense of pleasure. It was no better than awkward mimicry of the part, and more like a drawling imitation of Mrs. C. Kemble's genteel comedy than any thing else we have seen. The concluding penitential speech was an absolute sermon. We neither liked her manner of repeating 'Mimminee pimminee,' nor of describing the lady who rides round the ring in Hyde-park, nor of chucking Sir Peter under the chin, which was a great deal too coarse and familiar. There was throughout an equal want of delicacy and spirit, of ease and effect, of nature and art. It was in general flat and insipid, and where any thing more was attempted, it was overcharged and unpleasant.

Fawcett's Sir Peter Teazle was better than when we last saw it. He is an actor of much merit, but he has of late got into a strange way of slurring over his parts. Liston's Sir Benjamin Backbite was not very successful. Charles Kemble played Charles Surface very delightfully.

Guy Mannering, or the Gipsey's Prophecy, taken from the novel of that name, and brought out at Covent-Garden, is a very pleasing romantic drama. It is, we understand, from the pen of Mr. Terry, and reflects much credit on his taste and talents. The scenes between Miss Stephens, Miss Matthews, and Mr. Abbott, as Lucy Bertram, Julia Mannering, and Colonel Mannering, have a high degree of elegance and interest. Mrs. Egerton's Meg Merrilees was equal in force and nature to her Miller's Wife; and we cannot pay it a higher compliment. It makes the blood run cold. Mr. Higman played the chief Gipsey very well, and nothing could be better represented than the unfeeling, shuffling tricks and knavish impudence of the Gipsey Boy, by Master Williams. Liston's Dominie Sampson was *prodigious*; his talents are *prodigious*. The appearance and the interest he gave to the part were quite patriarchal. The unconscious simplicity of the humour was exquisite; it will give us a better opinion of the Scotch Clergy, and almost of the Scotch nation (if that were possible) while we live.

MR. KEAN

The Examiner. *March* 31, 1816.

A chasm has been produced in the amusements of Drury-Lane Theatre by the accident which has happened to Mr. Kean. He was to have played the Duke of Milan on Tuesday, but as he had not come to the Theatre at the time of the drawing up of the curtain, Mr. Rae came forward to propose another tragedy, Douglas. To this the audience did not assent, and wished to wait. Mr. Kean, however, not appearing, nor any tidings being heard of him, he was at length given up, and two farces substituted in his stead. Conjectures and rumours were afloat; and it was not till the next day that it was discovered that Mr. Kean having dined a few miles in the country, and returning at a very quick pace to keep his engagement at the Theatre, was thrown out of his gig, and had his arm dislocated, besides being stunned and very much bruised with the fall. On this accident a grave morning paper is pleased to be facetious. It observes that this is a very *serious* accident; that actors in general are liable to *serious* accidents; that the late Mr. Cooke used to meet with *serious* accidents; that it is a sad thing to be in the way of such accidents; and that it is to be hoped that Mr. Kean will meet with no more *serious* accidents. It is to be hoped that he will not—nor with any such profound observations upon them, if they should happen. Next to that spirit of bigotry which in a neighbouring country would deny actors christian burial after death, we hate that cant of criticism, which slurs over their characters while living with a half-witted jest. Actors are accused as a profession of being extravagant and intemperate. While they are said to be so as a piece of common cant, they are likely to continue so. But there is a sentence in Shakespear which should be stuck as a label in the mouths of the beadles and whippers-in of morality: 'The web of our life is of a mingled yarn: our virtues would be proud if our vices whipped them not, and our faults would despair if they were not cherished by our virtues.'

With respect to the extravagance of actors, as a traditional character, it is not to be wondered at: they live from hand to mouth; they plunge from want into luxury; they have no means of making money *breed*, and all professions that do not live by turning money into money, or have not a certainty of accumulating it in the end by parsimony, spend it. Uncertain of the future, they make sure of the present moment. This is not unwise. Chilled with poverty, steeped in contempt, they sometimes pass into the sunshine of fortune, and are lifted to the very pinnacle of public favour, yet even there cannot calculate on the continuance of success, but are, 'like the giddy sailor on the mast, ready with every blast to topple down into the fatal bowels of the deep!' Besides, if the young enthusiast who is smitten with the stage, and with the public as a mistress, were naturally a close *hunks*, he would become or remain a city clerk, instead of turning player. Again, with respect to the habit of convivial indulgence, an actor, to be a good one, must have a great spirit of enjoyment in himself, strong impulses, strong passions, and a strong sense of pleasure, for it is his business to imitate the passions and to communicate pleasure to others. A man of genius is not a machine. The neglected actor may be excused if he drinks oblivion of his disappointments; the successful one, if he quaffs the applause of the world, and enjoys the friendship of those who are the friends of the favourites of fortune, in draughts of nectar. There is no path so steep as that of fame; no labour so hard as the pursuit of excellence. The intellectual excitement inseparable from those professions which call forth all our sensibility to pleasure and pain, requires some corresponding physical excitement to support our failure, and not a little to allay the ferment of the spirits attendant on success. If there is any tendency to dissipation beyond this in the profession of a player, it is owing to the state of public opinion, which paragraphs like the one we have alluded to are not calculated to reform; and players are only not so *respectable* as a profession as they might be, because their profession is not *respected* as it ought to be.

There is something, we fear, impertinent and uncalled for in these remarks: the more so, as in the present instance the insinuation which they were meant to repel is wholly unfounded. We have it on very good authority, that Mr. Kean, since his engagement at Drury-Lane, and during his arduous and uninterrupted exertions in his profession, has never missed a single rehearsal, nor been absent a minute beyond the time for beginning his part.

MR. KEAN'S SHYLOCK

The Examiner.   *April* 7, 1816.

Mr. Kean's friends felt some unnecessary anxiety with respect to his reception in the part of Shylock, on Monday night at Drury-Lane, being his first appearance after his recovery from his accident, which we are glad to find has not been a very serious one. On his coming on the stage there was a loud burst of applause and welcome; but as this was mixed with some hisses, Mr. Kean came forward, and spoke nearly as follows:

'Ladies and Gentlemen, for the first time in my life I have been the unfortunate cause of disappointing the public amusement.

'That it is the only time, on these boards, I can appeal to your own recollection; and when you take into calculation the 265 times that I have had the honour to appear before you, according to the testimony of the Manager's books, you will, perhaps, be able to make some allowance.

'To your favour I owe all the reputation I enjoy.

'I rely on your candour, that prejudice shall not rob me of what your kindness has conferred upon me.'

This address was received with cordial cheers, and the play went forward without interruption. As soon as the curtain drew up, some persons had absurdly called out 'Kean, Kean,' though Shylock does not appear in the first scenes. This was construed into a call for 'God save the *King*: ' and the Duke of Gloucester's being in one of the stage-boxes seemed to account for this sudden effusion of loyalty,—a sentiment indeed always natural in the hearts of Englishmen, but at present not very noisy, and rather 'deep than loud.' For our own parts, we love the King according to law, but we cannot sing.

Shylock was the part in which Mr. Kean first sought the favour

294

of the town, and in which perhaps he chose for that reason to be reconciled to it, after the first slight misunderstanding. We were a little curious on this occasion to see the progress he has made in public opinion since that time; and on turning to our theatrical common-place book (there is nothing like a common-place book after all) found the following account of his first reception, copied from the most respectable of the Morning Papers: 'Mr. Kean (of whom report has spoken so highly) made his appearance at Drury-Lane in the character of Shylock. For *voice*, eye, action, and expression, no actor has come out for many years at all equal to him. The applause, from the first scene to the last, was general, loud, and uninterrupted. Indeed, the very first scene in which he comes on with Bassanio and Anthonio, shewed the master in his art, and at once decided the opinion of the audience. Perhaps it was the most perfect of any. Notwithstanding the complete success of Mr. Kean in Shylock, we question whether he will not become a greater favourite in other parts. There was a lightness and vigour in his tread, a buoyancy and elasticity of spirit, a fire and animation, which would accord better with almost any other character than with the morose, sullen, inward, inveterate, inflexible, malignity of Shylock. The character of Shylock is that of a man brooding over one idea, that of its wrongs, and bent on an unalterable purpose, that of revenge. In conveying a profound impression of this feeling, or in embodying the general conception of rigid and uncontroulable self-will, equally proof against every sentiment of humanity or prejudice of opinion, we have seen actors more successful than Mr. Kean. But in giving effect to the conflict of passions arising out of the contrast of situation, in varied vehemence of declamation, in keenness of sarcasm, in the rapidity of his transitions from one tone or feeling to another, in propriety and novelty of action, presenting a succession of striking pictures, and giving perpetually fresh shocks of delight and surprise, it would be difficult to single out a competitor. The fault of his acting was (if we may hazard an objection), an over-display of the resources of the art, which gave too much relief to the hard, impenetrable, dark ground-work of the character of Shylock. It would be needless to point out individual beauties, where almost every passage was received with equal and deserved applause. His style of acting is, if we may use the expression, more significant, more pregnant with meaning, more varied and alive in every part, than any we have almost ever witnessed. The character never stands still; there is no vacant pause in the action: the eye is never silent. It is not saying too much of Mr. Kean, though it is saying a great deal, that he has all that Mr. Kemble *wants* of perfection.'

The accounts in the other papers were not to be sure so favourable; and in the above criticism there are several errors. His voice, which is here praised, is very bad, though it must be confessed its defects appear less in Shylock than in most of his other characters. The critic appears also to have formed an overstrained idea of the gloomy character of Shylock, probably more from seeing other players perform it than from the text of Shakespear. Mr. Kean's manner is much nearer the mark. Shakespear could not easily divest his characters of their entire humanity: his Jew is more than half a Christian. Certainly, our sympathies are much oftener with him than with his enemies. He is honest in his vices; they are hypocrites in their virtues. In all his arguments and replies he has the advantage over them, by taking them on their own ground. Shylock (however some persons may suppose him bowed down by age, or deformed with malignity) never, that we can find, loses his elasticity and presence of mind. There is wonderful grace and ease in all the speeches in this play. 'I would not have parted with it (the jewel that he gave to Leah) for a *wilderness* of monkeys!' What a fine Hebraism! The character of Shylock is another instance of Shakespear's powers of identifying himself with the thoughts of men, their prejudices, and almost instincts.

THE ORATORIOS

The Examiner.   *April* 14, 1816.

The Oratorios are over, and we are not sorry for it. Not that we are not fond of music; on the contrary, there is nothing that affects us so much; but the note it sounds is of too high a sphere. It lifts the soul to heaven, but in so doing, it exhausts the faculties, draws off the ethereal and refined part of them, and we fall back to the earth more dull and lumpish than ever. Music is the breath of thought; the audible movement of the heart. It is, for the most part, a pure effusion of sentiment; the language of pleasure, abstracted from its exciting causes. But the human mind is so formed, that it cannot easily bear, for any length of time, an uninterrupted appeal to the sense of pleasure alone; we require the relief of objects and ideas; it may be said that the activity of the soul, of the voluptuous part of our nature, cannot keep pace with that of the understanding, which only discerns the outward differences of things. All passion exhausts the mind; and that kind of passion most, which presents no distinct object to the imagination. The eye may amuse itself for a whole day with the variety to be found in a florist's garden; but the

296

sense is soon cloyed with the smell of the sweetest flowers, and we throw them from us as if they had been weeds. The sounds of music are like perfumes, 'exhaling to the sky;' too sweet to last; that must be borne to us on the passing breeze, not pressed and held close to the sense; the warbling of heavenly voices in the air, not the ordinary language of men. If music is (as it is said to be) the language of angels, poetry is the most perfect language men can use: for poetry is music also, and has as much of the soft and voluptuous in its nature, as the hard and unyielding materials of our composition will bear. Music is colour without form; a soul without a body; a mistress whose face is veiled; an invisible goddess.

The Oratorios at Covent-Garden are in general much better than those at Drury-Lane: this year they have had Braham, Miss Stephens, Madam Marconi, and, if that were any great addition, Madame Mainville Fodor. Of this last lady it may be said, that she 'has her exits and her entrances,' and that is nearly all you know of her. She was encored in one song, 'Ah pardonna,' to her evident chagrin. Her airs of one kind scarcely make amends for her airs of another. Her voice is clear and forcible, and has a kind of deep internal volume, which seems to be artificially suppressed. Her hard, firm style of execution (something like the dragging of the painter's pencil) gives a greater relief to the occasional sweetness and power of tone which she displays. Her taste in singing is severe and fastidious; and this is, we suppose, the reason that a connoisseur of great eminence compared it to Titian's colouring. Madam Marconi, on the contrary, has a broad and full manner; sings with all her might, and pours out her whole soul and voice. There is something masculine, and we might say, rather vulgar, in her tones, if her native Italian or broken English did not prevent such a suggestion almost before it rises in the mind. Miss Stephens sang with more than her usual spirit, and was much applauded, particularly in 'The mower wets his scythe,' &c.; but we do not think her *forte* is in concert-music. Mr. Braham's certainly is; and his power is thrown away on the ballad airs which he sings in general on the stage. The sweetness of his voice becomes languishing and effeminate, unless where it is sustained by its depth and power. But on these occasions there is a rich mellifluous tone in his cadences, which is like that of bees swarming; his chest is dilated; he heaves the loud torrent of sound, like a load, from his heart; his voice rises in thunder, and his whole frame is inspired with the god! He sung Luther's Hymn very finely, with the exception of one quavering falsetto. This appears to our ignorant fancies at once the simplest and sublimest of compositions. The whole expresses merely the alternations of respiration, the heaving or drawing in of the breath, with the rising or sinking of hope or fear. It is music to which the dead might awake! On the last night of the Covent-Garden Oratorio, the beginning of Haydn's Creation was played. It is the accompaniment to the words, 'And God said let there be light,' &c. The adaptation of sound to express certain ideas, is most ingenious and admirable. The rising of the sun is described by a crashing and startling move-ment of sounds in all directions, like the effulgence of its rays sparkling through the sky; and the moon is made to rise to a slow and subdued symphony, like sound muffled, or like the moon emerging from a veil of mist, according to that description in Milton,—

> 'Till the moon
> Rising in clouded majesty, at length
> Apparent queen unveiled her peerless light,
> And o'er the dark her silver mantle threw.'

The stars also are represented twinkling in the blue abyss, by intervals of sweet sounds just audible. The art, however, by which this is done, is perhaps too little natural to please.

Mons. Drouet's performance on the flute was masterly, as far as we could judge. The execution of his variations on 'God save the King,' astonished and delighted the connoisseurs. Those on 'Hope told a flattering tale,' were also exquisite. We are, however, deep-versed in the sentiment of this last air; and we lost it in the light and fantastic movements of Mons. Drouet's execution. He belongs, we apprehend, to that class of musicians, whose ears are at their fingers' ends; but he is perhaps at the head. We profess, however, to be very ignorant in these matters, and speak under correction.

RICHARD III.

The Examiner. *April* 21, 1816.

The Managers of Covent-Garden Theatre have treated the public with two new Richards this season, Mr. Edwards, and Mr. Cobham. The first, his own good sense and modesty induced to withdraw, after the disapprobation of the public had been expressed on his first trial. Mr. Cobham, who is not 'made of penetrable stuff,' intends, we understand, to face the public out in the character. This is an experiment which will never answer. We shall take good care, however, not to be present at the fray. We do not blame Mr.

298

Cobham for the mortification and disappointment which we have received, but the Managers. Self-knowledge is a rare acquisition; but criticism upon others is a very easy task; and the Managers need merely have perceived as much of the matter as was obvious to every common spectator from the first moment of this actor's coming on, to know that it was quite impossible he should get through the part with ordinary decency. The only scene that was tolerable was the meeting with Lady Anne. But for his Richard—(Heaven save the mark)—it was a vile one—'unhousell'd, unanointed, unaneal'd, with all his imperfections on his head.' Not that this actor is without the physical requisites to play Richard: he raved, whined, grinned, stared, stamped, and rolled his eyes with incredible velocity, and all in the right place according to his cue, but in so extravagant and disjointed a manner, and with such a total want of common sense, decorum, or conception of the character, as to be perfectly ridiculous. We suspect that he has a wrong theory of his art. He has taken a lesson from Mr. Kean, whom he caricatures, and seems to suppose that to be familiar or violent is natural, and that to be natural is the perfection of acting. And so it is, if properly understood. But to play Richard naturally, is to play it as Richard would play it, not as Mr. Cobham would play it; he comes there to shew us not himself, but the tyrant and the king—not what he would do, but what another would do in such circumstances. Before he can do this he must become that other, and cease to be himself. Dignity is natural to certain stations, and grandeur of expression to certain feelings. In art, nature cannot exist without the highest art; it is a pure effort of the imagination, which throws the mind out of itself into the supposed situation of others, and enables it to feel and act there as if it were at home. The real Richard and the real Mr. Cobham are quite different things.

But we are glad to have done with this subject, and proceed to a more grateful one, which is to notice the Sir Pertinax Mac Sycophant of a Gentleman whose name has not yet been announced.[1] We have no hesitation in pronouncing him an acquisition to this Theatre. To compare him with Cooke in this character would be idle; for it was Cooke's very best character, and Cooke was one of the very best actors we have had on the stage. But he played the character throughout without a single failure, and with great judgment, great spirit, and great effect. In the scenes with Egerton, where he gives a loose to his natural feelings, he expressed all the turbulence and

---

[1] A Mr. Bibby, from the United States.

and we were afraid would have ended fatally; for Mrs. Bartley, as the Tragic Muse, was nearly upset by the breaking down of her car. We cannot go through the detail of this wretched burlesque. Mr. Stothard's late picture of the Characters of Shakespear was ingenious and satisfactory, because the figures seen together made picturesque groups, because painting presents but one moment of action, and because it is necessarily in dumb show. But this exhibition seemed intended as a travestie, to take off all the charm and the effect of the ideas associated with the several characters. It has satisfied us of the reality of dramatic illusion, by shewing the effect of such an exhibition entirely stripped of it. For example, Juliet is wheeled on in her tomb, which is broken open by her lover: she awakes, the tomb then moves forward, and Mr. S. Penley, not knowing what to do, throws himself upon the bier, and is wheeled off with her. Pope and Barnard come on as Lear and Mad Tom. They sit down on the ground, and Pope steals a crown of straw from his companion: Mad Tom then starts up, runs off the stage, and Pope after him, like Pantaloon in pursuit of the Clown. This is fulsome. We did not stay to see it out; and one consolation is, that we shall not be alive another century to see it repeated.

MR. KEMBLE'S SIR GILES OVERREACH

The Examiner.   *May* 5, 1816.

Why they put Mr. Kemble into the part of Sir Giles Overreach, at Covent-Garden Theatre, we cannot conceive: we should suppose he would not put himself there. Malvolio, though cross-gartered, did not set himself in the stocks. No doubt, it is the Managers' doing, who by rope-dancing, fire-works, play-bill puffs, and by every kind of quackery, seem determined to fill their pockets for the present, and disgust the public in the end, if the public were an animal capable of being disgusted by quackery. But

> 'Doubtless the pleasure is as great
> In being cheated as to cheat.'

We do not know why we promised last week to give some account of Mr. Kemble's Sir Giles, except that we dreaded the task then; and certainly our reluctance to speak on this subject has not decreased, the more we have thought upon it since. We have hardly ever experienced a more painful feeling than when, after the close of the play, the sanguine plaudits of Mr. Kemble's friends, and the circular discharge of hisses from the back of the pit, that came 'full volly

302

home,'—the music struck up, the ropes were fixed, and Madame Sachi ran up from the stage to the two-shilling gallery, and then ran down again, as fast as her legs could carry her, amidst the shouts of pit, boxes, and gallery!

> ' So fails, so languishes, and dies away
> All that this world is proud of. So
> Perish the roses and the crowns of kings,
> Sceptres and palms of all the mighty.'

We have here marred some fine lines of Mr. Wordsworth on the instability of human greatness, but it is no matter : for he does not seem to understand the sentiment himself. Mr. Kemble, then, having been thrust into the part, as we suppose, against his will, run the gauntlet of public opinion in it with a firmness and resignation worthy of a Confessor. He did not once shrink from his duty, nor make one effort to redeem his reputation, by ' affecting a virtue when he knew he had it not.' He seemed throughout to say to his instigators, *You have thrust me into this part, help me out of it, if you can ; for you see I cannot help myself.* We never saw signs of greater poverty, greater imbecility and decrepitude in Mr. Kemble, or in any other actor : it was Sir Giles in his dotage. It was all ' Well, well,' and, ' If you like it, have it so,' an indifference and disdain of what was to happen, a nicety about his means, a coldness as to his ends, much gentility and little nature. Was this Sir Giles Overreach ? Nothing could be more quaint and out-of-the-way. Mr. Kemble wanted the part to come to him, for he would not go out of his way to the part. He is, in fact, as shy of committing himself with nature, as a maid is of committing herself with a lover. All the proper forms and ceremonies must be complied with, before ' they two can be made one flesh.' Mr Kemble sacrifices too much to decorum. He is chiefly afraid of being contaminated by too close an identity with the characters he represents. This is the greatest vice in an actor, who ought never to *bilk* his part. He endeavours to raise Nature to the dignity of his own person and demeanour, and declines with a graceful smile and a waive of the hand, the ordinary services she might do him. We would advise him by all means to shake hands, to hug her close, and be friends, if we did not suspect it was too late—that the lady, owing to this coyness, has eloped, and is now in the situation of Dame Hellenore among the Satyrs.

The outrageousness of the conduct of Sir Giles is only to be excused by the violence of his passions, and the turbulence of his character. Mr. Kemble inverted this conception, and attempted to reconcile the character, by softening down the action. He ' aggravated

303

the part so, that he would seem like any sucking dove.' For example, nothing could exceed the coolness and *sang-froid* with which he raps Marall on the head with his cane, or spits at Lord Lovell: Lord Foppington himself never did any common-place indecency more insipidly. The only passage that pleased us, or that really called forth the powers of the actor, was his reproach to Mr. Justice Greedy: 'There is some fury in that *Gut*.' The indignity of the word called up all the dignity of the actor to meet it, and he guaranteed the word, though 'a word of naught,' according to the letter and spirit of the convention between them, with a good grace, in the true old English way. Either we mistake all Mr. Kemble's excellences, or they all disqualify him for this part. Sir Giles *hath a devil*; Mr. Kemble has none. Sir Giles is in a passion; Mr. Kemble is not. Sir Giles has no regard to appearances; Mr. Kemble has. It has been said of the Venus de Medicis, ' So stands the statue that enchants the world;' the same might have been said of Mr. Kemble. He is the very still-life and statuary of the stage; a perfect figure of a man; a petrifaction of sentiment, that heaves no sigh, and sheds no tear; an icicle upon the bust of Tragedy. With all his faults, he has powers and faculties which no one else on the stage has; why then does he not avail himself of them, instead of throwing himself upon the charity of criticism? Mr. Kemble has given the public great, incalculable pleasure; and does he know so little of the gratitude of the world as to trust to their generosity?

BERTRAM

The Examiner.   *May* 19, 1816.

The new tragedy of Bertram at Drury-Lane Theatre has entirely succeeded, and it has sufficient merit to deserve the success it has met with. We had read it before we saw it, and it on the whole disappointed us in the representation. Its beauties are rather those of language and sentiment than of action or situation. The interest flags very much during the last act, where the whole plot is known and inevitable. What it has of stage-effect is scenic and extraneous, as the view of the sea in a storm, the chorus of knights, &c. instead of arising out of the business of the play. We also object to the trick of introducing the little child twice to untie the knot of the catastrophe. One of these fantoccini exhibitions in the course of a tragedy is quite enough.

The general fault of this tragedy, and of other modern tragedies that we could mention, is, that it is a tragedy without business.

304

A VIEW OF THE ENGLISH STAGE

Aristotle, we believe, defines tragedy to be the representation of *a serious action*. Now here there is no action: there is neither cause nor effect. There is a want of that necessary connection between what happens, what is said, and what is done, in which we take the essence of dramatic invention to consist. It is a sentimental drama, it is a romantic drama, but it is not a tragedy, in the best sense of the word. That is to say, the passion described does not arise naturally out of the previous circumstances, nor lead necessarily to the consequences that follow. Mere sentiment is voluntary, fantastic, self-created, beginning and ending in itself; true passion is natural, irresistible, produced by powerful causes, and impelling the will to determinate actions. The old tragedy, if we understand it, is a display of the affections of the heart and the energies of the will; the modern romantic tragedy is a mixture of fanciful exaggeration and indolent sensibility; the former is founded on real calamities and real purposes: the latter courts distress, affects horror, indulges in all the luxury of woe, and nurses its languid thoughts, and dainty sympathies, to fill up the void of action. As the opera is filled with a sort of singing people, who translate every thing into music, the modern drama is filled with poets and their mistresses, who translate every thing into metaphor and sentiment. Bertram falls under this censure. It is a Winter's Tale, a Midsummer Night's Dream, but it is not Lear or Macbeth. The poet does not describe what his characters would feel in given circumstances, but lends them his own thoughts and feelings out of his general reflections on human nature, or general observation of certain objects. In a word, we hold for a truth, that a thoroughly good tragedy is an impossibility in a state of manners and literature where the poet and philosopher have got the better of the man; where the reality does not mould the imagination, but the imagination glosses over the reality; and where the unexpected stroke of true calamity, the biting edge of true passion, is blunted, sheathed, and lost, amidst the flowers of poetry strewed over unreal, unfelt distress, and the flimsy topics of artificial humanity prepared beforehand for all occasions. We are tired of this long-spun analysis; take an example:

'SCENE V.

A Gothic Apartment.

Imagine discovered sitting at a Table looking at a Picture.

Imogine. Yes,
'The limner's art may trace the absent feature,
And give the eye of distant weeping faith
To view the form of its idolatry:

> But oh ! the scenes 'mid which they met and parted—
> The thoughts, the recollections sweet and bitter—
> Th' Elysian dreams of lovers, when they loved—
> Who shall restore them ?
> Less lovely are the fugitive clouds of eve,
> And not more vanishing—if thou couldst speak,
> Dumb witness of the secret soul of Imogine,
> Thou might'st acquit the faith of woman kind—
> Since thou wert on my midnight pillow laid,
> Friend hath forsaken friend—the brotherly tie
> Been lightly loosed—the parted coldly met—
> Yea, mothers have with desperate hands wrought harm
> To little lives which their own bosoms lent.
> But woman still hath loved—if that indeed
> Woman e'er loved like me.'

This is very beautiful and affecting writing. The reader would suppose that it related to events woven into the web of the history; but no such thing. It is a purely voluntary or poetical fiction of possible calamity, arising out of the experience of the author, not of the heroine.

The whole of the character of Clotilda, her confidante, who enters immediately after, is superfluous. She merely serves for the heroine to vent the moods of her own mind upon, and to break her enthusiastic soliloquies into the appearance of a dialogue. There is no reason in the world for the confidence thus reposed in Clotilda, with respect to her love for the outlawed Bertram, but the eternal desire of talking. Neither does she at all explain the grounds of her marriage to Aldobrand, who her father was, or how his distresses induced her to renounce her former lover. The whole is an effusion of tender sentiments, sometimes very good and fine, but of which we neither know the origin, the circumstances, nor the object; for her passion for Bertram does not lead to any thing but the promise of an interview to part for ever, which promise is itself broken. Among other fine lines describing the situation of Imogine's mind, are the following:

> ' And yet some sorcery was wrought on me,
> For earlier things do seem as yesterday ;
> But I've no recollection of the hour
> They gave my hand to Aldobrand.'

Perhaps these lines would be more natural if spoken of the lady than by her. The descriptive style will allow things to be supposed or said of others, which cannot so well be believed or said by them. There is also a want of dramatic decorum in Bertram's description of

306

a monastic life addressed to the Prior. It should be a solitary
reflection.

> ' Yea, thus they live, if this may life be called,
> Where moving shadows mock the parts of men.
> Prayer follows study, study yields to prayer—
> Bell echoes bell, till wearied with the summons,
> The ear doth ache for that last welcome peal
> That tolls an end to listless vacancy.'

That part of the play where the chief interest should lie, namely, in
the scenes preceding the death of Aldobrand, is without any interest
at all, from the nature of the plot; for there is nothing left either to
hope or to fear; and not only is there no possibility of good, but
there is not even a choice of evils. The struggle of Imogine is a
mere alternation of senseless exclamations. Her declaring of her
husband, ' By heaven and all its hosts, he shall not perish,' is downright rant. She has no power to prevent his death; she has no
power even to will his safety, for he is armed with what she deems
an unjust power over the life of Bertram, and the whole interest of
the play centres in her love for this Bertram. Opposite interests
destroy one another in the drama, like opposite forces in mechanics.
The situation of Belvidera in Venice Preserved, where the love to her
father or her husband must be sacrificed, is quite different, for she not
only hopes to reconcile them, but actually does reconcile them. The
speech of Bertram to the Knights after he has killed Aldobrand, and
his drawing off the dead body, to contemplate it alone, have been
much admired, and there is certainly something grand and impressive
in the first suggestion of the idea; but we do not believe it is in
nature. We will venture a conjecture, that it is formed on a false
analogy to two other ideas, viz. to that of a wild beast carrying off
its prey with it to its den, and to the story which Fuseli has painted,
of a man sitting over the corpse of his murdered wife. Now we can
conceive that a man might wish to feast his eyes on the dead body of
a person whom he had loved, and conceive that there was no one else
' but they two left alone in the world,' but not that any one would
have this feeling with respect to an enemy whom he had killed.

Mr. Kean as Bertram did several things finely; what we liked
most was his delivery of the speech, ' The wretched have no country.'
Miss Somerville as Imogine was exceedingly interesting; she put us
in mind of Hogarth's Sigismunda. She is tall and elegant, and her
face is good, with some irregularities. Her voice is powerful, and
her tones romantic. Her mode of repeating the line,

> ' Th' Elysian dreams of lovers, *when they loved*,'

had the true poetico-metaphysical cadence, as if the sound and the sentiment would linger for ever on the ear. She might sit for the picture of a heroine of romance, whether with her form

> ' —————————decked in purple and in pall,
> When she goes forth, and thronging vassals kneel,
> And bending pages bear her footcloth well ; '

or whether the eye

> ' —————————beholds that lady in her bower,
> That is her hour of joy ; for then she weeps,
> Nor does her husband hear ! '

Bertram, or the Castle of St. Aldobrand, is written by an Irish Clergyman, whose name is Maturin. It is said to be his first successful production ; we sincerely hope it will not be the last.

ADELAIDE, OR THE EMIGRANTS

The Examiner.   (*Covent-Garden*) *May* 26, 1816.

A tragedy, to succeed, should be either uniformly excellent or uniformly dull. Either will do almost equally well. We are convinced that it would be possible to write a tragedy which should be a tissue of unintelligible common-places from beginning to end, in which not one word that is *said* shall be understood by the audience, and yet, provided appearances are saved, and nothing is *done* to trip up the heels of the imposture, it would go down. Adelaide, or the Emigrants, is an instance in point. If there had been one good passage in this play, it would infallibly have been damned. But it was all of a piece ; one absurdity justified another. The first scene was like the second, the second act no worse than the first, the third like the second, and so on to the end. The mind accommodates itself to circumstances. The author never once roused the indignation of his hearers by the disappointment of their expectations. He startled the slumbering furies of the pit by no dangerous inequalities. We were quite resigned by the middle of the third simile, and equally thankful when the whole was over. The language of this tragedy is made up of nonsense and indecency. Mixed metaphors abound in it. The 'torrent of passion rolls *along* precipices ; ' pleasure is said to gleam upon despair 'like moss upon the desolate rock ; ' the death of a hero is compared to the peak of a mountain setting in seas of glory, or some such dreadful simile, built up with ladders and scaffolding. Then the thunder and lightning are mingled with bursts of fury and

308

revenge in inextricable confusion; there are such unmeaning phrases as *contagious gentleness*, and the heroes and the heroine, in their transports, as a common practice, set both worlds at defiance.

The plot of this play is bad, for it is unintelligible in a great measure, and where it is not unintelligible, absurd. Count Lunenburg cannot marry Adelaide because ' his Emperor's frown ' has forbidden his marriage with the daughter of an Emigrant Nobleman; and so, to avoid this imperial frown, he betrays her into a pretended marriage, and thus intends to divide his time between war and a mistress. Hence all the distress and mischiefs which ensue; and though the morality of the affair is characteristic enough of the old school, yet neither the Emperor's frown nor the Count's levity seem sufficient reasons for harrowing up the feelings in the manner proposed by the author, and plunging us into the horrors of the French Revolution at the same time. The exiled St. Evremond saw ' his lawful monarch's bleeding head, and yet he prayed; ' he saw ' his castle walls crumbled into ashes by the devouring flames, and yet he prayed: ' but when he finds his daughter betrayed by one of his legitimate friends, he can ' pray no more.' His wife, the Countess, takes some comfort, and she builds her hope on a word, which, she says, is of great virtue, the word, ' perhaps.' ' It is the word which the slave utters as he stands upon the western shores, and looks towards Afric's climes—*Perhaps !* ' —Of the attention paid to costume, some idea may be formed by the circumstance, that in the church-yard where the catastrophe takes place, the inscriptions on the tomb-stones are all in German, though the people speak English. The rest is in the same style. The *Emigrants* is a political attempt to drench an English audience with French loyalty: now, French loyalty to the House of Bourbon, is a thing as little to our taste as Scotch loyalty to the House of Stuart; and when we find our political quacks preparing to pour their nauseous trash with false labels down our throats, we must ' throw it to the dogs: we 'll none of it.'

Mr. Young, as the injured Count, raved without meaning, and grew light-headed with great deliberation. Charles Kemble, in tragedy, only spoils a good face. Mr. Murray, as the old servant of the family, was ' as good as a prologue,' and his helpless horror at what is going forward exceedingly amusing.

Miss O'Neill's Adelaide, which we suppose was intended to be the chief attraction of the piece, was to us the most unpleasant part of it. She has powers which ought not to be thrown away, and yet she trifles with them. She wastes them equally on genteel comedy and vulgar tragedy. Her acting in Adelaide, which in other circumstances might have been impressive, was to us repulsive. The agonizing passion she expressed, required that our feelings should be wound up to the highest pitch, either by the imagination of the poet or the interest of the story, to meet it on equal terms. We are not in an ordinary mood prepared for the shrieks of mandrakes, for the rattles in the throat, for looks that drive the thoughts to madness. Miss O'Neill's acting is pure nature or passion: it is the prose of tragedy; for the poetry she must lean on her author. But strong passion must be invested with imagination by some one, either by the poet or the actor, before it can give delight, not to say, before it can be endured by the public. Her manner in the scene where she asks Lunenberg about her marriage, was much the same as when Monimia asks Polydore, ' Where did you rest last night ? ' Yet how different was the effect ! in the one, her frantic eagerness only corresponded with the interest already excited ; in the other, it shocked, because no interest had been excited. Miss O'Neill fills better than any one else the part assigned her by the author, but she does not *make* it, nor over-inform it with qualities which she is not bound to bring. She is, therefore, more dependent than any one else upon the character she has to represent; and as she originally owes her reputation to her powers of sensibility, she will perhaps owe its ultimate continuance to the cultivation of her taste in the choice of the characters in which she appears. The public are jealous of their favourites !

EVERY MAN IN HIS HUMOUR

The Examiner.   *June* 9, 1816.

Mr. Kean had for his benefit at Drury-Lane Theatre, on Wednesday, the Comedy of Every Man in his Humour. This play acts much better than it reads. It has been observed of Ben Jonson, that he painted not so much human nature as temporary manners, not the characters of men, but their *humours*, that is to say, peculiarities of phrase, modes of dress, gesture, &c. which becoming obsolete, and being in themselves altogether arbitrary and fantastical, have become unintelligible and uninteresting. Brainworm is a particularly dry and abstruse character. We neither know his business nor his motives ; his plots are as intricate as they are useless, and as the ignorance of those he imposes upon is wonderful. This is the impression in reading it. Yet from the bustle and activity of this character on the stage, the changes of dress, the variety of affected tones and gipsey jargon, and the limping, distorted gestures, it is a very amusing exhibition, as Mr. Munden plays it. Bobadil is the only actually striking character in the play, or which tells equally in the closet and

310

the theatre. The rest, Master Matthew, Master Stephen, Cob and
Cob's Wife, were living in the sixteenth century. But from the very
oddity of their appearance and behaviour, they have a very droll and
even picturesque effect when acted. It seems a revival of the dead.
We believe in their existence when we see them. As an example of
the power of the stage in giving reality and interest to what otherwise
would be without it, we might mention the scene in which Brainworm
praises Master Stephen's leg. The folly here is insipid, from its
seeming carried to an excess,—till we see it; and then we laugh the
more at it, the more incredible we thought it before.

The pathos in the principal character, Kitely, is 'as dry as the
remainder biscuit after a voyage.' There is, however, a certain good
sense, discrimination, or *logic of passion* in the part, which Mr. Kean
pointed in such a way as to give considerable force to it. In the
scene where he is about to confide the secret of his jealousy to his
servant, Thomas, he was exceedingly happy in the working himself
up to the execution of his design, and in the repeated failure of his
resolution. The reconciliation-scene with his wife had great spirit,
where he tells her, to shew his confidence, that 'she may sing, may
go to balls, may dance,' and the interruption of this sudden tide of
concession with the restriction—'though I had rather you did not do
all this'—was a master-stroke. It was perhaps the first time a
parenthesis was ever spoken on the stage as it ought to be. Mr. Kean
certainly often repeats this artifice of abrupt transition in the tones in
which he expresses different passions, and still it always pleases,—
we suppose, because it is natural. This gentleman is not only a good
actor in himself, but he is the cause of good acting in others. The
whole play was got up very effectually. Considerable praise is due
to the industry and talent shewn by Mr. Harley, in Captain Bobadil.
He did his best in it, and that was not ill. He delivered the
Captain's well-known proposal for the pacification of Europe, by
killing twenty of them each his man a day, with good emphasis and
discretion. Bobadil is undoubtedly the hero of the piece; his extravagant affectation carries the sympathy of the audience along with it,
and his final defeat and exposure, though exceedingly humorous, is
the only affecting circumstance in the play. Mr. Harley's fault in
this and other characters is, that he too frequently assumes mechanical
expressions of countenance and bye-tones of humour, which have not
any thing to do with the individual part. Mr. Hughes personified
Master Matthew to the life: he appeared 'like a man made after
supper of a cheese-paring.' Munden did Brainworm with laudable
alacrity. Oxberry's Master Stephen was very happily hit off;
nobody plays the traditional fool of the English stage so well; he

seems not only foolish, but fond of folly. The two young gentlemen, Master Well-bred and Master Edward Knowell, were the only insipid characters.

MRS. SIDDONS

The Examiner.   June 16, 1816.

Players should be immortal, if their own wishes or ours could make them so; but they are not. They not only die like other people, but like other people they cease to be young, and are no longer themselves, even while living. Their health, strength, beauty, voice, fails them; nor can they, without these advantages, perform the same feats, or command the same applause that they did when possessed of them. It is the common lot: players are only *not* exempt from it. Mrs. Siddons retired once from the stage: why should she return to it again? She cannot retire from it twice with dignity; and yet it is to be wished that she should do all things with dignity. Any loss of reputation to her, is a loss to the world. Has she not had enough of glory? The homage she has received is greater than that which is paid to Queens. The enthusiasm she excited had something idolatrous about it; she was regarded less with admiration than with wonder, as if a being of a superior order had dropped from another sphere to awe the world with the majesty of her appearance. She raised Tragedy to the skies, or brought it down from thence. It was something above nature. We can conceive of nothing grander. She embodied to our imagination the fables of mythology, of the heroic and deified mortals of elder time. She was not less than a goddess, or than a prophetess inspired by the gods. Power was seated on her brow, passion emanated from her breast as from a shrine. She was Tragedy personified. She was the stateliest ornament of the public mind. She was not only the idol of the people, she not only hushed the tumultuous shouts of the pit in breathless expectation, and quenched the blaze of surrounding beauty in silent tears, but to the retired and lonely student, through long years of solitude, her face has shone as if an eye had appeared from heaven; her name has been as if a voice had opened the chambers of the human heart, or as if a trumpet had awakened the sleeping and the dead. To have seen Mrs. Siddons, was an event in every one's life; and does she think we have forgot her? Or would she remind us of herself by shewing us what *she was not*? Or is she to continue on the stage to the very last, till all her grace and all her grandeur gone, shall leave behind them only a melancholy blank? Or is she merely to be played off as 'the baby of a girl' for a few nights?—'Rather than

312

so,' come, Genius of Gil Blas, thou that didst inspire him in an evil hour to perform his promise to the Archbishop of Grenada, ' and champion us to the utterance' of what we think on this occasion.

It is said that the Princess Charlotte has expressed a desire to see Mrs. Siddons in her best parts, and this, it is said, is a thing highly desirable. We do not know that the Princess has expressed any such wish, and we shall suppose that she has not, because we do not think it altogether a reasonable one. If the Princess Charlotte had expressed a wish to see Mr. Garrick, this would have been a thing highly desirable, but it would have been impossible; or if she had desired to see Mrs. Siddons *in her best days*, it would have been equally so; and yet without this, we do not think it desirable that she should see her at all. It is said to be desirable that a Princess should have a taste for the Fine Arts, and that this is best promoted by seeing the highest models of perfection. But it is of the first importance for Princes to acquire a taste for what is reasonable: and the second thing which it is desirable they should acquire, is a deference to public opinion: and we think neither of these objects likely to be promoted in the way proposed. If it was reasonable that Mrs. Siddons should retire from the stage three years ago, certainly those reasons have not diminished since, nor do we think Mrs. Siddons would consult what is due to her powers or her fame, in commencing a new career. If it is only intended that she should act a few nights in the presence of a particular person, this might be done as well in private. To all other applications she should answer —' Leave me to my repose.'

Mrs. Siddons always spoke as slow as she ought: she now speaks slower than she did. 'The line too labours, and the words move slow.' The machinery of the voice seems too ponderous for the power that wields it. There is too long a pause between each sentence, and between each word in each sentence. There is too much preparation. The stage waits for her. In the sleeping scene, she produced a different impression from what we expected. It was more laboured, and less natural. In coming on formerly, her eyes were open, but the sense was shut. She was like a person bewildered, and unconscious of what she did. She moved her lips involuntarily; all her gestures were involuntary and mechanical. At present she acts the part more with a view to effect. She repeats the action when she says, ' I tell you he cannot rise from his grave,' with both hands sawing the air, in the style of parliamentary oratory, the worst of all others. There was none of this weight or energy in the way she did the scene the first time we saw her, twenty years ago. She glided on and off the stage almost like an apparition. In the close of

313

the banquet scene, Mrs. Siddons condescended to an imitation which we were sorry for. She said, 'Go, go,' in the hurried familiar tone of common life, in the manner of Mr. Kean, and without any of that sustained and graceful spirit of conciliation towards her guests, which used to characterise her mode of doing it. Lastly, if Mrs. Siddons has to leave the stage again, Mr. Horace Twiss will write another farewell address for her: if she continues on it, we shall have to criticise her performances. We know which of these two evils we shall think the greatest.

Too much praise cannot be given to Mr. Kemble's performance of Macbeth. He was 'himself again,' and more than himself. His action was decided, his voice audible. His tones had occasionally indeed a learned quaintness, like the colouring of Poussin; but the effect of the whole was fine. His action in delivering the speech, 'To-morrow and to-morrow,' was particularly striking and expressive, as if he had stumbled by an accident on fate, and was baffled by the impenetrable obscurity of the future.—In that prodigious prosing paper, the Times, which seems to be written as well as printed by a steam-engine, Mr. Kemble is compared to the ruin of a magnificent temple, in which the divinity still resides. This is not the case. The temple is unimpaired; but the divinity is sometimes from home.

NEW ENGLISH OPERA-HOUSE

The Examiner.   *June* 23, 1816.

The New English Opera-House (late the Lyceum Theatre) in the Strand, opened on Saturday week. The carpenters are but just got out of it; and in our opinion they have made but an indifferent piece of work of it. It consists of lobbies and vacant spaces. The three tiers of boxes are raised so high above one another, that the house would look empty even if it were full, and at present it is not full, but empty. The second gallery, for fear of its crowding on the first, is thrown back to such an unconscionable height, that it seems like a balcony projecting from some other building, where the spectators do not pay for peeping. All this no doubt promotes the circulation of air, and keeps the Theatre cool and comfortable. Mr. Arnold's philosophy may be right, but our prejudices are strongly against it. Our notions of a summer theatre are, that it should look *smoking hot*, and feel more like a warm bath than a well. We like to see a summer theatre as crowded as a winter one, so that a breath of air is a luxury. We like to see the well-dressed company in the boxes languidly silent, and to hear the Gods noisy and quarrelling for want of room and breath—the cries of 'Throw him over!' becoming more loud and frequent as the weather gets farther on into the dog-days. We like all this, because we are used to it, and are as obstinately attached to old abuses in matters of amusement, as kings, judges, and legislators are in state affairs.

The New Theatre opened with Up all Night, or the Smugglers' Cave; a piece admirably well adapted as a succedaneum for keeping the house cool and airy. The third night there was nobody there. To say the truth, we never saw a duller performance. The Actors whom the Manager has got together, are both new and strange. They are most of them recruits from the country, and of that description which is known by the vulgar appellation of the *awkward squad.* Mr. Russell (from Edinburgh, not our old friend Jerry Sneak) is the only one amongst them who understands his exercise. Mr. Short and Mr. Isaacs are singers, and we fear not good ones. Mr. Short has white teeth, and Mr. Isaacs black eyes. We do not like the name of Mr. Huckel. There is also a Mrs. Henley, who plays the fat Landlady in the Beehive, of the size of life.—Mr. Lancaster, who played Filch in the Beggars' Opera, and Mrs. W. Penson, who played the part of Lucy Lockitt tolerably, and looked it intolerably well. There is also Mr. Bartley, who is Stage-manager, and who threatens to be very prominent this season. There is also, from the old corps, Wrench, the easiest of actors; and there is Fanny Kelly, who after all, is not herself a whole company. We miss little Knight, and several other of our summer friends.

The Winter Theatres.—We must, we suppose, for the present, take our leave of the winter performances. We lately saw at Covent-Garden Mr. Emery's Robert Tyke, in the School of Reform, of which we had heard a good deal, and which fully justified all that we had heard of its excellence. It is one of the most natural and powerful pieces of acting on the stage; it is the sublime of low tragedy. We should like to see any body do it better. The scene where, being brought before Lord Avondale as a robber, he dis-covers him to have been formerly an accomplice in villainy; that in which he gives an account of the death of his father, and goes off the stage calling for 'Brandy, brandy!' and that in which he finds this same father, whom he had supposed dead, alive again, are, in our judgment, master-pieces both of pathos and grandeur. We do not think all excellence is confined to walking upon stilts. We conceive that Mr. Emery shewed about as much genius in this part, which he performed for his benefit, as Mr. Liston did afterwards in singing the song of Ti, tum, ti; we cannot say more of it. Genius appears to

315

us to be a very *unclassical* quality. There is but a little of it in the world, but what there is, is always unlike itself and every thing else. Your imitators of the tragic, epic, and grand style, may be multiplied to any extent, as we raise regiments of grenadiers.

Mrs. Mardyn, after an absence of some weeks, has appeared again at Drury-Lane, in the new part of the Irish Widow, the charming Widow Brady ; and a most delightful representative she made of her —full of life and spirit, well-made, handsome, and good-natured. If it is a fault to be handsome, Mrs. Mardyn certainly deserves to be hissed off the stage.

THE JEALOUS WIFE

The Examiner.   *June* 30, 1816.

The performances at Drury-Lane Theatre closed for the season on Friday evening last, with the Jealous Wife, Sylvester Daggerwood, and the Mayor of Garratt. After the play Mr. Rae came forward, and in a neat address, not ill delivered, returned thanks to the public, in the name of the Managers and Performers, for the success with which their endeavours to afford rational amusement and to sustain the legitimate drama, had been attended.

The play-bills had announced Mrs. Davison for the part of Mrs. Oakley, in the Jealous Wife. We have seen nothing of this Lady of late, except when she personated the Comic Muse (for one night only), on the second centenary of Shakespear's death. The glimpses we catch of her are, in one sense,

'Like angels' visits, short, and far between.'

She was absent on the present occasion, and Mrs. Glover took the part of the well-drawn heroine of Colman's amusing and very instructive comedy. Mrs. Glover was not quite at home in the part. She represented the passions of the woman, but not the manners of the fine lady. She succeeds best in grave or violent parts, and has very little of the playful or delicate in her acting. If we were to hazard a general epithet for her style of performing, we should say that it amounts to the *formidable* ; her expression of passion is too hysterical, and habitually reminds one of hartshorn and water. On great occasions she displays the fury of a lioness who has lost her young, and in playing a queen or princess, deluges the theatre with her voice. Her Quaker in Wild Oats, on the contrary, is an inimitable piece of quiet acting. The demureness of the character, which takes away all temptation to be boisterous, leaves the justness of her conception in full force : and the simplicity of her Quaker dress is most agreeably relieved by the *embonpoint* of her person.

The comedy of the Jealous Wife was not upon the whole so well cast here as at Covent-Garden. Munden's Sir Harry Beagle was not to our taste. It was vulgarity in double-heaped measure. The part itself is a gross caricature, and Munden's playing caricature is something like *carrying coals to Newcastle*. Russell's Lord Trinket was also a failure : he can only play a modern jockey Nobleman : Lord Trinket is a fop of the old school.

Mr. Harley played Sylvester Daggerwood, in the entertainment which followed, well enough to make us regret our old favourite Bannister, and attempted some imitations, (one of Matthews in particular) which were pleasant and lively, but not very like.

The acting of Dowton and Russell, in Major Sturgeon and Jerry Sneak, is well known to our readers : at least we would advise all those who have not seen it, to go and see this perfect exhibition of comic talent. The strut, the bluster, the hollow swaggering, and turkey-cock swell of the Major, and Jerry's meekness, meanness, folly, good-nature, and hen-pecked air, are assuredly done to the life. The latter character is even better than the former, which is saying a bold word. Dowton's art is only an imitation of art, of an affected or assumed character ; but in Russell's Jerry you see the very soul of nature, in a fellow that is 'pigeon livered and lacks gall,' laid open and anatomized. You can see that his heart is no bigger than a pin, and his head as soft as a pippin. His whole aspect is chilled and frightened as if he had been dipped in a pond, and yet he looks as if he would like to be snug and comfortable, if he durst. He smiles as if he would be friends with you upon any terms ; and the tears come in his eyes because you will not let him. The tones of his voice are prophetic as the cuckoo's under-song. His words are made of water-gruel. The scene in which he tries to make a confidant of the Major is great ; and his song of 'Robinson Crusoe' as melancholy as the Island itself. The reconciliation-scene with his wife, and his exclamation over her, 'to think that I should make my Molly *veep*,' are pathetic, if the last stage of human infirmity is so. This farce appears to us to be both moral and entertaining ; yet it does not take. It is considered as an unjust satire on the city and the country at large, and there is a very frequent repetition of the word 'nonsense,' in the house during the performance. Mr. Dowton was even hissed, either from the upper boxes or gallery, in his speech recounting the marching of his corps 'from Brentford to Ealing, and from Ealing to Acton;' and several persons in the pit, who thought the whole *low*, were for going out. This shews well for the progress of civilisation. We suppose the manners described in the Mayor of Garratt have in the last forty years become obsolete, and the characters ideal: we have no longer either hen-pecked or brutal husbands, or domineering wives; the Miss Molly Jollops no longer wed Jerry Sneaks, or admire the brave Major Sturgeons on the other side of Temple Bar; all our soldiers have become heroes, and our magistrates respectable, and the farce of life is o'er!

THE MAN OF THE WORLD

The Examiner. *July 7, 1816.*

We are glad to find the Haymarket Theatre re-opened with some good actors from the Winter Theatres, besides recruits. On Monday was played the Man of the World, Sir Pertinax Mac-Sycophant by Mr. Terry. This part was lately performed by Mr. Bibby at Covent-Garden without success; and we apprehend that his failure was owing to the extreme purity and breadth of his Scotch accent. Mr. Terry avoided splitting on this rock, by sinking the Scotch brogue almost entirely, and thus this national caricature was softened into a more general and less offensive portrait of a common Man of the World. On the whole, Mr. Terry gave not only less of the costume and local colouring of the character, but less of the general force and spirit than the former gentleman. He however displayed his usual judgment and attention to his part, with less appearance of effort than he sometimes shews. If Mr. Terry would take rather less pains, he would be a better actor. He is exceedingly correct in the conception of his characters, but in the execution he often takes twice the time in bringing out his words that he ought, and lays double the emphasis on them that is necessary. In the present case, Mr. Terry, probably from feeling no great liking to his part, laid less stress on particular passages, and was more happy on that account. The scene in which he gives the account of his progress in life to his son Egerton, was one of the most effectual. Mrs. Glover's Lady Rodolpha Lumbercourt had considerable spirit and archness, as well as force. Of the new performers in it we cannot speak very favourably. The young gentleman who played Sydney, a Mr. Baker, seems really a clergyman by profession, and

318

to have left, rather imprudently, the prospect of a fellowship at Oxford or Cambridge. His voice and cadences are good; but they are fitter for the pulpit than the stage.

Mr. Watkinson, on Thursday played Sir Robert Bramble, in the Poor Gentleman, with a considerable share of that blunt native humour, and rustic gentility, which distinguish so large a class of characters on the English stage. We mean that sort of characters who usually appear in a brown bob-wig, and chocolate-coloured coat, with brass buttons. Of this class Mr. Watkinson, as far as we could judge on a first acquaintance, appears to be a very respectable, if not brilliant representative. A Miss Taylor made an elegant and interesting Emily, the daughter of the Poor Gentleman; and Mr. Foote played that personification of modern humanity, the Poor Gentleman himself. There is a tone of recitation in this actor's delivery, perhaps not ill suited to the whining sentimentality of the parts he has to play, but which is very tiresome to the ear. We might say to him as Caesar did to some one, 'Do you read or sing? If you sing, you sing very ill.' We must not omit to mention the part of Miss Lætitia Macnab, which was performed to the life by a Mrs. Kennedy of Covent-Garden Theatre, whom we never saw here before, but whom we shall certainly remember. Her hoop-petticoats, flying lappets, high head-dress, face, voice, and figure, reminded us but too well of that obsolete class of antiquated maidens of old families that flourished about fifty years ago, who had no idea of any thing but the self-importance which they derived from their ancestors, and of the personal attractions which were to be found in the ridiculousness of their dress. The effect was as surprising as it was painful. It was as if Miss Macnab had come in person from the grave. It was like the restoration of the Bourbons!

After this melancholy casualty, we had the Agreeable Surprise. Mrs. Gibbs played Cowslip delightfully. Fawcett was exceedingly laughable in Lingo; and would have been more so, if he had played it with more gravity. Fawcett's fault of late is, that he has not respect enough for his art. This is a pity; for his art is a very good art. At the scene between him and Mrs. Cheshire, (Mrs. Davenport), the house was in a roar. We never knew before that Lingo and Cowslip were descendants of Touchstone and Audrey. This is one of O'Keeffe's best farces, and his farces are the best in the world except Moliere's. O'Keeffe is (for he is still living) our English Moliere, and we here return him our most hearty thanks for all the hearty laughing he has given us. *C'est un bon garçon.*

319

There are in the Agreeable Surprise some of the most irresistible *double entendres* that can be conceived, and in Lingo's superb replication, 'A scholar! I was a master of scholars!' he has hit the height of the ridiculous.

MISS MERRY'S MANDANE

The Examiner.   *July* 21, 1816.

A young lady whose name is Miss Merry, has appeared with great applause in the part of Mandane, in Artaxerxes, at the New English Opera. Miss Merry is not tall, but there is something not ungraceful in her person: her face, without being regular, has a pleasing expression in it; her action is good, and often spirited; and her voice is excellent. The songs she has to sing in this character are delightful, and she sung them very delightfully. Her timidity on the first night of her appearing was so great, as almost to prevent her from going on. But her apprehensions, though they lessened the power of her voice, did not take from its sweetness. She appears to possess very great taste and skill; and to have not only a fine voice, but (what many singers want) an ear for music. Her tones are mellow, true, and varied; sometimes exquisitely broken by light, fluttering half-notes—at other times reposing on a deep-murmuring bass. The general style of her singing is equable, and unaffected; yet in one or two passages, we thought she added some extraneous and unnecessary ornaments, and (for a precious note or two) lost the charm of the expression, by sacrificing simplicity to execution. This objection struck us most in the manner in which Miss Merry sung the beautiful air, 'If o'er the cruel tyrant Love,' which is an irresistible appeal to the sentiments, and seems, in its genuine simplicity, above all art. This song, and particularly the last lines, 'What was my pride, is now my shame,' &c. ought to be sung, as we have heard them sung, as if the notes fell from her lips like the liquid drops from the bending flower, and her voice fluttered and died away with the expiring conflict of passion in her bosom. If vocal music has an advantage over instrumental, it is, we imagine, in this very particular; in the immediate communication between the words and the expression they suggest, between the voice and the soul of the singer, which ought to mould every tone, whether deep or tender, according to the impulse of true passion. Miss Merry's execution does not rest entirely upon the ground of expression: she is not always thinking of the subject. Her 'Soldier tired,' and 'Let not rage thy bosom firing,' were both admirable. Her voice has not the piercing softness of Miss Stephens's, its clear crystalline qualities. Neither has her style of singing the same originality, and simple pathos. Miss Stephens's voice and manner are her own : Miss Merry belongs to a class of singers, but that class is a very pleasing one, and she is at present at the head of it. She is an undoubted acquisition both to the New English Opera, and to the English stage.

Mr. Horn's Arbaces was very fine. He sings always in tune, and in an admirable *sostenuto* style. He keeps his voice (perhaps indeed) too much under him, and does not let it loose often enough. His manner of singing ' Water parted from the sea ' was of this internal and suppressed character. Though this may be the feeling suggested by part of the words, yet certainly in other parts the voice ought to be thrown out, and as it were, go a journey, like the water's course. Of the other performers we can say nothing favourable.

EXIT BY MISTAKE

The Examiner.   *July 28, 1816.*

We insert the following letter, which has been sent us, merely to show our impartiality :

' MR. EDITOR,—I have been to see the new Comedy Exit by Mistake, at the Theatre Royal Haymarket. As this piece is *sans* moral and *sans* interest, I am surprised at its being called a *Comedy*, for many of our old *Farces* are more worthy of the name. Perhaps the author fondly anticipated much pathos from Mrs. Kendal's scene with her son (Mr. Barnard), but it would have been much better if both mother and son had been omitted, for the latter is a hot-headed blockhead, who commits a most unjustifiable assault upon a *stranger*, in a *stranger's* house, by turning him out, which gross affront is in the last Act overlooked. In consequence of a letter about Mr. Roland's departure, accompanied by his will, it is supposed he had departed fron the *world* instead of the *country* where he was. This is the ' *Exit by Mistake*,' but the chief mistakes arise from the *entrances* of the performers. The executor hearing that Roland (Mr. Terry) is alive and in town, goes to an inn to meet him, but most unaccountably mistakes Mr. Rattletrap (Russel) an actor just arrived from America, for his own friend, and even calls the actor by the name of Rattletrap. Poor Mr. Roland, in order to recover his property, inquires for an attorney, and is told there 's one *below*. Soon after the executor enters, and though dressed in a *brown* coat, he is mistaken for an attorney. There are other inferior mistakes in the piece, but the greatest mistake is the author's—for it is a Farce instead of a Comedy. As the play-bills state, that this piece has since been applauded by ' brilliant and crowded audiences,' and that ' no orders can be admitted ; ' the proprietors have no right to complain of their rival, the Lyceum Theatre, except Mr. Arnold should produce a good Opera to

A VIEW OF THE ENGLISH STAGE

oppose this Farcical Comedy, and then the public will see the utility of rival theatres. Mr. Tokely's character in it (Crockery) is the same which the same gentleman performs in the author's 'Love and Gout,' with this difference, that in one he is a dissatisfied gentleman, and in the other a whining servant. Mr. Jones's character (Restless Absent) keeps him in motion the first two Acts, but in the last he is quite stationary.

'DRAMATICUS.

'*July* 25, 1816.'

We do not agree with Dramaticus on the subject of the piece, which he so resolutely condemns. He puts us a little (though not much) in mind of John Dennis, who drew his sword on the author of a successful tragedy, without any other provocation. As to the title of this play, to which our critic so vehemently objects, we leave him to settle that point with the author. We do not judge of plays, or of any thing else by their titles.

The writer says, the Proprietors of the Haymarket have no right to complain, 'except Mr. Arnold should produce a good Opera to oppose this Farcical Comedy, and then the public will see the utility of rival theatres.' We wish Mr. Arnold would lose no time in convincing the public. As we have not the same faith as our correspondent in the power of rival theatres in screwing up the wits of their opponents, we did not go to the new comedy of Exit by Mistake, expecting either a profound moral or high interest; and so far we were not disappointed. But with a good deal of absurdity, there is some whim in it: there are several very tolerable puns in it, and a sufficient stock of lively passing allusions. It is light and laughable, and does well enough for a summer theatre. The part of Crockery in particular is very droll, and to us quite new, for we are not acquainted with 'the dissatisfied gentleman,' his predecessor, in Love and Gout. Crockery is a foolish fat servant (personated exceedingly well by Mr. Tokely) who complains that every thing is altered since he went abroad with his master, 'cries all the way from Portsmouth, because the mile-stones are changed, and is in despair because an old pigstye has been converted into a dwelling-house.' This whimpering, maudlin philosopher, is as tenacious of innovation as the late Mr. Burke, and as great an admirer of *the good old times*, as the editor of a modern Journal. In one thing we agree with honest Crockery, where he does not like to see the sign of the Duke of Marlborough's head pulled down for the Duke of Wellington's; in the first place, because the Duke of Marlborough had a very good head, and the Duke of Wellington's is a mere sign-post; in the second, because we think it a more meritorious act to drive out the English Bourbons, the Stuarts, than

322

to restore the French Stuarts, the Bourbons, to the throne of *their* ancestors. So much for the politics of the Theatre.

There is another new piece, A Man in Mourning for Himself, come out at the new English Theatre, which, whether it is Comedy, Opera, or Farce, we do not know. But—*de mortuis nil nisi bonum.* So let it pass. But there is a Mr. Herring in it, whom we cannot pass by without notice. He is the oddest fish that has lately been landed on the stage. We are to thank Mr. Arnold for bringing him ashore. This *did* require some sagacity, some discrimination. We never saw any thing more amphibious,—with coat-pockets in the shape of fins, and a jowl like gills with the hook just taken out. He flounders and flounces upon the stage with the airs and genius of a Dutch plaise. His person detonates with boisterous wit and humour, and his voice goes off like a cracker near a sounding-board. With these preparatory qualifications, he played a valet who is his own master; and the jumble of high life below stairs was very complete. This gentleman's gentleman was very coarse and very mawkish; very blustering and very sheepish; and runs his head into scrapes without the slightest suspicion. We have never seen Mr. Herring before; but on this occasion he was, according to our tastes, in fine pickle and preservation.

The Beggar's Opera was performed on Thursday, when Miss Merry appeared in the part of Polly, and Mr. Horn as Captain Macheath. Miss Merry displayed great sweetness and taste in most of the songs, and her acting was pleasing, though she laboured under considerable embarrassment. We liked her 'Ponder well,' and 'My all's in my possession,' the best. She seemed to us not to be quite perfect either in 'Cease your funning,' or in the exquisite little air of 'He so teased me.' We have no doubt, however, that she will make in time a very interesting representative of one of the most interesting characters on the stage, for we hardly know any character more artless and amiable than Gay's Polly, except perhaps Shakespear's Imogen. And Polly has the advantage on the stage, for she *may be sung*, but Imogen cannot be *acted*.

Mr. Horn's Macheath was much better than what we have lately seen. He sung the songs well, with a little too much ornament for the profession of the Captain: and his air and manner, though they did not fall into the common error of vulgarity, were rather too precise and finical. Macheath should be a fine man and a gentleman, but he should be one of God Almighty's gentlemen, not a gentleman of the black rod. His gallantry and good-breeding should arise from

323

impulse, not from rule; not from the trammels of education, but from a soul generous, courageous, good-natured, aspiring, amorous. The class of the character is very difficult to hit. It is something between gusto and slang, like port-wine and brandy mixed. It is not the mere gentleman that should be represented, but the blackguard sublimated into the gentleman. This character is qualified in a highwayman, as it is qualified in a prince. We hope this is not a libel. Miss Kelly's Lucy was excellent. She is worthy to act Gay.

THE ITALIAN OPERA

The Examiner.   (*King's Theatre*) *August* 4, 1816.

In Schlegel's work on the Drama, there are the following remarks on the nature of the Opera:

'In Tragedy the chief object is the poetry, and every other thing is subordinate to it; but in the Opera, the poetry is merely an accessary, the means of connecting the different parts together, and it is almost buried under its associates. The best prescription for the composition of the text of an Opera is to give a poetical sketch, which may be afterwards filled up and coloured by the other arts. This anarchy of the arts, where music, dancing, and decoration endeavour to surpass each other by the most profuse display of dazzling charms, constitutes the very essence of the Opera. What sort of opera music would it be, where the words should receive a mere rythmical accompaniment of the simplest modulations? The fantastic magic of the Opera consists altogether in the luxurious competition of the different means, and in the perplexity of an over-flowing superfluity. This would at once be destroyed by an approximation to the severity of the ancient taste in any one point, even in that of costume; for the contrast would render the variety in all the other departments quite insupportable. The costume of the Opera ought to be dazzling, and overladen with ornaments; and hence many things which have been censured as unnatural, such as exhibiting heroes warbling and trilling in the excess of despondency, are perfectly justifiable. This fairy world is not peopled by real men, but by a singular kind of singing creatures. Neither is it any dis-advantage to us, that the Opera is conveyed in a language which is not generally understood; the text is altogether lost in the music, and the language, the most harmonious and musical, and which contains the greatest number of open vowels and distinct accents for recitative, is therefore the best.'

The foregoing remarks give the best account we have seen of that

324

splendid exhibition, the Italian Opera. These German critics can explain every thing, and upon any given occasion, *make the worse appear the better reason.* Their theories are always at variance with common sense, and we shall not in the present instance, undertake to decide between them. There is one thing, however, which we will venture to decide, which is, that the feelings of the English people must undergo some very elaborate process (metaphysical or practical) before they are thoroughly reconciled to this union of different elements, the consistency and harmony of which depends on their contradiction and discord. We take it, the English are so far from being an opera-going, that they are not even a play-going people, from constitution. You can hardly get them to speak their sentiments, much less to sing them, or to hear them sung with any real sympathy. The boxes, splendid as they are, and splendid as the appearance of those in them is, do not breathe a spirit of enjoyment. They are rather like the sick wards of luxury and idleness, where people of a certain class are condemned to perform the quarantine of fashion for the evening. The rest of the spectators are sulky and self-important, and the only idea which each person has in his head, seems to be that he is at the opera. Little interest is shewn in the singing or dancing, little pleasure appears to be derived from either, and the audience seem only to be stunned and stupified with wonder. The satisfaction which the English feel in this entertainment is very much *against the grain.* They are a people, jealous of being pleased in any way but their own.

We were particularly struck with the force of these remarks the other evening in the gallery, where our fellow-countrymen seemed to be only upon their good behaviour or self-defence against the ill-behaviour of others, some persons asserting their right of talking loud about their own affairs, and others resenting this, not as an interruption of their pleasures, but as an encroachment on their privileges. Soon after a Frenchman came in, and his eye at once fastened upon the ballet. At a particular air, he could no longer contain himself, but joined in chorus in an agreeable under-voice, as if he expected others to keep time to him, and exclaiming, while he wiped his forehead from an exuberance of satisfaction, his eyes glistening, and his face shining, ' *Ah c'est charmant, c'est charmant!* ' Now this, being ourselves English, we confess, gave us more pleasure than the opera or the ballet, in both of which, however, we felt a considerable degree of melancholy satisfaction, *selon la coutume de notre pays*—according to the custom of our country.

The opera was Cosi fan Tutti, with Mozart's music, and the ballet was the Dansomanie. The music of the first of these is really

325

enough (to borrow a phrase from a person who was also a great man in his way) 'to draw three souls out of one weaver:' and as to the ballet, it might make a Frenchman forget his country and all other things. This ballet is certainly the essence of a ballet. What a grace and a liveliness there is in it! What spirit and invention! What can exceed the ingenuity of the dance in which the favoured lover joins in with his mistress and the rival, and makes all sorts of advances to her, and receives her favours, her pressures of the hand, and even kisses, without being found out by the other, who thinks all these demonstrations of fondness intended for him! What an enthusiasm for art in the character of the master of the house, who is seized by the Dansomanie! What a noble and disinterested zeal in the pursuit and encouragement of his favourite science! What a mechanical sprightliness in all about him, particularly in the servant who throws down a whole equipage of china, while he is dancing with it on his head, and is rewarded by his master for this proof of devotion to his interests! What a sympathy throughout between the heels and the head, between the heart and the fingers' ends! The Minuet de la Cour, danced in full dresses, and with the well-known accompaniment of the music, put us in mind of the old chivalrous times of the Duke de Nemours and the Princess of Cleves, or of what really seems to us longer ago, the time when we ourselves used to be called out at school before the assembled taste and fashion of the neighbourhood, to go through this very dance with the partner whom we had selected for this purpose, and presented with a bunch of flowers on the occasion!

The Opera had less justice done it than the Ballet. The laughing Trio was spoiled by Mr. Naldi, who performs the part of an 'Old Philosopher' in it, but who is more like an impudent valet or *major-domo* of an hotel. We never saw any one so much at home; who seems so little conscious of the existence of any one but himself, and who throws his voice, his arms and legs about with such a total disregard of *bienseance*. The character is a kind of Opera Pandarus, who exposes the inconstancy of two young ladies, by entangling them in an intrigue with their own lovers in disguise. Mr. Braham, we are told, sings Mozart with a peculiar greatness of gusto. But this greatness of gusto does not appear to us the real excellence of Mozart. The song beginning *Secondate*, in which he and his friend (Signor Begri) call upon the gentle zephyrs by moonlight to favour their design, is exquisite, and 'floats upon the air, smoothing the raven down of darkness till it smiles.'

> 'And Silence wish'd, she might be never more
> Still to be so displaced.'

Madame Fodor's voice does not harmonize with the music of this composer. It is hard, metallic, and jars like the reverberation of a tight string. Mozart's music should seem to come from the air, and return to it. Madame Vestris is a pretty little figure, and is in this respect a contrast to Madame Fodor.

OLD CUSTOMS

The Examiner.   *August* 11, 1816.

We have suffered two disappointments this week, one in seeing a farce that was announced and acted at the English Opera, and the other in not seeing one that was announced and not acted at the Haymarket. We should hope that which is to come is the best; for the other is very bad, as we think. Old Customs is a farce or operetta, in which an uncle (Mr. Bartley) and his nephew (Mr. Wrench) court the same young lady (Miss L. Kelly). She prefers the nephew, from whom she has received several letters. These, with her answers, she sends to Mr. Bartley in a packet or basket, to convince him of her real sentiments, and of the impropriety of his prosecuting his rivalry to his nephew. In the mean time, it being Christmas or New Year's Day (we forget which), Bartley's servant (Russell) receives a visit from his old mother, who, in this season of compliments and presents, brings him a little sister in a basket, and leaves it to his care, while she goes to see her acquaintance in the village. Russell, after singing a ludicrous lullaby to the baby, goes out himself and leaves it in the basket on the table, a great and improbable neglect, no doubt, of his infant charge. His master (Bartley) soon after comes in, and receives the letter from his mistress (Miss L. Kelly) informing him of a present she has sent him *in a basket*, meaning her packet of love-letters, and apologizing for the abrupt method she has taken of unfolding the true state of her heart and progress of her affections. Bartley looks about for this important confidential basket, and finds that which the old woman had left with her son, with its explanatory contents. At this indecency of the young lady, and indignity offered to himself, he grows very much incensed, struts and frets about the stage, and when Miss L. Kelly herself, with her father and lover, comes to ask his decision upon the question after the clear evidence which she has sent him, nothing can come up to the violence of his rage and impatience, but the absurdity of the contrivance by which it is occasioned. His nephew (Mr. Wrench) provokes him still farther, by talking of a present which he has left with him that morning, an embryo production of his efforts

327

to please, meaning a manuscript comedy, but which Mr. Bartley confounds with the living Christmas-box in the basket. A strange scene of confusion ensues, in which every one is placed in as absurd and ridiculous a situation as possible, till Russell enters and brings about an unforeseen *denouement*, by giving an account of the adventures of himself and his little brother.

Such is the plot, and the wit is answerable to it. There was a good deal of laughing, and it is better to laugh at nonsense than at nothing. But really the humours of punch and the puppet-shew are sterling, legitimate, classical comedy, compared with the stuff of which the Muse of the new English Opera is weekly delivered. But it is in vain to admonish. The piece, we understand, has since been withdrawn.

MY LANDLADY'S NIGHT-GOWN

The Examiner.   *August* 18, 1816.

The new Farce at the Haymarket-Theatre, called My Landlady's Night-Gown, is made of very indifferent stuff. It is very tedious and nonsensical. Mr. Jones is the hero of the piece, and gives the title to it; for being closely pressed by some bailiffs, he suddenly slips on his Landlady's Night-gown, and escapes in disguise from his pursuers, by speaking in a feigned female voice to one of them, and knocking the other down by an exertion of his proper and natural prowess. Such is the story which he himself tells, to account for the oddity of his first appearance. Yet the apology is not necessary. Mr. Jones himself is always a greater oddity than his dress. There is something in his face and manner that bids equal defiance to disguise or ornament. The mind is affirmed by a great poet to be 'its own place:' and Nature, in making Mr. Jones, said to the tailor, You have no business here. Whether he plays my Lord Foppington in point-lace, or personates an old woman in My Landlady's Night-Gown, he is just the same lively, bustling, fidgetty, staring, queer-looking mortal; and the gradations of his metamorphosis from the nobleman to the footman are quite imperceptible. Yet he is an actor not without merit; the town like him, and he knows it; and as to ourselves, we have fewer objections to him the more we see of him. Use reconciles one to any thing. The only part of this entertainment which is at all entertaining, is the scene in which Russell, as the tailor, measures Jones for a new suit of clothes. This scene is not dull, but it is very gross, and the grossness is not carried off by a proportionable degree of wit. We could point out the

328

instances, but not with decency. So we shall let it alone. Tokely's character is very well, but not so good as Crockery. He is an actor of some humour, and he sometimes shews a happy conception of character; but we hope he will never play Sir Benjamin Backbite again.

New English Opera.

Miss Merry has disappointed us again, in not appearing in Rosetta. We may perhaps take our revenge, by not saying a word about her when she does come out. It was certainly a disappointment, though Miss Kelly played the part in her stead, who is a fine sensible girl, and sings not amiss. But there is that opening scene where Rosetta and Lucinda sit and sing with their song-books in their hands among the garden bowers and roses, for which we had screwed up our ears to a most critical anticipation of delight, not to be soothed but with the sweetest sounds. To enter into good acting, requires an effort; but to hear soft music is a pleasure without any trouble. Besides, we had seen Miss Stephens in Rosetta, and wanted to compare notes. How then, Miss Merry, could you disappoint us?

Mr. Horn executed the part of Young Meadows with his usual ability and propriety, both as an actor and a singer. We also think that Mr. Chatterley's Justice Woodcock was a very excellent piece of acting. The smile of recognition with which he turns round to his old flame Rosetta, in the last scene, told completely. Mrs. Grove's Deborah Woodcock reminded us of Mrs. Sparks's manner of acting it, which we take to be a high compliment.

Mr. Incledon appeared for the first time on this stage, as Hawthorn, and sung the usual songs with his well-known power and sweetness of voice. He is a true old English singer, and there is nobody who goes through a drinking song, a hunting song, or a sailor's song like him. He makes a very loud and agreeable noise without any meaning. At present he both speaks and sings as if he had a lozenge or a slice of marmalade in his mouth. If he could go to America and leave his voice behind him, it would be a great benefit—to the parent country.

CASTLE OF ANDALUSIA

The Examiner.   *(New English Opera) Sept.* 1, 1816.

We hear nothing of Miss Merry; and there is nothing else at this theatre that we wish to hear. Even Mr. Horn is nothing without her; he stands alone and unsupported; and the ear loses its relish and its power of judging of harmonious sounds, where it has nothing

329

but harshness and discordance to compare them with. We are sorry to include in this censure Miss Kelly, whose attempts to supply the place of *Prima Donna* of the English Opera, do great credit to her talents, industry, and good-nature, but still they have not given her a voice, which is indispensable to a singer, as singing is to an Opera. If the Managers think it merely necessary to get some one to *go through* the different songs in Artaxerxes, the Beggar's Opera, or Love in a Village, they might hire persons to read them through at a cheaper rate; and in either case, we fear they must equally have to hire the audience as well as the actors. Mr. Inceldon sung the duet of 'All's well,' the other night, with Mr. Horn, in the Castle of Andalusia, and has repeated it every evening since. Both singers were very much and deservedly applauded in it. Mr. Inceldon's voice is certainly a fine one, but its very excellence makes us regret that its modulation is not equal to its depth and compass. His best notes come from him involuntarily, or are often misplaced. The effect of his singing is something like standing near a music-seller's shop, where some idle person is trying the different instruments; the flute, the trumpet, the bass-viol, give forth their sounds of varied strength and sweetness, but without order or connection.

One of the novelties of the Castle of Andalusia, as got up at this theatre, was Mr. Herring's Pedrillo; an odd fish certainly, a very outlandish person, and whose acting is altogether incoherent and gross, but with a certain strong relish in it. It is only *too much* of a *good thing*. His oil has not salt enough to qualify it. He has a great power of exhibiting the ludicrous and absurd; but by its being either not like, or over-done, the ridicule falls upon himself instead of the character. Indeed he is literally to the comedian, what the caricaturist is to the painter; and his representation of footmen and fine gentlemen, is just such as we see in Gillray's shop-window. The same thing perhaps is not to be borne on the stage, though we laugh at it till we are obliged to hold our sides, in a caricature. We do not see, however, why this style of acting might not make a distinct species of itself, like the Italian *opera buffa*, with Scaramouch, Harlequin, and Pantaloon, among whom Mr. Herring would shine like a gold fish in a glass-case.

TWO WORDS

The Examiner.   *Sept.* 8, 1816.

It was the opinion of Colley Cibber, a tolerable judge of such matters, that in those degenerate days, the metropolis could only support one legitimate theatre, having a legitimate company, and acting legitimate plays. In the present improved state of the drama, which has 'gone like a crab backwards,' we are nearly of the same opinion, in summer time at least. We critics have been for the last two months like mice in an air-pump, gasping for breath, subsisting on a sort of theatrical half-allowance. We hate coalitions in politics, but we really wish the two little Theatres would club their stock of wit and humour into one. We should then have a very tight, compact little company, and crowded houses in the dog-days.

The new after-piece of 'Two Words,' at the English Opera, is a delightful little piece. It is a scene with robbers and midnight murder in it; and all such scenes are delightful to the reader or spectator. We can conceive nothing better managed than the plot of this. The spell-bound silence and dumb-show of Rose, the servant girl at the house in the forest, to which the benighted travellers come, has an inimitable effect; and to make it complete, it is played by Miss Kelly. The signals conveyed by the music of a lone flute in such a place, and at such a time, thrill through the ear, and almost suspend the breath. Mr. Short did not spoil the interest excited by the story, and both Mr. Wilkinson and Mrs. Grove did justice to the parts of the terrified servant, and the mischievous old house-keeper, who is a dextrous accomplice in the dreadful scene. The fault of the piece is, that the interest necessarily falls off in the second act, which makes it rather tiresome, though the second appearance of Miss Kelly in it, as the ward of Bartley at his great castle, is very ingeniously contrived, and occasions some droll perplexities to her lover, Don ——, whose life she has just saved from the hands of the assassins, only escaping from their vengeance herself by the arrival of her valorous guardian and a party of his soldiers. On the whole, this is the best novelty that has been brought out during the season at the English Opera, and we wish it every possible success.

Mr. Terry last week had for his benefit the Surrender of Calais. He played the part of Eustace de St. Pierre in it with judgment and energy, but without a pleasing effect. When Mr. Terry plays these tragic characters,

'The line too labours, and the thoughts move slow.'

He sticks in tragedy like a man in the mud; or to borrow a higher figure from a learned critic, 'he resembles a person walking on stilts in a morass.' We shall always be glad to lift him out of it into the common path of unpretending comedy : there he succeeds, and is himself. The Surrender of Calais is as interesting as a tragedy can be without poetry in it. It has considerable pathos, though of a kind which borders on the shocking too much. It requires accomplished actors to carry it off; but it was not, in the present instance, very heroically cast. The Haymarket Theatre inclines more to comedy than to tragedy; and there are several scenes in this tragedy (for such it really is *till it is over*), which, 'not to be hated,' should be seen at the greatest possible distance that the stage allows. One advantage, at least, of our overgrown theatres is, that they throw the most distressing objects into a milder historical perspective.

THE WONDER

The Examiner.   (*Covent Garden*) *Sept.* 15, 1816.

The Wonder is one of our good old English Comedies, which holds a happy medium between grossness and refinement. The plot is rich in intrigue, and the dialogue in *double entendre*, which however is so light and careless, as only to occasion a succession of agreeable alarms to the ears of delicacy. This genuine comedy, which is quite as pleasant to read as to see (for we have made the experiment within these few days, to our entire satisfaction) was written by an Englishwoman, before the sentimental, Ultra-Jacobinical German School, of which a short and amusing account has been lately given in the Courier, had spoiled us with their mawkish platonics and maudlin metaphysics. The soul is here with extreme simplicity considered as a mere accessary to the senses in love, and the conversation of bodies preferred to that of minds as much more entertaining. We do not subscribe our names to this opinion, but it is Mrs. Centlivre's, and we do not chuse to contradict a lady. The plot is admirably calculated for stage-effect, and kept up with prodigious ingenuity and vivacity to the end. The spectator is just beginning to be tired with the variety of stratagems that follow and perplex one another, when the whole difficulty is happily unravelled in the last scene. The *dove-tailing* of the incidents and situations (so that one unexpected surprise gives place to another, and the success of the plot is prevented by the unluckiest accident in the world happening in the very nick of time) supplies the place of any great force of character or sentiment. The time for the entrance of each person on the stage is the moment when they are least wanted, and when their arrival makes either themselves or somebody else look as foolish as possible. The Busy Body shews the same talent for invention and *coup-d'œil* for theatrical effect, and the laughableness of both comedies depends on a brilliant series of mis-timed exits and entrances. The Wonder is not,

332

however, without a moral; it exhibits a rare example of a woman keeping a secret, for the sake of a female friend, which she is under every temptation to break, and her resolution and fidelity are, after a number of mortifying accidents and fears, happily rewarded by the triumph both of her friendship and her love. The situation of Violante is more prominent than her character; or, at least, the character is more moral than entertaining. She is a young lady of great goodness of heart and firmness of principle, but who neither displays any great superiority of wit in extricating herself from the difficulties in which her regard for the safety of her friend involves her, nor of spirit in repelling the insinuations to which her reputation is exposed in the eyes of her lover. She submits to her situation with firmness of purpose and conscious reliance on her own innocence.

Miss Boyle, the young lady who appeared in this character on Friday, shewed herself not incompetent to its successful delineation. Her figure is tall, and her face, though her features are small, is pretty and expressive. Her articulation (for a first appearance) was remarkably distinct, and her voice is full and sweet. It is however rather sentimental than comic. She rounds her words too much, nor do they come 'trippingly from the tongue.' It is sufficient if the dialogue of genteel comedy comes with light-fluttering grace and gay animation from the lips; it should not come labouring up all the way from the heart. This young lady's general demeanour is easy and unaffected; and when she has overcome her timidity, we have no doubt she will give considerable spirit and dignity to the more serious scenes of the story. Her smile has much archness and expression; and we hope, from the promise of taste and talent which she gave through her whole performance, that she will prove an acquisition to the stage, in a line of comedy in which we are at present absolutely deficient. She was very favourably received throughout.

We do not think the play in general was well got up. Charles Kemble seemed to be rehearsing Don Felix with an eye to Macduff, or some face-making tragic character. He was only excellent in the drunken scene. Mrs. Gibbs at one time fairly took wing across the stage, and played the chamber-maid with too little restraint from vulgar decorums. Mr. Abbott never acts ill, but he does not answer to our idea of Colonel Briton. Emery's Gibby was sturdy enough, and seemed to prove what he himself says, that 'a Scotchman is not ashamed to shew his face any where.'

A VIEW OF THE ENGLISH STAGE

THE DISTRESSED MOTHER

The Examiner.   *September* 22, 1816.

A Mr. Macready appeared at Covent-Garden Theatre on Monday and Friday, in the character of Orestes, in the Distressed Mother, a bad play for the display of his powers, in which, however, he succeeded in making a decidedly favourable impression upon the audience. His voice is powerful in the highest degree, and at the same time possesses great harmony and modulation. His face is not equally calculated for the stage. He declaims better than any body we have lately heard. He is accused of being violent, and of wanting pathos. Neither of these objections is true. His manner of delivering the first speeches in this play was admirable, and the want of increasing interest afterwards was the fault of the author, rather than the actor. The fine suppressed tone in which he assented to Pyrrhus's command to convey the message to Hermione was a test of his variety of power, and brought down repeated acclamations from the house. We do not lay much stress on his mad-scene, though that was very good in its kind, for mad-scenes do not occur very often, and when they do, had in general better be omitted. We have not the slightest hesitation in saying, that Mr. Macready is by far the best tragic actor that has come out in our remembrance, with the exception of Mr. Kean. We however heartily wish him well out of this character of Orestes. It is a kind of forlorn hope in tragedy. There is nothing to be made of it on the English stage, beyond experiment. It is a trial, not a triumph. These French plays puzzle an English audience exceedingly. They cannot attend to the actor, for the difficulty they have in understanding the author. We think it wrong in any actor of great merit (which we hold Mr. Macready to be) to come out in an ambiguous character, to salve his reputation. An actor is like a man who throws himself from the top of a steeple by a rope. He should chuse the highest steeple he can find, that if he does not succeed in coming safe to the ground, he may break his neck at once, and so put himself and the spectators out of farther pain.

Ambrose Phillips's Distressed Mother is a very good translation from Racine's Andromache. It is an alternation of topics, of *pros* and *cons*, on the casuistry of domestic and state affairs, and produced a great effect of *ennui* on the audience. When you hear one of the speeches in these rhetorical tragedies, you know as well what will be the answer to it, as when you see the tide coming up the river—you know that it will return again. The other actors filled their parts with successful mediocrity.

We highly disapprove of the dresses worn on this occasion, and supposed to be the exact Greek costume. We do not know that the Greek heroes were dressed like women, or wore their long hair strait down their backs. Or even supposing that they did, this is not generally known or understood by the audience; and though the preservation of the ancient costume is a good thing, it is of more importance not to shock our present prejudices. The managers of Covent-Garden are not the Society of Antiquaries. The attention to costume is only necessary to preserve probability: in the present instance, it could only violate it, because there is nothing to lead the public opinion to expect such an exhibition. We know how the Turks are dressed, from seeing them in the streets; we know the costume of the Greek statues, from seeing casts in the shop-windows: we know that savages go naked, from reading voyages and travels: but we do not know that the Grecian Chiefs at the Siege of Troy were dressed as Mr. Charles Kemble, Mr. Abbott, and Mr. Macready were the other evening in the Distressed Mother. It is a discovery of the Managers; and they should have kept their secret to themselves.—The epithet in Homer, applied to the Grecian warriors, κάρη κομόωντες, is not any proof. It signifies not *long-haired*, but literally *bushy-headed*, which would come nearer to the common Brutus head, than this long dangling slip of hair. The oldest and most authentic models we have are the Elgin Marbles, and it is certain the Theseus is a *crop*. One would think this standard might satisfy the Committee of Managers in point of classical antiquity. But no such thing. They are much deeper in Greek costume and the history of the fabulous ages than those old-fashioned fellows, the Sculptors who lived in the time of Pericles. But we have said quite enough on this point.

Drury-Lane.

The chief novelties at this Theatre for the present week, have been a Mr. Bengough, from the Theatre Royal, Bath, and a Mrs. Knight, of the York Theatre, who have appeared in the characters of Baron Wildenheim and Agatha Friburg, in Lovers' Vows. Both have been successful. Mr. Bengough is an actor who shews considerable judgment and feeling, and who would produce more effect than he does, if he took less pains to produce it. The appearance of study takes from that of nature, and yet the expression of natural pathos is what he seems to excel in. He treads the stage well, and is, we think, an acquisition to the company.

We wonder the long-winded, heavy-handed writer in the Courier, who has been belabouring Bertram so woefully, does not fall foul of Lovers' Vows, as the quintessence of metaphysical licentiousness and

335

the ultra-Jacobinism of ultra-Jacobinical poetry. We think that everlasting writer might build thirty columns of lumbering criticisms, 'pointing to the skies,' on any single passage of this effusion of German sentiment and genius. We hope the worthy author will take this hint, and after he has exhausted upon this work the inexhaustible stores of his unspeakable discoveries and researches into the theory of mill-stones, we would recommend him to turn his pen to an almost forgotten play, called Remorse, at the bottom of which, if he will look narrowly, he will find 'a vaporous drop profound' of the same pernicious leaven; and by setting it fermenting, with the help of transcendental reasoning, and the mechanical operations of the spirit, may raise mists and clouds that will ascend above the moon, and turn the Courier office into a laundry!—Oh, we had forgot: Mrs. Mardyn played her old character of Amelia Wildenheim more charmingly than ever. She acts even with more grace and spirit than when she first came out in it, and looks as handsome as she used to do.

MISS BOYLE'S ROSALIND

The Examiner.   *October 6, 1816.*

We have had a considerable treat this week, in Miss Boyle's Rosalind, at Covent-Garden Theatre. It is one of the chastest and most pleasing pieces of comic acting we have seen for some time. We did not think much of her in Violante, which might be owing to the diffidence of a first appearance, or to the little she has to do in the character. But she rises with her characters, and really makes a very charming Rosalind. The words of Shakespear become her mouth, and come from it with a delicious freshness, which gives us back the sense. There should be in the tones of the voice, to repeat Shakespear's verses properly, something resembling the sound of musical glasses. He has himself given us his idea on this subject, where he says, 'How silver sweet sound lovers' tongues by night.' We were not satisfied with Miss Boyle's enunciation in Violante. It wanted lightness and grace. Her Rosalind was spoken with more effect, and with more gaiety at the same time. The sentiment seemed to infuse into her the true comic spirit, and her acting improved with the wit and vivacity of the passages she had to deliver. This would be a defect in a character of mere manners, like Lady Townley, where there is always supposed to be an air or affectation of a certain agreeable vivacity or fashionable tone; but in a character of nature, like Rosalind, who is supposed to speak only what she

336

thinks, and to express delight only as she feels it, it was a great beauty. Her eyes also became more sparkling, and her smile more significant, according to the *naiveté* and force of what she had to utter. The highest compliment we can pay her acting is by applying to it what Shakespear has somewhere said of poetry—

> ' Our poesy is a gum that issues
> From whence 'tis nourish'd. The fire i'th' flint
> Shews not till it be struck. Our gentle flame
> Provokes itself, and like the current flies
> Each bound in chafes.'

To realize this description would be the perfection of comic acting. We must not forget her Cuckoo-song; indeed we could not, if we would. It was quite delightful. The tone and manner in which she repeated the word Cuckoo, was as arch and provoking as possible, and seemed to grow more saucy every time by the repetition, but still, though it hovered very near them, it was restrained from passing the limits of delicacy and propriety. She was deservedly *encored* in it; though this circumstance seemed to throw her into some little confusion. We have, however, two faults to find, both of which may be easily remedied. The first is, that there is a tendency to a lisp in some of her words: the second is, that there is a trip in her gait, and too great a disposition to keep in motion while she is speaking, or to go up to the persons she is addressing, as if they were deaf. Both these are defects of inexperience: the two necessary qualities for any young actress to set out with, in the higher comedy, are liveliness and elegance, or in other words, feeling with delicacy, and these we think Miss Boyle possesses. We were a good deal pleased with Mr. Young's Jaques. He spoke several passages well, and is upon the whole an *improving* actor.

Mr. Macready's Bentevole, in the Italian Lover, is very highly spoken of. We only saw the last act of it, but it appeared to us to be very fine in its kind. It was natural, easy, and forcible. Indeed, we suspect some parts of it were too natural, that is, that Mr. Macready thought too much of what his feelings might dictate in such circumstances, rather than of what the circumstances must have dictated to him to do. We allude particularly to the half significant, half hysterical laugh, and distorted jocular leer, with his eyes towards the persons accusing him of the murder, when the evidence of his guilt comes out. Either the author did not intend him to behave in this manner, or he must have made the other parties on the stage interrupt him as a self-convicted criminal. His appeal to Manoah (the witness against him) to suppress the proofs which must be fatal to his honour and his life, was truly affecting. His resumption of a spirit of defiance was not sufficiently dignified, and was more like the self-sufficient swaggering airs of comedy, than the real grandeur of tragedy, which should always proceed from passion. Mr. Macready sometimes, to express uneasiness and agitation, composes his cravat, as he would in a drawing-room. This is, we think, neither graceful nor natural in extraordinary situations. His tones are equally powerful and flexible, varying with the greatest facility from the lowest to the highest pitch of the human voice.

MR. MACREADY'S OTHELLO

The Examiner.   *October* 13, 1816.

We have to speak this week of Mr. Macready's Othello, at Covent-Garden Theatre, and though it must be in favourable terms, it cannot be in very favourable ones. We have been rather spoiled for seeing any one else in this character, by Mr. Kean's performance of it, and also by having read the play itself lately. Mr. Macready was more than respectable in the part ; and he only failed because he attempted to excel. He did not, however, express the individual bursts of feeling, nor the deep and accumulating tide of passion which ought to be given in Othello. It may perhaps seem an extravagant illustration, but the idea which we think any actor ought to have of this character, to play it to the height of the poetical conception, is that of a majestic serpent wounded, writhing under its pain, stung to madness, and attempting by sudden darts, or coiling up its whole force, to wreak its vengeance on those about it, and falling at last a mighty victim under the redoubled strokes of its assailants. No one can admire more than we do the force of genius and passion which Mr. Kean shews in this part, but he is not stately enough for it. He plays it like a gipsey, and not like a Moor. We miss in Mr. Kean not the physiognomy, or the costume, so much as the *architectural* building up of the part. This character always puts us in mind of the line—

'Let Afric on its hundred thrones rejoice.'

It not only appears to hold commerce with meridian suns, and that its blood is made drunk with the heat of scorching skies ; but it indistinctly presents to us all the symbols of eastern magnificence. It wears a crown and turban, and stands before us like a tower. All this, it may be answered, is only saying that Mr. Kean is not so

338

A VIEW OF THE ENGLISH STAGE

tall as a tower: but any one, to play Othello properly, ought to look taller and grander than any tower. We shall see how Mr. Young will play it. But this is from our present purpose. Mr. Macready is tall enough for the part, and the looseness of his figure was rather in character with the flexibility of the South: but there were no sweeping outlines, no massy movements in his action.

The movements of passion in Othello (and the motions of the body should answer to those of the mind) resemble the heaving of the sea in a storm; there are no sharp, slight, angular transitions, or if there are any, they are subject to this general swell and commotion. Mr. Kean is sometimes too wedgy and determined; but Mr. Macready goes off like a shot, and startles our sense of hearing. One of these sudden explosions was when he is in such haste to answer the demands of the Senate on his services: 'I do agnise a natural hardness,' &c. as if he was impatient to exculpate himself from some charge, or wanted to take them at their word lest they should retract. There is nothing of this in Othello. He is calm and collected; and the reason why he is carried along with such vehemence by his passions when they are roused, is, that he is moved by their collected force. Another fault in Mr. Macready's conception was, that he whined and whimpered once or twice, and tried to affect the audience by affecting a pitiful sensibility, not consistent with the dignity and masculine imagination of the character: as where he repeated, 'No, not much moved,' and again, 'Othello's occupation's gone,' in a childish treble. The only part which should approach to this effeminate tenderness of complaint is his reflection, 'Yet, oh the pity of it, Iago, the pity of it!' What we liked best was his ejaculation, 'Swell, bosom, with thy fraught, *for 'tis of aspick's tongues.*' This was forcibly given, and as if his expression were choaked with the bitterness of passion. We do not know how he would have spoken the speech, 'Like to the Pontic sea that knows no ebb,' &c. which occurs just before, for it was left out. There was also something fine in his uneasiness and inward starting at the name of Cassio, but it was too often repeated, with a view to effect. Mr. Macready got most applause in such speeches as that addressed to Iago, 'Horror on horror's head accumulate!' This should be a lesson to him. He very injudiciously, we think, threw himself on a chair at the back of the stage, to deliver the farewell apostrophe to Content, and to the 'pride, pomp, and circumstance of glorious war.' This might be a relief to him, but it distressed the audience.—On the whole, we think Mr. Macready's powers are more adapted to the declamation than to the acting of

339

passion: that is, that he is a better orator than actor. As to
Mr. Young's Iago, 'we never saw a gentleman acted finer.' Mrs.
Faucit's Desdemona was very pretty. Mr. C. Kemble's Cassio
was excellent.

Drury-Lane.

The town has been entertained this week by seeing Mr. Stephen
Kemble in the part of Sir John Falstaff, as they were formerly with
seeing Mr. Lambert in his own person. We see no more reason
why Mr. Stephen Kemble should play Falstaff, than why Louis XVIII.
is qualified to fill a throne, because he is fat, and belongs to a
particular family. Every fat man cannot represent a great man.
The knight was fat; so is the player: the Emperor was fat, so is
the King who stands in his shoes. But there the comparison ends.
There is no sympathy in mind—in wit, parts, or discretion. Sir
John (and so we may say of the gentleman at St. Helena) 'had guts
in his brains.' The mind was the man. His body did not weigh
down his wit. His spirits shone through him. He was not a mere
paunch, a bag-pudding, a lump of lethargy, a huge falling sickness, an
imminent apoplexy, with water in the head.

The Managers of Drury-Lane, in providing a Sir John Falstaff
to satisfy the taste of the town, seem to ask only with Mr. Burke's
political carcass-butchers, 'How he cuts up in the cawl: how he
tallows in the kidneys!' We are afraid the Junto of Managers of
Drury-Lane are not much wiser than the junto of Managers of the
affairs of Europe. This, according to the luminous and voluminous
critic in the Courier, is because their affairs are not under the management of a single person. Would the same argument prove that the
affairs of Europe had better have been under the direction of one
man? 'The gods have not made' the writer in the Courier logical
as well as 'poetical.' By the rule above hinted at, every actor is
qualified to play Falstaff who is physically incapacitated to play any
other character. Sir John Falstaffs may be fatted up like prize oxen.
Nor does the evil in this case produce its own remedy, as where an
actor's success depends upon his own leanness and that of the part
he plays. Sir Richard Steele tells us (in one of the Tatlers) of a
poor actor in his time, who having nothing to do, fell away, and
became such a wretched meagre-looking object, that he was pitched
upon as a proper person to represent the starved Apothecary in
Romeo and Juliet. He did this so much to the life, that he was
repeatedly called upon to play it: but his person improving with his
circumstances, he was in a short time rendered unfit to play it with
the same effect as before, and laid aside. Having no other resource,

340

A VIEW OF THE ENGLISH STAGE

he accordingly fell away again with the loss of his part, and was again called upon to appear in it with his former reputation. Any one, on the contrary, who thrives in Falstaff, is always in an increasing capacity to overlay the part.—But we have done with this unpleasant subject.

THEATRICAL DEBUTS

The Examiner.   *October* 20, 1816.

There have been two theatrical or operatic debuts, to which we are in arrears, and of which we must say a word—Miss Mori's Rosetta in Love in a Village, at Covent-Garden, and Miss Keppel's Polly in the Beggar's Opera, at Drury-Lane. Both of them appeared to us to be indifferent. Miss Mori is by much the best singer of the two, but there is something exceedingly unprepossessing and hard both in her voice and manner. She sings without the least feeling, or lurking consciousness that such a thing is required in a singer. The notes proceed from her mouth as mechanically, as *unmitigated* by the sentiment, as if they came from the sharp hautboy or grating bassoon. We do not mean that her voice is disagreeable in itself, but it wants softness and sweetness of modulation. The words of the songs neither seem to tremble on her lips, nor play around her heart. Miss Mori did not look the character. Rosetta is to be sure a waiting-maid, but then she is also a young lady in disguise. There was no appearance of the *incognita* in Miss Mori. She seemed in downright earnest, like one of the country girls who come to be hired at the statute-fair. She was quite insensible of her situation, and came forward to prove herself a fine singer, as one of her fellow-servants might have done to answer to a charge of having stolen something. We never saw a *debutante* more at ease with the audience: we suppose she has played in the country. Miss Matthews, who is a good-natured girl, and wished to *patronize* her on so delicate an emergency, presently found there was no occasion for her services, and withdrew from the attempt with some trepidation.

If Miss Mori did not enchant us by her incomprehensible want of sensibility, neither did Miss Keppel by the affectation of it. Sensibility is a very pretty thing, but it will not do to make a plaything of, at least in public. It is not enough that an actress tries to atone for defects by throwing herself on the indulgence of the audience :— their eyes and ears must be satisfied, as well as their self-love. Miss Keppel acts with very little grace, and sings very much out of tune.

341

There were some attempts made to prejudice the audience against this young lady before she appeared : but they only had the effect which they deserved, of procuring a more flattering reception than she would otherwise have met with : but we do not think she will ever become a favourite with the town.

MR. KEMBLE'S CATO

The Examiner.   *October 27, 1816.*

Mr. Kemble has resumed his engagements at Covent-Garden Theatre for the season ; it is said in the play-bills, for the last time. There is something in the word *last*, that, 'being mortal,' we do not like on these occasions : but there is this of good in it, that it throws us back on past recollections, and when we are about to take leave of an old friend, we feel desirous to settle all accounts with him, and to see that the balance is not against us, on the score of gratitude. Mr. Kemble will, we think, find that the public are just, and his last season, if it is to be so, will not, we hope, be the least brilliant of his career. As his meridian was bright, so let his sunset be golden, and without a cloud. His reception in Cato, on Friday, was most flatter-ing, and he well deserved the cheering and cordial welcome which he received. His voice only failed him in strength ; but his tones, his looks, his gestures, were all that could be required in the character, He is the most classical of actors. He is the only one of the moderns, who both in figure and action approaches the beauty and grandeur of the antique. In the scene of the soliloquy, just before his death, he was rather inaudible, and indeed the speech itself is not worth hearing ; but his person, manner, and dress, seemed cast in the very mould of Roman elegance and dignity.

THE IRON CHEST

The Examiner.   *December 1, 1816.*

The Iron Chest is founded on the story of Caleb Williams, one of the best novels in the language, and the very best of the modern school : but the play itself is by no means the best play that ever was written, either in ancient or modern times, though really in modern times we do not know of any much better. Mr. Colman's serious style, which is in some measure an imitation of Shakespear's, is natural and flowing ; and there is a constant intermixture as in our elder drama, a *melange* of the tragic and comic ; but there is rather

342

a want of force and depth in the impassioned parts of his tragedies, and what there is of this kind, is impeded in its effect by the comic. The two plots (the serious and ludicrous) do not seem going on and gaining ground at the same time, but each part is intersected and crossed by the other, and has to set out again in the next scene, after being thwarted in the former one, like a person who has to begin a story over again in which he has been interrupted. In Shakespear, the comic parts serve only as a relief to the tragic. Colman's tragic scenes are not high-wrought enough to require any such relief; and this perhaps may be a sufficient reason why modern writers, who are so sparing of their own nerves, and those of their readers, should not be allowed to depart from the effeminate simplicity of the classic style. In Shakespear, again, the comic varieties are only an accompaniment to the loftier tragic movement: at least the only exception is in the part of Falstaff in Henry IV. which is not however a tragedy of any deep interest:—in Colman you do not know whether the comedy or tragedy is principal; whether he made the comic for the sake of the tragic, or the tragic for the sake of the comic; and you suspect he would be as likely as any of his contemporaries to parody his own most pathetic passages, just as Munden caricatures the natural touches of garrulous simplicity in old Adam Winterton, to make the galleries and boxes laugh. The great beauty of Caleb Williams is lost in the play. The interest of the novel arises chiefly from two things: the gradual working up of the curiosity of Caleb Williams with respect to the murder, by the incessant goading on of which he extorts the secret from Falkland, and then from the systematic persecution which he undergoes from his master, which at length urges him to reveal the secret to the world. Both these are very ingeniously left out by Mr. Colman, who jumps at a conclusion, but misses his end.

The history of the Iron Chest is well known to dramatic readers. Mr. Kemble either could not, or would not play the part of Sir Edward Mortimer (the Falkland of Mr. Godwin's novel)—he made nothing of it, or at least, made short work of it, for it was only played one night. He had a cough and a cold, and he hemmed and hawed, and whined and drivelled through the part in a marvellous manner. Mr. Colman was enraged at the ill-success of his piece, and charged it upon Kemble's acting, who he said did not do his best. Now we confess he generally tries to do his best, and if that best is no better, it is not his fault. We think the fault was in the part, which wants circumstantial dignity. Give Mr. Kemble only the *man* to play, why, he is nothing; give him the

A VIEW OF THE ENGLISH STAGE

paraphernalia of greatness, and he is great. He 'wears his heart in compliment extern.' He is the statue on the pedestal, that cannot come down without danger of shaming its worshippers; a figure that tells well with appropriate scenery and dresses; but not otherwise. Mr. Kemble contributes his own person to a tragedy—but only that. The poet must furnish all the rest, and make the other parts equally dignified and graceful, or Mr. Kemble will not help him out. He will not lend dignity to the mean, spirit to the familiar; he will not impart life and motion, passion and imagination, to all around him, for he has neither life nor motion, passion nor imagination in himself. He minds only the conduct of his own person, and leaves the piece to shift for itself. Not so Mr. Kean. 'Truly he hath a devil;' and if the fit comes over him too often, yet as tragedy is not the representation of *still-life*, we think this much better than being never roused at all. We like

> ' The fiery soul that working out its way,
> Fretted the pigmy body to decay,
> And o'er informed the tenement of clay.'

Mr. Kean has passion and energy enough to afford to lend it to the circumstances in which he is placed, without leaning upon them for support. He can make a dialogue between a master and a servant in common life, tragic, or infuse a sentiment into the Iron Chest. He is not afraid of being let down by his company. Formal dignity and studied grace are ridiculous, except in particular circumstances; passion and nature are every where the same, and these Mr. Kean carries with him into all his characters, and does not want the others. In the last, however, which are partly things of manner and assumption, he improves, as well as in the recitation of set speeches; for example, in the Soliloquy on Honour, in the present play. His description of the assassination of his rival to Wilford was admirable, and the description of his ' seeing his giant form roll before him in the dust,' was terrific and grand. In the picturesque expression of passion, by outward action, Mr. Kean is unrivalled. The transitions in this play, from calmness to deep despair, from concealed suspicion to open rage, from smooth decorous indifference to the convulsive agonies of remorse, gave Mr. Kean frequent opportunities for the display of his peculiar talents. The mixture of common-place familiarity and solemn injunction in his speeches to Wilford when in the presence o others, was what no other actor could give with the same felicity and force. The last scene of all—his coming to life again after his swooning at the fatal discovery of his guilt, and then falling back after a ghastly struggle, like a man waked from the

344

tomb, into despair and death in the arms of his mistress, was one of those consummations of the art, which those who have seen and have not felt them in this actor, may be assured that they have never seen or felt any thing in the course of their lives, and never will to the end of them.

MR. KEMBLE'S KING JOHN

The Examiner.   (*Covent Garden*) *December* 8, 1816.

We wish we had never seen Mr. Kean. He has destroyed the Kemble religion; and it is the religion in which we were brought up. Never again shall we behold Mr. Kemble with the same pleasure that we did, nor see Mr. Kean with the same pleasure that we have seen Mr. Kemble formerly. We used to admire Mr. Kemble's figure and manner, and had no idea that there was any want of art or nature. We feel the force and nature of Mr. Kean's acting, but then we feel the want of Mr. Kemble's person. Thus an old and delightful prejudice is destroyed, and no new enthusiasm, no second idolatry comes to take its place. Thus, by degrees, knowledge robs us of pleasure, and the cold icy hand of experience freezes up the warm current of the imagination, and crusts it over with unfeeling criticism. The knowledge we acquire of various kinds of excellence, as successive opportunities present themselves, leads us to acquire a combination of them which we never find realized in any individual, and all the consolation for the disappointment of our fastidious expectations is in a sort of fond and doating retrospect of the past. It is possible indeed that the force of prejudice might often kindly step in to suspend the chilling effects of experience, and we might be able to see an old favourite by a voluntary forgetfulness of other things, as we saw him twenty years ago; but his friends take care to prevent this, and by provoking invidious comparisons, and crying up their idol as a model of abstract perfection, force us to be ill-natured in our own defence.

We went to see Mr. Kemble's King John, and he became the part so well, in costume, look, and gesture, that if left to ourselves, we could have gone to sleep over it, and dreamt that it was fine, and 'when we waked, have cried to dream again.' But we were told that it was really fine, as fine as Garrick, as fine as Mrs. Siddons, as fine as Shakespear; so we rubbed our eyes and kept a sharp look out, but we saw nothing but a deliberate intention on the part of Mr. Kemble to act the part finely. And so he did in a certain sense, but not by any means as Shakespear wrote it, nor as it might be played. He did not harrow up the feelings, he did not electrify the sense: he did not enter into the nature of the part himself, nor consequently move others with terror or pity. The introduction to the scene with Hubert was certainly excellent: you saw instantly, and before a syllable was uttered, partly from the change of countenance, and partly from the arrangement of the scene, the purpose which had entered his mind to murder the young prince. But the remainder of this trying scene, though the execution was elaborate—painfully elaborate, and the outline well conceived, wanted the filling up, the true and master touches, the deep piercing heartfelt tones of nature. It was done well and skilfully, *according to the book of arithmetic;* but no more. Mr. Kemble, when he approaches Hubert to sound his disposition, puts on an insidious, insinuating, fawning aspect, and so he ought; but we think it should not be, though it was, that kind of wheedling smile, as if he was going to persuade him that the business he wished him to undertake was a mere jest; and his natural repugnance to it an idle prejudice, that might be carried off by a certain pleasant drollery of eye and manner. Mr. Kemble's look, to our apprehension, was exactly as if he had just caught the eye of some person of his acquaintance in the boxes, and was trying to suppress a rising smile at the metamorphosis he had undergone since dinner. Again, he changes his voice three several times, in repeating the name of Hubert; and the changes might be fine, but they did not vibrate on our feelings; so we cannot tell. They appeared to us like a tragic *voluntary*. Through almost the whole scene this celebrated actor did not seem to feel the part itself as it was set down for him, but to be considering how he ought to feel it, or how he should express by rule and method what he did not feel. He was sometimes slow, and sometimes hurried: sometimes familiar, and sometimes solemn: but always with an evident design and determination to be so. The varying tide of passion did not appear to burst from the source of nature in his breast, but to be drawn from a theatrical leaden cistern, and then directed through certain conduit-pipes and artificial channels, to fill the audience with well regulated and harmless sympathy.

We are afraid, judging from the effects of this representation, that ' man delight not us, nor woman neither : ' for we did not like Miss O'Neill's Constance better, nor so well as Mr. Kemble's King John. This character, more than any other of Shakespear's females, treads perhaps upon the verge of extravagance; the impatience of grief, combined with the violence of her temper, borders on insanity: her imagination grows light-headed. But still the boundary between poetry and phrensy is not passed: she is neither a virago nor mad.

346

Miss O'Neill gave more of the vulgar than the poetical side of the character. She generally does so of late. Mr. Charles Kemble in the Bastard, had the 'bulk, the thews, the sinews' of Falconbridge: would that he had had 'the spirit' too. There was one speech which he gave well—'Could Sir Robert make this leg?' And suiting the action to the word, as well he might, it had a great effect upon the house.

CORIOLANUS

The Examiner.   *December* 15, 1816.

Coriolanus has of late been repeatedly acted at Covent-Garden Theatre. Shakespear has in this play shewn himself well versed in history and state-affairs. Coriolanus is a storehouse of political common-places. Any one who studies it may save himself the trouble of reading Burke's Reflections, or Paine's Rights of Man, or the Debates in both Houses of Parliament since the French Revolution or our own. The arguments for and against aristocracy, or democracy, on the privileges of the few and the claims of the many, on liberty and slavery, power and the abuse of it, peace and war, are here very ably handled, with the spirit of a poet, and the acuteness of a philosopher. Shakespear himself seems to have had a leaning to the arbitrary side of the question, perhaps from some feeling of contempt for his own origin; and to have spared no occasion of baiting the rabble. What he says of them is very true: what he says of their betters is also very true, though he dwells less upon it. The cause of the people is indeed but ill calculated as a subject for poetry: it admits of rhetoric, which goes into argument and explanation, but it presents no immediate or distinct images to the mind, 'no jutting frieze, buttress, or coigne of vantage' for poetry 'to make its pendant bed and procreant cradle in.' The language of poetry naturally falls in with the language of power. The imagination is an exaggerating and exclusive faculty: it takes from one thing to add to another: it accumulates circumstances together to give the greatest possible effect to a favourite object. The understanding is a dividing and measuring faculty: it judges of things, not according to their immediate impression on the mind, but according to their relations to one another. The one is a monopolizing faculty, which seeks the greatest quantity of present excitement by inequality and disproportion; the other is a distributive faculty, which seeks the greatest quantity of ultimate good by justice and proportion. The one is an aristocratical, the other a republican faculty. The principle of poetry is a very anti-levelling principle. It aims at effect, it exists by contrast. It admits of no medium. It is every thing by excess. It rises above the ordinary standard of sufferings and crimes. It presents an imposing appearance. It shews its head turretted, crowned and crested. Its front is gilt and blood-stained. Before it, 'it carries noise, and behind it, it leaves tears.' It has its altars and its victims, sacrifices, human sacrifices. Kings, priests, nobles, are its train-bearers; tyrants and slaves its executioners—'Carnage is its daughter!' Poetry is right royal. It puts the individual for the species, the one above the infinite many, might before right. A lion hunting a flock of sheep or a herd of wild asses, is a more poetical object than they; and we even take part with the lordly beast, because our vanity, or some other feeling, makes us disposed to place ourselves in the situation of the strongest party. So we feel some concern for the poor citizens of Rome, when they meet together to compare their wants and grievances, till Coriolanus comes in, and, with blows and big words, drives this set of 'poor rats,' this rascal scum, to their homes and beggary, before him. There is nothing heroical in a multitude of miserable rogues not wishing to be starved, or complaining that they are like to be so; but when a single man comes forward to brave their cries, and to make them submit to the last indignities, from mere pride and self-will, our admiration of his prowess is immediately converted into contempt for their pusillanimity. The insolence of power is stronger than the plea of necessity. The tame submission to usurped authority, or even the natural resistance to it, has nothing to excite or flatter the imagination; it is the assumption of a right to insult or oppress others, that carries an imposing air of superiority with it. We had rather be the oppressor than the oppressed.

The love of power in ourselves, and the admiration of it in others, are both natural to man; the one makes him a tyrant, the other a slave. Wrong, dressed out in pride, pomp, and circumstance, has more attraction than abstract right.—Coriolanus complains of the fickleness of the people : yet the instant he cannot gratify his pride and obstinacy at their expense, he turns his arms against his country. If his country was not worth defending, why did he build his pride on its defence? He is a conqueror and a hero; he conquers other countries, and makes this a plea for enslaving his own; and when he is prevented from doing so, he leagues with its enemies to destroy his country. He rates the people 'as if he were a God to punish, and not a man of their infirmity.' He scoffs at one of their tribunes for maintaining their rites and franchises : 'Mark you his absolute *shall*?' not marking his own absolute *will* to take every thing from

348

them; his impatience of the slightest opposition to his own pretensions being in proportion to their arrogance and absurdity. If the great and powerful had the beneficence and wisdom of gods, then all this would have been well: if with greater knowledge of what is good for the people, they had as great a care for their interest as they have for their own; if they were seated above the world, sympathising with their welfare, but not feeling the passions of men, receiving neither good nor hurt from them, but bestowing their benefits as free gifts on them, they might then rule over them like another Providence. But this is not the case. Coriolanus is unwilling that the Senate should shew their 'cares' for the people, lest their 'cares' should be construed into 'fears,' to the subversion of all due authority; and he is no sooner disappointed in his schemes to deprive the people not only of the cares of the state, but of all power to redress themselves, than Volumnia is made madly to exclaim,

'Now the red pestilence strike all trades in Rome,
And occupations perish.'

This is but natural: it is but natural for a mother to have more regard for her son than for a whole city: but then the city should be left to take some care of itself. The care of the state cannot, we here see, be safely entrusted to maternal affection, or to the domestic charities of high life. The great have private feelings of their own, to which the interests of humanity and justice must courtesy. Their interests are so far from being the same as those of the community, that they are in direct and necessary opposition to them; their power is at the expense of our weakness; their riches, of our poverty; their pride, of our degradation; their splendour, of our wretchedness; their tyranny of our servitude. If they had the superior intelligence ascribed to them (which they have not) it would only render them so much more formidable; and from gods would convert them into devils.

The whole dramatic moral of Coriolanus is, that those who have little shall have less, and that those who have much shall take all that others have left. The people are poor, therefore they ought to be starved. They are slaves, therefore they ought to be beaten. They work hard, therefore they ought to be treated like beasts of burden. They are ignorant, therefore they ought not to be allowed to feel that they want food, or clothing, or rest, that they are enslaved, oppressed, and miserable. This is the logic of the imagination and the passions; which seek to aggrandize what excites admiration, and to heap contempt on misery, to raise power into tyranny, and to make tyranny absolute; to thrust down that which is low still lower, and to make wretches desperate: to exalt magistrates into kings, kings into gods; to degrade subjects to the rank of slaves, and slaves to the condition of brutes. The history of mankind is a romance, a mask, a tragedy constructed upon the principles of *poetical justice*; it is a noble or royal hunt, in which what is sport to the few, is death to the many, and in which the spectators halloo and encourage the strong to set upon the weak, and cry havoc in the chase, though they do not share in the spoil. We may depend upon it, that what men delight to read in books, they will put in practice in reality.

Mr. Kemble in the part of Coriolanus was as great as ever. Miss O'Neill as Volumnia was not so great as Mrs. Siddons. There is a *fleshiness*, if we may so say, about her whole manner, voice, and person, which does not suit the character of the Roman Matron. One of the most amusing things in the representation of this play is the contrast between Kemble and little Simmons. The former seems as if he would gibbet the latter on his nose, he looks so lofty. The fidgetting, uneasy, insignificant gestures of Simmons are perhaps a little caricatured; and Kemble's supercilious airs and *nonchalance* remind one of the unaccountable abstracted air, the contracted eyebrows and suspended chin of a man who is just going to sneeze.

THE MAN OF THE WORLD

The Examiner.   (*Covent-Garden*) *December* 29, 1816.

Mr. Henry Johnston (from the Glasgow Theatre) who came out some time ago in Sir Archy Mac Sarcasm, with much applause, appeared on Friday, in Sir Pertinax Mac Sycophant. During the first acts, he went through this highly, but finely coloured part, with great spirit and force: but in the midst of his account to his son Egerton, of the manner in which he rose in the world by *booing*, and by marrying an old dowager, 'like a surgeon's skeleton in a glass-case,' a certain disapprobation, not of the actor, but of the sentiments of the character, manifested itself through the house, which at this season of the year is not of a very refined composition; and some one cried out from the gallery for 'another play.' So little do the vulgar know of courts and the great world, that they are even shocked and disgusted at the satirical representation of them on the stage. This unexpected interruption given to the actor in the most prominent scene of the play, operated to damp his spirits considerably, nor did he rally completely again for the rest of the evening.

350

A VIEW OF THE ENGLISH STAGE

This is the second time that we have seen an actor fail in this character, not by any fault in himself, but by the fault of the Managers, in bringing them out in this part in the holiday season. The other was Mr. Bibby last year, certainly not inferior to Mr. Johnston in the conception or delineation of the sordid, gross, wily Scotchman : but who was equally or more unsuccessful, from the unintelligibility of the Scotch dialect and sentiments from the untutored and 'unclerkly' Christmas visitants. Upon the entrance indeed of Lord Castlereagh and some company of the higher classes, into the Prince's box, Mr. Johnston seemed to recover himself a little, and to appeal with more confidence from the ignorance of the rabble to these more judicious appreciators of the merits of his delineation of Macklin's idea of a modern statesman.

We wonder the Managers of either Theatre ever bring out a comedy relating to the artificial manners of high life, on occasions like the present. They ought either to have a tragedy and a panto-mime, or two pantomimes the same evening ; or a melo-drama, a puppet-show, and a pantomime. The common people like that which strikes their senses or their imagination : they do not like Comedy, because, if it is genteel, they do not understand the subject matter of which it treats—and if it relates to low manners and incidents, it has no novelty to recommend it. They like the dazzling and the wonder-ful. One of the objections constantly made by some persons who sat near us in the pit, to the play of the Man of the World, was, that the same scene continued through the whole play. This was a great disappointment to the pantomime appetite for rapid and wonderful changes of scenery, with which our dramatic novices had come fully prepared.

The pantomime, with Mr. Grimaldi, soon brought all to rights, and the audience drank in oblivion of all their grievances with the first tones of their old friend Joe's voice, for which indeed he might be supposed to have a patent. This great man (we really think him the greatest man we saw at the theatre last night) will not 'die and leave the world no copy,' as Shakespear has it, for his son is as like him in person as two peas. The new pantomime itself, or the 'Beggar of Bethnal-green,' is not a very good one. It has a clever dog and a rope-dancing monkey in it. The degeneracy of the modern stage threatens to be shortly redeemed by accomplished recruits from the four-footed creation. The monkey was hissed and encored, but this is the fate of all upstart candidates for popular applause, and we hope that *Monsieur* will console himself for this partial ill-will and prejudice manifested against him, by the reflection that envy is the shadow of merit.—Miss F. Dennett was the

351

Columbine, and played very prettily as the daughter of the Blind Beggar. But who shall describe the *pas de trois* by the three Miss Dennetts, 'ever charming, ever new,' and yet just the same as when we saw them before, and as we always wish to see them? If they were at all different from what they are, or from one another, it would be for the worse. The charm is in seeing the same grace, the same looks, the same motions, in three persons. They are a lovely reflection of one another. The colours in the rainbow are not more soft and harmonious ; the image of the halcyon reflected on the azure bosom of the smiling ocean is not more soft and delightful.

JANE SHORE

The Examiner.   (*Drury-Lane*) January 5, 1817.

Miss Somerville, who gave so interesting a promise of a fine tragic actress in the part of Imogine in Bertram, last year, appeared the other evening in Alicia in Jane Shore. We do not think Rowe's heroine so well adapted to the display of her powers as that of the modern poet. Miss Somerville is a very delightful sentimental actress, but she makes an indifferent scold. Alicia should be a shrew, and shrill-tongued : but Miss Somerville throws a pensive repentant tone over her bitterest imprecations against her rival, and her mode of recitation is one melancholy cadence of the whole voice, silvered over with sweet gleams of sound, like the moonbeams playing on the heaving ocean. When she should grow sharp and virulent, she only becomes more amiable and romantic, and tries in vain to be disagreeable. Though her voice is out of her controul, she yet succeeds in putting on a peevish dissatisfied look, which yet has too much of a mournful, sanctified cast. If Mr. Coleridge could write a tragedy for her, we should then see the Muse of the romantic drama exhibited in perfection. The fault of Miss Somerville, in short, is, that her delivery is too mannered, and her action without sufficient variety.

Mr. Bengough, as the Duke of Gloster, was in one or two scenes impressive, in others ridiculous. He has a singular kind of awkward energy and heavy animation about him. He works himself up occasionally to considerable force and spirit ; and then, as if frightened at his own efforts, his purpose fails him, and he sinks into an unaccountable vein of faltering insipidity. The great merit of Mr. Kean is his thorough decision and self-possession : he always knows what he means to do, and never flinches from doing it.

352

THE HUMOROUS LIEUTENANT

The Examiner.   *January* 26, 1817.

The Humorous Lieutenant, brought out on Saturday week at Covent-Garden, is a bad alteration from one of the most indifferent of Beaumont and Fletcher's plays. It went off very ill, and was as fairly damned as any thing at Covent-Garden could be. They have some *jus theatricum* here, which saves things and carries off appearances. So the play has been brought forward again, and its first failure attributed to the failure of the actress who played the part of Celia. That was certainly a failure, and an unexpected one; for the lady's accomplishments and attractions had been much spoken of, and perhaps justly. Of her talents for the stage, we shall say nothing; for we cannot say a word or syllable in their favour. Nor shall we say any thing against 'The Humorous Lieutenant:' for it passes under the name of Beaumont and Fletcher, 'whose utmost skirts of glory we behold gladly, and far off their steps adore:' and indeed it is at an immeasurable distance, and by a prodigious stretch of faith, that we see them at all in the Covent-Garden *refaccimento*. Mr. Liston plays the heroic Lieutenant in it; but we shall live to see him in the *mock-heroic* again!

TWO NEW BALLETS

The Examiner.   *February* 9, 1817.

There have been two new ballets this week, one at each Theatre. That at Drury-Lane, Patrick's Return, is one of the prettiest things we have seen a long time. The dancing and pantomime are very delightfully adapted to a number of old Irish melodies, which we are never tired of hearing.—Zephyr and Flora, at Covent-Garden, is too fine by half for our rude tastes. There are lusty lovers flying in the air, nests of winged Cupids, that start out of bulrushes, trees that lift up their branches like arms:—we suppose they will speak next like Virgil's wood. But in the midst of all these wonders, we have a more amiable wonder, the three Miss Dennetts, as nymphs,

> 'Whom lovely Venus at a birth
> To ivy-crowned Bacchus bore.'

They might represent Love, Hope, and Joy. There is one part in which they seem to dance on the strings of the harp which plays to them; the liquid sounds and the motion are the same. These young ladies put us in mind of Florizel's praise of Perdita:—

> 'When you do dance, I wish you a wave o' th' sea,
> That you might ever do nothing but that;
> Move still, still so, and own no other function.'

MR. BOOTH'S DUKE OF GLOSTER

The Examiner.   (*Covent-Garden*) *February* 16, 1817.

A Gentleman of the name of Booth, who we understand has been acting with considerable applause at Worthing and Brighton, came out in Richard Duke of Gloster, at this Theatre, on Wednesday. We do not know well what to think of his powers, till we see him in some part in which he is more himself. His face is adapted to tragic characters, and his voice wants neither strength nor musical expression. But almost the whole of his performance was an exact copy or parody of Mr. Kean's manner of doing the same part. It was a complete, but at the same time a successful piece of plagiarism. We do not think this kind of second-hand reputation can last upon the London boards for more than a character or two. In the country these *doubles* of the best London performers go down very well, for they are the best they can get, and they have not the originals to make invidious comparisons with. But it will hardly do to bring out the same entertainment that we can have as it is first served up at Drury-Lane, in a hashed state at Covent-Garden. We do not blame Mr. Booth for borrowing Mr. Kean's coat and feathers to appear in upon a first and trying occasion, but if he wishes to gain a permanent reputation, he must come forward in his own person. He must try to be original, and not content himself with treading in another's steps. We say this the rather, because, as far as we could judge, Mr. Booth, in point of execution did those passages the best, in which he now and then took leave of Mr. Kean's decided and extreme manner, and became more mild and tractable. Such was his recitation of the soliloquy on his own ambitious projects, and of that which occurs the night before the battle. In these he seemed to yield to the impulse of his own feelings, and to follow the natural tones and cadence of his voice. They were the best parts of his performance. The worst were those where he imitated, or rather caricatured Mr. Kean's hoarseness of delivery and violence of action, and affected an energy without seeming to feel it. Such were his repulse of Buckingham, his exclamation, 'What does he in the north,' &c. his telling the attendants to set down the corse of King Henry, &c. The scene with Lady Anne, on the contrary, which was of a softer and more insinuating kind, he was more successful in, and though still a palpable imitation of Mr. Kean, it had all the originality that imitation could have, for he seemed to feel it. His manner of saying 'good night,' and of answering, when he received the anonymous paper, 'A weak invention of the enemy,' we consider as mere tricks in the art, which no one but a professed mimic has a right to play. The dying scene was without effect.—The greatest drawback to Mr. Booth's acting is a perpetual strut, and unwieldy swagger in his ordinary gait and manner, which, though it may pass at Brighton for *grand, gracious, and magnificent,* even the lowest of the mob will laugh at in London. This is the third imitation of Mr. Kean we have seen attempted, and the only one that has not been a complete failure. The imitation of original genius is the *forlorn hope* of the candidates for fame :—its faults are so easily overdone, its graces are so hard to catch. A Kemble school we can understand : a Kean school is, we suspect, a contradiction in terms. Art may be taught, because it is learnt : Nature can neither be taught nor learnt. The secrets of Art may be said to have a common or *pass* key to unlock them ; the secrets of Nature have but one master-key—the heart.

Drury-Lane.

The charming afterpiece of Figaro, or the Follies of a Day, has been revived here, and revived with all its gloss and lustre. Miss Kelly, Mrs. Alsop, and Mrs. Orger, were all very happy in it. This play was written by a man who drank light French wines : in every line you see the brisk champaign frothing through green glasses. The beads rise sparkling to the surface and then evaporate. There is nothing in it to remember, and absolutely nothing to criticise ; but it is the triumph of animal spirits : while you see it, you seem to drink ether, or to inhale an atmosphere not bred of fogs or sea-coal fires. This is the secret of the charm of Figaro. It promotes the circulation of the blood, and assists digestion. We would by all means advise our readers to go and try the experiment. The best scene in it, is that in which the Page jumps from his concealment behind the arm-chair into the arm-chair itself. The beauty of this is in fact the perfect *heartfelt* indifference to detection ; and so of the rest.—We never saw Mr. Rae play better.

MR. BOOTH'S IAGO

The Examiner. (*Drury-Lane*) *February 23, 1817.*

The Managers of Covent-Garden Theatre, after having announced in the bills, that Mr. Booth's Richard the Third had met with a success unprecedented in the annals of histrionic fame, (which, to do them justice, was not the case), very disinterestedly declined engaging him at more than two pounds a week, as report speaks. Now we think they were wrong, either in puffing him so unmercifully, or in haggling with him so pitifully. It was either trifling with the public or with the actor. The consequence, as it has turned out, has been, that Mr. Booth, who was to start as 'the fell opposite' of Mr. Kean, has been taken by the hand by that gentleman, who was an old fellow-comedian of his in the country, and engaged at Drury-Lane at a salary of ten pounds per week. So we hear. And it was in evident allusion to this circumstance, that when Mr. Booth, as Iago, said on Thursday night, ' I know my price no less'—John Bull, who has very sympathetic pockets, gave a loud shout of triumph, which resounded all along the benches of the pit. We must say that Mr. Booth pleased us much more in Iago than in Richard. He was, it is true, well supported by Mr. Kean in Othello, but he also supported him better in that character than any one else we have seen play with him. The two rival actors hunt very well in couple. One thing which we did not expect, and which we think reconciled us to Mr. Booth's imitations, was, that they were here performed in the presence, and as it were with the permission of Mr. Kean. There is no fear of deception in the case. The original is there in person to answer for his identity, and 'give the world assurance of himself.' The original and the copy go together, like the substance and the shadow. But then there neither is nor can be any idea of competition, and so far we are satisfied. In fact, Mr. Booth's Iago was a very close and spirited repetition of Mr. Kean's manner of doing that part. It was indeed the most spirited copy we ever saw upon the stage, considering at the same time the scrupulous exactness with which he adhered to his model in the most trifling *minutiæ*. We need only mention as instances of similarity in the bye-play, Mr. Booth's mode of delivering the lines, ' My wit comes from my brains like birdlime,' or his significant, and we think improper pointing to the dead bodies, as he goes out in the last scene. The same remarks apply to his delivery, that we made last week. He has two voices; one his own, and the other Mr. Kean's. His delineation of Iago is more bustling and animated; Mr. Kean's is more close and cool. We suspect that Mr. Booth is not only a professed and deliberate imitator of Mr. Kean, but that he has in general the cameleon quality (we do not mean that of living upon air, as the Covent-Garden Managers supposed, but) of reflecting all objects that come in contact with him. We occasionally caught the mellow tones of Mr. Macready rising out of the thorough-bass of Mr. Kean's

A VIEW OF THE ENGLISH STAGE

guttural emphasis, and the flaunting, *degagé* robe of Mr. Young's oriental manner, flying off from the tight vest and tunic of the little ' bony prizer ' of the Drury-Lane Company.

Of Mr. Kean's Othello we have not room to speak as it deserves, nor have we the power if we had the room : it is beyond all praise. Any one who has not seen him in the third act of Othello (and seen him near) cannot have an idea of perfect tragic acting.

MR. BOOTH'S RICHARD

The Examiner.   (*Covent Garden*) *March* 2, 1817.

This Theatre was a scene of the greatest confusion and uproar we ever witnessed (not having been present at the O. P. rows) on Tuesday evening, in consequence of the re-appearance of Mr. Booth here, after he had entered into an engagement and performed at Drury-Lane. For our own parts, who are but simple diplomatists, either in theatricals or politics, the resentment and disapprobation of the audience appear to us to have been quite well-founded. The only fault we find with the expression of the public indignation is, that it was directed solely against Mr. Booth, whereas the Managers of the Theatre were entitled to the first and fullest share. Mr. Booth may have been only *their* dupe : they have wilfully trifled with the public, and tried to make a contemptible tool of a person belonging to a profession by which they exist, and from which they derive all their importance with the public. Their only excuse for inveigling an actor whom they refused to engage, from another Theatre where he had been engaged in consequence of such refusal, is, that by the rules of theatrical proceeding, one theatre has no right to engage an actor who has been in *treaty* for an engagement at the other, within a year after the breaking off of such treaty, without leave of the Managers. First, it appears that no such understanding exists, or is acted upon : that the pretext, as a mere pretext, is not true : secondly, such a mutual understanding, if it did exist, would be most unjust to the pro- fession, and an insult to the public. For at this rate, any Manager, by once entering into an agreement with an actor, may keep him dangling on his good pleasure for a year certain, may prevent his getting any other engagement, by saying that they are still in a progress of arrangement, though all arrangement is broken off, may deprive an ingenious and industrious man of his bread, and the public of the advantage of his talents, till the Managers, at the expiration of this probationary year of non-performance, once more grant him his *Habeas Corpus*, and release him from the restrictions and obligations

357

of his non-engagement. The obvious questions for the public to decide are these : Why, having announced Mr. Booth as a prodigy of success after his first appearance in Richard, the Managers declined to give Mr. Booth any but a very paltry salary ? In this they either deceived the town, or acted with injustice to Mr. Booth, because they thought him in their power. Why, the instant he was engaged at the other Theatre at a handsome salary, and on his own terms, and had played there with success, they wanted to have him back, employed threats as it should seem to induce him to return, and gave him a larger salary than he had even obtained at Drury-Lane? Whether, if he had not been engaged at the other theatre, they would have engaged him at their own upon the terms to which they have agreed to entice him back ? Whether, in short, in the whole pro-ceeding, they have had any regard either to professional merit, or to public gratification, or to any thing but their own cunning and self-interest ? The questions for Mr. Booth to answer are, why, after his treatment by the Covent-Garden Company, he applied to the Drury-Lane Company ; and why, after their liberal behaviour, he deserted back again, on the first overture, to the company that had discarded him ? Why he did not act on Saturday night, if he was able : or at any rate, state, to prevent the charge of duplicity, his new engage-ment with his old benefactors ? Whether, if Mr. Booth had not made this new arrangement, he would not have acted in spite of indisposition or weak nerves ? Lastly, whether the real motive which led Mr. Booth to fall in so unadvisedly with the renewed and barefaced proposals of the Covent-Garden Company, was not the renewed hope dawning in his breast, of still signalising himself, by dividing the town with Mr. Kean, instead of playing a second part to him, which is all he could ever hope to do on the same theatre ? But enough of this disagreeable and disgraceful affair. The only way to make it up with the public would be, as we are convinced, not by attempts at vindication, but by an open apology.

Drury-Lane.

The new farce of Frightened to Death, is the most amusing and original piece of invention that we have seen for a long time. The execution might be better, but the idea is good, and as far as we know, perfectly new. Harley, Jack Phantom, in a drunken bout, is beaten by the watch, and brought senseless to the house of his mistress, Mrs. Orger, who, in order to cure him of his frolics, determines to dress him up in an old wrapping-gown like a shroud, and persuade him that he is dead. When he awakes, he at first does

358

not recollect where he is : the first thing he sees is a letter from his friend to his mistress, giving an account of his sad catastrophe, and speaking of the manner in which order is to be taken for his burial. Soon after, his mistress and her maid come in in mourning, lament over his loss, and as has been agreed beforehand, take no notice of Phantom, who in vain presents himself before them, and thus is made to personate his own ghost. The servant, Mumps (Mr. Knight), who is in the secret, also comes in, and staggers Phantom's belief in his own identity still more, by neither seeing nor hearing him. The same machinery is played off upon him in a different mood by Munden's coming in, and taking him for a ghost. A very laughable dialogue and duct here take place between the Ghost and the Ghost-seer, the latter inquiring of him with great curiosity about his ancestors in the other world, and being desirous to cultivate an acquaintance with the living apparition, in the hope of obtaining some insight into the state of that state ' from which no traveller returns.' There was a foolish song about ' Kisses ' at the beginning, which excited some little displeasure, but the whole went off with great and deserved applause.

DOUBLE GALLANT

The Examiner.   (*Drury-Lane*) April 13, 1817.

Cibber's Comedy of the Double Gallant has been revived at this Theatre with considerable success. Pope did Cibber a great piece of injustice, when he appointed him to receive the crown of dulness. It was mere spleen in Pope ; and the provocation to it seems to have been an excess of flippant vivacity in the constitution of Cibber. That Cibber's Birth-day Odes were dull, seems to have been the common fault of the subject, rather than a particular objection to the poet. In his Apology for his own Life, he is one of the most amusing of coxcombs ; happy in conscious vanity, teeming with animal spirits, uniting the self-sufficiency of youth with the garrulity of age ; and in his plays he is not less entertaining and agreeably familiar with the audience. His personal character predominates indeed over the inventiveness of his muse ; but so far from being dull, he is every where light, fluttering, and airy. We could wish we had a few more such dull fellows ; they would contribute to make the world pass away more pleasantly ! Cibber, in short, though his name has been handed down to us as a bye-word of impudent pretension by the classical pen of his rival, who did not admit of any merit beyond the narrow circle of wit and friendship in which he moved, was a

359

gentleman and a scholar of the old school; a man of wit and
pleasantry in conversation; an excellent actor; an admirable dramatic
critic; and one of the best comic writers of his age. Instead of
being a *caput mortuum* of literature, (always excepting what is always
to be excepted, his Birth-day Odes), he had a vast deal of its spirit,
and too much of the froth. But the eye of ill-nature or prejudice,
which is attracted by the shining points of character in others,
generally transposes their good qualities, and absurdly denies them
the very excellences which excite its chagrin.—Cibber's Careless
Husband is a master-piece of easy gaiety; and his Double Gallant,
though it cannot rank in the first, may take its place in the second
class of comedies. It is full of character, bustle, and stage-effect.
It belongs to the composite style, and very happily mixes up the
comedy of intrigue, such as we see it in Mrs. Centlivre's Spanish
plots, with a tolerable share of the wit and sentiment of Congreve and
Vanburgh. As there is a good deal of wit, there is a spice of
wickedness in this play, which was the privilege of the good old style
of comedy, when vice, perhaps from being less common, was less
catching than it is at present. It was formerly a thing more to be
wondered at than imitated; and behind the rigid barriers of religion
and morality might be exposed freely, without the danger of any
serious practical consequences; but now that the safeguards of
wholesome prejudices are removed, we seem afraid to trust our
eyes or ears with a single situation or expression of a loose tendency,
as if the mere mention of licentiousness implied a conscious approbation of it, and the extreme delicacy of our moral sense would
be debauched by the bare suggestion of the possibility of vice. The
luscious vein of the dialogue in many of the scenes is stopped short
in the revived play, though not before we perceive its object—

> ————'In hidden mazes running,
> With wanton haste and giddy cunning!'

We noticed more than one of these *double meanings*, which however
passed off without any marks of reprobation, for unless they are made
pretty broad, the audience, from being accustomed to the cautious
purity of the modern drama, are not very expert in decyphering the
equivocal allusion.—All the characters in the Double Gallant are
very well kept up, and they were most of them well supported in the
representation. At-All and Lady Dainty are the two most prominent
characters in the original comedy, and those into which Cibber has
put most of his own nature and genius. They are the essence of
active impertinence and sickly affectation. At-All has three intrigues
upon his hands at once, and manages them all with the dexterity with

which an adept shuffles a pack of cards. His cool impudence is equal to his wonderful vivacity. He jumps, by mere volubility of tongue and limbs, under three several names into three several assignations with three several *incognitas*, whom he meets at the same house, as they happen to be mutual friends. He would succeed with them all, but that he is detected by them all round, and then he can hardly be said to fail, for he carries off the best of them at last (Mrs. Mardyn), who not being able to seduce him from her rivals by any other means, resorts to a disguise, and vanquishes him in love by disarming him in a duel. The scene in which At-All, who had made love to Clorinda as Colonel Standfast, is introduced to her by her cousin (who is also in love with him) as Mr. Freeman, and while he is disowning his personal identity, is surprised by the arrival of Lady Sadlife, to whom he had been making the same irresistible overtures, is one of the best *coup d'œils* of the theatre we have seen for a long time. Harley acts this character laughably, but not very judiciously. He bustles through it with the liveliness of a footman, not with the manners of a gentleman. He never changes his character with his dress, but still he is a pleasant fellow in himself, and is so happy in the applause he receives, that we are sorry to find any fault with him. Mrs. Alsop's Lady Dainty was a much better, but a much less agreeable piece of acting. The affected sensibility, the pretended disorders, the ridiculous admiration of novelty, and the languid caprices of this character, were given by the actress with an overpowering truth of effect. The mixture of folly, affectation, pride, insensibility, and spleen which constitute the character of the fine lady, as it existed in the days of Cibber, and is delineated in this comedy, is hardly to be tolerated in itself, with every advantage of grace, youth, beauty, dress, and fashion. But Mrs. Alsop gave only the inherent vice and ridiculous folly of the character, without any external accomplishments to conceal or adorn it. She has always the same painful 'frontlet' on : the same uneasy expression of face and person. Her affected distortions seemed to arise from real pain ; nor was her delight in mischief and absurdity counteracted by any palliating circumstances of elegance or beauty. A character of this description ought *only* to appeal to the understanding, and not to offend the senses. We do not know how to soften this censure ; but we will add, that Mrs. Alsop, in all her characters, shews sense, humour, and spirit.

Dowton and Miss Kelly, as Sir Solomon Sadlife and Wishwell, are two for a pair. We do not wish to see a better actor or actress. The effect which both these performers produce, is the best and strongest that can be, because they never try to produce an effect.

and is caught among its own echoes, that soften while they redouble the sound, and by its distant and varied accompaniment, soothes as much as it startles the ear. This short episode, which is included in four or five sentences printed in capital letters, is the only part of the opera which aims at the tragic: this part is not of a pure or unmixed species, but is very properly harmonised with the rest of the composition, by middle and reflected tones; and all the other scenes are of one uniform, but exquisite character, a profusion of delicate airs and graces. Except, then, where the author reluctantly gives place to the Ghost-statue, or rather compromises matters with him, this opera is Mozart all over; it is no more like Shakespear, than Claude Lorraine is like Rubens or Michael Angelo. It is idle to make the comparison. The personal character of the composer's mind, a light, airy, voluptuous spirit, is infused into every line of it; the intoxication of pleasure, the sunshine of hope, the dancing of the animal spirits, the bustle of action, the sinkings of tenderness and pity, are there, but nothing else. It is a kind of scented music; the ear imbibes an aromatic flavour from the sounds. It is like the breath of flowers; the sighing of balmy winds; or Zephyr with Flora playing; or the liquid notes of the nightingale wafted to the bosom of the bending rose. To show at once our taste or the want of it, the song of 'La ci darem' gives us, we confess, both in itself, and from the manner in which it is sung by Madame Fodor, more pleasure than all the rest of the opera put together. We could listen to this air for ever—with certain intervals: the first notes give a throb of expectation to the heart, the last linger on the sense. We *encore* it greedily, with a sort of childish impatience for new delight, and drink in the ethereal sounds, like draughts of earthly nectar. The heart is intoxicated through the ear; and feels in the tremulous accents of Zerlina's voice, all the varying emotions of tenderness, of doubt, of regret, and giddy rapture, as she resigns herself to her new lover. Madame Fodor's execution of her part of this duet was excellent. There is a clear, firm, silvery tone in her voice, like the reverberation of a tight-strung instrument, which by its contrast gives a peculiar effect to the more melting and subdued expression of particular passages, and which accords admirably with the idea of high health and spirits in the rustic character of Zerlina. We are tempted to say of her in this character, what Spenser says of Belphebe,

> '——And when she spake,
> Sweet words like dropping honey she did shed,
> And 'twixt the pearls and rubies softly brake
> A silver sound, that heav'nly music seem'd to make.'

She was less successful in the execution of the song to Massetto just after, 'Batte, batte, Massetto:' for she seemed to sing it as if she had hardly learned it by heart. To this, however, she gave a characteristic simplicity of expression; she appeared in the first part as if she would willingly stand like a lamb, *come agnellina*, to be beaten by her provoked lover, and afterwards, when she is reconciled to him, as if she was glad she had escaped a beating. Her song, *Vedrai carino*, promising him a remedy, when Massetto himself gets beaten by her, by offering him her heart, was charming, both from the execution of the air, and from the action with which she accompanied it.

Of the other performers we cannot speak so favourably. Signor Ambrogetti gave considerable life and spirit to the part of Don Giovanni; but we neither saw the dignified manners of the Spanish nobleman, nor the insinuating address of the voluptuary. He makes too free and violent a use of his legs and arms. He sung the air, *Finche dal vino*, in which he anticipates an addition to his list of mistresses from the success of his entertainment, with a sort of jovial turbulent vivacity, but without the least 'sense of amorous delight.' His only object seemed to be, to sing the words as loud and as fast as possible. Nor do we think he gave to Don Juan's serenade, *Deh vieni alla finestra*, any thing like the spirit of fluttering apprehension and tenderness which characterises the original music. Signor Ambrogetti's manner of acting in this scene was that of the successful and significant intriguer, but not of an intriguer—in love. Sensibility should be the ground-work of the expression: the cunning and address are only accessories.

Naldi's Laporello was much admired, and it was not without its merits, though we cannot say that it gave us much pleasure. His humour is coarse and boisterous, and is more that of a buffoon than a comic actor. He treats the audience with the same easy cavalier airs that an impudent waiter at a French table-d'hôte does the guests as they arrive. The gross familiarity of his behaviour to Donna Elvira, in the song where he makes out the list of his master's mistresses, was certainly not in character; nor is there any thing in the words or the music to justify it. The tone and air which he should assume are those of pretended sympathy, mixed with involuntary laughter, not of wanton undisguised insult.

Signor Crivelli and Madame Camporese did not add any particular prominence to the serious parts of Don Octavio, and Donna Anna. Signora Hughes's Donna Elvira was successful beyond what we could have supposed. This lady at the Italian Opera is respectable: on the English stage she was formidable. Signor Angrisani *doubles* the part of Massetto and the Ghost. In the former, he displayed much drollery and *naiveté*; and in the latter, he was as solemn, terrific, and mysterious as a ghost should be. A new translation accompanies the Opera House edition of Don Giovanni. It is very well executed. But as it is not in verse, it might have been more literal, without being less elegant.

THE CONQUEST OF TARANTO

The Examiner.   (*Covent Garden*) *April* 27, 1817.

The Conquest of Taranto continues to be acted here with a success proportionate to its merits. It is from the pen of Mr. Dimond, whose productions are well known to the public, and which have so strong a family-likeness, that from having seen any one of them, we may form a tolerably correct idea of the rest. *Ex uno omnes.* His pieces have upon the whole been exceedingly popular, and we think deservedly so; for they have all the merit that belongs to the style of the drama to which he has devoted his talents,—a style which is a great favourite with an immense majority of the play-going public. This style may be called the *purely romantic*; there is little or nothing classical in it. The author does not profess to provide a public entertainment at his own entire expence, and from his own proper funds, but contracts with the managers to get up a striking and impressive exhibition in conjunction with the scene-painter, the scene-shifter, the musical composer, the orchestra, the chorusses on the stage, and the *lungs* of the actors! It is a kind of *pic-nic* contribution, to which we sit down with a good appetite, and from which we come away quite satisfied, though our attention is somewhat distracted in the multitude of objects to which our gratitude is due for the pleasure we have received. The art of the romantic dramatist seems to be, to put ordinary characters in extraordinary situations, and to blend commonplace sentiments with picturesque scenery. The highest pathos is ushered in, and the mind prepared to indulge in all the luxury of woe, by the chaunting of music behind the scenes, as the blowing up of a mine of gunpowder gives the finishing stroke to the progress of the passions. The approach of a hero is announced by a blast of trumpets; the flute and flageolet breathe out the whole soul of the lover. Mr. Dimond is by no means jealous of the exclusive honours of the Tragic Muse; he is not at all disposed to make a monopoly of wit, genius, or reputation: he minds little but the conducting of his story to the end of the third act, and loses no

366

opportunity of playing the game into the hands of his theatrical associates, so that they may supply his deficiencies, and all together produce a perfect piece. In the Conquest of Taranto the scene lies almost the whole time upon the beautiful sea-coast of Spain, and we do not feel the lack of descriptive poetry, while the eye is regaled with one continued panorama. In a word, the author resembles those painters of history who pay more attention to their back-ground than their figures, to costume and drapery than to the expression of thought and sentiment.

The romantic drama, such as we have here described it, admits of various gradations, from the point where it unites with the pure tragic down to the melo-drame, and speaking pantomime, nor do we think that as it descends lower in its pretensions, its interest necessarily grows less. Where the regular drama studiously avails itself of the assistance of other arts, as painting and music, where the dialogue becomes the vehicle for connecting scenery, pantomime, and song in one dazzling and overpowering appeal to all our different faculties and senses, we are satisfied if the *tout ensemble* produces its effect, and do not enquire whether the work of the author alone, in a literary point of view, is proof against criticism. He is supposed to write for the stage 'with all appliances and means to boot,' not for the loneliness of the closet, and is little more than the ballet-master of the scene. He is not to enter into a competition with his assistants in the several departments of his art, but to avail himself of their resources. In the division of labour it is ridiculous to expect the same person to do the whole work. This would be double toil and trouble, and would, besides, answer no end. An appeal to the understanding or the imagination is superfluous, where the senses are assailed on all sides. What is the use of painting a landscape twice—to the ear as well as to the eye? What signify 'the golden cadences of verse,' when only employed to usher in a song? The gleams of wit or fancy glimmer but feebly on a stage blazing with phosphorus; and surely the Tragic Muse need not strain her voice so deep or high, while a poodle dog is barking fit to break his heart, in the most affecting part of the performance. We cannot attend to sounding epithets while a castle is tumbling about our ears, and it is sufficiently alarming to see an infant thrown from a precipice or hanging bridge into the foaming waves—reflections apart. Commonplace poetry is good enough as an accompaniment to all this; as very indifferent words are equally well set to the finest tunes.—So far then from joining in the common cry against Mr. Dimond's poetry as not rising above mediocrity, we should be sorry if he wrote better than he does. And what confirms us in this sentiment is, that those who have tried to do better have succeeded worse. The most ambitious writers of the modern romantic drama are Mr. Coleridge and Mr. Maturin. But in the Remorse of the one, all Mr. Coleridge's metaphysics are lost in moonshine; and in Bertram and Don Manuel, the genius of poetry crowned with faded flowers, and seated on the top of some high Gothic battlement, in vain breathes its votive accents amidst the sighing of the forest gale and the vespers of midnight monks. But enough of this.

There is considerable interest in the outline of the present play, and the events are ingeniously and impressively connected together, so as to excite and keep alive curiosity, and to produce striking situations. But to this production of external effect, character and probability are repeatedly sacrificed, and the actions which the different persons are made to perform, like stage-puppets, have no adequate motives. For instance, it is quite out of our common calculation of human nature, that Valencia (Mr. Macready) should betray his country to an enemy, because he is jealous of a rival in love; nor is there any thing in the previous character of Valencia to lead us to expect such an extreme violation of common sense and decency. Again, Rinaldo is betrayed to his dishonour, by acting contrary to orders and to his duty as a knight, at the first insidious suggestion of Valencia. The entrance of the Moors through the subterranean passage, and the blowing up of the palace while the court are preparing to give a sort of *fête champêtre* in the middle of a siege, is not only surprising but ridiculous. Great praise is due to Mr. Young as Aben Hamet, to Mr. Macready as Valencia, and to Mr. Booth as Rinaldo, for the force of their action, and the audibleness of their delivery:—perhaps for something more.—Miss Stephens, as Oriana's maid, sang several songs very prettily.

THE TOUCH-STONE

The Examiner.   (*Drury Lane*) *May* 11, 1817.

Mr. Kenney's new Comedy called the Touch-stone, or the World as it goes, has been acted here with great success. It possesses much liveliness and pleasantry in the incidents, and the dialogue is neat and pointed. The interest never flags, and is never wound up to a painful pitch. There are several *coups de théâtre*, which shew that Mr. Kenney is an adept in his art, and has the stage and the actors before him while he is writing in his closet. The character of Dinah Cropley, which is admirably sustained by Miss Kelly, is the chief attraction of the piece. The author has contrived situations

368

for this pretty little rustic, which bring out the exquisite *naiveté* and simple pathos of the actress in as great a degree as we ever saw them. Mr. Kenney, we understand, wrote this Comedy abroad; and there is a foreign air of homely contentment and natural gaiety about the character of poor Dinah, like the idea we have of Marivaux's *Paysanne parvenue*. She seemed to have fed her chickens and turned her spinning-wheel in France, under more genial and better-tempered skies. Perhaps, however, this may be a mere prejudice in our minds, arising from our having lately seen Miss Kelly in such characters taken from French pieces. Her lover, Harley, (Peregrine Paragon), is of undoubted home growth. He is a very romantic, generous, amorous sort of simpleton, while he is poor; and for want of knowing better, thinks himself incorruptible, till temptation falls in his way, and then he turns out a very knave: and only saves his credit in the end by one of those *last act* repentances which are more pleasing than probable. He is in the first instance a poor country schoolmaster, who is engaged to marry Dinah Cropley, the daughter of a neighbouring farmer. They cannot, however, obtain the consent of their landlord and his sister (Holland and Mrs. Harlowe), the one a town coquette, the other a commercial gambler; when just in the nick of time, news is brought that Holland is ruined by the failure of an extravagant speculation, and that a distant relation has left his whole fortune to Harley. The tables are now turned. Harley buys the mansion-house, furniture, and gardens, takes possession of them with highly amusing airs of upstart vanity and self-importance; is flattered by the Squire's sister, who discards and is discarded by a broken fortune-hunting lover of the name of Garnish (Wallack), makes proposals of marriage to her, and thinks no more of his old favourite Dinah. Garnish in the mean time finding the pliability of temper of Peregrine Paragon, Esq., and to make up for his disappointment in his own fortune-hunting scheme, sends for his sister (Mrs. Alsop) whom he introduces to the said Peregrine Paragon. The forward pretensions of the two new candidates for his hand, form an amusing contrast with the sanguine hopes and rejected addresses of the old possessor of his heart, and some very ridiculous scenes take place, with one very affecting one, in which Miss Kelly makes a last vain appeal to her lover's fidelity, and (Oxberry) her father watches the result with a mute wonderment and disappointed expectation infinitely natural, and well worth any body's seeing. By-and-bye it turns out that the fortune has been left not to Harley, but by a subsequent will to Miss Kelly, who is also a relation of the deceased, when instantly his two accomplished mistresses give over their persecution of him, their two brothers set off to make love to the new heiress, who exposes them both to the ridicule they deserve, and Harley, without knowing of the change of fortune, is moved by a letter he receives from her, to repent just in time to prove himself not altogether unworthy of her hand.

Such is the outline of this Comedy. Dowton acts the part of a friendly mediator, and spectator in the scene; and Hughes makes a very fit representative of a shuffling, officious, pettifogging attorney. The most unpleasant part of the play was the undisguised mercenary profligacy of the four characters of Wallack, Holland, Mrs. Alsop, and Mrs. Harlowe: and a precious *partie quarrée* they are. The scrapes into which their folly and cunning lead them are, however, very amusing, and their unprincipled selfishness is very deservedly punished at last.

THE LIBERTINE

The Examiner.   (*Covent Garden*) *May* 25, 1817.

The Libertine, an after-piece altered from Shadwell's play of that name, and founded on the story of Don Juan, with Mozart's music, was represented here on Tuesday evening. Almost every thing else was against it, but the music triumphed. Still it had but half a triumph, for the songs were not *encored*; and when an attempt was made by some rash over-weening enthusiasts to *encore* the enchanting airs of Mozart, that heavy German composer, 'that dull Beotian genius,' as he has been called by a lively verbal critic of our times, the English, disdaining this insult offered to our native talents, *hissed*—in the plenitude of their pampered grossness, and 'ignorant impatience' of foreign refinement and elegance, they hissed! We believe that unconscious patriotism has something to do with this as well as sheer stupidity: they think that a real taste for the Fine Arts, unless they are of British growth and manufacture, is a sign of dis-affection to the Government, and that there must be 'something rotten in the state of Denmark,' if their ears, as well as their hearts, are not true English. We have heard sailors' songs by Little Smith, and Yorkshire songs by Emery, and the Death of Nelson by Mr. Sinclair, *encored* again and again at Covent-Garden, so as almost 'to split the ears of the groundlings,' yet the other night they would not hear of *encoring* Miss Stephens, either in the Duet with Duruset, *La ci darem*, nor in the song appealing for his forgiveness, *Batte, Massetto*; yet at the Opera they tolerate Madame Fodor in repeating both these

370

songs, because they suppose it to be the etiquette, and would have you believe that they do not very warmly insist on the repetition of the last song she sings there, out of tenderness to the actress, not to spare their own ears, which are soon cloyed with sweetness, and delight in nothing but noise and fury.

We regard Miss Stephens's Zerlina as a failure, whether we compare her with Madame Fodor in the same part, or with herself in other parts. She undoubtedly sung her songs with much sweetness and simplicity, but her simplicity had something of insipidity in it; her tones wanted the fine, rich, *pulpy* essence of Madame Fodor's, the elastic impulse of health and high animal spirits; nor had her manner of giving the different airs that laughing, careless grace which gives to Madame Fodor's singing all the ease and spirit of conversation. There was some awkwardness necessarily arising from the transposition of the songs, particularly of the duet between Zerlina and Don Giovanni, which was given to Massetto, because Mr. Charles Kemble is not a singer, and which by this means lost its exquisite appropriateness of expression. Of Mr. Duruset's Massetto we shall only say, that it is not so good as Angrisani's. He would however have made a better representative of the statue of Don Pedro than Mr. Chapman, who is another gentleman who has not 'a singing face,' and whom it would therefore have been better to leave out of the Opera than the songs; particularly than that fine one, answering to *Di rider finira pria della Aurora*, which Mr. Chapman was mounted on horseback on purpose, it should seem, *neither to sing nor say*!

Mr. Charles Kemble did not play the Libertine well. Instead of the untractable, fiery spirit, the unreclaimable licentiousness of Don Giovanni, he was as tame as any saint;

'And of his port as meek as is a maid.'

He went through the different exploits of wickedness assigned him with evident marks of reluctance and contrition; and it seemed the height of injustice that so well meaning a young man, forced into acts of villainy against his will, should at last be seized upon as their lawful prize by fiends come hot from hell with flaming torches, and that he should sink into a lake of burning brimstone on a splendid car brought to receive him by the devil, in the likeness of a great dragon, writhing round and round upon a wheel of fire—an exquisite device of the Managers, superadded to the original story, and in striking harmony with Mozart's music! Mr. Liston's Leporello was not quite what we wished it. He played it in a mixed style between a burlesque imitation of the Italian Opera, and his own *inimitable*

371

manner. We like him best when he is his own great original, and copies only himself—

'None but himself can be his parallel.'

He did not sing the song of Madamira half so well, nor with half the impudence of Naldi. Indeed, all the performers seemed, instead of going their lengths on the occasion, to be upon their good behaviour, and instead of entering into their parts, to be thinking of the comparison between themselves and the performers at the Opera. We cannot say it was in their favour.

BARBAROSSA

The Examiner.   (*Drury-Lane*) *June* 1, 1817.

Mr. Kean had for his benefit on Monday, Barbarossa, and the musical after-piece of Paul and Virginia. In the tragedy there was nothing for him to do, and it is only when there is nothing for him to do, that he does nothing. The scene in which he throws off his disguise as a slave, and declares himself to be Achmet, the heir to the throne, which Barbarossa has usurped by the murder of his father, was the only one of any effect. We are sorry that Mr. Kean repeats this character *till further notice*. In Paul we liked him exceedingly : but we should have liked him better, if he had displayed fewer of the graces and intricacies of the art. The tremulous deliberation with which he introduced some of these ornamental flourishes, put us a little in mind of the perplexity of the lover in the Tatler, who was at a loss in addressing his mistress whether he should say,

'—And when your song you sing,
Your song you sing with so much art,'

Or,

'—And when your song you sing,
You sing your song with so much art.'

As Mr. Bickerstaff, who was applied to by the poet, declined deciding on this nice point, so we shall not decide whether Mr. Kean sung well or ill, but leave it to be settled by the connoisseurs and the ladies. His voice is clear, full, and sweet to a degree of tenderness. Miss Mangeon played Virginia, and in so doing, did not spoil one of the most pleasing recollections of our boyish reading days, which we have still treasured up 'in our heart's core, aye, in our best of hearts.'

372

A VIEW OF THE ENGLISH STAGE

MRS. SIDDONS'S LADY MACBETH

The Examiner.   *(Covent-Garden) June* 8, 1817.

Mrs. Siddons's appearance in Lady Macbeth at this Theatre on Thursday, drew immense crowds to every part of the house. We should suppose that more than half the number of persons were compelled to return without gaining admittance. We succeeded in gaining a seat in one of the back-boxes, and saw this wonderful performance at a distance, and consequently at a disadvantage. Though the distance of place is a disadvantage to a performance like Mrs. Siddons's Lady Macbeth, we question whether the distance of time at which we have formerly seen it is any. It is nearly twenty years since we first saw her in this character, and certainly the impression which we have still left on our minds from that first exhibition, is stronger than the one we received the other evening. The sublimity of Mrs. Siddons's acting is such, that the first impulse which it gives to the mind can never wear out, and we doubt whether this original and paramount impression is not weakened, rather than strengthened, by subsequent repetition. We do not read the tragedy of the Robbers twice; if we have seen Mrs. Siddons in Lady Macbeth only once, it is enough. The impression is stamped there for ever, and any after-experiments and critical enquiries only serve to fritter away and tamper with the sacredness of the early recollection. We see into the details of the character, its minute excellencies or defects, but the great masses, the gigantic proportions, are in some degree lost upon us by custom and familiarity. It is the first blow that staggers us; by gaining time we recover our self-possession. Mrs. Siddons's Lady Macbeth is little less appalling in its effects than the apparition of a preternatural being; but if we were accustomed to see a preternatural being constantly, our astonishment would by degrees diminish.

We do not know whether it is owing to the cause here stated, or to a falling-off in Mrs. Siddons's acting, but we certainly thought her performance the other night inferior to what it used to be. She speaks too slow, and her manner has not that decided, sweeping majesty, which used to characterise her as the Muse of Tragedy herself. Something of apparent indecision is perhaps attributable to the circumstance of her only acting at present on particular occasions. An actress who appears only once a-year cannot play so well as if she was in the habit of acting once a-week. We therefore wish Mrs. Siddons would either return to the stage, or retire from it altogether. By her present uncertain wavering between public and private life, she may diminish her reputation, while she can add nothing to it.

A VIEW OF THE ENGLISH STAGE

MR. MAYWOOD'S SHYLOCK

The Times.   *(Drury-Lane) September* 26, 1817.

Mr. Maywood, from the Theatre Royal Glasgow, of whom report had spoken highly, and we think not undeservedly so, appeared here in the part of Shylock. He was received throughout with very great applause; nor was there any part of his performance at which the slightest disapprobation was expressed. His figure is rather short; his face, though not regularly formed, expressive; his voice full, and capable of great depth of intonation; his attitudes firm and well conceived: the most spirited scene, we thought, was that in which Tubal brings him information of Antonio's losses and impending ruin, and of his daughter's waste of his money. His exclamation, 'Thank God! thank God!' on hearing of the shipwreck, was as animated as any thing we ever heard. In the last scene, the glare of malignity with which he eyed Antonio after his defeated revenge recoils upon his own head, was truly terrific. Upon the whole, we consider this gentleman as an acquisition to the tragic strength of the theatre; and are persuaded that what seemed the principal defect in his performance, an occasional want of decision of tone, and firmness of action, was attributable only to that diffidence which is natural to a young actor on his first appearance before a London audience, in a part of so much prominence, and which has been so ably filled of late.

MR. KEMBLE'S RETIREMENT

The Times.   *(Covent-Garden) June* 25, 1817.

Mr. Kemble took his leave of the Stage on Monday night, in the character of Coriolanus. On his first coming forward to pronounce his Farewell Address, he was received with a shout like thunder: on his retiring after it, the applause was long before it subsided entirely away. There is something in these partings with old public favourites exceedingly affecting. They teach us the shortness of human life, and the vanity of human pleasures. Our associations of admiration and delight with theatrical performers, are among our earliest recollections—among our last regrets. They are links that connect the beginning and the end of life together; *their* bright and giddy career of popularity measures the arch that spans our brief existence. It is near twenty years ago since we first saw Mr. Kemble in the same character — yet how short the interval seems! The impression appears as distinct as if it were of yesterday. In fact, intellectual objects, in proportion as they are lasting, may be said to shorten life. Time has no effect upon them. The petty and the

374

personal, that which appeals to our senses and our interests, is by degrees forgotten, and fades away into the distant obscurity of the past. The grand and the ideal, that which appeals to the imagination, can only perish with it, and remains with us, unimpaired in its lofty abstraction, from youth to age; as, wherever we go, we still see the same heavenly bodies shining over our heads! We forget numberless things that have happened to ourselves, one generation of follies after another; but not the first time of our seeing Mr. Kemble, nor shall we easily forget the last! Coriolanus, the character in which he took his leave of the Stage, was one of the first in which we remember to have seen him; and it was one in which we were not sorry to part with him, for we wished to see him appear like himself to the last. Nor was he wanting to himself on this occasion: he played the part as well as he ever did—with as much freshness and vigour. There was no abatement of spirit and energy—none of grace and dignity: his look, his action, his expression of the character, were the same as they ever were: they could not be finer. It is mere cant, to say that Mr. Kemble has quite fallen off of late—that he is not what he was: he may have fallen off in the opinion of some jealous admirers, because he is no longer in exclusive possession of the Stage: but in himself he has not fallen off a jot. Why then do we approve of his retiring? Because we do not wish him to wait till it is *necessary* for him to retire. On the last evening, he displayed the same excellences, and gave the same prominence to the very same passages, that he used to do. We might refer to his manner of doing obeisance to his mother in the triumphal procession in the second act, and to the scene with Aufidius in the last act, as among the most striking instances. The action with which he accompanied the proud taunt to Aufidius—

> 'Like an eagle in a dove-cote, I
> Flutter'd your Volscians in Corioli;
> Alone I did it——'

gave double force and beauty to the image. Again, where he waits for the coming of Aufidius in his rival's house, he stood at the foot of the statue of Mars, himself another Mars! In the reconciliation scene with his mother, which is the finest in the play, he was not equally impressive. Perhaps this was not the fault of Mr. Kemble, but of the stage itself, which can hardly do justice to such thoughts and sentiments as here occur:

> '———— My mother bows:
> As if Olympus to a mole-hill should
> In supplication nod.'

375

Mr. Kemble's voice seemed to faint and stagger, to be strained and cracked, under the weight of this majestic image : but, indeed, we know of no tones deep or full enough to bear along the swelling tide of sentiment it conveys ; nor can we conceive any thing in outward form to answer to it, except when Mrs. Siddons played the part of Volumnia.

We may on this occasion be expected to say a few words on the general merits of Mr. Kemble as an actor, and on the principal characters he performed ; in doing which, we shall

'————— Nothing extenuate,
Nor set down aught in malice.'

It has always appeared to us, that the range of characters in which Mr. Kemble more particularly shone, and was superior to every other actor, were those which consisted in the developement of some one solitary sentiment or exclusive passion. From a want of rapidity, of scope, and variety, he was often deficient in expressing the bustle and complication of different interests ; nor did he possess the faculty of overpowering the mind by sudden and irresistible bursts of passion : but in giving the habitual workings of a predominant feeling, as in Penruddock, or The Stranger, in Coriolanus, Cato, and some others, where all the passions move round a central point, and are governed by one master-key, he stood unrivalled. Penruddock, in The Wheel of Fortune, was one of his most correct and interesting performances, and one of the most perfect on the modern stage. The deeply-rooted, mild, pensive melancholy of the character, its embittered recollections, and dignified benevolence, were conveyed by Mr. Kemble with equal truth, elegance, and feeling. In The Stranger, again, which is in fact the same character, he brooded over the recollection of disappointed hope till it became a part of himself ; it sunk deeper into his mind the longer he dwelt upon it ; his regrets only became more profound as they became more durable. His person was moulded to the character. The weight of sentiment which oppressed him was never suspended : the spring at his heart was never lightened—it seemed as if his whole life had been a suppressed sigh ! So in Coriolanus, he exhibited the ruling passion with the same unshaken firmness, he preserved the same haughty dignity of demeanour, the same energy of will, and unbending sternness of temper throughout. He was swayed by a single impulse. His tenaciousness of purpose was only irritated by opposition ; he turned neither to the right nor the left ; the vehemence with which he moved forward increasing every instant, till it hurried him on to the catastrophe. In Leontes, also, in The Winter's Tale (a character he at one time played often),

376

the growing jealousy of the King, and the exclusive possession which this passion gradually obtains over his mind, were marked by him in the finest manner, particularly where he exclaims—

> ' —— Is whispering nothing ?
> Is leaning cheek to cheek ?   Is meeting noses ?
> Kissing with inside lip ?   Stopping the career
> Of laughter with a sigh (a note infallible
> Of breaking honesty) ?   Horsing foot on foot ?
> Skulking in corners ?   Wishing clocks more swift ?
> Hours minutes ?   The noon midnight ? and all eyes
> Blind with the pin and web, but their's ; their's only,
> That would unseen be wicked ?   Is this nothing ?
> Why then the world and that 's in 't is nothing,
> The covering sky is nothing, Bohemia 's nothing,
> My wife is nothing, if this be nothing ! '

In the course of this enumeration, every proof told stronger, and followed with quicker and harder strokes ; his conviction became more rivetted at every step of his progress ; and at the end, his mind, and 'every corporal agent,' appeared wound up to a phrenzy of despair.   In such characters, Mr. Kemble had no occasion to call to his aid either the resources of invention, or the tricks of the art : his success depended on the increasing intensity with which he dwelt on a given feeling, or enforced a passion that resisted all interference or control.

In Hamlet, on the contrary, Mr. Kemble in our judgment unavoidably failed from a want of flexibility, of that quick sensibility which yields to every motive, and is borne away with every breath of fancy, which is distracted in the multiplicity of its reflections, and lost in the uncertainty of its resolutions.   There is a perpetual undulation of feeling in the character of Hamlet ; but in Mr. Kemble's acting, 'there was neither variableness nor shadow of turning.'   He played it like a man in armour, with a determined inveteracy of purpose, in one undeviating straight line, which is as remote from the natural grace and indolent susceptibility of the character, as the sharp angles and abrupt starts to produce an effect which Mr. Kean throws into it.

In King John, which was one of Mr. Kemble's most admired parts, the transitions of feeling, though just and powerful, were prepared too long beforehand, and were too long in executing to produce their full effect.   The actor seemed waiting for some complicated machinery to enable him to make his next movement, instead of trusting to the true impulses of passion.   There was no sudden collision of opposite elements ; the golden flash of genius was not there ; 'the fire i' th' flint was cold,' for it was not struck.   If an image

377

could be constructed by magic art to play King John, it would play it in much the same manner that Mr. Kemble played it.

In Macbeth, Mr. Kemble was unequal to 'the tug and war' of the passions which assail him : he stood as it were at bay with fortune, and maintained his ground too steadily against 'fate and metaphysical aid;' instead of staggering and reeling under the appalling visions of the preternatural world, and having his frame wrenched from all the holds and resting places of his will, by the stronger power of imagination. In the latter scenes, however, he displayed great energy and spirit; and there was a fine melancholy retrospective tone in his manner of delivering the lines,

> 'My way of life has fallen into the sear, the yellow leaf,'

which smote upon the heart, and remained there ever after. His Richard III. wanted that tempest and whirlwind of the soul, that life and spirit, and dazzling rapidity of motion, which fills the stage, and burns in every part of it, when Mr. Kean performs this character. To Mr. Kean's acting in general, we might apply the lines of the poet, where he describes

> 'The fiery soul that, working out its way,
> Fretted the pigmy body to decay,
> And o'er-inform'd the tenement of clay.'

Mr. Kemble's manner, on the contrary, had always something dry, hard, and pedantic in it. 'You shall relish him more in the scholar than the soldier:' but his monotony did not fatigue, his formality did not displease; because there was always sense and meaning in what he did. The fineness of Mr. Kemble's figure may be supposed to have led to that statue-like appearance, which his acting was sometimes too apt to assume: as the diminutiveness of Mr. Kean's person has probably compelled him to bustle about too much, and to attempt to make up for the want of dignity of form, by the violence and contrast of his attitudes. If Mr. Kemble were to remain in the same posture for half an hour, his figure would only excite admiration: if Mr. Kean were to stand still only for a moment, the contrary effect would be apparent. One of the happiest and most spirited of all Mr. Kemble's performances, and in which even his defects were blended with his excellences to produce a perfect whole, was his Pierre. The dissolute indifference assumed by this character, to cover the darkness of his designs, and the fierceness of his revenge, accorded admirably with Mr. Kemble's natural manner; and the tone of morbid rancorous raillery, in which Pierre delights to indulge, was in unison with the actor's reluctant, contemptuous personifications

378

of gaiety, with the scornful spirit of his Comic Muse, which always laboured—*invita Minerva*—against the grain. Cato was another of those parts for which Mr. Kemble was peculiarly fitted by his physical advantages. There was nothing for him to do in this character, but to appear in it. It had all the dignity of still-life. It was a studied piece of classical costume—a conscious exhibition of elegantly disposed drapery, that was all: yet, as a mere display of personal and artificial grace, it was inimitable.

It has been suggested that Mr. Kemble chiefly excelled in his Roman characters, and among others in Brutus. If it be meant, that he excelled in those which imply a certain stoicism of feeling and energy of will, this we have already granted; but Brutus is not a character of this kind, and Mr. Kemble failed in it for that reason. Brutus is not a stoic, but a humane enthusiast. There is a tenderness of nature under the garb of assumed severity; an inward current of generous feelings, which burst out, in spite of circumstances, with bleeding freshness; a secret struggle of mind, and disagreement between his situation and his intentions; a lofty inflexibility of purpose, mingled with an effeminate abstractedness of thought, which Mr. Kemble did not give.

In short, we think the distinguishing excellence of his acting may be summed up in one word—*intensity*; in the seizing upon some one feeling or idea, in insisting upon it, in never letting it go, and in working it up, with a certain graceful consistency, and conscious grandeur of conception, to a very high degree of pathos or sublimity. If he had not the unexpected bursts of nature and genius, he had all the regularity of art; if he did not display the tumult and conflict of opposite passions in the soul, he gave the deepest and most permanent interest to the uninterrupted progress of individual feeling; and in embodying a high idea of certain characters, which belong rather to sentiment than passion, to energy of will, than to loftiness or to originality of imagination, he was the most excellent actor of his time. This praise of him is not exaggerated: the blame we have mixed with it is not invidious. We have only to add to both, the expression of our grateful remembrances and best wishes—Hail, and farewell!

End of A View of the English Stage.

ESSAYS ON THE ACTED DRAMA IN LONDON

CONTRIBUTED TO

THE LONDON MAGAZINE (1820)

BIBLIOGRAPHICAL NOTE

These essays, contributed to *The London Magazine* in 1820, have never been republished in their original form. A great part of them was included in the so-called 'second edition' of *A View of the English Stage* (see the bibliographical note to that work, *ante*, p. 170), but the essays were cut up and re-arranged, and many passages were left out altogether. In the present edition, all the essays are printed *verbatim* from *The London Magazine*, except that a part of Essay No. **VI.** and the whole of Essay No. **X.**, being plainly the work of another hand, have been omitted.

ESSAYS ON THE DRAMA

FROM

THE LONDON MAGAZINE, 1820

No. I

[*January*, 1820.

In commencing our account of the drama for the year 1820, and turning our eye back, as far as our personal recollection reaches, towards the conclusion of the last century, we do not think we should be justified, by the customary topics of comparison, or privileges of criticism, in making a general complaint of the degeneracy of the stage. Within our remembrance, at least, it has not fallen off to any alarming degree, either in the written or the acted performances. It has changed its style considerably in both these respects, but it does not follow that it has altogether deteriorated : it has shifted its ground, but has found its level. With respect to the pieces brought out, we have got striking melo-dramas for dull tragedies ; and short farces are better than long ones of five acts. The *semper varium et mutabile* of the poet, may be transferred to the stage, 'the inconstant stage,' without losing the original felicity of the application :—it has its necessary ebbs and flows, from its subjection to the influence of popular feeling, and the frailty of the materials of which it is composed, its own fleeting and shadowy essence and cannot be expected to remain for any great length of time stationary at the same point, either of perfection or debasement. Acting, in particular, which is the chief organ by which it addresses itself to the mind ;—the eye, tongue, hand by which it dazzles, charms, and seizes on the public attention—is an art that seems to contain in itself the seeds of perpetual renovation and decay, following in this respect the order of nature rather than the analogy of the productions of human intellect,—for whereas in the other arts of painting and poetry, the standard works of genius being permanent and accumulating, for awhile provoke emulation, but, in the end, overlay future efforts, and transmit only their defects to those that come after ; the exertions of the greatest actor die with him, leaving to his successors only the admiration of his name, and the aspiration after imaginary excellence : so that in effect 'no one generation of actors binds another ; ' the art is always setting out afresh on the stock of genius and nature, and the success depends (generally speaking) on accident, opportunity, and encouragement. The harvest of excellence (whatever it may be) is removed from the ground every twenty or thirty years, by Death's sickle ; and there is room left for another to sprout up and tower to an equal height, and spread into equal luxuriance—to 'dally with the wind, and court the sun'—according to the health and vigour of the stem, and the favourableness of the season. But books, pictures, remain like fixtures in the public mind ; beyond a certain point incumber the soil of living truth and nature ; and distort or stunt the growth of original genius. Again, the literary amateur may find employment for his time in reading old authors only, and exhaust his entire spleen in scouting new ones : but the lover of the stage cannot amuse himself, in his solitary fastidiousness, by sitting to witness a play got up by the departed ghosts of first-rate actors ; or be contented with the perusal of a collection of old play-bills :—he may extol Garrick, but he must go to see Kean ; and, in his own defence, must admire or at least tolerate what he sees, or stay away against his will. The theatrical critic may grumble a little, at first, at a new candidate for the favour of the town, and say how much better the part must have been done formerly by some actor whom he never saw ; but by degrees he makes a virtue of necessity, and submits to be pleased 'with coy, reluctant, amorous delay'—devoting his attention to the actual stage as he would to a living mistress, whom he selects as a matter of course from the beauties of the present, and not from those of the last age ! We think there is for this reason less pedantry and affectation (though not less party-feeling and personal prejudice) in judging of the stage than of most other subjects ; and we feel a sort of theoretical, as well as instinctive predilection for the faces of *play-going* people as among the most sociable, gossiping, good-natured, and humane members of society. In this point of view, as well as in others, the stage is a test and school of humanity. We do not much like any person or persons who do not like plays ; and for this reason, viz. that we imagine they cannot much like themselves or any one else. The really humane man (except in cases of unaccountable prejudices, which we do not think the most likely means to increase or preserve the natural amiableness of his disposition) is prone to the study of humanity. *Omnes boni et liberales* HUMANITATI *semper favemus.* He likes to see it brought home from the universality of precepts and general terms, to the reality of persons, of tones, and actions; and to have it raised from the grossness and familiarity of sense, to the lofty but striking platform of the imagination. He likes to see the face of man with the veil of time torn from it, and to feel the pulse of nature beating in all times and places alike. The smile of good-humoured surprise at folly, the tear of pity at misfortune, do not misbecome the face of man or woman. It is something delightful and instructive, to have seen Coriolanus or King John in the habiliments of Mr. Kemble, to have shaken hands almost with Othello in the person of Mr. Kean, to have cowered before the spirit of Lady Macbeth in the glance of Mrs. Siddons. The stage at once gives a body to our thoughts, and refinement and expansion to our sensible impressions. It has not the pride and remoteness of abstract science: it has not the petty egotism of vulgar life. It is particularly wanted in great cities (where it of course flourishes most) to take off from the dissatisfaction and *ennui*, that creep over our own pursuits from the indifference or contempt thrown upon them by others; and at the same time to reconcile our numberless discordant incommensurable feelings and interests together, by giving us an immediate and common topic to engage our attention, and to rally us round the standard of our common humanity. We never hate a face that we have seen in the pit: and Liston's laugh would be a cordial to wash down the oldest animosity of the most inveterate pit-critics.

The only drawback on the felicity and triumphant self-complacency of a play-goer's life, arises from the shortness of life itself. We miss the favourites, not of another age, but of our own—the idols of our youthful enthusiasm; and we cannot replace them by others. It does not shew that *these* are worse, because they are different from *those*: though they had been better, they would not have been so good to us. It is the penalty of our nature, from Adam downwards: so Milton makes our first ancestor exclaim,—

> ———'Should God create
> Another Eve, and I another rib afford,
> Yet loss of thee would never from my heart.'

We offer our best affections, our highest aspirations after the good and beautiful, on the altar of youth: it is well if, in our after-age, we can sometimes rekindle the almost extinguished flame, and inhale its dying fragrance like the breath of incense, of sweet-smelling flowers and gums, to detain the spirit of life, the ethereal guest, a little longer in its frail abode to cheer and soothe it with the pleasures of memory, not with those of hope. While we can do this, life is worth living for: when we can do it no longer, its spring will soon go down, and we had better not be!—Who shall give us Mrs. Siddons again, but in a waking dream, a beatific vision of past years, crowned with other hopes and other feelings, whose pomp is also faded, and their glory and their power gone! Who shall in our time (or can ever to the eye of fancy) fill the stage, like her, with the dignity of their persons, and the emanations of their minds? Or who shall sit majestic in the throne of tragedy—a Goddess, a prophetess and a Muse—from which the lightning of her eye flashed o'er the mind, startling its inmost thoughts—and the thunder of her voice circled through the labouring breast, rousing deep and scarce known feelings from their slumber? Who shall stalk over the stage of horrors, its presiding genius, or 'play the hostess,' at the banquetting scene of murder? Who shall walk in sleepless exstacy of soul, and haunt the mind's eye ever after, with the dread pageantry of suffering and of guilt? Who shall make tragedy once more stand with its feet upon the earth, and with its head raised above the skies, weeping tears and blood? That loss is not to be repaired. While the stage lasts, there will never be another Mrs. Siddons! Tragedy seemed to set with her; and the rest are but blazing comets or fiery exhalations.—It is pride and happiness enough for us to have lived at the same time with her, and one person more! But enough on this subject. Those feelings that we are most anxious to do justice to, are those to which it is impossible we ever should!

To turn to something less serious. We have not the same pomp of tragedy nor the same gentility, variety, and correctness in comedy. There was the gay, fluttering, hair-brained Lewis; he that was called 'Gentleman Lewis,'—all life, and fashion, and volubility, and whim; the greatest comic *mannerist* that perhaps ever lived; whose head seemed to be in his heels, and his wit at his fingers' ends: who never let the stage stand still, and made your heart light and your head giddy with his infinite vivacity, and bustle, and hey-day animal spirits. We wonder how Death ever caught him in his mad, whirling career, or ever fixed his volatile spirit in a dull *caput mortuum* of dust and ashes? Nobody could break open a door, or jump over a table, or scale a ladder, or twirl a cocked hat, or dangle a cane, or play a jockey-nobleman, or a nobleman's jockey, like him. He was at Covent Garden. With him was Quick, who made an excellent self-important, busy, strutting, money-getting citizen; or crusty old guardian, in a brown suit and a bob wig. There was also Munden, who was as good an actor then, as he is now; and Fawcett, who was at that time a much better one than he is at present. He, of late, seems to slur over his parts, wishes to merge the actor in the manager, and is grown serious before retiring from the stage. But a few years back (when he ran the race of popularity with Jack Bannister) nobody could give the *view holla* of a fox-hunting country squire like him; and he sung AMO AMAS, as Lingo in the Agreeable Surprise, in a style of pathos to melt the heart of the young apprentices in the two shilling gallery. But he appears to have grown averse to his profession, and indifferent to the applause he might acquire himself, and to the pleasures he used to give to others. In turbulent and pragmatical characters, and in all that cast of parts which may be called the *slang* language of comedy, he hardly had his equal. Perhaps he might consider this walk of his art as beneath his ambition; but, in our judgment, whatever a man can do best, is worth his doing. At the same house was little Simmons, who remained there till lately, like a veteran at his post, till he fell down a flight of steps and broke his neck, without any one's seeming to know or care about the matter. Though one of those 'who had gladdened life,' his death by no means 'eclipsed the gaiety of nations.' The public are not grateful. They make an effort of generosity, collect all their reluctant admiration into a heap, and offer it up with servile ostentation at the shrine of some great name, which they think reflects back its lustre on the worshippers. Or, like fashionable creditors, they pay their debts of honour for the *eclat* of the thing, and neglect the claims of humbler but sterling merit; such as was that of Simmons, one of the most correct, pointed, *naive*, and whimsical comic actors, we have for a long time had, or are likely to have again. He was not a buffoon, but a real actor. He did not play *himself*, nor play tricks, but played the part the author had assigned him. This was the great merit of the good old style of acting. He fitted into it like a brilliant into the setting of a ring, or as the ring fits the finger. We shall look for him often in Filch, in which his appearance was a continual *double entendre*, with one eye leering at his neighbour's pockets, and the other turned to the gallows :—also in the spangled Beau Mordecai, in Moses, in which he had all the precision, the pragmaticalness, and impenetrable secresy of the Jew money-lender; and in my Lord Sands, where he had all the stage to himself, and seemed to fill it by the singular insignificance of his person, and the infinite airs he gave himself. We shall look for him in these and many other parts, but in vain, or for any one equal to him.

At the other house, there was King, whose acting left a taste on the palate, sharp and sweet like a quince; with an old, hard, rough, withered face, like a John-apple, puckered up into a thousand wrinkles; with shrewd hints and tart replies; ' with nods and becks and wreathed smiles;' who was the real amorous, wheedling, or hasty, choleric, peremptory old gentleman in Sir Peter Teazle and Sir Anthony Absolute; and the true, that is, the pretended, clown in Touchstone, with wit sprouting from his head like a pair of ass's ears, and folly perched on his cap like the horned owl. There was Parsons too, whom we just remember like a worn-out 'suit of office' in Elbow; and Dodd in Acres, who had the most extraordinary way of hitching in a meaning, or subsiding into blank folly with the best grace in nature; and whose courage seemed literally to ooze out of his fingers in the preparations for the duel. There was Suett, the delightful old croaker, the everlasting Dicky Gossip of the stage; and, with him, Jack Bannister, whose gaiety, good humour, cordial feeling, and natural spirits, shone through his characters, and lighted them up like a transparency. Bannister did not go out of himself to take possession of his part, but put it on over his ordinary dress, like a *surtout*, snug, warm, and comfortable. He let his personal character appear through; and it was one great charm of his acting. In Lenitive, in the Prize, when the beau is ingrafted on the apothecary, he came out of his shell like the aurelia out of the grub; and surely never lighted on the stage, which he hardly seemed to touch, a more delightful vision —gilding, and cheering the motley sphere he just began to move in— shining like a gilded pill, fluttering like a piece of gold-leaf, gaudy as a butterfly, loud as a grasshopper, full of life, and laughter, and joy. His Scrub, in which he spouts a torrent of home-brewed ale against the ceiling, in a sudden fit of laughter at the waggeries of his brother Martin;—his Son-in-law; his part in the Grandmother; his Autolycus; his Colonel Feignwell; and his Walter in the Children in the Wood, were all admirable. Most of his characters were exactly fitted for him—for his good-humoured smile, his buoyant activity, his kind heart, and his honest face: and no one else could do them so well, because no one else could play Jack Bannister. He was, some time since, seen casting a wistful eye at Drury-lane theatre, and no doubt thinking of past times: others who also cast a wistful eye at it, do not forget him when they think of old and happy times! There were Bob and Jack Palmer, the Brass and Dick of the Confederacy; the one the pattern of an elder, the other of a younger brother. There was Wewitzer, the trustiest of Swiss valets, and the most 'secret Tattle' of the stage. There was, and there still is, Irish Johnstone, with his supple knees, his hat twisted round in his hand, his good-humoured laugh, his arched eye-brows, his insinuating leer, and his lubricated *brogue*, curling round the ear like a well oiled mustachio. These were all the men. Then there was

Miss Farren, with her fine-lady airs and graces, with that elegant turn of her head, and motion of her fan, and tripping of her tongue; and Miss Pope, the very picture of a Duenna, a maiden lady, or an antiquated dowager—the latter spring of beauty, the second childhood of vanity, more quaint, fantastic, and old-fashioned, more pert, frothy, and light-headed than any thing that can be imagined; embalmed in the follies, preserved in the spirit of affectation of the last age:— and then add to these, Mrs. Jordan, the child of nature, whose voice was a cordial to the heart, because it came from it, rich, full, like the luscious juice of the ripe grape; to hear whose laugh was to drink nectar; whose smile 'made a sunshine,' not 'in the shady place,' but amidst dazzling lights and in glad theatres:—who 'talked far above singing,' and whose singing was like the twang of Cupid's bow. Her person was large, soft, and generous like her soul. It has been attempted to compare Miss Kelly to her. There is no comparison. Miss Kelly is a shrewd, clever, arch, lively girl; tingles all over with suppressed sensibility; licks her lips at mischief, bites her words in two, or lets a sly meaning out of the corners of her eyes; is fidgetty with curiosity, or unable to stand still for spite:—she is always uneasy and always interesting; but Mrs. Jordan was all exuberance and grace, 'her bounty was as boundless as the sea; her love as deep.' It was her capacity for enjoyment, and the contrast she presented to every thing sharp, angular, and peevish, that communicated the same genial heartfelt satisfaction to the spectator. Her Nell, for instance, was right royal like her liquor, and wrapped up in measureless content with lambs' wool. Miss Kelly is a dextrous knowing chambermaid: Mrs. Jordan had nothing dexterous or knowing about her. She was Cleopatra turned into an oyster-wench, without knowing that she was Cleopatra, or caring that she was an oyster-wench. An oyster-wench, such as she was, would have been equal to a Cleopatra; and an Antony would not have deserted her for the empire of the world!

From the favourite actors of a few years back, we turn to those of the present day: and we shall speak of them, not with grudging or stinted praise.

The first of these in tragedy is Mr. Kean. To show that we do not conceive that tragedy regularly declines in every successive generation, we shall say, that we do not think there has been in our remembrance any tragic performer (with the exception of Mrs. Siddons) equal to Mr. Kean. Nor, except in voice and person, and the conscious ease and dignity naturally resulting from those advantages, do we know that even Mrs. Siddons was greater. In truth of nature and force of passion, in discrimination and originality, we see no inferiority to any one on the part of Mr. Kean: but there is an insignificance of figure, and a hoarseness of voice, that necessarily *vulgarize*, or diminish our idea of the characters he plays: and perhaps to this may be added, a want of a certain correspondent elevation and magnitude of thought, of which Mrs. Siddons's noble form seemed to be only the natural mould and receptacle. Her nature seemed always above the circumstances with which she had to struggle: her soul to be greater than the passion labouring in her breast. Grandeur was the cradle in which her genius was rocked: for *her* to be, was to be sublime! She did the greatest things with child-like ease: her powers seemed never tasked to the utmost, and always as if she had inexhaustible resources still in reserve. The least word she uttered seemed to float to the end of the stage: the least motion of her hand seemed to command awe and obedience. Mr. Kean is all effort, all violence, all extreme passion: he is possessed with a fury, a demon that leaves him no repose, no time for thought, or room for imagination. He perhaps screws himself up to as intense a degree of feeling as Mrs. Siddons, strikes home with as sure and as hard a blow as she did, but he does this by straining every nerve, and winding up every faculty to this single point alone: and as he does it by an effort himself, the spectator follows him by an effort also. Our sympathy in a manner ceases with the actual impression, and does not leave the same grand and permanent image of itself behind. The Othello furnishes almost the only exception to these remarks. The solemn and beautiful manner in which he pronounces the farewell soliloquy, is worth all gladiatorship and pantomime in the world. His Sir Giles is his most equal and energetic character: but it is too equal, too energetic from the beginning to the end. There is no reason that he should have the same eagerness, the same *impetus* at the commencement as at the close of his career: he should not have the fierceness of the wild beast till he is goaded to madness by the hunters. Sir Giles Mompesson (supposed to be the original character) we dare say, took things more quietly, and only grew desperate with his fortunes. Cooke played the general casting of the character better in this respect: but without the same fine breaks and turns of passion. Cooke indeed, compared to Kean, had only the *slang* and *bravado* of tragedy. Neither can we think Mr. Kemble equal to him, with all his study, his grace, and classic dignity of form. He was the statue of perfect tragedy, not the living soul. Mrs. Siddons combined the advantage of form and other organic requisites with nature and passion: Mr. Kemble has the external requisites, (at least of face and figure) without the internal workings of the soul: Mr.

Kean has the last without the first, and, if we must make our election between the two, we think the *vis tragica* must take precedence of every thing else. Mr. Kean, in a word, appears to us a test, an *experimentum crucis*, to shew the triumph of genius over physical defects, of nature over art, of passion over affectation, and of originality over common-place monotony.—Next to Mr. Kean, the greatest tragic performer now on the stage is undoubtedly Miss O'Neill. She cannot take rank by the side of her great predecessor, but neither can any other actress be at all compared with her. If we had not seen Mrs. Siddons, we should not certainly have been able to conceive any thing finer than some of her characters, such as Belvidera, Isabella in the Fatal Marriage, Mrs. Beverly, and Mrs. Haller, which (as she at first played them) in tenderness of sensibility, and the simple force of passion, could not be surpassed. She has, however, of late, carried the expression of mental agony and distress to a degree of physical horror that is painful to behold, and which is particularly repulsive in a person of her delicacy of frame and truly feminine appearance.—Mrs. Bunn is a beautiful and interesting actress in the sentimental drama; and in the part of Queen Elizabeth, in Schiller's Tragedy of Mary Stuart, which she played lately, gave, in the agitation of her form, the distracted thoughts painted in her looks, and the deep but fine and mellow tones of her voice, earnest of higher excellence than she has yet displayed. Her voice is one of the finest on the stage. It resembles the deep murmur of a hive of bees in spring-tide, and the words drop like honey from her lips.—Mr. Macready is, in our opinion, a truly spirited and impassioned declaimer, with a noble voice, and great fervour of manner; but, we apprehend, his *forte* is rather in giving a loose to the tide of enthusiastic feeling or sentiment, than in embodying individual character, or discriminating the diversity of the passions. There is a gaiety and tip-toe elevation in his personal deportment, which Mr. Kean has not, but in other more essential points there is no room for competition. Of his Coriolanus and Richard, we may have to speak in detail hereafter.

We shall conclude this introductory sketch with a few words on the comic actors. Emery at Covent Garden might be said to be the best *provincial* actor on the London boards. In his line of rustic characters he is a perfect actor. He would be a bold critic who should undertake to show that in his own walk Emery ever did any thing wrong. His Hodge is an absolute reality; and his Lockitt is as sullen, as gloomy, and impenetrable as the prison walls of which he is the keeper. His Robert Tyke is the sublime of tragedy in low life.—Mr. Liston has more comic humour, more power of face, and a more genial and happy vein of folly, than any other actor we remember. His farce is not caricature : his drollery oozes out of his features, and trickles down his face : his voice is a pitch-pipe for laughter. He does some characters but indifferently, others respectably ; but when he *puts himself whole* into a jest, it is unrivalled.—Munden with all his merit, his whim, his imagination, and with his broad effects, is a caricaturist in the comparison. He distorts his features to the utmost stretch of grimace, and trolls his voice about with his tongue in the most extraordinary manner, but he does all this with an evident view to the audience : whereas Liston's style of acting is the unconscious and involuntary ; he indulges his own risibility or absurd humours to please himself, and the odd noises he makes come from him as naturally as the bleating of a sheep.—Elliston is an actor of great merit, and of a very agreeable class : there is a joyousness in his look, his voice, and manner ; he treads the stage as if it was his ' best-found, and latest as well as earliest choice ; ' writes himself comedian in any book, warrant, or acquittance ; hits the town between wind and water, between farce and tragedy ; touches the string of a mock heroic sentiment with due pathos and vivacity ; and makes the best strolling gentleman, or needy poet, on the stage. His Rover is excellent : so is his Duke in the Honeymoon ; and in Matrimony he is best of all.—Dowton is a genuine and excellent comedian ; and, in speaking of his Major Sturgeon, we cannot pass over, in disdainful silence, Russell's Jerry Sneak, and Mrs. Harlowe's Miss Molly Jollop. Oxberry is an actor of a strong rather than of a pleasant comic vein (his Mawworm is particularly emphatical). Harley pleases others, for he seems pleased himself ; and little Knight, in the simplicity and good nature of the country lad, is inimitable.

Of the particular parts in which these and other performers display their talents to advantage, we must speak in future articles on this subject ; as well as of the merits of the modern drama itself ; the management of our theatres ; and a variety of other topics, to which we propose to give the best attention in our power—determined neither to ' extenuate, nor set down aught in malice.'

L. M.

No. II

[*February*, 1820.

Since we wrote a former article on this subject, the stage has lost one of its principal ornaments and fairest supports, in the person of Miss O'Neill. As Miss Somerville changed her name for that of

392

Mrs. Bunn, and still remains on the stage, so Miss O'Neill has altered hers for Mrs. Beecher, and has, we fear, quitted us for good and all. 'There were two upon the house-top: one was taken, and the other was left!' Though, on our own accounts, we do not think this 'a consummation devoutly to be wished,' yet we cannot say we are sorry on her's. Hymen has, in this instance, with his flaming torch and saffron robe, borne a favourite actress from us, and held her fast, beyond the seas and sounding shores, 'to our moist vows denied': but, whatever complaints or repinings have been heard on the occasion, we think Miss O'Neill was in the right to do as she has done. *Fast bind fast find,* is an old proverb, and a good one, and is no doubt applicable to both sexes, and on both sides of the water. A husband, like death, cancels all other claims, and we think, more especially, any imaginary and imperfect obligations, (with a clipt sixpence, and clap hands and a bargain) to the stage or to the town. Miss O'Neill, (for so her name may yet linger on our tongues) made good her retreat in time from the world's 'slippery turns,' and we are glad that she has done so. It is better to retire from the stage, when young, with fame and fortune, than to have to return to it when old (as Mrs. Crawfurd, Mrs. Abington, and so many others have done) in poverty, neglect, and scorn. There is no marriage for better and for worse to the public; it is but a 'Mr. Limberham, or Kind Keeper,' at the very best: it does not tie itself to worship its favourites, or 'with its worldly goods them endow,' through good report, or evil report, in sickness or in health, 'till death them do part.' No such thing is even thought of: they must be always young, always beautiful, and dazzling, and allowed to be so; or they are instantly discarded, and they pass from their full-blown pride, and the purple light that irradiates them, into 'the list of weeds, and worn-out faces.' If a servant of the theatre dismisses himself without due warning, it makes a great deal of idle talk: but, on the other hand, does the theatre never dismiss one of its servants without formal notice, and is any thing then said about it? How many old favourites of the town—that many-headed abstraction, with new opinions, whims, and follies ever sprouting from its teeming brain; how many decayed veterans of the stage, do we remember, in the last ten or twenty years, laid aside 'in monumental mockery'; thrown from the pinnacle of prosperity and popularity, to pine in poverty and obscurity, their names forgotten, or staring in large capitals, asking for a benefit at some minor theatre! How many of these are to be seen, walking about with shrunk shanks and tattered hose, avoiding the eye of the stranger whom they suppose to have known them in better days; straggling through the streets with faultering steps, and on some hopeless errand,—with sinking hearts, or heart-broken long ago:—engaged, dismissed again, tampered with, tantalised, trifled with, pelted, hooted, scorned, unpitied: performing quarantine at a distance from the centre of all their hopes and wishes, as if their names were a stain on their former reputations;—or perhaps received once more,—tolerated, endured out of charity, in the very places that they once adorned and gladdened by their presence!—And all this, often without any fault in themselves, any misconduct, any change, but in the taste and humour of the audience; or from their own imprudence, in not guarding (while they had the opportunity) against the ingratitude and treachery of that very public, that claims them as its property, and would make them its slaves and puppets for life—or during pleasure! We might make out a long list of superannuated pensioners on public patronage, who have had the last grudging pittance of favour withdrawn from them, but that it could do no sort of good, and that we would not expose the names themselves to the gaze and wonder of vulgar curiosity. We are only not sorry that Miss O'Neill has put it out of the power of the Nobility, the Gentry, and her Friends in general, to add her name to the splendid, tarnished list; and that she cannot, like so many of her predecessors, be chopped and changed, and hacked, and banded about, in tragedy, or in comedy, in farce or in pantomime, in dance or song, at the Surry, or the Cobourg, or the Sans Pareil Theatres; or even be sent to mingle her silvery cadences with Mr. Kean's hoarse notes at Old Drury!

Before, however, we take leave of her for ever in that capacity in which she has so often delighted, and so often astonished us, we must be excused in saying a few parting words of that excellence, which, for the future, can be known (how very imperfectly!) only by description, and be remembered only as an enchanting dream. We believe that ladies, even after the marriage ceremony, sign their maiden names in the church-register: we hope that Miss O'Neill will not refuse to subscribe, in the same manner, to our critical jurisdiction, for the last time that we shall have to exercise it upon her.

Miss O'Neill was in size of the middle form: her complexion was fair: and her person not inelegant. She stooped somewhat in the shoulders, but not so as to destroy grace or dignity:—in moving across the stage, she dragged a little in her step, with some want of firmness and elasticity. The action of her hands and arms, however (one of the least common, and therefore, we suppose, one of the most difficult accomplishments an actor or actress has to acquire) was perfectly just, simple and expressive. They either remained in

394

unconscious repose by her side, or, if employed, it was to anticipate or confirm the language of the eye and tongue. There was no affectation, no unmeaning display, or awkward deficiency in her gesticulation; but her body and mind seemed to be under the guidance of the same impulse, to move in concert, and to be moulded into unity of effect by a certain natural grace, earnestness, and good sense. The contour of her face was nearly oval; and her features approached to the regularity of the Grecian outline. The expression of them was confined either to the extremity of pain and agony, or to habitual softness and placidity, with an occasional smile of great sweetness. Her voice was deep, clear, and mellow, capable of the most forcible exertion, but, in ordinary speaking, 'gentle and low, an excellent thing in woman!' She, however, owed comparatively little to physical qualifications: there was nothing in her face, voice, or person, sufficiently striking to have obtruded her into notice, or to have been a factitious substitute for other requisites. Her external advantages were merely the medium through which her internal powers displayed their refulgence, without obstruction or refraction (with the exception hereafter to be stated): they were the passive instruments, which her powerful and delicate sensibility wielded, with the utmost propriety, ease, and effect. Her excellence (unrivalled by any actress since Mrs. Siddons) consisted in truth of nature, and force of passion. Her correctness did not seem the effect of art or study, but of instinctive sympathy, of a conformity of mind and disposition to the character she was playing, as if she had unconsciously become the very person. There were no catching lights, no pointed hits, no theatrical tricks, no female arts resorted to, in her best or general style of acting: there was a singleness, an entireness, and harmony in it, that gave it a double charm as well as a double power. It rested on the centre of its own feelings. Her style of acting was smooth, round, polished, and classical, like a marble statue; self-supported, and self-involved; owing its resemblance to life, to the truth of imitation; not to startling movements, and restless contortion, but returning continually within the softened line of beauty and nature. Her manner was, in this respect, the opposite of Mr. Kean's, of whom no man can say (either in a good or in a bad sense) that he is like a marble statue, but of whom it may be said, with some appearance of truth, that he is like a paste-board figure, the little, uncouth, disproportioned parts of which, children pull awry, twitch, and jerk about in fifty odd and unaccountable directions, to laugh at—or like the mock figure of Harlequin, that is stuck against the wall, and pulled in pieces, and fastened together again, with twenty idle, pantomimic, eccentric absurdities! Or he seems to have St. Antony's fire in his veins, St. Vitus's dance in his limbs, and a devil tugging at every part:—one shrugging his shoulders, another wagging his head, another hobbling in his legs, another tapping his breast; one straining his voice till it is ready to crack, another suddenly, and surprisingly, dropping it down into an inaudible whisper, which is made distinct and clear by the '*bravos*' in the pit, and the shouts of the gallery. There was not any of this paltry patch-work, these vulgar snatches at applause, these stops, and starts, and breaks, in Miss O'Neill's performance, which was sober, sedate, and free from pretence and mummery. We regret her loss the more, and fear we shall have to regret it more deeply every day. In a word, Mr. Kean's acting is like an anarchy of the passions, in which each upstart humour, or phrensy of the moment, is struggling to get violent possession of some bit or corner of his fiery soul and pigmy body—to jostle out, and lord it over, the rest of the rabble of short-lived, and furious purposes. Miss O'Neill seemed perfect mistress of her own thoughts, and if she was not indeed the rightful queen of tragedy, she had at least all the decorum, grace, and self-possession of one of the Maids of Honour waiting around its throne.—Miss O'Neill might have played, to the greatest advantage, in one of the tragedies of Sophocles, which are the perfection of the stately, elegant, and simple drama of the Greeks; we cannot conceive of Mr. Kean making a part of any such classical group. Perhaps, however, we may magnify his defects in this particular, as we have been accused of over-rating his general merits. We do not think it an easy matter 'to praise him, or blame him too much.' We have never heard any thing to alter the opinion we always entertained of him: he can only do it himself—by his own acting. While we owe it to him to speak largely of his genius and his powers, we owe it to the public to protest against the eccentricities of the one, or the abuses of the other.

To return from this digression. With all the purity and simplicity, Miss O'Neill possessed the utmost force of tragedy. Her soul was like the sea, calm, beautiful, smiling, smooth, and yielding; but the storm of adversity lashed it into foam, laid bare its centre, or heaved its billows against the skies. She could repose on gentleness, or dissolve in tenderness, and at the same time give herself up to all the agonies of woe. She could express fond affection, pity, rage, despair, madness. She felt all these passions in their simple and undefinable elements only. She felt them as a woman,—as a mistress, as a wife, a mother, or a friend. She seemed to have the most exquisite sense of the pressure of those soft ties, that were woven round her heart, and that bound her to her place in society; and the rending them asunder appeared to give a proportionable revulsion to her frame, and

396

disorder to her thoughts. There was nothing in her acting of a preternatural or *ideal* cast—that could lift the mind above mortality, or
might be fancied to descend from another sphere. But she gave the
full, the true, and unalloyed expression, to all that is common, obvious,
and heart-felt in the charities of private life, and in the conflict of
female virtue and attachment with the hardest trials and intolerable
griefs. She did not work herself up to the extremity of passion, by
questioning with her own thoughts; or raise herself above circumstances, by ascending the platform of imagination; or arm herself
against fate, by strengthening her will to meet it: no, she yielded to
calamity, she gave herself up entire, and with entire devotion, to her
unconquerable despair:—it was the tide of anguish swelling in her
own breast, that overflowed to the breasts of the audience, and filled
their eyes with tears as the loud torrent projects itself from the cliff
to the abyss below, and bears everything before it in its resistless
course. The source of her command over public sympathy, lay, in
short, in the intense conception, and unrestrained expression, of what
she, and every other woman, of natural sensibility would feel in given
circumstances, in which she, and every other woman, was liable to
be placed. Her Belvidera, Isabella, Mrs. Beverley, etc. were all
characters of this strictly feminine class of heroines, and she played
them to the life. They were made of softness and suffering. We
recollect the first time we saw her in Belvidera, when the manner in
which she threw herself into the arms of Jaffier, before they part, was
as if her heart would have leaped out of her bosom, if she had not
done so. It staggered the spectator like a blow. Again, her first
meeting with Biron, in Isabella, was no less admirable and impressive.
She looked at, she saw, she knew him: her surprise, her joy were
painted in her face, and woke every nerve to rapture. She seemed
to have perfected all that her art could do. But the sudden alteration
of her look and manner, the shuddering and recoil within herself,
when she recovers from her surprise, and recollects her situation,
married to another,—at once on the verge of ecstacy and perdition,—
baffled description, and threw all that she had before done in the
shade,—'like to another morn, risen on mid noon.' We could
mention many other instances, but they are still too fresh in the
memory of our readers to make it necessary. It must be confessed,
as perhaps the only drawback on Miss O'Neill's merit, or on the
pleasure derived from seeing her, that she sometimes carried the
expression of grief, or agony of mind, to a degree of physical horror
that could hardly be borne. Her shrieks, in the concluding scenes
of some of her parts, were like those of mandrakes, and you stopped
your ears against them: her looks were of 'moody madness, laughing

wild, amidst severest woe,' and you turned your eyes from them; for they seemed to sear like the lightening. Her eye-balls rolled in her head: her words rattled in her throat. This was carrying reality too far. The sufferings of the body are no longer proper for dramatic exhibition when they become objects of painful attention in themselves, and are not merely indications of what passes in the mind —comments and interpreters of the moral sense within. The effect was the more ungrateful from the very contrast (as we before hinted) between this lady's form and delicate complexion, and the violent conflict into which she was thrown. She seemed like the little flower, not the knotted oak, contending with the pitiless storm. There appeared no reason why she should 'mar that whiter skin of her's than snow, or monumental alabaster,' or rend and dishevel, with ruthless hand, those graceful locks, fairer than the opening day. But these were faults arising from pushing truth and nature to an excess, and we should, at present, be glad to see 'the best virtues' of others make even an approach to them. Her common style of speaking had a certain mild and equable intonation, not quite free from *manner*, but in the more impassioned parts, she became proportionably natural, bold, and varied. In comedy, Miss O'Neill did not, in our judgment, excel: her *forte* was the serious. Had we never seen her play anything but Lady Teazle, we should not have felt the regret at parting with her, which we now do, in common with every lover of genius, and of the genuine drama.

But it is high time that we should turn from the actors we have lost, to those that still remain amongst us.—Among the novelties of the season are, of course, the two Pantomimes, which, lest we should forget them at last, we shall mention in the first place. We cannot say that we exactly relish the taking Don Quixote as the subject of a Pantomime. The knight was battered and bruised enough in his life-time, without undergoing a gratuitous penance at this time of day. With all our good-will to Mr. Grimaldi, we have a greater affection for Sancho Panza, and do not want to see him metamorphosed into anything but himself. Indeed we cannot spoil Don Quixote; but neither need we try to do it.—Jack and the Bean Stalk is the legitimate growth of the Christmas holidays, and the winter Theatres. The wonders of the necromancer are equalled by the surprising arts of the mechanist. The favoured Bean Stalk grows and ascends the skies, as it did to our infant imaginations, and as if it would never have done growing; and Ogres and Ogresses become familiar to our senses, as to our early fears, in the enchanted palace of Drury-lane Theatre. Seeing is sometimes believing. It is worth going to a good Pantomime, if it was for no other reason than to hear the

398

children from school laugh at it, till they are ready to split their sides. What we can no longer enjoy, or wonder at ourselves, it is well to take at the rebound, in the reflection of happy faces, and in the echo of joyous mirth. These little real folks are even better than the fantastical beings, and poetic visions, we see upon the stage!

We are sorry we cannot say anything to reverse the judgment passed upon a new comedy, called *Gallantry*, or *Adventures at Madrid*, brought out at this Theatre in the beginning of the month. It was *a comedy of intrigue*; and, in conformity with the idea of this style of invention, was decorated with a wearisome display of Spanish costume, and enriched with an unmeaning catalogue of enamoured Dons, and disdainful or neglected Donnas. The plot was intricate, so as to become unintelligible, mechanical, and improbable. Every contrivance ' had its brother, and half the story just reflects the other.' There was a strange and insurmountable coincidence of antithetical blunders and epigrammatic accidents. The author's invention seemed to *run on all fours*, to cut out the different compartments of his fable, like the figures in a country-dance, to answer to one another : or he made all his characters turn the tables on one another, without knowing it. Thus, if a lady sends a letter very innocently to the lover of another, her own lover writes a letter to the mistress of his imaginary rival ; if an old fellow falls in love with a young lady, this turns out to be his son's intended bride ; and in this manner the game of cross-purposes is easily kept up, and the plot is diversified by the rule of contraries throughout. There was little attempt at wit in this piece (what little there is was flat and shallow, as well as gross), and there was no attempt at interest or sentiment, except in the character of Constantia, which was well played by Mrs. West, but very ill supported by the author. Mr. Barnard was her lover ; and we must say that this gentleman spoils any intrigue in which he is engaged, if it soars above a chambermaid. He plays an impudent, self-sufficient valet, with good emphasis and discretion, or can get through an under-steward very well ; but he cannot act the hero or look the gentleman. There is a cast of parts, for which Mr. Barnard is really qualified ; and we are unwilling to see him taken out of them, both for his sake and our own. The play was altogether ill got up : it indeed called out the strength of the house, but there was either nothing for them to do, or their parts became them as little as their dresses. Mr. Harley, for instance, who is always so lively in himself, and who so often enlivens others, was put to play a villainous grave Spanish Don, who is full of stratagem and deliberate knavery ; and he popped, and wriggled, and fidgetted on and off the stage, nodding his airy plumes, and shaking the powdered locks, in which he had been bedizened out, like the figure of Pug we have seen at Bartlemy-Fair, or in Hogarth's picture of the same little chuckling favourite, in Fashion in High Life. The fault was not in Mr. Harley, who always does his best to please, but in the cut of his clothes, and the cast of his part. Russel had no business in the play. He looked like an Alguazil, not like a Madrid gallant. Instead of meddling with the Spanish cavalier, and strutting about with a feather in his hat and a sword by his side, he should be *At Home* every night of his life, in Jerry Sneak: he is abroad in almost every other character! Munden made nothing of an amorous, superannuated, wheedling old lord: and, making nothing of the part 'as it was set down for him,' he tried, now and then, to thrust in a little caricature of his own, and to insinuate a bye-joke to the galleries. Munden's is not 'the courtier's or the lover's melancholy;' but a quaint, fantastical, uncouth, irresistible humour of his own, and he must be strangely grouped, or disposed of, on the theatrical canvass, to lose all his effect. Munden is not a sickly, vapid, decayed inamorato, fit to make his approaches to his mistress's eyebrows, in good set terms, or with cringing manners: he is a sturdy grotesque—a wild exotic, not a faded passion flower. He does not belong to any class, fashionable or vulgar. He is himself alone: and should only personate those extraordinary and marked characters, that Gilray painted, and O'Keeffe drew. Dowton and Knight were pieces of supererogation in the comedy of Gallantry; and Mrs. Harlowe is only happy in those parts which are meant to be unequivocally repulsive. Miss Kelly was neatly tucked up, in a Spanish bodice and petticoat; and had to carry several messages on or off the stage, in which she succeeded. The play languished on to the end of the fifth act, and then died a natural death. The only chance which it had of escaping was from one or two dramatic situations, borrowed from well-known plays, but disfigured and deprived of their effect, that they might pass for new. One of these was, where Mrs. West, as Constantia, retires from her antiquated lover (Munden) on his knees, in the middle of a speech, profuse of sentiments and compliments, and leaves her maid, Mrs. Harlowe, to receive the reversion of his protestations: the old gallant not discovering his mistake, till he is interrupted by the entrance of company. Mrs. Edwin delivered an Epilogue with some spirit, but its appeals to the favour of the audience only bespoke repeated condemnation. After the curtain dropped, Mr. Elliston, who had performed a part in the piece, came forward to announce that it was withdrawn; but, in submitting to the pleasure of the House, he seemed disposed to dispute the soundness of their taste. He said, 'It was a difficult thing to write a good comedy; perhaps a more difficult thing to judge of one.' Critics as we are, we cannot make up our minds to that opinion. Or we might say in answer, 'It is an easy thing to write a bad comedy; a more easy thing to judge of one.'[1] Be that as it may (for we do not wish to be drawn into a literary or metaphysical controversy with the present manager of Drury Lane,) we do not see what it was to the purpose. Does Mr. Elliston mean to infer, that, because it is a difficult thing to judge of a good comedy, he is a better judge than anyone else, or than the great majority of the audience, who had pronounced sentence upon this? Suppose the comedy had succeeded, as completely as it failed, and that a single individual in the pit had got up to say, that he differed from everyone present, and that his uncalled-for opinion was to be put in competition with the voice of the House, would not Mr. Elliston have thought it a great piece of impertinence and presumption? Why then should he commit the same folly himself?

At Covent Garden there have been two new debutants, Mr. Nathan as Henry Bertram, in Guy Mannering, and Miss Wensley as Rosalind. The first was a decided failure. We do not know what Mr. Nathan's powers of voice or execution in a room may be: but he has evidently not the capacity of sending out a sufficient volume of articulate sound to fill a large theatre: neither is his manner of speaking, nor his action, at all fitted for the stage. Miss Wensley's Rosalind was well received, and has been repeated. Her face and figure are agreeable; her voice has considerable sweetness and flexibility; and her manner of performing the part itself, was arch, graceful, and lively; though this young lady (who we understand had not appeared before on any stage) was withheld from giving herself up entirely to the character, by a natural and amiable timidity. We heartily wish she may succeed, and have no fear but she will.[2] Miss Tree has lately made a valuable addition to the musical strength of Covent Garden. She sings delightfully in company with Miss Stephens; and in the Comedy of Errors almost puzzles the town, as she does Antipholis of Syracuse, which to prefer: *Magis pares quam similes.* She is quite different, both in quality of voice and style of execution, from our old favourite; and it is this difference that completes the charm of their singing. Her tones are as firm, deep, and mellow, as Miss Stephens's are clear and sweet. Her ear is as true as it is possible to be; and the sustained manner in which she dwells upon

---

[1] ''Tis hard to say, if greater want of skill
    Appear in writing, or in judging ill.'   *Pope.*

[2] This young lady has since acted Beatrice in 'Much Ado About Nothing,' with considerable applause.

a note, is as delightful as the airy fluttering grace with which Miss Stephens varies, and sportively plays with it. The singing of the one may be compared perhaps to a continued stream of honeyed sound, while that of the other is like the tremulous bubbles that float and rise above its surface. Or Miss Tree's singing has the consistency, the lengthened tenuity or breadth of tone, drawn from a well-strung violin, as Miss Stephens's resembles the light, liquid, echoing accompaniments of the harp or lute. Of both together, it may be said, when they join their efforts in a single composition, that 'All is grace above, while all is strength below.' It is a treat to which of late we have been seldom accustomed.

MR. KEAN'S CORIOLANUS.—Mr. Kean's acting is not of the patrician order; he is one of the people, and what might be termed a *radical* performer. He can do all that may become a man 'of our infirmity,' 'to relish all as sharply, passioned as we;' but he cannot play a God, or one who fancies himself a God, and who is sublime, not in the strength of his own feelings, but in his contempt for those of others, and in his imaginary superiority to them. That is, he cannot play Coriolanus so well as he plays some other characters, or as we have seen it played often. Wherever there was a struggle of feelings, a momentary ebullition of pity, or remorse, or anguish, wherever nature resumed her wonted rights, Mr. Kean was equal to himself, and superior to every one else; but the prevailing characteristics of the part are inordinate self-opinion, and haughty elevation of soul, that aspire above competition or controul, as the tall rock lifts its head above the skies, and is not bent or shattered by the storm, beautiful in its unconquered strength, terrible in its unaltered repose. Mr. Kean, instead of 'keeping his state,' instead of remaining fixed and immoveable (for the most part) on his pedestal of pride, seemed impatient of this mock-dignity, this *still-life* assumption of superiority; burst too often from the trammels of precedent, and the *routine* of etiquette, which should have confined him; and descended into the common arena of man, to make good his pretensions by the energy with which he contended for them, and to prove the hollowness of his supposed indifference to the opinion of others by the excessive significance and studied variations of the scorn and disgust he expressed for it. The intolerable airs and aristocratical pretensions of which he is the slave, and to which he falls a victim, did not seem *legitimate* in him, but upstart, turbulent, and vulgar. Thus his haughty answer to the mob who banish him—'I banish you'—was given with all the virulence of execration, and rage of impotent despair, as if he had to strain every nerve and faculty of soul to shake off the contamination of their hated power over him, instead of being delivered with calm, majestic self-possession, as if he remained rooted to the spot, and his least motion, word, or look, must scatter them like chaff or scum from his presence! The most effective scene was that in which he stands for the Consulship, and begs for 'the most sweet voices' of the people whom he loathes; and the most ineffective was that in which he is reluctantly reconciled to, and over-come by the entreaties of, his mother. This decisive and affecting interview passed off as if nothing had happened, and was conducted with diplomatic gravity and skill. The casting of the other parts was a climax in bathos. Mr. Gattie was Menenius, the friend of Coriolanus, and Mr. Penley Tullus Aufidius, his mortal foe. Mr. Pope should have played the part. One would think there were processions and ovations enough in this play, as it was acted in John Kemble's time; but besides these, there were introduced others of the same sort, some of which were lengthened out as if they would reach all the way to the Circus; and there was a sham-fight, of melodramatic effect, in the second scene, in which Mr. Kean had like to have lost his voice. There was throughout a continual din of—

'Guns, drums, trumpets, blunderbuss, and thunder.'

or what was very like it. In the middle of an important scene, the tinkling of the stage-bell was employed to announce a flourish of trumpets—a thing which even Mr. Glossup would not hear of, whatever the act of parliament might say to enforce such a puppet-show accompaniment. There is very bad management in all this; and yet Mr. Elliston is the manager.

No. III

MINOR THEATRES.—This is a subject on which we shall treat, with satisfaction to ourselves, and, we hope, to the edification of the reader. Indeed, we are not a little vain of the article we propose to write on this occasion; and we feel the pen in our hands flutter its feathered down with more than its usual specific levity, at the thought of the idle, careless career before it. No Theatre-Royal oppresses the imagination, and entombs it in a mausoleum of massy pride; no manager's pompous pretensions choak up the lively current of our blood: no long-announced performance, big with expectation, comes to nothing, and yet compels us gravely to record its failure, and compose its epitaph. We have here 'ample scope and verge enough;' we pick and chuse as we will, light where we please, and stay no longer than we have a mind—saying 'this I like, that I loath, as one

Happy are we who look on and admire; and happy, we think, must they be who are so looked at and admired; and sometimes we begin to feel uneasy till we can ourselves mingle in the gay, busy, talking, fluttering, powdered, painted, perfumed, peruked, quaintly-accoutred throng of coxcombs and coquettes,—of tragedy heroes or heroines, —in good earnest; or turn stage-players and represent them in jest, with all the impertinent and consequential airs of the originals!

It is no insignificant epoch in one's life the first time that odd-looking thing, a play-bill, is left at our door in a little market-town in the country (say W—m in S——shire). The Manager, somewhat fatter and more erect, 'as Manager beseems,' than the rest of his Company, with more of the man of business, and not less of the coxcomb, in his strut and manner, knocks at the door with the end of a walking cane (a badge of office!) and a bundle of papers under his arm; presents one of them printed in large capitals, with a respectful bow and a familiar shrug; hopes to give satisfaction in the town; hints at the liberal encouragement they received at W——ch, the last place they stopped at; had every possible facility afforded by the Magistrates; supped one evening with the Rev. Mr. J——s, a dissenting clergyman, and really a very well-informed, agreeable, sensible man, full of anecdote—no illiberal prejudices against the profession :—then talks of the strength of his company, with a careless mention of his own favourite line—his benefit fixed for an early day, but would do himself the honour to leave farther particulars at a future opportunity—speaks of the stage as an elegant amusement, that most agreeably enlivened a spare evening or two in the week, and, under proper management (to which he himself paid the most assiduous attention) might be made of the greatest assistance to the cause of virtue and humanity—had seen Mr. Garrick act the last night but one before his retiring from the stage—had himself had offers from the London boards, and indeed could not say he had given up all thoughts of one day surprising them—as it was, had no reason to repine—Mrs. F—— tolerably advanced in life—his eldest son a prodigious turn for the higher walks of tragedy—had said perhaps too much of himself—had given universal satisfaction—hoped that the young gentleman and lady, at least, would attend on the following evening, when the West-Indian would be performed at the market-hall, with the farce of No Song No Supper—and so having played his part, withdraws in the full persuasion of having made a favourable impression, and of meeting with every encouragement the place affords! Thus he passes from house to house, and goes through the routine of topic after topic, with that sort of modest assurance, which is indispensable in the manager of a country theatre.

This fellow, who floats over the troubles of life as the froth above the idle wave, with all his little expedients and disappointments, with pawned paste-buckles, mortgaged scenery, empty exchequer, and rebellious orchestra, is not of all men the most miserable:—he is little less happy than a king, though not much better off than a beggar. He has little to think of, much to do, more to say; and is accompanied, in his incessant daily round of trifling occupations, with a never-failing sense of authority and self-importance, the one thing needful (above all others) to the heart of man. This however is their man of business in the company; he is a sort of fixture in their little state; like Nebuchadnezzar's image, but half of earth and half of finer metal: he is not ' of imagination all compact:' he is not, like the rest of his aspiring crew, a feeder upon air, a drinker of applause, tricked out in vanity and in nothing else; he is not quite mad, nor quite happy. The whining Romeo, who goes supperless to bed, and on his pallet of straw dreams of a crown of laurel, of waving hand-kerchiefs, of bright eyes, and billet-doux breathing boundless love: the ranting Richard, whose infuriate execrations are drowned in the shouts of the all-ruling pit; he who, without a coat to his back, or a groat in his purse, snatches at Cato's robe, and binds the diadem of Cæsar on his brow;—these are the men that Fancy has chosen for herself, and placed above the reach of fortune, and almost of fate. They take no thought for the morrow. What is it to them what they shall eat, or what they shall drink, or how they shall be clothed? ' Their mind to them a kingdom is.'—It is not a poor ten shillings a week, their share in the profits of the theatre, with which they have to pay for bed, board, and lodging, that bounds their wealth. They share (and not unequally) in all the wealth, the pomp, and pleasures of the world. They wield sceptres, conquer kingdoms, court princesses, are clothed in purple, and fare sumptuously every night. They taste, in imagination, ' of all earth's bliss, both living and loving:' whatever has been most the admiration or most the envy of mankind, they, for a moment, in their own eyes, and in the eyes of others, become. The poet fancies others to be this or that; the player fancies himself to be all that the poet but describes. A little rouge makes him a lover, a plume of feathers a hero, a brazen crown an emperor. Where will you buy rank, office, supreme delights, so cheap as at his shop of fancy? Is it nothing to dream whenever we please, and *seem* whatever we desire? Is real greatness, is real prosperity, more than what it seems? Where shall we find, or where shall the votary of the stage find, Fortunatus's Wishing Cap, but in the wardrobe which we laugh at: or borrow the philosopher's stone but from the *property-man* of the theatre? He has discovered the true Elixir of Life, which is freedom from care : he quaffs the pure *aurum potabile*, which is popular applause. He who is smit with the love of this *ideal* existence, cannot be weaned from it. Hoot him from the stage, and he will stay to sweep the lobbies or shift the scenes. Offer him twice the salary to go into a counting-house, or stand behind a counter, and he will return to poverty, steeped in contempt, but eked out with fancy, at the end of a week. Make a laughing-stock of an actress, lower her salary, tell her she is too tall, awkward, stupid, and ugly ; try to get rid of her all you can—she will remain, only to hear herself courted, to listen to the echo of her borrowed name, to live but one short minute in the lap of vanity and tinsel shew. Will you give a man an additional ten shillings a week, and ask him to resign the fancied wealth of the world, which he 'by his so potent art' can conjure up, and glad his eyes, and fill his heart with it? When a little change of dress, and the muttering a few talismanic words, make all the difference between the vagabond and the hero, what signifies the interval so easily passed? Would you not yourself consent to be alternately a beggar and a king, but that you have not the secret skill to be so? The player has that 'happy alchemy of mind :'—why then would you reduce him to an equality with yourself?—The moral of this reasoning is known and felt, though it may be gainsayed. Wherever the players come, they send a welcome before them, and leave an air in the place behind them.[1] They shed a light upon the day, that does not very soon pass off. See how they glitter along the street, wandering, not where business but the bent of pleasure takes them, like mealy-coated butterflies, or insects flitting in the sun. They seem another, happier, idler race of mortals, prolonging the carelessness of childhood to old age, floating down the stream of life, or wafted by the wanton breeze to their final place of rest. We remember one (we must make the reader acquainted with him) who once overtook us loitering by 'Severn's sedgy side,' on a fine May morning, with a score of play-bills streaming from his pockets, for the use of the neighbouring villages, and a music-score in his hand, which he sung blithe and clear, advancing with light step and a loud voice ! With a sprightly *bon jour*, he passed on, carolling to the echo of the babbling stream, brisk as a bird, gay as a mote, swift as an arrow from a twanging bow, heart-whole, and with shining face that shot back the sun's broad rays !—What is become of this favourite of mirth and song? Has care touched him? Has death tripped up his heels? Has an

[1] So the old song joyously celebrates their arrival :—
'The beggars are coming to town,
Some in rags, and some in jags, and some in velvet gowns.'

indigestion imprisoned him, and all his gaiety, in a living dungeon? Or is he himself lost and buried amidst the rubbish of one of our larger, or else of one of our Minor Theatres?

> ——' Alas! how changed from him,
> That life of pleasure, and that soul of whim!'

But as this was no doubt the height of his ambition, why should we wish to debar him of it?

This brings us back, after our intended digression, to the subject from whence we set out,—the smaller theatres of the metropolis; which we visited lately, in hopes to find in them a romantic contrast to the presumptuous and exclusive pretensions of the legitimate drama, and to revive some of the associations of our youth above described. —The first attempt we made was at the Cobourg, and we were completely baulked. Judge of our disappointment. This was not owing, we protest, to any fault or perversity of our own; to the crust and scales of formality which had grown over us; to the panoply of criticism in which we go armed, and which made us inaccessible to 'pleasure's finest point;' or to the *cheveux-de-fris* of objections, which cut us off from all cordial participation in what was going forward on the stage. No such thing. We went not only willing, but determined to be pleased. We had laid aside the pedantry of rules, the petulance of sarcasm, and had hoped to open once more, by stealth, the source of sacred tears, of bubbling laughter, and concealed sighs. We were not formidable. On the contrary, we were 'made of penetrable stuff.' Stooping from our pride of place, we were ready to be equally delighted with a clown in a pantomime, or a lord-mayor in a tragedy. We were all attention, simplicity, and enthusiasm. But we saw neither attention, simplicity, nor enthusiasm in any body else; and our whole scheme of voluntary delusion and social enjoyment was cut up by the roots. The play was indifferent, but that was nothing. The acting was bad, but that was nothing. The audience were low, but that was nothing. It was the heartless indifference and hearty contempt shown by the performers for their parts, and by the audience for the players and the play, that disgusted us with all of them. Instead of the rude, naked, undisguised expression of curiosity and wonder, of overflowing vanity and unbridled egotism, there was nothing but an exhibition of the most petulant cockneyism and vulgar slang. All our former notions and theories were turned topsy-turvy. The genius of St. George's Fields prevailed, and you felt yourself in a bridewell, or a brothel, amidst Jew-boys, pickpockets, prostitutes, and mountebanks, instead of being in the precincts of Mount Parnassus, or in the company of the Muses.

The object was not to admire or to excel, but to vilify and degrade every thing. The audience did not hiss the actors (that would have implied a serious feeling of disapprobation, and something like a disappointed wish to be pleased) but they laughed, hooted at, nick-named, pelted them with oranges and witticisms, to show their unruly contempt for them and their art; while the performers, to be even with the audience, evidently slurred their parts, as if ashamed to be thought to take any interest in them, laughed in one another's faces, and in that of their friends in the pit, and most effectually marred the process of theatrical illusion, by turning the whole into a most unprincipled burlesque. We cannot help thinking that some part of this indecency and licentiousness is to be traced to the diminutive size of these theatres, and to the close contact into which these unmannerly censors come with the objects of their ignorant and unfeeling scorn. Familiarity breeds contempt. By too narrow an inspection, you take away that fine, hazy medium of abstraction, by which (in moderation) a play is best set off: you are, as it were, admitted behind the scenes; ' see the puppets dallying; ' shake hands, across the orchestra, with an actor whom you know, or take one you do not like by the beard, with equal impropriety :—you distinguish the paint, the individual features, the texture of the dresses, the patch-work and machinery by which the whole is made up; and this in some measure destroys the effect, distracts attention, suspends the interest, and makes you disposed to quarrel with the actors as impostors, and 'not the men you took them for.' You here see Mr. Booth, in Brutus, with every motion of his face *articulated*, with his under-jaws grinding out sentences, and his upper-lip twitching at words and syllables, as if a needle and thread had been passed through each corner of it, and the *gude wife* still continued sewing at her work :—you perceive the contortion and barrenness of his expression (in which there is only one form of bent brows, and close pent-up mouth for all occasions) the parsimony of his figure is exposed, and the refuse tones of his voice fall with undiminished vulgarity on the pained ear :—you have Mr. Higman as Prior Aymer in Ivanhoe, who used to play the Gipsey so well at Covent-garden in Guy Mannering, and who certainly is an admirable bass singer: you have Mr. Stanley, from the Theatre-Royal, Bath, and whom we thought an interesting actor there (such as poor Wilson might have been who trod the same boards, and with whom our readers will remember that Miss Lydia Melford, in Humphrey Clinker, fell in love) :—you have Mr. Barrymore, that old and deserving favourite with the public in the best days of Mrs. Siddons and of John Kemble, superintending, we believe, the whole, from a little oval window in a stage-box, like

Mr. Bentham eying the hopeful circle of delinquents in his Panopticon:—and, to sum up all in one word, you have here Mr. H. Kemble, whose hereditary gravity is put to the last test, by the yells and grins of the remorseless rabble.

'My soul turn from them!'—'Turn we to survey' where the Miss Dennetts, at the Adelphi Theatre, (which should once more from them be called the *Sans Pareil*) weave the airy, the harmonious, liquid dance. Of each of them it might be said, and we believe has been said—

> ' Her, lovely Venus at a birth
> With two Sister Graces more
> To ivy-crowned Bacchus bore.'

Such figures, no doubt, gave rise to the fables of ancient mythology, and might be worshipped. They revive the ideas of classic grace, life, and joy. They do not seem like taught dancers, Columbines, and figurantes on an artificial stage; but come bounding forward like nymphs in vales of Arcady, or, like Italian shepherdesses, join in a lovely group of easy gracefulness, while 'vernal airs attune the trembling leaves' to their soft motions. If they were nothing in themselves, they would be complete in one another. Each owes a double grace, youth, and beauty, to her reflection in the other two. It is the principle of proportion or harmony personified. To deny their merit or criticise their style, is to be blind and dead to the felicities of art and nature. Not to feel the force of their united charms (united, yet divided, different, and yet the same), is not to see the beauty of 'three red roses on a stalk,'—or of the mingled hues of the rainbow, or of the halcyon's breast, reflected in the stream,—or 'the witchery of the soft blue sky,' or grace in the waving of the branch of a tree, or tenderness in the bending of a flower, or liveliness in the motion of a wave of the sea. We shall not try to defend them against the dancing-school critics; there is another school, different from that of the *pied a plomb* and *pirouette* cant, the school of taste and nature. In this school, the Miss Dennetts are (to say the least) delicious novices. Theirs is the only performance on the stage (we include the Opera) that gives the uninitiated spectator an idea that dancing can be an emanation of instinctive gaiety, or express the language of sentiment. We might shew them to the Count Stendhal, who speaks so feelingly of the beauties of a dance by Italian peasant girls, as our three English Graces; and we might add, as a farther proof of national liberality and public taste, that they had been discarded from one of our larger, to take refuge in one of our petty theatres, on a disagreement about a pound a week in their joint salaries. Yet we suppose if these young ladies were to marry, and not volunteer to put ten thousand pounds in the pockets of some liberally disposed manager, we should hear a very pitiful story of their ingratitude to their patrons and the public. It is the way of the world. There is a Mr. Reeve at this theatre (the Adelphi in the Strand) of whom report had spoken highly in his particular department as a mimic, and in whom we were considerably disappointed. He is not so good as Matthews, who, after all, is by no means a *fac-simile* of those he pretends to represent. We knew most of Mr. Reeve's likenesses, and that is the utmost we can say in their praise ; for we thought them very bad ones. They were very slight, and yet contrived to be very disagreeable. Farren was the most amusing, from a certain oddity of voice and manner in the ingenious and eccentric original. Harley, again, was not at all the thing. There was something of the external dress and deportment, but none of the spirit, the frothy essence. He made him out a great burly swaggering ruffian, instead of being what he is—a pleasant, fidgetty person, pert as a jack-daw, light as a grasshopper. In short, from having seen Mr. Reeve, no one would wish to see Mr. Harley, though there is no one who has seen him but wishes to see him again ; and, though mimicry has the privilege of turning into ridicule the loftier pretensions of tragic heroes, we believe it always endeavours to set off the livelier peculiarities of comic ones in the most agreeable light. Mr. Kean was bad enough. It might have been coarse and repulsive enough, and yet like ; but it wanted point and energy, and this was inexcusable. We have heard much of ludicrous and admirable imitations of Mr. Kean's acting. But the only person who ever caricatures Mr. Kean well, or from whose exaggerations he has any thing to fear, is himself. There are several other actors at the Adelphi who are, and must continue to be, nameless. There are also some better known to the town, as Mr. Wilkinson, Mrs. Alsop, etc. This lady has lost none of her exuberant and piquant vivacity by her change of situation. She also looks much the same : and as you see her near, this circumstance is by no means to her advantage. The truth is, that there are not good actors or agreeable actresses enough in town to make one really good company (by which we mean a company able to get up any one really good play throughout) and of course there are not a sufficient number (unless by a miracle) to divide into eight or ten different establishments.

Of the Haymarket and Lyceum, which come more properly under the head of *Summer Theatres*, it is not at present ' our hint to speak ' ; but we may shortly take a peep into the Surrey and East London

Theatres,[1] and enlarge upon them as we see cause. Of the latter it is sufficient to observe, that Mr. Rae is the principal tragic actor there, and Mr. Peter Moore the chief manager. After this, is it to be wondered at that Covent-garden is almost deserted, and that Mr. Elliston cannot yet afford to give up the practice of puffing at the bottom of his play-bills!

The larger, as well as the smaller, theatres have been closed during the greater part of the last month. There has been one new piece, the *Antiquary*, brought out at Covent-garden, since our last report. It is founded, as our readers will suppose, on the admirable novel of that name by the author of Waverley, but it is only a slight sketch of the story and characters, and not, we think, equal to the former popular melo-dramas taken from the same prolific source. The characters in general were not very intelligibly brought out, nor very strikingly cast. Liston made but an indifferent Mr. Jonathan Old-buck. He was dressed in a snuff-coloured coat and plain bob-wig, and that was all. It was quaint and dry, and accordingly inefficient, and quite unlike his admirable portrait of Dominie Sampson, which is one of the finest pieces of acting on the stage, both for humour and feeling, invention and expression. The little odd ways and anti-quarian whims and crochets of Mr. Oldbuck, even were they as well managed in the drama as they are exquisitely hit off in the novel, would hardly tell in Liston's hands. Emery made an impressive Edie Ochiltree ; but he was somewhat too powerful a preacher, and too sturdy a beggar. Mr. Abbott personated the haughty, petulant Captain MacIntire to a great nicety of resemblance. Mr. Duruset as young Lovell 'warbled' in a manner that Jacques would not have found fault with. Miss Stephens sang one or two airs very sweetly, and was complimented at the end very rapturously and unexpectedly by the *ungallant* Mr. Oldbuck. The scene on the sea-shore, where she is in danger of being overtaken by the tide, with her father and old Edie, had an admirable effect, as far as the imitation of the rolling of the waves of the sea on a London stage could produce admiration. The part of old Elspith of Craigie Burn Wood was strikingly per-formed by Mrs. Fawcett, who, indeed, acts whatever she undertakes well ; and the scene with Lord Glenallan, in which she unfolds to

[1] The story of the Heart of Midlothian was, we understand, got up at the Surrey Theatre last year by Mr. Dibdin, in the most creditable style. A Miss Taylor, we hear, made an inimitable Jenny Deans, Miss Copeland was surprising as Madge Wildfire, Mrs. Dibdin as Queen Caroline, was also said to be a complete piece of royal wax-work, and Dumbydikes was done to the life. Would we had seen them so done ; but we can answer for these things positively on no authority but our own. If they make as good a thing of Ivanhoe, they will do more than the author has done.

him the dreadful story of his life, was given at much length and with considerable effect. But what can come up to the sublime, heart-breaking pathos, the terrific painting of the original work? The story of this unhappy feudal lord is the most harrowing in all these novels (rich as they are in the materials of nature and passion) : and the description of the old woman, who had been a principal subordinate instrument in the tragedy, is done with a more masterly and withering hand than any other. Her death-like appearance, her strange existence, like one hovering between this world and the next, or like a speaking corpse; her fixed attitude, her complete forgetfulness of every thing but the one subject that loads her thoughts, her preternatural self-possession on that, her prophetic and awful denunciations, her clay-cold and shrivelled body, consumed and kept alive by a wasting fire within, are all given with a subtlety, a truth, a boldness and originality of conception, that were never, perhaps, surpassed. But the author does not want our praise; nor can we withhold from him our admiration.

Mr. Kean, the week before we saw him in Coriolanus, played Othello; and as we would always prefer bearing testimony to his genius, to recording his comparative failures, we will here express our opinion of his performance of this character in the words of a contemporary journal, a short time back :—

Mr. Kean's Othello is, we suppose, the finest piece of acting in the world. It is impossible either to describe or praise it adequately. We have never seen any actor so wrought upon, so 'perplexed in the extreme.' The energy of passion, as it expresses itself in action, is not the most terrific part : it is the agony of his soul, showing itself in looks and tones of voice. In one part, where he listens in dumb despair to the fiend-like insinuations of Iago, he presented the very face, the marble aspect of Dante's Count Ugolino. On his fixed eye-lids, 'horror sat plumed.' In another part, where a gleam of hope or of tenderness returns to subdue the tumult of his passions, his voice broke in faltering accents from his over-charged breast. His lips might be said less to utter words, than to distil drops of blood, gushing from his heart. An instance of this was in his pronunciation of the line, 'of one that loved not wisely but too well.' The whole of this last speech was indeed given with exquisite force and beauty. We only object to the virulence with which he delivers the last line, and with which he stabs himself—a virulence which Othello would neither feel against himself at the moment, nor against the 'turbaned Turk' (whom he had slain) at such a distance of time. His exclamation on seeing his wife, 'I cannot think but Desdemona's honest,' was, 'the glorious triumph of exceeding love'; a thought flashing conviction on his mind, and irradiating his countenance with joy, like sudden sunshine. In fact, almost every scene or sentence in this extraordinary exhibition is a master-piece of natural passion. The convulsed motion of the hands, and the involuntary swelling

414

of the veins in the forehead in some of the most painful situations, should not only suggest topics of critical panegyric, but might furnish studies to the painter or anatomist.

No. IV

[*April*, 1820.

The age we live in is critical, didactic, paradoxical, romantic, but it is not dramatic. This, if any, is its weak side: it is there that modern literature does not run on all fours, nor triumph over the periods that are past; it halts on one leg; and is fairly distanced by long-acknowledged excellence, as well as by long-forgotten efforts of the same kind. Our ancestors could write a tragedy two hundred years ago; they could write a comedy one hundred years ago; why cannot we do the same now? It is hard to say; but so it is. When we give it as our opinion, that this is not 'the high and palmy state' of the productions of the stage, we would be understood to signify, that there has hardly been a good tragedy or a good comedy written within the last fifty years, that is, since the time of Home's Douglas, and Sheridan's School for Scandal; and when we speak of a good tragedy or comedy, we mean one that will be thought so fifty years hence. Not that we would have it supposed, that a work, to be worth any thing, must last always: what we have said above of works that have fallen into unmerited decay, through the lapse of time, and mutation of circumstances, would show the contrary: but we think that a play that only runs its one-and-twenty nights, that does not reach beyond the life of an actor, or the fashion of a single generation, may be fairly set down as good for nothing, to any purposes of criticism, or serious admiration. Time seems to have its circle as well as the globe we inhabit; the loftiest eminences, by degrees, sink beneath the horizon; the greatest works are lost sight of in the end, and cannot be restored; but those that disappear at the first step we take, or are hidden by the first object that intervenes, can, in either case, be of no real magnitude or importance. We have never seen the highest range of mountains in the world; nor are the longest-lived works intelligible to us (from the difference both of language and manners) at this day: but the name of the Andes, like that of old, blind Homer, serves us on this side of the globe, and at the lag-end of time, to repeat and wonder at; and that we have ever heard of either is alone sufficient proof of the vastness of the one, and of the sublimity of the other! Without waiting for the final award, or gradual oblivion of slow-revolving ages, we may be bold to say of our writers for the stage, during the last twenty or thirty years, as

Pope is reported to have said of Ben Jonson's, somewhat unadvisedly, 'What trash are *their* works, taken altogether!' We would not deny or depreciate merit, wherever we find it, in individuals, or in classes: for instance, we grant that all the pantomimes are good in which Mr. Grimaldi plays the clown; and that the melodrames have been excellent, when Mr. Farley had a hand in them; and that the farces could not be damned if Munden showed his face in them; and that O'Keeffe's could not fail with an audience that had a mind to laugh: but having mentioned these, and added a few more to our private list (for it might be invidious to specify particularly No Song no Supper, the Prize, Goldfinch, Robert Tyke, or Lubin Log, &c. &c.), we really are at a loss to proceed with the more legitimate and higher productions of the modern drama. Are there not then Mr. Coleridge's Remorse, Mr. Maturin's Bertram, Mr. Milman's Fazio, and many others? There are; but we do not know that they make any difference in the question. The poverty indeed of our present dramatic genius cannot be made appear more fully than by this, that whatever it has to show of *profound*, is of German taste and origin; and that what little it can boast of *elegant*, though light and vain, is taken from *petite* pieces of Parisian mould.

We have been long trying to find out the meaning of all this, and at last we think we have succeeded. The cause of the evil complained of, like the root of so many other grievances and complaints, lies in the French revolution. That event has rivetted all eyes, and distracted all hearts; and, like people staring at a comet, in the panic and confusion in which we have been huddled together, we have not had time to laugh at one another's defects, or to condole over one another's misfortunes. We have become a nation of politicians and newsmongers; our inquiries in the streets are no less than after the health of Europe; and in men's faces, we may see strange matters written,—the rise of stocks, the loss of battles, the fall of kingdoms, and the death of kings. The Muse, meanwhile, droops in byecorners of the mind, and is forced to take up with the refuse of our thoughts. Our attention has been turned, by the current of events, to the general nature of men and things; and we cannot call it heartily back to individual caprices, or head-strong passions, which are the nerves and sinews of Comedy and Tragedy. What is an individual man to a nation? Or what is a nation to an abstract principle? The affairs of the world are spread out before us, as in a map; we sit with the newspaper, and a pair of compasses in our hand, to measure out provinces, and to dispose of thrones; we 'look abroad into universality,' feel in circles of latitude and longitude, and cannot contract the grasp of our minds to scan with nice scrutiny particular foibles, or to be engrossed by any single suffering. What we gain in extent, we lose in force and depth. A general and speculative interest absorbs the corroding poison, and takes out the sting of our more circumscribed and fiercer passions. We are become public creatures; 'are embowelled of our natural entrails, and stuffed,' as Mr. Burke has it in his high-flown phrase, 'with paltry blurred sheets of paper about the rights of man,' or the rights of legitimacy. We break our sleep to argue a question; a piece of news spoils our appetite for dinner. We are not so solicitous after our own success as the success of a cause. Our thoughts, feelings, distresses, are about what no way concerns us, more than it concerns any body else, like those of the Upholsterer, ridiculed as a new species of character in the Tatler: but we are become a nation of upholsterers. We participate in the general progress of intellect, and the large vicissitudes of human affairs; but the hugest private sorrow looks dwarfish and puerile. In the sovereignty of our minds, we make mankind our quarry; and, in the scope of our ambitious thoughts, hunt for prey through the four quarters of the world. In a word, literature and civilization have abstracted man from himself so far, that his existence is no longer *dramatic*; and the press has been the ruin of the stage, unless we are greatly deceived.

If a bias to abstraction is evidently, then, the reigning spirit of the age, dramatic poetry must be allowed to be most irreconcileable with this spirit; it is essentially individual and concrete, both in form and in power. It is the closest imitation of nature; it has a body of truth; it is 'a counterfeit presentment' of reality; for it brings forward certain characters to act and speak for themselves, in the most trying and singular circumstances. It is not enough for them to declaim on certain general topics, however forcibly or learnedly—this is merely oratory, and this any other characters might do as well, in any other circumstances: nor is it sufficient for the poet to furnish the colours and forms of style and fancy out of his own store, however inexhaustible; for if he merely makes them express his own feelings, and the idle effusions of his own breast, he had better speak in his own person, without any of those troublesome 'interlocutions between Lucius and Caius.' The tragic poet (to be truly such) can only deliver the sentiments of given persons, placed in given circumstances; and in order to make what so proceeds from their mouths, at once proper to them and interesting to the audience, their characters must be powerfully marked: their passions, which are the subject-matter of which they treat, must be worked up to

the highest pitch of intensity; and the circumstances which give force
and direction to them must be stamped with the utmost distinctness
and vividness in every line. Within the circle of dramatic character
and natural passion, each individual is to feel as keenly, as profoundly,
as rapidly as possible, but he is not to feel beyond it, for others or
for the whole. Each character, on the contrary, must be a kind of
centre of repulsion to the rest; and it is their hostile interests, brought
into collision, that must tug at their heart-strings, and call forth every
faculty of thought, of speech, and action. They must not be represented like a set of profiles, looking all the same way, nor with their
faces turned round to the audience; but in dire contention with each
other: their words, like their swords, must strike fire from one
another,—must inflict the wound, and pour in the poison. The
poet, to do justice to his undertaking, must not only identify himself
with each, but must take part with all by turns, 'to relish all as
sharply, passioned as they;'—must feel scorn, pity, love, hate, anger,
remorse, revenge, ambition, in their most sudden and fierce extremes,
—must not only have these passions rooted in his mind, but must be
alive to every circumstance affecting them, to every accident of
which advantage can be taken to gratify or exasperate them; a word
must kindle the dormant spark into a flame; an unforeseen event must
overturn his whole being *in conceipt*; it is from the excess of passion
that he must borrow the activity of his imagination; he must mould
the sound of his verse to its fluctuations and caprices, and build up
the whole superstructure of his fable on the deep and strict foundations of nature. But surely it is hardly to be thought that the poet
should feel for others in this way, when they have ceased almost to
feel for themselves; when the mind is turned habitually out of itself
to general, speculative truth, and possibilities of good, and when, in
fact, the processes of the understanding, analytical distinctions, and
verbal disputes, have superseded all personal and local attachments
and antipathies, and have, in a manner, put a stop to the pulsation
of the heart—quenched the fever in the blood—the madness in the
brain;—when we are more in love with a theory than a mistress,
and would only crush to atoms those who are of an opposite party
to ourselves in taste, philosophy, or politics. The folds of self-love,
arising out of natural instincts, connections, and circumstances, have
not wound themselves exclusively and unconsciously enough round
the human mind to furnish the matter of impassioned poetry in real
life: much less are we to expect the poet, without observation of its
effects on others, or experience of them in himself, to supply the
imaginary form out of vague topics, general reflections, far-fetched
tropes, affected sentiments, and fine writing. To move the world,

he must have a place to fix the levers of invention upon. The poet (let his genius be what it will) can only act by sympathy with the public mind and manners of his age; but these are, at present, not in sympathy, but in opposition to dramatic poetry. Therefore, we have no dramatic poets. It would be strange indeed (under favour be it spoken) if in the same period of time that produced the Political Justice or the Edinburgh Review, there should be found such an 'unfeathered, two-legged thing' as a real tragedy poet.

But it may be answered, that the author of the Enquiry concerning Political Justice, is himself a writer of romances, and the author of Caleb Williams. We hearken to the suggestion, and will take this and one or two other eminent examples, to show how far we fall short of the goal we aim at. 'You may wear your *bays* with a difference.' Mr. Godwin has written an admirable and almost unrivalled novel (nay, more than one)—he has also written two tragedies, and failed. We can hardly think it would have been possible for him to have failed, but on the principle here stated; viz. that it was impossible for him to succeed. His genius is wholly adverse to the stage. As an author, as a novel writer, he may be considered as a philosophical recluse, a closet-hero. He cannot be denied to possess the *constructive* organ, to have originality and invention in an extraordinary degree : but he does not construct according to nature; his invention is not dramatic. He takes a character or a passion, and works it out to the utmost possible extravagance, and palliates or urges it on by every resource of the understanding, or by every species of plausible sophistry; but in doing this, he may be said to be only spinning a subtle theory, to be maintaining a wild paradox, as much as when he extends a philosophical and abstract principle into all its ramifications, and builds an entire and exclusive system of feeling and action on a single daring view of human nature. 'He sits in the centre' of his web, and 'enjoys' not 'bright day,' but a kind of gloomy grandeur. His characters stand alone, self-created, and self-supported, without communication with, or reaction upon, any other (except in the single instance of Caleb Williams himself) :—the passions are not excited, qualified, or irritated by circumstances, but moulded by the will of the writer, like clay in the hands of the potter. Mr. Godwin's imagination works like the power of steam, with inconceivable and incessant expansive force ; but it is all in one direction, mechanical and uniform. By its help, he weaves gigantic figures, and unfolds terrific situations; but they are like the cloudy pageantry that hangs over the edge of day, and the prodigious offspring of his brain have neither fellow nor competitor in the scene of his imagination. They require a clear stage to themselves. They do not enter the lists with other men : nor are actuated by the ordinary wheels, pulleys, and machinery of society : they are at issue with themselves, and at war with the nature of things. Falkland, St. Leon, Mandeville, are studies for us to contemplate, not men that we can sympathise with. They move in an orbit of their own, urged on by restless thought and morbid sentiment, on which the antagonist powers of sense, habit, circumstances, and opinion have no influence whatever. The arguments addressed to them are idle and ineffectual. You might as well argue with a madman, or talk to the winds. But this is not the nature of dramatic writing. Mr. Godwin, to succeed in tragedy, should compose it almost entirely of long and repeated soliloquies, like the Prometheus of Æschylus ; and his dialogues, properly translated, would turn out to be monologues, as we see in the Iron Chest.[1]

The same, or similar, remarks would apply to Mr. Wordsworth's hankering after the drama. We understand, that, like Mr. Godwin, the author of the Lyric Ballads formerly made the attempt, and did not receive encouragement to proceed. We cannot say positively : but we much suspect that the writer would be for having all the talk to himself. His moody sensibility would eat into the plot like a cancer, and bespeak both sides of the dialogue for its own share. Mr. Wordsworth (we are satisfied with him, be it remembered, as he is), is not a man to go out of himself into the feelings of any one else ; much less, to act the part of a variety of characters. He is not, like Bottom, ready to play the lady, the lover, and the lion. His poetry is a virtual proscription passed upon the promiscuous nature of the drama. He sees nothing but himself in the universe : or if he leans with a kindly feeling to any thing else, he would impart to the most uninteresting things the fulness of his own sentiments, and elevate the most insignificant characters into the foremost rank, —before kings, or heroes, or lords, or wits,—because they do not interfere with his own sense of self-importance. He has none of the bye-play, the varying points of view, the venturous magnanimity of dramatic fiction. He thinks the opening of the leaves of a daisy, or the perfume of a hedge (not of a garden) rose, matters of consequence enough for him to notice them ; but he thinks the ' daily intercourse of all this unintelligible world,' its cares, its crimes, its noise, love, war, ambition, (what else ?) mere vanity and vexation of spirit, with which a great poet cannot condescend to disturb the

[1] Miss Baillie has much of the power and spirit of dramatic writing, and not the less because, as a woman, she has been placed out of the vortex of philosophical and political extravagances.

420

bright, serene, and solemn current of his thoughts. This lofty indifference and contempt for his *dramatis personæ* would not be the most likely means to make them interesting to the audience. We fear Mr. Wordsworth's poetical egotism would prevent his writing a tragedy. Yet we have above made the dissipation and rarefaction of this spirit in society, the bar to dramatic excellence. Egotism is of different sorts ; and he would not compliment the literary and artificial state of manners so much, as to suppose it quite free from this principle. But it is not allied at present to imagination or passion. It is sordid, servile, inert, a compound of dulness, vanity, and interest. That which is the source of dramatic excellence, is like a mountain spring, full of life and impetuosity, sparkling with light, thundering down precipices, winding along narrow defiles ; or

> ' Like a wild overflow, that sweeps before him
> A golden stack, and with it shakes down bridges,
> Cracks the strong hearts of pines, whose cable roots
> Held out a thousand storms, a thousand thunders,
> And so, made mightier, takes whole villages
> Upon his back, and, in that heat of pride,
> Charges strong towns, towers, castles, palaces,
> And lays them desolate.'

The other sort is a stagnant, gilded puddle. Mr. Wordsworth has measured it from side to side. ' 'Tis three feet long and two feet wide.'—Lord Byron's patrician haughtiness and monastic seclusion are, we think, no less hostile than the levelling spirit of Mr. Wordsworth's Muse, to the endless gradations, variety, and complicated ideas or *mixed modes* of this sort of composition. Yet we have read Manfred.

But what shall we say of Mr. Coleridge, who is the author not only of a successful but a meritorious tragedy ? We may say of him what he has said of Mr. Maturin, that he is of the transcendental German school. He is a florid poet, and an ingenious metaphysician, who mistakes scholastic speculations for the intricate windings of the passions, and assigns possible reasons instead of actual motives for the excesses of his characters. He gives us studied special-pleadings for involuntary bursts of feeling, and the needless strain of tinkling sentiments for the point-blank language of nature. His Remorse is a spurious tragedy. Take the following passage, and then ask, whether the charge of sophistry and paradox, and dangerous morality, to startle the audience, in lieu of more legitimate methods of exciting their sympathy, which he brings against the author of Bertram, may not be retorted on his own head. Ordonio is made to defend

first attempt of Mr. Scott (we wish the writer would either declare himself, or give himself a *nom de guerre*, that we might speak of him without either a periphrasis or impertinence) it is, we say, Mr. Scott's first attempt on English ground, and it is, we think, only a comparative, but comparatively with himself, a decided failure. There are some few scenes in it, and one or two extraneous characters, equal to what he has before written; but we think they are, *in comparison*, few; and by being so distinctly detached as they are, from the general groundwork (so that no two persons taking the work to dramatise would not pitch upon the same incidents and individuals to bring forward on the stage) show that the other parts of the story are without proportionable prominence and interest. In the other novels it was not so. The variety, the continued interest, the crowded groups, the ever-changing features distracted attention, and perplexed the choice: the difficulty was not what to select, but what to reject. All was new, and all was equally, or nearly equally, good—teeming with life and throbbing with interest. But here, no one, if called upon for a preference, can miss pointing out Friar Tuck in his cell, and the Jew and his daughter Rebecca. These remain, and stand out after the perusal, as above water mark; when the rest are washed away and forgotten. For want of the same pulse, the same veins of nature circling throughout, the body of the work is cold and colourless. The author does not feel himself at home; and tries to make up for cordial sympathy and bold action, by the minute details of his subject—by finishing his Saxon draperies, or furbishing up the armour of his Normans, with equal care and indifference—so that we seem turning over a book of antiquarian prints, instead of the pages of an admired novel-writer. In fact, we conceive, as a point of speculative criticism, that the genius of the author of Waverley, however lofty, and however extensive, still has certain discernible limits; that it is strictly national; that it is traditional; that it relies on actual manners and external badges of character; that it insists on costume and dialect; and is one of individual character and situation, rather than of general nature. This was some time doubtful: but the present work 'gives evidence of it.' Compare his Rob Roy with Robin Hood. What rich Highland blood flows through the veins of the one; colours his hair, freckles his skin, bounds in his step, swells in his heart, kindles in his eye: what poor waterish puddle creeps through the soul of Locksley; and what a lazy, listless figure he makes in his coat of Lincoln-green, like a figure to let, in the novel of Ivanhoe! Mr. T. Cooke, of the Theatre Royal, Drury-lane, does not make him much more insipid. Mr. Scott slights and slurs our archer good. His imagination mounts

424

with Rob Roy, among his native wilds and cliffs, like an eagle to its lordly nest: but it cannot take shelter with Robin Hood and *his* crew of outlaws in the Forest of Merry Sherwood: 'his affections do not that way tend.' Like a good patriot and an honest man, he feels not the same interest in old English history, as in Scottish tradition; the one is not bound up with his early impressions, with his local knowledge, with his personal attachments, like the other; and we may be allowed to say, that our author's genius soars to its enviable and exclusive height from the depth of his prejudices. He has described Scottish manners, scenery, and history so well, and made them so interesting to others, from his complete knowledge and intense love of his country. Why should we expect him to describe English manners and events as well? On his native soil, within that hallowed circle of his warm affections and his keen observation, no one will pretend to cope with him. He has there a wide and noble range, over which his pen 'holds sovereign sway and masterdom;' to wit, over the Highlands and the Lowlands, and the Tolbooth and the good town of Edinburgh, with 'a far cry to Lochiel,' over gleaming lake and valley, and the bare mountain-path, over all ranks and classes of his countrymen, high and low, and over all that has happened to them for the last five hundred years, recorded in history, tradition, or old song. These he may challenge for himself; and if he throws down his gauntlet, no one but a madman will dare to take it up. But on this side the Tweed we have others as good as he. The genius of that magic stream may say to him, 'Hitherto shalt thou come, but no further.' We have novels and romances of our own as good as Ivanhoe; and we will venture to predict, that the more this admirable and all but universal genius extends his rapid and unresisted career on this side the border, the more he will lose in reputation, and in real strength—

> ' Like kings who lose the conquests gain'd before,
> By vain ambition still to make them more.'

How feeble, how slight, how unsatisfactory and disjointed, did the adaptations from Guy Mannering, Rob Roy, and the Antiquary appear, contrasted with the story we had read! The play of Ivanhoe at Covent Garden, on the contrary, seems to give all (or nearly so), that we remember distinctly in the novel; and the Hebrew, which constantly wanders from it, without any apparent object or meaning, yet does so without exciting much indignation or regret. We have in both the scene, the indispensable scene, at the hermitage of Copmanhurst, between the Black Knight, and

Robin Hood's jolly Friar (which, however, has not half the effect on the stage that it has in reading, though Mr. Emery plays the Friar, and sings a jolly stave for him admirably well at Covent Garden)—we have the trial of Rebecca, and the threat to put her father to the torture, almost carried into execution at the castle of Torquilstone; we have the siege and demolition of the castle itself; we have the fair Rowena at one house, in her own proper shape; and at the other, metamorphosed into the fairer and more lovely Israelite; and at both we have Cedric the Saxon, Gurth the swine-herd, and Wamba the jester, and Brian de Bois-Guilbert; and what more would any one require in reason? The details, however, of all these personages and transactions are much more accurately given, and more skilfully connected in Ivanhoe than in the Hebrew, and the former play is better got up than the latter, in all the characters, with the exception of one, which it is needless to mention. Yet, why should we not, envy apart? Mr. Farren played Isaac of York, well; Mr. Kean played the Hebrew still better. As for the rest, Charles Kemble played the same character at one house that Mr. Penley, Jun. did at the other: Mr. Emery was Friar Tuck at Covent Garden, Mr. Oxberry at Drury Lane: Mr. Macready was Sir Reginald Front de Bœuf, a character exactly fitted for his impetuous action, and his smothered tremulous tones, which we cannot say of his other representative, Mr. Hamblin, though we have nothing to say against him: Miss Foote looked the beautiful Rebecca (all but the raven locks and dark eye-lashes) which Mrs. West played but insipidly, with Miss Carew to help her: and Mrs. Fawcett was the wretched, but terrific daughter of the race of Torquilstone, a character omitted at the other house. As a literary composition, we have nothing to offer on Ivanhoe; but the Hebrew (which is published, and which is from the pen of Mr. Soane, the author of some former pieces which have been well received), requires a word or two of remark. As a play, it is ill-constructed, without propor-tion or connection. As a poem, it has its beauties, and those we think neither mean nor few. It is disjointed, without dramatic decorum, and sometimes even to a ludicrous degree: as where a principal hero, on hearing the sound of a horn or trumpet, jumps on a table to look out of a window, and receives an arrow in his breast from one of the besiegers, on which he is carried out apparently lifeless; and yet he is presently after introduced again, as well as if no such accident had happened. But notwithstanding this, and many other errors of the same kind, and a weakness and languor in the general progress of the story, there are individual touches of nature and passion, which we can account for in no other way so satisfactorily as by imagining the author to be a man of genius. The flowers of poetry interspersed were often sad, but beautiful—

'Like to that sanguine flower inscribed with woe'—

the turns and starts of passion in feeble and wronged old age, were often delicate and striking. Among these we might mention the Jew's comparison of his own feelings on receiving an unexpected kindness, to the cold and icy current of the river frozen by the winter, but melting in the genial warmth of the sun: his refusal, in the wanderings of his intellect, to go to witness his daughter's death in company with any one else; 'No: thou art not my child, I'll go alone:' and the fine conception of his hearing, in the deep and silent abstraction of his despair (before any one else), the sound of the trampling of the champion's steed, who comes to rescue her from destruction, which is, however, nearly ruined and rendered ridiculous by Mr. Penley's running in with armour on from the farthest end of the stage, as fast as his legs can carry him. Upon the whole, this character, compared to the rough draught in the novel, is like a curiously finished miniature, done after a bold and noble design. For the dark, massy beard, and coarse weather-beaten figure, which we attribute to Isaac of York, we have a few sprinkled grey hairs, and the shrivelled, tottering frame of the Hebrew; and Mr. Kean's acting in it, in several places, was such as to terrify us when we find from the play-bills that he is soon to act Lear. Of the two plays, we would then recommend it to our readers to go to see Ivanhoe at Covent Garden: but for ourselves, we would rather see the Hebrew a second time at Drury Lane, though every time we go there it costs us three and sixpence more than at the other house—a serious sum! Notwithstanding this repeated and heavy defalcation from our revenue, which really hurts our vanity not less than our interest, we must do the Manager the justice to say, that we never laughed more heartily than we did at his Sir Charles and Lady Racket the other night. 'Unkindness may do much,' but it is not a little matter that will hinder us from laughing as long and as loud as any body, 'to the very top of our lungs,' at so rich a treat as Three Weeks after Marriage. Mr. Elliston never shines to more advantage than in light, genteel farce, after Mr. Kean's tragedy. 'Do you think I'll sleep with a woman that doesn't know what's trumps?' It was irresistible. It might have been *encored* with few dissentient voices, and with no greater violation of established custom than the distributing three different performers, Mr. Connor, Mr. Yates, and Mrs. Davenport, in the pit and boxes, to hold a dialogue with a person on the stage, in the introductory interlude of The Manager in Distress at Covent Garden. We, however, do not object to this novelty, if nobody else does, and if it is not repeated; and it certainly did not put us in an ill humour for seeing Mr. Jones's 'Too Late for Dinner.' Mr. Jones is much such an author as he is an actor—wild, but agreeable, going all lengths without making much progress, determined to please, and succeeding by dint of noise, bustle, whim, and nonsense. There is neither much plot, nor much point in the new farce; but it tells, and keeps the house laughing by a sort of absurd extravagance and good humour. Besides, Mr. Jones plays in it himself, and exerts himself with his wonted alacrity; so do Mr. Liston, Mr. Emery, Mrs. Davenport, and Miss Foote. The author has, indeed, cut out a cockney character for Liston (who is the *Magnus Apollo* of farce writers), as good as our old friend Lubin Log; and the scene in which he comes in stuffing buns, and talking at the same time, till he nearly chokes himself in the double operation, is one that would do for Hogarth to paint, if he were alive; or, as he is not, for Mr. Wilkie. Emery is a country bumpkin, who is learning French, to fit himself for travel into foreign parts; and his Yorkshire dialect and foreign jargon, jumbled together, have a very odd effect. But Mr. Emery's acting, we are sorry to say, is not a subject for criticism: it is always just what it ought to be; and it is impossible to praise it sufficiently, because there is never any opportunity for finding fault with it. To criticise him, would be like criticising the countryman, who carried the pig under his cloak. He is always the very character he undertakes to represent; we mean, in his favourite and general cast of acting.

No. V

[*May*, 1820.

We don't know where to begin this article—whether with Mr. Matthews and his Country Cousins; or with Harlequin *versus* Shakespear; or Cinderella and the Little Glass Slipper; or the story of Goody Two-Shoes and the Fate of Calas, at the Summer Theatre of Sadler's Wells; or with Mr. Booth's Lear, which we have seen with great pleasure; or with Mr. Kean's, which is a greater pleasure to come, (so we anticipate) and which we see is put off to the last moment, lest, we suppose, as the play-bills announce, 'the immortal Shakespear should meet with opponents.' And why should the immortal Shakespear meet with opponents in this case? Nobody can tell. But to prevent so terrible and unlooked-for a catastrophe,

428

and to protect the property of the theatre at so alarming a crisis from cries of 'fire,' the Manager has thought it his duty 'to suspend the Free List during the representation, the public press excepted.' As we have not the mortification of the exclusion, nor the benefit of the exception, we care little about the matter, but as a curiosity in theatrical diplomacy. The anxiety of the Manager about the double trust committed to him, the property of a great theatre, and the fame of a great poet, is exemplary; and the precautions he uses for their preservation, no less admirable and efficacious:—so that, if the tragedy of King Lear should pass muster for a night or two, without suffering the greatest indignities, it will be owing to the *suspension of the Free List*: if Mr. Kean should ride triumphant in a sea of passion, the king of sorrows, and drown his audience in a flood of tears, it will be owing to the *suspension of the Free List*: if the heart-rending tragedy of the immortal bard, as it was originally written, does not meet with the same untoward fate as the speaking pantomime of the late Mr. Garrick deceased, 'altered by a professional gentleman of great abilities,' it will be owing to the *suspension of the Free List*. In a word, if the glory of the 'great heir of fame' does not totter to its base at the representation of his noblest work, nor the property of the theatre tumble about our ears the very first night, we shall have to thank Mr. Elliston's timely care in the *suspension of the Free List*! 'Strange that an old poet's memory should be as mortal as a new manager's wits!' This bold anticipation and defiance of opposition, where none can be expected, is not very politic, though it may be very valiant. It is bringing into litigation an unencumbered estate (we mean that part of it relating to the character of Shakspear) of which we are in full and quiet possession. It is not only waking the sleeping lion, but kicking him. Mr. Elliston's shutting his doors in the face of the Free List is like Don Quixote's throwing open the cages of the wild beasts in the caravan, and insisting that they should come out and fight him. If the Free List were that formidable and ill-disposed body of sworn foes to Shakspear, that 'tasteless monster that the world ne'er saw,' and into which the manager's officious zeal for the interests of the theatre would convert them, it were best to let them alone, and not court their hostility by invidious and impracticable disqualifications. If they are determined to *damn* Shakspear, there is no help for it: if they hold no such antipathy to him, 'if that they love the gentle bard,' why should their 'unhoused, free condition, be put in circumscription and confine,' during the Manager's pleasure? We are in no great pain for the deathless renown of Shakspear: but we really entertain apprehensions that these Berlin and Milan decrees (in imitation of a great man) which our arbitrary theatrical dictator is in the habit of issuing at the bottom of his play-bills, may be of no service to the life-renters of Drury-lane. We hear a report (which we do not believe, and shall be happy to contradict) that the Drury-Lane Management have put in a claim to the exclusive representation of Lear, and have proposed to suspend the performance at the other house. This we think too much, even for the gratuitous and imposing pretensions of Mr. Elliston. We shall, at this rate, soon see stuck up about the town, —'Shakspear performed at this theatre, for a few nights only, by permission of the Manager of Drury-Lane!' Why, this would be a sweeping clause indeed, a master-stroke at the liberty of the stage. It cannot be. It is 'as if he would confine the interminable.' He may seat himself in the manager's chair, like the lady in the lobster, but the tide of Shakspear's genius must be allowed to take its full scope, and overflow, like the Nile, the banks on either side of Russell Street. Our poet is national, not private property. The *quondam* proprietor of the Circus cannot catch this mighty Proteus to make a Harlequin of him: it is not in the bond, that he should not now let any one else but Mr. Kean play Shakspear, as he once objected to let it play at all! We suspect this idle report must have arisen, not from any hint of an injunction, on the part of Mr. Elliston, against 'a beard so old and white' as Mr. Booth's; but as a critical reproof to the Covent-Garden Managers, for reviving Nahum Tate's Lear, instead of the original text; and as a friendly suggestion to them instantly to deprive Cordelia of her lover—and to exclude the Free List '*lest the immortal Shakspear should meet with opponents!*' But we have said enough on this ridiculous subject.

We proceed to another; Mr. Matthews's Country Cousins. This is the third season that this gentleman has entertained the town successfully, and we trust profitably to himself, by a *melange* of imitations, songs, narrative, and ventriloquism, entirely of his own getting up. For one man to be able to amuse the public, or, as the phrase is, to *draw houses*, night after night, by a display of his own resources and feats of comic dexterity alone, shews great variety and piquancy of talent. The Country Cousins is popular, like the rest: the audiences are, at this present speaking, somewhat thinner, but they do not laugh the less. We do not regret that Mr. Matthews has been transferred from the common stage to a stage of his own. He himself complained, at first, (as the cause of this removal) that he had not regular opportunities afforded him at Covent Garden for appearing in legitimate comedy, which was the chief object of his study and his ambition. If it were not the most ridiculous of all things to expect self-knowledge from any man, this ground of complaint would be sufficiently curious. Mr. Matthews was seldom or never put into any characters but those of mimicry and burlesque by the managers of Covent Garden: into what characters has he put himself since he has been upon his own hands? why, seldom or never into any but those of mimicry and burlesque. We remember on some former occasion throwing out a friendly discouragement of Mr. Matthews's undertaking the part of Rover in Wild Oats, (as not exactly fitted to his peculiar cast of acting) which we had reason to think was not received in good part: yet how did he himself propose to make it palatable, and how did he really contrive to make it tolerable, to the audience?—By the introduction of Imitations of all the actors on the London boards. It is not easy to give a character of a man (without making a fool of him) with which he shall be satisfied: but actors are in general so infatuated with applause, or sore from disappointment, that they are, of all men, the least accessible to reason. We critics are a sort of people whom they very strangely look upon as in a state of natural hostility with them. A person who undertakes to give an account of the acted drama in London, may be supposed to be led to this by some fondness for, and some knowledge of, the stage: here then 'there's sympathy' between the actor and the critic. He praises the good, he holds out a warning to the bad. The last may have cause to complain, but the first do not thank you a bit the more. You cheer them in the path of glory, shew them where to pluck fresh laurels, or teach them to shun the precipice, on which their hopes may be dashed to pieces: you devote your time and attention to them; are romantic, gay, witty, profound in adorning their art with every embellishment you have in store to make it interesting to others; you occupy the eyes and ears of the town with their names and affairs; weigh their merits and defects in daily, weekly, monthly scales, with as much preparation and formality as if the fate of the world depended on their failure or success; and yet they seem to suppose that your whole business and only object are to degrade and vilify them in public estimation. What you say in praise of any individual, is set down to the score of his merit: what you say of others, in common justice to yourself, is considered as a mere effusion of spleen, stupidity, and spite—as if you took a particular pleasure in torturing their feelings. Yet, upon second thoughts, there may be some ground for all this. We do not like to have a physician feel our pulse, shake his head, and prescribe a regimen: many persons have objection to sit for their pictures, and there is, perhaps, something in the very fact of being criticised, to which human nature is not easily reconciled. To have every word you speak scanned, every look scrutinised,—never to be sure whether you are right or wrong; to have it said that this was too high, that too low; to be abused by one person for the very same thing that another 'applauds you to the very echo, that does applaud again;' to have it hinted that one's very best effort only just wanted something to make it perfect; and that certain other parts which we thought tolerable, were not to be endured; to be taken in pieces in this manner, turned inside out, to be had up at a self-elected tribunal of impertinence, — tried, condemned, and acquitted every night, — to hear the solemn defence, the ridiculous accusation,—to be subjected to a living anatomy,—to be made the text of a perpetual running commentary,—to be set up in an antithesis, to be played upon in an alliteration,—to have one's faults separated from one's virtues, like the sheep from the goats by the good shepherd,—to be shorn bare and have a mark set upon one,—to be bewitched and bedevilled by the critics,—to lie at the mercy of every puny whipster, and not be suffered to know whether one stands on one's head or one's heels till he tells one how—has, to be sure, something very perplexing and very provoking in it; and it is not so much to be wondered at that the subjects of this kind of critical handling undergo the operation with so little patience as they do. They particularly hate those writers who pretend to patronize them, for this takes away even the privilege of resentment.

An actor, again, is seldom satisfied with being extolled for what he is, unless you admire him for being what he is not. A great tragic actress thinks herself particularly happy in comedy, and it is a sort of misprision of treason not to say so. Your pen may grow wanton in praise of the broad farcical humour of a low comedian; but if you do not cry him up for the fine gentleman, he threatens to leave the stage. Most of our best comic performers came out in tragedy as their favourite line; and Mr. Matthews does not think it enough to enliven a whole theatre with his powers of drollery, and whim, and personal transformation, unless by way of preface and apology he first delivers an epitaph on those talents for the legitimate drama which were so prematurely buried at Covent Garden Theatre! —If we were to speak our minds, we should say, that Mr. Matthews shines particularly, neither as an actor, nor a mimic of actors, but that his forte is a certain general tact, and versatility of comic power. You would say, he is a clever performer: you would guess he is a cleverer man. His talents are not pure, but mixed. He is best when he is his own prompter, manager, and performer, orchestra, and scene-shifter; and, perhaps, to make the thing complete, the audience should be of his own providing too.—If we had never known any thing more of Mr. Matthews than the account we have heard of his imitating the interior of a German family, the wife lying a-bed grumbling at her husband's staying out, the husband's return home drunk, and the little child's *padding* across the room to get to its own bed as soon as it hears him, we should set him down for a man of genius. These felicitous strokes are, however, casual and intermittent in him :—they proceed from him rather by chance than design, and are followed up by others equally gross and superficial. Mr. Matthews wants taste, or has been spoiled by the taste of the town, whom 'he must live to please, and please to live.' His talent, though limited, is of a lively and vigorous fibre; capable of a succession of shifts and disguises; he is *up to* a number of good things— single hits here and there; but by the suddenness and abruptness of his turns, he surprises and shocks oftener than he satisfies. His wit does not move the muscles of the mind, but, like some practical joker, gives one a good rap on the knuckles, or a lively box on the ear. He serves up a *pic-nic* entertainment of scraps and odd ends (some of them, we must say, old ones). He is like a host, who will not let us swallow a mouthful, but offers us something else, and directly after brings us the same dish again. He is in a continual hurry and disquietude to please, and destroys half the effect by trying to increase it. He is afraid to trust for a moment to the language of nature and character, and wants to translate it into pantomime and grimace, like a writing-master, who for the letter *I* has the hieroglyphic of an eye staring you in the face. Mr. Matthews may be said to have taken tythe of half the talents of the stage and of the town; yet his variety is not always charming. There is something dry and meagre in his jokes : they do not lard the lean earth as he walks; but seem as if they might be written upon parchment. His humour, in short, is not like digging into a fine Stilton cheese, but is more like the scrapings of Shapsugar.—As an actor, we think he cannot rise higher than a waiter, (certainly not a dumb one,) or than Mr. Wiggins. In this last character, in particular, by a certain panic-struck expression of countenance at the persecution of which the hen-pecked husband is the victim, and by the huge unwieldy helplessness of his person, unable to escape from it and from the rabble of boys at his heels, he excites shouts of laughter, and hits off the humour of the thing to an exact perfection. In general, his performance is of that kind which implies manual dexterity, or an assumption of bodily defect, rather than mental capacity : take from Mr. Matthews's drollest parts an odd shuffle in the gait, a restless volubility of speech and motion, a sudden suppression of features, or the continual repetition of some cant phrase with unabated vigour, and you reduce him to almost total insignificance, and a state of still life. He is not therefore like—

> ' A clock that wants both hands,
> As useless when it goes as when it stands : '

for only keep him going, and he bustles about the stage to some purpose. As a mimic of other actors, Mr. Matthews fails as often as he succeeds (we call it a failure, when it is with difficulty we can distinguish the person intended,) and when he succeeds, it is more by seizing upon some peculiarity, or exaggerating some defect, than by hitting upon the true character or prominent features. He gabbles like Incledon, or croaks like Suett, or lisps like Young ; but when he attempts the expressive silver-tongued cadences of John Kemble, it is the shadow of a shade. If we did not know the contrary, we should suppose he had never heard the original, but was imitating some one who had. His best imitations are taken from something characteristic or absurd that has struck his fancy, or occurred to his observation in real life—such as a chattering footman, a drunken coachman, a surly traveller, or a garrulous old Scotchwoman. This last we would fix upon as Mr. Matthews's *chef-d'œuvre*. It was a portrait of common nature, equal to Wilkie or Teniers—as faithful, as simple, as delicately humorous, and with a slight dash of pathos ; but without one particle of caricature, of vulgarity, or ill-nature. We see no reason why the ingenious artist should not show his Country Cousins a gallery of such portraits, and of no others, once a year. ' He might exhibit it every night for a month, and we should go to see it every night ! ' [1] What has impressed itself on our memory as the next best thing to this exquisite piece of genuine painting, was the broad joke of the abrupt proposal of a mutton-chop to the man who is sea-sick, and the convulsive marks of abhorrence with which it is received. The representation also of the tavern-beau in the Country Cousins, who is about to swallow a lighted-candle for a glass of brandy and water, as he is going drunk to bed, is well feigned and admirably humoured ; with many more, too long to mention. It is more to our performer's credit to suppose that the songs which he sings with such rapidity and vivacity of effect are not of his own composing ; and, as to his ventriloquism, it is yet in its infancy. The fault of these exhibitions—that which appears ' first, midst, and last ' in them, is that they turn too much upon caricaturing the most common-place and worn-out topics of ridicule—the blunders of

---

[1] We have given this sentence in marks of quotation, and yet it is our own. We should put a stop to the practices of ' such petty larceny rogues '—but that it is not worth while.

Frenchmen in speaking English, — the mispronunciations of the cockney dialect, the ignorance of Country Cousins, and the impertinence and foppery of relations in town. It would seem too likely from the uniform texture of these pieces, that Mr. Matthews had passed his whole time in climbing to the top of the Monument, or had never been out of a tavern, or a stage-coach, a Margate-hoy or a Dover packet-boat. We do not deny the merit of some of the cross-readings out of the two languages; but certainly we think the quantity of French and English jargon put into the mouths of French and English travellers all through these imitations, must lessen their popularity instead of increasing it, as two-thirds of Mr. Matthews's auditors, we should imagine, cannot know the point on which the jest turns. We grant that John Bull is always very willing to laugh at Mounseer, if he knew why or how—perhaps, even without knowing how or why! But we thought many of the jokes of this kind, however well contrived or intended, miscarried in their passage through the pit, and long before they reached the two shilling gallery.

A new pantomime, called *Shakspear versus Harlequin*, has been produced at Drury-lane Theatre. It is called 'a speaking pantomime:' we had rather it had said nothing. It is better to act folly than to talk it. The heels and wand and motley coat of Harlequin are sacred to nonsense; but the words, the cap and wings of Mercury (who was here also made the representative of Shakspear) are worthy of a better use. The essence of pantomime is practical absurdity, keeping the wits in constant chase, coming upon one by surprise, and starting off again before you can arrest the fleeting phantom: the essence of this piece was prosing stupidity remaining like a mawkish fixture on the stage, and overcoming your impatience by the force of *ennui*. A speaking pantomime (such as this one) is not unlike a flying waggon: but we do not want a pantomime to move in minuet-time, nor to have Harlequin's light wand changed into a leaden mace. If we must have a series of shocks and surprises, of violations of probability, common sense, and nature, to keep the brain and senses in a whirl, let us, at least, have them hot and hot, let them 'charge on heaps, that we may lose distinction in *absurdity*,' and not have time to doze and yawn over them, in the intervals of the battle. The bringing Harlequin to the test of reason resembles the old story of hedging in the cuckoo, and surpasses the united genius of the late Mr. Garrick (to whom this dull farce is ascribed) and of the professional gentleman who has fitted the above productions of 'the olden times' (*viz.* those of the late Mr. Garrick) to modern taste! After all, though Harlequin is tried by three grave judges, who are very unnecessarily metamorphosed into three old women, no competi-

DRAMATIC ESSAYS

tion, no collision takes place between him and the genius of Shakspear, unless Mr. T. Cooke's playing very cleverly on a variety of musical instruments, so as to ravish the heart of Miss Dolly Snip (Madam Vestris) can be construed into so many proofs of the superiority of Shakspear's Muse! Again, Mr. Harley, as Harlequin, and Mr. Oxberry (as a country clown) get up into a tree to see the sport, from which it was as difficult to dislodge them as owls from an ivy-bush; and the sport is to see Joey Snip, the tailor, have his head cut off, and walk with it about the stage, and, unlike the sign of the good woman, talk without his tongue. The slicing off a blackamoor's head or two with the stroke of a scymitar, provided the thing is done quickly, and instantly got out of sight, we do not much object to; but we do not like to have a ghastly spectre of this sort placed before us for a whole evening, as the heads of the rebel Scotch lords were stuck on Temple-bar for half a century. It may be well said indeed, *Quod sic mihi ostendis incredulus odi.* Perhaps this exhibition of posthumous horror and impertinence might be meant as a sly hit at the ghost of Hamlet.

'See o'er the stage the ghost of *Munden* stalks.'

If so, we cry the Manager mercy. We must add, that the strength of the theatre was put in requisition for this piece, and if it could have been saved, it would. Miss Tree, to enliven so many dreary objects, danced a *pas seul.* We would rather see this young lady dance round a may-pole at a country wake or fair.

'But thou, oh Hope, with eyes so fair,
What was thy enchanting measure?
Still it whisper'd promised pleasure,
And bade the lovely scenes at distance hail:'—

We could not help repeating these lines as we saw the youngest of the Miss Dennetts, the tallest of the three, resume the part of Cinderella at Covent Garden,—restored, like Psyche, to her late-lost home, and transformed by the little hump-backed fairy, from a poor house-maid to a bright princess, drinking pleasure and treading air. This is a consummation more devoutly to be wished than the changing of a pipkin into a sign-post, or a wheel-barrow into a china-shop. A Fairy Tale is the true history of the human heart—it is a dream of youth realized! How many country-girls have fancied themselves princesses, nay, what country-girl ever was there that, some time or other, did not? A Fairy Tale is what the world would be, if every one had their wishes or their deserts, if our power

436

and our passions were equal.   We cannot be at a loss for a thousand
bad translations of the story of Cinderella, if we look around us in
the boxes.   But the real imitation is on the stage.   If we could
always see the flowers open in the spring, or hear soft music, or see
Cinderella dance, or dream we did, life itself would be a Fairy Tale.
If the three Miss Dennetts are a little less like one another than they
were, on the other hand, we must say that Miss Eliza Dennett (what
a pretty name) is much improved, combines a little cluster of graces
in her own person, and ' in herself sums all delight.'   She has learned
to add precision to ease, and firmness of movement to the utmost
harmony of form.   In the scene where Cinderella is introduced at
court and is led out to dance by the enamoured prince, she bows as
if she had a diadem on her head, moves as if she had just burst from
fetters of roses, folds her arms as the vine curls its tendrils, and
hurries from the scene, after the loss of her faithless slipper, as if she
had to run a race with the winds.   We had only one thing to desire,
that she and her lover, instead of the new ballet, had danced the
Minuet de la Cour with the Gavot, as they do in the Dansomanie ;
that we might have called the Minuet de la Cour divine, and the
Gavot heavenly, and exclaimed once more, with more than artificial
rapture—' Such were the joys of our dancing days ! '   We do not
despair of seeing this alteration adopted, as our recommendations are
sometimes attended to : and in that case we shall feel.—But the
mechanical anticipation of an involuntary burst of sentiment in supposed circumstances is in vile taste, and we leave it to lords and
pettifoggers.   We hate to copy them : but we like to steal from
Spenser.   Here is a passage descriptive of dancing, and of the delights
of love, of youth, and beauty which sometimes surround it, and of the
eternal echo which they leave in the ear of fancy.   The Managers
of Covent-Garden may perhaps apply it to their own enchanted
palace : we have nothing to do with the passage but to quote it.

> ' They say that Venus, when she did dispose
>   Herself to pleasure, used to resort
> Unto this place, and therein to repose
> And rest herself as in a gladsome port,
> Or with the Graces there to play and sport :
> That even her own Cytheron, though in it
> She used most to keep her royal court,
> And in her sovereign majesty to sit,
> She in regard hereof refus'd and thought unfit.
>
> Unto this place, when as the Elfin knight
> Approach'd, him seemed that the merry sound
> Of a shrill pipe he playing heard on hight,

And many feet fast thumping th' hollow ground,
That through the woods their echo did rebound.
He nigher drew to weet what it mote be :
There he a troop of ladies dancing found
Full merrily, and making gladful glee,
And in the midst a shepherd piping he did see.

All they without were ranged in a ring,
And danced round ; but in the midst of them
Three other ladies did both dance and sing,
The whilst the rest them round about did hem,
And like a girlond did encompass them,
And in the midst of those same three was placed
Another damsel, as a precious gem,
Amidst a ring most richly well enchaced,
That with her goodly presence all the rest much graced.

Look how the crown which Ariadne wore
Upon her ivory forehead, that same day
That Theseus her unto her bridal bore
(When the bold Centaurs made that bloody fray
With the fierce Lapiths that did him dismay)
Being now placed in the firmament,
Through the bright heaven doth her beams display,
And is unto the stars an ornament ;
Which round her move in order excellent.

Such was the beauty of this goodly band,
Whose sundry shape were here too long to tell :
But she that in the midst of them did stand,
Seem'd all the rest in beauty to excel,
Crown'd with a rosy girlond, that right well
Did her beseem.   And ever as the crew
About her danc'd, sweet flow'rs that far did smell,
And fragrant odours, they upon her threw,
But most of all, those three did her with gifts endue.

Those were the Graces, daughters of delight,
Handmaids of Venus, which are wont to haunt
Upon this hill, and dance there day and night :
Those three to men all gifts of grace do grant ;
And all that Venus in herself doth vaunt,
Is borrowed of them.   But that fair one,
That in the midst was placed paravant,
Was she to whom that shepherd piped alone,
That made him pipe so merrily, as never none.'

Faery Queen, Book vi. Canto 10.

On the subject of the pantomime and the miscellaneous Drama, we have two words to add, *viz.* that we have been to see the Heart of Midlothian at the Surrey Theatre, of which we spoke by hearsay in our last but one, and which answered our warmest expectations; and that we took a pleasant stroll up to the Aquatic Theatre of Sadler's Wells, and after dining at the Sir Hugh Middleton's Head, saw a very pretty play-house, Goody Two Shoes, the Monastery, and the Fate of Calas. Goody Two Shoes was played first, on the evening we were there, because Mr. Grimaldi and Mr. Barnes were in it, and they were obliged afterwards to perform in the pantomime at Covent Garden. Did Miss Vallancy go with them? Otherwise, we should like to have seen her again in the course of the evening. All that we could see to praise in the Monastery was its faithfulness to the original, and the acting of Mr. and Mrs. Stanley. We hope that under the management of a gentleman (Mr. Howard Paine,) so well acquainted with both departments of his undertaking, the literary and dramatic, this theatre will soon flourish in all the pride of summer. We had nearly omitted to notice a new Hamlet, that came out at Drury-lane a few weeks ago, who, it appeared to us, would have made the prettiest Hamlet we have seen, if he had been only equal to the part. Indeed he looked it to perfection; he had an elegant figure with a thoughtful face; and on the ordinary conduct and conception of the character, was at once the gentleman and scholar. In the more declamatory and impassioned scenes, however, his voice totally broke down under him, and he did not repeat the part as was given out; for he was the next morning pierced through with the feathered arrows of criticism, as if his breast had been a target. The gentlemen-critics of the daily press have not, in general, their cue on the first night of a performer's appearance. If he fails, they fall upon him without mercy; if he succeeds, they are almost afraid to say so, lest others should say that they were wrong. They pretend (some of them) to lead public opinion and yet have no opinion of their own. They dare not boldly and distinctly declare their opinion of a new dramatic experiment, and the reason is, their convictions are not clear enough to warrant their placing any confidence in them, till they are confirmed by being put to the vote. The first quality of a good critic is courage; but mental courage, like bodily, is the result of conscious strength. Some of the Vampyre crew, indeed, retreat from the dimness and inanity of their perceptions, into the solid darkness of their prejudices, and the crude consistence of their ever-rankling spite; and, in that strong-hold of dirt and cob-webs, are impervious to every ray of sense or reason. We might leave them, if they had themselves been contented to remain, in their narrow, gloomy cells, the proper hiding-place of ignorance and bigotry; but when they come out into the blaze of noon,

> 'Shut their blue-fringed lids, and hold them close,
> And hooting at the glorious sun in heaven,
> Cry out, where is it?'—

it is time to stop their ominous flight, and send them back to that life of sloth and pride, where the poison of dull-eyed envy preys only upon itself.

There was a want of proper spirit and gallantry shown the other day in the critical reception of Mr. Booth's Lear. It was not thought that he would make any thing of it, and therefore it was not said that he did. Because he was on his trial, he was not to have a hearing. Because he was *not* 'the most favoured actor of the day,' he was to have no favour at all shown him. *Fiat justitia, ruat cælum.* When Mr. Booth does nothing but make wry faces and odd harsh noises in a character, in imitation of Mr. Kean, we will say, that he does it ill: but when he plays it as he did Lear, we will say that he does it not ill, but well, and that in prejudging him, we have been mistaken. It does not lessen Mr. Macready in our opinion, that (as we understand) he refused this character in obstinate despair of doing it justice: but if this was a proof of modesty and judgment in him, it certainly ought to raise our idea of Mr. Booth's talents, that he was able to get through it in the way he did. Where failure would have been so fatal and so marked, it was a sufficient triumph even to a proud ambition not to fail. If the part in our adventurous actor's hands wanted something of the breadth and majesty of Lear, it did not want for life or spirit, or a human interest. If he did not give the torrent and whirlwind of the passion, he had plenty of its gusts and flaws. Without his crown, or even the faded image of one, circling his brow, he bustled about the stage with a restlessness and impetuosity of feeling that kept expectation continually awake and gratified the attention which had been so excited. There was no feebleness, and no vulgarity in any part of Mr. Booth's acting, but it was animated, vigorous, and pathetic throughout. The audience, we are sure, the first night, thought and felt as we did. In the exclamation, 'I am every inch a king,' his energy rose to dignity: again, in his reiteration of Gloucester's epithet of 'the *fiery* Duke,' applied to his son-in-law, his manifest impatience, and increasing irritability, showed that Mr. Booth had felt the full force of that beautiful passage in which his own half-conscious infirmity is played off so finely on the ill-fated old king; and in the scenes with Edgar as mad Tom, where his wits begin to unsettle, the distraction and alienation

440

of his mind, wandering from its own thoughts to catch hold of a clue less painful, and yet broken and entangled like them, were pourtrayed with equal skill and delicacy. In the more set speeches, as in the curse on his daughters, Mr. Booth, we thought, comparatively failed ; but where action was to come in aid of the sentiment and point the meaning, he was almost uniformly correct and impressive. In fact, it is only when the poet's language is explained by the comment of gesture or some sudden change of look, or situation—that is, when tragedy is enlivened by pantomime, that it becomes intelligible to the greater part of the audience ; and we do not see how an actor can be supposed to do those things well which are almost abstractions in his art, and in which he is not encouraged by the sympathy or corrected by the judgment of his hearers. We observed, that the finest touches of thought, of poetry and nature in this play, which were not set off by the accompaniment of show and bustle, passed in profound silence, and without the smallest notice. The sublimity of repose is one in which our play-house frequenters do not seem to be proficients, and the players may be excused, if they do not always cultivate (as we might wish) this occult and mysterious branch of their profession. Of Mr. C. Kemble's Edgar we cannot speak in terms of too high praise. In the supposed mad-scenes, his conception and delivery of the part excited the warmest approbation ; his fine face and figure admirably relieved the horror of the situations ; and, whenever we see Mad Tom played (which is not often), we should wish to see it played by him. The rest of the play was very respectably got up, and all we could object to was the interspersion of the love-scenes by Tate. The happy ending, and the triumph and dotage of the poor old king in repeating again and again, ' Cordelia's Queen, Cordelia's Queen,' were perhaps allowable concessions to the feelings of the audience.

HENRI QUATRE.—There are two lines in a modern poem which we often repeat to ourselves—

> ''Twas Lancelot of the Lake, a bright romance,
> That like a trumpet made young spirits dance : '

and we were much disposed to apply them to this romantic, light and elegant drama. We prophesy that the Managers and the public have a splendid career before them for the season. *This will do.* We saw it in the first opening scene, a view near Paris, the clearest, the most sparkling, the most vivid we ever saw. ' Ah ! brilliant land ! ah ! sunny, cloudless skies ! Not all the ink, that has been shed to blacken thee, can blot thy shining face ! Not all the blood that has been spilt to enslave thee can choke up thy living breath ! ' If we can thus be transported to another and a gayer region, and made to drink the warmth and lustre of another climate by the painter's magic art, what can we desire more ?—What the pencil had in this case done, the poet's pen did not undo : what the author had written, the actors did not spoil. They *do* order these things well at Covent Garden. We never saw a piece better got up in all its parts, nor one more adapted to the taste of the town in scenery, in dresses, in songs, in passing allusions, in popular sentiments; nor one that went off with less *ennui*, or with more continual bursts of flattering applause. The writing (as far as it was French) was, as might be expected, lively and sentimental : as far as we could perceive Mr. Morton to have had a hand in it, it consisted of strong touches of obvious nature, and showed a perfect understanding with the actors and the audience. The characters were strikingly conceived, and admirably sustained. Mr. Macready's Henri Quatre was (we think) his very happiest effort. There was an originality, a raciness in it that hit our palates. With something, nay, with much of the stiffness and abruptness of one of 'the invincible knights of old,' used to march in rusty armour, there was at the same time the ease, the grace and gallantry of an accomplished courtier. 'He is ten times handsomer,' says the fair Jocrisse, 'than Uncle Jervais,' and according to her husband's comment, 'Handsome is that handsome does.' There was a spirit of kindness blended with authority in his tones and in his actions ; he was humane, and yet a king and a soldier. Some of the sentiments put into his mouth were worthy of the attention of princes, if they had time for serious reflection, and called forth loud and repeated plaudits. Henry professed his desire to reign by love not fear in the hearts of his subjects ; and quoted a saying of his mother's on the mode of effecting this purpose, that 'a pound of honey would draw more flies than a ton of vinegar.' We seemed suddenly and unaccountably carried back to the heroic times of camps and courts, in the company of this good-natured, high spirited, old fashioned monarch, and his favourite counsellor, Sully, a pattern of sound thinking and plain-speaking, who was characteristically represented by Mr. Egerton. It is his business to prevent the king from doing anything wrong,—'no sinecure,' as he honestly declares. We like these bitter jests ; and we found that others were of our thinking, though they flew about as thick as hail. We should have thought this piece more likely to have been imported from Spain than France, at the present crisis of affairs. At any rate, Mr. Morton has given a truly English version of it. Mr. Emery played a blunt, rough old soldier (Moustache,) well, who is afterwards appointed keeper of a prison—'Because,' he says to his sovereign, 'you think me a savage.' 'No!' (is the answer,)

442

'but because with the courage and rough outside of a lion you have
the heart of a man.' The scenes in which Charles Kemble, as
Eugene de Biron, is committed to his charge under sentence of death
—is liberated by him to perform a last act of friendship and of
affection, and returns on his parole of honour to meet his fate (from
which however he is delivered by having, in his night's adventure,
saved the lives of Henri and Sully, who had been attacked by
assassins in a forest hard by) are among the most interesting of the
story. We do not enter into the details of the plot, because we hope
all our readers will go to see this piece, and it is anticipating a
pleasure to come. Besides, we are bad hands at getting up a plot,
and should on that account make but indifferent ministers of state.
But the whole was delightful. Miss M. Tree was delightful as the
village representative of the fair Gabrielle; Mr. Liston was happy as
the husband of Jocrisse, 'whom the king had deigned to salute,' and
to put a diamond ring on her finger, which was to introduce them to
the Louvre in their wooden shoes on his coronation day.—Miss
Stephens sung sweetly; Mr. Fawcett was at home in the old general;
Irish Johnstone blundered in his own beautiful *brogue*, and every thing
was as it should be. We like things to succeed in this manner: that
they do not always do so, is assuredly no fault of ours.

I.,

No. VI

[*June*, 1820.

Mr. Kean's Lear.—We need not say how much our expectations
had been previously excited to see Mr. Kean in this character, and
we are sorry to be obliged to add, that they were very considerably
disappointed. We had hoped to witness something of the same effect
produced upon an audience that Garrick is reported to have done in
the part, which made Dr. Johnson resolve never to see him repeat it
—the impression was so terrific and overwhelming. If we should
make the same rash vow never to see Mr. Kean's Lear again, it
would not be from the intensity and excess, but from the deficiency
and desultoriness of the interest excited. To give some idea of the
manner in which this character might, and ought to be, made to seize
upon the feelings of an audience, we have heard it mentioned, that
once, when Garrick was in the middle of the mad-scene, his crown of
straw came off, which circumstance, though it would have been fatal
to a common actor, did not produce the smallest interruption, or even
notice in the house. On another occasion, while he was kneeling to
repeat the curse, the first row in the pit stood up in order to see him

better ; the second row, not willing to lose the precious moments by remonstrating, stood up too ; and so, by a tacit movement, the entire pit rose to hear the withering imprecation, while the whole passed in such cautious silence, that you might have heard a pin drop. John Kemble (that old campaigner) was also very great in the curse : so we have heard, from very good authorities ; and we put implicit faith in them.—What led us to look for the greatest things from Mr. Kean in the present instance, was his own opinion, on which we have a strong reliance. It was always his favourite part. We have understood he has been heard to say, that ' he was very much obliged to the London audiences for the good opinion they had hitherto expressed of him, but that when they came to see him over the dead body of Cordelia, they would have quite a different notion of the matter.' As it happens, they have not yet had an opportunity of seeing him over the dead body of Cordelia : for, after all, our versatile Manager has acted Tate's Lear instead of Shakspear's : and it was suggested, that perhaps Mr. Kean played the whole ill *out of spite*, as he could not have it his own way—a hint to which we lent a willing ear, for we would rather think Mr. Kean the most spiteful man, than not the best actor, in the world ! The impression, however, made on our minds was, that, instead of its being his master-piece, he was to seek in many parts of the character ;—that the general conception was often perverse, or feeble ; and that there were only two or three places where he could be said to electrify the house. It is altogether inferior to his Othello. Yet, if he had even played it equal to that, all we could have said of Mr. Kean would have been that he was a very wonderful man ;—and such we certainly think him as it is. Into the bursts, and starts, and torrent of the passion in Othello, this excellent actor appeared to have flung himself completely : there was all the fitful fever of the blood, the jealous madness of the brain : his heart seemed to bleed with anguish, while his tongue dropped broken, imperfect accents of woe ; but there is something (we don't know how) in the gigantic, outspread sorrows of Lear, that seems to elude his grasp, and baffle his attempts at comprehension. The passion in Othello pours along, so to speak, like a river, torments itself in restless eddies, or is hurled from its dizzy height, like a sounding cataract. That in Lear is more like a sea, swelling, chafing, raging, without bound, without hope, without beacon, or anchor. Torn from the hold of his affections and fixed purposes, he floats a mighty wreck in the wide world of sorrows. Othello's causes of complaint are more distinct and pointed, and he has a desperate, a maddening remedy for them in his revenge. But Lear's injuries are without provocation, and admit of no alleviation or atonement. They are strange, bewilder-

444

ing, overwhelming : they wrench asunder, and stun the whole frame : they 'accumulate horrors on horror's head,' and yet leave the mind impotent of resources, cut off, proscribed, anathematised from the common hope of good to itself, or ill to others—amazed at its own situation, but unable to avert it, scarce daring to look at, or to weep over it.   The action of the mind, however, under this load of disabling circumstances, is brought out in the play in the most masterly and triumphant manner : it staggers under them, but it does not yield.   The character is cemented of human strength and human weaknesses (the firmer for the mixture) :—abandoned of fortune, of nature, of reason, and without any energy of purpose, or power of action left,—with the grounds of all hope and comfort failing under it, —but sustained, reared to a majestic height out of the yawning abyss, by the force of the affections, the imagination, and the cords of the human heart—it stands a proud monument, in the gap of nature, over barbarous cruelty and filial ingratitude.   We had thought that Mr. Kean would take possession of this time-worn, venerable figure, 'that has outlasted a thousand storms, a thousand winters,' and, like the gods of old, when their oracles were about to speak, shake it with present inspiration :—that he would set up a living copy of it on the stage : but he failed, either from insurmountable difficulties, or from his own sense of the magnitude of the undertaking.   There are pieces of ancient granite that turn the edge of any modern chisel : so perhaps the genius of no living actor can be expected to cope with Lear.   Mr. Kean chipped off a bit of the character here and there : but he did not pierce the solid substance, nor move the entire mass.— Indeed, he did not go the right way about it.   He was too violent at first, and too tame afterwards.   He sunk from unmixed rage to mere dotage.   Thus (to leave this general description, and come to particulars) he made the well-known curse a piece of downright rant. He 'tore it to tatters, to very rags,' and made it, from beginning to end, an explosion of ungovernable physical rage, without solemnity, or elevation.   Here it is ; and let the reader judge for himself whether it should be so served.

> 'Hear, Nature, hear ; dear goddess, hear a father !
> Suspend thy purpose, if thou didst intend
> To make this creature fruitful :
> Into her womb convey sterility,
> Dry up in her the organs of increase,
> And from her derogate body never spring
> A babe to honour her ! If she must teem,
> Create her child of spleen, that it may live,
> And be a thwart disnatur'd torment to her :

Let it stamp wrinkles in her brow of youth,
With cadent tears fret channels in her cheeks;
Turn all her mother's pains and benefits
To laughter and contempt; that she may feel,
How sharper than a serpent's tooth it is
To have a thankless child.'

Now this should not certainly be spoken in a fit of drunken choler, without any ' compunctious visitings of nature,' without any relentings of tenderness, as if it was a mere speech of hate, directed against a person to whom he had the most rooted and unalterable aversion. The very bitterness of the imprecations is prompted by, and turns upon, an allusion to the fondest recollections : it is an excess of indignation, but that indignation, from the depth of its source, conjures up the dearest images of love : it is from these that the brimming cup of anguish overflows ; and the voice, in going over them, should falter, and be choked with other feelings besides anger. The curse in Lear should not be *scolded*, but recited as a Hymn to the Penates ! Lear is not a Timon. From the action and attitude into which Mr. Kean put himself to repeat this passage, we had augured a different result. He threw himself on his knees ; lifted up his arms like withered stumps ; threw his head quite back, and in that position, as if severed from all that held him to society, breathed a heart-struck prayer, like the figure of a man obtruncated !—It was the only moment worthy of himself, and of the character.

In the former part of the scene, where Lear, in answer to the cool didactic reasoning of Gonerill, asks, ' Are you our daughter ? ' &c., Mr. Kean, we thought, failed from a contrary defect. The suppression of passion should not amount to immobility : that intensity of feeling of which the slightest intimation is supposed to convey everything, should not seem to convey nothing. There is a difference between ordinary familiarity and the *sublime* of familiarity. The mind may be staggered by a blow too great for it to bear, and may not recover itself for a moment or two ; but this state of suspense of its faculties, ' like a phantasma, or a hideous dream,' should not assume the appearance of indifference, or *still-life*. We do not think Mr. Kean kept this distinction (though it is one in which he is often very happy) sufficiently marked in the foregoing question to his daughter, nor in the speech which follows immediately after, as a confirmation of the same sentiment of incredulity and surprise.

' Does any here know me ? This is not Lear :
Does Lear walk thus ? speak thus ? where are his eyes ?
Either his notion weakens, his discernings
Are lethargied—Ha ! waking—'tis not so ;

Who is it that can tell me who I am ?
Lear's shadow ? I would learn ; for by the marks
Of sovereignty, of knowledge, and of reason,
I should be false persuaded I had daughters.
Your name, fair gentlewoman ? '—

These fearful interrogatories, which stand ready to start away on the brink of madness, should not certainly be asked like a common question, nor a dry sarcasm. If Mr. Kean did not speak them so, we beg his pardon.—In what comes after this, in the apostrophe to Ingratitude, in the sudden call for his horses, in the defence of the character of his train as ' men of choice and rarest parts,' and in the recurrence to Cordelia's ' most small fault,' there are plenty of stops to play upon, all the varieties of agony, of anger and impatience, of asserted dignity and tender regret—Mr. Kean struck but two notes all through, the highest and the lowest.

This scene of Lear with Gonerill, in the first act, is only to be paralleled by the doubly terrific one between him and Regan and Gonerill in the second act. To call it a decided failure would be saying what we do not think : to call it a splendid success would be saying so no less. Mr. Kean did not appear to us to set his back fairly to his task, or to trust implicitly to his author, but to be trying experiments upon the audience, and waiting to see the result. We never saw this daring actor want confidence before, but he seemed to cower and hesitate before the public eye in the present instance, and to be looking out for the effect of what he did, while he was doing it. In the ironical remonstrance to Regan, for example :

' Dear daughter, I confess that I am old—
Age is unnecessary, &c.'

he might be said to be waiting for the report of the House to know how low he should bend his knee in mimic reverence, how far he should sink his voice into the tones of feebleness, despondency, and mendicancy. But, if ever, it was upon *this* occasion that he ought to have raised himself above criticism, and sat enthroned (in the towering contemplations of his own mind) with Genius and Nature. They alone (and not the critic's eye, nor the tumultuous voices of the pit) are the true judges of Lear ! If he had trusted only to these, his own counsellors and bosom friends, we see no limit to the effect he might have produced. But he did not give any particular effect to the exclamation—

——' Beloved Regan,
Thy sister's naught : oh, Regan, she hath tied
Sharp-tooth'd unkindness, like a vulture here : '

nor to the assurance that he will not return to her again—

> ' Never, Regan :
> She hath abated me of half my train,
> Look'd black upon me ; struck me with her tongue,
> Most serpent-like, upon the very heart.
> All the stored vengeances of heaven fall
> On her ingrateful top ! '

nor to the description of his two daughters' looks—

> ——' Her eyes are fierce ; but thine
> Do comfort, and not burn : '

nor to that last sublime appeal to the heavens on seeing Gonerill approach—

> ' Oh, heav'ns !
> If you do love old men, if your sweet sway
> Hallow obedience, if yourselves are old,
> Make it your cause, send down, and take my part.
> Art not asham'd to look upon this beard ?
> Oh, Regan, will you take her by the hand ? '

One would think there are tones, and looks, and gestures, answerable to these words, to thrill and harrow up the thoughts, to ' appal the guilty, and make mad the free,' or that might ' create a soul under the ribs of death ! ' But we did not see, or hear them. It was Mr. Kean's business to furnish them : it would have been ours to feel them, if he had ! It is not enough that Lear's crosses and perplexities are expressed by single strokes. There should be an agglomeration of horrors, closing him in like a phalanx. His speech should be thick with the fulness of his agony. His face should, as it were, encrust and stiffen into amazement at his multiplied afflictions. A single image of ruin is nothing—there should be a growing desolation all around him. His wrongs should seem enlarged tenfold through the solid atmosphere of his despair—his thoughts should be vast and lucid, like the sun when he declines—He should be ' a huge dumb heap ' of woe ! The most that Mr. Kean did was to make some single hits here and there ; but these did not tell, because they were separated from the main body and movement of the passion. They might be compared to interlineations of the character, rather than parts of the text. In the sudden reiteration of the epithet—'*fiery* quality of the Duke,' applied to Cornwall by Gloucester, at which his jealousy blazes out to extravagance, we thought Mr. Kean feeble and indecisive : but in breaking away at the conclusion of the scene, ' I will do such things : what they are, yet I know not ; but they shall

be the terrors of the earth,'—he made one of those tremendous bursts
of energy and grandeur, which shed a redeeming glory round every
character he plays.

Mr. Kean's performance of the remainder of the character, when
the king's intellects begin to fail him, and are, at last, quite disordered,
was curious and quaint, rather than impressive or natural. There
appeared a degree of perversity in all this—a determination to give
the passages in a way in which nobody else would give them, and in
which nobody else would expect them to be given. But singularity
is not always excellence. Why, for instance, should our actor lower
his voice in the soliloquy in the third act, ' Blow winds, and crack
your cheeks,' &c. in which the tumult of Lear's thoughts, and the
extravagance of his expressions, seem almost contending with the
violence of the storm? We can conceive no reason but that it was
contrary to the practice of most actors hitherto. Mr. Rae's manner
of mouthing the passage would have been 'more germane to the
matter.' In asking his companion—

> ' How dost, my boy ? Art cold ?
> I 'm cold myself '——

there was a shrinking of the frame, and a chill glance of the eye, like
the shivering of an ague-fit: but no other feeling surmounted the
physical expression. On meeting with Edgar, as Mad Tom, Lear
wildly exclaims, with infinite beauty and pathos, ' Didst thou give all
to thy daughters, and art thou come to this?' And again, presently
after, he repeats, ' What, have his daughters brought him to this
pass? Couldst thou save nothing? Didst thou give 'em all?'—
questions which imply a strong possession, the eager indulgence of
a favourite idea which has just struck his heated fancy; but which
Mr. Kean pronounced in a feeble, sceptical, querulous under-tone, as
if wanting information as to some ordinary occasion of insignificant
distress. We do not admire these cross-readings of a work like
Lear. They may be very well when the actor's ingenuity, however
paradoxical, is more amusing than the author's sense : but it is not so
in this case. From some such miscalculation, or desire of finding out
a clue to the character, other than ' was set down ' for him, Mr.
Kean did not display his usual resources and felicitous spirit in these
terrific scenes :—he drivelled, and looked vacant, and moved his lips,
so as not to be heard, and did nothing, and appeared, at times, as if
he would quite forget himself. The pauses were too long; the
indications of remote meaning were too significant to be well understood. The spectator was big with expectation of seeing some
extraordinary means employed : but the general result did not

correspond to the waste of preparation. In a subsequent part, Mr. Kean did not give to the reply of Lear, 'Aye, every inch a king!' —the same vehemence and emphasis that Mr. Booth did; and in this he was justified: for, in the text, it is an exclamation of indignant irony, not of conscious superiority; and he immediately adds with deep disdain, to prove the nothingness of his pretensions—

> 'When I do stare, see how the subject quakes.'

Almost the only passage in which Mr. Kean obtained his usual heart-felt tribute, was in his interview with Cordelia, after he awakes from sleep, and has been restored to his senses.

> 'Pray, do not mock me:
> I am a very foolish fond old man,
> Fourscore and upward; and to deal plainly,
> I fear, I am not in my perfect mind.
> Methinks, I should know you, and know this man;
> Yet I am doubtful; for I'm mainly ignorant
> What place this is; and all the skill I have
> Remembers not these garments; nay, I know not
> Where I did lodge last night. *Do not laugh at me,*
> *For, as I am a man, I think this lady*
> *To be my child Cordelia.*
>   *Cordelia.* And so I am; I am.'

In uttering the last words, Mr. Kean staggered faintly into Cordelia's arms, and his sobs of tenderness, and his ecstasy of joy commingled, drew streaming tears from the brightest eyes,

> 'Which sacred pity had engender'd there.'

Mr. Rae was very effective in the part of Edgar, and was received with very great applause. If this gentleman could rein in a certain 'false gallop' in his voice and gait, he would be a most respectable addition, from the spirit and impressiveness of his declamation, to the general strength of any theatre, and we heartily congratulate him on his return to Drury-lane.—Mrs. West made an interesting representative of Cordelia. In all parts of plaintive tenderness, she is an excellent actress. We could have spared the love-scenes—and one of her lovers, Mr. Hamblin. Mr. Holland was great in Gloster. In short, what is he not great in, that requires a great deal of sturdy prosing, an 'honest, sonsy, bawzont face,' and a lamentably broken-down, hale, wholesome, hearty voice, that seems 'incapable of its own distress?' We like his jovial, well-meaning way of going about his parts. We can afford, out of his good cheer, and lively aspect, and his manner of bestriding the stage, to be made melancholy by

him at any time, without being a bit the worse for it. Mr. Dowton's
Kent was not at all good : it was a downright discarded serving-man.
Mr. Russel, in the absence of the Fool, played the zany in the
Steward.   The tragedy was, in general, got up better than we
expected.

Artaxerxes.—We believe that this is the most beautiful opera in
the world, though we have great authorities against us : but we do
not believe, that it is better acted now than it ever was, though we
have no less an authority for us, were we disposed to be of that
opinion, than the Manager himself.   The *Cognoscenti,* he tells us,
hold that this Musical Drama was never so got up before as it is at
present ; *viz.*, by Mr. Braham, Mr. Incledon, Miss Carew, and the
pretty little Madame Vestris.   There is no degree of excellence,
however high, with which this Opera could be played, that we should
not hail with delight ; and we would at any time go ten miles on foot,
only to see it played as we formerly did.   The time we allude to, was
when Miss Stephens first came out in Mandane, when Miss Rennell
(who is since dead) played Artaxerxes, when Mr. Incledon played
the same part he does still, better than he does at present, when Miss
Carew was the fair Semira, who listens no less delightfully than she
sings, and some one (we forget who) played Arbaces, not very well.
As to Mr. Braham, he was not there, nor was he wanted ;—for we
prefer the music of Arne, to Mr. Braham's, and Mr. Braham willingly gives us none but his own.   He has omitted some of the most
exquisite airs in Artaxerxes to introduce others of his own composing ;
—and where he has not done this, he might as well, for he so over-
loads, embellishes, accompanies, and flourishes over the original songs
that one would hardly know them again.   Can anything be more
tantalising than to hear him sing 'Water parted from the sea ?'
Instead of one continued stream of plaintive sound, labouring from
the heart with fond emotion, and still murmuring as it flows, it was
one incessant exhibition of frothy affectation and sparkling pretence ;
as if the only ambition of the singer, and the only advantage he could
derive from the power and flexibility of his voice, was to run away
at every opportunity from the music and the sentiment.   Does
Mr. Braham suppose that the finest pieces of composition were only
invented, and modulated into their faultless perfection, for him to
play tricks with, to make *ad libitum* experiments of his powers of
execution upon them, and to use the *score* of the musician only as the
rope-dancer does his rope, to vault up and down on,—to shew off his
pirouettes and his summersaults, and to perform feats of impossibility ?
This celebrated person's favourite style of singing is like bad Opera-
dancing, of which not grace, but trick is the constant character.   So

DRAMATIC ESSAYS

Mr. Braham's object is not to please but astonish his hearers—to do what is difficult and absurd, not what is worth doing—to unfold the richness, depth, sweetness, and variety of his tones, not to touch the chords of sentiment. In fact, it is the essence of all perverted art, to display art, and carry itself to the opposite extreme from nature, lest it should be mistaken for her, instead of returning back to and identifying itself as much as possible with nature (both as means and end) that they may seem inseparable, and no one discern the difference. The accomplished singer, whom we are criticising, too often puts himself in the place of his subject. He mistakes the object of the public. We do not go to the theatre to admire him, to hear him *tune* his voice like an instrument for sale. We go to be delighted with certain 'concords of sweet sounds,' which strike certain springs in unison in the human breast. These things are found united in nature, and in the works of the greatest masters, such as Arne and Mozart. What they have joined together, why will Mr. Braham put asunder? Why will he pour forth, for instance, as in this very song which he murdered, a volume of sound in one note, like the deep thunder, or the loud water-fall, and in the next, without any change of circumstance, try to thrill the ear by an excess of the softest and most voluptuous effeminacy? There is no reason why he should—but that he *can*, and is allowed to do so. Mr. Braham, we know, complains that the fault is not in his own taste, but in the vitiated ear of the town which he is obliged (much against his will) to pamper with trills, quavers, crotchets, *falsetios*, *bravuras*, and all the idle brood of affectation and sickly sensibility. He might have been taught a lesson to the contrary, a year or two ago, when he sung with Miss Stephens at Covent-Garden; and never surely was the difference of two styles more marked, or the triumph of good taste over bad more complete. Mr. Braham could not plead want of skill, of power, of practice: it was the difference of style only; and Miss Stephens's simple, artless manner, gave nothing but pure pleasure, while Mr. Braham's ornamental, laboured, complicated, or tortured execution, excited feelings of mingled astonishment, regret, and disappointment. There is Miss Tree again, who is another instance. What is it that gives such a superiority to her singing? Nothing but its truth, its seriousness, its sincerity. She has no capricios, plays no fantastic tricks; but seems as much in the power, at the mercy of the composer, as a musical instrument: her lips transmit the notes she has by heart, as the Æolian harp is stirred by the murmuring wind; and her voice seems to brood over, and become enamoured of the sentiment. But simplicity, we believe, will not do alone without sentiment, and we suspect Mr. Braham of a want of

452

sentiment. He apparently sings, as far as the passion is concerned, from the marginal directions, *con furio, con strepito, adagio,* etc., which are but indifferent helps to expression; and where a performer cannot fasten instinctively on the sympathy of his hearers, he has no better resource than to make an appeal to their wonder. To confess the extent of our insensibility, or our prejudice, we do not admire Mr. Braham's 'Mild as the moonbeams,' which is in his most lisping and languishing, nor his 'Wallace,' which is in his most heroic manner. What we like best, is his Oratorio style of singing, and that is the most manly, the most direct, and the least an abuse of the great powers which both Nature and Art have given to him. Having said so much of Mr. Braham, we will say nothing of Mr. Incledon. Miss Carew, as Mandane, warbled like a nightingale, and held her head on one side like a peacock; of Madame Vestris, we repeat that she is pretty. Indeed, we liked her the best of the four.

T.

No. VII

[*July*, 1820.

The Drama is a subject of which we could give a very entertaining account once a month, if there were no plays acted all the year. But, as some artists have said of Nature, 'the Theatres put us out.' The only article we have written on this matter that has given us entire satisfaction—(we answer, be it observed, for nobody but ourselves)—is the one we wrote in the winter, when, in consequence of two great public calamities, the theatres were closed for some weeks together. We seized that lucky opportunity, to take a peep into the raree-show of our own fancies,—the moods of our own minds, —and a very pretty little kaleidoscope it made. Our readers, we are sure, remember the description. Our head is stuffed full of recollections on the subject of the Drama, some of older, some of later date, but all treasured up with more or less fondness; we, in short, love it, and what we love, we can talk of for ever. We love it as well as Mr. Weathercock loves maccaroni; as Mr. Croker loves the Quarterly Review, and the Quarterly Review the Edinburgh; as Kings love Queens; and Scotchmen love their country. But, as happens in some of these instances, we love it best at a distance. We like to be a hundred miles off from the Acted Drama in London, and to get a friend (who may be depended on) to give an account of it for us; which we read, at our leisure, under the shade of a clump of lime-trees. What is the use indeed of coming to town, merely to

DRAMATIC ESSAYS

discover that Mr. Elliston is 'fat, fair, and forty,' and becomes silk hose worse than fleecy hosiery?

'Odious, in *satin*! 'Twould a saint provoke!'

We had rather stay where we are, and think how young, how genteel, how sprightly Lewis was at seventy! Garrick too was fat and pursy; but who ever perceived it through that airy soul of his, that life of mind, that bore him up 'like little wanton boys that swim on bladders?' Or why should we take coach to prevent our friend and coadjutor, of the whimsical name,—that Bucolical Juvenile, the Sir Piercie Shafton of the London Magazine,—from carrying off his Mysie Happer, the bewitching Miss Brunton, from our critical advances, and forestalling our praises of the grey twinkling eyes, the large white teeth, and querulous catechising voice of this accomplished little rustic? We shall leave him in full possession of his prize;— she shall be his *Protection*, and he shall be her *Audacity*: but we cannot consent to give up to his agreeable importunity our right and interest in the Miss Dennetts—the fair, the 'inexpressive three.' We will not erase their names from our pages, but twine them in cypher, as they are 'written in our heart's tables,'—though they do not dance at the Opera! We have not this gentleman's exquisitely happy knack in the geography of criticism: nor do we carry a map of London in our pockets to make out an exact scale of merit and *virtù*; nor judge of black eyes, a white cheek, and so forth, by the bills of mortality. We do not hate pathos because it is found in the Borough; our taste (such as it is) can cross the water, by any of the four bridges, in search of spirit and nature; we can make up our minds to beauty even at Whitechapel! Our friend and correspondent, Janus, grieves and wonders at this. He asks us why we do not express his sentiments instead of our own? and we answer, 'It is because we are not you.' He runs away from vulgar places and people, as from the plague; swoons at the mention of the Royal Cobourg; mimics his barber's pronunciation of *Ashley's*; and is afraid to trust himself at Sadler's Wells, lest his clothes should be covered with gingerbread, and spoiled with the smell of gin and tobacco. Now we, in our turn, laugh at all this. We are never afraid of being confounded with the vulgar; nor is our time taken up in thinking of what is ungenteel, and persuading ourselves that we are mightily superior to it. The gentlemen in the gallery, in Fielding's time, thought every thing *low*; and our friend, Mr. Weathercock, presents his compliments to us, and tells us we are wrong in condescending to any thing beneath 'Milanie's foot of fire.' We have no notion of condescending in any thing we write about: we seek for

454

truth and beauty wherever we can find them, and think that with these we are safe from contamination. 'Entire affection scorneth nicer hands.' Our comparative negligence, in this respect, probably arises from the difference that exists between our dress and that of our correspondent. A good judge has said, 'a man's mind is parcel of his fortunes,'—and a man's taste is part of his dress. If we wore 'diamond rings on our fingers, antique cameos in our breast-pins, cambric pocket-handkerchiefs breathing forth Attargul, and pale lemon-coloured kid gloves,' our perceptions might be strangely altered. We might then think Mr. Young 'the perfect gentleman both on and off the stage,' and consider Mr. Jones's 'cut-steel watch chain quite refreshing.' As it is, we differ from him on most of the above points. Yet, for any thing we see to the contrary, we might safely have staid in the country another month, and deputed the modern Euphuist, as our tire-man of the theatre, to adjust Mr. Kemble's boots, to tie on Mr. Abbott's sash to his liking, to dry Miss Stephens's bonnet, and dye Miss Tree's stockings any colour but blue :—but we heard from good authority that there was a new tragedy worth seeing, and also that it was written by an old friend of ours. *That* there was no resisting. So 'we came, saw, and were satisfied.'—Virginius is a good play :—we repeat it. It is a real tragedy ; a sound historical painting. Mr. Knowles has taken the facts as he found them, and expressed the feelings that would naturally arise out of the occasion. Strange to say, in this age of poetical egotism, the author, in writing his play, has been thinking of Virginius and his daughter, more than of himself ! This is the true imagination, to put yourself in the place of others, and to feel and speak for them. Our unpretending poet travels along the high road of nature and the human heart ; and does not turn aside to pluck pastoral flowers in primrose lanes, or hunt gilded butterflies over enamelled meads, breathless and exhausted ;—nor does he, with vain ambition, 'strike his lofty head against the stars.' So far indeed, he may thank the Gods for not having made him poetical. Some cold, formal, affected, and interested critics have not known what to make of this. It was not what *they* would have done. One finds fault with the style as poor, because it is not inflated. Another can see nothing in it, because it is not interlarded with modern metaphysical theories, unknown to the ancients. A third declares that it is all borrowed from Shakspear, because it is true to nature. A fourth pronounces it a superior kind of melodrame, because it pleases the public. The two last things to which the dull and envious ever think of attributing the success of any work (and yet the only ones to which genuine success is attributable), are Genius and Nature. The one they hate, and of the other they are ignorant. The same critics who despise and slur the Virginius of Covent Garden, praise the Virginius and the David Rizzio of Drury Lane, because (as it should appear) there is nothing in *them* to rouse their dormant spleen, stung equally by merit or success, and to mortify their own ridiculous, inordinate, and hopeless vanity. Their praise is of a piece with their censure; and equally from what they applaud and what they condemn, you perceive the principle of their perverse judgments. They are soothed with flatness and failure, and doat over them with parental fondness; but what is above their strength, and demands their admiration, they shrink from with loathing, and an oppressive sense of their own imbecility: and what they dare not openly condemn, they would willingly secrete from the public ear! We have described this class of critics more than once, but they breed still: all that we can do is to sweep them from our path as often as we meet with them, and to remove their dirt and cobwebs as fast as they proceed from the same noisome source. Besides the merits of Virginius as a literary composition, it is admirably adapted to the stage. It presents a succession of pictures. We might suppose each scene almost to be copied from a beautiful bas-relief, or to have formed a group on some antique vase. ''Tis the taste of the ancients, 'tis classical lore.' But it is a speaking and a living picture we are called upon to witness. These figures so strikingly, so simply, so harmoniously combined, start into life and action, and breathe forth words, the soul of passion—inflamed with anger, or melting with tenderness. Several passages of great beauty were cited in a former article on this subject; but we might mention in addition, the fine imaginative apostrophe of Virginius to his daughter, when the story of her birth is questioned:

> 'I never saw you look so like your mother
> In all my life '—

the exquisite lines ending,

> . . . 'The lie
> Is most unfruitful then, that makes the flower—
> The very flow'r our bed connubial grew
> To prove its barrenness '——

or the sudden and impatient answer of Virginius to Numitorius, who asks if the slave will swear Virginia is her child—

> 'To be sure she will ! Is she not his slave ?'

or again, the dignified reply to his brother, who reminds him it is time to hasten to the Forum,

> 'Let the Forum wait for us !'

This is the true language of nature and passion; and all that we can wish for, or require, in dramatic writing. If such language is not poetical, it is the fault of poets, who do not write as the heart dictates! We have seen plays that produced much more tumultuous applause; none scarcely that excited more sincere sympathy. There were no clap-traps, no sentiments that were the understood signals for making a violent uproar; but we heard every one near us express heartfelt and unqualified approbation; and tears more precious supplied the place of loud huzzas. Each spectator appeared to appeal to, and to judge from the feelings of his own breast, not from vulgar clamour; and we trust the success will be more lasting and secure, as its foundations are laid in the deep and proud humility of nature. Mr. Knowles owes every thing, that an author can owe, to the actors; and they owed every thing to their attention to truth and to real feeling. Mr. Macready's Virginius is his best and most faultless performance,—at once the least laboured and the most effectual. His fine, manly voice sends forth soothing, impassioned tones, that seem to linger round, or burst with terrific grandeur from the home of his heart. Mr. Kemble's Icilius was heroic, spirited, fervid, the Roman warrior and lover; and Miss Foote was 'the freeborn Roman maid,' with a little bit, a delightful little bit, of the English school-girl in her acting. We incline to the *ideal* of our own country-women after all, when they are so young, so innocent, so handsome. We are both pleased and sorry to hear a report which threatens us with the loss of so great a favourite; and one chief source of our regret will be, that she will no longer play Virginia. The scenery allotted to this tragedy encumbered the stage, and the simplicity of the play. Temples and pictured monuments adorned the scene, which were not in existence till five hundred years after the date of the story; and the ruins of the Capitol, of Constantine's arch, and the temple of Jupiter Stator, frowned at once on the death of Virginia, and the decline and fall of the Roman empire. As to the dresses, we leave them to our deputy of the wardrobe; but, we believe, they were got right at last, with some trouble. In the printed play, we observe a number of passages marked with inverted commas, which are omitted in the representation. This is the case almost uniformly wherever the words 'Tyranny,' or 'Liberty,' occur. Is this done by authority, or is it prudence in the author, '*lest the courtiers offended should be?*' Is the name of Liberty to be struck out of the English language, and are we not to hate tyrants even in an old Roman play? 'Let the galled jade wince: our withers are unwrung.' We turn to a pleasanter topic, and are glad to find an old and early friend unaltered in sentiment as he is unspoiled by success:—the same boy-poet, after a lapse of years, as when we first knew him; unconscious of the wreath he has woven round his brow, laughing and talking of his play just as if it had been written by any body else, and as simple-hearted, downright, and honest as the unblemished work he has produced ! [1]

We saw Mr. Kean at his benefit at the risk of our limbs, and are sorry for the accident that happened to himself in the course of the evening. We have longed ever since we saw Mr. Kean—that is, any time these six years—to see him jump through a trap-door— hearing he could do it. 'Why are those things hid? Is this a time to conceal virtues?' said we to ourselves. What was our disappointment, then, when on the point of this consummation of our wishes—just in the moment of the projection of our hopes—when dancing with Miss Valancy too, he broke the tendon Achilles, and down fell all our promised pleasure, our castles in the air! Good-reader, it was not the jump through the trap-door that we wished literally to see; but the leap from Othello to Harlequin. What a jump! What an interval, what a gulph to pass! What an elasticity of soul and body too—what a diversity of capacity in the same diminutive person! To be Othello, a man should be all passion, abstraction, imagination: to be Harlequin, he should have his wits in his heels, and in his fingers' ends! To be both, is impossible, or miraculous. Each doubles the wonder of the other; and in judging of the aggregate amount of merit, we must proceed, not by the rules of addition, but multiply Harlequin's lightness into Othello's gravity, and the result will give us the sum total of Mr. Kean's abilities. What a spring, what an expansive force of mind, what an untamed vigour, to rise to such a height from such a lowness; to tower like a Phoenix from its ashes; to ascend like a pyramid of fire! Why, what a complex piece of machinery is here; what an involution of faculties, circle within circle, that enables the same individual to make a summersault, and that swells the veins of his forehead with true artificial passion, and that turns him to a marble statue with thought! It is not being educated in the fourth form of St. Paul's school, or cast in the antique mould of the high Roman fashion, that can do this; but it is genius alone that can raise a man thus above his first origin, and make him thus various from himself! It is bestriding the microcosm of man like a Colossus, and, by uniting the extremes of the chain of being, seemingly implies all the intermediate links. We do not think much of Mr. Kean's singing: we could, with a little practice and tuition, sing nearly as well our-

[1] Generosity and simplicity are not the characteristic virtues of poets. It has been disputed whether 'an honest man is the noblest work of God.' But we think an honest poet is so.

selves : as for his dancing, it is but *so so*, and anybody can dance :
his fencing is good, nervous, firm, fibrous, like that of a new pocket
Hercules :—but for his jumping through a hole in the wall,—clean
through, head over heels, like a shot out of culverin—'by Heavens,
it would have been great !' This we fully expected at his hands,
and 'in this expectation we were baulked.' Just as our critical
expectations were on tip-toe, Mr. Kean suddenly strained his
ancle :—as it were to spite us ;—we went out in dudgeon, and were
near missing his Imitations, which would not have signified much if
we had. They were tolerable, indifferent, pretty good, but not the
thing. Mr. Matthews's or Mr. Yates's are better. They were
softened down, and fastidious. Kemble was not very like. Incledon
and Braham were the best, and Munden was very middling. The
after-piece of the Admirable Crichton, in which he was to do all
this, was neither historical nor dramatic. The character, which
might have given excellent opportunities for the display of a variety
of extraordinary accomplishments in the real progress of the story,
was ill-conceived and ill-managed. He was made either a pedagogue
or an antic. In himself, he was dull and grave, instead of being
high-spirited, volatile, and self-sufficient ; and to show off his abilities,
he was put into masquerade. We did not like it at all ; though, from
the prologue, we had expected more point and daring. Mr. Kean's
Jaffier was fine, and in some parts admirable. This indeed, is only
to say that he played it. But it was not one of his finest parts, nor
indeed one in which we expected him to shine pre-eminently : but
on that we had not depended, for we never know beforehand what he
will do best or worst. He is one of those wandering fires, whose
orbit is not calculable by any known rules of criticism. Mr.
Elliston's Pierre, was, we are happy to say, a spirited and effectual
performance. We must not forget to add that Mrs. M'Gibbon's
Belvidera was excellent, declaimed with impassioned propriety, and
acted with dignity and grace.

'And what of this new opera of David Rizzio, that the *New
Times* makes such a rout about ?'—Nothing. 'Nothing can come
of nothing.' We truly and strictly could not make a word of sense
of it. We wonder whose it can be. It is praised too in the
Chronicle ; but that is no matter. The story promised much ; the
music, the old Scotch tunes, more. They were both completely *trans-
mographied*,—they melted into thin air. The author set aside the
one, and the composers (of whom there are no less than five)
the other. This required some ingenuity. The plot turns altogether
upon this, that Rizzio (Braham) is supposed and made to be in love
with Lady Mary Livingstone (Miss Carew), and by warbling out

her Christian name in ballads in the open air, is imagined, by Darnley and the rest, to be in love with Mary, Queen of Scots (Mrs. West), from which strange misinterpretation all the mischief and confusion ensue. We fancy there is no foundation for this in tradition or old records. The author has indeed reversed the method of the writer of the Scotch Novels, for, instead of building as much as possible on facts and history, he has built as little as possible on them—and has produced just the contrary effect of the Great Unknown, that is, has spun a tissue of incidents and sentiments out of his own head, worth nothing, unmeaning, feeble, languid, disjointed, and for the most part, incomprehensible. Most of the scenes in the two first acts, consisted of the Exits and Entrances of single persons, who only appeared to deliver an introductory speech, and sing a song, and then vanished before any one else could come on to entrap them into a dialogue—a delicate evasion of the wily dramatist! Mr. Barnard repeated these Operatic soliloquies so often, as to be almost hissed off the stage, and Miss Povey (his sweetheart) by coming to his relief half a minute after he was gone, did not much mend the matter, either by the charms of her voice or person. This young lady is pretty, and sings agreeably enough, but we do not see what she can have to do with romantic sentiments or situations. Some of those in which she was placed, would require the utmost delicacy of the most accomplished heroine to carry them off without an obtrusive sense of impropriety. For instance, after warbling a ditty to the desert air of Holyrood House, she retires into a summer-house hard by, to keep an assignation with the persuasive Mr. Barnard, and is presently surprised and carried off, instead of the silver-voiced Carew, by a band of ruffians, who—on her making many exclamations, and repeating 'Oh! dear me!' and saying she only came to meet a young man—reply very laconically, 'Aye, you came to meet one young man, and now you have met with four—that's better!' In the last scene, the catastrophe is brought about by Rizzio's being discovered by the conspirators at a magnificent entertainment in the apartment of the Queen, which confirms their former suspicions and infuriates their revenge ; and he is hurried from her frantic embraces, which display all the tenderness of a mistress, rather than the attachment of a sovereign, to be despatched in the adjoining chamber. His assassins find their error too late, when, from the passionate declaration of Lady Mary Livingstone that she is his wife, they are convinced of his and the Queen's innocence. The lesson to be drawn from this fiction, seems to be, that ladies (whether Princesses or not) who defy opinion, must take the consequences of their infatuated self-indulgence, or involve others in ruin : for the presumption is, that no woman in her senses will risk her character, unless she has a further object in view, namely, to gratify her passions. This was not, however, the inference drawn by the generality of the audience; for several passages, construed in allusion to passing events, were loudly and triumphantly cheered. They, indeed, saved the piece from final and absolute damnation, for it drooped from the beginning, and to the end, and had no other interest than what arose from the occasional parallelism of political situations. Mr. Braham (as David Rizzio) disappointed us much. He sung the airs he had probably himself selected, without any affectation indeed—'softly sweet in Lydian measures'—but without any effect whatever upon our ears; he fell into simplicity and insipidity, plump together, ten thousand fathoms down. The other singers acquitted themselves very well, but there was nothing to excite an interest in itself, or to answer the previous expectations arising from the title of the piece. We had hoped to have been treated to some old Scotch airs, at least: but the joint-composers seemed to have a strong aversion to any thing connected with the sound of a bagpipe. This we suppose is a symptom of the progress of a more refined taste among us. The causes of our want of sympathy with it have been explained above. The piece has been repeated once or twice since.

Giovanni in London has been transferred to this theatre (Drury Lane) from the Olympic. It was a favourite with the town there; it has become a favourite with the town here. There is something in burlesque that pleases. We like to see the great degraded to a level with the little. The humour is extravagant and coarse, but it is certainly droll; and we never check our inclinations to laugh, when we have an opportunity given us. We have not laughed so heartily a long time, as at seeing the meddlesome lawyer tossed in a blanket in the King's Bench; and we should imagine there is a natural and inevitable connection between the performance of that gentle salutary mode of discipline, and the titillation of the lungs of the spectators. Madame Vestris played, sung, and looked the incorrigible Don John very prettily and spiritedly; but, we confess, we had rather see her petticoated than in a Spanish doublet and hose, hat and feather. Yet she gave a life to the scene, and Pluto relented as she sung. There is a pulpy softness and ripeness in her lips, a roseate hue, like the leaves of the damask rose, a luscious honeyed sound in her voice, a depth and fulness too, as if it were clogged with its own sweets, a languid archness, an Italian lustre in her eye, an enchanting smile, a mouth—shall we go on? No. But she is more bewitching even than Miss Brunton. Yet we like to see her best in petticoats. It cannot be denied that Mrs. Gould (late Miss Burrell)

461

of the Olympic, who played it first, was the girl to play Giovanni in London. She had a hooked nose, large staring eyes, a manlike voice, a tall person, a strut that became a rake.

> 'She forgot to be a woman : changed fear, and niceness,
> (The hand maids of all women, or more truly
>   Woman its pretty-self) into a waggish courage ;
> Ready in gibes, quick answered, saucy, and
>   As quarrellous as the weasel.'

All this Madame Vestris attempts ; but in spite of her efforts to the contrary, she shrinks back into feminine softness and delicacy, and her heart evidently fails her, and flutters, 'like a new ta'en sparrow,' in the midst of all her pretended swaggering and determination to brazen the matter out. On the night we saw this afterpiece, Mr. Knight played Leporello, instead of Mr. Harley : so that we can praise neither. L.

No. VIII

August, 1820.

It is now the middle of July, when we are by turns drenched with showers and scorched with sun-beams : the winter theatres are closed, and the summer ones have just opened, soon to close again—

> 'Like marigolds with the sun's eye.'

We are not, however, in the number of those who deprecate the shortness of the summer season, as one of the miseries of human life, or who think little theatres better than big. We like a play-house in proportion to the number of happy human faces it contains (and a play-house seldom contains many wretched ones)—and again we like a play best when we do not see the faces of the actors too near. We do not want to be informed, as at the little theatre in the Haymarket, that part of the rich humour of Mr. Liston's face arises from his having lost a tooth in front, nor to see Mr. Jones's eyes roll more meteorous than ever. At the larger theatres we only discover that the ladies paint red : at the smaller ones we can distinguish when they paint white. We see defects enough at a distance, and we can always get near enough (in the pit) to see the beauties. Those who go to the boxes do not go to see the play, but to make a figure, and be thought something of themselves (so far they probably succeed, at least in their own opinion) : and if the Gods cannot hear, they make themselves heard. We do not like *private theatricals.* We like every thing to be what it is. We

462

have no fancy for seeing the actors look like part of the audience, nor for seeing the pit invade the boxes, nor the boxes shake hands with the galleries. We are for a proper distinction of ranks—at the theatre. While we are laughing at the broad farcical humour of the Agreeable Surprise, or critically examining Mrs. Mardyn's dress in the Will, we do not care to be disturbed by some idle whisper, or mumbling disapprobation of an old beau, or antiquated dowager in a high head-dress, close at our ear, but in a different part of the house.—Mr. Arnold has taken care of this at the New English Opera-house in the Strand, of which he is proprietor and patentee. The 'Great Vulgar and the Small' (as Cowley has it) are there kept at a respectful distance. The boxes are perched up so high above the pit, that it gives you a head-ache to look up at the beauty and fashion that nightly adorn them with their thin and scattered constellations; and then the gallery is 'raised so high above all height,' it is nearly impossible for the eye to scale it, while a little miserable shabby upper-gallery is partitioned off with an iron railing, through which the poor one-shilling devils look like half-starved prisoners in the Fleet, and are a constant butt of ridicule to the genteeler rabble beneath them. Then again (so vast is Mr. Arnold's genius for separating and combining), you have a Saloon, a sweet pastoral retreat, where any love-sick melancholy swain, or romantic nymph, may take a rural walk to Primrose-hill, or Chalk-farm, by the side of painted purling streams, and sickly flowering shrubs, without once going out of the walls of the theatre:—

> 'Such tricks hath strong Imagination!'

If the Haymarket has been praised by a contemporary critic (of whom we might say, that he is *alter et idem*) for being as hot as an oven in the midst of the dog-days; the Lyceum, on the other hand, is as cool as a well; and much might, we think, be said on both sides. As a matter of taste, or fancy, or prejudice, (we shall not pretend to say which) we do not greatly like the new English Opera-house. The house is *new*, the pieces are *new*, the company are *new*, and we do not know what to make of any of them. As to the things that are acted there, they are a sort of pert, patched-up, insipid, flippant attempt at mediocrity. They are like the odd-ends and scraps of all the rejected pieces, which have come into the manager's possession in virtue of his office for a length of time; and which he has stitched and tacked together in such a way that neither the authors nor the public can know any thing of the matter. They are a condensed essence of all the vapid stuff that has been suppressed at home or acted abroad for a number of years last past. Visions of farces, operas, and interludes, thin, blue, fluttering, gawzy appearances, mock the empty sight, elude the public comprehension, and the critic's grasp. The worst of these slender, wire-drawn productions is, that there is nothing to praise in them, nor any thing to condemn. They 'present no mark' to friend or foe. 'You may as well take aim at the edge of a pen-knife,' as try to pick any thing out of them. They are trifling, tedious, frivolous, and vexatious. The best is, they do not last long, and 'one bubble' (to borrow an illusion from an eloquent divine, in treating on a graver subject) 'knocks another on the head, and both rush together into oblivion!'—Miss Kelly is here; she might as well be a hundred miles off. She is not good at child's play, at the *make-believe* fine-lady, or the *make-believe* waiting-maid. Hers is *bonâ fide* downright acting, and she must have something to do, in order to do it properly. She is too clever and too knowing to act a part totally without meaning, such as that lately given her in the Promissory Note. Such was not her Yarico. Ah! there were tones, and looks, and piercing sighs in her representation of the fond, injured, sun-burnt Indian maid, that make it difficult to think of her in any inferior part, or to speak slightingly of any theatre in which she is concerned: but critics, as it has been said of judges, must not give way to their feelings. There is Wrench here too, as easy as an old glove, the same careless, hair-brained, idle, impudent, good humoured, lackadaisical sort of a gentleman as ever; there is Harley too, who has not been spoiled by the town, since we first saw him here:—then there is Mr. Rowbotham, a grave young man, a new hand, very like the real, the prudent Mr. Thomas Inkle: *encore un coup*, we have Mr. Bartley, who, if not a new hand, is fresh returned from America, and as much at home on these boards as before he went abroad: in the Governor of Barbadoes, he had quite a Transatlantic look with him: there is also Mr. Westbourn (we think he is at this house) and a Mr. Wilkinson, and a Mr. Richardson (whose names and persons we are apt to confound together), and Mr. Pearman (whom it is not possible to mistake for any one else) and Miss Stevenson (a very provoking young thing), and Miss Love, and Mrs. Grove, and a whole *Sylva Critica* of actors and actresses, of whom the very nomenclature terrifies us. We give it up in despair: and so humbly take our leave of the New English Opera house for the season!—'We had rather be taxed for silence, than checked for speech.'

At the other house, to which we 'do more favourably incline,' both from old associations and immediate liking. though there are some raw recruits (picked up we don't know where), there is a large and powerful detachment from the veteran corps of Covent

Garden; Terry, Jones, Mrs. Gibbs, Liston, Mr. and Mrs. Charles Kemble, J. Russel, Farley, and Mrs. Mardyn and Madame Vestris from Drury-Lane, and last, Miss R. Corri, from the Opera House. —In fact, it is our opinion that there is theatrical strength enough in this town only to set up one good summer or one good winter theatre. Competition may be necessary to prevent negligence and abuse, but the result of this distribution of the *corps dramatique* into different companies, is, that we never, or very rarely indeed, see a play well acted in all its parts. At Drury-Lane there is only one tragic actor, Mr. Kean: all the rest are supernumeraries. No one, we apprehend, would ever cross the threshold to see Mr. Pope's Iago, or Mr. Elliston's Richmond, or Mr. Rae's Bassanio, or Mr. Hamblin, or Mr. Penley, or Mr. Fisher, or Mr. Philips, who plays the King in Hamlet: though, 'in the catalogue they go for actors.' In comedy, Drury-Lane is better off: yet, they cannot get up a real sterling comedy, for want of actors and actresses to fill the parts of *gentlemen* and *ladies*. Miss Kelly is the best comic actress on either stage, but she is only an appendage to the real fine lady, Millamant's Mrs. Mincing, 'to curl her hair so crisp and pure': in cases of necessity, they have no one but Mr. Penley, jun. to top the part of Lord Foppington: Mr. Munden is their Sir Peter Teazle, and Mr. Elliston is his own Lord Townley. But they really hit off a modern comedy, such as Wild Oats, which is a mixture of farce and romantic sentiment, to an exact perfection. At Covent-Garden they lately had one great tragic actress, Miss O'Neill; and two or three actors who were highly respectable, at least in second-rate tragic characters. At present, the female throne in tragedy is vacant; and of the men 'who rant and fret their hour upon the stage,' Mr. Macready is the only one who draws houses, or who finds admirers. He shines most, however, in the pathos of domestic life; and we still want to see tragedy, 'turretted, crowned, and crested, with its front gilt, and blood-stained,' stooping from the skies (not raised from the earth) as it did in the person of John Kemble. He is now quaffing health and burgundy in the south of France. He perhaps finds the air that blows from the 'vine-covered hills' wholesomer than that of a crowded house; and the lengthened murmurs of the Mediterranean shores more soothing to the soul, than the deep thunders of the pit. Or does he sometimes recline his lofty, laurelled head upon the sea-beat beach, and unlocking the cells of memory, listen to the rolling Pæans, the loud never-to-be-forgotten plaudits of enraptured multitudes, that mingle with the music of the waves,

'And murmur as the Ocean murmurs near?'

Or does he still 'sigh his soul towards England' and the busy hum of Covent-Garden? If we thought so, (but that we dread all returns from Elba) we would say to him, 'Come back, and once more bid Britannia rival old Greece and Rome!'—Or where is Mr. Young now? There is an opening for *his* pretensions too.—If the Drury-Lane company are deficient in genteel comedy, we fear that Covent-Garden cannot help them out in this respect. Mr. W. Farren is the only exception to the sweeping clause we were going to insert against them. He plays the old gentleman, the antiquated beau of the last age, very much after the fashion that we remember to have seen in our younger days, and that is quite a singular excellence in this. Is it that Mr. Farren has caught glimpses of this character in real life, hovering in the horizon of the sister kingdom, which has been long banished from this? They have their Castle Rack-rents, their moats and ditches, still extant in remote parts of the interior: and perhaps in famed Dublin city, the *cheveux-de-fris* of dress, the trellis-work of lace and ruffles, the masked battery of compliment, the port-cullises of formal speech, the whole artillery of sighs and ogling, with all the appendages and proper costume of the ancient regime, and paraphernalia of the *preux chevalier*, may have been kept up in a state of lively decrepitude and smiling dilapidation, in a few straggling instances from the last century, which Mr. Farren had seen. The present age produces nothing of the sort; and so, according to our theory, Mr. Farren does not play the young gentleman or modern man of fashion, though he is himself a young man. For the rest, comedy is in a rich, thriving state at Covent-Garden, as far as the lower kind of comic humour is concerned; but it is like an ill-baked pudding, where all the plums sink to the bottom. Emery and Liston, the two best, are of this description: Jones is a caricaturist; and Terry, in his graver parts, is not a comedian, but a moralist.—Even a junction of the two companies into one would hardly furnish out one set of players competent to do justice to any of the standard productions of the English stage in tragedy or comedy: what a hopeful project it must be then to start a few more play-houses in the heart of the metropolis as nurseries of histrionic talent, still more to divide and dissipate what little concentration of genius we have, and still more to weaken and distract public patronage? As to the argument in favour of two or more theatres from the necessity of competition, we shall not dispute it; but the actual benefits are not so visible to our dim eyes as to some others. There is a competition in what is bad as well as in what is good: the race of popularity is as often gained by tripping up the heels of your antagonist, as by pressing forward yourself: there is a com-

466

petition in running an indifferent piece, or a piece indifferently acted, to prevent the success of the same piece at the other house; and there is a competition in puffing, as Mr. Elliston can witness.—No, there we confess, he leaves all competition behind!

The two pleasantest pieces we have seen this season at the Haymarket are the Green Man, and Pigeons and Crows. They were both to us an Agreeable Surprise; for we had not seen them when they were brought out last year, or the year before. The first is moral and pointed; the latter more lively and quaint. The Green Man abounds in laconic good sense: in Pigeons and Crows there is as edifying a vein of nonsense. We do not know the author of this last piece (to whom we confess ourselves obliged for two mirthful, thoughtless evenings), but we understand that the Green Man is adapted by Mr. Jones from a French *petite pièce*, which was itself taken from a German novel, we believe one of Kotzebue's. The sentiments indeed are evidently of that romantic, levelling cast, which formerly abounded in the writings of the *ci-devant* philanthropic enthusiast. The principal character in it is that of the Green Man himself, who is a benevolent, blunt-spoken, friendly cynic. The only joke of the character consists in his being dressed all in green— he has a green coat, a green waistcoat and breeches, green stockings, a green hat, a green pocket handkerchief, and a green watch. This gives rise to many pleasant allusions; and indeed, from the manner in which the peculiarity of his personal appearance affects our notion of his personal identity, he looks like a talking suit of clothes, a sermonizing and sententious vegetable. Mr. Terry performs the part admirably, and seems himself transformed into 'a brother of the groves.' He does not aggravate the author's meaning too much, but gives just as much point as was intended, and passes on to what comes next, as naturally, and with that sort of manner and unconscious interest which a man really takes in his own, or other people's affairs. Mr. Terry's acting always shows vigour and good sense. His only fault is, that he is too jealous of himself, and strives to do better than well. In the Green Man he was quite at home, and quite at his ease; and made every one else feel equally so. Mr. Jones is an overstarched French fop in this play, full of foreign grimace and affectation, of which, however, he is cured by his passion for the fair ward of the Green Man (Miss Leigh, a very pleasing new actress), who does not at all tolerate such impertinence, and he afterwards turns out (*dandyism* apart) a very good sort of a humane character. Perhaps, enough has never been made on the stage of the frequent contradiction in this respect between outside appearances and sterling qualities within. We carry our prejudices both for and against dress too far. It is no rule either way. A fop is not necessarily a fool, nor without feeling. A man may even wear stays, and not be effeminate; or a pink coat, without making his friends blush for him. The celebrated beau, Hervey, threw the scavenger that ridiculed him into his own mud-cart; and a person in our own time, who has carried extravagance of dress and appearance to a very great pitch indeed, is, in reality, a very good-natured, sensible, modest man. The fault, in such cases, is neither in the head nor heart, but in the cut of a coat-collar, or the size of a pair of whiskers.—Farley and J. Russell were Major Dumpling and Captain Bibber in the same piece: and a scene of high farce they made of it. The one is an officer in the army, the *local militia*; the other is an officer in the navy. The one excels in eating, the other in drinking. The one is most at home in the kitchen, the other in the cellar. The one is fat, huge, and unwieldy; the other, dapper, tight, and bustling. Farley is an actor with whose merit, in such parts, the public are well acquainted: Russel is one who will be liked more, the more he is known. Both in Captain Bibber, Blondeau, the French showman in Pigeons and Crows, and in Silvester Daggerwood, he has acquitted himself with great applause, and entered into the humour, eccentricity, and peculiar distinctions of his characters, with spirit and fidelity. His mimicry is also good, and he sings a French rondeau, or a sailor's ditty, *con amore*. The part of Major Dumpling was originally played by Mr. Tokely. It was one of three parts (Crockery and Peter Pastoral were the other two) for which he seemed born, and having rolled himself up in them, like the silk-worm, he died. Poor Tokely! He relished his parts; with Crockery doated over an old sign-post, or wept with honest Peter over a green leaf.

> 'His tears were tears of oil and gladness.'

But he also relished his morning's draught, and sipped the sweets till he was drowned in a butt of whiskey. The said fair-looking, round-faced, pot-bellied, uncouth, awkward, out-of-the-way, unmeaning, inimitable Crockery, or Peter Pastoral, or Major Dumpling, was the very little child that, in the year 1796, Kemble used to carry off triumphantly on his arm in the original performance of Pizarro! Thinking of these things, may we not say, *sic transit gloria mundi*? So flies the stage away, and life flies after it as fast!—Mrs. Gibbs, 'that horse-whipping woman,' in Teazing made Easy, does not, however, wear the willow on his account, but looks as smiling, as good-humoured, as buxom, as in the natural and professional life-time of Mr. Tokely, and drinks her bowl of cream as Cowslip, and expresses her liking of a roast-duck with the same resignation of flesh and spirit as ever.

Mr. Liston in Pigeons and Crows plays the part of Sir Peter Pigwiggin, knight, alderman, and pin-maker. What a name, what a person, and what a representative! We never saw Mr. Liston's countenance in better preservation; that is, it seems tumbling all in pieces with indescribable emotions, and a thousand odd twitches, and unaccountable absurdities, oozing out at every pore. His jaws seem to ache with laughter: his eyes look out of his head with wonder: his face is unctuous all over and bathed with jests; the tip of his nose is tickled with conceit of himself, and his teeth chatter in his head in the eager insinuation of a plot: his forehead speaks, and his wig (not every particular hair, but the whole bewildered bushy mass) 'stands on end as life were in it.' In the scene with his dulcinea (Miss Leigh) his approaches are the height of self-complacent, *cockney* courtship; his rhymes on his own projected marriage,

> 'What a thing!
> Bless the King!'

would make any man (who is not so already) loyal, and his laughing in the glass when he is told by mistake that Miss's mamma is eighteen, and his convulsive distortions as he recovers from his first surprise, and the choking effects of it, out-Hogarth Hogarth!

> 'Let those laugh now who never laugh'd before,
> And those who still have laugh'd, now laugh the more.'

The scene where he is told he is poisoned, and his interview with the drunken apothecary (Mr. Williams), though excellent in themselves, were not so good: for Liston does not play so well to any one else, as he does to himself. The rest of the characters were well supported. Jones, as the younger Pigwiggin, alias Captain Neville, the lover of Liston's fair inamorata, 'does a little bit of fidgets' very well. He is sprightly, voluble, knowing, and pleasant; and is the life of a small theatre, only that he is now and then a little too obstreperous; but he keeps up the interest of his part, and that is every thing. The audience delight to hear his 'View Halloa' before he comes on the stage (which is a sure sign of their opinion), and expect to be amused for the next ten minutes. If an actor can excite hope, and not disappoint it, what can he do more? Mr. Russell, as the little French showman, Mr. Farley as Mr. Wadd, and Mr. Connor as a blundering Irish servant, all sustained their parts with great eclat: and so did the ladies. The scene where Jones deceives two of his creditors, Russell and Farley, by appointing each to pay the other, had a very laughable effect ; but the stratagem is borrowed from Congreve, who indeed was not the very worst source to borrow from.

The house was crowded to excess to see the new appearances in the Beggar's Opera; Madame Vestris's Captain Macheath, Miss R. Corri's Polly, and Mrs. Charles Kemble's Lucy, which last, indeed, is an old friend with a new face. Mrs. Kemble was the best Lucy we ever saw (not excepting Miss Kelly, who is also much at home in this part), and she retains all the spirit of her original performances. Miss Kelly plays Lucy as naturally, perhaps more so ; but Mrs. Kemble does it more characteristically. She has no ' compunctious visitings' of delicacy, but her mind seems hardened against the walls that enclose it. She is Lockitt's daughter, the child of a prison ; the true virago, that is to be the foil to the gentle spirit of Polly. The air with which she throws the rat to the cat in the song has a *gusto* worthy of one of Michael Angelo's Sybils; a box on the ear from her right hand is no jesting matter. Her rage and sullenness are of the true unmitigated stamp, and her affected civilities to her fair rival are a parody (as the author intended) on the friend-ships of courts.—Madame Vestris, as the Captain, almost shrunk before her, like Viola before her enraged enemies. Indeed, she played the part very prettily, with great vivacity and an agreeable swagger, cocking her hat, throwing back her shoulders, and making a free use of a rattan-cane, like Little Pickle, but she did not look like the hero, or the highwayman, if this was desirable in her case. If, however, she turned Macheath into a *petit-maitre*, she did not play it like Mr. Incledon or Mr. Cooke, or Mr. Braham, or Mr. Young, or any one else we have seen in it, which is no small commendation. Miss Corri sang *Cease your funning*, and one or two other songs, with sweetness and effect; but, in general, she was more like a modern made-up boarding-school girl, than the artless and elegant Polly. She lisps and looks pretty. The other parts were very respectably filled, but some of the best scenes (we are sorry to say it) were left out.   T.

No. IX

[*September*, 1820.

DRURY LANE.—The following is a play-bill of this theatre, for which we paid two-pence on the spot, to verify the fact—as some well-disposed persons, to prevent mistakes, purchase libellous or blasphemous publications from their necessitous or desperate vendors.

Theatre Royal, Drury Lane.—Agreeably to the former advertisement, this theatre is now open for the last performances of Mr. Kean, before his positive departure for America. This evening, Saturday, August 19, 1820, his Majesty's servants will perform Shakespear's tragedy of Othello. Duke of Venice, Mr. Thompson; Brabantio, Mr. Powell; Gratiano, Mr. Carr; Lodovico, Mr. Vining; Montano, Mr. Jeffries; Othello, Mr. Kean—(his last appearance in that character); Cassio, Mr. Bromley—(his first appearance in that character); Roderigo, Mr. Russell; Iago, Junius Brutus Booth; Leonardo, Mr. Hudson; Julio, Mr. Raymond; Manco, Mr. Moreton; Paulo, Mr. Read; Giovanni, Mr. Starmer; Luca, Mr. Randall; Desdemona, Mrs. W. West; Emilia, Mrs. Egerton—This theatre overflows every night. The patentees cannot condescend to enter into a competition of scurrility which is only fitted for minor theatres—what their powers really are, will be, without any public appeal, legally decided in November next, and any gasconade can only be supposed to be caused by cunning or poverty.—After which, the farce of Modern Antiques, &c.

A more impudent puff, and heartless piece of bravado than this, we do not remember to have witnessed. *This theatre does not overflow every night.* As to the competition of scurrility, which the manager declines, it is he who has commenced it. The minor theatres—that is, one of them—to wit, the Lyceum—put forth a very proper and well-grounded remonstrance against this portentous opening of the winter theatre in the middle of the dog-days, to scorch up the dry, meagre, hasty harvest of the summer ones:—at which our mighty manager sets up his back, like the great cat, Rodilardus; scornfully rejects their appeal to the public; says he will pounce upon them in November with the law in his hands; and that, in the mean time, all they can do to interest the public in their favour by a plain statement of facts, ' can only be supposed to be caused by *cunning* or *poverty*.' This is pretty well for a manager who has been so *thanked* as Mr. Elliston! His own committee may laud him for bullying other theatres, but the public will have a feeling for his weaker rivals, though the angry comedian ' should threaten to swallow them up quick,' and vaunt of his action of battery against them, without any public appeal, ' when wind and rain beat dark November down.' This sorry manager, ' dressed ' (to use the words of the immortal bard, whom he so modestly and liberally patronises) ' dressed in a little brief authority, plays such fantastic tricks before high Heaven,' —not ' as make the angels weep,'—but his own candle-snuffers laugh, and his own scene-shifters blush. He ought to be ashamed of himself. Why, what a beggarly account of wretched actors, what an exposure of the nakedness of the land, have we in this very play-bill, which is issued forth with such a mixture of pomp and imbecility! Mr. Kean's name, indeed, stands pre-eminent in lordly capitals, in defiance of Mr. Dowton's resentment,—and Junius Brutus Booth, in his way, scorns to be *Mistered*! But all the rest are, we suppose—Mr. Elliston's friends. They are happy in the favour of the manager, and in the total ignorance of the town! Mr. Kean, we grant, is in himself a host; a sturdy column, supporting the tottering, tragic dome of Drury-Lane! What will it be when this main, this sole striking pillar is taken away—'You take my house, when you do take the prop that holds my house'—when the patentees shall have nothing to look to for salvation but the puffing of the Great Lessee, and his genius for law, which we grant may rival the Widow Black-acre's— and when the cries of Othello, of Macbeth, of Richard, and Sir Giles, in the last agonies of their despair, shall be lost, through all the long winter months, 'over a vast and unhearing ocean?' Mr. Elliston, instead of taking so much pains to announce his own approaching dissolution, had better let Mr. Kean pass in silence, and take his *positive departure for America* without the pasting of placards, and the dust and clatter of a law-suit in Westminster Hall. It is not becoming in him, W. R. Elliston, Esq., comedian, formerly pro- prietor of the Surrey and the Olympic, and author of a pamphlet on the unwarrantable encroachments of the Theatres-royal, now to insult over the plea of self-defence and self-preservation, set up by his brethren of the minor play-houses, as the resource of 'poverty and cunning!'—'It is not friendly, it is not gentlemanly. The profession, as well as Mr. Arnold, may blame him for it:' but the patentees will no doubt thank him at their next quarterly meeting.

Mr. Kean's Othello the other night did not quite answer our over-wrought expectations. He played it *with variations*; and therefore, necessarily worse. There is but one perfect way of playing Othello, and that was the way in which he used to play it. To see him in this character at his best, may be reckoned among the consolations of the human mind. It is to feel our hearts bleed by sympathy with another; it is to vent a world of sighs for another's sorrows; to have the loaded bosom 'cleansed of that perilous stuff that weighs upon the soul,' by witnessing the struggles and the mortal strokes that 'flesh is heir to.' We often seek this deliverance from private woes through the actor's obstetric art; and it is hard when he disappoints us, either from indifference or wilfulness. Mr. Kean did not repeat his admired farewell apostrophe to Content, with that fine 'organ-stop' that he used,—as if his inmost vows and wishes were ascending to the canopy of Heaven, and their sounding echo were heard upon the earth like distant thunder,—but in a querulous, whining, sobbing tone, which we do not think right. Othello's spirit

472

does not sink under, but supports itself on the retrospect of the past; and we should hear the lofty murmurs of his departing hopes, his ambition and his glory, borne onward majestically 'to the passing wind.' He pronounced the 'not a jot, not a jot,' as an hysteric exclamation, not with the sudden stillness of fixed despair. As we have seen him do this part before, his lips uttered the words, but they produced and were caused by no corresponding emotion in his breast. They were breath just playing on the surface of his mind, but that did not penetrate to the soul. His manner of saying to Cassio, 'But never more be officer of mine,' was in a tone truly terrific, magnificent, prophetic; and the only alteration we remarked as an improvement. We have adverted to this subject here, because we think Mr. Kean cannot wisely outdo himself. He is always sufficiently original, sufficiently in extremes, and when he attempts to vary from himself, and go still farther, we think he has no alternative but to run into extravagance. It is true it may be said of him that he is—

> ' Never so sure our passion to create,
> As when he treads the brink of all we hate—'

but still one step over the precipice is destruction. We also fear that the critical soil of America is slippery ground. Jonathan is inclined to the safe side of things, even in matters of taste and fancy. They are a little formal and common-place in those parts. They do not like liberties in morals, nor excuse poetical licenses. They do not tolerate the privileges of birth, or readily sanction those of genius. A very little excess above the water-mark of mediocrity is with them quite enough. Mr. Kean will do well not to offend by extraordinary efforts, or dazzling eccentricities. He should be the Washington of actors, the modern Fabius. If he had been educated in the fourth form of St. Paul's school, like some other top-tragedians that we know, we should say to him, in classic terms, *in medio tutissimus ibis.* ' Remember that they hiss the Beggar's Opera in America. If they do not spare Captain Macheath, do you think they will spare you? Play off no pranks in the United States. Do not think to redeem great vices by great virtues. They are inexorable to the one, and insensible to the other. Reserve all works of supererogation till you come back, and have safely run the gauntlet of New York, of Philadelphia, of Baltimore, and Boston. Think how Mr. Young would act,—and act with a little more meaning, and a little less pomp than he would—who, we are assured on credible authority, is that model of indifference that the New World would worship and bow down before.'—We have made bold to offer this advice, because we wish well to Mr. Kean; and because we wish to think as well as

possible of a republican public. We watch both him and them
' with the rooted malice of a friend.' We have thus paid our respects
to Old Drury in holiday-time; and thought we had already taken
leave of the New English Opera-House for the season. But there
were Two Words to that bargain. The farce with this title is a
very lively little thing, worth going to see; and the new Dramatic
Romance (or whatever it is called) of the Vampyre is, upon the
whole, the most splendid *spectacle* we have ever seen. It is taken
from a French piece, founded on the celebrated story so long bandied
about between Lord Byron, Mr. Shelley, and Dr. Polidori, which
last turned out to be the true author. As a mere fiction, and as a
fiction attributed to Lord Byron, whose genius is chartered for the
land of horrors, the original story passed well enough: but on the
stage it is a little shocking to the feelings, and incongruous to the
sense, to see a spirit in human shape,—in the shape of a real Earl,
and, what is more, of a *Scotch* Earl—going about seeking whom it
may marry and then devour, to lengthen out its own abhorred and
anomalous being. Allowing for the preternatural atrocity of the
fable, the situations were well imagined and supported: the acting of
Mr. T. P. Cooke (from the Surry Theatre) was spirited and imposing, and certainly Mrs. W. H. Chatterley, as the daughter of his
friend the Baron, (Mr. Bartley), and his destined bride, bid fair to be
a very delectable victim. She is however saved in a surprizing
manner, after a rapid succession of interesting events, to the great joy
of the spectator. The scenery of this piece is its greatest charm, and
it is inimitable. We have seen sparkling and overpowering effects of
this kind before; but to the splendour of a transparency were here
added all the harmony and mellowness of the finest painting. We
do not speak of the vision at the beginning, or of that at the end of
the piece,—though these were admirably managed,—so much as of
the representation of the effects of moonlight on the water and on the
person of the dying knight. The hue of the sea-green waves, floating
in the pale beam under an arch-way of grey weather-beaten rocks, and
with the light of a torch glaring over the milder radiance, was in as
fine keeping and strict truth as Claude or Rembrandt, and would
satisfy, we think, the most fastidious artist's eye. It lulled the sense
of sight as the fancied sound of the dashing waters soothed the
imagination. In the scene where the moonlight fell on the dying
form of Ruthven (the Vampire) it was like a fairy glory, forming a
palace of emerald light: the body seemed to drink its balmy essence,
and to revive in it without a miracle. The line,

' See how the moon sleeps with Endymion,'

474

came into the mind from the beauty and gorgeousness of the picture, notwithstanding the repugnance of every circumstance and feeling. This melodrame succeeds very well; and it succeeds in spite of Mr. Kean's last nights, and without Miss Kelly!

At the Hay-market there has been a new comedy, called 'the Diamond Ring, or Exchange no Robbery.' It is said to be by Mr. Theodore Hook. We should not wonder. The morality, and the sentiment are very flat, and very offensive; we mean, all the half platonic, half serious love scenes between Sir Lennox Leinster, (Mr. Conner), and Lady Cranberry (Mrs. Mardyn). This actress,— young, handsome, and full of spirit as she is, and as the character she represents is supposed to be,—and married to an old husband, who is always grumbling, and complaining,—does not appear fitted to be engaged in half an amour; nor as if she would excuse Sir Lennox for being 'figurative,' in that way. Her conduct is at least equivocal, and without any ostensible motive but a gross one, which yet she does not acknowledge to herself. A Milan commission would inevitably have ruined her, even though Sir Lennox had been a less likely man than a well-looking, impudent, Irish Baronet. His personal pretensions are certainly formidable to her jealous spouse (Mr. Terry, an Adonis of sixty)—though it is hard to find out the charms in his conversation that recommend him so powerfully to the friendship of the lady. He has one joke, one flower of rhetoric, interspersed through all his discourse, witty or amorous—the cant phrase, 'You'll excuse my being figurative.' His metaphorical turn would not however have been excused, but for the matter-of-fact notions and accomplishments of Mr. Liston—who plays a *bona fide* pot boy in the comic group, the supposed son of old Cranberry, but the real and proper off-spring of old Swipes, the landlord of The Pig and Gridiron. This hopeful young gentleman has been palmed upon his pretended father, (to the no small mortification and dismay of both parties) instead of the intrepid Lieutenant Littleworth (Mr. Barnard) the true heir to the Cranberry estate and honours. Liston, as young Swipes, has nothing genteel about him; not even the wish to be so. His inclinations are low. Thus he likes to drink with the butler; makes a young blackamore, whom he calls 'snowdrop,' drunk with claret, and is in love with Miss Polly Watts, who has red hair, a red face, and red elbows. He has vowed to elope with her before that day week, and make her Mrs. C., and would no doubt have been as good as his word if the secret of his birth had not been discovered by his mother-in-law, in revenge for a matrimonial squabble; and the whole ends, as a three-act piece should do—abruptly but agreeably. Mr. Liston's acting in such a character as we have described, it is needless to add, was infinitely droll, and Terry was a father worthy (*pro tempore*) of such a son.

The Manager of the English Opera House on Monday, 21st ult. brought out an occasional farce against the Manager of Drury-Lane, called Patent Seasons ; deprecating the encroachments of the winter theatres, and predicting that, in consequence, 'the English Opera would soon be a Beggar's Opera.' His hits at his overbearing rival were good, and *told*; but the confession of the weakness and 'poverty,' which Mr. Elliston had thrown in his teeth, rather served to damp than excite the enthusiasm of the audience. Every one is inclined to run away from a falling house ; and of all appeals, that to humanity should be the last. The town may be bullied, ridiculed, wheedled, *puffed* out of their time and money, but to ask them to sink their patronage in a bankrupt concern, is to betray an ignorance of the world, who sympathise with the prosperous, and laugh at injustice. Generosity is the last infirmity of the public mind. Pity is a frail ground of popularity : and 'misery doth part the flux of company.' If you want the assistance of others, put a good face upon the matter, and conceal it from them that you want it. Do not whine and look piteous in their faces, or they will treat you like a dog. The 170 families that Mr. Arnold tells us depend upon his minor theatre for support are not 'Russian sufferers,' nor sufferers in a triumphant cause. Talk of 170 distressed families dependent on a distressed manager (not an autocrat of one vast theatre) and the sound hangs like a mill-stone on the imagination, 'or load to sink a navy.' The audience slink away, one by one, willing to slip their necks out of it. *Charity is cold.*

The Manager of the English Opera House, however, does not stand alone in his difficulties. The theatres in general seem to totter, and feel the hand of decay. Even the King's Theatre, we understand, has manifested signs of decrepitude, and 'palsied eld,' and stopped,—we do not say its payments, but its performances. Of all the theatres, we should feel the least compassion for the deserted saloons and tattered hangings of the Italian Opera. We should rather indeed see it flourish, as it has long flourished, in splendour and in honour : we do not like 'to see a void made in the Drama : any ruin on the face of the land.' But this would touch us the least. We might be disposed to write its epitaph, not its elegy.

L.

No. XI

[*December,* 1820.

'At last he rose, and twitched his mantle blue :
To-morrow to fresh fields and pastures new.'

Why was not this No. xii. instead of No. xi. of the Acted
Drama in London ? Had we but seen No. xii. at the head of our
article for December, we had been happy, 'as broad and casing as
the general air, whole as the marble, founded as the rock,' but now
we are 'cooped and cabined in by saucy doubts and fears.' Had
No. xi. been ready in time, we should have been irreproachable 'in
act and complement extern,' which is with us every thing. Punctu-
ality is 'the immediate jewel of our souls.' We leave it to others to
be shrewd, ingenious, witty and wise ; to think deeply, and write
finely ; it is enough for us to be exactly dull. The categories of
number and *quantity* are what we chiefly delight in ; for on these
depend (by arithmetical computation) the pounds, shillings, and pence.
We suspect that those writers only trouble their heads about fame,
who cannot get any thing more substantial for what they write ; and
are in fact equally at a loss for 'solid pudding or for empty praise.'
That is not the case with us. We have money in our purse, and
reputation—to spare. Nothing troubles us but that our article on the
drama was wanting for November—on this point we are inconsolable.
No more delight in regularity—no more undisturbed complacency in
the sense of arduous duty conscientiously discharged—no more confidence in meeting our Editors—no more implicit expectation of our
monthly decisions on the part of the public ! As the Italian poet for
one error of the press, in a poem presented to the Pope, died of
chagrin, so we for one deficiency in this series of Dramatic Criticisms
(complete but for that) must resign ! We have no other way left to
appease our scrupulous sense of critical punctilio. That there was but
one link wanting, is no matter—

'Tenth or ten thousandth break the chain alike.'

There was one Number (the eleventh) of the London Magazine, of
which the curious reader turned over the pages with eager haste, and
found no Drama—a thing never to be remedied ! It was no fault of
ours that it was so. A friend hath done this. The author of the
the Calendar of Nature (a pleasing and punctual performance) has
spoiled our Calendar of Art, and robbed us of that golden rigol of
periodical praise, that we had in fancy 'bound our brows withal.'
With the month our contribution to the stock of literary amusement
and scientific intelligence returned without fail. In January, we gave

an account of all the actors we had ever seen or heard of. In February, we confined ouselves to Miss O'Neill. In March, we expatiated at large on the Minor Theatres, and took great delight in the three Miss Dennetts. In April (being at Ilminster, a pretty town in the Vale of Taunton, and thence passing on to the Lamb at Hindon, a dreary spot), we proved at these two places, sitting in an arm-chair by a sea-coal fire, very satisfactorily, and without fear of contradiction,—neither Mr. Maturin, Mr. Shiel, nor Mr. Milman being present,—that no modern author could write a tragedy. In May, we wrote an article which filled the proper number of columns, though we forget what it was about. In June, we had to show that a modern author had written a tragedy (Virginius)—an opinion, which, though it overset our theory, we are by no means desirous to retract. We still say, that that play is better than Bertram, though Mr. Maturin, in the Preface to Melmoth, says it is not. As in June we were not dry, neither in July were we droughty. We found something to say in this and the following month without being much indebted to the actors or actresses, though, if Miss Tree came out in either of those months, we ought to recollect it, and mark the event with *a white stone*. We had rather hear her sing in ordinary cases than Miss Stephens, though not in extraordinary ones. By the bye, when will that little pouting[1] slut, with crystalline eyes and voice, return to us from the sister island? The Dublin critics hardly pretend to keep her to themselves, on the ground that they (like the Edinburgh wags) are better judges and patrons of merit, than we of famous London town.—The Irish are impudent : but they are not so impudent as the Scotch. This is a digression. To proceed.—In August, we had a skirmish with the facetious and biting Janus, of versatile memory, on his assumed superiority in dramatic taste and skill, when we corrected him for his contempt of court—and the Miss

---

[1] 'Or mouth with slumbery pout.' *Keats's Endymion.*
The phrase might be applied to Miss Stephens : though it is a vile phrase, worse than Hamlet's 'beautified' applied to Ophelia. Indeed it has been remarked that Mr. Keats resembles Shakspeare in the novelty and eccentricity of his combinations of style. If so, it is the only thing in which he is like Shakspeare : and yet Mr. Keats, whose misfortune and crime it is, like Milton, to have been born in London, is a much better poet than Mr. Wilson, or his Patroclus Mr. Lockart ; nay, further, if Sir Walter Scott (the sly Ulysses of the Auld Reekie school,) had written many of the passages in Mr. Keats's poems, they would have been quoted as the most beautiful in his works. We do not here (on the banks of the Thames) damn the Scotch novels in the lump, because the writer is a *Sawney Scot*. But the sweet Edinburgh wits damn Mr. Keats's lines in the lump, because he is born in London. 'Oh Scotland, judge of England, what a treasure hast thou in one fair son, and one fair son-in-law, neither of whom (by all accounts) thou lovest passing well !'

478

Dennetts, our wards in criticism. In September, we got an able article written for us; for we flatter ourselves, that we not only say good things ourselves, but are the cause of them in others. In October, we called Mr. Elliston to task for taking, in his vocation of manager, improper liberties with the public. But in November, (may that dark month stand aye accursed in the Calendar!) we failed, and failed, as how? Our friend, the ingenious writer aforesaid (one of the most ingenious and sharp-witted men of his age, but not so remarkable for the virtue of *reliability* as Mr. Coleridge's friend, the poet-laureate), was to take a mutton-chop with us, and afterwards we were to go to the play, and club our forces in a criticism—but he never came, *we* never went to the play (The Stranger with Charles Kemble as the hero, and a new Mrs. Haller), and the criticism was never written. The Drama of the LONDON MAGAZINE for that month is left a blank!—We were in hopes that our other contributors might have been proportionably on the alert; but, on the contrary, we were sorry to hear it remarked by more than one person, that the Magazine for November was, on the whole, dull. There was no TABLE-TALK, for instance, an article which we take up immediately after we have perused our own, and seldom lay it down till we get to the end of it, though we think the papers too long. We are glad to see the notice from the redoubtable LION's HEAD of No. v. for the present Number, for we understand that a Cockney, in clandestine correspondence with Blackwood, on looking for it in the last, and finding it *missing*, had sent off instant word, that the writer 'was expelled' from the LONDON MAGAZINE. We are sure we should be sorry for that.

If theatrical criticisms were only written when there is something worth writing about, it would be hard upon us who live by them. Are we not to receive our quarter's salary (like Mr. Croker in the piping time of peace) because Mrs. Siddons has left the stage, and 'has not left her peer;' or because John Kemble will not return to it with renewed health and vigour, to prop a falling house, and falling art; or because Mr. Kean has gone to America; or because Mr. Wallack has arrived from that country? No; the duller the stage grows, the gayer and more edifying must we become in ourselves: the less we have to say about that, the more room we have to talk about other things. Now would be the time for Mr. Coleridge to turn his talents to account, and write for the stage, when there is no topic to confine his pen, or, 'constrain his genius by mastery.' 'With mighty wings outspread, his imagination might brood over the void and make it pregnant.' Under the assumed head of the Drama, he might unfold the whole mysteries of Swedenborg, or ascend the third heaven of invention with Jacob Behmen: he might write a

479

treatise on all the unknown sciences, and finish the Encyclopedia Metropolitana in a pocket form:—nay, he might bring to a satisfactory close his own dissertation on the difference between the Imagination and the Fancy,[1] before, in all probability, another great actor appears, or another tragedy or comedy is written. He is the man of all others to swim on empty bladders in a sea, without shore or soundings: to drive an empty stage-coach without passengers or lading, and arrive behind his time; to write marginal notes without a text; to look into a millstone to foster the rising genius of the age; to 'see merit in the chaos of its elements, and discern perfection in the great obscurity of nothing,' as his most favourite author, Sir Thomas Brown, has it on another occasion. Alas! we have no such creative talents: we cannot amplify, expand, raise our flimsy discourse, as the gaseous matter fills and lifts the round, glittering, slow-sailing balloon, to 'the up-turned eyes of wondering mortals.' Here is our bill of fare for the month, our list of memoranda—*The French dancers—Farren's Deaf Lover—Macready's Zanga—Mr. Cooper's Romeo. A new farce, not acted a second time—Wallace, a tragedy,—and Mr. Wallack's Hamlet.* Who can make any thing of such a beggarly account as this? Not we. Yet as poets at a pinch invoke the Muse, so we, for once, will invoke Mr. Coleridge's better genius, and thus we hear him talk, diverting our attention from the players and the play.

'The French, my dear H——,' would he begin, 'are not a people of imagination. They have so little, that you cannot persuade them to conceive it possible that they have none. They have no poetry, no such thing as genius, from the age of Louis xiv. It was that, their boasted Augustan age, which stamped them French, which put the seal upon their character, and from that time nothing has grown up original or luxuriant, or spontaneous among them; the whole has been cast in a mould, and that a bad one. Montaigne and Rabelais (their two greatest men, the one for thought, and the other for imaginative humour, — for the distinction between imagination and fancy holds in ludicrous as well as serious composition) I consider as Franks rather than Frenchmen, for in their time the national literature was not *set*, was neither mounted on stilts, nor buckramed in stays. Wit they had too, if I could persuade myself that Moliere was a genuine Frenchman, but I cannot help suspecting that his mother played his reputed father false, and that an Englishman begot him. I am sure his genius is English; and his wit not of the Parisian cut. As a proof of this, see how his most extravagant

[1] The Fancy is not used here in the sense of Mr. Peter Corcoran, but in a sense peculiar to Mr. Coleridge, and hitherto undefined by him.

farces, the Mock-doctor, Barnaby Brittle, &c. take with us. What can be more to the taste of our *bourgeoisie*, more adapted to our native tooth, than his Country Wife, which Wycherly did little else than translate into English? What success a translator of Racine into our vernacular tongue would meet with, I leave you to guess. His tragedies are not poetry, are not passion, are not imagination : they are a parcel of set speeches, of epigrammatic conceits, of declamatory phrases, without any of the glow, and glancing rapidity, and principle of fusion in the mind of the poet, to agglomerate them into grandeur, or blend them into harmony. The principle of the imagination resembles the emblem of the serpent, by which the ancients typified wisdom and the universe, with undulating folds, for ever varying and for ever flowing into itself,—circular, and without beginning or end. The definite, the fixed, is death : the principle of life is the indefinite, the growing, the moving, the continuous. But every thing in French poetry is cut up into shreds and patches, little flowers of poetry, with tickets and labels to them, as when the daughters of Jason minced and hacked their old father into collops—we have the *disjecta membra poetæ*—not the entire and living man. The spirit of genuine poetry should inform the whole work, should breathe through, and move, and agitate the complete mass, as the soul informs and moves the limbs of a man, or as the vital principle (whatever it be) permeates the veins of the loftiest trees, building up the trunk, and extending the branches to the sun and winds of heaven, and shooting out into fruit and flowers. This is the progress of nature and of genius. This is the true poetic faculty ; or that which the Greeks literally called ποιησις. But a French play (I think it is Schlegel, who somewhere makes the comparison, though I had myself, before I ever read Schlegel, made the same remark) is like a child's garden set with slips of branches and flowers, stuck in the ground, not growing in it. We may weave a gaudy garland in this manner, but it withers in an hour : while the products of genius and nature give out their odours to the gale, and spread their tints in the sun's eye, age after age—

> "Outlast a thousand storms, a thousand winters,
> Free from the Sirian star, free from the thunder stroke,"

and flourish in immortal youth and beauty. Every thing French is, in the way of it, frittered into parts : every thing is therefore dead and ineffective. French poetry is just like chopped logic : nothing comes of it. There is no life of mind : neither the birth nor genera-tion of knowledge. It is all patch-work, all sharp points and angles, all superficial. They receive, and give out sensation, too readily for it ever to amount to a sentiment. They cannot even dance, as you may see. There is, I am sure you will agree, no expression, no grace in their dancing. Littleness, point, is what damns them in all they do. With all their vivacity, and animal spirits, they dance not like men and women under the impression of certain emotions, but like puppets; they twirl round like *tourniquets*. Not to feel, and not to think, is all they know of this art or any other. You might swear that a nation that danced in that manner would never produce a true poet or philosopher. They have it not in them. There is not the principle of cause and effect. They make a sudden turn because there is no reason for it: they stop short, or move fast, only because you expect something else. Their style of dancing is difficult: would it were impossible.'[1] (By this time several persons in the pit had turned round to listen to this uninterrupted discourse, and our eloquent friend went on, rather raising his voice with a *Paulo majora canamus*.) 'Look at that Mademoiselle Milanie with "the foot of fire," as she is called. You might contrive a paste-board figure, with the help of strings or wires, to do all, and more, than she does—to point the toe, to raise the leg, to jerk the body, to run like wild-fire. Antics are not grace: to dance is not to move against time. My dear H——, if you could see a dance by some Italian peasant-girls in the Campagna of Rome, as I have, I am sure your good taste and good sense would approve it. They came forward slow and smiling, but as if their limbs were steeped in luxury, and every motion seemed an echo of the music, and the heavens looked on serener as they trod. You are right about the Miss Dennetts, though you have all the cant-phrases against you. It is true, they break down in some of their steps, but it is like "the lily drooping on its stalk green," or like "the flowers Proserpina let fall from Dis's waggon." Those who cannot see grace in the youth and inexperience of these charming girls, would see no beauty in a cluster of hyacinths, bent with the morning dew. To shew at once what is, and is not French, there is Mademoiselle Hullin, she is Dutch. Nay, she is just like a Dutch doll, as round-faced, as rosy, and looks for all the world as if her limbs were made of wax-work, and would take in pieces, but not as if she could move them of her own accord. Alas, poor tender thing! As to the men, I confess' (this was said to me in an audible whisper, lest it might be construed into a breach of confidence) 'I should like, as Southey says, to have them *hamstrung*!'—(At this moment Monsieur Hullin *Pere* looked as if this charitable operation was about to be performed on him by an extra-official warrant from the poet-laureate.)

---

[1] This expression is borrowed from Dr. Johnson. However, as Dr. Johnson is not a German critic, Mr. C. need not be supposed to acknowledge it.

'Pray, H——, have you seen Macready's Zanga?'

'Yes.'

'And what do you think of it?'

'I did not like it much.'

'Nor I.—Macready has talents and a magnificent voice, but he is, I fear, too improving an actor to be a man of genius. That little ill-looking vagabond Kean never improved in any thing. In some things he could not, and in others he would not. The only parts of M.'s Zanga that I liked (which of course I only half-liked) were some things in imitation of the *extremely natural manner* of Kean, and his address to Alonzo, urging him, as the greatest triumph of his self-denial, to sacrifice

> " A wife, a bride, a mistress unenjoyed— "

where his voice rose exulting on the sentiment, like the thunder that clothes the neck of the war-horse. The person that pleased me most in this play was Mrs. Sterling: she did justice to her part—a thing not easy to do. I like Macready's Wallace better than his Zanga, though the play is not a good one, and it is difficult for the actor to find out the author's meaning. I would not judge harshly of a first attempt, but the faults of youthful genius are exuberance, and a continual desire of novelty: now the faults of this play are tameness, common-place, and clap-traps. It is said to be written by young Walker, the son of the Westminster orator. If so, his friend, Mr. Cobbett, will probably write a Theatrical Examiner of it in his next week's Political Register. What, I would ask, can be worse, more out of character and costume, than to make Wallace drop his sword to have his throat cut by Menteith, merely because the latter has proved himself (what he suspected) a traitor and a villain, and then console himself for this voluntary martyrdom by a sentimental farewell to the rocks and mountains of his native country! This effeminate softness and wretched cant did not belong to the age, the country, or the hero. In this scene, however, Mr. Macready shone much; and in the attitude in which he stood after letting his sword fall, he displayed extreme grace and feeling. It was as if he had let his best friend, his trusty sword, drop like a serpent from his hand. Macready's figure is awkward, but his attitudes are graceful and well composed.—Don't you think so?'—

I answered, yes; and he then ran on in his usual manner, by inquiring into the metaphysical distinction between the grace of form, and the grace that arises from motion (as for instance, you may move a square form in a circular or waving line), and illustrated this subtle observation at great length and with much happiness. He asked me

how it was, that Mr. Farren in the farce of the Deaf Lover, played
the old gentleman so well, and failed so entirely in the young gallant.
I said I could not tell. He then tried at a solution himself, in which
I could not follow him so as to give the precise point of his argument.
He afterwards defined to me, and those about us, the merits of
Mr. Cooper and Mr. Wallack, classing the first as a respectable, and
the last as a second-rate actor; with large grounds and learned definitions of his meaning on both points; and, as the lights were by this
time nearly out, and the audience (except his immediate auditors)
going away, he reluctantly 'ended,'

> 'But in Adam's ear so pleasing left his voice,'

that I quite forgot I had to write my article on the Drama the next
day; nor without his imaginary aid should I have been able to wind
up my accounts for the year, as Mr. Matthews gets through his AT
HOME by the help of a little awkward ventriloquism.

W. H.

November 21, 1820.

NOTES

NOTES

LECTURES ON THE ENGLISH COMIC WRITERS

THESE Lectures were delivered at the Surrey Institution, in Blackfriars Road, in 1818, after the completion of the course on the English Poets (see vol. v.). Some particulars as to their delivery will be found in Talfourd's edition of Lamb's *Letters* (see Mr. W. C. Hazlitt's reprint, Bohn, I. 38 *et seq*.), and in Patmore's *My Friends and Acquaintance*. See also Mr. W. C. Hazlitt's *Four Generations of a Literary Family* (vol. I. pp. 121-2), where the opinions of Beckford and Thackeray are referred to. In the third edition of the Lectures (see Bibliographical Note) several passages 'collected by the author, apparently with a view to a reprint of the volume,' were interpolated. Two of these passages are taken from a long letter (published in full in the Appendix to these notes) which Hazlitt contributed to *The Morning Chronicle*, Oct. 15, 1813. The rest are taken from prefatory notices which he contributed to William Oxberry's *The New English Drama* (20 vols. 1818-1825), and are printed in the following notes.

LECTURE I. INTRODUCTORY

8. *The Tale of Slaukenbergius*. *Tristram Shandy*, vol. IV.
9. ' *There is something in the misfortunes,*' *etc.* Rochefoucault, *Maximes et Réflexions Morales*, CCXLI.
   ' *They were talking,*' *etc.* Farquhar's *Beaux' Stratagem*, Act III. Sc. I.
   Lord Foppington. In *The Relapse* of Vanbrugh. See *post*, p. 82.
10. *Aretine laughed himself to death, etc.* The story is that while laughing at the jest Aretine fell from a stool and was killed.
    Sir Thomas More jested, etc. More bade the executioner stay till he had put aside his beard, ' for that,' he said, ' had never committed treason.'
    Rabelais and Wycherley. 'When Rabelais,' says Bacon (Apophthegms), 'the great jester of France, lay on his death-bed, and they gave him the extreme unction, a familiar friend came to him afterwards, and asked him how he did ? Rabelais answered, " Even going my journey, they have greased my boots already." ' But his last words, uttered ' avec un éclat de rire,' were : ' Tirez le rideau, la farce est jouée.' It is said that Wycherley, on the night before he died, made his young wife promise that she would never marry an old man again. See a letter from Pope to Blount, Jan. 21, 1715-6 (*Works*, ed. Elwin and Courthope, VI. 366). Pope, after telling the story, adds : 'I cannot help remarking that sickness, which often destroys both wit and wisdom, yet seldom has power to remove that talent which we call humour.'
    The dialogue between Aimwell and Cibbot. The *Beaux' Stratagem*, Act III. Sc. 2.
    Mr. Emery's Robert Tyke. In Thomas Morton's *School of Reform* (1805). Cf. *post*, p. 391.

488

NOTES

20. *'Soul-killing lies,' etc.* Lamb, *John Woodvil*, Act II.
21. *'The instance might be painful,' etc. Letters of Junius*, Letter XLIX.
   'And ever,' etc. L'Allegro, 135-6.
   The reply of the author, etc. This was Richard Owen Cambridge (1717-1802), contributor to Edward Moore's *The World* (1753-1756).
   'Full of sound and fury,' etc. Macbeth, Act V. Sc. 5.
   'For thin partitions,' etc. Dryden, *Absalom and Achitophel*, Part I. 164.
   Mr. Curran. Curran had died on October 14, 1817.
22. *Haeret lateri, etc. Æneid*, IV. 73.
   The Duke of Buckingham's saying. 'And give me leave to tell your lordships, by the way, that statutes are not like women, for they are not one jot the worse for being old.' Speech on the Dissolution of Parliament, 1676. The speech was included by Hazlitt in his *Eloquence of the British Senate.* See vol. III. p. 399.
   Mr. Addison, indeed, etc. The Spectator, No. 61.
   Mandrake. In Farquhar's *The Twin Rivals*, Act II. Sc. 2.
   Sir Hugh Evans. The Merry Wives of Windsor, Act I. Sc. 1.
23. *'From the sublime,' etc.* 'Du sublime au ridicule il n'y a qu'un pas.' Attributed to Napoleon. Thomas Paine had, however, said the same thing in his *Age of Reason*, Part II.
24. *Mr. Canning's Court Parodies, etc.* In the *Anti-Jacobin* (1797-1798). Southey was the victim of two of the best known of these parodies, the *Inscription for the door of the Cell in Newgate where Mrs. Brownrigg, the Prentice-cide, was confined previous to her execution,* and *The Friend of Humanity and the Knife-Grinder.*
   The Rejected Addresses. By James and Horace Smith, published in 1812. The parody of Crabbe was by James Smith.
   Lear and the Fool. The references in this paragraph are to *King Lear*, Act I. Sc. 4.
   'Tis with our judgments,' etc. Pope, *Essay on Criticism*, 9-10.
25. *'He is the cause,' etc.* Cf. 'I am not only witty in myself, but the cause that wit is in other men.' *Henry IV.*, Part II., Act I. Sc. 2.
   'That perilous stuff,' etc. Macbeth, Act V. Sc. 3.
   'Imitate humanity,' etc. Hamlet, Act III. Sc. 2.
26. *Barrow's celebrated description.* See Isaac Barrow's (1630-77) sermon 'Against Foolish Talking and Jesting.'
27. *'Who did essay,' etc. The Faerie Queene*, Book II., Canto VI., St. 7.
28. *Barnaby Brittle.* See *post*, note to p. 481.
29. *The strictures of Rousseau.* Lettre à M. D'Alembert. *Petits Chefs-d'œuvre* (ed. Firmin-Didot), pp. 405 *et seq.*
   An exquisite . . . defence. See *La Critique de l'École des Femmes*, Sc. 6.
   'An equal want,' etc. 'But equally a want of books and men.' Wordsworth, *Poems dedicated to National Independence and Liberty*, xv., Sonnet beginning 'Great men have been among us ; hands that penned,' etc.

LECTURE II. ON SHAKSPEARE AND BEN JONSON

30. *Dr. Johnson thought, etc.* See his *Preface to Shakespeare* (*Works*, Oxford, 1825, vol. V. p. 113).
   'Smit with the love of sacred song.' Paradise Lost, III. 29.
31. *There is but one, etc.* Hazlitt is recalling Dryden's line, 'within that circle none must walk but he.' (Prologue to *The Tempest.*)

LECTURES ON THE COMIC WRITERS

LECTURE III. ON COWLEY, BUTLER, SUCKLING, ETHEREGE, ETC.

NOTES

55. '*Inimitable on earth*,' etc. *Paradise Lost*, III. 508-9.

Suckling. Sir John Suckling (1609-1642). Johnson refers to him in his *Life of Cowley* as one of the 'immediate successors' of the metaphysical poets, but adds : 'Suckling neither improved versification, nor abounded in conceits. The fashionable style remained chiefly with Cowley ; Suckling could not reach it, and Milton disdained it.'

57. *Cowley.* Cf. vol. v. p. 372.

'*The Phœnix Pindar*,' etc. *The Praise of Pindar*, l. 2.

'*Sailing with supreme dominion*,' etc. Gray, *The Progress of Poesy*, III. 3.

58. *He compares Bacon to Moses.* 'Bacon, like Moses, led us forth at last.' *To the Royal Society.*

60. *Cowley's Essays.* Published in 1668.

61. *Cutter of Coleman Street.* *The Guardian* acted at Cambridge in 1641 and printed in 1650, afterwards re-written and produced at Lincoln's Inn Fields as 'Cutter of Coleman Street' in 1661.

62. '*Call you this backing your friends ?*' *Henry IV.*, Part I., Act II. Sc. 4.

Butler's Hudibras. The three Parts of *Hudibras* appeared in 1662, 1663, and 1678 respectively.

Dr. Campbell. Dr. George Campbell (1719-1796) published his *Philosophy of Rhetoric* in 1776.

'*Narrow his mind*,' etc. Goldsmith's *Retaliation*, 31-2.

Dr. Zachary Grey. Zachary Grey's (1688-1766) edition of *Hudibras* appeared in 1744.

63. Note. (1) Part II., Canto II. 297-8 ; and II., I. 617-20 ; (2) II., I. 273-4 ; (3) I., II. 255-6 ; (4) I., II. 109-10 ; (5) I., II. 225-6 ; I., I. 241-252 ; and I., I. 375-8.

64. Note. (1) Part II. Canto II. 831-2, and II. III. 107-8 ; (2) II. II. 421-2 ; (3) I. I. 59-60 ; (4) II. III. 809-10 ; (5) I. II. 1099-1102.

65. '*Pilloried*,' etc. Cowper, *Hope*, 556.

'*As one grain of wheat*,' etc. *Merchant of Venice*, Act I. Sc. I.

The account of Sidrophel and Whackum. *Hudibras*, Part II. Canto III.

Note. '*Thus stopp'd*,' etc. *Hudibras*, Part I. Canto III. 951-2. '*And setting his right foot*,' etc. I. III. 82-4. '*At this the knight*,' etc. II. II. 541-4. '*The knight himself*,' etc. I. II. 1123-6. '*And raised*,' etc. I. II. 95-6. '*And Hudibras*,' etc. II. II. 661-2. '*Both thought*,' etc. II. II. 577-90.

67. *The burlesque description*, etc. *Hudibras*, Part I. Canto II. 1129, *et seq.*

'*As when an owl*,' etc. *Ibid.* I. III. 403-6.

'*The queen of night*,' etc. *Ibid.* III. I. 1321-6.

Butler's Remains. *The Genuine Remains in Verse and Prose of Mr. Samuel Butler*, not published till 1759.

'*Reduce all tragedy*,' etc. Butler, *Upon Critics*, 17-42.

68. *Etherege.* Sir George Etherege (1635 ?-1691) wrote three comedies, *The Comical Revenge, or Love in a Tub* (1664), *She Would if she Could* (1667), and *The Man of Mode, or Sir Fopling Flutter* (1676). The last was a great favourite of Hazlitt's, and is constantly referred to by him.

'*Tames his wild heart*,' etc. *Much Ado About Nothing*, Act III. Sc. I.

'*Like the morn*,' etc. *Paradise Lost*, v. 310-11.

The Wild Gallant. First performed February 1662-3. See Act II. Sc. I.

69. *Sir Martin Mar-all.* Produced in 1667, and founded on a translation by the Duke of Newcastle of Molière's *L'Étourdi*. *The Busy Body*, by Mrs. Centlivre, appeared in 1709.

Otway's comedies. *The Cheats of Scapin* (adapted from Molière) (1677), *Friendship in Fashion* (1678), *The Soldier's Fortune* (1681), and *The Atheist* (1684).

493

LECTURES ON THE COMIC WRITERS

85. *Mr. Burke's courtly and chivalrous observation.* 'That chastity of honour . . . under which vice itself lost half its evil, by losing all its grossness.' *Reflections on the Revolution in France* (*Select Works,* ed. Payne, II. 89).

86. '*Now, dear madam,*' *etc. Sir Harry Wildair,* Act IV. Sc. 2.

88. *The dialogue between Cherry and Archer.* See *The Beaux' Stratagem* (produced 1707), Act II. Sc. 3.

89. *The Recruiting Officer.* 1706.
   Catastrophe of this play. See Farquhar's Dedication.
   Love and a Bottle, 1699 ; *The Twin Rivals,* 1702.
   Farquhar's Letters. Originally published in 1702 under the title of 'Love and Business.'
   Dennis's Remarks, etc. Dennis's *Remarks upon Cato* appeared in 1713.
   His View of the English Stage. Jeremy Collier's *Short View of the Immorality and Profaneness of the English Stage* (1697-8).

90. '*Shews vice,*' *etc.* Cf. 'To show virtue her own feature, scorn her own image.' *Hamlet,* Act III. Sc. 2.
   '*Denote a foregone conclusion.*' *Othello,* Act III. Sc. 3.
   Colley Cibber's Life, etc. Cf. the second essay 'On Actors and Acting' in *The Round Table,* vol. I. p. 156.

91. '*Let no rude hand,*' *etc.* Wordsworth, *Ellen Irwin,* St. 7.
   '*Die and leave the world no copy.*' *Twelfth Night,* Act I. Sc. 5.

LECTURE V. ON THE PERIODICAL ESSAYISTS

'*The proper study,*' *etc.* Pope, *Essay on Man,* II. 2.
'*Comes home to the business,*' *etc.* Bacon, dedication of the *Essays.*
'*Quicquid agunt homines,*' *etc.* These words of Juvenal (*Sat.* I. 85-6) formed the motto of the first 40 numbers of *The Tatler.*
'*Holds the mirror,*' *etc. Hamlet,* Act III. Sc. 2.
'*The act* [art] *and practic part,*' *etc. Henry V.,* Act I. Sc. 1.

92. '*The web of our life,*' *etc. All's Well that Ends Well,* Act IV. Sc. 3.
   '*Quid sit pulchrum,*' *etc.* Horace, Epistles, I. 2, ll. 3-4.
   Montaigne. The *Essais* of Michael de Montaigne (1533-1592), were published, Books I. and II. in 1580, Book III. in 1588.

93. '*Pour out all as plain,*' *etc.* Pope, *Imitations of Horace,* Sat. I. 51-2.
   Note. 'What made (say Montaigne, or more sage Charron !) Otho a warrior, Cromwell a buffoon.'
   Pope, *Moral Essays,* I. 87-8.

   De la Sagesse, the chief work of Montaigne's friend Pierre Charron (1541-1603), appeared in 1601.

94. '*Pereant isti,*' *etc.* Ælius Donatus, St. Jerome, *Commentary on Ecclesiastes,* Cap. I.
   Charles Cotton. Cotton's translation of Montaigne was published in three volumes in 1685, and has frequently been reprinted, the latest edition being that of Mr. W. C. Hazlitt (republished 1902). The earlier version by John Florio (1603) has been included in the *Tudor Translations* (1893) and in the *Temple Classics* (1897).
   '*The book in the world,*' *etc.* Cotton's translation was dedicated to George Savile, Marquis of Halifax, who, in his reply, addressed to Cotton, spoke of the *Essays* as 'the book in the world I am best entertained with.'
   Cowley, etc. Abraham Cowley's *Several Discourses by way of Essays in Prose and Verse* were appended to the collected edition of his works in 1668 ; Sir

496

NOTES

William Temple's (1628-1699) essays entitled *Miscellanea* were published in 1680 and 1692 ; Lord Shaftesbury's (1671-1713) *Moralists* in 1709, and *Characteristics* in 1711.

94. Note. *Nam quodcumque, etc.* Lucretius, III. 752-3.

95. ' *The perfect spy o' th' time.*' *Macbeth*, Act III. Sc. 1.
The Tatler. The first number of the *Tatler* appeared on April 12, 1709, the last on January 2, 1711. The papers were re-issued in two forms, one in 8vo., one in 12mo., in 1710-11. Nearly the whole of this paragraph and the next is taken from an essay in *The Examiner* (March 5, 1815), re-printed in *The Round Table.* See vol. 1. pp. 7-10, and the notes thereon.

96. Note. No. 86, not No. 125, of *The Tatler.*
Mr. Lilly's shop-windows. Charles Lillie, the perfumer's at the corner of Beaufort Buildings in the Strand.
Will Estcourt or Tom Durfey. Richard Estcourt (1668-1712), actor and dramatist, and Tom D'Urfey (1653-1723), the dramatist and song-writer, are constantly referred to in *The Tatler.*

97. *The Spectator.* The *Spectator* ran from March 1, 1711, to December 6, 1712, and from June 18, 1714, to December 20, 1714. The collected edition appeared in 8 vols., 1712-15.
' *The whiteness of her hand.*' ' She has certainly the finest hand of any woman in the world.' *The Spectator*, No. 113.

98. ' *He has a widow in his line of life.*' *The Spectator*, No. 130.
His falling asleep in church, etc. The Spectator, No. 112. John Williams should be ' one John Matthews.'

99. *The Guardian.* March 12, 1713, to October 1713. Of the 176 numbers Steele contributed 82, and Addison 53, papers.

100. *The Rambler.* March 20, 1749-50, to March 14, 1752.
' *Give us pause.*' *Hamlet*, Act III. Sc. 1.

101. ' *The elephant,*' etc. *Paradise Lost*, IV. 345-7.

102. ' *If he were to write,*' etc. Boswell's *Life of Johnson* (ed. G. B. Hill), II. 231.
Abused Milton and patronised Lauder. See Boswell's *Life of Johnson* (ed. G. B. Hill), I. 228-31.

103. ' *The king of good fellows,*' etc. Burns, *Auld Rob Morris*, l. 2.
' *Inventory of all he said.*' Cf. ' And ta'en an inventory of what they are.' Ben Jonson, *The Alchemist*, Act III. Sc. 2.
' *Does he wind,*' etc. Boswell's *Life of Johnson* (ed. G. B. Hill), II. 260.
' *If that fellow Burke,*' etc. *Ibid.* II. 450.
' *What, is it you,*' etc. *Ibid.* I. 250.
' *Now I think I am,*' etc. *Ibid.* II. 362.
His quitting the society, etc. Ibid. I. 201.
His dining with Wilkes. Ibid. III. 64 et seq.
His sitting with the young ladies. Ibid. II. 120.
His carrying the unfortunate victim, etc. Ibid. IV. 321.

104. *An act which realises the parable of the good Samaritan.* Sergeant Talfourd, in his account of these Lectures, speaks of the insensibility of the bulk of the audience, and adds : ' He [Hazlitt] once had a more edifying advantage over them. He was enumerating the humanities which endeared Dr. Johnson to his mind, and at the close of an agreeable catalogue mentioned as last and noblest " his carrying the poor victim of disease and dissipation on his back through Fleet Street," at which a titter arose from some who were struck by the picture as ludicrous, and a murmur from others who deemed the allusion unfit for ears polite : he paused for an instant, and then added, in his sturdiest and most impressive manner—" an act which realizes the

PAGE

parable of the Good Samaritan "—at which his moral, and his delicate hearers shrank, rebuked, into deep silence.' *Lamb's Letters* (ed. **W. C.** Hazlitt), I. 39-40.

104. '*Where they,*' etc. Gray's *Elegy*, The Epitaph.

The Adventurer. Nov. 7, 1752, to March 9, 1754. John Hawkesworth (1715-1773) was the chief contributor.

The World. Jan. 4, 1753, to Dec. 30, 1756.

The Connoisseur. Jan. 31, 1754, to Sept. 30, 1756.

One good idea, etc. Hazlitt referrs to a paper by Edward Moore which appeared in *The World* (No. 176), not, as he says, in *The Connoisseur.*

Citizen of the World. Republished (from the *Public Ledger* and elsewhere) in 2 vols., 1762.

' *Go about to cozen,*' etc. *Merchant of Venice,* Act II. Sc. 9.

The Persian Letters. Lord Lyttelton's *Letters from a Persian in England to his friend at Ispahan,* 1735.

'*The bonzes,*' etc. The *Citizen of the World,* Letter X.

105. '*Edinburgh. We are positive,*' etc. Ibid. Letter V.

Beau Tibbs. Ibid. Letters XXIX., LIV., LV., and LXXI.

The Lounger and The Mirror. The *Mirror* appeared in Edinburgh from Jan. 23, 1779, to May 27, 1780 ; *The Lounger* from Feb. 5, 1785, to Jan. 6, 1786. Henry Mackenzie was the chief contributor to both.

La Roche. The *Mirror,* Nos. 42, 43, and 44.

Le Fevre. *Tristram Shandy,* VI. chaps. 6 *et seq.*

The Man of the World. By Henry Mackenzie (1745-1831), published in 1773.

Julia de Roubigné. Published in 1777.

Rosamond Gray. See Lamb's *Poems, Plays, and Essays,* ed. Ainger, Notes to *Rosamund Gray,* p. 391.

The Man of Feeling. Published in 1771.

LECTURE VI. ON THE ENGLISH NOVELISTS

The whole of this Lecture down to the end of the paragraph on p. 125 is taken with but few variations from an article in *The Edinburgh Review* for Feb. 1815, on 'Standard Novels and Romances,' ostensibly a review of Madame D'Arblay's *The Wanderer.*

PAGE

106. '*Be mine to read,*' etc. Gray, in a letter to Richard West, April 1742 (*Letters,* ed. Tovey, I. 97).

'*Something more divine in it.*' Hazlitt is perhaps recalling a passage in Bacon's *Advancement of Learning* (II. iv. 2) : 'So as poesy serveth and conferreth to delectation, magnanimity, and morality, . . . it may seem deservedly to have some participation of divineness,' etc.

107. *Fielding in speaking,* etc. *Joseph Andrews,* Book III. chap. 1.

The description . . . given by Mr. Burke. *Reflections on the Revolution in France* (*Select Works,* ed. Payne, II. 92-3).

Echard ' *On the Contempt of the Clergy.*' John Eachard's (1636 ?-1697) *The Grounds and Occasions of the Contempt of the Clergy and Religion enquired into,* published in 1670 and frequently reprinted.

'*Worthy of all acceptation.*' 1 *Timothy,* I. 15.

The Lecture which Lady Booby reads, etc. *Joseph Andrews,* Book IV. chap. 3.

Blackstone or De Lolme. Sir William Blackstone's (1723-1780) *Commentaries on the Laws of England* appeared in 1765-9, John Louis De Lolme's (1740 ?-1807) *The Constitution of England*, in French 1771, in English 1775.

108. *What I have said upon it*, etc. In *The Edinburgh Review*. See *ante*, note to p. 106.

Don Quixote. Part I., 1605 ; Part II., 1615.

'The long-forgotten order of chivalry.' 'The long-neglected and almost extinguished order of knight-errantry.' *Don Quixote* (trans. Jarvis), Part I., Book IV. chap. 28.

'Witch the world,' etc. *Henry IV.*, Part I., Act IV. Sc. 1.

109. *'Oh, what delicate wooden spoons,'* etc. *Don Quixote*, Part II., Book IV. chap. 67.

The curate confidentially informing Don Quixote, etc. *Ibid.*

Our adventurer afterwards, etc. *Ibid.*

110. *'Still prompts,'* etc. Pope, *Essay on Man*, IV. 3-4.

'Singing the ancient ballad of Roncesvalles.' *Don Quixote*, Part II., Book I. chap. 9.

Marcella. Ibid. Part I., Book I. chaps. 12 and 13.

His Galatea, etc. *Galatea*, 1585 ; *Persiles and Sigismunda*, 1616.

111. *Gusman D'Alfarache.* By Mateo Aleman, published in 1599.

Lazarillo de Tormes. Attributed to Diego Hurtado de Mendoza (1503-1575), published in 1553.

Gil Blas. The *Histoire de Gil Blas de Santillane* of Alain-René le Sage (1668-1747) appeared in 4 vols., 1715-1735.

112. *Smollett is more like Gil Blas.* In the Preface to *Roderick Random* he admitted his obligation to Le Sage.

113. *Tom Jones.* Published in 1749.

114. *'I was never so handsome,'* etc. *Tom Jones*, Book XVII. chap. 4.

The story of Tom Jones, etc. Cf. the well-known dictum of Coleridge (*Table Talk*, July 5, 1834), 'Upon my word, I think the Œdipus Tyrannus, the Alchemist, and Tom Jones, the three most perfect plots ever planned.'

Amelia and Joseph Andrews. Published in 1751 and 1742 respectively.

Amelia, and the hashed mutton. Cf. Hazlitt's essay 'A Farewell to Essay-writing,' from which it appears that the article in the *Edinburgh Review* from which this lecture is taken was the result of a 'sharply-seasoned and well-sustained' discussion with Lamb, kept up till midnight.

115. *Roderick Random.* Published in 1748, when Smollett was 27 ; *Tom Jones* was published in 1749, when Fielding was 42.

116. *Intus et in cute.* Persius, *Satires*, III. 30.

117. *Peregrine Pickle . . . and Launcelot Graves.* 1751 and 1762 respectively.

Humphrey Clinker and Count Fathom. 1771 and 1753 respectively.

Richardson. The three novels of Samuel Richardson (1689-1761) appeared as follows : *Pamela* in 1740 ; *Clarissa Harlowe* in 1747-8 ; *Sir Charles Grandison* in 1753.

119. *Dr. Johnson . . . when he said*, etc. Boswell's *Life of Johnson* (ed. G. B. Hill), II. 174.

120. *'Books are a real world,'* etc. Wordsworth, *Personal Talk*, St. 3.

Sterne. Laurence Sterne's (1713-1768) *Tristram Shandy* appeared in 9 vols. 1759-1767, and *A Sentimental Journey* (2 vols.) in 1768.

121. *Goldsmith . . . should call him*, etc. Boswell's *Life of Johnson* (ed. G. B. Hill), II. 222.

123. *'Have kept the even tenor of their way.'* Gray's *Elegy*, 76.

Evelina, Cecilia, and Camilla. By Frances Burney, Madame D'Arblay (1752-1840), published respectively in 1778, 1782, and 1796.

123. *Mrs. Radcliffe.* Ann Radcliffe (1764-1822), author of *The Romance of the Forest* (1791), *The Mysteries of Udolpho* (1794), etc.

'*Enchantments drear.*' *Il Penseroso,* 119.

Mrs. Inchbald. Elizabeth Inchbald (1753-1821), novelist, dramatist, and actress. Her *Nature and Art* appeared in 1796, *A Simple Story* in 1791.

Miss Edgeworth. Maria Edgeworth (1767-1849). *Castle Rackrent* appeared in 1800.

Meadows. In *The Wanderer.*

Note. *The Fool of Quality,* by Henry Brooke (1766) ; *David Simple,* by Sarah Fielding (1744) ; and *Sidney Biddulph,* by Mrs. Sheridan (1761).

124. *It has been said of Shakspeare, etc.* By Pope. See Hazlitt's *Characters of Shakespear's Plays,* vol. I. p. 171 and note.

'*There is nothing so true as habit.*' Windham, Speech on the Conduct of the Duke of York, *Speeches,* III. 205, March 14, 1809.

125. '*Stand so* [not] *upon the order,' etc. Macbeth,* Act III. Sc. 4.

The green silken threads, etc. Don Quixote, Part II. IV. Chap. 58.

The Wanderer. 1814.

'*The gossamer,' etc. Romeo and Juliet,* Act II. Sc. 6.

127. *The Castle of Otranto.* By Horace Walpole (1764).

Quod sic mihi, etc. Horace, *Ars Poetica,* 188.

The Recess, by Sophia Lee (1785) ; *The Old English Baron,* by Clara Reeve, originally published in 1777 under the title of '*The Champion of Virtue, a Gothic Story.*'

'*Dismal treatises.*' *Macbeth,* Act V. Sc. 5.

The Monk, by Matthew Gregory Lewis, published in 1795 as '*Ambrosio, or the Monk.*'

'*All the luxury of woe.*' Moore, *Juvenile Poems,* stanzas headed '*Anacreontic,*' beginning '*Press the grape, and let it pour,*' etc.

128. '*His chamber,' etc. The Faerie Queene,* Book II. Canto IX. St. 50.

129. '*Familiar in our mouths,' etc. Henry V.,* Act IV. Sc. 3.

130. *The author of Caleb Williams.* William Godwin (1756-1836). *Caleb Williams* appeared in 1794, *St. Leon* in 1799, *Mandeville* in 1817.

'*Action is momentary,' etc.* These lines are slightly misquoted from Wordsworth's tragedy, *The Borderer.* See note to vol. IV., p. 276.

132. *Political Justice. An Inquiry concerning Political Justice and its Influence on Morals and Happiness,* 1793.

'*Where his treasure,' etc. St. Matthew,* vi. 21.

LECTURE VII. ON THE WORKS OF HOGARTH—ON THE GRAND AND FAMILIAR STYLE OF PAINTING

A great part of this lecture is taken from two papers in *The Examiner,* republished in *The Round Table.* See vol. I. pp. 25-31, and notes thereon.

133. *Hogarth.* William Hogarth (1697-1764).

'*Instinct in every part.*' Cf. '*Instinct through all proportions low and high.*' *Paradise Lost,* XI. 562.

'*Other pictures we see, Hogarth's we read.*' '*Other pictures we look at,—his prints we read.*' Lamb's *Essay on the Genius and Character of Hogarth,* referred to below, p. 138.

Not long ago. In 1814.

NOTES

134. '*Of amber-lidded snuff-box,*' etc. Pope's *Rape of the Lock*, IV. 123.
134. '*A person, and a smooth dispose,*' etc. *Othello*, Act I. Sc. 3.
      '*Vice loses half,*' etc. Burke, *Reflections on the Revolution in France* (*Select Works*, ed. Payne, II. 89).
137. '*All the mutually reflected charities.*' Burke, *Reflections on the Revolution in France* (*Select Works*, ed. Payne, II. 40).
      '*Frequent and full,*' etc. *Paradise Lost*, I. 795-7.
138. *Mr. Lamb's Essay.* Published in *The Reflector* (1811) and reprinted in *Poems, Plays and Essays* (ed. Ainger).
      What distinguishes, etc. The remainder of the lecture from this point had not appeared in *The Examiner* or *The Round Table.*
139. *Mr. Wilkie.* David Wilkie (1785-1841), Royal Academician 1811, knighted 1836.
      Teniers. David Teniers, the younger (1610-1690).
      '*To shew vice,*' etc. Adapted from *Hamlet*, Act III. Sc. 2.
140. '*The very error of the time.*' Cf. 'The very error of the moon,' *Othello*, Act V. Sc. 2.
      '*Your lungs,*' etc. *As You Like It*, Act II. Sc. 7.
      Bagnigge Wells. Sadler's Wells. Hazlitt refers to Hogarth's 'Evening,' one of the four 'Times of Day.'
142. *Parson Ford.* Johnson's cousin, Cornelius Ford. See Boswell's *Life of Johnson* (ed. G. B. Hill), I. 49. The figure in Hogarth's picture has also been identified with 'Orator' Henley.
143. '*Die of a rose,*' etc. Pope, *Essay on Man*, I, 200.
      In the manner of Ackerman's dresses for May. Moore, *Horace, Ode XI., Lib. 2. Freely translated by the Pr—ce R—g—t.*
144. '*The Charming Betsy Careless.*' See the last of the series of 'The Rake's Progress,' the scene in Bedlam. One of the lunatics has scratched the name on the bannisters.
      '*Stray-gifts of love and beauty.*' Wordsworth, *Stray Pleasures.*
145. *Sir Joshua Reynolds.* See *Table-Talk*, vol. VI. p. 131 *et seq.*
146. '*Conformed to this world,*' etc. Romans, xii. 2.
      '*Give to airy nothing,*' etc. *A Midsummer Night's Dream*, Act V. Sc. 1.
      '*Ignorant present.*' *Macbeth*, Act I. Sc. 5.
      Note. '*Nay, nay,*' etc. 'Na, na ! not that way, not that way, the head to the east.' *Guy Mannering*, chap. 55.
148. *It is many years since, etc.* About 1798, at St. Neots, in Huntingdonshire. Cf. the essay 'On Going a Journey' in *Table-Talk*, vol. VI. p. 185.
      '*How was I then uplifted.*' *Troilus and Cressida*, Act III. Sc. 2.
      '*Temples not made with hands,*' etc. 2 Corinthians, v. 1.
      In the Louvre. In 1802, when the Louvre still contained the spoils of Buonaparte's conquests. Cf. *Table-Talk*, vol. VI. pp. 15 *et seq.* and notes thereon.
      '*All eyes shall see me,*' etc. Cf. Romans, xiv. 11.
149. There '*stood the statue,*' etc. 'So stands the statue that enchants the world.' Thomson, *The Seasons*, Summer, 1347. The statue is the Venus of Medici.
      '*There was old Proteus,*' etc. Wordsworth's Sonnet, 'The world is too much with us,' adapted.
      The stay, the guide, etc. An unacknowledged quotation from Wordsworth's *Lines composed a few miles above Tintern Abbey*, 109-110.
      '*Smoothed the raven down,*' etc. *Comus*, 251.

LECTURES ON THE COMIC WRITERS

LECTURE VIII. ON THE COMIC WRITERS OF THE LAST CENTURY

Much of the early part of this Lecture is taken from a paper in *The Examiner* (Aug. 20, 1815), republished in *The Round Table*. See vol. I. pp. 10-14, and notes.

PAGE

150. '*Where it must live,*' etc. *Othello,* Act II. Sc. 4.

'*To see ourselves,*' etc. Burns, *To a Louse.*

151. '*Present no mark to the foeman.*' *Henry IV.,* Part II., Act III. Sc. 2. *Wart* should be *Shadow.*

152. *The authority of Sterne, etc.* See *Tristram Shandy,* I. 21.

l. 22. In the third edition a passage is interpolated from Hazlitt's letter to *The Morning Chronicle,* Oct. 15, 1813.

'*The ring,*' etc. Pope, *Moral Essays,* III. 309-10.

Angelica, etc. All these characters are in Congreve's *Love for Love.*

The compliments which Pope paid to his friends. Cf. the essay 'On Persons one would wish to have seen,' where some of these compliments are quoted.

153. *The loves of the plants and the triangles.* Erasmus Darwin's poem 'The Loves of the Plants' (1789) was the subject of Canning's famous parody 'The Loves of the Triangles' in *The Anti-Jacobin.*

Berinthias and Alitheas. Berinthia in Vanbrugh's *The Relapse*; Alithea in Wycherley's *The Country Wife.*

Beppo, etc. Lord Byron's *Beppo* (1818), Campbell's *Gertrude of Wyoming* (1809), Scott's *Lady of the Lake* (1810). Madame De Staël's *Corinne* appeared in 1807.

l. 17. In the third edition a long passage from Hazlitt's letter to *The Morning Chronicle* is here inserted.

'*That sevenfold fence.*' See note to vol. I. p. 13, and cf. *A Reply to Malthus,* vol. IV. p. 101.

154. '*Mr. Smirk, you are a brisk man.*' Foote's *The Minor,* Act II.

'*Almost afraid to know itself.*' *Macbeth,* Act IV. Sc. 3.

Mr. Farren. William Farren (1786-1861). Lord Ogleby in Colman and Garrick's *The Clandestine Marriage* was one of his best parts.

Note. See vol. I. p. 313.

155. *Jeremy Collier.* Jeremy Collier's (1650-1726) *Short View of the Immorality and Profaneness of the English Stage* appeared in March 1697-8.

Mrs. Centlivre. Susannah Centlivre (1667 ?-1723). *The Busy Body* appeared in 1709, *The Wonder* in 1714.

156. *The scene near the end.* *The Wonder,* Act V. Sc. 2.

'*Roast me these Violantes.*' *Ibid.* Act II. Sc. 1.

156. In the third edition the following account of *The Busy Body,* taken from Oxberry's *The New English Drama* (Vol. VI.) is inserted :

'"The Busy Body" is a comedy that has now held possession of the stage above a hundred years (the best test of excellence) ; and the merit that has enabled it to do so, consists in the ingenuity of the contrivance, the liveliness of the plot, and the striking effect of the situations. Mrs. Centlivre, in this and her other plays, could do nothing without a stratagem; but she could do everything with one. She delights in putting her *dramatis personae* continually at their wit's end, and in helping them off with a new evasion ; and the subtlety of her resources is in proportion to

NOTES

the criticalness of the situation and the shortness of the notice for resorting
to an expedient. Twenty times, in seeing or reading one of her plays, your
pulse beats quick, and you become restless and apprehensive for the event ;
but with a fine theatrical sleight of hand, she lets you off, undoes the knot
of the difficulty, and you breathe freely again, and have a hearty laugh
into the bargain. In short, with her knowledge of chambermaids' tricks,
and insight into the intricate foldings of lovers' hearts, she plays with the
events of comedy, as a juggler shuffles about a pack of cards, to serve his
own purposes, and to the surprise of the spectator. This is one of the
most delightful employments of the dramatic art. It costs nothing—but
a voluntary tax on the inventive powers of the author ; and it produces,
when successfully done, profit and praise to one party, and pleasure to all.
To show the extent and importance of theatrical amusements (which some
grave persons would decry altogether, and which no one can extol too
highly), a friend of ours,[1] whose name will be as well known to posterity as
it is to his contemporaries, was not long ago mentioning, that one of the
earliest and most memorable impressions ever made on his mind, was the
seeing " Venice Preserved " acted in a country town when he was only nine
years old. But he added, that an elderly lady who took him to see it,
lamented, notwithstanding the wonder and delight he had experienced, that
instead of " Venice Preserved," they had not gone to see " The Busy Body,"
which had been acted the night before. This was fifty years ago, since
which, and for fifty years before that, it has been acted a thousand times
in town and country, giving delight to the old, the young, and middle-aged,
passing the time carelessly, and affording matter for agreeable reflection
afterwards, making us think ourselves, and wish to be thought, the men
equal to Sir George Airy in grace and spirit, the women to Miranda and
Isabinda in love and beauty, and all of us superior to Marplot in wit.
Among the scenes that might be mentioned in this comedy, as striking
instances of happy stage effect, are Miranda's contrivance to escape from
Sir George, by making him turn his back upon her to hear her confession
of love, and the ludicrous attitude in which he is left waiting for the
rest of her speech after the lady has vanished ; his offer of the hundred
pounds to her guardian to make love to her in his presence, and when she
receives him in dumb show, his answering for both ; his situation concealed
behind the chimney-screen ; his supposed metamorphosis into a monkey,
and his deliverance from thence in that character by the interference of
Marplot ; Mrs. Patch's sudden conversion of the mysterious love letter
into a charm for the toothache, and the whole of Marplot's meddling and
blunders. The last character is taken from Dryden and the Duchess of
Newcastle ; and is, indeed, the only attempt at character in the play. It
is amusing and superficial. We see little of the puzzled perplexity of his
brain, but his actions are absurd enough. He whiffles about the stage
with considerable volubility, and makes a very lively automaton. Sir
George Airy sets out for a scene or two in a spirited manner, but afterwards
the character evaporates in the name ; and he becomes as commonplace as
his friend Charles, who merely laments over his misfortunes, or gets out
of them by following the suggestions of his valet or his valet's mistress.
Miranda is the heroine of the piece, and has a right to be so ; for she is a
beauty and an heiress. Her friend has less to recommend her ; but who

---

[1] This was Godwin, who saw *Venice Preserved* at Norwich. See Kegan Paul,
William Godwin: His Friends and Contemporaries, I. 10.

can refuse to fall in love with her name ? What volumes of sighs, what a
world of love, is breathed in the very sound alone—the letters that form
the charming name of Isabinda.'

157. *'The one cries Mum,'* etc. *The Merry Wives of Windsor,* Act 5. Sc. 2.
Note. See first edition (1714), pp. 35-6.

158. *'Some soul of goodness,'* etc. *Henry V.,* Act iv. Sc. 1.
His Funeral. Produced in 1701.
'All the milk of human kindness.' *Macbeth,* Act 1. Sc. 5.
The Conscious Lovers. 1722. Hazlitt refers to Act iii. Sc. 1.
Parson Adams against me. See *Joseph Andrews,* Book iii. chap. 11.
Addison's Drummer. 1715.
'An Hour after Marriage.' *Three Hours after Marriage* (1717), the joint
production of Gay, Pope, and Arbuthnot.
'An alligator stuff'd.' *Romeo and Juliet,* Act v. Sc. 1.
Gay's What-d'ye-call-it. 1715.
'Polly.' Published in 1728. The representation was forbidden by the Court.
Last line but one. In the third edition Hazlitt's essay 'On the Beggar's
Opera' (see vol. 1. pp. 65-6) is here introduced.

159. *The Mock Doctor.* 1732.
Tom Thumb. Afterwards called *The Tragedy of Tragedies, or the Life and
Death of Tom Thumb the Great* (1730 ; additional Act, 1731).
Lord Grizzle. In *Tom Thumb.*
'Like those hanging locks,' etc. Fletcher, *The Faithful Shepherdess,* Act 1. Sc. 2.
'Fell of hair,' etc. *Macbeth,* Act v. Sc. 5.
'Hey for Doctor's Commons.' *Tragedy of Tragedies, etc.,* Act ii. Sc. 5.
'From the sublime,' etc. See *ante,* note to p. 23.
Lubin Log. In James Kenney's farce, *Love, Law, and Physic,* produced 1812.
See *ante,* p. 192.
The Widow's Choice. Allingham's *Who Wins, or The Widow's Choice,* 1808.
'Is high fantastical.' *Twelfth Night,* Act 1. Sc. 1.

160. *The hero of the Dunciad.* Cibber was substituted for Theobald as the King of
Dulness in consequence of his famous letter to Pope, published in 1742.
'By merit raised,' etc. *Paradise Lost,* ii. 5-6.
His Apology for his own Life. Published in 1740. Cf. *The Round Table,*
vol. 1. pp. 156-7.
His account of his waiting, etc. *An Apology, etc.,* 2nd ed. 1740, chap. iii. pp.
59-60.
Mr. Burke's celebrated apostrophe. *Reflections on the Revolution in France* (*Select
Works,* ed. Payne, ii. 89).
Kynaston, etc. See vol. 1. notes to pp. 156-7.

161. *His Careless Husband.* 1704.
His Double Gallant. 1707. The play was revived in 1817 and noticed by
Hazlitt. See *ante,* pp. 359-362.
'In hidden mazes,' etc. Misquoted from *L'Allegro,* 141-2.

162. *His Nonjuror.* 1717. Isaac Bickerstaff's *The Hypocrite* was produced in
1768.
Love's Last Shift. Colley Cibber's first play, produced in 1694. For
Southerne's remark to Cibber, see *An Apology for the Life of Colley Cibber,*
p. 173.
l. 34. In the third edition a great part of Hazlitt's article on *The Hypocrite*
(see *A View of the English Stage, ante,* p. 245) is inserted here. The
passage is also in Oxberry's *New English Drama,* vol. 1.
Love in a Riddle. 1729.

504

NOTES

163. *The Suspicious Husband,* 1747, *The Jealous Wife,* 1761, *The Clandestine Marriage,* 1766.

l. 15. In the third edition the following passage on *The Jealous Wife,* taken from Oxberry's *The New English Drama* (Vol. 1.) is here inserted :—

'Colman, the elder, was the translator of Terence : and the "Jealous Wife" is a classical play. The plot is regular, the characters well supported, and the moral the best in the world. The dialogue has more sense than wit. The ludicrous arises from the skilful development of the characters, and the absurdities they commit in their own persons, rather than from the smart reflections which are made upon them by others. Thus nothing can be more ridiculous or more instructive than the scenes of which Mrs. Oakly is the heroine, yet they are all serious and unconscious : she exposes herself to our contempt and ridicule by the part she acts, by the airs she gives herself, and the fantastic behaviour in the situations in which she is placed. In other words, the character is pure comedy, not satire. Congreve's comedies for the most part are satires, in which, from an exuberance of wit, the different speakers play off the sharp-pointed raillery on one another's foibles, real or supposed. The best and most genuine kind of comedy, because the most dramatic, is that of character or humour, in which the persons introduced upon the stage are left to betray their own folly by their words and actions. The progressive winding up of the story of the present comedy is excellently managed. The jealousy and hysteric violence of Mrs. Oakly increase every moment, as the pretext for them becomes more and more frivolous. The attention is kept alive by our doubts about Oakly's wavering (but in the end triumphant) firmness ; and the arch insinuations and well-concerted home-thrusts of the Major heighten the comic interest of the scene. There is only one circumstance on which this veteran bachelor's freedom of speech might have thrown a little more light, namely, that the married lady's jealousy is in truth only a pretence for the exercise of her domineering spirit in general ; so that we are left at last in some uncertainty as to the turn which this humour may take, and as to the future repose of her husband, though the affair of Miss Russet is satisfactorily cleared up. The under-plot of the two lovers is very ingeniously fitted into the principal one, and is not without interest in itself. Charles Oakly is a spirited, well-meaning, thoughtless young fellow, and Harriet Russet is an amiable romantic girl, in that very common, but always romantic situation —in love. Her persecution from the addresses of Lord Trinket and Sir Harry Beagle fans the gentle flame which had been kindled just a year before in her breast, produces the adventures and cross-purposes of the plot, and at last reconciles her to, and throws her into the arms of her lover, in spite of her resentment for his misconduct and apparent want of delicacy. The figure which Lord Trinket and Lady Freelove make in the piece is as odious and contemptible as it is possible for people in that class of life (and for no others) to make. The insolence, the meanness, the affectation, the hollowness, the want of humanity, sincerity, principle, and delicacy, are such as can only be found where artificial rank and station in society supersede not merely a regard to propriety of conduct, but the necessity even of an attention to appearances. The morality of the stage has (we are ready to hope) told in that direction as well as others, has, in some measure suppressed the suffocating pretensions and flaunting affectation of vice and folly in "persons of honour," and, as it were, humanised rank and file. The pictures drawn of the finished depravity of such characters in high life, in the old comedies and novels, can hardly have been thrown away upon the persons themselves, any more than upon the world at large. Little Terence O'Cutler, the delicious *protégé* of Lord Trinket and Lady Freelove, is a fit instrument for them to use, and follows in the train of such principals as naturally and assuredly as their shadow. Sir Harry Beagle is a coarse, but striking character of a thorough-bred fox-hunting country squire. He has but one idea in his head, but one sentiment in his heart— and that is his stud. This idea haunts his imagination, tinges or imbues every other object, and accounts for his whole phraseology, appearance, costume, and conduct. Sir Harry's ruling passion is varied very ingeniously, and often turned to a very ludicrous account. There is a necessary monotony in the humour, which arises from a want of more than one idea, but the obviousness of the jest almost makes up for the recurrence of it ; if the means of exciting mirth are mechanical, the effect is sure ; and to say that a hearty laugh is cheaply purchased, is not a serious objection against it. When an author is terribly conscious of plagiarism, he seldom confesses it ; when the obligation does not press his conscience, he sometimes does. Colman, in the advertisement to the first edition of the " Jealous Wife," apologises for the freedom which he has used in borrowing from " Tom Jones." In reading this modest excuse, though we have seen the play several times, we could not imagine what part of the plot was taken from Fielding. We did not suspect that Miss Russet was Sophia Western, and that old Russet and Sir Harry Beagle between them somehow represented Squire Western and young Blifil. But so it is ! The outline of the plot and some of the characters are certainly the same, but the filling up destroys the likeness. There is all in the novel that there is in the play, but there is so much in the novel that is not in the play, that the total impression is quite different, and loses even an appearance of resemblance. In the same manner, though a profile or a shade of a face is exactly the same as the original, we with difficulty recognise it from the absence of so many other particulars. Colman might have kept his own secret, and no one would have been the wiser for it.'

163. *The elder Colman's translation of Terence.* Published in 1765.
Bickerstaff's plays. *Love in a Village,* 1763, *The Maid of the Mill,* 1765, and *The Hypocrite* are the best known.
Mrs. Cowley's comedy, etc. Hannah Cowley's (1743?-1809) *The Belle's Stratagem* appeared in 1780, *Who's the Dupe ?* in 1779.
164. *Goldsmith's Good-natured Man,* 1768 ; *She Stoops to Conquer,* 1773.

In the third edition the following account of *She Stoops to Conquer* from Oxberry's *The New English Drama* (Vol. IV.) is here inserted :—

'It, however, bears the stamp of the author's genius, which was an indefinable mixture of the original and imitative. His plot, characters, and incidents are all apparently new ; and yet, when you come to look into them, they are all old, with little variation or disguise : that is, the author sedulously avoided the beaten, vulgar path, and sought for singularity, but found it rather in the unhackneyed and eccentric inventions of those who had gone before him, than in his own stores. The " Vicar of Wakefield," which abounds more than any of his works in delightful and original traits, is still very much borrowed, in its general tone and outline, from Fielding's " Joseph Andrews." Again, the characters and adventures of Tony Lumpkin, and the ridiculous conduct of his mother, in the present comedy, are a counterpart (even to the incident of the theft of the jewels) of those of the Widow Blackacre and her booby son in Wycherley's " Plain Dealer."

NOTES

'This sort of plagiarism, which gives us a repetition of new and striking pictures of human life, is much to be preferred to the dull routine of trite, vapid, every-day common-places ; but it is more dangerous, as the stealing of pictures or family plate, where the property can be immediately identified, is more liable to detection than the stealing of bank-notes, or the current coin of the realm. Dr. Johnson's sarcasm against some writer, that his "singularity was not his excellence," cannot be applied to Goldsmith's writings in general ; but we are not sure whether it might not in severity be applied to " She Stoops to Conquer." The incidents and characters are many of them exceedingly amusing ; but they are so, a little at the expense of probability and *bienseance*. Tony Lumpkin is a very essential and unquestionably comic personage ; but certainly his absurdities or his humours fail of none of their effect for want of being carried far enough. He is in his own sex what a hoyden is in the other. He is that vulgar nick-name, a *hobbety-hoy*, dramatised ; forward and sheepish, mischievous and idle, cunning and stupid, with the vices of the man and the follies of the boy ; fond of low company, and giving himself all the airs of consequence of the young squire. His vacant delight in playing at cup and ball, and his impenetrable confusion and obstinate gravity in spelling the letter, drew fresh beauties from Mr. Liston's face. Young Marlow's bashfulness in the scenes with his mistress is, when well acted, irresistibly ludicrous ; but still nothing can quite overcome our incredulity as to the existence of such a character in the present day, and in the rank of life, and with the education which Marlow is supposed to have had. It is a highly amusing caricature, a ridiculous fancy, but no more. One of the finest and most delicate touches of character is in the transition from the modest gentleman's manner with his mistress, to the easy and agreeable tone of familiarity with the supposed chambermaid, which was not total and abrupt, but exactly such in kind and degree as such a character of natural reserve and constitutional timidity would undergo from the change of circumstances. Of the other characters in the piece, the most amusing are Tony Lumpkin's associates at the Three Pigeons ; and of these we profess the greatest partiality for the important showman who declares that " his bear dances to none but the genteelest of tunes, ' Water parted from the Sea,' or the minuet in ' Ariadne ' ! " [1] This is certainly the " high-fantastical " [2] of low comedy.'

164. *Murphy's plays, etc.* Arthur Murphy's (1730-1805) *All in the Wrong*, 1761, and *Know Your Own Mind*, 1778.

Both his principal pieces, etc. There seems to be some inaccuracy here. Colman's *Jealous Wife* was produced in February 1761, Murphy's *All in the Wrong* in June of the same year. *The School for Scandal*, however, appeared a month later than Murphy's *Know Your Own Mind*, viz., in May 1777.

The School for Scandal, 1777, *The Rivals*, 1775, *The Duenna*, 1775, and *The Critic*, 1779.

Cumberland. Richard Cumberland (1732-1811), the dramatist, whose *West Indian* (1771) and *The Wheel of Fortune* (1795) are referred to below, p. 166.

'Dragged the struggling,' etc. Goldsmith, *The Traveller*, l. 190.

165. *Miss Farren.* Elizabeth Farren (1759 ?-1829), Countess of Derby. She played Lady Teazle on the occasion of her last appearance, April 8, 1797.

Matthew Bramble and his sister. In *Humphry Clinker*.

' He had damnable iteration in him.' Henry IV., Part I., Act 1. Sc. 2.

---

[1] *She Stoops to Conquer*, Act 1.   [2] *Twelfth Night*, Act 1. Sc. 1.

LECTURES ON THE COMIC WRITERS

165, l. 36. In the third edition Hazlitt's description of *The Rivals,* from Oxberry's *The New English Drama* (Vol. i.) is inserted here :—

'The "Rivals" is one of the most agreeable comedies we have. In the elegance and brilliancy of the dialogue, in a certain animation of moral sentiment, and in the masterly *dénouement* of the fable, the "School for Scandal" is superior ; but the "Rivals" has more life and action in it, and abounds in a greater number of whimsical characters, unexpected incidents, and absurd contrasts of situation. The effect of the "School for Scandal" is something like reading a collection of epigrams, that of the "Rivals" is more like reading a novel. In the first you are always at the toilette or in the drawing-room ; in the last you pass into the open air, and take a turn in King's Mead. The interest is kept alive in the one play by smart repartees, in the other by startling rencontres : in the one we laugh at the satirical descriptions of the speakers, in the other the situation of their persons on the stage is irresistibly ludicrous. Thus the interviews between Lucy and Sir Lucius O'Trigger, between Acres and his friend Jack, who is at once his confidant and his rival ; between Mrs. Malaprop and the lover of her niece as Captain Absolute, and between the young lady and the same person as the pretended Ensign Beverley, tell from the mere *double entendre* of the scene, and from the ignorance of the parties of one another's persons and designs. There is no source of dramatic effect more complete than this species of practical satire (in which our author seems to have been an adept), where one character in the piece is made a fool of and turned into ridicule to his face, by the very person whom he is trying to over-reach.

'There is scarcely a more delightful play than the "Rivals" when it is well acted, or one that goes off more indifferently when it is not. The humour is of so broad and farcical a kind, that if not thoroughly entered into and carried off by the tone and manner of the performers, it fails of effect from its obtrusiveness, and becomes flat from eccentricity. The absurdities brought forward are of that artificial, affected, and preposterous description, that we in some measure require to have the evidence of our senses to see the persons themselves "jetting under the advance plumes of their folly,"[1] before we can entirely believe in their existence, or derive pleasure from their exposure. If the extravagance of the poet's conception is not supported by the downright reality of the representation, our credulity is staggered and falls to the ground.

'For instance, Acres should be as odd a compound in external appearance as he is of the author's brain. He must look like a very notable mixture of the lively coxcomb and the blundering blockhead, to reconcile us to his continued impertinence and senseless flippancy. Acres is a mere conventional character, a gay, fluttering automaton, constructed upon mechanical principles, and pushed, as it were, by the logic of wit and a strict keeping in the pursuit of the ridiculous, into follies and fopperies which his natural thoughtlessness would never have dreamt of. Acres does not say or do what such a half-witted young gentleman would say or do of his own head, but what he might be led to do or say with such a prompter as Sheridan at his elbow to tutor him in absurdity—to make a butt of him first, and laugh at him afterwards. Thus his presence of mind in persisting in his allegorical swearing, "Odds triggers and flints,"[2] in the duel scene, when he is trembling all over with cowardice, is quite out of character, but it keeps up the preconcerted jest. In proportion, therefore, as the author has over-

---

[1] Cf. *Twelfth Night,* Act ii. Sc. 5.   [2] *The Rivals,* Act v. Sc. 3.

done the part, it calls for a greater effort of animal spirits, and a peculiar aptitude of genius in the actor to go through with it, to humour the extravagance, and to seem to take a real and cordial delight in caricaturing himself. Dodd[1] was the only actor we remember who realised this ideal combination of volatility and phlegm, of slowness of understanding with levity of purpose, of vacancy of thought and vivacity of gesture. Acres' affected phrases and apish manners used to sit upon this inimitable actor with the same sort of bumpkin grace and conscious self-complacency as the new cut of his clothes. In general, this character is made little of on the stage ; and when left to shift for itself, seems as vapid as it is forced.

'Mrs. Malaprop is another portrait of the same overcharged description. The chief drollery of this extraordinary personage consists of her unaccountable and systematic misapplication of hard words. How she should know the words, and not their meaning, is a little odd. In reading the play we are amused with such a series of ridiculous blunders, just as we are with a series of puns or cross-readings. But to keep up the farce upon the stage, besides "a nice derangement of epitaphs,"[2] the imagination must have the assistance of a stately array of grave pretensions, and a most formidable establishment of countenance, with all the vulgar self-sufficiency of pride and ignorance, before it can give full credit to this learned tissue of technical absurdity.

'As to Miss Lydia Languish, she is not easily done to the life. She is a delightful compound of extravagance and *naïveté*. She is fond and froward, practical and chimerical, hot and cold in a breath. She is that kind of fruit which drops into the mouth before it is ripe. She must have a husband, but she will not have one without an elopement. This young lady is at an age and of a disposition to throw herself into the arms of the first handsome young fellow she meets ; but she repents and grows sullen, like a spoiled child, when she finds that nobody hinders her. She should have all the physiognomical marks of a true boarding-school, novel-reading Miss about her, and some others into the bargain. Sir Anthony's description hardly comes up to the truth. She should have large, rolling eyes ; pouting, disdainful lips ; a pale, clear complexion ; an oval chin, an arching neck, and a profusion of dark ringlets falling down upon it, or she will never answer to our ideas of the charming sentimental hoyden, who is the heroine of the play.

'Faulkland is a refined study of a very common disagreeable character, actuated by an unceasing spirit of contradiction, who perversely seizes every idle pretext for making himself and others miserable ; or querulous enthusiast, determined on disappointment, and enamoured with suspicion. He is without excuse ; nor is it without some difficulty that we endure his self-tormenting follies, through our partiality for Julia, the amiable, unresisting victim of his gloomy caprice.

'Sir Anthony Absolute and his son are the most sterling characters of the play. The tetchy, positive, impatient, overbearing, but warm and generous character of the one, and the gallant, determined spirit, adroit address, and dry humour of the other, are admirably set off against each other. The two scenes in which they contend about the proposed match, in the first of which the indignant lover is as choleric and rash as the old gentleman is furious and obstinate, and in the latter of which the son affects such a cool indifference and dutiful submission to his father, from having found out that it is the mistress of his choice whom he is to be compelled to marry,

---

[1] James William Dodd (1740?-1796). [2] *The Rivals*, Act III. Sc. 3.

are masterpieces both of wit, humour, and character. Sir Anthony Absolute is an evident copy after Smollett's kind-hearted, high-spirited Matthew Bramble, as Mrs. Malaprop is after the redoubted linguist, Mrs. Tabitha Bramble ; and, indeed the whole tone, as well as the local scenery of the " Rivals," reminds the reader of " Humphry Clinker." Sheridan had a right to borrow ; and he made use of this privilege, not sparingly, both in this and in his other plays. His Acres, as well in the general character as in particular scenes, is a *mannered* imitation of Sir Andrew Ague-cheek.

' Fag, Lucy, and Sir Lucius O'Trigger, though subordinate agents in the plot of the " Rivals," are not the less amusing on that account. Fag wears his master's wit, as he does his lace, at second-hand ; Lucy is an edifying specimen of simplicity in a chambermaid, and Sir Lucius is an honest fortune-hunting Hibernian, who means well to himself, and no harm to anybody else. They are also traditional characters, common to the stage ; but they are drawn with all the life and spirit of originals.

' This appears, indeed, to have been the peculiar *forte* and the great praise of our author's genius, that he could imitate with the spirit of an inventor. There is hardly a character, we believe, or a marked situation in any of his works, of which there are not distinct traces to be found in his predecessors. But though the groundwork and texture of his materials was little more than what he found already existing in the models of acknowledged excellence, yet he constantly varied or improved upon their suggestions with masterly skill and ingenuity. He applied what he thus borrowed, with a sparkling effect and rare felicity, to different circumstances, and adapted it with peculiar elegance to the prevailing taste of the age. He was the farthest possible from a servile plagiarist. He wrote in imitation of Congreve, Vanbrugh, or Wycherley, as those persons would have written in continuation of themselves, had they lived at the same time with him. There is no excellence of former writers of which he has not availed himself, and which he has not converted to his own purposes, with equal spirit and success. He had great acuteness and knowledge of the world ; and if he did not create his own characters, he compared them with their prototypes in nature, and understood their bearings and qualities, before he undertook to make a different use of them. He had wit, fancy, sentiment at command, enabling him to place the thoughts of others in new lights of his own, which reflected back an added lustre on the originals : whatever he touched, he adorned with all the ease, grace, and brilliancy of his style. If he ranks only as a man of second-rate genius, he was assuredly a man of first-rate talents. He was the most classical and the most popular dramatic writer of his age. The works he has left behind him will remain as monuments of his fame, for the delight and instruction of posterity.

' Mr. Sheridan not only excelled as a comic writer, but was also an eminent orator, and a disinterested patriot. As a public speaker, he was distinguished by acuteness of observation and pointed wit, more than by impassioned eloquence, or powerful and comprehensive reasoning. Considering him with reference to his conversational talents, his merits as a comic writer, and as a political character, he was perhaps the most accomplished person of his time.

> " Take him for all in all,
> We shall not look upon his like again." '[1]

[1] *Hamlet*, Act I. Sc. 2.

165. '*Had I a heart,*' etc. *The Duenna*, Act I. Sc. 5.
166. '*Half thy malice,*' etc. *Ibid.* Act III. Sc. I.
That on the Begum's affairs. June 3, 6, 10, 13, 1788.
One who has all the ability, etc. Hazlitt refers to Thomas Moore, whose *Life of Sheridan*, however, did not appear till 1825.
Macklin's Man of the World. Charles Macklin's (1697?-1797) *The Man of the World*, first produced in London in 1781. For George Frederick Cooke's (1756-1811) acting in the part of Sir Pertinax Macsycophant see Leigh Hunt's *Critical Essays on the Performers of the London Theatres* (1807), pp. 220-1.
Mr. Holcroft. See Hazlitt's *Memoirs of the Life of Thomas Holcroft*, vol. II. pp. 121-4 of the present edition.
l. 38. In the third edition the following account of *The West Indian* from Oxberry's *The New English Drama* (Vol. I.) is interpolated :—

'As to the "West Indian," it is a play that from the time of its first appearing has continued to hold possession of the stage, with just enough merit to keep it there, and no striking faults to drive it thence. It is above mediocrity. There is an agreeable vein of good humour and animal spirits running through it that does not suffer it to sink into downright insipidity, nor ever excites any very high degree of interest or delight. Wit there is none, and hardly an attempt at humour, except in the character of Major O' Flaherty, who would not be recognised as a genuine Irishman but by virtue of his representative on the stage. His blunders and conduct are not such as would proceed from the good-natured unthinking impetuosity of such a person as O' Flaherty is intended to be : but they are such as the author might sit down and try to invent for him. It is not an Irish character, but a character playing the Irishman ; not a hasty, warm-hearted, hair-brained fellow, stumbling on mistakes by accident either in his words and actions, but a very complaisant gentleman, looking out for them by design, to humour the opinion which you entertain of him, and who is to make himself a national butt for the audience to laugh at. The "West Indian" himself (Belcour) is certainly the support of the piece. There is something interesting in the idea of seeing a young fellow of high animal spirits, a handsome fortune, and considerable generosity of feeling, launched from the other side of the world (with the additional impetus that the distance would give him) to run the gauntlet of the follies and vices of the town, to fall into scrapes only to get out of them, and who is full of professions of attachment to virtues which he does not practise, and of repentance for offences which he has not committed. It is the same character as Charles Surface in the "School for Scandal," with an infusion of the romantic from his transatlantic origin, and an additional excuse for his extravagances in the tropical temperature of his blood.

'The language of this play is elegant but common-place : the speakers seem in general more intent on adjusting their periods than on settling their affairs. The sentiments aspire to liberality. They are amiably mawkish, and as often as they incline to paradox, have a rapid sort of petulance about them, which excites neither our sympathy nor our esteem. The plot is a good plot. It is well laid, decently distributed through the course of five acts, and wound up at last to its final catastrophe in a single sentence.'

The Mayor of Garratt. Samuel Foote's (1720-1777), produced in 1764.
John O'Keeffe's (1747-1833) *The Agreeable Surprise*, 1781.

PAGE

167. *Mother Cole, etc.* Mrs. Cole and Smirk are both in *The Minor* (1760). Hazlitt may have been thinking of Puff in *Taste* (1752).

The acting of Dowton, etc. See *A View of the English Stage, ante*, p. 317, from which this passage is taken.

'*Pigeon-livered,*' etc. *Hamlet*, Act II. Sc. 2.

168. *Peter Pindar.* John Wolcot (1738-1819). *Sir Joseph Banks and the Emperor of Morocco* was published in 1788. The first of his *Lyric Odes to the Royal Academicians* appeared in 1782, and his *Ode upon Ode, or a Peep at St. James's and Instructions to a celebrated Laureat, being a Comic Account of the Visit of the Sovereign to Whitbread's Brewery*, in 1787.

'*Faint picture,*' etc. Adapted from *Hamlet*, Act v. Sc. 1.

Like his own expiring taper. Hazlitt seems to refer to some verses of Wolcot's, entitled 'To My Candle.' See *Pindar's Works* (1816), vol. II. p. 399.

A VIEW OF THE ENGLISH STAGE

IN this work, published in 1818, Hazlitt collected the greater part of the theatrical criticisms which he had contributed successively to *The Morning Chronicle, The Champion, The Examiner*, and *The Times*. His first article in *The Morning Chronicle* appeared on October 18, 1813 (see *ante*, p. 192), and the last on May 27, 1814 (see *ante*, p. 195). In his essay, 'On Patronage and Puffing' (*Table Talk*, vol. v. pp. 292, *et seq.*), Hazlitt gives an account of his theatrical criticisms in the *Chronicle*. He thought himself that they were the best articles in the series (see *ante*, p. 174), and they are at any rate of exceptional interest inasmuch as they deal for the most part with the first appearances of Edmund Kean in London. His first article in *The Champion*, then edited by John Scott, appeared on August 14, 1814 (see p. 196), and the last on January 8, 1815 (see p. 208). Early in 1815 he became the regular dramatic critic of *The Examiner*. Leigh Hunt, the editor, had intended to resume theatrical criticism after his release from prison in February, but his attention was diverted to politics by the return of Buonaparte from Elba. Hazlitt's first article (except for two notices of Kean's *Iago*, July 24 and August 7, 1814) appeared on March 19, 1815 (see p. 221), the last on June 8, 1817 (see p. 373). By far the greater part of Hazlitt's articles in *The Morning Chronicle, The Champion*, and *The Examiner* were included by him in *A View of the English Stage*. Some passages, however, and, we think, some articles, he did omit (especially from *The Examiner* of 1817). In the following notes passages omitted from articles included in *A View* are printed in full; articles omitted from *A View* are shortly summarised, if it is pretty clear from internal evidence that they were written by Hazlitt. Owing to want of space these articles cannot be printed in the present volume, but those which are clearly Hazlitt's will be found among fugitive writings in a later volume, together with some notices (deemed certainly his) from *The Times*. Hazlitt seems to have been the dramatic critic, or one of the dramatic critics, of *The Times* from the summer of 1817 till the spring of 1818, but only two of his articles (pp. 374, *et seq.*) were included in *A View of the English Stage*. These appeared in September 1817, near the beginning of his term of office. Hazlitt's reason for including so few of his *Times* articles is not known. An examination of the dramatic notices in *The Times* during the period in question suggests (1) that there were at least two regular dramatic critics on the staff, (2) that Hazlitt chiefly confined himself to Shakespearian and other plays of established reputation, and (3) that he practically ceased to write at the end of 1817. The following may be mentioned among the more important articles, which may, with varying degrees of probability, be ascribed to Hazlitt :—

NOTES

School for Scandal (Munden as Sir Peter Teazle), September 8, 1817; Young's
Hamlet, September 9; *As You Like It* (Miss Brunton as Rosalind), September 20;
Maywood's Zanga, October 3; Cibber's *The Refusal, or The Ladies' Philosophy*,
October 6; Kean's Richard III., October 7; *The Wonder, or A Woman Keeps a
Secret*, October 9; *Venice Preserved*, October 10; Kean's Macbeth, October 21;
Othello (Kean as Othello, Maywood as Iago), October 27; *Venice Preserved* (Miss
O'Neill as Belvidera), December 2; *The Honey Moon*, December 3; Fisher's
Hamlet, December 11; Kean's Macbeth, December 16; *King John* (Miss O'Neill
as Constance), December 18.

Reference should be made (1) to Mr. William Archer's Introduction to a Selection of Hazlitt's *Dramatic Essays* (ed. Archer and Lowe, 1895), and (2) to the
companion-volume of Leigh Hunt's *Dramatic Essays* (ed. Archer and Lowe, 1894).

PAGE

173. *Rochefoucault, etc.   Maximes et Réflexions Morales*, cccxii.
  ' *The brief chronicles of the time.*' *Hamlet*, Act II. Sc. 2.
  ' *Hold the mirror,*' etc. *Ibid.* Act. III. Sc. 2.
  ' *Imitate humanity,*' etc. *Ibid.*
  Zoffany's pictures. John Zoffany (1733-1810), a native of Ratisbon, came
    to England in 1758, and soon became noted for his pictures of Garrick and
    other actors in character. Several of these are preserved at the Garrick
    Club.
  Colley Cibber's Life. Cf. *ante*, pp. 160-1.

174. *A perverse caricature.* Hazlitt refers to the character of Marmozet in
    Peregrine Pickle (1751). The quarrel between Garrick and Smollett was
    afterwards made up.
  In different newspapers. See *ante*, introductory note to p. 169.
  ' *The secrets of the prison-house.*' *Hamlet*, Act I. Sc. 5.
  The editor of which, etc. Thomas Barnes was editor of *The Times* when
    Hazlitt was theatrical critic, but the reference is probably to the proprietor,
    John Walter the Second.
  Too prolix on the subject of the Bourbons. Hazlitt probably refers to his
    brother-in-law, Dr., afterwards Sir John Stoddart, who was dismissed
    from the editorship of *The Times* early in 1817, in consequence of the
    violence of his writings on French affairs. Stoddart immediately started
    The Day and New Times, the title of which was altered in 1818 to *The New
    Times.*
  ' *One who loved,*' etc. *Othello*, Act v. Sc. 2.

175. ' *Some quantity,*' etc. A composite quotation from *Hamlet*, Act III. Sc. 2, and
    Romeo and Juliet, Act v. Sc. 1.
  Mr. Perry. James Perry (1756-1821), proprietor and editor of *The Morning
    Chronicle.*
  ' *Screw the courage,*' etc. *Macbeth*, Act I. Sc. 7.

176. ' *Pritchard's genteel,*' etc. Churchill, *The Rosciad,* 852, the reference being
    to Hannah Pritchard (1711-1768), the actress who played Johnson's
    Irene.
  Swiss bodyguards. The famous corps, constituted in 1616, who had shown
    such fidelity to Louis XVI. during the attack on the Tuileries on August 10,
    1792.
  ' *Pigmy body,*' etc. Dryden, *Absalom and Achitophel*, I. 157-8.
  The Fudge family in Paris (1818), Letter II. 116-123.

177. ' *A master of scholars.*' Cf. *ante*, p. 167.

178. *The Characters of Shakespear's Plays.* A second edition had just been pub-
    lished. Hazlitt certainly availed himself to the full of the license which

he frankly claims in this paragraph. An attempt has been made in the present edition to indicate the source of his essays and criticisms, and also the various publications into which they were afterwards transferred.

179. *Mr. Kean's Shylock.* Edmund Kean (1787-1833) had already acted many important parts in the provinces. At Dorchester one of his performances had been witnessed by Arnold, the stage manager of Drury Lane, through whom an engagement was made with the management of that theatre. Kean insisted on playing Shylock, and though the management and his fellow-actors were incredulous as to his powers, his success was undisputed. Henceforward his many triumphs in London were associated with the Drury Lane Theatre, except for a short period from 1827 to 1829, when his services were transferred to Covent Garden. For a later account of his Shylock, see *ante*, pp. 294-6.

180. l. 8. In *The Morning Chronicle* Hazlitt adds: 'After the play we were rejoiced to see the sterling farce of *The Apprentice*[1] revived, in which Mr. Bannister was eminently successful.'

Miss Smith. The assumed maiden name of the actress who married George Bartley, the actor, on August 24, 1814. She made her first appearance in London in 1805. She suffered by comparison with Mrs. Siddons, and later with Miss O'Neill.

Rae. Alexander Rae (1782-1820), after acting for a season at the Haymarket in 1806, made his first appearance at Drury Lane on November 12, 1812. Kean quickly eclipsed him in tragedy, though he maintained the reputation of being a good Hamlet.

'*Far-darting*' eye.

'And covetous of Shakspeare's beauty seen
In every flash of his far-beaming eye.'

COWPER, *The Task*, III. 601-2.

181. '*But I was born so high*,' etc. *Richard III.*, Act I. Sc. 3.

The miserable medley acted for Richard III. The work chiefly of Colley Cibber, published in 1700.

Cooke. George Frederick Cooke (1756-1811). His first appearance in London (Covent Garden, October 31, 1801) was in this part, which remained one of his best impersonations.

'*Stand all apart*,' etc. *Richard III.* (Cibber's version).

182. '*The golden rigol*,' etc. *Ibid.* Interpolated from *Henry IV.*, Part II. Act IV. Sc. 5:

'———— This is a sleep
That from this golden rigol hath divorced
So many English kings.'

'*Chop off his head.*' See *post*, note to p. 201.

last line. In *The Morning Chronicle* Hazlitt proceeds: 'His fall, however, was too rapid. Nothing but a sword passed through the heart could occasion such a fall. With his innate spirit of *Richard* he would struggle with his fate to the last moment of ebbing life. But on the whole the performance was the most perfect of any thing that has been witnessed since the days of Garrick. The play was got up with great skill. The scenes were all painted with strict regard to historic truth. There had evidently been research as to identity of place, for the views of the Tower, of Crosby House, etc. were, in the eye of the best judges, considered as

[1] By Arthur Murphy (1756).

504

faithful representations according to the descriptions handed down to us. The cast of the play was also good. Green-room report says that Miss Smith refused the part of the *Queen*, as not great enough *forsooth* for her superior talents, although Mrs. Siddons, Mrs. Pope,[1] Mrs. Crauford[2] and others felt it to their honour to display their powers in the character. In the present case the absence of Miss Smith was not a misfortune, for Mrs. Glover[3] gave to the fine scene with her children, a force and feeling that drew from the audience the most sympathetic testimonies of applause. Miss Boyce made a very interesting and elegant representative of *Lady Anne*. We sincerely congratulate the public on the great accession to the theatrical art which they have obtained in the talents of Mr. Kean. The experience of Saturday night convinces us that he acts from his own mental resources, and that he has organs to give effect to his comprehension of character. We never saw such admirable use made of the eye, of the lip, and generally of the muscles. We could judge of what he would have been if his voice had been clear from hoarseness; and we trust he will not repeat the difficult part till he has overcome his cold. We understand, he is shortly to appear in *Don John*, in *The Chances*. We know no character so exactly suited to his powers.'

183. '*I am myself alone.*' *Richard III.* (Cibber's version).
'*I am not i' the vein.*' *Richard III.* Act IV. Sc. 2.
'*His grace looks cheerfully,*' etc. *Ibid.* Act III. Sc. 4.
184. '*Take him for all in all,* etc. *Hamlet*, Act I. Sc. 2.
Mr. Wroughton. Richard Wroughton (1748-1822), the main part of whose career closed in 1798. He returned to the stage two years later, and continued to act till 1815.
Mrs. Glover. Julia Glover (1779-1850), the daughter of an actor named Betterton, a favourite actress who had made her first appearance in London in 1797.
'*For in the very torrent,*' etc. *Hamlet*, Act III. Sc. 2.
Shakespear Gallery. Hazlitt refers to the well known Shakespeare Gallery projected and carried out by Alderman Boydell between 1786 and 1802.
185. *Mr. Kean's Hamlet.* Drury Lane, March 12, 1814.
'*A young and princely novice.*' *Richard III.*, Act I. Sc. 4.
186. '*That has no relish,*' etc. *Hamlet*, Act III. Sc. 2.
'*That noble and liberal casuist.*' Charles Lamb refers to the old English Dramatists as ' those noble and liberal casuists.' *Poems, Plays and Essays* (ed. Ainger), p. 248.
'*Out of joint.*' *Hamlet*, Act I. Sc. 5.
'*Come then,*' etc. Pope, *Moral Essays*, II. 17-20.
187. '*A wave of the sea.*' *A Winter's Tale*, Act IV. Sc. 4.
'*That within,*' etc. *Hamlet*, Act I. Sc. 2.
'*Weakness and melancholy.*' *Ibid.* Act II. Sc. 2.
'*'Tis I, Hamlet the Dane.*' *Ibid.* Act V. Sc. 1.
188. '*I'll call thee,*' etc. *Ibid,* Act I. Sc. 4.
'*The rugged Pyrrhus.*' *Ibid.* Act II. Sc. 2.
'*Bordered on the verge,*' etc. Cf. Pope, *Moral Essays*, II. 51-2.

---

[1] Elizabeth Pope (1744?-1797) wife of Alexander Pope the actor. She made her first appearance in 1768 and became famous in a wide range of parts.
[2] Better known as Mrs. Barry. Ann Spranger Barry (1734-1801) first appeared at Drury Lane in 1767-8, and soon acquired a great reputation both in tragedy and comedy. She married Spranger Barry the actor in 1768.
[3] See *post*, note to p. 184.

A VIEW OF THE ENGLISH STAGE

189. *Mr. Raymond's Representation, etc.* For Raymond, at this time acting manager at Drury Lane, see Leigh Hunt's *Critical Essays* (1807), pp. 29-32.

Mr. Dowton. William Dowton (1764-1851), one of the chief comedians of the Drury Lane company, made his first appearance in London in 1796 and retired in 1840.

'*Flows on to the Propontic,*' etc. This and the other quotations in this notice are from *Othello*, Act III. Sc. 3.

The rest of the play, etc. Pope played Iago, Miss Smith Desdemona and Mrs. Glover Emilia.

190. '*A consummation,*' etc. Adapted from *Hamlet*, Act III. Sc. 1.

Antony and Cleopatra. This version was attributed to Kemble.

191. '*The barge,*' etc. *Antony and Cleopatra*, Act II. Sc. 2.

192. '*He's speaking now,*' etc. Ibid. Act I. Sc. 5.

'*It is my birth-day,*' etc. Ibid. Act III. Sc. 13.

Mrs. Faucit. Harriet Faucit, the mother of Helen Faucit, had made her first appearance, on October 7, as Desdemona.

Mr. Terry. Daniel Terry (1780?-1829), who appeared in Edinburgh in 1809 and in London in 1813. He is chiefly remembered as an intimate friend and correspondent of Sir Walter Scott, many of whose novels he adapted for the stage.

Artaxerxes. By Thomas Augustine Arne (1710-1778), originally produced in 1762. The words were translated from Metastasio's 'Artaserse.'

Miss Stephens. Catherine Stephens (1794-1882), a great favourite with Hazlitt who here notices her first important appearance on the stage. She was popular not only on the stage but in the concert-room. She retired in 1835 and in 1838 married the fifth earl of Essex.

193. *Catalani.* Angelica Catalani (1779-1849), the greatest *prima donna* of her time.

Mr. Liston's acting, etc. See *ante*, pp. 159-60.

The Beggar's Opera. See the essay 'On Patronage and Puffing' in *Table-Talk* (Vol. VI. pp. 292-3), where Hazlitt gives an interesting account of the writing of this article, 'the last,' he says, 'I ever wrote with any pleasure to myself.' Cf. also *The Round Table*, (Vol. I. pp. 65-6) for an account of *The Beggar's Opera*, which Hazlitt was never tired of praising.

'*O'erstepping,*' etc. *Hamlet*, Act III. Sc. 2.

194. '*Woman is* [Virgins are] *like,*' etc. *The Beggar's Opera*, Act I.

'*There is some soul,*' etc. *Henry V.*, Act IV. Sc. 1.

'*Hussey, hussey,*' etc. *The Beggar's Opera*, Act I.

'*Cease your funning.*' Ibid. Act II. Sc. 2.

195. *Described by Molière.* In *La Critique de l'École des Femmes*, Sc. 6.

Mrs. Liston's person. Miss Tyer (d. 1854), who married Liston in 1807, was of diminutive stature. She retired from the stage when her husband left Covent Garden in 1822.

Richard Cœur de Lion. The version (1786) by General Burgoyne of Sedaine's *Richard Cœur de Lion*, produced in Paris in 1784.

Oh, Richard! etc. This song in the original opera 'O Richard! O mon Roi!' had enjoyed great popularity in France before the Revolution.

196. *Miss Foote.* Maria Foote (1797?-1867), 'a very pretty woman and a very pleasing actress,' according to Genest. Some circumstances of her private life, alluded to by Hazlitt elsewhere, increased her popularity with the public. She retired in 1831, and in the same year married the fourth Earl of Harrington.

196. *Amanthus.* In Mrs. Inchbald's *Child of Nature.*
'*Youthful poet's fancy,*' etc. Rowe, *The Fair Penitent*, Act III. Sc. 1.
197. *Madame Grassini.* Josephina Grassini (1773-1850), a contralto singer who first appeared in London in 1803. Cf. De Quincey's *Confessions of an English Opium Eater* (*Works*, ed. Masson, III. 389).
Signor Tramezzani. A favourite Italian tenor. 'To a beautiful voice he joined delicate apprehension, intense feeling and rich expression.' (*Dictionary of Musicians*, 1824.)
'*Might create,*' etc. *Comus*, 562.
198. *The Genius of Scotland.* Hazlitt is perhaps thinking of Sir Pertinax Macsycophant in Macklin's *The Man of the World*, who 'always booed, and booed, and booed, as it were by instinct.' (Act III. Sc. 1.)
M. Vestris. *The Champion* reads : 'M. Vestris, who made an able-bodied representative of *Zephyr* in the ballet, appears to us to be the Conway among dancers.'
Miss O'Neill's Juliet. For Eliza O'Neill (1791-1872), afterwards Lady Becher, see *The Round Table*, vol. I., note to p. 156, and many references in the present volume.
The Gamester, etc. Edward Moore's tragedy, first produced in 1753.
199. *Palmer.* John Palmer (1742 ?-1798), 'Plausible Jack,' the original Joseph Surface. See Lamb's Essay 'On Some of the Old Actors.'
Isabella. In *Isabella; or the Fatal Marriage* (1758), Garrick's version of Thomas Southerne's *The Fatal Marriage* (1694).
'*Sweet is the dew,*' etc. Cf. vol. I. p. 91 (*The Round Table*).
200. '*And Romeo banished.*' *Romeo and Juliet*, Act III. Sc. 2.
'*Festering in his shroud.*' *Ibid.* Act IV. Sc. 3.
'*The last scene,*' etc. In Garrick's version (1750) of *Romeo and Juliet*.
'*I have forgot,*' etc. *Romeo and Juliet*, Act II. Sc. 2.
Mr. Jones's Mercutio. Richard Jones (1779-1851), known as 'Gentleman Jones,' a good actor of farces.
Mr. Conway's Romeo. William Augustus Conway (1789-1828) first appeared in London in 1813, when he captivated Mrs. Piozzi, who is said to have offered to marry him. He continued to act in London and at Bath (sometimes playing important parts) till 1821, when he was driven from the English stage by an anonymous attack. In 1823 he went to America where, after acting with success and delivering religious discourses, he drowned himself in 1828. Hazlitt has somewhat softened the asperities of this paragraph. See *The Champion*, October 16, 1814.
'*The very beadle,*' etc. 'A very beadle to a humorous sigh.' *Love's Labour's Lost*, Act III. Sc. 1.
Mr. Coates's absurdities. Robert Coates (1772-1848), the wealthy 'Amateur of Fashion,' who was known as 'Romeo Coates' from his representations of Romeo, the first of which took place at Bath in 1810.
Mr. Kean's Richard. Drury Lane, October 3, 1814.
201. '*Chop off his head.*' 'Off with his head ! So much for Buckingham !' Act IV. Sc. 3 of Cibber's 'miserable medley.' See *ante*, p. 181.
'*I fear no uncles,*' etc. *Richard III.*, Act III. Sc. 1.
203. '*Inexplicable dumb show and noise.*' *Hamlet*, Act III. Sc. 2.
Captain Barclay. Robert Barclay Allardice (1779-1854), generally known as 'Captain Barclay,' famous for his feats of pedestrianism, the most remarkable of which was walking one mile in each of 1000 successive hours, which he accomplished in the summer of 1809 at Newmarket.

Bets amounting in the aggregate to £100,000 are said to have been made in connection with this feat.

204. '*With her best nurse,*' etc. *Comus*, 377-80.

Mr. *Kean's Macbeth.* November 5, 1814.

205. '*Real hearts,*' etc. Burke, *Reflections on the Revolution in France* (*Select Works*, ed. Payne, II. 101).

'*Fate and metaphysical aid.*' *Macbeth*, Act I. Sc. 5.

206. '*Direness is thus,*' etc. *Ibid.* Act V. Sc. 5.

'*Troubled with thick-coming fancies.*' *Ibid.* Act V. Sc. 3.

'*Subject* [servile] *to all the skyey influences.*' *Measure for Measure*, Act III. Sc. 1.

207. '*Lost too poorly in himself.*' *Macbeth*, Act II. Sc. 2.

'*My way of life,*' etc. *Ibid.* Act V. Sc. 3.

'*Then, oh farewell,*' etc. *Othello*, Act III. Sc. 3.

'*To consider too curiously.*' *Hamlet*, Act V. Sc. 1.

208. Mr. *Kean's Romeo.* January 2, 1815.

'*Added a cubit,*' etc. *St. Matthew*, vi. 27.

'*As musical,*' etc. *Comus*, 477.

Luke. In Sir James Bland Burgess's *Riches; or, The Wife and Brother*, founded on Massinger's *The City Madam*, and produced in 1810.

209. *Garrick and Barry.* Garrick and Spranger Barry (1719-1777) were rival Romeos. In 1750 the play was acted twelve consecutive nights both at Drury Lane and Covent Garden. See Dr. Doran's *Annals of the English Stage* (ed. Lowe), II. 122-3, where the remark quoted by Hazlitt is attributed to 'a lady who did not pretend to be a critic, and who was guided by her feelings.'

'*The silver sound,*' etc. '*How silver-sweet sound lovers' tongues by night,*' *Romeo and Juliet*, Act II. Sc. 2.

210. '*What said my man,*' etc. *Ibid.* Act V. Sc. 3.

211. *Mrs. Beverley.* In Edward Moore's *The Gamester*.

'*As one,*' etc. *Hamlet*, Act III. Sc. 2.

l. 36. In *The Champion* Hazlitt proceeded as follows : 'To return to Mr. Kean. We would, if we had any influence with him, advise him to give one thorough reading to Shakspeare, without any regard to the prompt-book, or to his own cue, or to the effect he is likely to produce on the pit or gallery. If he does this, not with a view to his profession, but as a study of human nature in general, he will, we trust, find his account in it, quite as much as in keeping company with "the great vulgar, or the small." [1] He will find there all that he wants, as well as all that he has :—sunshine and gloom, repose as well as energy, pleasure mixed up with pain, love and hatred, thought, feeling, and action, lofty imagination, with point and accuracy, general character with particular traits, and all that distinguishes the infinite variety of nature. He will then find that the interest of *Macbeth* does not end with the dagger scene, and that *Hamlet* is a fine character in the closet, and might be made so on the stage, *by being understood*. He may then hope to do justice to Shakspeare, and when he does this, he need not fear but that his fame will last.'

Mr. *Kean's Iago.* Cf. *ante*, p. 190.

212. '*Hedged in,*' etc. Adapted from *Hamlet*, Act IV. Sc. 5.

In contempt of mankind. Hazlitt refers to a passage of Burke's. See *Political Essays*, vol. III. p. 32 and note.

213. '*Play the dog,*' etc. *Henry VI.*, Part III., Act V. Sc. 6.

214. *Plausibility of a confessor. The Examiner* has the following note on this

---

[1] Cowley, Horace, *Odes*, III. 1.

passage : 'Iago is a Jesuit out of orders, and ought to wear black. Mr. Kean had on a red coat (certainly not "the costume of his crime," which is hypocrisy), and conducted the whole affair with the easy intrepidity of a young volunteer officer, who undertakes to seduce a bar-maid at an inn.'

214. '*His cue*,' etc. *King Lear*, Act I. Sc. 2.

215. '*Who has that heart so pure*,' etc. *Othello*, Act III. Sc. 3.

216. '*What a full fortune*,' etc. *Othello*, Act I. Sc. 1.
'*Here is her father's house*,' etc. *Ibid.* Act I. Sc. 1.
Ode to Indifference. By Mrs. Frances Greville, Fanny Burney's godmother.
'*What is the reason*,' etc. *Othello*, Act I. Sc. 1.

217. '*I cannot believe*,' etc. *Ibid.* Act II. Sc. 1.
'*And yet how nature*,' etc. *Ibid.* Act III. Sc. 3.
'*Nearly are allied*,' etc. Dryden, *Absalom and Achitophel*, I. 163-4.
'*Who knows all quantities* [qualities], etc. *Othello*, Act III. Sc. 3. In *The Examiner* the following note is appended to this passage :—

'If *Desdemona* really "saw her husband's visage in his mind," [1] or fell in love with the abstract idea of "his virtues and his valiant parts," [2] she was the only woman on record, either before or since, who ever did so. Shakespeare's want of penetration in supposing that those are the sort of things that gain the affections, might perhaps have drawn a smile from the ladies, if honest *Iago* had not checked it by suggesting a different explanation. It should seem by this, as if the rankness and gross impropriety of the personal connection, the difference in age, features, colour, constitution, instead of being the obstacle, had been the motive of the refinement of her choice, and had, by beginning at the wrong end, subdued her to the amiable qualities of her lord. *Iago* is indeed a most learned and irrefragable doctor on the subject of love, which he defines to be "merely a lust of the blood, and a permission of the will." [3] The idea that love has its source in moral or intellectual excellence, in good nature or good sense, or has any connection with sentiment or refinement of any kind, is one of those preposterous and wilful errors, which ought to be extirpated for the sake of those few persons who alone are likely to suffer by it, whose romantic generosity and delicacy ought not to be sacrificed to the baseness of their nature, but who treading securely the flowery path, marked out for them by poets and moralists, the licensed artificers of fraud and lies, are dashed to pieces down the precipice, and perish without help.' In the following number of *The Examiner* (August 14, 1814) Leigh Hunt, then in Surrey Gaol, wrote a long reply to this characteristic passage. In the number for September 4, the dramatic critic of *The Examiner* replied to Hazlitt's article on the character of Iago. A letter from Hazlitt by way of rejoinder appeared on September 11 (see Appendix to these notes). The critic replied (closing the controversy) on September 18.

218. '*Oh gentle lady*,' etc. *Othello*, Act II. Sc. 1.
'*The milk of human kindness.*' *Macbeth*, Act I. Sc. 5.
'*Least relish of salvation*,' etc. *Hamlet*, Act III. Sc. 3.
'*Oh, you are well tuned now*,' etc. *Othello*, Act II. Sc. 1.
'*Though in the trade of war*,' etc. *Ibid.* Act I. Sc. 2.

219. '*My noble lord*,' etc. *Ibid.* Act III. Sc. 3.
'*It is not written in the bond.*' *The Merchant of Venice*, Act IV. Sc. 1.

220. '*Though I perchance*,' etc. *Othello*, Act III. Sc. 3.
'*O grace*,' etc. *Ibid.*

[1] *Othello*, Act I. Sc. 3.
[2] 'His honours and his valiant parts.' *Ibid.*   [3] *Ibid.*

220. '*This may do something*,' etc.   *Ibid*.
     '*I did say so*,' etc.   *Ibid*.
221. '*Work on*,' etc.   *Ibid*. Act IV. Sc. I.
     How is it, General,' etc.   *Ibid*.
     '*Look on the tragic loading*,' etc.   *Ibid*. Act v. Sc. 2.
     Mr. Kean's Richard II.   Shakespeare's play with considerable alterations and additions (by Wroughton), produced March 9, 1815, and acted thirteen times.   This is the first paper which Hazlitt wrote as regular dramatic critic of *The Examiner*.   Leigh Hunt, the editor, who was released from prison in February 1815, had intended to take up this work, and had begun the year (while still in Surrey gaol) by contributing a series of articles on the principal actors and actresses of the day.   He had also written one ' Theatrical Examiner ' (February 26, on Kean's Richard III.) before he was compelled by the stirring events of the 'hundred days' to devote all his attention to politics.   Thus the work of dramatic critic, as well as the carrying out of the 'Round Table' scheme, fell to Hazlitt. Cf. the advertisement to *The Round Table* (Vol I. p. xxxi.).
     We are in the number, etc.   Cf. Lamb's essay ' On the tragedies of Shakspere considered with reference to their fitness for stage representation,' originally published in *The Reflector* (1811).
222. *Inexpressible* [inexplicable] *dumb-show and noise.*'   *Hamlet*, Act III. Sc. 2.
     ' *Segnius per aures*,' etc.   Horace, *Ars Poetica*, 180.
     Mr. Kean . . . in very many passages, etc.   Cf. Coleridge's well-known saying (*Table Talk*, April 27, 1823) : 'To see him [Kean] act, is like reading Shakspere by flashes of lightning.'
223. ' *Overdone or come tardy of* [off]'   *Hamlet*, Act III. Sc. 2.
224. '*Why on thy knee*,' etc.   *Richard II.*, Act III. Sc. 3.
     '*Oh that I were a mockery king*,' etc.   *Ibid*. Act IV. Sc. I.
     The Editor of this Paper.   Leigh Hunt first saw Kean as Richard III., and wrote a criticism in *The Examiner* (February 26, 1815) to which Hazlitt refers.
     Mr. Pope.   Alexander Pope (1763-1835) from 1785 till 1827 acted an immense number of parts both at Drury Lane and Covent Garden.
     Mr. Holland.   Charles Holland (1768-1849?), nephew of the better known Charles Holland (1733-1769), Garrick's friend, first appeared at Drury Lane in 1796.
     Idly tacked on to the conclusion.   'For Mrs. Bartley to rant and whine in,' *The Examiner* adds.
     The Unknown Guest.   Produced on March 29, 1815, and attributed to Arnold, the manager.
     Mr. Arnold.   Samuel James Arnold (1774-1852) in 1809 opened the Lyceum Theatre as the English Opera House, of which he was manager for many years.   He was manager at Drury Lane from 1812 to 1815.
225. '*More honoured*,' etc.   *Hamlet*, Act I. Sc. 4.
     Mr. Kelly.   Michael Kelly (1764?-1826), after singing abroad chiefly in Italy and Vienna, first appeared in 1787 at Drury Lane of which he became musical director.
     Mr. Braham.   See vol. VII., note to p. 70.
226. *Mr. Phillips.*   Thomas Philipps (1774-1841), the composer, who first appeared in London in 1796.
     Mrs. Dickons.   Maria Dickons (1770?-1833) appeared at Covent Garden as Miss Poole (her maiden name) in 1793.   She joined the Drury Lane company in 1811 and retired about 1820.

520

NOTES

226. *Miss Kelly.* Frances Maria Kelly (1790-1882), a niece of Michael Kelly, appeared at Drury Lane as early as 1798 and was chiefly associated with that theatre during her long career as an actress. She retired in 1835 and devoted herself to the training of young actresses. She was a great friend of the Lambs and the heroine of Elia's *Barbara S——.* The present volume shows how greatly Hazlitt admired her acting.

   Mr. Knight. Edward Knight (1774-1826), 'Little Knight,' a regular member of the Drury Lane company from 1812.

227. *Love in Limbo.* Attributed to Millingen.

   Zembuca. Zembuca, or the Net-Maker and his Wife, by Pocock.

   Mr. Kean's Zanga. At Drury Lane, May 24, 1815.

   The Revenge. By Edward Young, produced in 1721.

228. '*I knew you could not bear it.*' Act iv. Sc. 1.

   '*And so is my revenge.*' Act v. Sc. 2.

   Oxberry. William Oxberry (1784-1824), one of the regular Drury Lane comedians. His *Dramatic Biography* (5 vols. 1820-1826) was edited after his death by his widow.

229. *Mr. Bannister's Farewell.* June 1, 1815. Hazlitt had already published part of this article in *The Round Table,* (vol. i. p. 155).

   The World. By James Kenney, produced in 1808.

   The Children in the Wood. By Thomas Morton, music by Dr. Samuel Arnold, produced in 1793.

   Mr. Gattie. Henry Gattie (1774-1844), a member of the Drury Lane company from 1813 till his retirement in 1833.

   The Honey-Moon. By John Tobin (1770-1804), produced in 1805.

   Mrs. Davison. Maria Rebecca Davison (1780?-1858) appeared at Drury Lane (as Miss Duncan) in 1804, and was chiefly associated with that theatre for a number of years.

   Decamp. See *post,* note to p. 247.

   We do not wonder, etc. This passage to the end is in *The Round Table.* See vol. i. pp. 155-6 and notes.

230. *Comus.* Produced April 28, 1815, and acted fourteen times.

231. '*Of mask and antique pageantry.*' *L'Allegro,* 128.

   '*A marvellous proper man.*' *Richard III.,* Act i. Sc. 2.

   Mr. Duruset. J. B. Durusett, 'an agreeable tenor singer' at Covent Garden. He was regarded as the principal male singer during the absence of John Sinclair from that theatre.

   '*Magic circle.*'

         Cf. 'But Shakespear's magic could not copied be ;
            Within that circle none durst walk but he.'

                 Dryden, Prologue to *The Tempest,* 19-20.

   '*This evening late,*' etc. *Comus,* 540 *et seq.*

232. '*Two such I saw,*' etc. *Ibid.* 291 *et seq.*

233. '*Royal fortitude.*' '——— whose mind ensued,
            Through perilous war, with regal fortitude.'

   Wordsworth's Sonnet, 'November, 1813,' published in 1815. In the note Hazlitt probably refers to the omission of *The Evening Walk* (1793), which was not republished till 1837.

   Mr. Kean's Leon. June 20, 1815.

   Leon. In Fletcher's *Rule a Wife and Have a Wife.*

234. *Mr. Bartley.* George Bartley (1782?-1858) first appeared at Drury Lane in 1802, and became manager of Covent Garden in 1829.

234. '*Double deafness.*' Cf. 'But yield to double darkness nigh at hand.'
Samson Agonistes, 593.
The Shakespear Gallery. Cf. *ante*, note to p. 184.

235. '*The gay creatures*,' etc. *Comus*, 299.
Messrs. Young, etc. Charles Mayne Young (1777-1856), who succeeded
Kemble as the chief tragedian at Covent Garden, and retired in 1832;
William Abbott (1789-1843), a member of the Covent Garden company
for many years from 1812; John Emery (1777-1822), one of the best
actors of his time, especially in rustic parts, associated almost entirely with
Covent Garden from 1798 till his death; Sarah Booth (1793-1867), who
first appeared at Covent Garden in 1810.
'*Tis much.*' *Cymbeline*, Act I. Sc. 6.

236. *Airy shapes*, etc. Cf. *Paradise Lost*, I. 775 *et seq.*
Mr. Grimaldi's Orson. In *Valentine and Orson*, the part in which Joseph
Grimaldi (1779-1837) made his first appearance (1806) at Covent Garden.
'*Tricksy spirit.*' *The Tempest*, Act v. Sc. 1.

237. *Mrs. Bland.* Maria Theresa Bland (1769-1838), who made her first
appearance at Drury Lane (as Miss Romanzini) in 1786. Hazlitt heard
her in Liverpool in 1792. See vol. VII. p. 193.
'*After the songs of Apollo.*' *Love's Labour's Lost*, Act v. Sc. 2.
My Wife! What Wife? By Barrett, produced July 25, 1815.
'*Keep such a dreadful pudder* [pother],' etc. *King Lear*, Act III. Sc. 2.

238. '*Good Mr. Tokely* [Master Brook],' etc. *The Merry Wives of Windsor*, Act II.
Sc. 2.
'*In the likeness of a sigh.*' *Romeo and Juliet*, Act II. Sc. 1.

239. *Mr. Meggett.* This actor from Edinburgh made his first appearance at the
Haymarket on July 19, 1815. Genest (VIII. 486) says that he was
'cruelly used by the bigotted admirers of Kean.'
The Mountaineers. By George Colman the younger, produced in 1795.
Mr. Harley's Fidget. In *The Boarding House*, a musical farce by Samuel
Beazley (1786-1851), first produced on August 26, 1811.
Mr. Harley. John Pritt Harley (1786-1858) made his first appearance in
London at the English Opera House in July, 1815. Soon afterwards he
joined the company at Drury Lane, where he remained till 1835, and made
a great reputation as a comic actor and singer.
The Blue Stocking. Moore's *M.P.*, or *the Blue-Stocking* (1811).

240. *Mr. Wallack.* James William Wallack (1791 ?-1864), a versatile actor well
known for many years both in London and America.
Mrs. Harlowe. Sarah Harlowe (1765-1852), a low comedy actress who first
appeared at Covent Garden in 1790.
'*Warbled*,' etc. Cf. 'In amorous ditties all a summer's day.' *Paradise
Lost*, I. 449.
'*As one incapable*,' etc. *Hamlet*, Act IV. Sc. 7.
The Iron Chest. By George Colman the younger, produced by Kemble in
1796.

241. *The Squire of Dames.* *The Faerie Queene*, Book III. Canto VII. The giantess
was Argante.
Mr. Capel Lofft. Capell Lofft (1751-1824), a well-known politician and
miscellaneous writer, the patron of the poet Bloomfield and Napoleon.
The letter referred to by Hazlitt appeared in *The Morning Chronicle*,
August 3, 1815.
Mr. Foote. An actor from Edinburgh who had made his first appearance in
London on July 18, 1815.

NOTES

242. *Mr. Gyngell.* Gyngell's 'Exhibition of the original Fantoccini, the Microcosm, the Moving Panorama,' etc. was on view at this time at the theatre in Catherine Street.

Living in London. Attributed to Jameson, produced August 5, 1815.

'*Want of decency,' etc.* The Earl of Roscommon's *Essay on Translated Verse,* 114.

243. *Quod sit, etc.* Horace, *Ars Poetica,* 188.

The King's Proxy. By Samuel James Arnold.

Plato. The Republic, Book VII.

244. *Mr. and Mrs. T. Cooke.* Thomas Simpson Cooke (1782-1848), who composed the music for *The King's Proxy.*

l. 23. *The Examiner* proceeds to quote from *The Morning Chronicle* a favourable notice of a new musical farce (by E. P. Knight) entitled *A Chip of the Old Block, or, The Village Festival,* and adds : 'This account is from the *Chronicle.* It is much too favourable. The piece is one of the most wretched we have seen. A statute fair would be more entertaining. The political claptraps were so barefaced as to be hissed. Matthews sung a song with that kind of humour and effect of which our readers will easily form an idea.'

The Maid and the Magpie. Arnold's version, produced August 21, 1815.

245. *The Hypocrite.* By Isaac Bickerstaffe, first produced in 1768.

246. '*Sleek o'er his rugged looks.' Macbeth,* Act III. Sc. 2.

Major Sturgeon. In Foote's *The Mayor of Garratt.*

Mrs. Sparks. See Leigh Hunt's *Dramatic Essays* (ed. Archer and Lowe), p. 177.

Mrs. Orger. Mary Ann Orger (1788-1849) appeared at Drury Lane in 1808. She was the wife of Thomas Orger, a Quaker.

247. '*Has honours,' etc.* Cf. 'Some have greatness thrust upon 'em.' *Twelfth Night,* Act II. Sc. 5.

Mr. Decamp. De Camp (Mrs. Charles Kemble's brother) had played Isidore in Coleridge's *Remorse* (January 23, 1813). For another failure of his see Lamb's *Letters* (ed. W. C. Hazlitt), I. 377.

Mr. Edwards's Richard III. September 25, 1815.

'*Sole sway and sovereignty.'* Cf. 'Give solely sovereign sway.' *Macbeth,* Act I. Sc. 5.

248. *Mr. Incledon.* Charles Incledon (1763-1826), the tenor, a good singer but a bad actor, appeared at Covent Garden from 1790 till 1815.

249. *Lovers' Vows.* Mrs. Inchbald's version of Kotzebue's *Natural Son,* first produced at Covent Garden, 1798, revived at Drury Lane, September 26, 1815.

Mrs. Mardyn. Mrs. Mardyn had been very successful in Dublin. A false report was afterwards spread that she had eloped with Byron. See Byron's *Letters and Journals* (ed. Prothero), III. 217, and Mrs. Baron Wilson's *Our Actresses,* I. 198-207.

Mr. Dowton . . . for the first time. October 5, 1815.

'*Merry jest.' Titus Andronicus,* Act V. Sc. 2.

250. *Mr. Lovegrove.* William Lovegrove (1778-1816), who made his reputation at Bath, and appeared in London in 1810.

Wewitzer. Ralph Wewitzer (1748-1825), who had had a long career, chiefly in secondary parts. This was one of his last appearances.

l. 18. *The Examiner* article continues : 'The new farce [at Covent Garden, October 5, 1815], called *The Farce-Writer,* has been very successful ; we wish we could add deservedly so. It is a happy instance of lively dulness.

The wit consists entirely in the loco-motion of the actors. It is a very badly written pantomime.'

250. *The School for Scandal.* September 27, 1815.

Little Simmons. Samuel Simmons (1777?-1819), a regular member of the Covent Garden company from 1796, and very successful as a comedian. Moses in *The School for Scandal* was one of his parts.

'*Cast some longing,*' etc. Gray's *Elegy*, St. 22.

251. *Fawcett.* John Fawcett (1768-1837), for many years manager of Covent Garden.

Mrs. Gibbs. For an account of this actress, said to have been the wife of George Colman the younger, see Mrs. Baron Wilson's *Our Actresses*, I. 83-90.

Mr. Blanchard. William Blanchard (1769-1835), one of the Covent Garden comedians. See Leigh Hunt's *Critical Essays*, p. 122.

Mr. Farley. Charles Farley (1771-1859), actor, dramatist, and stage-manager.

last line. *The Examiner* continues : 'Miss O'Neill has resumed her engagement at this house, and plays her usual characters to crowded audiences with even increased effect. We should attempt to describe her excellency in some of them, but that we feel ourselves unable to do her even tolerable justice.'

252. *Mrs. Alsop's Rosalind.* Covent Garden, October 18, 1815. Mrs. Alsop did not continue long on the stage. She was the daughter of Mrs. Jordan and Richard Daly, the Irish theatrical manager.

'*No more like,*' etc. Cf. *Hamlet*, Act I. Sc. 2.

Her Nell. In *The Devil to Pay.*

The Will. By F. Reynolds, produced in 1797.

253. *John Du Bart.* October 25, 1815. The piece, attributed to Pocock, seems to have been founded on an exploit of the French naval hero, Jean Barth (1651-1702).

That which took place in Hyde Park. Hazlitt refers to the extraordinary thanksgiving jubilee, which took place in London on August 1, 1814, and following days. Part of the programme consisted of a sham fight on the Serpentine.

254. *Mr. Bishop.* Afterwards Sir Henry Rowley Bishop (1786-1855), the composer.

'*Guns, drums,*' etc. Pope, *Satires*, I. 26.

The Beggar's Opera. October 28, 1815. Cf. *ante*, pp. 193-5.

Miss Nash. Miss Nash had played Polly at Bath, November 4, 1813, a performance described by Genest as 'very good.'

255. *Mrs. Davenport.* Mary Ann Davenport (1765?-1843) first appeared at Covent Garden in 1794.

256. l. 15. *The Examiner* adds : 'A new farce has been brought out at Drury-Lane in the course of the week, called *Twenty per Cent.* It has succeeded very well. A voluble lying knave of a servant in it by Mr. Harley, who plays this class of characters well, is its chief attraction. It is deficient in plot, but not without pleasantry. It is improbable, lively, and short.' The farce was by T. Dibdin.

Miss O'Neill's Elwina. Covent Garden, November 11. Hannah More's *Percy* was produced in 1778.

l. 15. The *Theatrical Examiner* for November 12, 1815, on Kean's Bajazet, and Mrs. Mardyn and Mrs. Alsop in *The Country Girl,* is clearly Hazlitt's.

257. *There is one short word,* etc. 'Fudge.' See *The Vicar of Wakefield,* chap. xi.

NOTES

258. l. 24. *The Examiner* continues : 'Miss Stephens has appeared twice in *Polly*, and once in *Rosetta*. She looks better than she did last year, and, if possible, sings better. Of the new Farce at Drury-Lane [*Who's Who?* or *The Double Imposture*], we have only room to add, that there is one good scene in it, in which Munden and Harley made a very grotesque contrast, with some tolerable equivoques ; all the rest is a tissue of the most tedious and gross improbabilities. The author's wit appeared to have been *elicited and expended* in the same moment.'

Where to Find a Friend. By Leigh, produced at Drury Lane November 23, 1815.

260. *Johnstone.* John Henry Johnstone (1749-1828), a member of the Drury Lane company from 1803 to 1820. He began his career as a singer.

'*The milk of human kindness.*' *Macbeth*, Act I. Sc. v.

261. *Cymon.* Garrick's play was produced in 1767.

'*Sweet Passion of Love*,' Act III. Sc. 2.

'*It is silly sooth*,' etc. *Twelfth Night*, Act II. Sc. 4.

'*Now I am seventy-two.*' *Cymon*, Act II. Sc. 3.

'*Split the ears*,' etc. *Hamlet*, Act III. Sc. 2.

262. *What's a Man of Fashion?* 'An indifferent farce' (according to Genest) by Reynolds.

263. '*With pleased attention*,' etc. Collins, *Epistle to Sir Thomas Hanmer*, 59-63. Collins is referring to Fletcher.

'*Where did you rest last night?*' *The Orphan*, Act IV. Sc. 3.

'*A cubit from his stature.*' Cf. *St. Matthew*, vi. 27.

The Honey-Moon. By John Tobin (1805).

'*He still plays the dog.*' Cf. *Henry VI.*, Part III. Act v. Sc. 6.

last line. *The Examiner* adds : 'Mrs. Marden [Mardyn] played *Miss Hoyden* on Wednesday in the admirable comedy of the *Trip to Scarborough*. She seemed to consult her own genius in it less than the admonitions of some critics. There was accordingly less to find fault with, but we like her better when she takes her full swing.

'If to her share some trifling errors fall,
Look in her face, and you'll forget them all.'[1]

Mr. Penley's *Lord Foppington* had very considerable merit.

264. *The Merchant of Bruges.* A version by Douglas Kinnaird, Byron's friend, of Fletcher's comedy, *The Beggar's Bush.*

'*That every petty lord*,' etc. For this and the other passages quoted see *The Beggar's Bush*, Act II. Sc. 3.

266. l. 17. In *The Examiner* the article continued as follows : 'The new musical farce, *My Spouse and I*, continues to be acted with deserved applause. It is by much the best thing brought out this season. It has a great deal of all that is necessary to a good farce, point, character, humour, and incident. It was admirably supported. Harley played a lively character of the bustling Fawcett-cast very happily. He may now stick very comfortably in the skirts of public favour, if he does not chuse to fling himself out of them. The only faults of this piece are, that it is too long in the second act, and that Miss Kelly continues somewhat too long in breeches, for the purposes of decorum. Mr. Barnard, as a country lad, played very well, and was deservedly encored in a song, "But not for me the merry bells." This piece is described by Genest as "an indifferent musical farce by C. Dibdin, Jun."'

[1] Pope, *The Rape of the Lock*, II. 17-18.

525

266. *Smiles and Tears.* By Mrs. Charles Kemble (Maria Theresa De Camp, 1774-1838), produced December 12, 1815.
268. *Lucy Lockitt.* In *The Beggar's Opera.*
    Deaf and Dumb. A version (1801) of Bouilly's *Abbé de l'Épée.*
    Father and Daughter. Mrs. Opie's (1769-1853) first publication (1801).
    l. 29. In *The Examiner* Hazlitt adds : 'Mr. Liston spoke an indifferent epilogue inimitably well.'
    George Barnwell. Cf. *The Round Table,* vol. i. p. 154.
    '*A custom more honoured,*' etc. *Hamlet,* Act. i. Sc. 4.
269. '*These odds more even.*' Cf. *Measure for Measure,* Act iii. Sc. 1.
    '*A good hater.*' See Boswell's *Life of Johnson* (ed. G. B. Hill), i. 190, n. 1.
    '*He is the fitter for heaven.*' *George Barnwell,* Act iii. Sc. 3.
    '*Could he lay,*' etc. *Ibid.* Act iv. Sc. 1.
270. l. 10. *The Examiner* concludes : 'Both Pantomimes are indifferent. That at Drury-Lane consists in endless flights of magpies up to the ceiling, and that at Covent-Garden stays too long in China. The latter part was better where Mr. Grimaldi comes in, and lets off a culverin at his enemies, and sings a serenade to his mistress in concert with *Grimalkin.* We were glad, right glad, to see Mr. Grimaldi again. There was (some weeks back) an ugly report that Mr. Grimaldi was dead. We would not believe it ; we did not like to ask any one the question, but we watched the public countenance for the intimation of an event which "would have eclipsed the gaiety of nations."[1] We looked at the faces we met in the street, but there were no signs of general sadness ; no one stopped his acquaintance to say, that a man of genius was no more. Here indeed he is again, safe and sound, and as pleasant as ever. As without the gentleman at St. Helena, there is an end of politics in Europe ; so without the clown at Sadler's Wells, there must be an end of pantomimes in this country !'
    The Busy Body. Mrs. Centlivre's comedy (1709).
    '*His voice,*' etc. *As You Like It,* Act ii. Sc. 7.
271. *Barnes.* 'Mrs. Barnes from Exeter.' December 29, 1815.
    '*The divine Desdemona.*' *Othello,* Act ii. Sc. 1.
    '*That flows on,*' etc. *Ibid.* Act iii. Sc. 3.
    Zanga or Bajazet. In Young's *The Revenge* and Rowe's *Tamerlane* respectively.
272. '*Then, oh, farewell!*' For this and the other *Othello* quotations see *ante,* p. 189.
    A New Way to Pay Old Debts. Sir Giles Overreach was one of Kean's greatest parts. See Doran's *Annals of the English Stage* (ed. Lowe), iii. 390-1.
    It has been considered, etc. Part of this passage was repeated in *The Round Table.* See vol. i. pp. 156-7, and notes.
273. '*Two at a time,*' etc. *The Beggar's Opera,* Act iii. Sc. 4.
    Edwin. John Edwin, the elder (1749-1790), one of the great comedians of his day.
274. '*His fortune swells him,*' etc. *A New Way to Pay Old Debts,* Act v. Sc. 1.
    '*Come hither, Marall,*' etc. *Ibid.,* Act ii. Sc. 1.
    '*I'm feeble,*' etc. *Ibid.*
    A Midsummer Night's Dream. As altered by Reynolds, and produced January 17, 1816.
    We hope we have not been, etc. Hazlitt probably refers to the concluding paragraph of one of his *Round Table* essays. See vol. i. p. 64.

[1] See Johnson's *Lives of the Poets,* Life of Edmund Smith.

NOTES

275. '*Injurious Hermia*,' etc. *A Midsummer Night's Dream*, Act III. Sc. 2.

277. '*Is he not moved*,' etc. *A New Way to Pay Old Debts*, Act IV. Sc. 1.
'*Lord,—Right Honourable Lord*.' *Ibid.* Act II. Sc. 1, and Act III. Sc. 2.
'*Do themselves homage*.' *Othello*, Act I. Sc. 1.
'*It came twanging off*.' *A New Way to Pay Old Debts*, Act III. Sc. 2.

278. *Love for Love.* January 23, 1816.
Munden's Foresight. Cf. *ante*, p. 71.
Parsons. William Parsons (1736-1795), 'the comic Roscius.' Foresight
was one of his best parts.
'*School's up*,' etc. An interpolation apparently.

279. '*A great sea-porpoise*.' '*You great sea-calf*,' Miss Prue says to him (Act III.
Sc. 7).
'*And pray sister*,' etc. Act II. Sc. 9.
The Anglade Family. Accusation, or The Family of D'Anglade, adapted from
the French by J. H. Payne, and produced February 1, 1816.
The Maid and the Magpye. Cf. *ante*, p. 244.

280. note. Lavalette, after the second Bourbon restoration in 1815, was, along
with Ney, condemned to death, but escaped by changing clothes with his
wife. Cf. vol. III. p. 157 and note.

281. *The same drama.* The Covent Garden version (February 1) was by James
Kenney.
Mathews. Charles Mathews (1776-1835), one of the best comedians, and
the greatest mimic of his time. Hazlitt's admiration of him was not
enthusiastic.
Charles Kemble. Charles Kemble (1775-1854), the younger brother of
Mrs. Siddons and John Philip Kemble, first appeared in London in 1794,
and retired in 1840.
Measure for Measure. Covent Garden, February 8, 1816.
Lectures on Dramatic Literature, etc. Cf. vol. I. (*Characters of Shakespear's
Plays*), p. 346 and note.

282. '*The cowl*,' etc. Cf. '*All hoods make not monks*.' *Henry VIII.*,
Act III. Sc. 1.
'*If I do lose thee*,' etc. *Measure for Measure*, Act III. Sc. 1.

283. '*To lie in cold obstruction*,' etc. *Ibid.*
'*Careless*,' etc. *Ibid.* Act IV. Sc. 2.
'*He has been drinking hard*,' etc. *Ibid.* Act IV. Sc. 3.
'*A dish of some three-pence*.' *Ibid.* Act II. Sc. 1.
'*There is some soul*,' etc. *Henry V.*, Act IV. Sc. 1.
Society for the Suppression of Vice. See vol. I. p. 60, and note.

284. '*The enemies of the human race*.' The phrase was applied to Buonaparte. Cf.
vol. IX. p. 321.
'*Oh fie, fie*.' *Measure for Measure*, Act III. Sc. 1.
Vetus. See vol. III. pp. 57 *et seq.*, and notes.
'*Marall, come hither, Marall*.' See *ante*, note to p. 274.

285. l. 35. In *The Examiner* the article concludes: '*Rosina* has been acted at this
theatre to introduce the two Miss Halfords in the characters of *Rosina* and
Phœbe. They have both of them succeeded, and equally well. If they
are not a pair of Sirens, they are very pretty singers. Miss E. Halford is
the tallest, and Miss S. Halford the fattest of the two.'

286. '*The mob are so pleased*,' etc. *The Recruiting Officer*, Act I. Sc. 1.
'*Oh, the wonderful works of Nature*.' *Ibid.* Act II. Sc. 3.
'*Well, Tummy*.' *Ibid.*

287. l. 6. In *The Examiner* the article concludes as follows: '*The new farce of*

What Next? is very broad, very improbable, but if better managed, might have been made very laughable. The plot turns entirely on the disguise assumed by a nephew to personate his uncle, which leads to several ridiculous surprises and blunders, and the carrying on and the disentangling of the plot is effected with much more violence than art. It was once or twice in danger, but it hurried on so rapidly from absurdity to absurdity, that it at last distanced the critics. Even as a farce, it is too crude and coarse ever to become a very great favourite.' 'A moderate Farce by T. Dibdin' (Genest), produced at Drury Lane, Feb. 29.

287. *The Fair Penitent.* By Nicholas Rowe (1674-1718), produced in 1703. On the present occasion Charles Kemble played Lothario.
'*A Muse of fire*,' etc.   Henry V., Prologue.
An awkward imitator of Shakespear.' See *Tom Jones*, Book IX. chap. I.

288. '*Which to be hated*,' etc.   Pope's *Essay on Man*, II. 218.
'*It was the day*,' etc.   The Fair Penitent, Act III. Sc. I.
Last line. The article in *The Examiner* concludes with a brief reference to the re-appearance of Braham in *Israel in Egypt*, and gives the speech addressed by him to the audience, who had received him with some signs of disapprobation.

289. *The Duke of Milan.* Published in 1623.
'*Which felt a stain*,' etc.   Burke, *Reflections on the Revolution in France* (*Select Works*, ed. Payne, II. 89).

290. '*Proud to die*,' etc.   The Duke of Milan, Act V. Sc. 2.
'*Some widow's curse*,' etc.   See *ante*, note to p. 274.
'*By orphans' tears*.'   See *ante*, note to p. 277.

291. l. 5.   Add : 'Mr. Bartley spoke a new prologue on the occasion, which was well received.'
Miss O'Neill's Lady Teazle. In *The Examiner* this article begins as follows : 'Miss O'Neill [we beg pardon of the Board of Green Cloth, and are almost afraid that this style of theatrical criticism may not be quite consistent with the principles of subordination and the scale of respectability about to be established in Europe; for we read in the *Examiner* of last week the following paragraph : "At Berlin, orders have been given by the police to leave out the titles of Mr., Mrs., and Miss, prefixed to the names of public actors. The females are to take the name of *frou*. Accordingly we see the part of Desdemona, in Shakespeare's tragedy of *Othello*, is given out to be played by *frou* (woman) Schrok." This is as it should be, and legitimate. But to proceed till further orders in the usual style].'
Miss Farren. Elizabeth Farren (1759-1829), who first played in London in 1777, retired in 1797, and in the same year married the 12th Earl of Derby. Cf. *ante*, p. 389. Her last appearance was in the character of Lady Teazle.

292. *Mrs. Egerton.* Sarah Egerton (1782-1847) first appeared in London in 1811, and retired in 1835. Mrs. Baron Wilson (*Our Actresses*, I. 79) relates that on the occasion here referred to by Hazlitt she played Meg Merrilies in place of Emery, who 'refused to put on petticoats.'
The late Mr. Cooke. George Frederick Cooke (1756-1811) was frequently too intoxicated to appear on the stage. See *ante*, note to p. 207.

293. '*The web of our life*,' etc.   All's Well that Ends Well, Act IV. Sc. 3.
'*Like the giddy sailor*,' etc.   Misquoted from *Richard III.*, Act III. Sc. 4.

294. '*Deep than loud*.'   Cf. 'Curses, not loud, but deep.'   *Macbeth*, Act V. Sc. 3.

295. *The following account.*   See *ante*, pp. 179-80.

296. '*I would not have parted with it*,' etc.   The Merchant of Venice, Act III. Sc. I.

NOTES

297. *'Exhaling to the sky.'* Cf. 'No natural exhalation in the sky.' *King John*, Act III. Sc. 4.

Madame Mainville Fodor. Josephine Fodor-Mainvielle (b. 1793). This was her first, or one of her first appearances in London. She retired from the stage in 1833.

'*Has her exits,' etc. As You Like It*, Act II. Sc. 7.

298. *'Till the moon,' etc. Paradise Lost*, IV. 607 *et seq.*

'*Hope told a flattering tale.'* An anonymous song set to music by Paisiello.

Mons. Drouet. Louis François Philippe Drouet (1792-1873).

l. 29. *The Examiner* continues : '*Drury Lane.*—A young lady has appeared at this theatre in the character of *Cecilia* in the *Chapter of Accidents* : but from the insipidity of the character in which she chose to appear, we know no more of her powers of acting than before we saw her. Both her face and voice are pleasing.' The lady was Miss Murray. Sophia Lee's comedy *The Chapter of Accidents* was produced in 1780.

Mr. Cobham. April 15, 1816. Thomas Cobham (1786-1842) failed on this occasion, but became 'a hero to transpontine audiences.'

'*Made of penetrable stuff.' Hamlet*, Act III. Sc. 4.

299. '*Unhousell'd,' etc. Ibid.* Act I. Sc. 5.

Sir Pertinax MacSycophant. In Macklin's *The Man of the World* (1781). Bibby appeared on April 16, 1816.

Egerton. Daniel Egerton (1772-1835), 'long the performer of "cruel uncles" and "flinty-hearted fathers"' at Covent Garden. He married Sarah Fisher, for whom see *ante*, p. 292.

300. *Miss Grimani.* Miss Grimani from Bath played Juliet, April 23, 1816.

'*How silver sweet,' etc. Romeo and Juliet*, Act II. Sc. 2.

'*The midnight bell,' etc. King John*, Act III. Sc. 3.

'*Gentle tassel.'* 'To lure this tassel-gentle back again.' *Romeo and Juliet*, Act II. Sc. 2.

301. *Garrick's Ode on Shakespear.* Written for the famous Shakespeare Jubilee at Stratford in 1769.

'*Vesuvius in an eruption,' etc.* Gray, Letter to Warton, August 8, 1749. See *Letters* (ed. Tovey), I. 201.

'*I was ready to sink for him,' etc. Ibid.*

302. l. 20. In *The Examiner* Hazlitt continues as follows : 'But any one who chuses may see the celebration of the centenary of Shakspeare's death to-day, (which is Thursday) on Saturday or on Tuesday next, at Covent-Garden Theatre. They kill him there as often as the town pleases.——We cannot speak favourably of either of the new after-pieces, *Who wants a Wife?* and *Pitcairn's Island.* The one is contrived for Mr. Liston to make foolish love in ; and the other for Mr. Smith to play that land-monster, a singing, swaggering, good-natured, honest, blackguard English Jack Tar, a sort of animal that ought never to come ashore, or as soon as it does, ought to go to sea again.'

'*Doubtless the pleasure,' etc. Hudibras*, Part II., Canto III., 1-2.

'*Full volly home.'* Cf. 'But rattling nonsense in full volleys breaks,' Pope, *An Essay on Criticism*, 628. Cf. *King Lear*, Act V. Sc. 3, l. 174.

303. *Madame Sacchi.* Madame Sacchi's 'astonishing performances' on the tight rope were introduced 'for the accommodation of the crowds of applicants' who desired to witness them.

'*So fails,' etc.* See *The Excursion*, Book VII., 975 *et seq.*

'*Affecting a virtue.'* 'Assume a virtue, if you have it not.' *Hamlet*, Act III. Sc. 4.

A VIEW OF THE ENGLISH STAGE

303. '*They two can be made one flesh.*' Cf. *Genesis* ii. 24.
Dame Hellenore. *The Faerie Queene*, Book III. Canto X.
'*Aggravated*,' etc. *A Midsummer Night's Dream*, Act I. Sc. 2.

304. '*There is some fury*,' etc. *A New Way to Pay Old Debts*, Act IV. Sc. 1.
'*A word of naught.*' Cf. 'You must say "paragon"; a paramour is, God
bless us, a thing of naught.' *A Midsummer Night's Dream*, Act IV. Sc. 2.
'*So stands the statue*,' etc. Thomson, *The Seasons*, Summer, 1347.
l. 24. Hazlitt concluded his article in *The Examiner* as follows : 'He must
be sent to Coventry or St. Helena !'

305. *Bertram.* By the Rev. Charles Robert Maturin (1782-1824), author of *Melmoth
the Wanderer* (1820). *Bertram* had previously been recommended by Scott to
Kemble who declined it. Coleridge attacked it in *The Courier* and in *Bio-
graphia Literaria*. See Dykes Campbell's *Samuel Taylor Coleridge*, p.223, note 1.
Aristotle, etc. Part of the famous definition of tragedy in the *Poetics*.
'*Yes, the limner's art*,' etc. *Bertram*, Act I. Sc. 5.

306. '*And yet some sorcery*,' etc. *Ibid.*

307. '*Yea, thus they live*,' etc. *Ibid.* Act III. Sc. 2.
'*By heaven*,' etc. *Ibid.* Act IV. Sc. 2.
The speech of Bertram. *Ibid.* Act V. Sc. 2.
'*The wretched have no country.* *Ibid.* Act II. Sc. 3.
Miss Somerville. Margaret Agnes Somerville (1799-1883), whose first
appearance Hazlitt notices here. In 1819 she married Alfred Bunn, the
theatrical manager. Her subsequent appearances were fitful, and she
retired at an early age.

308. '*Decked in purple*,' etc. *Ibid.* Act I. Sc. 5.
'*Beholds that lady*,' etc. *Ibid.*
l. 13. In *The Examiner* Hazlitt adds : 'Covent-Garden. We have seen
Miss O'Neill's *Mrs. Oakley*. It is much better than her *Lady Teazle*, and yet
it is not good. Her comedy is only tragedy *diluted*. It wants the true spirit.'
Adelaide, or the Emigrants. The first play of Richard Lalor Sheil (1791-
1851). It had been brought out at Dublin in 1814.

309. '*Throw it to the dogs*,' etc. *Macbeth*, Act V. Sc. 3.
Mr. Murray. Charles Murray (1754-1821), after acquiring considerable
reputation in the provinces, appeared at Covent Garden in 1796.

310. '*Where did you rest last night.*' See *ante*, note to p. 263.
l. 22. In *The Examiner* the article concludes with a long account of the
plot of *Bertram*.
It has been observed of Ben Jonson, etc. Cf. *ante*, note to p. 42.

311. '*As dry*,' etc. *As You Like It*, Act II. Sc. 7.
'*Like a man*,' etc. *Henry IV.*, Part II., Act III. Sc. 2.

312. '*The baby of a girl.* *Macbeth*, Act III. Sc. 4.
'*Rather than so*,' etc. *Ibid.* Act III. Sc. 1.

313. *The Princess Charlotte.* The only daughter of the Prince Regent, and a great
favourite of the nation's. She married (May 2, 1816) Prince Leopold of
Saxe-Coburg, and died November 5, 1817.
'*Leave me to my repose.* 'Leave me, leave me to repose.' Gray. *The
Vegtam's Kivitha ; or the Descent of Odin.*
'*The line too labours*,' etc. Pope, *An Essay on Criticism*, 371.
'*I tell you*,' etc. *Macbeth*, Act V. Sc. 1.

314. '*Go, go.*' In the banquet scene presumably, Act III. Sc. 4.
Mr. Horace Twiss. Horace Twiss (1787-1849), the biographer of Lord
Eldon, was a nephew of Mrs. Siddons and wrote for her an address which
she delivered on taking her farewell of the stage, June 29, 1812.

NOTES

314. '*Himself again.*' *Richard III.* (Cibber's version).
'*Tomorrow and tomorrow.*' *Macbeth*, Act v. Sc. 5.
Printed by a steam-engine. See vol. III., p. 158 (*Political Essays*).
315. *Up all Night, or the Smuggler's Cave.* By Matthew Peter King (1773-1823) first produced in 1809 (words by S. J. Arnold).
Mr. Russell from Edinburgh. Hazlitt distinguishes him from Samuel Thomas Russell (1769?-1845), great as Jerry Sneak.
The Beehive. A musical farce by John Gideon Millingen (1782-1862), produced in 1811.
Wrench. Benjamin Wrench (1778-1843), after playing at Bath and York, appeared in London in 1809 and became a well-known comedian at Drury Lane, The Lyceum and Covent Garden.
The School of Reform. By Thomas Morton, produced in 1805.
316. *The Irish Widow.* By Garrick, produced in 1772.
l. 10. Hazlitt, in concluding his article in *The Examiner*, declares his disbelief of the rumours relating to Mrs. Mardyn (see *ante*, note to p. 249), and publishes a long letter from her addressed to the editor of the *Morning Chronicle*, indignantly denying them.
The Jealous Wife. By George Colman the elder, produced in 1761.
Sylvester Daggerwood. By George Colman the younger, first acted in 1795 as 'New Hay at the Old Market.'
'*Like angels' visits,*' etc. See vol. IV., note to p. 346 (*The Spirit of the Age*).
Wild Oats. O'Keeffe's comedy, produced in 1794.
317. *The acting of Dowton and Russell.* This paragraph is repeated in *Lectures on the Comic Writers.* See *ante*, pp. 167-8.
319. *The Poor Gentleman.* By George Colman the younger, produced in 1802.
The Agreeable Surprise. Cf. Hazlitt's account of this farce, *ante*, pp. 166-7.
320. l. 4. Hazlitt continues in *The Examiner* : 'We saw Miss Matthews's name in the bills, but as it was her benefit night at Covent-Garden, her entrance in the afterpiece was an agreeable surprise to us.—*English Opera.* A gentleman of the name of Horn has re-appeared with much and deserved applause at this Theatre, in the part of the *Seraskier*. His voice and style of singing are good, and his action spirited and superior to that of singers in general. We hope soon to say more of him.' Charles Edward Horn (1786-1849), the composer of 'Cherry Ripe,' 'I know a bank,' etc.
Artaxerxes. Cf. *ante*, pp. 192-3.
321. *Exit by Mistake.* 'A pretty good comedy in 3 acts, by Jameson' (Genest).
322. *John Dennis.* Hazlitt probably refers to John Dennis's 'Remarks upon Cato,' 1713.
The editor of a modern journal. Probably Hazlitt's brother-in-law, Dr., afterwards Sir John Stoddart.
323. *The Beggar's Opera.* Cf. *ante*, pp. 193-5. Polly's famous song, 'Oh, ponder well ! be not severe,' etc. (Act I.), is said to have turned the tide in favour of the opera at its first representation, January 29, 1728.
324. *Schlegel's work on the Drama.* See Lecture IV. *Lectures on Dramatic Art and Literature* (trans. John Black, ed. 1900), p. 64.
325. *Selon la coutume de notre pays.* See vol. I. note to p. 100.
Cosi fan Tutti. Mozart's Opera, 1788.
Dansomanie. By Étienne Nicolas Méhul (1763-1817), produced in Paris, 1800.
326. '*To draw three souls,*' etc. *Twelfth Night,* Act II. Sc. 3.
Mr. Naldi. Giuseppe Naldi (1770-1820), who first appeared in London in 1806.

326. *Pandarus.* In *Troilus and Cressida.*

    Signor Begri. Presumably Pierre Ignace Begrey (1783-1863), who appeared in London, 1815-1822.

    '*Floats upon the air*,' etc. Loosely quoted from *Comus*, 249-251.

    '*And silence*,' etc. *Ibid.* 557-560.

327. *Madame Vestris.* Lucia Elizabeth Bartolozzi (1797-1856), granddaughter of the engraver, and the wife, first (1813) of Armand Vestris, a dancer at the King's Theatre, and second (1838), of Charles James Mathews. She first appeared in London in 1815, and retired in 1854. Mrs. Baron Wilson (*Our Actresses*, II. 184) describes her as 'the fair Syren, who, for nearly a quarter of a century, has fascinated the whole kingdom by her talent and beauty.'

    Miss L. Kelly. The younger sister of Frances Maria Kelly, born 1795.

328. l. 13. In *The Examiner* the article concludes as follows : '*Love in a Village* is put off till Thursday next, and Mr. Incledon is to perform in *Artaxerxes* on Tuesday. Mr. Horn played the *Seraskier* in the *Siege of Belgrade* on Friday, and sung the songs, particularly 'My heart with love is beating' with great truth and effect. Mr. Russell's *Leopold* was very lively. It is not necessary to say that Miss Kelly's *Lilla* was good, for all that she does is so. The Duke and Duchess of Gloucester were present, and were very cordially greeted by the audience. After the play, God save the King was repeatedly called for, and at length sung, with an additional, occasional, and complimentary verse by Mr. Arnold :—

> " Long may the Royal Line,
> Proud Star of Brunswick shine ;
> While thus we sing,
> Joy may thy Daughter share,
> Blest by a Nation's pray'r,
> Blest be the Royal Pair ;
> God save the King."

    'At the Haymarket, where the same Illustrious Personages appeared for the first time in public (since their marriage) the night before, the following stanza was introduced :—

> " Great George ! thy people's voice
> Now hails thy daughter's choice
> Till echoes ring :
> This shout still rends the air,
> May she prove blest as fair !
> Long live the noble pair !
> God save the King." '

    My Landlady's Night-Gown. My Landlady's Gown (August 10, 1816), by Walley Chamberlain Oulton (1770 ?-1820 ?).

    '*Its own place.*' *Paradise Lost*, I. 254.

329. l. 4. In *The Examiner* Hazlitt proceeds : 'A Miss Ives played a little plump chambermaid prettily enough. *The Jealous Wife* was acted at this Theatre on Monday. Mr. Meggett played *Mr. Oakley* but indifferently. He seemed to be at hawk and buzzard between insipid comedy and pompous tragedy. It was not the thing. Mr. Terry's *Major Oakley* we like very much. Mrs. Glover, who played *Mrs. Oakley*, is really too big for this little theatre. The stage cannot contain her, and her violent airs. Miss Taylor was *Miss Russet*, and looked like a very nice, runaway school-girl. Barnard played her lover, and got through the part very well.'

NOTES

329. *Rosetta.* In Bickerstaffe's *Love in a Village.*

    Mr. Chatterley. William Symonds Chatterley (1787-1822). Justice Woodcock was his best character.

    Castle of Andalusia. A comic opera by O'Keeffe, produced in 1782.

330. l. 36. The article in *The Examiner* continues : '*Haymarket-Theatre.* The new farce in one act, called *The Fair Deserter*, succeeds very well here. It preserves the unities of time, place, and action, with the most perfect regularity. The merit of it is confined to the plot, and to the pretended changes of character by the changes of dress, which succeed one another with the rapidity and with something of the ingenuity of a pantomime. Mr. Duruset, a young officer of musical habits, wishes to release Miss MacAlpine from the power of her guardian, who is determined to marry her the next day. The young lady is kept under lock and key, and the difficulty is to get her out of the house. For this purpose Tokely, servant to Duruset, contrives to make the cook of the family drunk at an alehouse, where he leaves him, and carries off his official paraphernalia, his night-cap, apron, and long knife, in a bundle to his master. The old guardian (Watkinson) comes out with his lawyer from the house, and Tokely, presenting himself as the drunken cook, is let in. He, however, takes the key of the street door with him, which he shuts to, and as this intercepts the return of the old gentleman to his house, Tokely is forced to get out of the window by a ladder to fetch a blacksmith. He presently returns himself, in the character of the blacksmith, unlocks the door, but on the other's refusing him a guinea for his trouble, locks it again, and walks off in spite of all remonstrances. The guardian is now compelled to ascend the ladder himself as well as he can : and while he is engaged in this ticklish adventure, the young Gallant and his mischievous Valet return with a couple of sentries whom Duruset orders to seize the poor old Guardian as a robber, and upon his declaring who and what he is, he is immediately charged by the lover with concealing a Deserter in his house, who is presently brought out, and is in fact his ward, disguised in a young officer's uniform, which Tokely had given to her for that purpose. Tokely now returns dressed as an officer, and pretending to be the father of the young gentleman, with much blustering and little probability, persuades the guardian to consent to the match between his (adopted) son and the young lady, who has just been arrested as the Deserter, and who, upon this, throwing aside her disguise, the affair is concluded, to the satisfaction of every body but the old guardian, and the curtain drops. The bustle of this little piece keeps it alive : there is nothing good either in the writing or the acting of it.'

331. '*Gone like a crab,*' etc. *Hamlet*, Act II. Sc. 2.

    Mr. Terry last week, etc. At the Haymarket, on August 27, 1816.

    The Surrender of Calais. By George Colman the younger (1791).

    '*The line too labours,*' etc. Cf. *ante*, note to p. 313.

    '*He resembles a person,*' etc. Schlegel on Dryden. See *Lectures on Dramatic Literature* (trans. John Black, ed. 1900), p. 479.

332. '*Not to be hated.*' Cf. *ante*, note to p. 288.

    The Wonder. Mrs. Centlivre's (1714), Covent Garden, Sep. 13, 1816.

    The Busy Body. 1709.

333. '*Trippingly from* [on] *the tongue.*' *Hamlet*, Act III. Sc. 2.

    '*A Scotsman is not ashamed,*' etc. *The Wonder*, Act V. Sc. 1.

334. *The Distressed Mother.* Originally produced in 1712. Hazlitt here notices the first appearance in London of William Charles Macready (1793-1873), Covent Garden, Sep. 16, 1816.

---

[1] *Macbeth*, Act v. Sc. 5.

misinformed : and shall be glad to say so, if possible, in our next.' The article concludes with an account of Kean quoted from *The Edinburgh Courant.*

342. '*Being mortal.*' *A Midsummer Night's Dream*, Act II. Sc. 1.

l. 27. In *The Examiner* the article continues as follows : 'After the play, we saw the *Broken Sword*, which is a melodrame of some interest, for it has a dumb boy, a murderer, and an innocent person suspected of being the perpetrator of the crime, in it : but it is a very ill-digested and ill-conducted piece. The introduction to the principal events is very tedious and round about, and the incidents themselves, when they arrive, come in very great disorder, and shock from their improbability and want of necessary connection as much as from their own nature. Mr. Terry played the part of a murderer with considerable gravity. We do not know at all how he came to get into so awkward a situation. The piece is, we understand, from common report, by Mr. Dimond.[1] It is by no means one of his best. For he is a very impressive as well as a prolific writer in this way, and would do still better, if he would mind his fine writing less, and get on faster to the business of the story. Mr. Farley was highly interesting as *Estevan*, the servant who is unjustly accused of the murder of his master ; in fact, he always plays this class of characters admirably, both as to feeling and effect ; and Miss Lupino played the dumb *Florio* very prettily. In the first act, there was a dance by the Miss Dennets.[2] If our readers have not seen this dance, we hope they will, and that they will *encore* it, which is the etiquette. Certainly, it is the prettiest thing in the world, except the performers in it. They are quite charming. They are three kindred Graces cast in the same mould : a little Trinity of innocent delights, dancing in their "trinal simplicities below."[3] They are like "three red roses on a stalk ;"[4] and in the *pas de trois* which they dance twice over, they are as it were twined and woven into garlands and festoons of blushing flowers, such as "Proserpine let fall from Dis's waggon."[5] You can hardly distinguish them from one another, they are at first so alike in shape, age, air, look : so that the pleasure you receive from one is blended with the delight you receive from the other two, in a sort of provoking, pleasing confusion. Milton was thinking of them when he wrote the lines :—

> 'Whom lovely Venus at a birth,
> With two Sister Graces more,
> To ivy-crowned Bacchus bore."[6]

Yet after all we have a preference, but we will not say which it is, whether the tallest or the shortest, the fairest or the darkest, of this lovely, laughing trio, more gay and joyous than *Mozart's.*—"But pray, dear sir, could you not give us a little bit of a hint which of us it is you like the very, very best ?"—Yes, yes, you rogue, you know very well it's you, but don't say a word of it to either of your sisters.' The theatrical criticisms during November were written by Leigh Hunt.

The Iron Chest. By George Colman the younger (1796), revived at Drury Lane, November 23, 1816.

343. *Adam Winterton.* A character in *The Iron Chest.*

---

[1] William Dimond of Bath, the author of a great number of plays.
[2] Cf. *ante*, pp. 411-12.
[3] Cf. 'In their trinal triplicities on hye.' *The Faerie Queene*, Book I. Canto I. St. 38.
[4] Cf. 'Their lips were four red roses on a stalk.' *Richard III.*, Act IV. Sc. 3.
[5] *A Winter's Tale*, Act IV. Sc. 4.   [6] *L'Allegro*, 14 *et seq.*

A VIEW OF THE ENGLISH STAGE

343. *Mr. Colman was enraged, etc.* He wrote an angry preface which was suppressed after the first edition.

344. *'Wears his heart,' etc.* Adapted from *Othello*, Act I. Sc. 1.
'*The fiery soul,' etc.* Dryden, *Absalom and Achitophel*, Part I., 156-8.

345. l. 5. In *The Examiner* the article concludes as follows : 'The new farce, *Laugh to Day and Cry Tomorrow* [by E. P. Knight], met as it deserved a very indifferent reception. It was a series of awkward clap-traps about the glory of Old England, and the good-nature of English audiences. Munden was the only thing in it not *damnable.*'
Mr. Kemble's King John. December 3, 1816.
'*When we waked,' etc.* The Tempest, Act III. Sc. 2.

346. *According to the book of arithmetic.* More commonly 'according to Cocker.'
'*Man delight*' [delights],' etc. *Hamlet*, Act II. Sc. 2.

347. '*Bulk, the thews,' etc.* Misquoted from *Henry IV.*, Part II., Act III. Sc. 2.
'*Could Sir Robert,' etc.* King John, Act I. Sc. 1.
Coriolanus. November 28 and 30, 1816. For the rest of this article, except the last paragraph, see vol. I. pp. 214-6 (*Characters of Shakespear's Plays*) and notes thereon.

350. l. 21. In *The Examiner* the article concludes as follows : 'There have been two new farces this week : one at each house. One was saved and one was damned. One was justly damned, and the other unjustly saved. *Nota Bene*, or *The Two Dr. Fungus's*, shot up and disappeared in one night, notwithstanding the inimitable acting and well-oiled humour of Oxberry in one scene, where he makes bumpkin forward love to Mrs. Orger in a style equal to Liston. *Love and Toothache*, though there is neither Love nor Toothache in it, is as disagreeable as the one and as foolish as the other. One farce consists of a succession of low incidents without a plot, and the other is one tedious and improbable incident without a plot. The changing of the two signs, or Nota Benes of the two Fungus's, barber and doctor, in the first, is better than anything in the last. The only difference is, that at the one house they contrive to have their pieces cast, and get them condemned at the other. Yet this is a saying without any meaning ; for in the present case they were both got up as well as they could be.— We almost despair of ever seeing another good farce. Mr. H——, thou wert damned. Bright shone the morning on the play-bills that announced thy appearance, and the streets were filled with the buzz of persons asking one another if they would go to see Mr. H——, and answering that they would certainly ; but before night the gaiety, not of the author, but of his friends and the town, was eclipsed, for thou wert damned ! Hadst thou been anonymous, thou mightst have been immortal ! But thou didst come to an untimely end, for thy tricks and for want of a better name to pass them off (as the old joke of Divine Right passes current under the *alias* of Legitimacy)—and since that time nothing worth naming has been offered to the stage !' Hazlitt refers again to Lamb's farce ' Mr. H——' in his essay ' On Great and Little Things.' See vol. VI. p. 232 and notes. The passage above, beginning ' Mr. H——, thou wert damned' down to ' for want of a better name to pass them off' was prefixed to the farce by Lamb, when he published it in 1818.
The Man of the World. Revived December 27, 1816.
Mr. Henry Johnston. Henry Erskine Johnston, (1777-1830?), the ' Scottish Roscius.'
Sir Archy Mac Sarcasm. In Macklin's *Love à-la-Mode* (1793) revived at Covent Garden, with Johnston as Sir Archy, on December 10, 1816.

NOTES

351. ‘*Die and leave,*’ etc.   *Twelfth Night,* Act I. Sc. 5.
352. ‘*Ever charming,*’ etc.   Dyer, *Grongar Hill,* l. 103.
   Jane Shore.   January 2, 1817.   Rowe’s tragedy was first produced in 1713.
   In *The Examiner* Hazlitt concludes this article as follows :—‘ We think the
   tragedy of *Jane Shore,* which is founded on the dreadful calamity of hunger,
   is hardly proper to be represented in these starving times ; and it ought
   to be prohibited by the Lord Chamberlain, on a principle of decorum.   Of
   Mrs. Alsop, who is said to have an engagement at this theatre, we have
   spoken at the time when she appeared at the other house.   Those who
   have before not witnessed her performance, will now probably have an
   opportunity of seeing her in company with Mrs. Mardyn, and may judge
   whether the laborious comparison we attempted between her and that lady
   was well or ill-founded.   We see little alteration or improvement in her.
   Her figure and face are against her ; otherwise she is certainly a very
   spirited little actress, and her voice is excellent.   Her singing, however,
   does not correspond with what you would expect from her speaking tones.
   It wants volume and clearness.   Mrs. Alsop’s laugh sometimes puts us a
   little in mind of her mother : and those parts of the character of *Violante*
   in which she succeeded best were the most joyous and exulting ones : her
   expression of distress is truly distressing.   Miss Kelly played *Flora* ; and it
   was the only time we ever saw her fail.   She seemed to be playing tricks
   with the chambermaid : now those kind of people are as much in earnest
   in their absurdities as any other class of people in the world, and the
   great beauty of Miss Kelly’s acting in all other instances is, that it is more
   in downright earnest than any other acting in the world.   We hope she
   does not think of growing fantastical, and *operatic.*   The new pantomime
   is very poor.’
   The *Theatrical Examiners* of January 12 and January 19, 1817 are
   clearly Hazlitt’s.   The first is a notice of Cherry’s *The Soldier’s Daughter,*
   revived at Covent Garden, January 8, 1817, and contains a severe criticism of
   Miss O’Neill as a comic actress.   The second is a notice of Cimarosa’s
   Penelope and the comic Ballet *Dansomanie* at the King’s Theatre, and
   concludes with a long quotation from Colley Cibber’s *Life* on the introduction of opera into England.
353. *The Humorous Lieutenant.*   In *The Examiner* the article from which this notice
   is taken begins with a long account (probably by Hazlitt) of Southerne’s
   Oroonoko revived at Drury Lane January 20, 1817 with Kean as Oroonoko
   and Miss Somerville as Imoinda.   *The Humorous Lieutenant* (January 18)
   was ‘ a bad alteration ’ by Frederic Reynolds.   Celia was played by ‘ a Young
   Lady, 1st appearance on any stage.’
   ‘*Whose utmost skirts,*’ etc.   *Paradise Lost,* XI. 332-3.
   l. 20.   The *Theatrical Examiner* of February 2, 1817 in which are noticed
   John Philip Kemble’s farce *The Pannel,* revived at Drury Lane January 29,
   1816 and a melodrama (attributed to Pocock) *The Ravens, or the Force of
   Conscience,* acted at Covent Garden January 24, 1817, is clearly Hazlitt’s.
   The article contains a comparison between the Drury Lane and Covent
   Garden companies.
   Two New Ballets.   From a *Theatrical Examiner* which begins with an
   account of Mozart’s *Nozze di Figaro* not at all in Hazlitt’s manner.
   Like Virgil’s wood.   *Æneid,* III. 37-40.
   ‘*Whom lovely Venus,*’ etc.   *L’Allegro,* 14 *et seq.*
354. ‘*When you do dance,*’ etc.   *A Winter’s Tale,* Act IV. Sc. 4.
   Booth.   Junius Brutus Booth (1796-1852), whose first important appearances

in London are noticed in this and the two following articles. The last years of his life were spent in America.

'*What does he* [do they] *in the north.*' *Richard III.*, Act IV. Sc. 4.

355. '*A weak invention,*' etc. Cf. 'A thing devised by the enemy.' *Richard III.*, Act V. Sc. 3.

Figaro. Holcroft's *The Follies of a Day; or, the Marriage of Figaro* (1784).

356. '*The fell opposite.*' Vaguely Shakesperian. Cf. *Twelfth Night*, Act III. Sc. 4, and *Hamlet*, Act V. Sc. 2.

'*I know my price no less.*' *Othello*, Act I. Sc. I.

'*Give the world,*' etc. *Hamlet*, Act III. Sc. 4.

'*My wit comes,*' etc. Misquoted from *Othello*, Act II. Sc. I.

357. *The O. P. rows.* The old price riots at the new Covent Garden Theatre in 1809.

358. *Frightened to Death.* A musical farce by Oulton.

359. '*From which,*' etc. *Hamlet*, Act III. Sc. I.

l. 19. The *Theatrical Examiner* for the following week (March 9, 1817) contains a notice (possibly by Hazlitt) of *The Heir of Vironi, or Honesty the Best Policy* (Covent Garden, February 27), and of 'Mr. Booth's imitations of Mr. Kean.' With this exception The *Theatrical Examiners* down to March 13 are by Leigh Hunt.

Cibber. Cf. *ante*, pp. 160-2.

360. '*In hidden mazes,*' etc. Misquoted from *L'Allegro*, 141-2.

361. '*Frontlet.*' *King Lear*, Act I. Sc. 4.

362. *The Inn-Keeper's Daughter.* By George Soane (1790-1860).

363. '*Airs from heaven,*' etc. *Hamlet*, Act I. Sc. 4.

364. '*And when she spake,*' etc. *The Faerie Queene*, II. iii. 24.

365. *Signor Ambrogetti.* Giuseppe Ambrogetti was in London 1817-1821.

'*Sense of amorous delight.*' 'The spirit of love and amorous delight.' *Paradise Lost*, VIII. 477.

Signor Crivelli, etc. Gaetano Crivelli (1774-1836), a tenor; Violante Camporese (b. 1785), a soprano; Carlo Angrisani (b. *circa* 1760), a bass.

366. l. 6. The *Theatrical Examiner* concludes with an 'Anecdote relating to the Overture of *Don Giovanni*,' and a reference to *Elphi Bey*, 'a tedious and insipid' romantic drama (Drury Lane, April 17).

Ex uno omnes. 'Ab uno disce omnes.' *Æneid*, II. 65-6.

367. '*With all appliances,*' etc. *Henry IV.*, Part II. Act III. Sc. I.

'*The golden cadences,*' etc. 'Golden cadence of poesy.' *Love's Labour's Lost*, Act IV. Sc. 2.

368. l. 29. The *Theatrical Examiner* of May 4, 1817, clearly by Hazlitt, contains a notice of *Johnny Gilpin* (Drury Lane, April 28), and a brief reference to Mrs. Hill's Lady Macbeth (April 29). *Johnny Gilpin* is described as 'very poorly got up.'

369. *Holland.* Charles Holland (1768-1849?) played at Drury Lane 1796-1820.

370. l. 14. The *Theatrical Examiner* concludes as follows : 'We have not room to say much of the new tragedy of *The Apostate*,[1] for which we are not sorry, as we should have little good to say of it. The poetry does not rise to the merit of common-place, and the tragic situations are too violent, frequent, and improbable. It is full of a succession of self-inflicted horrors. Miss O'Neill played the heroine of the piece, whose affectation and meddling

[1] By Richard Lalor Sheil.

imbecility occasion all the mischief, and played it shockingly well. Mr. Young's *Malec* was in his best and most imposing manner. The best things in *The Apostate* were the palpable hits at the Inquisition and Ferdinand the Beloved, which were taken loudly and tumultuously by the house, a circumstance which occasioned more horror in that wretched infatuated devoted tool of despotism, the Editor of *The New Times*,[1] than all the other horrors of the piece. The Dungeons of the Holy Inquisition, whips, racks, and slow fires, kindled by legitimate hands, excite no horror in his breast ; but that a British public still revolt at these things, that that fine word Legitimacy has not polluted their souls and poisoned their very senses with the slime and filth of slavery and superstition, this writhes his brain and plants scorpions in his mind, and makes his flesh crawl and shrink in agony from the last expression of manhood and humanity in an English audience, as if a serpent had wound round his heart !'

The *Theatrical Examiner* of May 18, 1817, in which is described a second visit to *Don Giovanni*, and Kean's *Eustace de St. Pierre* in *The Surrender of Calais*, is clearly Hazlitt's.

370. '*Something rotten*,' etc. *Hamlet*, Act I. Sc. 4.

Mr. Sinclair. John Sinclair (1791-1857), tenor singer.

'*To split the ears*,' etc. *Hamlet*, Act III. Sc. 2.

371. '*And of his port*,' etc. *The Canterbury Tales*, Prologue, 69.

372. '*None but himself*,' etc. Lewis Theobald, *The Double Falsehood*.

l. 9. The article in *The Examiner* concludes : ' Drury Lane. The farce of *The Romp*[2] was revived here, and we hope will be continued, for we like to laugh when we can. Mrs. Alsop does the part of *Priscilla Tomboy*, and is all but her mother in it. Knight is clever enough as *Watty Cockney* ; and the piece, upon the whole, went off with great *éclat*, allowing for the badness of the times, for our want of genius for comedy, and of taste for farce.'

Barbarossa. By John Brown (1715-1766), author of *An Estimate of the Manners and Principles of the Times* (1757). *Barbarossa* was produced in 1754, *Athelstane*, the author's other tragedy, in 1756.

Paul and Virginia. A musical drama by James Cobb (1756-1818), produced in 1800.

'*And when your song*,' etc. *The Tatler*, No. 163 (by Addison).

'*In our heart's core*,' etc. *Hamlet*, Act III. Sc. 2.

last line. The *Theatrical Examiner* concludes as follows :—'*Covent Garden.* Mr. Kemble played *Posthumus* here on Friday. At present, to use a favourite pun, all his characters are posthumous ; he plays them repeatedly after *the last time*. We hate all suspense : and we therefore wish Mr. Kemble would go, or let it alone. We had much rather, for ourselves, that he staid ; for there is no one to fill his place on the stage. The mould is broken in which he was cast. His *Posthumus* is a very successful piece of acting. It alternately displays that repulsive stately dignity of manner, or that intense vehemence of action, in which the body and the mind strain with eager impotence after a certain object of disappointed passion, for which Mr. Kemble is peculiarly distinguished. In the scenes with *Iachimo* he was particularly happy, and threw from him the imputations and even the proofs of *Imogen's* inconstancy with a fine manly graceful scorn. The burst of inconsolable passion when the conviction of his

---

[1] Dr. John Stoddart, who had left *The Times* early in 1817, and started *The Day and New Times*, afterwards known as *The New Times*.

[2] Founded on Bickerstaffe's *Love in the City*, and first produced 1781.

treacherous rival's success is forced upon him, was nearly as fine as his smothered indignation and impatience of the least suggestion against his mistress's purity of character, had before been. In the concluding scene he failed. When he comes forward to brave *Iachimo*, and as it were to sink him to the earth by his very presence—'Behold him here '—his voice and manner wanted force and impetuosity. Mr. Kemble executes a surprise in the most premeditated and least unexpected manner possible. What was said the other day in praise of this accomplished actor, might be converted into an objection to him : he has been too much used to figure " on tesselated pavements, when a fall would be fatal " to himself as well as others. He therefore manages the movements of his person with as much care as if he were a marble statue, and as if the least trip in his gait, or discomposure of his balance, would be sure to fracture some of his limbs. Mr. Terry was *Bellarius,* and recited some of the most beautiful passages in the world like the bellman's verses. His voice is not " musical as is Apollo's lute," but "harsh and crabbed as dull fools suppose." [1] Mr. Young made a very respectable *Iachimo,* and Miss Foote lisped through the part of *Imogen* very prettily. The rest of the characters were very poorly cast.—Oh ! we had forgot Mr. Liston's *Cloten* : a sign that it is not so good as his *Lord Grizzle,* or *Lubin Log,* or a dozen more exquisite characters that he plays. It would, however, have been very well, if he had not *whisked* off the stage at the end of each scene, "to set on some quantity of barren spectators to laugh." [2] The serenade at *Imogen's* window was very beautiful, and was *encored,*—we suspect, contrary to the etiquette of the regular drama. But we take a greater delight in fine music than in etiquette.'

373. *Mrs. Siddons's Lady Macbeth.* The *Theatrical Examiner,* from which this notice is taken, opens with a notice (possibly by Hazlitt) of Paer's opera *Agnese,* at the King's Theatre. Mrs. Siddons played Lady Macbeth on June 5, 1817, with J. P. Kemble as Macbeth and Charles Kemble as Macduff. After this date the theatrical criticism of *The Examiner* was taken over by Leigh Hunt, and Hazlitt began to write for *The Times.*

374. ' *Thank God,*' etc. *The Merchant of Venice,* Act iii. Sc. 1.
Mr. Kemble's retirement. Covent Garden, June 23, 1817.

375. ' *Like an eagle,*' etc. *Coriolanus,* Act v. Sc. 6.
' *My mother bows,*' etc. *Ibid.* Act v. Sc. 3.

376. ' *Nothing extenuate,*' etc. *Othello,* Act v. Sc. 2.

377. ' *Is whispering,*' etc. *A Winter's Tale,* Act i. Sc. 2.
' *Every* [each] *corporal agent.*' *Macbeth,* Act i. Sc. 7.
' *There was neither variableness,*' etc. *St. James,* i. 17.
' *The fire i' th' flint,*' etc. *Timon of Athens,* Act i. Sc. 1.

378. ' *My way of life,*' etc. *Macbeth,* Act v. Sc. 3.
' *The fiery soul,*' etc. Dryden, *Absalom and Achitophel,* i. 156-8.
' *You shall relish,*' etc. Cf. *Othello,* Act ii. Sc. 1.

379. ' *The tug and war.*' Cf. ' Then was the tug of war.' Lee, *Alexander the Great,* Act iv. Sc. 2.
' *Fate and metaphysical aid.*' *Macbeth,* Act i. Sc. 5.
Invita Minerva. Horace, *Ars Poetica,* 385.

---

[1] *Comus,* 476-7.   [2] *Hamlet,* Act iii. Sc. 2.

NOTES

ESSAYS ON THE DRAMA FROM *THE LONDON MAGAZINE*, 1820.

383. *Semper varium et mutabile.* Virgil, *Æneid*, IV. 569.
   'The stage, the inconstant stage.' Cf. 'The moon, the inconstant moon.' *Romeo and Juliet*, Act II. Sc. 2.
384. 'To dally with the wind,' etc. Cf. *Richard III.*, Act I. Sc. 3.
   'With coy [sweet] reluctant,' etc. *Paradise Lost*, IV. 311.
385. 'Should God create,' etc. *Paradise Lost*, IX. 911-13.
386. 'Play the hostess.' Cf. 'Ourself will mingle with society, and play the humble host. Our hostess keeps her state,' etc. *Macbeth*, Act III. Sc. 4.
387. *Eclipsed the gaiety, etc.* Cf. *ante*, note to p. 270.
   Beau Mordecai. In Macklin's *Love à-la Mode*, brought out in 1760.
   Lord Sands. In *King Henry VIII.*
   'With nods and becks,' etc. *L'Allegro*, 28.
388. 'Secret Tattle.' In Congreve's *Love for Love*.
389. 'Made a sunshine,' etc. *The Faerie Queene*, I. iii. 4.
   'Talked far above singing.' Beaumont and Fletcher, *Philaster*, Act V. Sc. 5.
   'Her bounty,' etc. *Romeo and Juliet*, Act II. Sc. 2.
   Her Nell. In Coffey's *The Devil to Pay* (1731).
392. 'Extenuate,' etc. *Othello*, Act V. Sc. 2.
393. 'There were two,' etc. Cf. *St. Luke*, xvii. 31 *et seq.*
   'A consummation,' etc. *Hamlet*, Act III. Sc. 1.
   'To our moist vows denied.' *Lycidas*, 159.
   'Slippery turns,' etc. *Coriolanus*, Act IV. Sc. 4.
   'Mr. Limberham,' etc. Dryden's *The Kind Keeper; or, Mr. Limberham* (1680).
   'With its worldly goods,' etc. *The Book of Common Prayer*, Marriage Service.
   'The list of weeds,' etc. Jeremy Taylor, *Holy Dying*, Chap. I. § 2.
   'In monumental mockery.' *Troilus and Cressida*, Act III. Sc. 3.
394. *The Surrey, etc.* The Surrey Theatre, in Blackfriars Road, opened in 1782; The Cobourg Theatre, Waterloo Bridge Road, opened in 1818; The Sans Pareil, better known as The Adelphi Theatre, in the Strand, opened in 1806.
395. 'Gentle and low,' etc. *King Lear*, Act V. Sc. 3.
397. 'Like to another morn, etc.' *Paradise Lost*, V. 310-11.
   'Moody madness,' etc. Gray, Ode, *On a Distant Prospect of Eton College*, 79-80.
398. 'Mar [scar] that whiter skin,' etc. *Othello*, Act V. Sc. 2.
399. *Gallantry, or Adventures at Madrid.* Jan. 15, 1820; acted only once.
   'Had its brother,' etc. Cf. Pope, *Moral Essays*, IV. 117-8.
400. 'As it was set down for him.' *Hamlet*, Act III. Sc. 2.
   'The courtier's or the lover's melancholy.' Cf. *As You Like It*, Act IV. Sc. 1.
   Gilray. James Gillray (1757-1815), the caricaturist.
   Mrs. Edwin. Elizabeth Rebecca Richards (1771 ?-1854) first appeared at Covent Garden 1789; married in 1791 John Edwin the younger.
401. *Magis pares, etc.* Cf. 'Similia omnia magis visa hominibus, quam paria.' Livy, XLV. 43.
   Note 1. Pope's *Essay on Criticism*, 1-2.
402. 'All is grace above,' etc. 'Thus all below is strength, and all above is grace.' Dryden, *Epistle to Congreve*, 19.
   'To relish all,' etc. *The Tempest*, Act V. Sc. 1.

DRAMATIC ESSAYS

PAGE
402. *' I banish you.'* *Coriolanus,* Act III. Sc. 3.
'*The most sweet voices.'* *Ibid.* Act II. Sc. 3.
403. '*Guns, drums,'* etc. Pope, *Satires,* I. 26.
'*Ample scope [room],'* etc. Gray, *The Bard,* 5.
404. '*Constrained by mastery.'* Cf. *post,* note to p. 479.
'*Speculative,'* etc. *Othello,* Act I. Sc. 3.
'*There he arriving,'* etc. *Muiopotmos,* St. XXII. and XXVII.
405. '*Like greyhound on the slip.'* *Henry V.,* Act III. Sc. 1.
'*The full eyes,'* etc. Jeremy Taylor, *Holy Dying,* Chap. I. § 2.
'*Embalmed with odours.'* *Paradise Lost,* II. 843.
'*A wide O.'* Cf. ' Why should you fall into so deep an O ?' *Romeo and Juliet,* Act III. Sc. 3.
'*Come, let me clutch thee.'* *Macbeth,* Act II. Sc. 1.
'*Those gay creatures,'* etc. *Comus,* 299-301.
406. *W—m.* Wem.
The Rev. Mr. J——s. The author's son fills this blank with the name of Jenkins.
407. '*Of imagination all compact.'* *A Midsummer Night's Dream,* Act V. Sc. 1.
'*Their mind to them,'* etc. Sir Edward Dyer's ' My mynde to me a kyngdome is,' set to music by Byrd in 1588.
'*Of all earth's bliss,'* etc. From Lamb's version of Thekla's song in *Wallenstein* (Part I., The Piccolomini). See Coleridge's *Poetical Works* (ed. J. D. Campbell), 648.
408. '*By his so potent art.'* *The Tempest,* Act V. Sc. 1.
'*Happy alchemy of mind.'* See vol. v., note to p. 107.
'*Severn's sedgy side.'* ' Gentle Severn's sedgy bank.' *Henry IV.,* Part I., Act I. Sc. 3.
' Note. ' *The beggars are coming,'* etc. From the old song beginning, ' Hark, hark, the dogs do bark,' etc.
409. '*Alas! how changed,'* etc. Pope, *Moral Essays,* III. 305-6.
'*Made of penetrable stuff.'* *Hamlet,* Act III. Sc. 4.
410. '*See the puppets dallying.'* *Ibid.* Act III. Sc. 2.
Mr. Stanley. Stanley had been well known at Bath, and had appeared for a short time at Drury Lane. Genest (VIII. 693) describes him as ' a very good actor for a provincial theatre, and a fair actor for London.'
411. *Panopticon.* Cf. vol. IV., note to p. 197.
'*My soul turn from them.'* Goldsmith, *The Traveller,* 165.
'*Her, lovely Venus,'* etc. *L'Allegro,* 14-16.
'*Vernal airs,'* etc. *Paradise Lost,* IV. 264-6.
'*Three red roses,'* etc. Cf. *Richard III.,* Act IV. Sc. 3.
'*The witchery,'* etc. Wordsworth, *Peter Bell* (Part I.), l. 265.
412. *Mr. Reeve.* John Reeve (1799-1838), a mimic and comedian, chiefly associated with the Adelphi.
'*Our hint to speak.'* *Othello,* Act I. Sc. 3.
413. *Mr. Peter Moore.* Peter Moore (1753-1828), member of parliament and company promoter. He was at one time one of the managers of Drury Lane Theatre.
The Antiquary. A musical play in three acts by Daniel Terry, Jan. 25, 1820.
'*Warbled.'* ' Come, warble, come.' *As You Like It,* Act II. Sc. 5.
Note. *The Surrey Theatre.* The Surrey Theatre had been taken by Thomas John Dibdin (1771-1841) in 1816.
414. '*Perplexed in the extreme.'* *Othello,* Act V. Sc. 2.
'*Horror sat plumed.'* *Paradise Lost,* IV. 989.

542

NOTES

414. '*Of one that loved,*' etc. *Othello,* Act v. Sc. 2.
'*Turbaned Turk,*' *Ibid.* Act v. Sc. 2.
'*I cannot think,*' etc. *Ibid.* Act III. Sc. 3.
'*The glorious triumph* [trial],' etc. *Paradise Lost,* IX. 961.
415. '*The high and palmy state.*' *Hamlet,* Act I. Sc. I.
416. *Mr. Milman's Fazio.* Produced at Covent Garden, Feb. 5, 1818.
'*Look abroad,*' etc. Bacon, *The Advancement of Learning,* Book I., III. 6.
417. '*Are embowelled,*' etc. Burke, *Reflections on the Revolution in France (Select Works,* ed. Payne, II. 101).
The Upholsterer. Cf. *ante,* p. 96.
'*A counterfeit presentment.*' *Hamlet,* Act III. Sc. 4.
418. '*To relish,*' etc. Cf. *ante,* p. 402.
419. '*Unfeathered, two-legged thing.*' Dryden, *Absalom and Achitophel,* I. 170.
'*You may wear,*' etc. *Hamlet,* Act Iv. Sc. 5.
'*He sits in the centre,*' etc. *Comus,* 382-3.
420. *Mr. Wordsworth's hankering after the drama.* Wordsworth's tragedy, *The Borderers,* composed in 1795-6, and soon afterwards refused by the Covent Garden management, was not published till 1842.
'*The daily intercourse,*' etc. Quoted vaguely from Wordsworth's *Lines composed a few miles above Tintern Abbey.*
note. Joanna Baillie (1762-1851), whose *Plays on the Passions* had appeared in 3 vols. 1798-1812.
421. '*Like a wild overflow,*' etc. Beaumont and Fletcher, *Philaster,* Act v. Sc. 3.
'*'Tis three feet long,*' etc. Wordsworth, *The Thorn,* (l. 33), as published in *Lyrical Ballads* (1798).
422. '*What? if one reptile,*' etc. *Remorse,* Act III. Sc. 2.
423. *The Hebrew.* By George Soane (1790-1860).
'*I had as lief,*' etc. *Hamlet,* Act III. Sc. 2.
'*Instinct with fire.*' *Paradise Lost,* II. 937.
Disjecta [disjecti] *membra poetae.* Horace, *Satires,* I. 4, 62.
425. '*His affections,*' etc. *Hamlet,* Act III. Sc. I.
'*Holds sovereign sway.*' *Macbeth,* Act I. Sc. 5.
'*A far cry to Lochiel.*' 'It's a far cry to Lochow.' See *Rob Roy,* note to chap. 29.
'*Hitherto shalt thou come,*' etc. *Job,* xxxviii. 11.
'*Like kings,*' etc. Pope, *An Essay on Criticism,* 64-5.
427. *Like to that sanguine flower,*' etc. *Lycidas,* 106.
'*Unkindness,*' etc. *Othello,* Act Iv. Sc. 2.
Three Weeks after Marriage. Arthur Murphy's comedy, produced in 1776.
Mr. Connor. Charles Connor (d. 1826), Irish comedian.
428. *The Manager in Distress.* By George Colman the elder.
'*Too Late for Dinner.*' A farce by Richard Jones the actor.
429. '*Great heir of fame.*' Milton, *On Shakespeare.* l. 5.
'*Strange that,*' etc. Cf. 'Then there's hope a great man's memory may outlive his life half a year.' *Hamlet,* Act III. Sc. 2.
Don Quixote's throwing open the cages, etc. *Don Quixote,* Part II., Book I. Chap. 17.
'*Tasteless monster,*' etc. 'A faultless monster whom the world ne'er saw.' John Sheffield, Duke of Buckinghamshire, *Essay on Poetry.*
'*If that they love,*' etc. Cf. 'But that I love the gentle Desdemona,' etc. *Othello,* Act I. Sc. 2.

543

DRAMATIC ESSAYS

PAGE

Berlin and Milan decrees. Of Napoleon, 1806 and 1807.

430. *Like the lady in the lobster.* Cf. Herrick's *Hesperides*, No. 224 (The Faerie Temple).

' *As if he would confine,' etc. Samson Agonistes*, 307.

' *A beard so old and white.*' ''Gainst a head so old and white as this.' *King Lear*, Act III. Sc. 2.

Nahum Tate's Lear. Produced in 1681.

431. '*There's sympathy.*' *The Merry Wives of Windsor*, Act II. Sc. 1.

432. '*Applauds you,' etc. Macbeth*, Act v. Sc. 3.

433. '*He must live to please,' etc.* Johnson, Prologue at the opening of Drury Lane Theatre, 1747, l. 54.

'*Lard the lean earth,' etc. Henry IV.* Part I., Act II. Sc. 2.

434. '*First, midst, and last.*' Cf. *Paradise Lost*, v. 165.

435. *Shakspear versus Harlequin.* An alteration of *Harlequin's Invasion* produced in 1759.

'*Charge on heaps,' etc.* Cf. *Troilus and Cressida*, Act III. Sc. 2.

436. *Quod sic mihi, etc.* Horace, *Ars Poetica*, 188.

'*See o'er the stage,' etc.* Cf. Thomson, *The Seasons*, winter, 646.

'*But thou, oh Hope,' etc.* Collins, Ode, *The Passions*, 29-32.

439. *Sir Hugh Middleton's Head.* The sign of this inn, opposite Sadler's Wells, figures in Hogarth's *Evening*.

440. '*Shut their blue-fringed lids,' etc.* Coleridge, *Fears in Solitude*, 84-6.

Mr. Booth's Lear. Covent Garden, April 13, 1820.

'*I am every inch a King. King Lear*, Act IV. Sc. 6.

'*The fiery Duke. Ibid.* Act II. Sc. 4.

441. *Henri Quatre.* A musical romance in three acts by Thomas Morton.

''*Twas Lancelot,' etc.* Leigh Hunt, *The Story of Rimini.*

'*Ah! brilliant land,' etc.* To this quotation the Editor of *The London Magazine* prints the following note : 'Does our Correspondent here refer to the ink he has himself shed in severe criticism of the French National Character.'

442. '*The invincible knights of old.*' Wordsworth's Sonnet, 'It is not to be thought of,' etc.

Miss M. Tree. Ann Maria Tree (1801-1862), afterwards Mrs. Bradshaw, made her first appearance at Covent Garden in 1818.

The present crisis of affairs. Hazlitt alludes to the Revolution in Spain. in 1820.

445. '*Accumulate horrors,' etc. Othello*, Act III. Sc. 3.

'*That has outlasted,' etc.* Misquoted from Beaumont and Fletcher's *Philaster*, Act v. Sc. 3.

'*Tore it to tatters,' etc. Hamlet*, Act III. Sc. 2.

'*Hear, Nature, hear,' etc.* The quotations from *King Lear* in this paragraph are from Act I. Sc. 4.

446. '*Compunctious visitings of nature.*' *Macbeth*, Act I. Sc. 5.

'*Like a phantasma,' etc. Julius Caesar*, Act II. Sc. 1.

447. '*Dear daughter,' etc. King Lear*, Act II. Sc. 4.

'*Beloved Regan,' etc. Ibid.* Act II. Sc. 4.

448. '*Appal the guilty,' etc.* Misquoted from *Hamlet*, Act II. Sc. 2.

'*Create a soul,' etc. Comus*, 562.

'*The fiery quality,' etc. King Lear*, Act II. Sc. 4.

'*I will do such things,' etc. Ibid.* Act II. Sc. 4.

449. '*Blow winds,' etc. Ibid.* Act III. Sc. 2.

'*More germane,' etc. Hamlet*, Act v. Sc. 2.

NOTES

449. '*How dost*,' etc. *King Lear*, Act III. Sc. 2.
   '*Didst thou give all*,' etc. *Ibid*. Act III. Sc. 3.
   '*What, have his daughters*,' etc. *Ibid*. Act III. Sc. 3.
   '*Was set down*.' *Hamlet*, Act III. Sc. 2.

450. '*Aye, every inch a king*.' *King Lear*, Act IV. Sc. 6.
   '*When I do stare*,' etc. *Ibid*. Act IV. Sc. 6.
   '*Pray do not mock me*.' *Ibid*. Act IV. Sc. 6.
   '*Which sacred pity*, etc.' *As You Like It*, Act II. Sc. 7.
   '*False gallop*.' *Ibid*. Act III. Sc. 2.
   '*Honest sonsy*,' etc. Burns, *Address to a Haggis*, I.

451. *Artaxerxes*. Cf. *ante*, pp. 192-3.

452. '*Concords of sweet sounds*.' *The Merchant of Venice*, Act V. Sc. 1.

453. l. 15. In *The London Magazine* the article concludes with a notice (signed '*X*.') of a new after-piece at Drury Lane, entitled *The Lady and the Devil*, and a flattering notice of *Virginius* at Covent Garden. Neither of these notices is written in Hazlitt's manner, and it is evident from his later account of Knowles's tragedy (see pp. 455, *et seq*.) that the notice of *Virginius* at any rate is the work of another hand. It would seem that after seeing Kean in *King Lear* Hazlitt retired for a time to Winterslow.
   The only article, etc. Hazlitt probably refers to his third article, published in the March number (*ante*, pp. 403, *et seq*.), which was probably written while the theatres were closed in consequence of the deaths of the Duke of Kent (d. January 23, 1820) and George III. (d. January 29, 1820).
   Mr. Weathercock. Thomas Griffiths Wainewright (1794-1852), afterwards well known as a forger and murderer, was at this time a regular contributor to *The London Magazine*, chiefly under the pseudonym of Janus Weathercock. His contributions were for the most part on the Fine Arts, but in the number for June 1820 (*Janus's Jumble*, chap. III.) he wrote some remarks on the theatres, in the course of which he chaffed '*Mr. Drama*' (*i.e.* Hazlitt) on some of his theatrical criticisms, and especially on his article on the minor theatres published in March. To these remarks Hazlitt replies in the present essay. For Wainewright himself see the biographical introduction to Mr. W. C. Hazlitt's edition (1880) of his contributions to *The London Magazine*, and Mr. Bertram Dobell's *Sidelights on Charles Lamb* (1903).

454. '*Odious in satin*,' etc. '*Odious ! in woollen ! 'twould a saint provoke*.' Pope, *Moral Essays*, I. 246.
   '*Like little wanton boys*,' etc. *Henry VIII*. Act III. Sc. 2.
   '*Inexpressive three*.' Cf. '*Unexpressive she*.' *As You Like It*, Act III. Sc. 2, '*Written in our heart's tables*.' *All's Well that Ends Well*, Act I. Sc. 1.

455. '*Entire affection scorneth* [hateth],' etc. *The Faerie Queene*, Book I. Canto VIII. St. 40.
   '*A man's mind*,' etc. '*Men's judgements are a parcel of their fortunes*.' *Antony and Cleopatra*, Act III. Sc. 13.
   '*Diamond rings*,' etc. etc. Hazlitt quotes from Wainewright's article.
   '*We came*,' etc. A hasty adaptation, presumably, of the famous '*Veni, vidi, vici*.'
   Virginius. James Sheridan Knowles's (1784-1862) *Virginius* was produced at Covent Garden on May 17, 1820.
   '*Strike his lofty head*,' etc. '*Sublimi feriam sidera vertice*.' Horace, *Odes*, I. 1. 36.

456. *The Virginius and the David Rizzio, etc.* Another *Virginius*, with Kean in the title *rôle*, was produced at Drury Lane on May 29, 1820, *David*

DRAMATIC ESSAYS

Rizzio, an opera by Colonel Hamilton, appeared at the same theatre on June 17.

A former article. See *ante*, note to p. 453.

'*I never saw you*,' etc. *Virginius*, Act iv. Sc. 1.

'*The lie*,' etc. *Ibid.* Act iv. Sc. 2.

'*To be sure she will*,' etc. *Ibid.* Act iv. Sc. 2.

'*Let the forum wait for us!*' *Ibid.* Act iv. Sc. 1.

'*The freeborn Roman maid.*' Varied slightly from phrases applied to Virginia in the play.

457. '*Lest the courtiers*,' etc. *The Beggar's Opera*, Act ii. Sc. 2.

'*Let the galled jade*,' etc. *Hamlet*, Act iii. Sc. 2.

458. '*Why are those things hid*,' etc. *Twelfth Night*, Act i. Sc. 3.

Mr. Kean at his benefit. June 12, 1820. The play was *Venice Preserved*, followed by *The Admirable Crichton*.

Educated in the fourth form, etc. A gibe at Elliston, who was educated at St. Paul's School.

Cast in the antique mould, etc. The reference is to Kemble.

note. '*An honest man*,' etc. Pope, *Essay on Man*, iv. 248.

459. '*In this expectation*,' etc. Cf. 'This was looked for at your hand, and this was balked.' *Twelfth Night*, Act iii. Sc. 2.

'*Nothing can come of nothing.*' 'De nihilo nihil.' Persius, *Satires*, iii. 84.

460. *Miss Povey.* Born in 1804, and appeared first at Drury Lane in 1817.

461. '*Softly sweet in Lydian measures.*' Dryden, *Alexander's Feast*, 97.

Giovanni in London. By William Thomas Moncrieff (1794-1857), originally produced at the Olympic on December 26, 1817.

462. '*She forgot to be a woman*,' etc. Misquoted from *Cymbeline*, Act iii. Sc. 4.

'*Like a new ta'en sparrow.*' *Troilus and Cressida*, Act iii. Sc. 2.

'*Like marigolds*,' etc. Cf. 'The marigold, that goes to bed wi' the sun,' etc. *A Winter's Tale*, Act iv. Sc. 4.

463. The '*Great Vulgar and the Small.*' Cowley, Horace, *Odes*, iii. 1.

'*Raised so high*,' etc. Cf. 'High throned above all highth.' *Paradise Lost*, iii. 58.

'*Such tricks*,' etc. *A Midsummer Night's Dream*, Act v. Sc. 1.

464. '*Present no mark.*' *Henry IV.*, Part II. Act iii. Sc. 2.

'*You may as well*,' etc. *Ibid.* Act iii. Sc. 2.

'*One bubble*,' etc. Jeremy Taylor, *Holy Dying*, Chap. 1. § 1.

Her Yarico. In Colman's *Inkle and Yarico* (1787).

'*We had rather*,' etc. Adapted from *All's Well that Ends Well*, Act i. Sc. 1.

465. '*In the catalogue*,' etc. Cf. 'Ay, in the catalogue ye go for men.' *Macbeth*, Act iii. Sc. 1.

'*To curl her hair*,' etc. See Congreve's *The Way of the World*, Act. ii. Sc. 5.

465. '*Who rant and fret*,' etc. Misquoted from *Macbeth*, Act v. Sc. 5.

'*Vine-covered hills.*' 'From the vine-cover'd hills and gay valleys of France.' From lines 'written in 1788' by William Roscoe (1753-1831). The lines were partly parodied by Canning and Frere in *The Anti-Jacobin* ('La Sainte Guillotine') : 'From the blood-bedew'd valleys and mountains of France.' Cf. vol. vi. p. 189 (*Table Talk*).

'*And murmur*,' etc. Landor, *Gebir*, Book I.

466. '*Sigh his soul*,' etc. Cf. 'And sighed his soul towards the Grecian tents.' *The Merchant of Venice*, Act v. Sc. 1.

467. '*A brother of the groves.*' Hazlitt perhaps recalls Wordsworth's line, 'A brother of the dancing leaves' (*The Green Linnet*, 34). As originally

published (*Poems*, 1807, II. 81), the line ran, 'A Brother of the Leaves he seems,' which is still nearer to Hazlitt's phrase.

468. *Crockery and Peter Pastoral.* In *Exit by Mistake* and *Teazing Made Easy* respectively.

'*His tears,*' etc.

Cf. 'The tears which came to Matthew's eyes
Were tears of light, the oil of gladness.'

Wordsworth, *Matthew*, as published in *Lyrical Ballads*, 1800, vol. II. p. 121.
'*Sic transit,*' etc. Thomas à Kempis, *De Imitatione Christi*, I. 3, 6.

469. '*Stands on end,*' etc. Misquoted from *Macbeth*, Act v. Sc. 5.
'*Let those laugh,*' etc.

Cf. 'Let those love now, who never lov'd before ;
Let those who always lov'd, now love the more.'

Parnell, *The Vigil of Venus.*

470. '*Compunctious visitings.*' *Macbeth*, Act I. Sc. 5.
Little Pickle. In *The Spoilt Child.*

471. *The great cat, Rodilardus.* In Rabelais. See *Pantagruel*, IV. 67.
'*Dressed in a little brief authority,*' etc. *Measure for Measure*, Act II. Sc. 2.

472. '*You take my house,*' etc. *The Merchant of Venice*, Act IV. Sc. 1.
'*Cleansed,*' etc. *Macbeth*, Act v. Sc. 3.
'*Flesh is heir to.*' *Hamlet*, Act III. Sc. 1.

473. '*Not a jot,*' etc. *Othello*, Act III. Sc. 3.
'*But never more,*' etc. *Ibid.* Act II. Sc. 3.
'*Never so sure,*' etc. Pope, *Moral Essays*, II. 51-2.
'*In medio,*' etc. Ovid, *Metamorphoses*, II. 137.
They hiss the Beggar's Opera in America. *The Times* of Dec. 10, 1817, quotes from New York papers dated Oct. 27 an account of the refusal of a New York audience to hear *The Beggar's Opera.*

474. *The Vampyre.* By James Robinson Planché (1796-1880), adapted from 'Le Vampire.'
The celebrated story. 'The Vampyre,' by John William Polidori (1795-1821), was published in 1819. Byron had intended to write a story on the same subject. See *Letters and Journals*, ed. Prothero, III. 446-453, and IV. 286 and 296.
'*See how the moon,*' etc. *The Merchant of Venice*, Act v. Sc. 1.

475. '*The Diamond Ring.*' Adapted by Theodore Hook from *He would be a Soldier* (1786), and produced Aug. 12, 1820.

476. '*Misery,*' etc. *As You Like It*, Act II. Sc. 1.
'*A load,*' etc. *Henry VIII.*, Act III. Sc. 2.
'*Palsied eld.*' *Measure for Measure*, Act III. Sc. 1.

477. '*At last he rose,*' etc. *Lycidas*, 192-3.
'*As broad,*' etc. Misquoted from *Macbeth*, Act III. Sc. 4.
'*In act,*' etc. *Othello*, Act I. Sc. 1.
'*The immediate jewel,*' etc. *Ibid.*, Act III. Sc. 3.
'*Solid pudding,*' etc. Pope, *The Dunciad*, I. 54.
'*Tenth,*' etc. Pope, *Essay on Man*, I. 246.
The Calendar of Nature. Hazlitt seems to refer to Leigh Hunt's *The Months*, originally published in the *Literary Pocket Book*, 1819-20, and there described as a 'Calendar of the Seasons.'
'*Bound our brows withal.*' 'To grace thy brows withal.' *Richard III.*, Act v. Sc. 5.

DRAMATIC ESSAYS

In January, etc. It will be noticed that Hazlitt does not give an accurate account of the dates and subjects of his articles.

478. *'Being at Illminster,' etc.* Possibly on a visit to John Hunt, who had retired to the neighbourhood of Taunton. Mr. W. C. Hazlitt mentions (*Memoirs*, I. xviii.) a report that Hazlitt contributed for a short time to the *Taunton Courier*.

Note. *'Or mouth,' etc. Endymion*, II. 405-6.

Note. *'Beautified.' Hamlet*, Act II. Sc. 2.

Note. *'Oh Scotland,' etc.* Cf. 'O Jephthah, judge of Israel,' etc. *Hamlet*, Act II. Sc. 2.

479. *An able article written for us.* No. x., published in the October (not September) number.

No Table-Talk. The *Table-Talks* were of course the work of Hazlitt himself.

The Lion's Head. The name given to two or three editorial paragraphs prefixed to *The London Magazine*. In the number for November, 1820, the editor announced for the next number 'a *chef d'œuvre* of a *Table Talk*—the best yet, we think.' This was No. v. 'On the Pleasure of Painting.'

'Has not left her peer.' Lycidas, 9.

'Constrain his genius,' etc. Cf. 'That Love will not submit to be controlled by mastery.' Wordsworth, *The Excursion*, VI. 163-4.

'With mighty wings,' etc. Paradise Lost, I. 20-22.

480. *Encyclopædia Metropolitana.* The publication of this work began in 1817. Coleridge drew up the scheme, and contributed the 'Preliminary Treatise on Method.'

Note. Hazlitt refers to *The Fancy: a Selection from the Poetical Remains of the late Peter Corcoran, of Gray's Inn, Student at Law*, a 'jeu d'esprit' by John Hamilton Reynolds, reviewed in *The London Magazine*, July 1820.

'The up-turned eyes,' etc. Romeo and Juliet, Act II. Sc. 2.

481. *Barnaby Brittle.* Founded on Molière's *George Dandin*, and produced at Covent Garden in 1791.

Disjecta membra poetæ. 'Disjecti membra poëtæ.' Horace, *Satires*, I. 4-62.

'Outlasts a thousand storms,' etc. Beaumont and Fletcher's *Philaster*, Act v. Sc. 3.

482. *Paulo majora canamus.* Virgil, *Eclogues*, IV. 1.

'The lily drooping,' etc. Cf. 'Than is the lilie upon his stalke grene.' *The Canterbury Tales*, The Knighte's Tale, 1036.

'The flowers,' etc. A Winter's Tale, Act IV. Sc. 4.

Note. See Boswell's *Life of Johnson*, ed. G. B. Hill, II. 409 n.

483. *Macready's Zanga.* Macready first appeared as Zanga in Young's *Revenge* on October 30, 1820.

'A wife,' etc. The Revenge, Act IV. Sc. 1.

Wallace. By C. E. Walker, November 14, 1820.

484. *The Deaf Lover.* By Frederick Pilon (1750-1788), originally produced in 1780 and revived at Covent Garden in 1819.

'But in Adam's ear,' etc. Paradise Lost, VIII. 1-2.

APPENDIX

APPENDIX

I

(*See introductory note on p.* 487)

ON MODERN COMEDY

To the EDITOR of the MORNING CHRONICLE.

Sɪʀ,—I believe it seldom happens that we confess ourselves to be in the dark on any subject, till we are pretty well persuaded that no one else is able to dispel the gloom in which we are involved. Convinced, that where our own sagacity has failed, all further search must be vain, we resign ourselves implicitly to all the self-complacency of conscious ignorance, and are very little obliged to any one, who comes to disturb our intellectual repose. Something of this kind appears to have happened to your Correspondent on the subject of the Drama. Indeed, Sir, I should have been very cautious of attempting to remove the heap of doubts and difficulties which seemed to oppress him, but that I thought so obvious a truth as the connection between the manners of the age and comedy could not startle 'the plainest understanding;' but the moment this obvious truth is pointed out to him, he complains that he is 'dazzled with excess of light,'[1] and puts a ready moveable screen of common places before him to keep it out. And then, Sir, I observe, that to fortify himself in his scruples, and lest he should be forced to give up his sceptical solution of sceptical doubts, he has confounded characters with you, Sir, by a dextrous ventriloquism puts his sentiments into your mouth, and has contrived to get the balance into his own hands, and 'smiles delighted with the eternal poise.'[2]

After complimenting the writer of a former article, by saying that '*his* powers have not languished in the dense atmosphere of logic and criticism,' (a compliment which I am ready to return with equal sincerity), your Correspondent proceeds— 'We confess it did not occur to us, that it is because so many excellent comedies have been written that so few are written at present. To our plain understanding, on the first statement of this circumstance, a conclusion directly the reverse would have presented itself. We should have been inclined to apply in this instance the analogy which we find to hold in almost every other, that relative perfection is only the result of repeated efforts, and that, as in the case of an individual artist, till his powers are impaired by age, every successive attempt is in general an improvement on the preceding, so in the art itself what has once been well done, usually leads to something better.'—On this passage I might observe, first, that I am always apt to distrust these modest pretensions to plain understanding. They signify nothing more than that an opinion is contrary to our own, and that we will not take the trouble to examine it. And besides, we all of us refine as much and as well as we are able; only we are not willing that others should refine more than we do. Secondly, Sir, the analogy to which your

----
[1] 'Blasted with excess of light.' Gray, *The Progress of Poesy,* ɪɪɪ. 2, 7.
[2] Cowper, *The Task,* ɪᴠ. 486.

APPENDIX

Correspondent appeals in support of his hypothesis, that the arts are uniformly progressive, totally fails ; it applies to science, and not to art.

Farther, your Correspondent observes, 'That the production of many good comedies should render us more severe towards bad ones, and bad poets more averse from exposing themselves, would appear much more likely than that exactly the reverse of all this should happen. We naturally expect from a landlord, who at the commencement of a repast regales us with elegant wines, that he will not place homely ale or insipid porter before us towards the end of it. It was D'Alembert, we believe, who suggested as a great improvement in modern literature, that all our books should be collected together every fifty years, for the purpose of making a bonfire of them,' &c. All this may be very true, but I really do not see what it has to do with the question.

'For true no-meaning puzzles more than wit.' [1]

I am afraid he will think I am at cross-purposes with his theories, but it is really because they appear to me at cross-purposes with facts. For instance, the bad poets do not in the present case seem very backward to expose themselves ; but what is it that hinders the good ones (rising like so many Phœnixes out of the ashes of their predecessors) from claiming the admiration that is due to them ? Surely, if every succeeding writer improved upon the last, and 'what was once well done always led to something better,' the managers would not damp the rising flame. The progress of comedy among us appears to have been just the reverse of what your Correspondent would have anticipated ; namely, from elegant wines to insipid porter, and our critic (if I mistake him not), would make the matter still worse by diluting this insipid stuff with water, in order that it may become still more tasteless, and according to him, more elegant and refined. Our elder comic writers provided choice wines, strong liquors and rich viands of all kinds for the entertainment of the public, while our author, seated at the full banquet, like Christopher Sly at the Duke's table, calls out incessantly for 'a pot of the smallest ale.' [2] As to the project of D'Alembert, I have no great objection to it. Only I would propose as a compromise that we should let our present stock remain on hand, and that nothing but reviews and newspaper criticisms should be written for the next fifty years, by which means I shall keep possession of Jonson, Farquhar, Wycherley, Congreve, and Smollett, and in the mean time your correspondent may take a surfeit of Mr. Tobin's *Honey Moon*, *The Duenna* (for whom I have a great respect), and Madame de Stael. I cannot, however, agree with him in the building up of his chronological ladder of taste. Congreve did not improve upon Wycherley, because he was not indebted to him, and Sheridan was indebted to Congreve without improving upon him. Your Correspondent, Sir, writes very well about these authors, but as if he had not read them. As to the hardship of which he complains, that our fathers should have laughed for themselves and for us too, it is but the common course of nature. It is not a misfortune peculiar to ourselves. Even Madame de Stael is forced to go a hundred and fifty years back, for an author to insult the English with, on their want of comic genius, and of the knowledge of those traits peculiar to the refinements of French manners, but which *yet paint human nature in every country*. I agree with your Correspondent in his first letter, that though we cannot write good Comedies, we can assign good reasons why they are not written ; and I think we have, between us, made out the reason of the present want of dramatic writers, though I doubt if we should, both of us together, make even half a Menander. But he will have all the advantages on his side, and be as merry as he is wise. Why, after he has laughed folly out of countenance, is he determined to laugh at her as much as ever, and to

[1] Pope, *Moral Essays*, ii. 114.   [2] *The Taming of the Shrew*, Induction, Sc. 2.

552

APPENDIX

make good sense or absurdity equally subservient to his spleen? He is bent on laughing at all events—at every thing or nothing; and if he does not find things ridiculous, he will make them so. The fantastic resolution of *Biron*, 'to laugh a twelvemonth in an hospital,'[1] does not exceed the preposterous ambition of your Correspondent, to extract the soul of mirth out of the schools of philosophy. We cannot expect to reconcile opposite things. If he or I were to put ourselves into the stage, to go from Salisbury to London, I dare say we should not meet with the same number of odd accidents or ludicrous distresses on the road, that befel *Parson Adams*; but why, if we get into a common vehicle, and submit to the conveniences of modern travelling, do we complain of the want of adventures? Modern manners may be compared to a modern stage-coach : our limbs may be a little cramped with the confinement, and we may grow drowsy ; but we arrive safe, without any very amusing or any very sad accident, at our journey's end. But your Correspondent sees nothing in the progress of modern manners and characters but a vague, abstract progression from grossness to refinement, marked on a graduated scale of human perfectibility. This sweeping distinction appears to him to explain satisfactorily the whole difference between all sorts of manners, and all kinds and degrees of dramatic excellence. These two words stand him instead of other ideas on the texture of society, or the nature of the dramatic art. He is not, however, quite consistent on this subject, for in one place he says, that 'the stock of folly in the world is in no danger of being diminished,' and in the next sentence, that there is a progression in society, an age of grossness and an age of refinement, and he only wonders that the progress of the stage does not keep pace with it. Now the reason why I do not share his wonder is, that though I think the quantity of dull, dry, serious, incorrigible folly in the world is in no danger of being diminished, yet I think the stock of lively, dramatic, entertaining, laughable folly is, and necessarily must be, diminished by the progress of that *mechanical* refinement which consists in throwing our follies, as it were, into a common stock, and moulding them in the same general form. Our peculiarities have become insipid sameness ; our eccentricity servile imitation ; our wit, wisdom at second-hand ; our prejudices indifference ; our feelings not our own ; our distinguishing characteristic the want of all character. We are become a nation of authors and readers, and even this distinction is confounded by the mediation of the reviewers. We all follow the same profession, which is criticism, each individual is every thing but himself, not one but all mankind's epitome, and the gradations of vice and virtue, of sense and folly, of refinement and grossness of character, seem lost in a kind of intellectual *hermaphroditism*. But on this *tabula rasa*, according to your Correspondent, the most lively and sparkling hues of comedy may be laid. His present reasoning gives a very different turn to the question he at first proposed. He appears to have set out with a theory of his own about the production of comic excellence, in which it was entirely regulated by the state of the market, and to have supposed that as long as authors continued to write plays, and managers to accept them, that is, so long as the thing answered in the way of trade, Comedy would go on pretty much as it had hitherto done, to the end of the world. But finding that this was not exactly the case, he takes his stand near the avenues leading to the manager's door, and happening to see a young man of worth and talents, with great knowledge of the world, and of the refinements of polished society, come out with his piece in his hand, and a face of disappointment, he is no longer at a loss for the secret of the decline of Comedy among us, and proceeds cautiously to hint his discovery to the world. But it being suggested to him that the change of manners, produced partly by the stage itself, and the total disappearance of the characters which before formed the very life and

[1] *Love's Labour's Lost*, Act v. Sc. 2.

553

APPENDIX

soul of Comedy, might have something to do with the decline of the Stage, he will not hear a word of it, but says, that this circumstance, so far from shewing why our modern Comedies *are not so good* as the old ones, proves that they *ought to be better*; that the more we are become like one another, or like nothing, the less distinction of character we have, the greater discrimination must it require to bring it out; that the less ridiculous our manners become, the more scope do they afford for art and ingenuity in discovering our weak sides and shades of infirmity; and that the greatest sameness and monotony must in the end produce the most exquisite variety. For a plain man, this is very well. It is on the same principle, that some writers have contended that Scotland is more fertile than England, the excellence of the crop being in proportion to the barrenness of the soil. What a pity it is, that so ingenious a theory should not have the facts on its side; and that the perfection of satire should not be found to keep pace with the want of materials. It is rather too much to assume on a mere hypothesis, that the present manners are equally favourable to the production of the highest comic excellence, till they do produce it. Even in France, where encouragement is given to the noblest and most successful exertions of genius by the sure prospect of profit to yourself or your descendants, every time your piece is acted in any corner of the empire, to the latest posterity, we find the best critics going back to the grossness and illiberality of the age of Louis xiv. for the production of the best comedies; which is rather extraordinary, considering the infinitely refined state of manners in France, and the infinite encouragement given to dramatic talent. But has it never occurred to your Correspondent, as a solution of this difficulty, that there is a difference between refinement and imbecility, between general knowledge and personal elegance, between metaphysical subtlety and stage-effect? Does he think all manners, all kinds of folly, and all shades of character equally fit for dramatic representation? Does he not perceive that there is a point where minuteness of distinction becomes laborious foolery, and where the slenderness of the materials must baffle the skill and destroy the exertions of the artist? He insists, indeed, on pulling off the mask of folly, by some ingenious device, though she has been stripped of it long ago; and forced to compose her features into a decent appearance of gravity; and he next proceeds to apply a microscope of a new construction, to detect the freckles on her face and inequalities in her skin, in order to communicate his amusing discoveries to the audience, as some philosophical lecturer does the result of his chemical experiments on the decomposition of substances to the admiring circle. There is no end of this. Your Correspondent confesses that 'we are drilled into a sort of stupid decorum and apparent uniformity,' but this he converts into an advantage. His penetrating eye is infinitely delighted with the picturesque appearance of so many imperceptible deviations from a right line, and mathematical inclinations from the perpendicular. The picture of the Flamborough Family, painted with each an orange in his hand, must have been a masterpiece of nice discrimination and graceful inflection. Upon this principle of going to work the wrong way, and of making something out of nothing, we must reverse all our rules of taste and common sense. No Comedy can be perfect till the *dramatis personæ* might be reversed without creating much confusion: or the ingredients of character ought to be so blended and poured repeatedly from one vessel into another that the difference would be perceptible only to the finest palate. Thus, if Molière had lived in the present day, he would not have drawn his Avare, his Tartuffe and his Misanthrope with those strong touches and violent contrasts which he has done, but with those delicate traits which are common to human nature in general, that is, his Miser without avarice, his Hypocrite without design, and his Misanthrope without disgust at the vices of mankind. Or instead of the heroines of his *School for Women* (*Alithea* and *Miss Peggy*, which Wycherley has

554

APPENDIX

contrived to make the English understand) we should have had two sentimental young ladies brought up much in the same way, with nice shades of difference, which we should have been hardly able to distinguish, subscribing to the same circulating library, reading the same novels and poems, one preferring Gertrude of Wyoming to The Lady of the Lake, and the other The Lady of the Lake to Gertrude of Wyoming, differing in their opinions on points of taste or systems of mineralogy, and delivering dissertations on the arts with Corinna of Italy.

Considering the difficulty of the task which by our author's own account is thus imposed upon modern writers, may we not suppose this very difficulty to have operated to deter them from the pursuit of dramatic excellence. But I suspect that your Correspondent has taken up his complaint of the deficiency of refined Comedy too hastily, and that he need not despair of finding some modelled upon his favourite principles. Guided by his theory he should have sought them out in their remote obscurity, and have obtruded them on the public eye. He might have formed a new era of criticism, and have claimed the same merit as Voltaire, when he discovered that the English had one good Tragedy, *Cato.* Your Correspondent, availing himself of the idea that frivolity, taste, and elegance are the same, might have shewn how much superior *The Heiress* of Burgoyne was to *The Confederacy*, or *The Way of the World*, and *The Basil* of *Miss Bailey*, to *Romeo and Juliet.* He would have found ample scope in the blooming desert for endless discoveries—of beauties of the most shadowy kind, of fancies ' wan that hang the pensive head,' [1] of evanescent smiles, and sighs that breathe not, of delicacy that shrinks from the touch, and feebleness that scarce supports itself, an elaborate vacuity of all thought, and an artificial dearth of sense, spirit, wit and character ! I can assure your Correspondent, there has been no want of Comedies to his taste ; but the taste of the public was not so far advanced. It was found necessary to appeal to something more palpable : and so, in this interval of want of characters in real life, the actors amuse themselves with taking off one another.

But your Correspondent will have it that there are different degrees of refinement in wit and pleasantry, and he seems to suppose that the best of our old Comedies are no better than the coarse jests of a set of country clowns—a sort of *comedies bourgeoises*, compared with the admirable productions which might and ought to be written. Even our modern dramatists, he suspects, are not so familiar with high life as they ought to be. ' They have not seen the Court, and if they have not seen the Court their manner must be damnable.' [2] Leaving him to settle this last point with the poetical Lords and Ladies of the present day, I am afraid he has himself fallen into the very error he complains of, and would degrade genteel Comedy from a high Court Lady into a literary prostitute. What does he mean by refinement ? Does he find none in *Millamant*, and her morning dreams, in *Sir Roger de Coverly* and his widow ? Did not Congreve, Wycherley, and Suckling approach tolerably near ' the ring of mimic Statesmen, and their merry King ? ' [3] Does he suppose that their fine ladies were mere rustics, because they did not compose metaphysical treatises, or their fine gentlemen inexperienced tyros, because they had not been initiated into the infinitely refined society of Paris and of Baron Grimm ? Is there no distinction between an Angelica, and a Miss Prue, a Valentine, a Tattle, and a Ben ? Where in the annals of modern literature will he find anything more refined, more deliberate, more abstracted in vice than the Nobleman in Amelia ? Are not the compliments which Pope paid to his friends, [4] to St. John, Murray, and Cornbury, equal in taste and elegance to those which passed between the French philosophers and their patrons ?—Are there no traits in Sterne ?—Is not Richardson minute enough ?—Must we part

[1] *L'Allegro*, 147.   [2] *As You Like It*, Act III. Sc. 2.   [3] Pope, *Moral Essays*, III., 309-10.
[4] Cf. the essay ' Of persons one would wish to have seen.'

555

APPENDIX

with Sophia Western and Clarissa for the loves of the plants and the triangles ?— The beauty of these writers in general was, that they gave every kind and gradation of character, and they did this, because their portraits were taken from life. They were true to nature, full of meaning, perfectly understood and executed in every part. Their coarseness was not mere vulgarity, their refinement was not a mere negation of precision. They refined *upon* characters, instead of refining them *away*. Their refinement consisted in working out the parts, not in leaving a vague outline. They painted human nature as it was, and as they saw it with individual character and circumstances, not human nature in general, abstracted from time, place and circumstance. Strength and refinement are so far from being incompatible, that they assist each other, as the hardest bodies admit of the finest touches and the brightest polish. But there are some minds that never understand any thing, but by a negation of its opposite. There is a strength without refinement, which is grossness, as there is a refinement without strength or effect, which is insipidity. Neither are grossness and refinement of manners inconsistent with each other in the same period. The grossness of one class adds to the refinement of another, by circumscribing it, by rendering the feeling more pointed and exquisite, by irritating our self-love, &c. There can be no great refinement of character where there is no distinction of persons. The character of a gentleman is a *relative term*. The diffusion of knowledge, of artificial and intellectual equality, tends to level this distinction, and to confound that nice perception and high sense of honour, which arises from conspicuousness of situation, and a perpetual attention to personal propriety and the claims of personal respect. Your Correspondent, I think, mistakes refinement of individual character for general knowledge and intellectual sublety, with which it has little more to do than with the dexterity of a rope-dancer or juggler. The age of chivalry is gone with the improvements in the art of war, which superseded personal courage, and the character of a gentleman must disappear with those refinements in intellect which render the advantages of rank and situation common almost to any one. The bag-wig and sword followed the helmet and the spear, when these outward insignia no longer implied a real superiority, and were a distinction without a difference. Even the grossness of a state of mixed and various manners receives a degree of refinement from contrast and opposition, by being defined and implicated with circumstances. The *Upholsterer* in *The Tatler* is not a mere vulgar politician. His intense feeling of interest and curiosity about what does not at all concern him, displays itself in the smallest things, assumes the most eccentric forms, and the peculiarity of his absurdity masks itself under various shifts and evasions, which the same folly, when it becomes epidemic and universal as it has since done, would not have occasion to resort to. In general it is only in a state of mere barbarism or indiscriminate refinement that we are to look for extreme grossness or complete insipidity. Our modern dramatists indeed have happily contrived to unite both extremes. *Omne tulit punctum.*[1] On a soft ground of sentiment they have daubed in the gross absurdities of modern manners void of character, have blended metaphysical waiting maids with jockey noblemen, and the humours of the four in hand club, and fill up the piece by some vile and illiberal caricature of particular individuals known on the town.

To return once more to your Correspondent, who condemns all this as much as I do. He is for refining Comedy into a pure intellectual abstraction, the shadow of a shade. Will he forgive me if I suggest, as an addition to his theory, that the drama in general might be constructed on the same abstruse and philosophical principles. As he imagines that the finest Comedies may be formed without individual character, so the deepest Tragedies might be composed without real

[1] Horace, *Ars Poetica*, 343.

APPENDIX

passion. The slightest and most ridiculous distresses might be improved by the help of art and metaphysical aid, into the most affecting scenes. A young man might naturally be introduced as the hero of a philosophic drama, who had lost the gold medal for a prize poem ; or a young lady, whose verses had been severely criticized in the reviews. Nothing could come amiss to this rage for speculative refinement ; or the actors might be supposed to come forward, not in any character, but as a sort of Chorus, reciting speeches on the general miseries of human life, or reading alternately a passage out of Seneca's Morals or Voltaire's Candide. This might by some be thought a great improvement on English Tragedy, or even on the French.

In fact, Sir, the whole of our author's reasoning proceeds on a total misconception of the nature of the Drama itself. It confounds philosophy with poetry, laboured analysis with intuitive perception, general truth with individual observation. He makes the comic muse a dealer in riddles, and an expounder of hieroglyphics, and a taste for dramatic excellence, a species of the second sight. He would have the Drama to be the most remote, and it is the most substantial and real of all things. It represents not only looks, but motion and speech. The painter gives only the former, looks without action or speech, and the mere writer only the latter, words without looks or action. Its business and its use is to express the thoughts and character in the most striking and instantaneous manner, in the manner most like reality. It conveys them in all their truth and subtlety, but in all their force and with all possible effect. It brings them into action, obtrudes them on the sight, embodies them in habits, in gestures, in dress, in circumstances, and in speech. It renders every thing overt and ostensible, and presents human nature not in its elementary principles or by general reflections, but exhibits its essential quality in all their variety of combination, and furnishes subjects for perpetual reflection.

But the instant we begin to refine and generalise beyond a certain point, we are reduced to abstraction, and compelled to see things, not as individuals, or as connected with action and circumstances, but as universal truths, applicable in a degree to all things, and in their extent to none, which therefore it would be absurd to predicate of individuals, or to represent to the senses. The habit, too, of detaching these abstract species and fragments of nature, destroys the power of combining them in complex characters, in every degree of force and variety. The concrete and the abstract cannot co-exist in the same mind. We accordingly find, that to genuine comedy succeed satire and novels, the one dealing in general character and description, and the other making out particulars by the assistance of narrative and comment. Afterwards come traits, and collections of anecdotes, bon mots, topics, and quotations, &c. which are applicable to any one, and are just as good told of one person as another. Thus the trio in the Memoirs of M. Grimm, attributed to three celebrated characters, on the death of a fourth, might have the names reversed, and would lose nothing of its effect. In general these traits, which are so much admired, are a sort of systematic libels on human nature, which make up, by their malice and *acuteness*, for their want of wit and sense.

I have already taken notice of the quotation from Madame de Stael, with which your Correspondent concludes. I can only oppose to it the authority of Sterne and Sir Richard Steele, who thought that the excellence of the English in comedy was in a great measure owing to the originality and variety of character among them [See Sentimental Journey, and Tatler, No.   .][1] With respect to that extreme refinement of taste which the fair Author arrogates to the French, they are neither entirely without it, nor have they so much as they think. The

[1] Hazlitt has omitted the number. The reference is perhaps to No. 42.

APPENDIX

two most refined things in the world are the story of the Falcon in Boccacio, and the character of Griselda in Chaucer, of neither of which the French would have the smallest conception, because they do not depend on traits, or minute circumstances, or turns of expression, but in infinite simplicity and truth, and an everlasting sentiment. We might retort upon Mad. de Stael what she sometimes says in her own defence, That we understand all in other writers that is worth understanding. As to Moliere, he is quite out of the present question ; he lived long before the era of French philosophy and refinement, and is besides almost an English author, quite a *barbare*, in all in which he excels. He was unquestionably one of the greatest comic geniuses that ever lived, a man of infinite wit, gaiety, and invention, full of life and laughter, the very soul of mirth and whim. But it cannot be denied, that his plays are in general mere farces, without real nature or refined character, totally void of probability. They could not be carried on a moment without a perfect collusion between the parties, to wink at impossibilities, by contradicting and acting in defiance of all common sense. For instance, take the *Medecin malgre lui*, in which a common wood-cutter voluntarily takes upon himself, and supports through a long play, the character of a learned physician, without exciting the least suspicion, but which is, notwithstanding the absurdity of the plot, one of the most laughable and truly comic things that can be imagined. The rest of his lighter pieces are of the same description—mere gratuitous fictions and exaggerations of nature. As to his serious Comedies, as the *Tartuffe* and *Misanthrope*, nothing can be more objectionable, and the chief objection to them is that nothing is more hard than to read them through. They have all the improbability and extravagance of the rest, united with all the tedious common-place prosing of French declamation. What can exceed the absurdity of the *Misanthrope*, who leaves his mistress after every proof of her attachment and constancy, merely because she will not submit to the *technical formality* of going to live with him in a desert ? The characters which she gives of her friends in the beginning of the play are very admirable satires, but not Comedy. The same remarks apply in a greater degree to the *Tartuffe*. The long speeches and reasonings in this Play may be very good logic, or rhetoric, or philosophy, or any thing but Comedy. They are dull pompous casuistry. The improbability is monstrous. This play is indeed invaluable, as a lasting monument of the credulity of the French to all verbal professions of virtue or wisdom, and its existence can only be accounted for from that astonishing and tyrannical predominance which words exercise over things in the mind of every Frenchman.

In short, Sir, I conceive, that neither M. de Stael nor your Correspondent has hit upon the true theory of refinement. To suppose that we can go on refining for ever with vivacity and effect, embodying vague abstractions, and particularising flimsy generalities,—'shewing the very body of the age, its form and pressure,'[1] though it has neither form nor pressure left,—seems to me the height of speculative absurdity. That undefined 'frivolous space,' beyond which Madame de Stael regards as 'the region of taste and elegance,' is, indeed, nothing but the very Limbo of Vanity, the land of chiromancy and occult conceit, and paradise of fools, where, according to your correspondent,

> 'None yet, but store hereafter from the earth
> Shall, like aerial vapours, upward rise
> Of all things transitory and vain.'[2]

I am, Sir, your humble servant,   H.

[1] *Hamlet*, Act III. Sc. 2.   *Paradise Lost*, III. 444-6.

558

APPENDIX

II

(See note to p. 217.)

ON MR KEAN'S IAGO

Mr. Examiner,—I was not at all aware that in the remarks which I offered on Mr. Kean's *Iago* my opinions would clash with those already expressed by the respectable writer of the Theatrical Examiner : for I did not mean to object to 'the gay and careless air which Mr. Kean threw over his representation of that arch villain,' but to its being nothing but carelessness and gaiety ; and I thought it perfectly consistent with a high degree of admiration of this extraordinary actor, to suppose that he might have carried an ingenious and original idea of the character to a paradoxical extreme. In some respects, your Correspondent seems to have mistaken what I have said ; for he observes that I have entered into an analysis to shew, 'that *Iago* is a malignant being, who hates his fellow-creatures, and doats on mischief and crime as the best means of annoying the objects of his hate.' Now this is the very reverse of what I intended to shew ; for so far from thinking that *Iago* is 'a ruffian or a savage, who pursues wickedness for its own sake,' I am ready to allow that he is a pleasant amusing sort of gentleman, but with an over-activity of mind that is dangerous to himself and others ; that so far from hating his fellow-creatures, he is perfectly regardless of them, except as they may afford him food for the exercise of his spleen, and that 'he doats on mischief and crime,' not 'as the best means of annoying the objects of his hate,' but as necessary to keep himself in that strong state of excitement which his natural constitution requires, or, to express it proverbially, in *perpetual hot water*. Iago is a man who will not suffer himself or any one else to be at rest ; he has an insatiable craving after action, and action of the most violent kind. His conduct and motives require some explanation ; but they cannot be accounted for from his interest or his passions,—his love of himself, or hatred of those who are the objects of his persecution : these are both of them only the occasional pretext for his cruelty, and are in fact both of them subservient to his love of power and mischievous irritability. I repeat, that I consider this sort of unprincipled self-will as a very different thing from common malignity ; but I conceive it also just as remote from indifference or levity. In one word, the malice of *Iago* is not *personal*, but *intellectual*. Mr. Kean very properly got rid of the brutal ferocity which had been considered as the principle of the character, and then left it without any principle at all. He has mistaken the want of moral feeling, which is inseparable from the part, for constitutional ease and general indifference, which are just as incompatible with it. Mr. Kean's idea seems to have been, that the most perfect callousness ought to accompany the utmost degree of inhumanity ; and so far as relates to callousness to moral considerations, this is true ; but that is not the question. If our Ancient had no other object or principle of action but his indifference to the feelings of others, he gives himself a great deal of trouble to no purpose. If he has nothing else to set him in motion, he had much better remain quiet than be broken on the rack. Mere carelessness and gaiety, then, do not account for the character. But Mr. Kean acted it with nearly the same easy air with which Mr. Braham sings a song in an opera, or with which a comic actor delivers a side-speech in an after-piece.

But the character of *Iago*, says your Correspondent, has nothing to do with the

APPENDIX

manner of acting it. We are to look to the business of the play. Is this then so
very pleasant, or is the part which *Iago* undertakes and executes the perfection of
easy comedy ? I should conceive quite the contrary. The rest of what your
Correspondent says on this subject is ' ingenious, but not convincing.' It amounts
to this, that *Iago* is a hypocrite, and that a hypocrite should always be gay. This
must depend upon circumstances. *Tartuffe* was a hypocrite, yet he was not gay :
Joseph Surface was a hypocrite, but grave and plausible : *Blifil* was a hypocrite, but
cold, formal and reserved. The hypocrite is naturally grave, that is, thoughtful,
and dissatisfied with things as they are, plotting doubtful schemes for his own
advancement and the ruin of others, studying far-fetched evasions, double-minded
and double-faced.—Now all this is an effort, and one that is often attended with
disagreeable consequences ; and it seems more in character that a man whose
invention is thus kept on the rack, and his feelings under painful restraint, should
rather strive to hide the wrinkle rising on his brow, and the malice at his heart,
under an honest concern for his friend, or the serene and regulated smile of steady
virtue, than that he should wear the light-hearted look and easy gaiety of thoughtless constitutional good humour. The presumption therefore is not in favour of
the lively, laughing, comic mien of hypocrisy. Gravity is its most obvious
resource, and, with submission, it is quite as effectual a one. But it seems, that
if *Iago* had worn this tremendous mask, ' the gay and idle world would have had
nothing to do with him.' Why, indeed, if he had only intended to figure at a
carnival or a ridotto, to dance with the women or drink with the men, this
objection might be very true. But *Iago* has a different scene to act in, and has
other thoughts in his contemplation. One would suppose that *Othello* contained no
other adventures than those which are to be met with in *Anstey's Bath Guide*,[1] or
in one of *Miss Burney's* novels. The smooth smiling surface of the world of
fashion is not the element he delights to move in : he is the busy meddling fiend
' who rides in the whirlwind, and directs the storm,'[2] triumphing over the scattered
wrecks, and listening to the shrieks of death. I cannot help thinking that Mr.
Kean's *Iago* must be wrong, for it seems to have abstracted your Correspondent
entirely from the subject of the play. Indeed it is one great proof of Mr. Kean's
powers, but which at the same time blinds the audience to his defects, that they
think of little else in any play but of the part he acts. ' What ! a gallant Venetian
turned into a musty philosopher ! Go away, and beg the reversion of Diogenes'
tub ! Go away, the coxcomb *Roderigo* will think you mighty dull, and will
answer your requests for money with a yawn ; the cheerful spirited *Cassio* will
choose some pleasanter companion to sing with him over his cups ; the fiery
Othello will fear lest his philosophic Ancient will be less valorously incautious in
the day of battle, and that he will not storm a fort with the usual uncalculating
intrepidity.' Now, the coxcomb *Roderigo* would probably have answered his
demands for money with a yawn, though he had been ever so facetious a companion,
if he had not thought him useful to his affairs. He employs him as a man of
business, as a dextrous, cunning, plotting rogue, who is to betray his master and
debauch his wife, an occupation for which his good humour or apparent want
of thought would not particularly qualify him. An accomplice in knavery ought
always to be a solemn rogue, and withal a casuist, for he thus becomes our better
conscience, and gives a sanction to the roguery. *Cassio* does not invite *Iago* to
drink with him, but is prevailed upon against his will to join him ; and *Othello*
himself owes his misfortunes, in the first instance, to his having repulsed the
applications of *Iago* to be made his lieutenant. He himself affects to be blunt
and unmannerly in his conversation with *Desdemona*. There is no appearance of

[1] Christopher Anstey's (1724-1805) *New Bath Guide* (1766).
[2] Addison, *The Campaign*, 292.

560

APPENDIX

any cordiality towards him in *Othello*, nor of his having been a general favourite (for such persons are not usually liked), nor of his having ever been employed but for his understanding and discretion. He every where owes his success to his intellectual superiority, and not to the pleasantness of his manners. At no time does *Othello* put implicit confidence in *Iago's* personal character, but demands his proofs ; or when he founds his faith on his integrity, it is from the gravity of his manner : 'Therefore these stops of thine fright me the more,' *etc.*[1]

Your Correspondent appeals to the manners of women of the town, to prove that 'there is a fascination in an open manner.' I do not see what this has to do with *Iago*. Those who promise to give only pleasure, do not of course put on a melancholy face, or ape the tragic muse. The Sirens would not lull their victims by the prophetic menaces of the Furies. *Iago* did not profess to be the harbinger of welcome news. The reference to Milton's *Satan* and *Lovelace* is equally misplaced. If *Iago* had himself endeavoured to seduce *Desdemona*, the cases would have been parallel. *Lovelace* had to seduce a virtuous woman to pleasure, by presenting images of pleasure, by fascinating her senses, and by keeping out of sight every appearance of danger or disaster. *Iago*, on the contrary, shews to *Othello* that he has 'a monster in his thought' ;[2] and it is his object to make him believe this by dumb show, by the knitting of his brows, by stops and starts, *etc.* before he is willing to commit himself by words. Milton's devil also could only succeed by raising up the most voluptuous and delightful expectations in the mind of Eve, and by himself presenting an example of the divine effects produced by eating of the tree of knowledge. Gloom and gravity were here out of the question. Yet how does Milton describe the behaviour of this arch-hypocrite, when he is about to complete his purpose ?

> 'She scarce had said, though brief, when now more bold
> The Tempter, but with shew of zeal and love
> To man and indignation at his wrong,
> New part puts on, and as to passion moved,
> Fluctuates disturb'd yet comely and in act
> Rais'd, as of some great matter to begin,
> As when of old some orator renown'd
> In Athens or free Rome, where eloquence
> Flourish'd, since mute, to some great cause address'd,
> Stood in himself collected, while each part,
> Motion, each act, won audience ere the tongue ;
> Sometimes in height began, as no delay
> Of preface brooking through his zeal of right ;
> So standing, moving, or to height upgrown,
> The Tempter all-impassion'd thus began :'[3]

If this impassioned manner was justifiable here, where the serpent had only to persuade Eve to her imagined good, how much more was it proper in *Iago*, who had to tempt *Othello* to his damnation ? When he hints to *Othello* that his wife is unfaithful to him—when he tells his proofs, at which *Othello* swoons, when he advises him to strangle her, and undertakes to dispatch *Cassio* from his zeal in 'wronged Othello's service,'[4] should he do this with a smiling face, or a face of indifference ? If a man drinks or sings with me, he may perhaps drink or sing much as Mr. Kean drinks or sings with *Roderigo* and *Cassio* : if he bids me good day, or wishes me a pleasant journey, a frank and careless manner will well become him ; but if he assures me that I am on the edge of a precipice, or way-

---

[1] Act III. Sc. 3   [2] *Ibid.*   [3] *Paradise Lost*, IX. 664-678.   [4] Act III. Sc. 3.

APPENDIX

laid by assassins, or that some tremendous evil has befallen me, with the same fascinating gaiety of countenance and manner, I shall be little disposed to credit either his sincerity or friendship or common sense.

Your Correspondent accounts for the security and hilarity of *Iago*, in such circumstances, from his sense of superiority and his certainty of success. First, this is not the account given in the text, which I should prefer to any other authority on the subject. Secondly, if he was quite certain of the success of his experiment, it was not worth the making, for the only provocation to it was the danger and difficulty of the enterprise ; and at any rate, whatever were his feelings, the appearance of anxiety and earnestness was necessary to the accomplishment of his purpose. 'He should assume a virtue, if he had it not.'[1] Besides, the success of his experiment was not of that kind even which has been called *negative* success, but proved of a very tragical complexion both to himself and others. I can recollect nothing more to add, without repeating what I have before said, which I am afraid would be to no purpose. I am, Sir, your obedient servant, **W. H.**

[1] *Hamlet*, Act III. Sc. 4.

Edinburgh : Printed by T. and A. CONSTABLE